Fights for the Cl

The Men and Their Times
(Volume II)

Fred Henning

Alpha Editions

This Edition Published in 2020

ISBN: 9789354211225

Design and Setting By
Alpha Editions
www.alphaedis.com
Email – info@alphaedis.com

MEMOIRS

OF

THE PRIZE RING.

VOL. II.

CHAPTER I.

TOM CRIBB AND BOB GREGSON. — ONE THOUSAND GUINEAS
AND CHAMPIONSHIP.—A RARE OLD CARD.—A MONSTER
MEETING AT MOULSEY HURST.

In our first volume we mentioned the competition as
to the division of the inner ring tickets for the great fight
between the men whose names appear above. It will be
worth while once more referring to those pieces of paste-
board, as they are now extremely rare, for they are said
to be the very first used for ring admission since the days
of Figg and Broughton, a facsimile of which we printed
in our first volume. We regret that we cannot reproduce
this also in facsimile and in colour, but the lettering is
taken from one which we had an opportunity of seeing
some few years ago, and which formerly belonged to
Tom Jones, the popular Master of the Ceremonies at
the Fives Court.

It was quite an artistic bit of printing, and measured
about 5in by 3½in. One side, printed in red on a
blue ground (Gregson's colours), has the figures of two
men in fighting attitude, and underneath in lines of
blue (Cribb's colours) are the following words.

GREAT DISPLAY OF ENGLISH BOXING.
Tom Cribb and Bob Gregson.
For the Championship
AND
One Thousand Guineas.

Tom Belcher and Bill Copley.
For the Championship of the Middle-Weights
and 400 Guineas.
and
Dogherty and Power
(Tom Jones' Novice) for a Purse.

On the other side of the card was printed in black letters on a yellow ground (Tom Belcher's colours) the following:—

Admit the Bearer to the
INNER RING,
On Tuesday, October 27, 1808,
Within Fifty Miles of London.
This Day is called the Feast of Crispin.

The framer of the above card, who put in the last line, must have had some knowledge of the bard. It was the anniversary of the battle of Agincourt, and nearly fifty years after the fight between Cribb and Gregson came October 25 as another red letter day in our annals of England. That date is the anniversary of the Balaclava charge.

But to our muttons. A few days before the fight the hosts of the sporting houses sent in their returns for tickets sold, when it was discovered that not less than 400 had been disposed of at three guineas each. This was an unexpected match, and, of course, did not represent nearly the number that would be disposed of by the provincial visitors, who were sure to come up in strong force, besides tickets that would be sold on the ground. It was quite clear then that some provision would have to be made to accommodate such a host in the inner ring. Mr. John Johnson therefore called in Bill Gibbons, who, it will be remembered, usually took charge of the ring on special occasions, and consulted him as to what should be done. This astute gentleman, always with an eye to business, declared that the only possibly way out of the difficulty would be to engage not less than sixty ring constables, recruited from the

pugilistic ranks, and to fit up a kind of amphitheatre
for the gents to sit or stand upon. Asked what the cost
would be, Master William declared that it could not be
done for less than 12s. per nob. Now on 450 this would
come to no less a sum than £270, which Mr. Jackson
considered exceedingly excessive. However, Gibbons
stuck to his price, and obtained it, although it is
fair to say that only a small amount of it came out of
the combatants' money, Mr. Akers, a generous sport,
and some dozen wealthy amateurs subscribing liberally.

Having settled this, Jackson informed Gibbons that
the place would be Moulsey Hurst, advising that it
should be kept as secret as possible, although he believed
that the Surrey magistrates would not interfere, for
some influence had been brought to bear.

On the Monday evening there set forth from London,
under the superintendence of Caleb Baldwin and Bill
Gibbons, some dozen waggons laden with strong planks,
quartering, saws, hammers, and nails, quite an army
of carpenters. Their destination was Moulsey Hurst.
Fortunately the weather was fine, and they worked all
night, disturbing not a little the sleepers in the small
village hard by with their ceaseless hammering, and
looking like so many " will o' the wisps " as they dodged
about with their lanterns and torches. Soon after daylight the work was complete. They had constructed rows
of strong planks on three sides of the ring, each six inches
higher than the other from the front row, that being
sufficient distance from the ring to enable a line of
people to sit upon the grass. Behind, the vehicles and
horsemen could look well over the heads of those in the
inner ring, and indeed it was really by all accounts an
excellent amphitheatre.

"Before nine o'clock in the morning," one account
says, "crowds began to pour on to the ground. Men
on horseback, men on foot, and men and women in
vehicles of every kind, from the fashionable phaeton
and the lordly barouche to the humbler ' shay,' and the
decidedly democratic donkey-cart."

Tom Cribb was driven over by Tommy Onslow on a
coach with a large and lively party, including John
Gully. Finding it impossible to take the high road on
account of its crowded state, the celebrated whip tooled
his team through country lanes, beneath the shade of
the russet leaves, through Sutton Green, Picfort, and
Wisley, when he struck the high road at Byfleet. Once
more leaving the road, other lanes brought them to the
south gate of Oatlands Park, across which lovely place
they drove, emerging at Walton, thence to Hurst.
There a halt was made for refreshments and to change

the team, which had been sent down on the previous
day. Of course, they were loudly cheered when they
arrived upon the ground, which was done just as Tom
Belcher and Cropley entered the ring.   Within ten
minutes of his opponent's arrival Bob Gregson and
party were also there in time to see the middle-weight
battle.

Without going into a long list of those present, it will
be necessary only to say that the most aristocratic supporters of the Ring were there, and to mention Byron,
who had come with Lord Annesley.

After Tom Belcher had defeated Copley in thirty-four
rounds, lasting fifty minutes (an account of the battle
not finding a place here), the *pièce de résistance* was
placed before the company assembled.   Bill Gibbons
with Tom Jones examined and tightened up the ropes,
when after beating down the turf, which had been
somewhat disturbed by the men's spiked shoes, everything was ready for the big event.

Tom Cribb was the first to "shy his cady" into the
roped arena, and followed by Gully and Gibbons (who
were to act respectively as second and bottle-holder) was
at once in the ring.   There was a ringing cheer for
Cribb, and hardly had that subsided when Gregson,
with Jem Belcher and Ben Richmond joined the others.
It would appear to have been a most amicable meeting,
for the seconds and bottle-holders, as well as the
principals, shook hands heartily, which brought forth
more applause from the multitude.

It must have been an exciting moment when Jackson
stood beside the ring, watch in hand, awaiting the
signal that all was ready, and called "Time."   Both
men jumped from their corners simultaneously, and
once more shook hands, but very quickly this time, for
there was no time to pause.   We have described both
the men's physique on former occasions; but chroniclers
say that never did two men look more perfect, and
they must have been fine specimens of the *genus* athlete.

The report says: "Gregson's splendidly developed
figure carried off his height so well that few who did
not know it would have been inclined to credit him with
the full 6ft 1½in, although it was easier to believe in his
weight, which was on this day exactly 15½st.   Tom,
although three inches shorter, was only 18lb lighter,
so that which he lost in height he made up in
massiveness.   He stood on his pins as firm as a rock,
with both hands held right over the face.   Cribb
looked as cool and collected as ever, his pleasant mug
not showing the slightest sign that he ever realised
the presence of the numerous spectators, who were

shouting and clamouring for him to begin. Gregson,
on the other hand, seemed somewhat nervous and
worried with the sun, which was shining in his eyes."

There was apparently very little difference in the
betting at the opening of the fight, the very slight odds
of guineas to pounds being on Cribb. Bob was the first
to open the ball with a try with the left, being much out

TOM CRIBB.
(From a contemporary print.)

of distance. Tom was also short with his return, and
it was palpable that they had not taken measure at the
start. After slight sparring, they closed, and Gregson
managed to force Cribb underneath him; but no
damage was done.

In the second round Cribb settled down to work. He
showed great activity, particularly about the legs. He
popped in one with the right and another with the left,

avoiding the returns most cleverly. Then, before Bob
knew where he was, he delivered a slashing blow on the
cheek that laid it open, and it bled profusely, never
staying throughout the whole fight, and causing his
second no end of trouble. Gregson showing slight
ill-temper, then rushed in and tried to land blow after
blow at Tom's neck. The latter was too clever for
him, however, and it was a good job for Cribb, for the
power put into the efforts was so great that one might
have knocked him right out. Then a sharp rally ensued
at close quarters, ending with Gregson being thrown
very heavily.

Offers after this of 3 to 2 on Cribb were made. Before
coming up for the next round, Gregson gulped down a
tumbler of brandy—rather early in the battle, we should
say, to administer stimulants in such quantity.

It seemed to sharpen him up a bit, however, for he let
go and caught Tom a nasty smack under the ear ; but the
latter quietly retreated, and Bob, eager to repeat the dose,
followed in a very incautious manner, when Cribb opened
fire and landed him full on the gashed cheek, which
caused him in turn to beat a retreat. Tom, not to be
denied though, followed up, and splash, splash, went his
fist upon the gaping wound until Gregson, half-stunned
and smarting with the pain, fell to the ground.

But such are the fortunes of war, in the very next
bout the tables might easily have been turned, had
Gregson been a good general. We read that his very first
blow was a terrific one upon Tom's temple, delivered
with such force that Cribb reeled, and for a few seconds
was quite dazed, and certainly did not know what he
was about. Now, had his opponent followed this up
quickly with effective hitting, the fight might have been
settled then and there in his favour. But instead of
doing so we read that he wasted time in sparring, thus
enabling Cribb to beat a retreat to the ropes. Belcher
shouted to his man, " Now, Bob, now's your time,
my lad," and then Gregson rushed at his man. It was,
however, too late. Cribb had recovered somewhat, and
was able to defend himself ; but after a rally received a
nasty smack on the side of the head, which really must
have been a knock-down blow.

The betting had by this time veered round in favour
of the North countryman ; but both men had received a
deal of punishment, they had pelted each other with
such determination and effect.

Without going into the details of all the rounds, a
record of which we have before us, it will be enough to
say that Tom Cribb put forth all his science, and
Gregson all his strength, but he judged his distance

badly and was undoubtedly out manœuvred by his opponent. Tom became once more a very hot favourite, 2 to 1 being laid on him. Yet shortly afterwards he received a slight reverse, and the wagering went back to 6 to 4. It must be remembered that both were fighting for more than profit, they were fighting for glory and honour—for the title of Champion of England.

When the thirteenth round had been reached it was anybody's battle, but the punishment that both had received was beginning to tell. Cribb was bleeding profusely from three cuts on the forehead, the blood from which poured into his eyes and well nigh blinded him. Yet he was as cool as the proverbial cucumber. On one occasion Bob caught his man a fearful thump on the temple which seemed to finish the fight. The excitement must have been intense. Cribb lay all of a heap motionless, and Gully and Gibbons rushed to the centre of the ring and carried him to his corner. "It's all over!" yelled a hundred voices. "Not yet!" came from a hundred more. Restoratives were given, and Cribb, with a sigh and a vacant stare, was placed upon his feet just at the last moment as Mr. Jackson called out "Time!"

Fortunately for Tom his antagonist was little better; he could walk but slowly to the scratch, he was so weak. Exhorted by Belcher, however, he made desperate efforts, and eventually knocked Cribb down and fell upon him heavily. "Ten to one against Tom Cribb!" yelled the multitude, and everybody thought it was all over. Not so, though; he came tottering up to the call of "Time!" It was (one account says) "the merest toss up which man would be the first to cry a go, and some of the amateurs who were interested financially were for ordering them out of the ring and dividing the stakes. But they neither of them had any notion of being satisfied with less than victory, and as soon as possible they closed. By a good stroke of fortune Cribb contrived to throw Gregson in such a manner that not only did his own weight in falling seem to knock all the breath out of Bob's body, but his leg was twisted under him in such a manner as to hurt him very seriously. He was picked up quickly and placed on his second's knee, and at the call of "Time" he tried to rise, but his head fell forward, and he whispered to Belcher, "I can do no more, I am fairly licked."

Up went the sponge, and Tom Cribb was proclaimed Champion of England.

Captain Barclay presented the new Champion with £150 on the spot, as soon as he recovered (for he had fallen down insensible directly he knew that he had won), and John Jackson subscribed a handsome sum for Bob Gregson, who had been so unfortunate in all his battles. The latter was taken to the King's Head at Hampton Court, and Cribb was conveyed to the Fox Inn at the same town. Both remained there quietly for a couple of days, when they came to town.

Tom Cribb will appear several times again upon these pages; but we must say farewell to Bob Gregson, who never entered the roped arena again. With the money that was subscribed, and by the help of friends, he became landlord of the Castle Tavern, Holborn, now called the Napier. He might have done well there had he been a prudent man. As it was, he lived there for six years, and entertained some of the best patrons of the Ring. His extravagance, however, led him to bankruptcy, and he was turned out of the celebrated hostelry in 1814. It seems that he then went over to Ireland, and eventually opened a boxing saloon in Dublin. Coming to London in 1819, he took a benefit at the theatre in Catherine Street, Strand, which is now the *Echo* office. Returning to Dublin he became landlord of the Punch House, Moor Street. But misfortune, brought about by his own imprudence, followed him, and he did no good. After getting into a shocking state of poverty he came to Liverpool, where he died in the November of 1824, unknown and without a friend near him. Such was the end of one of the most ardent aspirants for the title of Champion of England.

CHAPTER II.

A SPELL OF INACTIVITY.—BETTER TO LEAVE WELL ALONE.
JEM BELCHER AND TOM CRIBB.—THEIR SECOND BATTLE.
—DEATH OF JEM BELCHER.

AND now we come to that which will certainly not
make one of the brightest chapters of our history of the
Champions. Yet it must be told, for it concerns one of
the most remarkable fighters of all who won the coveted
title. It is the record of the final and undoubtedly
most inglorious fight of Jem Belcher.

It will be remembered that the last time the Bristolian
figured upon these pages was when we described his
meeting and defeat by Tom Cribb upon April 8,
1807, when they fought at Moulsey Hurst, before an
immense assemblage of patricians and plebeians, including royalty itself in the person of the Duke of
Clarence, afterwards William IV., and all the leading
lights of the sporting world. It was an exciting event,
for the company had witnessed the once incomparable
and invincible Jem Belcher—the quondam Napoleon of
the Ring—taken from the arena a beaten man, vanquished by the all-powerful arm of the stalwart Tom
Cribb. They had seen science and skill give way to
superior strength and endurance. It had been a thrilling
and sensational fight, and many believed that Belcher
would have won had it not been for the artfulness of Will
Warr, Tom Cribb's second, who took from John Gully a
bet of 5 to 1. Gully, it will be remembered, was seconding
the Bristolian. The artful William, after taking the bet,
insisted upon the money being staked. This gave the
men a minute's extra time, and enabled Cribb to come
round after that fearful blow Jem had administered in
the eighteenth round, which caused Cribb to fall like a
lump of lead, quite stupefied. Anyhow, had it not been
for Warr and his bet, it is doubtful whether Tom could
have responded to the call of " Time."

Belcher had, however, in delivering that blow, sprained
his wrist, and was unable to use his right again, and
besides that he had received a dreadful hit upon his only

good eye, which confused his sight. Jem attributed his
defeat entirely to the accident to his wrist, and was so
satisfied of his ability to thrash Cribb that he vowed he
would never rest until he had turned the tables upon the
conqueror.

It will be remembered that John Gully, after his second
victory over Bob Gregson, had resigned the Championship and finally retired from the Ring into private life.
The defeated Gregson considered himself to have a rever-
sionary interest in the Belt, but had found a ready rival
to dispute his claim in the person of Tom Cribb. The
sporting world was divided in opinion as to the merits
of the two men. Some maintained that Tom, who had
only once been beaten in his seven engagements, was
incomparably superior to Gregson, who, whatever he
might have done amongst the yokels of Lancashire, had
lost his battles in the metropolitan school. Others
thought that the herculean Bob, although overmatched
by Gully, would prove too good for Cribb. So the match
was made, it being understood that they should fight for
the Championship of England and the Belt. The battle
we described fully in our last chapter. The Marquis of
Tweedale was Bob's backer, and Mr. Paul Methuen
Cribb's. This was a desperate battle, which took place
upon Moulsey Hurst on the 25th of October, 1808.
Indeed, it was a very near thing, as our readers will
recollect ; the terrible punishment inflicted by each
being great. They were both bled and sent to their hotels
at Hampton, with doctors in attendance, and were not
permitted to leave until the next day. Anyhow, Cribb had
asserted himself Champion, having defeated all the best,
with the exception of the "Game Chicken" and John
Gully, and both those heroes had bidden farewell to the
arena.

Naturally the question arose, who was to try conclusions with the newly-fledged Champion? To the astonishment of the sporting world the answer came from a most
unexpected quarter. Jem Belcher threw down the
gauntlet and challenged Cribb's title to the Championship. It seemed as if the Napoleon of the Ring
could not bear anybody but a Bristolian to hold the
title. His grandfather was the celebrated John Slack,
and had he not introduced his fellow-townsman, the
"Game Chicken," to hold it after he had won it, and
from whom he vainly endeavoured to recover it? And
that was Belcher's first mistake. He never should have
met "The Chicken," but finished his career in the ring
after his defeat of Firby, the "Young Ruffian," when he
had an unbroken career of prosperity.

Now Jem Belcher, who had seconded Gregson, and lost

heavily over his defeat, had the old feeling for revenge come over him, and within a fortnight of Cribb's victory over the Lancastrian he had challenged, to the astonishment, as we have said, of the whole sporting world, the Champion to fight him for £200 and the Belt. Jem's old friend, John Cullington, of the Black Bull, Tottenham Court Road, who had lost heavily over his fight with the "Game Chicken," implored Belcher not to enter the ring again, and all his true friends pointed out the madness for a man who was minus an eye, had neglected himself sadly, and whose stamina was on the wane, to try conclusions with a man of Cribb's splendid physique. Nothing, however, irritated Belcher so much as having his decline or infirmities pointed out to him, and he declared that if he could find nobody to support him he would stake the money himself, even if he sold up his hostelry to do so. Fortunately for him, however, there was one who stood by him, and he was no less a celebrity than Lord Barrymore, brother to our old friend who, years before, was mixed up with Hooper the Tinman, and, as we have described, met with a tragic end. His noble patron was about the only man, though, that believed in him, whilst Cribb, of course, after his recent defeat of Gregson, and having won the proud title, had any number of friends and supporters, Mr. Paul Methuen and Captain Barclay coming readily forward with the stake money, and opening the betting with offers of 7 to 4 on Cribb.

It may be mentioned here that at this period Captain Barclay had just accepted a wager from Lieutenant Wedderburne Webster that he would not walk 1,000 miles in 1,000 consecutive hours, at the rate of a mile in each hour—a match which, as all the sporting world knows, was won by the gallant Captain in the following June, and which even now, in the days of great feats in pedestrianism, is looked upon as a wonderful performance. The Captain took Cribb away with him to Yorkshire, where he himself looked after his training, for it will be remembered that Barclay had some extraordinary methods of preparing a man for a contest, which rarely failed.

Belcher, who was accompanied by Dan Mendoza and brother Tom, took his breathings at Jem's old quarters, Virginia Water, making the Wheatsheaf their home. Everything went well, and those who visited the ex-Champion declared that he was magnificently fit and in the highest spirits.

The eventful day having arrived, that being February 1, 1809, hundreds tramped out of London to the battle-field, which was Epsom Downs. Before daylight

the roads so familiar to visitors to the City and Suburban and Derby were crowded, and later on the strings
of vehicles making their way in the same direction told
the early risers *en route* that some affair of great moment
was about to take place. Tom Cribb had come up with
Captain Barclay the day before from Yorkshire, and was
driven down to Epsom, accompanied by several friends.
There was quite a representative party of sporting nobs,
too. His Royal Highness the Duke of York (then
Commander-in-Chief) was present, as were Lord Barrymore, Marquis of Tweedale, Lords Yarmouth, Craven,
Brooke, Ogle, Mr. Paul Methuen, Lieut. Wedderburne
Webster, the Hons. Berkeley and Keppel Craven, besides
others too numerous to mention.

Dan Mendoza and Bob Clarke officiated for Jem Belcher
as second and bottle-holder respectively; whilst Bill
Gibbons and the veteran Joe Ward did the like for Tom
Cribb. And here it may be mentioned that curiously
enough Bill Gibbons had seconded Belcher in all his
successful conquests; but owing to a personal quarrel
Bill deserted him, and never was Jem once a winner
again. It was the habit of Gibbons to proudly call
attention to this fact. Mr. Jackson was, as usual on all
important occasions like this, appointed referee, and
everything being in readiness, the combatants were at
12.45 p.m. summoned from their corners to once more
decide who should be entitled to the Belt.

Cribb looked the picture of health, and was in what
then would be considered good condition, although
he weighed upwards of 14st, and at the present
time would have been thought a bit too "beefy." He
stood 5ft 10½in. and his ponderous, broad-built frame
made him appear formidable before his more slightly-
built adversary, for Jem Belcher, who stood 5ft 11½in.
and weighed 11st 10lb, was more of the slim-built
athlete. Here is a description of one who knew the ex-
Champion:—" Though graceful and finely proportioned,
he had none of those muscular exaggerations in his
form when stripped, and still less when attired, which
go, in the artistic as well as the popular notion, to make
up a Hercules.

Naturally, the loss of an eye was a disfigurement;
but, as he faced his powerful adversary, he was a
model of grace in his attitude and symmetry of form.
The silence was almost painful as the men began to spar.
For quite half a minute there was not a single attempt
at a blow, when Belcher, in his dashing, old, quick style,
lashed out with left and right. The first Cribb stopped,
but the latter found its way to the body with a spank
that could be heard all around the ring. Tom was stopped

on the return, and as they closed, Belcher, to avoid the expenditure of his strength by wrestling, slipped to the ground.

In the second round, we are told that Cribb threw aside his usual caution and dashed in somewhat recklessly, and although he landed heavily on the ribs, Jem returned with his smart one, two, but there was little force exhibited, and Cribb could not be kept out, but closed in and threw Jem heavily. Our informant writes : " It was noticeable that scarcely any cheering followed this successful stroke of Cribb's. Popular sympathy was now with Belcher, and showed itself by the silence which reigned round the ring, broken only by expressions of pity and regret at the sight of Jem's attitude and beautiful style of hitting, recalled memories of his glorious prime, and forced home the painful contrast between what he had been *then* and what he was *now.*"

In the third round, though, it seems that Belcher had all the best of it, and undoubtedly returned to his old form of hard hitting, for we read that he advanced in that bold, dashing fashion which had of yore been such a conspicuous feature of his fighting. Tom retreated with caution, but Jem sprang in at him and sent home two terrific blows—one on the body, the other under the left ear, the very spot where Gregson had planted some of his most tremendous and effective hits three months before.

Belcher then shot in a couple more heavy blows at long range; when Cribb, finding that at outfighting he had no chance with his nimble adversary, closed, regardless of a smack on the nose, which turned on the claret again. and once more the ex-Champion was thrown.

In the fourth round the betting was 5 to 1 on Cribb, for again Belcher went to ground, and he was palpably tired and winded thus early in the battle. In the next bout, however, Jem showed all his old brilliancy of delivery, sending both hands into Tom's face with wonderful rapidity and decision. Unfortunately in doing this he lamed his right hand as he did in his former fight, and Cribb, seeing something was wrong, rallied, hit Belcher back, closed and threw him. Again silence prevailed, for the sympathy was still with Jem.

We cannot afford space to describe this the last of Jem Belcher's battles in full, so we will content ourselves by quoting the succeeding round as graphically told, and then give a brief summary of the remainder of the fight. This account shows what a splendid exponent of the art Jem Belcher was to the very last:—" When Belcher came up for the sixth round he was panting like a hunted

hare, and, feeling his weakness, instead of attacking as
usual, retreated. 'Follow him up, Tom. Now's your
chance. He's dead beat. Follow him up and mill him,'
shouted Cribb's friends, in a state of frantic excitement.
Tom stirred his slow stumps, and in two seconds had
Jem pinned up against the ropes, where he gave him
some heavy hits in the body, the crowd all the while
yelling and shouting like demons, some urging Cribb to
hit harder, other calling to Jem either to go down or
make an effort to get free. Belcher chose the latter
course; with a quick movement he slipped to one side,
and as Tom turned to face him let out with his right,
regardless of the injury it had sustained, and with all
his force caught Cribb on the sore place under the left
ear. Tom reeled from the terrific blow, the blood
streamed down his neck, and for a moment he was
utterly dazed. 'Now, Jem, you've got him,' roared Dan
Mendoza, and Belcher springing in, closed, spun his
massive foe round, and gave him a splendid cross-buttock.
Then there went up a shout from Jem's admirers. 'Jem
will win! Jem will win!' was the cry from a thousand
voices." Again did Belcher hit Tom Cribb all over the
ring, and even the latter's backers, Captain Barclay and
Mr. Paul Methuen, have misgivings as to the result of
the fight. Jem hit Tom when, where, and as often as he
liked, sent him about the ring like a shuttlecock, and
wound up by closing, evidently intending another cross-
buttock, but Cribb, bothered and confused, had sense
enough to slip to the ground. Once more the cries came
that Belcher would win.

But Jem's second, Dan Mendoza, knew better, for this
last effort had pumped him completely out, and it was
only by the administration of a good drink of brandy
that he was able to respond to the call of "Time." He
had shot his bolt. Tom Cribb saw it at a glance, and
dropping the defensive went in boldly. Yet Belcher's
defence was so marvellous and his tactics so grand that
he was enabled to prolong the contest until the thirty-
first round. Still his heroic resistance could not secure
him victory. His right forearm was black and blue
from bruises acquired in making his defence, and it was
evident that before long he would be unable to use it,
while his hands were practically useless.

Then Lord Barrymore, the Marquis of Tweeddale,
John Cullington, and several other old friends came to the
ropes and begged him to give in, as it was a physical
impossibility to win with his hands in such a dreadful
state. Very reluctantly Jem consented, and offered his
swollen fist to Cribb, in token of surrender, after a
contest of forty minutes.

So ended Jem Belcher's career in the ring. Sorrowfully he quitted the field of his renown, regretful at having tempted fortune in defiance of his friends' advice, and of Nature herself, who had deserted him.

After this defeat, which he seemed to take much to heart, his spirits entirely deserted him, and he became gloomy and morose. Again, domestically, he was by no means happy, for he had the worst of all wives to try a man's temper and to sour his days—a woman who was passionately jealous, and of a shrewish disposition, nagging and complaining of everything, great or little.

Jem had left the Jolly Brewers, in Wardour Street, and gone to the Coach and Horses, a smaller house in Soho. His customers fell away, for he was no longer the bright, jovial, animated Jem Belcher of old. He would sit for hours without speaking, would drink heavily, and became taciturn and depressed. He became very ill, and his once magnificent athletic figure shrank to a mere nothing. He was the shadow only of the great gladiator. At last, with only his two faithful friends by his side, he passed into shadowland on Tuesday, July 30, 1811, in the thirty-first year of his age.

After his death his many old friends and the fickle public thought of his greatness, and never had there been seen such a following at a pugilist's funeral, nor has there been since, we should be safe in saying, if we except that of Tom Sayers. He was buried on the Sunday following his death, in the Marylebone burial ground, and an immense concourse of people were present to pay respect to the most brilliant fighter that ever did battle on the green turf of old England. To those who have the patience to search, the half obliterated inscription may now be seen upon the gravestone. It is a modest epitaph, and is follows :—

In Memory of
JAMES BELCHER,
Late of St. Anne's Parish, Soho,
Who died
The 30th of July, 1811 :
Aged 30.
Universally regretted by all who knew him.

Jem Belcher—the Napoleon of the Ring, as he was aptly called, not only for his facial resemblance to the great Corsican, but for his similarity as a tactician in battle— was undoubtedly the finest fighter that ever lived, and although we have the pleasurable task of introducing several more famous gladiators, none will compare for brilliancy, grace, precision in attack, and science in defence with James Belcher.

CHAPTER III.

INTRODUCING THE BLACK.—DOWN IN OLE VARGINNY.—HIS
ROMANTIC CAREER.—MOLYNEUX CHALLENGES CRIBB.

Two years all but two months had elapsed before the
Champion, Tom Cribb, was on the war-path again. It
was a long period of inactivity, but the warrior, after
his defeat of Bob Gregson and Jem Belcher, as related
in our last two chapters, had earned for himself such a
reputation as a determined natural fighter, with no small
amount of science thrown in, that few dared to dream
of trying conclusions with him, and he was for the
whole of that period permitted to rest upon his laurels.

In the meanwhile Tom had taken unto himself a wife,
and had told more than one friend that it was his intention to give up pugilism and settle quietly down to business, for he was the victor in eight battles, had only been
defeated once, and had held the Championship for two
years. There was, however, an extraordinary individual, who for some time had been a conspicuous
figure in the fistic circles of the metropolis, who had
come to England with an express determination to fight
his way to the top of the tree. His name was Molyneux,
and he was located at Bill Richmond's house, the Horse
and Dolphin, in St. Martin's Street. A pure African,
as black as the master of Hades, was this lump of
ebony, and as ugly as sin, as will be seen by our
portrait, which is taken from an oil painting, for which
he sat.

But before we introduce this gentleman, who is to
play a very important part amongst the Fights for the
Championship, it will be as well to trace back his origin
and briefly sketch his somewhat romantic career, and
how he won the opportunity to get to England in order
to pit himself against the Champion of England.

In the latter part of last century there lived in Virginia a wealthy planter named Molyneux. He belonged
to what they call the "First Families of Virginia,"
that is to say, he was a descendant from one of the
English aristocratic houses to which King Charles had
wisely granted lands on an extensive scale in the States.

This Virginian planter was descended from the Molyneux family, of which in England at the present time, the Earl of Sefton is the head. In 1784, the master of this Virginian estate was the fifth Molyneux who had succeeded to it. As everybody knows, slavery was the order of the day, and infants born upon the estates had to be kept and looked after until they were old enough to work, when they could be sold or employed where they were born.

Now in this particular year, 1784, was born a piccaninny as black as a lump of coal, and the Molyneuxs being particularly kind to their slaves, the infant grew up hale and hearty, and developed into as fine a specimen of ebony manhood as it would be possible to conceive —that is to say, so far as muscular form went, for his face was anything but prepossessing. He became the constant companion of young Algernon Molyneux, a gay spark, son of the planter, and a reckless, dissipated youth, who aped the vices of the English aristocracy of the period, and was particularly fond of sport, prize-fighting coming in for much of his patronage. These matches were common enough amongst the niggers, who were compelled to stand up and slash at each other for the amusement of their masters, who frequently had very high stakes upon the result. Young Algernon had taken a great fancy to the nigger lad, whose name was Tom, for he had found him very useful as a body guard, and he had twice backed him to beat others older and more experienced than he with the fists.

Algernon Molyneux, whilst with a gay set in Richmond, where his father had a town house, and a number of these gay young sparks met, and the conversation turned upon fighting, when one named Peyton, a young planter, whose father had recently died and left him a considerable amount of money, offered to back one of his slaves named Abe, against any black in Virginia. Molyneux, who was more than half intoxicated at the time, immediately accepted the challenge, and nominated Tom. Stakes were posted and bets were made, and in the morning, Master Algernon, when he came to his senses, was rather shocked to find that he stood to lose no less a sum than a hundred thousand dollars. Now, he was none too wealthy, and such a sum as this would have been quite out of his reach, whilst his father would never have countenanced such business. It was too late to retire then, however, so he determined to risk it. In the first place his object was to get time, so that Tom could be properly trained. That having been accomplished, and everything settled that the men should fight in two months from the signing of articles, his next business was to turn his attention to Tom. It so happened that in Richmond was a man named Davis, a sailor from Bristol, whom Molyneux had met, and who had been a third-class pugilist in his native city, but said to be very smart with his fists. Davis was at once sought, and being quite willing for a consideration to look after the Black, was at once engaged, and Tom was placed under his care, with orders to do everything he was told.

This he did to the letter, and so far as docility went Davis had nothing to complain about. In fact, Tom was too docile, and the ex-pugilist found that he could not—try what he would—wake the young nigger up. He was as dull as ditch water, and nothing could be done with him. In despair Davis went to young Algernon Molyneux, and told him the state of affairs. The young planter was exasperated, and threatened to flog Tom into activity But the Bristol man had another idea altogether, and said that flogging would be quite out of the question. "Promise him his freedom and a hundred dollars if he wins, and I'll stake my existence that young Tom will thrash any nigger in the country," was Davis' advice. Struck with the sense of the advice given, Molyneux acted upon it, and in a few days Tom was a different being. His spirits were overflowing, he stuck to his training, and outgeneralled the old pugilist with the gloves in a most wonderful manner.

Well, to cut a long story short, Tom met Abe and beat him easily. and young Molyneux, delighted with his fine haul, made Tom a present of 500 dols. and secured for him his freedom. We need hardly conjecture that this was a *ruse* on Davis' part to procure the man his liberty, and the two set forth for New York the closest of friends.

For nearly five years Tom, who had taken the name of Molyneux, lived in New York, and during that period he fought several battles; but we have no means of discovering with whom, or for what amounts. Both the battles and the men must have been of some importance, as in the year 1809 we find the Black assuming the title of "Champion of America," and he would appear to be the first man to call himself such.

What became of Davis we are unable to say; but Molyneux, who had, of course, heard much of the British prize-ring, and of Cribb, the Champion, in particular, determined to make his way to London and challenge the great fighter for the Championship of the World.

So in the year 1809 we find the sable gladiator in the metropolis with little money in his pocket, but with

the heroic determination to whip the Champion. No
doubt he had met some English pugilist in New York,
who had instructed him where to go and what to do
upon his arrival in London, for he made direct for Bill
Richmond's house, the Horse and Dolphin, in St.
Martin's Street, Leicester Square. It will be remembered that Bill Richmond was a black, who had been
most successful in the ring, but had been defeated by
Tom Cribb

TOM MOLYNEUX.

Molyneux received apparently a hearty welcome, for
we learn that he at once made himself at home, and took
up his quarters at Richmond's hostelry. He was not
long in telling his host the purport of his visit; but
although Bill appreciated his ambition and confidence, he
paused before recommending him to throw down a
challenge to such a man as Tom Cribb, who had given
him a taste of his quality. Besides, he did not believe
for a moment that anybody would be likely to put down
the money for an unknown, as it must be remembered
that we were at this period in very little touch with our

American cousins, and knew little or nothing of their
fighting displays, which, indeed, so far as the Ring went
then, had no notoriety. Bill Richmond, however,
thought it out carefully, for he was desirous that somebody should be found to take down Tom Cribb's colours,
and what a bit of satisfaction it would have been to
Bill if one of his own colour could be found to accomplish the feat. In the first place, he determined that the
stranger should have a go with a trial horse. But then
came the difficulty; Belcher and Gregson were out of the
question, Nicholls and Horton also had retired, Maddox
was too old, Richmond himself could not very well be
backer and opponent, so Bill ruminated and bided his
time.

At length an opportunity came for him to make his
bow before the British sporting public, although it was
a quiet affair. Bill Richmond had offered to back his
"dark horse against any inferior man," as he put it,
which we suppose meant that he was willing to pit him
against any but the top sawyers. Anyhow, on Monday,
the 4th of June, 1809, when the battle money was handed
over to Dutch Sam for his fight with Mr. Medley, Tom
Cribb met Richmond and asked him if he would still
back the Black. Bill said that he certainly would against
Tom's novice for fifty pounds a-side. The match was
made, and the fight fixed to come off on Tuesday, 24th
of July.

There does not appear to have been much interest
created over the affair, for not even an excursion into
the country was arranged, it having been decided to
fight at six o'clock in the morning, and the place selected
was Tothill Fields, Westminster, where it was hoped
that the little affair would be over before people were up.

It was a small crowd that gathered to watch the
battle, although there was a sprinkling of Corinthians
(no doubt present at Tom Cribb's instigation) who had
an up-all-nightish-look about them. The novice was a
young fellow from Bristol, named Burrows, a *protégé*
of Cribb's, and he was waited on by Tom himself and
his brother George, whilst the Black was attended by
Bill Richmond and Clarke. It looked at first a horse
to a gooseberry on the Englishman, for he was at least
three inches taller than Molyneux, and apparently a
heavier and stronger man. But the Black at once took
the lead both as a boxer and a wrestler, whilst his punishing powers were considerably superior. Burrows, however, must have been a game man, for he came up time
after time in a most determined manner, until sixty-five
minutes had expired, when, according to one account,
"there was not a feature of Burrows' face distinguish-

able. When the breath had been shaken out of his body and both his eyes closed, Cribb threw up the sponge, and Molyneux's first attempt on English soil had proved a victory. Opinions were much divided about the ability of the Virginian, but one gentleman present, Lord George Sackville, a younger brother of the Duke of Dorset, said that the Black was equal to anything on the list.

Indeed, so much did his lordship think of Molyneux, that he promised Richmond that if he could get a line for him, *i.e.*, another battle with a first-class man, he would with pleasure put up the money for the Black to fight for the Championship. Again there was a difficulty in selecting a man good enough to test the merits of Molyneux severely. To do this Cribb's list of former opponents was most carefully scanned. There was only one man worth attention, and he was Tom Blake, or "Tom Tough," as he was called, with whom Cribb had fought in 1805, it being his second contest in the ring. He was nearly forty years of age, but he had just returned from a two years' cruise, and was as hard as nails, with a constitution unimpaired, and splendidly preserved by his seafaring life.

The sailor boy was by no means unwilling to oblige Molyneux or anybody else apparently, for he had been at home long enough to squander all his "lashings" of prize money, and was literally without a shot in his locker. When he received Bill Richmond's invitation to fight for 100 guineas a-side, he went straight off to Tom Cribb and informed him that he was quite ready to oblige that gentleman, but was at the same time unable to find the money. The Champion, who was beginning to get curious about the Black, soon set his mind to rest, and promised that he would get the money put up, and a meeting having been convened at Bob Gregson's, the Castle, the match was made, and the day fixed for August 21.

Tothill Fields, which was the celebrated Caleb Baldwin's special domain, was quite out of the question this time, for several swells expressed their desire to be present. What an extraordinary place that must have been at the time, not only as a battle-field principally used by ambitious novices who were in hopes of being recognised by the Fancy; but it was there that bull-baiting, badger drawing, dog fights, dog races, ratting, sparring, fighting, and sports of all kinds, in the getting up of which Bill Gibbons and Caleb (known as the Westminster Champion) divided the reputation of being the most proficient masters of their time.

So Tothill Fields was no place for my lords and dukes.

Molyneux's second fight was therefore arranged to take place at Epple Bay, near Margate, and on a broiling hot day in August—the hottest of the year, it was said—without the slightest sea-breeze to temper the fierce rays of the sun, the men entered the ring, the Black revelling in the sunshine, while Tom Tough, so says the report, " literally mopped his head with his bandana."

To give details of the fight would be out of place here. The sailor fought magnificently, but the Black proved too much for him, and on several occasions bashed down his guard with the left and struck him full in the face with the right. Molyneux, it is said, seemed to have his tropical blood boiling with fury, and rushed on his man in a truly ferocious manner. One blow at the finish landed so heavily on his temple that he fell as if he had been shot, and Tom Cribb ordered the sponge to be thrown up in token of Blake's defeat.

It is said that the sailor, when he came to, was in a fearful state of mind; that he turned to the Champion and cried, "Tom, I don't mind being licked by you, but to think that I should have been beaten by that black thief!" Then Tom Cribb solaced him by replying that " Never mind, old fellow, I'll thrash him for you before you're much older. In the meanwhile Massa was going all over the place declaring that his next victory would make him Champion ; but Cribb took no notice of his idle boast, and looked down upon him with contempt.

Poor Tom Tough never fought again. He was shortly after stricken down with paralysis and was lodged in Greenwich Hospital, where he told his stories of fights by land and sea.

As might be imagined, Bill Richmond, after Molyneux's second victory, and the way in which he did it, thought his dream at last would be realised, and that the Champion's time had come. But Cribb, although he became very angry at the boasting of the nigger at the Horse and Dolphin, was not inclined to take the initiative; for, as we have said, he had recently got married and had invested his money in a small coal merchant's business, having determined not to enter the ring again. He was still Champion, because he had not formally retired, and there appeared to be nobody capable of taking the title away from him until the Black appeared upon the scene so mysteriously.

Quite half a century had passed away without a foreigner making a bid for the Championship, and it would have been strange, indeed, if it had fallen to a Black. Our readers will remember in our early records of the Ring we have spoken of Bob Whitaker, who beat the Venetian Gondolier, and of Jack Slack, who thrashed

the herculean Frenchman, Pettit. Then there was
Tom Juchan, the pavior, said to be a Swiss. He was
a good fighter, and had not Bill Darts defeated him,
his name might have figured amongst our champions.
Since then none but natives of the United Kingdom had
contended for the Belt, and nobody believed that it was
not from France, Germany, or Italy that formidable
rivals of the British bruiser would arrive, but from the
despised African negroes.

Bill Richmond (who, by the bye, was not a pure
negro) was the first man to show how apt with his fists
is a man of colour; but it was Tom Molyneux who made
us fully realise the fact that of all foreigners the
African negro is gifted by nature with qualities which
rendered him a formidable rival to the British prize-
fighter. We have since Molyneux had scores of dusky
gladiators, some of them comparable with our best
exponents, and whose names will be mentioned as our
history progresses; but Molyneux stands out boldly as
one of the best, if not the best, of all times.

But to return to our muttons. Within a month
of the second victory of the Black, Bill Richmond
induced Molyneux to throw down the gauntlet, and he
publicly challenged any man to fight him for the Championship.

This was too much for Tom Cribb, and he instantly
responded, accepting. But the details of the making
of the match and the battle itself, we must reserve for
another chapter.

CHAPTER IV.

A BLOT ON THE ESCUTCHEON.—TOM CRIBB AND TOM MOLY-

NEUX.—DISGRACEFUL BATTLE FOR THE BELT.

In our last we introduced the Black, Mr. Thomas
Molyneux, to our readers, who had come over from
" ole Virginny " with the heroic determination of
" whipping creation," and if possible matching himself
against the very best man in this country. This, as we
have told, he succeeded after no little difficulty in doing,
and the fight between the dusky one and Tom Cribb,
then Champion of England, was dated to come off on
the 18th of December, 1810.

Everybody was naturally much interested over this
novel match, although Cribb himself looked upon the
new comer as, and boldly asserted him to be, an "ebony
impostor." There was one absentee, however, whom
everybody would have liked to see upon the spot,
and that was Tom's backer and adherent, the genial
Captain Barclay. Two days after his great thousand
miles match, to which we have already referred, the
gallant Captain had started to join the ill-fated and
inglorious expedition to Walcheren, as aide-de-camp to
the Marquis of Huntly. Seldom, if ever, has a more
formidable expedition left Great Britain, and had it
been conducted with vigour and directed by skill, it
might have shaken the empire of Napoleon to its
foundations. But the Earl of Chatham, who was in
command, was an incompetent noodle. He kept the
troops, to the number of 40,000, manœuvring about on
the marshes of Walcheren, for no less a time than five
months, until 7,000 perished with fever and ague, whilst
more than half that survived were unfit for service.

Our old friend Captain Barclay, although he had, as
our readers will remember, an iron frame and constitution, was not proof against the effect of these swamps,

and when he returned his health was so shattered that he was glad to get away to Scotland in order to pull himself together, although the big fight that we are about to relate had a great attraction for him, and he did not relish the idea of deserting his favourite, Tom Cribb. However, Tom had plenty of aristocratic supporters, as we have already shown, and Bill Richmond, the brother Black, stood steadfastly by Molyneux.

Of the preliminaries we spoke in our last chapter, so we shall devote the best part of this to a description of the fight itself, which, although a blot upon the history of our Championships, must be told, for it was one of the most desperate, although unfair, battles fought in the roped arena. Indeed, there are few chapters in the history of the Prize Ring less creditable than that which records the heroic efforts of Thomas Molyneux, the Black, to gain the Championship of England, and we cannot help wondering where was the British manliness and fair play, the boast of the lovers of true sport. But we are anticipating; let us give an account of this disgraceful exhibition and its results.

It must not be forgotten that at this period a black man was not looked upon quite so much as a brother as at the present time, and he was shunned generally by most people. So, as the day drew near, the excitement increased, and it began to dawn upon those who followed the matter that actually a black man was making a bid for the Championship of England, and the awful thought suggested itself—supposing the dusky one should win? What a fearful disgrace it would be to England! Indeed, the talk in sporting circles was of nothing but the coming fight.

So that the Corinthians, who at that time affected Brighton a great deal, should be accommodated, the field of battle selected was Coptall Common, near East Grinstead, about half way between London and Brighton. Hundreds of swells poured into the towns close to the spot selected, and beds on the eve of the battle could not be had for love or money. Tom Cribb arrived on the previous day, and put up at the Crown, rooms having been taken by one of his backers, Lord Stradbroke, who was before this Sir John Rous, father of the Admiral of that ilk, the "Dictator of the Turf." Bill Richmond had provided rooms for Molyneux at the Dorset Arms.

The morning of Thursday, December 18, 1810, according to all accounts, was about as bad as it could be for a prize-fight, for the weather was windy and bitterly cold, whilst the rain came down in torrents, making the roads in a dreadful state, and the bye-lanes

leading to the common almost impassable. Still, the
weather appears not to have damped the ardour of the
sports, if it did their jackets, for the cry was " Still they
come " from all points of the compass, and the vehicular
attendance was enormous, whilst the number of spectators, when everything was arranged, was computed at
not less than 5,000.

Bill Gibbons, as usual, fitted up the arena, providing
a 24ft ring, and Mr. John Jackson, who superintended,
had the vehicles ranged round in a large circle some six
deep, leaving plenty of space for the pedestrians to take
up their position between the carriages and the outer
ring, the space at the other side of which, and close to
the arena, being liberally scattered with straw, was
reserved for the " nobs " who were willing to pay for
the luxury of a seat.

It is worth noting that there were no less than four
ex-Champions present, viz., Dan Mendoza, John Jackson, Jem Belcher, and John Gully, and the aristocratic
patrons of the Ring were too numerous to mention
here. Royalty, however, was conspicuous on this occasion by its absence, for neither of the Princes of the Blood
could with decency enter an appearance, for the Princess
Amelia had recently died, and the King was hopelessly
mad. It is asserted, however, that the Prince of Wales
sent his factotum, Jack Ratford, with instructions to
that worthy to note every detail of the battle, and at
once post off to his Highness when all was over with a
faithful account.

But to the fight. Molyneux is the first to make his
bow to those assembled, as at a quarter to twelve he
is driven up in a close carriage and, quickly striding
through the wet to the ring-side, he defiantly throws his
travelling-cap within the ropes. Immediately this is
done, Tom Cribb emerges from the inside of Lord Stradbroke's drag, and a loud cheer bursts forth from the five
thousand throats of the spectators, making a wonderful
contrast to the comparative silence with which the Black
was received.

Another shout rends the air as the two men eye each
other and shake hands before retiring to their corners
for the purpose of allowing their seconds to disrobe
them. In the Champion's corner are the familiar features
of John Gully and Joe Ward ; whilst, in that of the
Black, Bill Richmond and Paddington Jones are acting
as valets.

That fine old white-headed sportsman, Sir Thomas
Apreece, has been appointed referee, whilst the umpires
are Lord Archibald Hamilton and Colonel Barton. It
is exactly half-past twelve when Sir Thomas calls

CRIBB AND MOLYNEUX.
(From an old print.)

3

" Time," and at the word there is a silence around the
ring that is truly painful. Then both step steadily
towards each other, and each accepts the proffered hand
as a mark of courtesy before commencing this desperate
and bloody battle, which is to decide, not only who is to
be Champion of England, but Champion of the World.

Molyneux's ferocious look upon his unprepossessing
face is repulsive; yet there is a look of confidence in the
expression that undoubtedly proves that he means to do
or die. He is certainly a formidable warrior. His
height, we learn, is 5ft 8½in. His frame is obviously
powerful, and exceedingly muscular. His weight is
14st 3lb, or only one pound less than the Champion, who
is in height 2¼in taller, yet the Black looks the bigger
man.

" His arms," says one chronicler who was present,
" were of wondrous length and roundness of form."

Cribb, with that sturdy and solid calm, faces his
ebony antagonist with that dogged determination which
always characterised his battles. They both take stock
of one another, eying from head to foot, and commence
to open, the Black looking with a fiery glare, whilst
Cribb's eyes are immovable. For half a minute, which
appears like ten times as long, their eyes are fixed, the
slow movement of their arms alone tells that they are
animate.

Then suddenly a quick movement takes place as the
Black lets go the right and cleverly lands on the Champion's ribs. It is not a severe blow, and Cribb like
lightning counters with both hands upon the head, and
follows with a third upon the body. There is a look of
amazement upon the face of the Black, for he has been
informed that the Champion was slow at delivery. This,
however, undeceives him, and he is more cautious.
Creeping up to within distance, Molyneux closes and
encircles Tom with his long, black, snake-like arms.
But the sturdy West-countryman is as immovable as a
statue, and the Black, with his muscles standing out like
whip-cord in his endeavours to move him, fails, and
Cribb as quick as thought shifts his foot, gives him the
crook, and down he goes heavily, There is a tremendous
outburst of cheering for the Britisher, and the Black
has received a nasty taste of the Champion.

The excitement now is intense; but there is more to
come, for it is palpable that both men are intent upon
fighting, for they have warmed to their work. They
start in grand style, and fierce and furious is the rally
that opens the second round. It is now easy to see the
different styles of the men. Molyneux seems to beat
down his blows, and although they come with the force

of a sledge-hammer, they are more easily stopped, and those that do get there fall upon the thickest part of Tom's skull, and that has often been compared to granite. Tom's blows, on the other hand, are straight from the shoulder, and delivered with such force that they do far more execution. Yet these fearful deliveries seem to do little damage to the adamantine visage of the nigger, whose skin seems as hard as rhinoceros hide. The Black gains first blood by inflicting a cut over Tom's lip; but Cribb at once scores the second event, for he brings his fist with such force against Molyneux's head that he causes him to measure his full length on the earth.

Now the cheering for Cribb beggars description. Four to one on the Englishman is on offer all round the ring. But Cribb does not share the sanguine opinion of his supporters, it is evident, by regarding his serious visage. Without doubt he considers the herculean negro a tougher morsel than he bargained for, and he means to be very cautious. He, therefore, commences to fight on the retreat, much to the surprise of those who were laying the odds. The men have been fighting twenty minutes, and the Champion has really gained no advantage. Indeed, the courage and determination of Molyneux are beginning to be, if not appreciated, certainly dreaded, and again comes the question, "Should the Black win, after all!"

One thing is greatly in favour of the Champion. The cold rain is having an effect upon his antagonist, and he now and again has fits of shuddering, whilst the encouragement when he does succeed in getting home a blow is nothing. Cribb gets in two to one of the Black's blows, and the already ugly visage of the latter begins to assume hideous proportions; yet his heart is in the right place, and he strikes Tom down upon his knees round after round. The power and ferocity of the negro are undoubtedly tiring the Englishman out, and if Tom does not check him in some aggressive manner the belt may yet go to the man of colour. It is too dreadful to contemplate, yet there is an uneasiness about those assembled that tells plainly that there is great anxiety. So great an advantage does Molyneux gain in each succeeding round, and so painfully weak becomes the Champion, that at the close of the twenty-second round the tables are changed, and Bill Richmond yells out, "Four to one on Molyneux!"

But now let us take one of the graphic descriptions of the progress of the battle. Our chronicler says:— "Here was a startling state of affairs! Was the terrible Black, who had already completely upset all the calcula- tions of the knowing ones, going to win after all? It looked like it. Horrible, maddening as the thought was, there was no stifling it. The grim possibility stared them in the face. The extraordinary agitation of that vast concourse defies all attempt at description. Those who were seated on the roofs of the drags or the tops of the chaises rose to their feet trembling with excitement. Those who were on the ground stood on tip-toe and, with strained eyes and craned necks, tried with feverish anxiety to see what was going on in Cribb's corner. Then as soon as 'Time' was called (and even old Sir Thomas' voice faltered as he gave the summons, so agitated was he at the prospect of England's disgrace) the excitement ran high. The moment Cribb was lifted to his feet burst forth a cry that was almost pathetic in its earnestness, 'Now, Tom, now, for God's sake, don't let the nigger beat you. Go for him, Tom, go for him; Old England for ever.' "

It would appear, though, that Cribb needed no advice, for he was, although decidedly weak, the coolest man present on the field that day, and had never for a moment lost his head.

The Black, however, was furious at the prospect of success, and, encouraged by his brother negro, Bill Richmond, dashed in and rained blows that were terrible upon Cribb's bleeding face. In the twenty-eighth round Thomas Molyneux *fairly won the fight.* Tom Cribb could not come to time, and Sir Thomas Apreece allowed the half-minute to elapse, and summoned the men three times. Still Cribb could not come, and the Black awaited the award of victory, his just due, in the centre of the Ring. But during the excitement Joe Ward rushed across the ring to Bill Richmond, and accused him of having placed two bullets in the Black's fist. This was, of course, indignantly denied, and Molyneux was requested to open his hands, proving that nothing was there.

The ruse, however, succeeded, and gave Cribb the opportunity to come round. As they faced each other again the Champion dodged his man, and by good luck succeeded in knocking him down. The shouts were terrific, and Cribb's name was on every lip. Yet nobody was quite prepared for what was about to happen. The cold had at last taken serious effect upon the nigger. He was seized with violent shivering, and all at once he seemed to collapse. Cribb, seeing his opponent's condition, felt that now was his time, and pulling all his remaining strength together, dashed in at his foe, knocking him down. In the next round, however, the Black caught his man round the waist and threw him heavily, but in doing so pitched over him, and bringing his head in contact with one of the stakes, he lay there upon his back in a semi-stunned state.

When Molyneux was set up for the next round, he staggered, and could hardly lift his arms. Cribb struck him in the throat, and down he went again like a log of wood. The crowd with almost one voice shouted, "Cribb wins!" and as they faced each other again, before Tom could hit the Black he fell from sheer weakness. "Foul! foul!" was the frantic cry of the crowd. Before, however, the referee could be appealed to, Molyneux feebly lifted his hand and said to his second, "Massa Richmond, me can fight no more."

And so Tom Cribb was lucky enough to remain Champion of England; but a more unfairly fought battle for the Championship had never—up to that period, at any rate—been witnessed.

CHAPTER V.

A BIG NIGHT AT THE FIVES COURT.—MOLYNEUX AS A GAY LOTHARIO.—THE MATCH FOR THE SECOND BATTLE WITH CRIBB.

AFTER the great battle between the Black and the Champion described in the last chapter, there was a pause in matters pugilistic, and Tom Cribb had quite a life of inactivity. He had netted over the affair, however, a nice little sum, nearly a thousand pounds, and was of course the hero of the hour.

To add to the Champion's well-lined purse, too, a benefit at the Fives Court was arranged by some of the aristocratic patrons of the Ring. It is a curious fact that benefits are always organised for those who are not in need—the bigger the position the bigger the benefit—and no matter whether it be in the dramatic, sporting, or musical world it is invariably a question, to put it in vulgar but very expressive language, "greasing the fatted sow."

So on January 29, 1811, only six or seven weeks after
the Champion's victory over Molyneux, St. Martin
Street, Leicester Square, where the Fives Court was
situated, presented a most animated appearance. The
thoroughfare was blocked by a swearing, seething mass
of humanity struggling to get near to the entrance o'
the courts. Their struggles, pushing, and desperate
endeavours, however, to get near the entrance were in
vain, for inside the great sporting establishment the
people were packed like sardines in a box, the doors
were closed, and it would have been impossible to have
admitted another soul into the place.

Still the pushing and crushing continued, until the
mob got so noisy that it assumed the proportions of a
riot.

Here is an account of the delightful state of affairs:
" Blows were given and returned, heads were punched,
hats knocked over their wearers' eyes, and there seemed
every prospect of a free fight when suddenly a prolonged
burst of cheering from one section of the crowd
attracted the attention of all, and every eye was
directed to a window at some distance from the
ground opening from the building known far and wide
as the Fives Court. ' It's Cribb himself,' shouted a
hundred voices. ' He's going to speak. Silence!
Silence! Bravo, Tom!' There was no mistake
about it. Anybody who had once seen the Champion's
leonine but good-natured visage could see that it was he.
Presently silence was sufficiently restored for those near
to catch what he said. ' Gentlemen,' said Cribb, in his
suavest tones. ' I am very sorry for you; but I assure
you, upon my honour, that the court is full in every
part ; there's not even a foot of standing room left. I
am very grateful for this token of your good wishes to
me, and I only regret that the court is not twice the
size. But as it isn't, I hope you will go away quietly,
and I shall take it as a great personal favour if you
will do so ' This neat and diplomatic speech—prompted
by Mr. Paul Methuen, who stood behind Cribb unseen
by the crowd—had the desired effect. The mob gave
three cheers for Tom Cribb, and then began to dis-
perse as good humouredly as was compatible with the
disappointment they could not help feeling."

And now our readers will ask why all this exceptional
excitement? As we have said, it was Tom Cribb's
benefit, and there was to be a grand display, whilst it
was announced that the Champion would declare
whether he intended to meet Molyneux a second time or
retire from the Ring. That was quite enough to create
the extraordinary interest ; but it was also rumoured

that Bob Gregson would bring forth his big Lancashire lad, about whom so much had been talked. Then there was to be a set-to between the Champion and Tom Belcher, between Dan Dogherty and George Silverthorne (who had fought a desperate battle a few weeks before), and Molyneux and Bill Richmond were to spar together.

We are told that never since it had been built had the Fives Court seen such a company, "dukes, marquises, earls, right honourables, and Members of Parliament were massed together shoulder to shoulder. Upwards of 3,000 persons paid for admission." The excitement reached its height when Cribb stepped upon the platform to return thanks for the manner in which his patrons had so generously supported him, for everybody was burning to know what his intentions were in respect to the future.

The Champion briefly explained his position. He said that he accepted Molyneux's challenge — (loud cheers)—but declined to fight for a smaller stake than 500 guineas — *i.e.*, 250 a-side. Molyneux was not prepared to put down such a sum at once, so the understanding was that the match was to remain open for twelve months, Cribb pledging himself to fight the black at any time within that period, providing the sum stipulated was forthcoming. This statement did not give universal satisfaction, for many thought that the champion had no right to fix the amount at so high a figure, and when Molyneux appeared on the stage in company with his mentor, Bill Richmond, he received quite an ovation. The latter explained that although his man for the moment could not find the money, he had little doubt that it would be forthcoming within the twelve months, for his man had determined to have a second turn with the champion. In the meanwhile Molyneux was open to fight anybody breathing for £100 a-side.

Now Bob Gregson had brought his novice to Cribb's benefit purposely to get him matched, and had openly stated that he was prepared to back him against anybody bar three men. So anxious inquiries went round as to who the three were—whether Molyneux was included. Bob Gregson explained that the three men who were barred were Tom Cribb, John Gully, and himself. So it was arranged that on the following morning the men should meet at Bob's coffee house, in Holborn, and articles should be drawn up.

Gregson at this time had become very popular, and the tavern which he kept, afterwards known as the Castle and now as the Napier, was the most celebrated

rendezvous amongst sportsmen in London. Besides
Bob himself was a great favourite, and, amongst other
accomplishments, he could rattle off verses by the yard.
He was, in fact, called the "Laureate of the Ring."
Tom Moore in his satirical verses entitled "Tom Cribb's
Memorial to Congress," thus refers ironically to
Gregson's pugilistic laureateship :—

> A pause ensued, till cries of Gregson
> Brought Bob, the poet, on his legs soon.
> My eyes, how prettily Bob writes !
> Talk of your camels, hogs, and crabs,
> And twenty more such Pidcock frights,
> Bob's worth a hundred of these dabs :
> For a short turn up at a sonnet,
> A round of odes or pastoral bout ;
> All Lombard Street to ninepence on it
> Bob's the boy would clean them out.

We have before us now some of Bob Gregson's verses,
but we do not think they are worth quoting. Nevertheless if he was a failure as a pugilist, and as a poet, Bob
was a decided success as a host, and at the celebrated
tavern in Holborn all the nobs patronised him, and on
the day following Cribb's benefit the house was crowded.
About noon Molyneux and Bill Richmond appeared and
were introduced to Gregson's novice. His name was
Heskin Rimmer, a Lancashire lad, who had "coom oop
t' Lunnon " to seek his fortune in the prize ring, having
vanquished all comers in the North. He was a
big, strapping chap, and Bob Gregson had great faith
in him.

Although it was quite early, there were many swells
who had dropped in after their exercise with the foils
or gloves at John Jackson's in Bond-street, and amongst
those present we read were the Marquis of Tweeddale
(an old backer of Gregson's when he fought Gully), and
Lieutenant Wedderburn Webster. Everything looked
like plain sailing until it came to a question as to the
amount cf the stakes, when Gregson thought fifty
guineas quite enough for his *protégé* to start with.
Richmond, however, would not hear of anything less
than double that amount. It was pointed out that
Rimmer was a novice, to which Bill retorted that
Molyneux was *not*, and that if he were good enough to
fight Cribb for the championship and 250 guineas a-side,
he was too good to fight anybody else for less than one
hundred guineas a-side. The Marquis of Tweeddale
remarked that he was a beaten man, and that put him
on a level with the novice. This could not be accepted
by the black party, so negotiations were broken off.

We have gone into this matter, because it proves how

at this particular period prize fighting had lost favour with the sports of the period. Where was the old liberality of the Ring? How was it that there was this tightening of purse-strings? Time was not so long since when, as our readers will remember, the sinews of war were always forthcoming to any amount, and wealthy sports did not grudge fifty or a hundred pounds to bring off a good match. Here are a few of the big amounts netted in the Prize Ring: Tom Johnson made £5,000 over his victory over Perrins; Mendoza cleared £1,000 by his last battle with Humphries; Tom Cribb, as we have already stated, made £900 out of his triumph over Molyneux, yet for the Black himself they found it impossible to raise a single hundred.

It was argued that the reason for the patrons of the Prize Ring being less generous was because money was tight. The prolonged strain and drain of the war with France, the injuries done to our commerce by French privateers, and the general rise in the price of all necessaries of life, made even wealthy men look closer at a guinea before they parted with it than they had been wont to do. So the Prize Ring languished, and its enemies rejoiced.

However, on April 2, Molyneux became sufficiently appreciated to have given him a benefit at the Fives Court, and about a thousand spectators attended. The Black had a set-to with Isaac Bittoon, Tom Belcher, and Ben Burn. The *Morning Chronicle* of the following day, referring to Molyneux's exhibition, and the above-named pugilist says "none were able to make any impression on him." "Gregson's Lancashire man hits with power, and showed some courage and strength. In fact, Rimmer so pleased his friends that they took heart of grace, and backed him that same evening to fight Molyneux for a hundred guineas a-side within a month, the stakes to be put down at Bill Richmond's on Wednesday, April 17."

The latter took Molyneux away immediately after the match was ratified on a touring expedition through the Midlands, and, to quote the *Chronicle*, once more, returned to London "laden with treasure," from which we may infer the business they did was exceptionally good. Tuesday, May 21, was the day fixed for the fight, and the Black went into Kent to train. Then came an extraordinary paragraph in the above-named sporting paper—"Molyneux is to receive the hand of a fair young captivating widow in Kent on Sunday next."

This startling announcement bewildered the Fancy. How could any man who was to fight within a few

weeks be mad enough to commence his training by
marriage? A honeymoon would be a nice preparation
indeed for a prize-fight! Anyhow it turned out to be a
fact that a buxom widow at Lee, near Blackheath,
really had taken such a fancy to his ugly black visage,
or perhaps his athletic ebony physique, to yield to his
embraces, and would have wedded him had not two of
her brothers taken her off by force.

The match (we mean that between Rimmer and
Molynenx, not with the widow) created great interest,
for we read in the daily papers on the day before the
fight—which was, as we have said, May 21, 1811—the
following paragraph:—

"MOLYNEUX AND RIMMER.—This *inviting* fight on this
inviting day is likely to afford more *hard-hitting* than
any match in the annals of pugilism. Independent of
the large stakes between the *amateurs of milling*, a purse
has been made in the City to present the victor with as
many quarters of lottery tickets as they may fight
rounds. This will produce a severe contest to obtain a
quarter each of the sixty capitals of £20,000, &c., &c., to
be all drawn for on Tuesday, the 4th of June, the birth-
day of our beloved Sovereign."

The battle, the details of which, not being a Championship fight, has no place here, came off at Moulsey
Hurst, and resulted in a brilliant victory for Molyneux,
although foul play was again attempted, so that the
Black should be robbed of his deserts, as was done in
his fight with Cribb. The ring was broken into by
Rimmer's friends, and was not cleared for at least
twenty minutes, giving the white man time to recover if
he could. But there was little fight in him after this,
and, although they contested six more rounds, Bob
Gregson had ultimately to give in for his *protégé*.

After this there was no getting away from the fact
that the Black had proved himself a formidable antagonist to any man in England, and nobody dared take up
the gauntlet that he immediately threw down. Tom
Cribb, it seems, had thought better of his promise to try
conclusions again with the ebony one, to fight him within
the year. He had got married and settled down as a
coal merchant, and hesitated to risk his reputation and
upset his business by entering the Ring again. However, strong pressure was brought to bear upon him,
and he yielded rather than let the Championship of
England pass into the possession of a foreigner, and he
a coloured man. Tom, however, insisted that, to com-
pensate him for loss in business, the stakes should be
increased to 300 guineas.

This was agreed to, and a meeting was convened to

take place at the house of Bill Richmond, the Hare and Dolphin, in St. Martin's Lane, to settle the details. There must have been a most representative company present on that memorable occasion, for we read that amongst the distinguished patrons of the Ring were Sir Henry Smyth, Mr. Thirlwell Harrison, the Hon. Berkeley Craven, Lord Yarmouth, Lord Pomfret, the Marquis of Queensberry, Captain Barclay, Sir Clement Brigg, Mr. Paul Methuen, the Earl of Sefton, Sir Bellingham Graham, Lord Barrymore, Sir Francis Baynton, General Grosvenor, Lord Archibald Hamilton, General Barton, and many other well-known sportsmen. Most of these gentlemen were up for the Ascot races, but their presence at the Hare and Dolphin proved conclusively that the Ring had not lost its patrons, and that although there had been a lull in matters pugilistic, interest was reviving with the coming great fight.

The meeting is very fully reported in the journals of the day, but it will not be necessary to give full details of the discussion. Suffice it to say that John Jackson was voted to the chair, and he stated that the arrangement was that Thomas Cribb and Thomas Molyneux should fight, for 300 guineas a-side, upon a wooden stage 25ft square, at some spot hereinafter to be named on the North Road, not less than 100 miles from London, on September 28, 1811; that each man should be on the stage punctually at twelve o'clock; that half-minute time should be strictly observed except when either man was hit off the stage, in which case a minute should be allowed. That 100 guineas a-side should be staked with Mr. John Jackson that evening, and the remainder be made good on July 27.

These terms were put into writing, when Cribb affixed his signature, whilst Molyneux put his mark to the articles. Then Captain Barclay placed 100 guineas upon the table, and Bill Richmond covered the same for the Black. So at last the great match which had taken so long to arrange was made—a match which was to create greater excitement and interest perhaps than any since the time of Figg down to the great international encounter between Tom Sayers and Heenan in later years.

At first there was little betting, for the Bill Richmond school were not overburdened with cash; indeed, they had raised the hundred guinea deposit by means of a loan, Bill being joint security with a Mr. Scholefield, a fishmonger in Bond Street. To find the balance and repay the loan the party looked forward to a successful tour through the country with Molyneux, which Richmond had arranged for his protégé.

As time went on, however, the wagering became exceedingly heavy, for some of the swells who had seen the stubborn stand which the Black had made with the Champion at their first meeting fancied that, given fair play (which was certain on the coming occasion), might turn the tables. It is stated in a paragraph which appeared in the *Morning Chronicle* of July 31 that upwards of £50,000 was at that time wagered on the result of the great battle, which was significant proof that public opinion had changed since the first fight. Many remembered too, that at one time during the battle on the 19th of the previous December at Copthall Common, the odds were 4 to 1 on the Black, and that as a matter of fact he really won the fight.

But of the progress made by the men in training, and the details of the great contest, we must reserve for another chapter.

CHAPTER VI.

CAPTAIN BARCLAY'S NOTES ON TRAINING.—THE BLACK IN BAD HANDS.—TOM CRIBB AND MOLYNEUX. — THEIR SECOND DESPERATE BATTLE FOR SIX HUNDRED POUNDS.

ALL having been satisfactorily arranged for the second meeting between the great gladiators, as described in our previous chapter, Captain Barclay, Cribb's principal backer, who had stuck to the champion through thick and thin, proceeded to put Tom through his preparation. The gallant Captain who, it will be remembered, was a great athlete and the most extraordinary pedestrian of his time, had peculiar ideas as to training. That his method was successful nobody can deny; but the kind of work he put himself through and all those under his charge was, to say the least of it, severe, and would be quite contradictory to the system adopted at the present time. The Captain and his charge, we read, left London on the 2nd of July, and travelled by easy stages to Ury, Barclay's ancestral seat in Aberdeenshire. Arrived there, he commenced operations upon his man at once. So extraordinary was the treatment that perhaps it will be better to quote the celebrated pedestrian's own words as to the method adopted :

"Cribb," he says, "weighed upwards of 16st on his arrival at Ury, and from his mode of living in London, and the confinement of a crowded city, he had become corpulent, big-bellied, full of gross humours, and short-breathed, and it was with difficulty that he could walk ten miles. He first went through a course of physic, which consisted of four doses; but for two weeks he walked about as he pleased, and generally traversed the woods and plantations with a fowling-piece in his hand; the reports of his gun resounded everywhere through the groves and hollows of that delightful place, to the great terror of the magpies and the woodpigeon.

"After amusing himself in this way for about a fortnight, he then commenced his regular walking exercise, which at first was about ten or twelve miles a day. It was soon after increased to eighteen or twenty, and he ran regularly, morning and evening, a quarter of a mile at the top of his speed. In consequence of his physic and exercise, his weight was reduced in the course of five weeks from 16st to 14st 9lb. At this period he commenced his sweats, and took three during the month he remained at Ury afterwards; and his weight was gradually reduced to 13st 5lb, which was ascertained to be his pitch of condition, as he would not reduce further without weakening. During the course of his training the Champion went twice to the Highlands and took strong exercise. He walked to Mar Lodge, which is about sixty miles from Ury, where he arrived at dinner on the second day, being now able to go thirty miles a day with ease, and probably he could have walked twice as far if it had been necessary.

"He remained in the Highlands about a week each time, and amused himself with shooting. The principal advantage which he derived from these expeditions was the severe exercise he was obliged to undergo. He improved more in strength and wind by these journeys in the Highlands than by any other part of the training process.

"Cribb was altogether about eleven weeks under training, but he remained only nine weeks at Ury. Besides his regular exercise, he was occasionally employed in sparring at Stonehaven, where he gave lessons in the pugilistic art. He was not allowed much rest, but was constantly occupied in some active employment. He enjoyed good spirits, being at that time fully convinced that he should beat his antagonist."

It would seem then that Master Thomas Cribb had a
"high old time" with his patron, Captain Barclay, and
we may be sure that the victualling department was on
the very best model, although the Captain does not tell
us whether he allowed his protégé wine or whisky.
Cribb, however, on his return stated that he was made
to follow the plough, and fill a dung-cart; in fact, do
regular farm labourers' work. Indeed, the champion is
said to have stated more than once that he would
sooner have fought Molyneux twice over than have gone
through such a terrible course of training again. Anyhow, his patron got him into splendid condition, and
when he came back to London he was as hard as
nails.

Poor Molyneux, however, had no such opportunity of
preparation. As we have stated, he had to combine
business with training in order to get the money
together to pay off the loans he had contracted in
order to get his stake money together. He, Bill Richmond, and Tom Belcher went round the country giving
exhibitions of sparring. So general was the excitement
over the fight, though, that crowds came to see the
Black, and their tour was eminently successful, Bill
Richmond raking in considerably more money than
was necessary to pay back what he had borrowed.
Speaking of their exhibitions at York, the *Morning
Chronicle* says:—"They were unable to satisfy the
public appetite, although they gave exhibitions of
sparring three or four times a day; yet the
room in which they exhibited was insufficient
to accommodate the people who flocked into
the city from all parts of the country." So exceedingly
lucrative was this touring that Bill Richmond appears
to have lost his head, and thought a good deal more
about making money out of the business than training
his man for the greatest event of his life. To keep the
Black going and in a good temper his patron was
obliged to indulge him in all his whims and passions.
These were many, for Molyneux felt that he was so
strong that nothing on earth could affect his constitution.

It is true that Bill Richmond stopped the touring business about a fortnight before the battle, and took his man
to Hayes, near Hillingham Heath, and gave him
some hard work, whilst he knocked off his dissipations.
But it was too late to get the Black into proper condition. Yet everybody who saw him was struck with
his marvellous physique and tremendous hitting power,
and he found many supporters. The betting was 2 to 1
on Cribb (as quoted at Tattersall's), evens that the fight

lasted over three-quarters of an hour, and 6 to 4 that Cribb gave the first knock-down blow.

The Champion won the toss for the privilege of naming the place, and Lincolnshire was selected, but not until after a deal of wrangling, which at one time threatened to knock the whole business on the head. On the 23rd of September Cribb left Easingwold, in Yorkshire, to which little town he had walked with Captain Barclay from Ury, and journeyed on to Sleaford, in Lincolnshire, making the Red Lion his headquarters. On the same day Molyneux arrived at Grantham, and put up at the Royal Oak.

Directly it became known in what locality the battle was to take place there was such a rush on the Northern road for hotel accommodation that had never been known before. The spot finally selected was Thiselton Gap, in the parish of Wymondham, in the county of Leicester, eight miles from Grantham, and close to Crown Point, where the three counties of Leicester, Lincolnshire, and Rutland meet. To make things as safe as possible a stubble field had been engaged from a farmer, who charged the rather high figure of £50. There is a story told that when they came to fit up the stage the old farmer declined to let them do so until he got his money. Captain Barclay handed him a cheque, but the old chap shook his head and refused the piece of worthless paper, and it was not until Mr. George Marriot, of Melton, whom he knew, put his name to the cheque that the wary old agriculturist would permit them to proceed.

On the Saturday, September 28, 1811, around that platform was gathered one of the greatest and most distinguished crowds that ever witnessed a prize fight. We have no space for the names of the noblemen and famous sports who were present. It must have been a wonderful sight. This is how an eye witness describes the scene:—" The stage, which was twenty-five feet square, was erected in a stubble field, surrounded first by a roped ring in order to prevent any interruption by the crowd, and, secondly, by as well-framed, and supported a circle of pedestrians as were, perhaps, ever witnessed, notwithstanding the great distance from the metropolis. The first row of these, as usual upon most occasions lying down, the second kneeling, and the rest standing up. Outside these again were numerous horsemen, some seated, while others more eager stood circus-like on their saddles. These were intermixed with every description of carriage, gig, barouche, buggy, cart, and waggon. The display of sporting men, from the peer on the box of the

four-in-hand to the rustic in clouted shoes, made as
perfect a picture as the Fancy can well conceive.
Every fighting man of note, every pugilistic amateur,
was to be seen there."

Dick Christian, the celebrated huntsman of the
Quorn, was present, and he must have been conspicuous
as one of the "circus-like horsemen," for he has
written of that memorable day :—" I was on horseback
—a mare of my own. (I gave Mr. Harper eighty pounds
for her) not ten yards off them. I was crowded in, and
I drawed my legs up and stood on top of the saddle all
the time they were fighting. I'd hard work to get them
down again."

But let us in fancy stand beside the ring. What
excitement and enthusiasm there is at exactly twelve
o'clock. Tom Cribb steps upon the stage, accompanied
by his friend John Gully and Joe Ward. How they
cheer the Champion. What must the feelings of the
Black be as he also mounts the platform? There is no
encouragement for him. He is received almost in silence.
But Bill Richmond and Bill Gibbons, who accompany
him, whisper some cheery words, and he forces
a smile to his dusky face, and his white teeth flash in
the sunlight. Mr. John Jackson, all smiles, and with a
word for everybody, is appointed referee, and the
colours are tied to the ropes, Tom Cribb sporting the
old blue bird's'eye, and the Black's fogle being crimson
and orange.

It is exactly eighteen minutes past twelve when Mr.
John Jackson gives the word to begin, and as they stand
before us there is a fine opportunity of casting the critic's
eye over them. Never has Tom Cribb looked in such
magnificent condition. The Captain has done his work
admirably, and no mistake. He is trained to the ounce.
We are told that his precise weight is 13st 6lb, which is
quite a stone less than when he last fought Molyneux,
whilst his height is 5ft 10½in. Every muscle stands out
upon his powerful frame as if carved in ivory, and his
white polished skin flashes under the sun.

But look at Molyneux. What a contrast! He is as
gross as a man could well be who had taken no exercise
for months, and the fat hangs about his back and belly
in rolls. We hear, too, on the best authority, that Bill
Richmond has even allowed him that morning only a few
hours ago to devour a boiled chicken and an apple pie,
which he has insisted upon washing down with half a
gallon of porter. If this be true, what a poor chance
he must have with the mighty Cribb, who is a picture
of perfect manhood in the pink of condition.

They waste little time in sparring, for it is evident

that the Black intends to bid for an early victory or reverse, for to the astonishment of all he rushes with such fury and determination at the Champion, that Tom has difficulty in avoiding the blows that are swinging in at his face. As cool as ever with that calmness and self possession which has characterised all his encounters throughout, he keeps the attack off and then planting a blow full on the throat, down goes Molyneux with a thud upon the wooden floor.

There is a very serious expression upon the Champion's face as he comes up to renew the contest, and he frowns as Bill Richmond rushes across the ring and claims for his man first blood. It is perfectly true, the crimson fluid is running from the corner of Cribb's mouth, for one of the random hits of the Black has struck him sharply, and his lips are cut. Adopting the same tactics, Molyneux again dashes in with terrific fury, and a tremendous rally is the result. The champion is playing for the body, and is evidently taking advantage of the Black's want of condition, so that he shall be winded while the latter is making for a knock-out blow at the head. Crack goes one on Tom's face, and a lump the size of an egg is raised upon Cribb's cheek. They come together and grip, and a tremendous struggle ensues. The Black, however, proves stronger than his opponent, and Tom is thrown violently upon the boards. There is a silence around which is only broken by a shout here and there to lay the shortened odds of 6 to 4.

Then a murmur goes through the multitude as Cribb comes up for the third round, for it is obvious that one eye is all but closed, whilst blood is trickling from nose and mouth. The Black, on the other hand, shows not the slightest mark; but his chest is heaving, and it is palpable that the exertion and want of condition is beginning to tell. Yet his determination is so great that he once more dashes in, and a fiercer rally than ever takes place, Cribb directing his attention still to the body, Molyneux to the head. At length they close, and again the Black hugs his man, and throws him to the ground with great violence. Now the hoots and shrieks of the crowd are diabolical. They are cursing the Black and using such language that Bill Richmond is evidently anxious, and feels that so strong is the opinion against his man that they would sooner smash up the stage than let this Black beat the Champion. It is disgraceful on the part of some of those present; but the feeling is so much in favour of the Champion that reason and fairplay seem to have deserted them.

Captain Barclay is very anxious, for he leaves his

carriage, and going to Cribb's corner, implores him to alter his tactics and fight on the defensive. John Gully lances Tom's eye, and he is again sent up to meet his dusky ferocious foeman. Cribb, however, does not think it yet time to take the captain's advice, for he meets his man, and again a rally ensues. Molyneux is so successful with the left that he plants blow after blow upon Tom's face. Both the Champion's eyes are now damaged, and he is bleeding profusely. But Molyneux is evidently in great distress, for his chest and sides are heaving heavily. Cribb smiles at such a favourable omen, and renews the rally with a heroism perhaps never excelled. Every blow is by him now most adroitly timed. Hits in abundance are exchanged, Cribb still fighting at the " mark " and the Black at the head. This Black is a terrible fighter. What would he be had he been properly trained and could boast the condition of the Champion? He must have carried all before him. Even now he takes the lead, and his hitting is terrific. There is that same feeling going around the ring that existed during the first fight—Could it be possible that the foreigner was going to win after all? He doesn't seem to mind the punches he receives on the body, and he certainly gets the best of the exchanges. The Champion reels before his fearful blows, and one of them on the side of the head sends him over. As he falls, Molyneux hits him again in the face, and he goes heavily to the floor. There are loud cries of "Foul! Foul!" but the hit was perfectly legitimate, and the umpires agree that they must fight on.

Now at length it is seen that Molyneux's want of training is showing itself. Truly he has shot his bolt. His wind has almost gone. He is cowed too by the treatment he is receiving, and by the language of the mob that is against him. Still with the ferocity begot by despair he makes another desperate rush. Cribb now adopts Captain Barclay's advice, and fights on the retreat. Drawing his adversary to within distance, Tom now jobbs him mercilessly in the face until the Black gets frantic with rage, and seems for the moment almost paralysed. He has lost all control over himself. He again rushes in and swings his arms about like flails. Tom waits his opportunity and delivers the left full on the throat, and down goes Molyneux.

In the eighth round Cribb gets the Black's head in chancery and fibbs him terribly before he releases him. The spectators shriek with delight. The Black is dead beat, yet, with expiring strength, he makes a tremendous rush; but Cribb meets him with a fearful blow, the

power of which is doubly increased in force by the
Black's impetuous advance.   There is a noise as the
crack of a whip, and Molyneux falls upon the boards
like a log of wood. *His jaw is broken.* Still, the plucky
fellow comes up to the scratch again, but only to be
more punished, and at length staggers back and falls
helplessly beaten.

Thus fell the mighty Black. In less than twenty
minutes he was defeated. Everybody was surprised
that the battle should have lasted so short a time,
especially as Molyneux showed equal science and
infinitely greater strength than the Champion in the
first few rounds.   It was his want of condition which
lost him the battle, and Bill Richmond was more to
blame than anybody concerned.

The poor fellow, with bruised body and fractured jaw,
was carried almost in a senseless state to a carriage, and
driven to the Royal Oak, Grantham, where medical aid
was sought.   Tom Cribb, who was very much distressed,
although not so seriously injured, was taken by Captain
Barclay to the Red Lion, Sleaford, and put to bed,
where we will leave him until we re-introduce him to
our readers in the next chapter.

CHAPTER VII.

GREAT MEETING AT BOB GREGSON'S.—PRESENTATION OF THE
CUP.—LAST OF TOM CRIBB.—HIS MONUMENT AT WOOLWICH.

After the great battle at Thistleton Gap, which we
described in the last chapter, the excitement amongst
the 20,000 people present was intense. That the heroic
Black should have been beaten in so short a time
was astounding. Nevertheless, if the contest had been
disappointing, there was no doubt about the interest of
it whilst it lasted. Even Captain Barclay, who had the
most implicit confidence in Tom Cribb, trembled once
or twice as to the result.

On the following day, Sunday, September 29, 1811, Tom Cribb left the Red Lion in a carriage drawn by four horses decorated with the Champion's colours, and proceeded through Grantham, in company with his patron, Captain Barclay, and old Joe Ward. The reception they met with beggars description. They called at the Royal Oak, where they found poor Molyneux in bed, suffering fearfully from the injury to his jaw and bruises upon the body. He was unable to speak, but his glance of pleasure as he took his opponent's hand and listened to some words of kindness and sympathy spoke volumes.

Next day they arrived in town, and there another great ovation awaited them. The news of their approach had fled like wildfire, and all along St. Martin's Lane to Great St. Andrew's Street, Seven Dials, where the Champion lived, the crowd was enormous and the cheering tremendous. So thick were they that it was with difficulty the carriage could pass along. At length Cribb got to his door, where his smiling wife received him. For days afterwards, whenever he went out a cheering mob followed him, and he was certainly the hero of the hour. But he received more substantial tokens of regard, for the whole of the battle-money (600 guineas) was presented to him, together with more than 400 in bets and presents. Captain Barclay won no less a sum than £10,000, whilst Cribb's old master, Mr. Sant, the coal merchant, and brother to the well-known brewer of Wandsworth, netted over £2,000. Tom's father-in-law, who carried on business as a baker in the Borough, staked everything he possessed on the result, even mortgaged the lease of his house, raking together £1,500, all of which went on his son-in-law at an average of 3 to 1. Amongst other bets, Bob Gregson won a curious wager. It was a complete suit of clothes, shirt, cravat, &c., with a walking-stick, gloves, and a guinea in every pocket.

Naturally a banquet was given in honour of the victory of the Champion, and this was held at Bob's Chop House, in Holborn, where all the swell sports attended. In order to show how slangy some of the reports of those affairs were, we will quote the *Morning Chronicle* account, which appeared the next day:—

"A MILLING GRUBBING MATCH.—Tom Cribb having promised his friend Bob a turn, he took the chair at Gregson's at a *game* dinner on Monday evening (Oct. 7, 1811), surrounded by threescore as *prime swell coves* as any in the milling Fancy. After a sumptuous *twisting match*, and the usual loyal toasts had been given, the chairman was *officed* for a *chaunt;* but not possessing

vocal abilities, it was *stowed*, and a *sw.ll* delighted the
company in the Champion's stead. A toast was next
given: 'Tom Cribb, the Champion of England, who
has nobly and successfully competed for the laurels of
native championship against a Moor in a main.' Three
times three. Here the Champion made his *début* as an
orator, and after *lushing* a bit by way of clearing the
pipes, he gave a bit of a stave about his principles, in
rhetoric more *energetic* than *elegant*. At times he *wanted
words* to express himself; but he disdained to *cut* it,
and in his *classic* style confounded his auditory. his
language at times being unintelligible from the desire
of rapid delivery, even to the compiler of Harding's
'Slang Dictionary,' or Walker's English. The speech
was received with unbounded applause, bravos, &c."

Then the account goes on to say that "the Champion
give the health of his friend Gully, after that of Captain
Barclay had been drunk. Bob Gregson tipped his
customers a *rum chaunt* about the mill, and proposed
the health of Mr. John Jackson, which was uproariously
drunk with three times three. Another *chaunt*, which
was penned on the morning previous to the dinner, was
professionally sung rumpty; and the following toast
was proposed with three times three, and enthusiastically drunk: 'Sir Harry Smyth, Thirlwall Harrison,
Esq., and the patrician band who nobly support British
pugilism.'"

The following are the words of the song composed by
Bob Gregson, and sung after the dinner to the air of
"Jolly Young Waterman:"

Pray, haven't you heard of a jolly young coalheaver,
  Who over at Hungerford used for to ply,
His mawleys he used with such skill and dexterity,
  Winning each mill, sir, and blacking each eye.
    He sparred so neat and he fought so steadily,
    He hit so straight and he won so readily,
And now he's a coal-merchant, why should he care
  Tho' his dealings are black, yet his actions are fair?

To mention the time that he won by hard milling,
  'Tis useless to tell unto anyone here;
For tho' no Adonis, he's very nigh killing,
  His arguments have such an *effect* on the *ear*.
    He hit half round and he fought so steadily,
    He milled away and won so readily,
Then why should this coal-merchant ever know care,
Tho' his dealings are black, his actions are fair.

A cove in the black line, he showed opposition,
  So Tommy determined to give him a turn;
And Molyneux made him a bold proposition,

But since he has found that his coal wouldn't burn.
For he sparred so neat and fought so steadily,
He hit so straight and won so readily,
Then why should this coal-merchant ever know care,
When he's Champion of England, and now fills the chair.

Our reporter goes on to say : " Several good songs were
sung, followed by toasts, and bumpers had so often gone
round that *Mr. Maltby* was getting on board, but *Sir
Oliver's* resplendence conducted the company home
before twelve in good order. The evening was spent
with the utmost conviviality. The Champion will take
the chair again some time next week, to receive a subscription tankard adorned with emblems of his victories,
which has been set on foot by Gregson, and which has
been most liberally subscribed to."

By the above account this meeting must have been a
rare jollification; but to read the particulars of the
dinner given on the 11th of December of the same year,
for the purpose of presenting Cribb with the eighty-
guinea silver cup, the latter must have excelled it both
in attendance and conviviality. The chair was taken on
this occasion by the celebrated actor, John Emery, of
Covent Garden Theatre, who was one of the most
brilliant men of his time. Not only was he a fine
actor, but his paintings hung on the walls of the Royal
Academy, and he wrote and composed many excellent
songs, which he sang with a good tenor voice. Besides
all these accomplishments, John Emery was an
enthusiast in sporting matters, especially driving
four-in-hand. Without going into the particulars of
this meeting at Gregson's, we must have something to
say about the presentation, for Tom Cribb valued the
cup more than any of his other trophies.

After dinner the chairman proposed the health of
Tom Cribb, the Champion of England, and delivered the
following address:—

" Thomas Cribb,—I have the honour this day of
being the representative of a numerous and most
respectable body of your friends, and though I am by no
means qualified to attempt the undertaking that has
devolved upon me by a vote of the subscribers, yet the
cause will, I am confident, prove a sufficient excuse for
my want of ability. You are requested to accept this
cup as a tribute of respect for the uniform valour and
integrity you have shown in your several combats, but
most particularly for the additional proof of native
skill and manly intrepidity displayed by you in your
last battle, when the cause rested not merely upon individual fame, but for the pugilistic reputation of your
native country, in contending with a formidable foreign

antagonist. In that combat you gave proof that the innovating hand of a foreigner when lifted against a son of Britannia must not only be aided by the strength of a lion but the heart also. The fame you have so well earned has been by manly and upright conduct, and such conduct, I have no doubt, will ever mark your very creditable retirement from the Ring or stage of pugilism. However intoxicated the cup or its contents may at any future period make you, I am sufficiently persuaded the gentlemen present, and the sons of John Bull in general, will never consider you have a *cup* too much."

By the above it will be seen that Tom Cribb had determined upon retirement from the Ring. True, his battles had been few, but the two last with Molyneux proved him to be a man of exceptional mettle, and with a heart, as Mr. Emery inferred, as big as a lion's. That his earlier battles were between men of second-class we are prepared to admit, and that he had not the science of a Jem Belcher goes without saying. Yet we think that some of his eminent critics were somewhat captious, and feel that they went a little too far in their condemnation of the Champion.

Professor John Wilson, " Christopher North," one of the finest all-round athletes and judges, besides one of the most eminent writers of the period, sums Cribb up in the following manner :—" I'm no enemy of Cribb's; but lives there a man so base as to say that he has not been indebted more to fortune than to bravery and skill in all his battles? Was he not fast losing his first fight with Jem Belcher when that finished pugilist's hands gave way? Was not the Monops (one-eyed) out of condition in the second contest? When Gregson by a chance fall could not come to time, Cribb was dead beaten, and ' Bob of Wigan, Ring-honoured Lancaster,' was comparatively fresh and able to renew the combat? What Briton will dare to say that Molyneux did not win the first battle with the Champion? It seemed otherwise to the umpires; but neither Europe nor America was to be so satisfied, and as my friend Leigh Hunt has lately expressed a wish that Napoleon may be liberated from St. Helena that he may fight the battle of Waterloo over again with Wellington, so do I wish that Pluto would send us back Molyneux to try his fortunes once more with Tom Cribb. My own opinion is that judgment would be reversed in both cases."

Professor Wilson was not the only expert who took exception to Cribb's performances, for the editor of the *Fancy Gazette* wrote :—

" He was a slow, heavy fighter, not such a hero as Jem, always on the defensive, milling on the retreat,

and so forth. All that is very well in its way; but there
is nothing grand, sublime, magnificent in it. The
Champion of England ought to fight after another
fashion. Reflect on Cribb's victories, and after all they
were no great shakes. George Maddox was a good boxer,
but not a first-rate pugilist—old and stale, and lighter
than Cribb—yet he stood before him a couple of hours.
Ikey Pig was a great big awkward coward. Jem
Belcher's constitution, as I have said, was utterly ruined.
Richmond capered and scarcely fought. Gregson had
been knocked to pieces by Gully, and his wind was broken
bellows. And Molyneux, I maintain, beat Cribb; curse
me, if he did not! So did little Nichols, and fifty men
on the list could have licked Horton. So much for the
Champion."

In spite of these adverse opinions, Tom Cribb was a
very popular Champion, and he retired with many friends
and admirers. We have already said that he had, after
his fight with Belcher, taken a coal business; but
he was never very successful in trade, and when he
left the Ring his old friends, who were publicans and
tradesmen, ordered coals, thinking it quite a favour
conferred upon the ex-Champion, and many never
thought of paying. Tom was a bad business man, and
sued his customers indiscriminately, thereby losing
his trade, and was eventually ruined.

Still he had many rich friends, and they came
forward and enabled him to set up as a publican, his
first house being the King's Arms, Duke Street, St.
James'. After a brief occupancy he went to the Golden
Lion, in the Borough Market, and thence to the Union
Arms, Panton Street, Haymarket. This house became
one of the most popular sporting houses in London. It
was here that " Tom Cribb's Parlour," that became
famous all over the kingdom, was established, and which
was made notorious by Pierce Egan's work entitled
"Tom and Jerry," an illustration from which we give.
There Tom would be found with his " yard of clay "
and his glass of " daffy " any evening, surrounded not
only by sportsmen, but by poets, artists, actors, and
men of letters. Tom Cribb's parlour was a favourite
place of resort for such eminent men as Jack Emery,
John Reeves, William Hazlett, Tommy Moore, and Lord
Byron. We have already alluded to the great poet's
journal, in which he mentions Cribb, for the ex-Champion was a great favourite of Byron's, and he writes
about him in several of his works.

The parlour was first represented upon the stage at
the Adelphi, and who has not seen it reproduced many a
time since? It was the most successful sporting scene

TOM CRIBB'S PARLOUR, UNION ARMS, PANTON STREET, HAYMARKET.

ever put up at any theatre. For eleven years he held
the title of Champion, and during the whole time never
raised his hands, with the exception of a dust-up with
Jack Carter.

It was not until 1822 that he took his great farewell
benefit at the Fives' Court, which we shall describe in
our introduction of Tom Spring, when that worthy took
the title of Champion of England from Tom Cribb, to
defend against all comers. We shall also have to relate
how Cribb had the honour of sparring before the
monarchs and princes who visited England.

But let us deal with his career in the present chapter,
so far as his movements were to the end. After relinquishing the Championship, Tom Cribb did fairly well
at his house, the Union Arms ; but after many years his
life was embittered by domestic troubles, and he suffered
severe pecuniary losses, chiefly through lending money,
and, becoming responsible for relatives, he was obliged
to give up his tavern. His last appearance before the
public was at the Westminster Baths, on the 12th of
November, 1840, or twenty-nine years after his battle
with Molyneux. This was a benefit got up for him by
the Pugilistic Association. He then retired to the house
of his son, a baker, in High Street, Woolwich, where one
friend frequently visited. That was Tom Spring, and
when Cribb was well enough to come to London he
would always be found at the Castle, in Holborn, then
kept by Spring, where there was an arm-chair next the
fireplace always at the disposal of the old pugilist.

Pain, disease, and worry, though, wore the ex-champion
down to a mere skeleton. What a change from George
Burrow's description of him in " Lavengro," as he
appeared at the parlour of the Union Arms, " with his
huge, massive figure, and face wonderfully like that of
a lion !"

He was attacked by his last illness in the early part of
1848, and he lay at his son's house dying in the
early summer. Tom Spring and many other old comrades in arms constantly visited him, and mine host of
the Castle gives a description of a touching little scene
that was enacted in the dying man's room.

They were alone, and the spirit of the brave old
gladiator seemed suddenly to glow in his breast, like an
expiring light. Poor old Tom sat up in bed, and, with
eyes lit up with momentary excitement, struck out right
and left, showing " how battles were won." " Ah !"
said Spring, " you have not forgotten days of yore."
" No," said Cribb, " there's the action, but the steam has
gone," and he fell back exhausted.

He died on the 11th of May, 1848, when he was within

two months of his sixty-seventh year. There was an
enormous concourse of people at the funeral, amongst
them many red-coated warriors and blue-jackets, who
attended to pay their last respects to the brave Englishman.

A few years after his death it was thought that a
monument should be erected to mark his resting-place,
and a subscription list was started, to which all the

TOM CRIBB'S GRAVE AT WOOLWICH.

foremost sportsmen throughout the kingdom contributed.

It was not, however, until the 30th of April, 1854,
that the monument, an illustration of which we give,
was erected over Cribb's grave. Here is a description
of it :—" The design represents the British Lion
grieving over the remains of the dead hero. The paw

of the lion rests on a funeral urn over which is lightly thrown the Belt which was presented to Cribb as Champion of England. The inscription is simply, ' Sacred to the memory of Thomas Cribb ; born July 8th, 1781, died May 11th, 1848.' On the plinth beneath are the words : ' Respect the ashes of the brave !' "

Far above all others stands this colossal tomb of the dead Champion, sculptured from a solid block of Portland stone, weighing no less than twenty tons. It is the most impressive of all in that forest of grave-stones in Woolwich Churchyard, and can be distinctly discerned by those passing up or down river. It is a fitting monument to the brave-hearted, honest gladiator, who, if not the most scientific fighter whose name is upon our long list of Champions, certainly possessed in no ordinary degree that stubborn determination and in-domitable pluck which have made Britain what she is to-day.

CHAPTER VIII.

AN EVENING AT THE FIVES COURT. — INTRODUCING TOM SPRING.—TOM AS A BARGE BOY.—HIS LOVE FOR THE LADIES.—HE APPEARS IN THE CIRCUS RING.—SPRING'S FIRST BATTLE.

SIX years after Tom Cribb's last battle in the Ring, that with Molyneux, described in our previous chapter, a benefit to Josh Hudson (one of the best men who ever shaped in the arena), was given at the Fives Court. Cribb (who, it will be remembered, remained Champion, for nobody dared come forward to contest the title) appeared, and altogether, judging from the accounts before us, it was a very lively evening.

Without going into details of the entertainment, we must be satisfied with the description of one little inci-dent—an incident which had the effect of introducing to the notice of the Fancy a man who was destined to play an exceedingly prominent part in the fights for the Championship, and whose name will be ever associated with the Ring.

On this particular evening (which, by-the-bye, was

August 15, 1817), Tom Cribb came to the famous arena in St. Martin's Street, accompanied by a young man, a stranger to all present save Paddington Jones, who shook hands with him as he entered with the Champion. The youth during the entertainment attracted considerable attention. We are told that " he was singularly quiet and demure, and his face had the freshness of the rustic rose. He was besides nearly six feet high, had a graceful carriage, and, so far as one could judge from appearances, was also well endowed with muscular strength." During a lull in the proceedings, a great rugged-faced man jumped upon the stage and challenged anybody to have a bout with him. Nobody seemed inclined, as most of the stars of the Ring had done their turns, when Cribb and his young friend were observed to be in earnest conversation. The youth, amidst general applause, then arose, and, slipping off his coat and shirt, entered the ring. When the Champion's *protégé* had stripped, a murmur of admiration ran through the hall, for it was at once seen that his form was of the delicacy and beauty of development quite equal to the promise of his face.

At it they went without ceremony ; but the contrast in the two styles was very great. The Yorkshireman (for the challenger was no other than Jack Stringer, a horse-dealer, who fancied himself a deal, but had never fought in the ring proper) was all fire and flurry, and kept dashing in rashly. His young opponent, on the contrary, took things as coolly as an old hand, most skilfully stopping all the blows of his antagonist until the latter tired, when the youth set about the infuriated one, and with straight hitting, and in splendid style, brought the contest to a close.

The audience were delighted, and the cry was : " Name, name." The young man, however, quietly dressed himself again, and calmly sat down beside Cribb. Such an impression had he made, though, that the demand was kept up to know who he was, and the noise was deafening. At length Paddington Jones, the master of the ceremonies, stood up, and when comparative silence was restored, in a loud voice shouted " Young Spring ! Young Spring !" At this the audience, one account says, did not know how to take it, whether in earnest or as a joke upon the part of Jones. The appropriateness of the name struck everybody so much that there were loud cheers, followed by laughter, for the youth presented such a fresh appearance and had such a rosy face. This name, which Paddington Jones so happily gave him at the Fives Court (although we think that it had been pre-arranged by the Champion), stuck to him through the whole of his career.

His real name was, however, Thomas Winter, and as he will play an important part in our sketches of the Champions, it will be well to give a brief history of what induced him to leave home and make his appearance upon the metropolitan sparring stage. The family of the Winters were known for several generations in the little hamlet of Fownhope, in Herefordshire, where they had carried on the business of butchers and farmers combined. They were fairly prosperous, very hardworking, and much-respected people. Some of them had gone into the town of Hereford; and an uncle of Tom's kept a large bookseller's shop there. Spring (for that is the name he will go by in these pages) was a fine, athletic man, full of adventure and gallantry, and before he was in his twenty-second year had made love to the daughter of a rich wine merchant of Hereford. The girl, to her parents' great annoyance, returned the affection, and they were secretly married. The future Champion's mother, by all accounts, was a graceful, handsome, well-educated woman, and, as will be seen from our portrait, Tom thus inherited good looks from both parents. Mr. Winter, Tom's father, naturally intended him to follow his own business ; but as quite a boy he had determined not to remain in his native village, but that he would seek adventure by land or sea. It must be remembered that at this period the recruiting-sergeants were scouring the country for men to fight the " Monster Boney," and the smart uniforms and bright streamers, together with the exciting stories he had overheard, induced him as a boy of twelve to beg that he might be taken as a drummer-boy. No doubt he would have gone too, had not his father discovered it in time and given the sergeant a good thrashing for daring to decoy children. However, young Tom was determined not to bury his life at Fownhope, so he bolted from home and took a job on a coal barge that used to sail from the Forest of Dean to Hereford. His mother was in great distress, thinking that he had been drowned whilst swimming in the river Wye.

After three months or so, during which time he suffered very cruel treatment, however, he was discovered at Hereford and sent home. He had had a sickener, so remained with his parents, working in the slaughter-house and upon the farm for some years, growing up to be an exceedingly fine fellow. One of Spring's biographers says :—" He was sober and industrious ; in fact, had but one weakness, and that leaned to virtue's side. Tom was ' desperate fond of the ladies.' It was, however, not so much his own fault, for, to tell the truth, he was as much sought after as seeking. His elegant and respectable face, his fine manly form, joined to an obliging and almost chivalric temper, had made him the favourite cavalier of all the country dames of the neighbourhood."

His biographer goes on to state that one October, during the fair time at Hereford, an incident occurred which undoubtedly altered the career of one of England's

TOM SPRING.

From a drawing by G. Sharples, in 1822.

greatest boxers. At one of the dancing-houses a great fellow, standing over six feet, became jealous of Tom for having waltzed a little too freely with the girl whom he had brought there. A quarrel ensued, and they came to blows. All was, of course, confusion in the dance room, and the shrieks of the ladies called everybody's attention. Amongst those present were George Cooper and Sam Robinson, the Black, both celebrated pugilists of their time, who had been giving sparring exhibitions at the theatre. Seeing that this was no place for a fight they interfered, and appealed to them to desist before the ladies, and as it was then nearly midnight, to bottle up their feelings until the following day. This they agreed upon, and Cooper promised that he would take the arrangements into his own hands, and everything should be done in proper form. The time appointed was three o'clock next day, in a field a short distance out of the town. Everything was ready, and at the time appointed the men stood before each other, George Cooper seconding Spring, and Robinson his opponent.

It is not our intention to describe this battle. It lasted a considerable time, for Tom's antagonist was burly and tough ;. about fifteen rounds were got through, during which Spring blinded his man, but came out comparatively unscathed himself. So delighted were the professionals with Tom's performance, that they wished him to join the troupe at once, offering him £3 a-week. But Spring had to reluctantly refuse, for his father had met with an accident, and his mother was seriously ill.

On Cooper's return to the metropolis he did not forget to sing the praises of the young Hereford man though, and quite excited the curiosity of Tom Cribb and the other leading lights, amongst them George Head, who was one of the best judges of boxing then living. Now George was about to take out a sparring show during the coming year, and he determined upon visiting Hereford and judging for himself what this so-called marvel really might be. In due course, therefore, Head arrived at the cathedral town, and had no difficulty in finding Tom, for he came to their show the first night they opened. The short time since Cooper had been away many things had happened to Spring. His mother had died, and he had a shrewd suspicion that his father intended to marry again. To make a long story short, Head engaged the novice for his company, and he proved more than a match for any of them, save himself. They travelled about a good deal, and visited Bristol, where Tom's style of boxing was much admired, and ultimately returned to London, where the company was broken up.

Before this, however, Spring had made the acquaintance of Tom Cribb, who took a wonderful fancy to the young pugilist, and invited him to stay at his house. Just about this time his introduction to the metropolitan Fancy took place at Josh Hudson's benefit, which we have already described.

The Champion took to him wonderfully, and set himself the task of training him for the Ring, whilst a romantic friendship, unequalled in the annals of pugilism, sprang up. Cribb would not listen to his return to the paternal home, but kept him, and to this timely aid Tom looked back with a lifelong gratitude. When Spring spoke of Cribb it was as " my old dad," and Tom would talk about the youngster as " my boy."

They had on more than one occasion tried to get a match on with Stringer, with whom he had boxed at the Fives Court; but it never came to anything, and Spring was anxious about getting a living. It so happened that one of the Astley family, whose celebrated circus stood until recently in the Westminster Bridge Road, was present at the benefit, and was much struck by young Spring's appearance, and the pleasing figure he had cut with the Yorkshireman, that he gave him a three months' engagment to appear at the circus. He made himself very conspicuous there, and the papers spoke in the highest terms of his performances. Meanwhile, whether through jealousy or annoyance at having been shown up by the novice, Jack Stringer at length felt that he must have a cut at Tom, and, having had a present of fifteen guineas, he put a challenge to Spring to fight for that amount in the *Weekly Dispatch*. Tom was quite eager to take it up; but Cribb advised him strongly not to commence fighting for so ridiculously small an amount, and Captain Barclay offered to put down thirty guineas if Spring would find ten, and advised him to also put in a challenge to Stringer to fight him for forty guineas a-side. The latter replied with another advertisement in the *Dispatch*, in which he plainly informed the world that Spring was no more or less than a coward, who wanted to escape fighting under the pretence of demanding more money. " But," continued the challenger, " he shall not escape, even by that means. The E—— of L—— is determined to back me for the sum named, and I am now ready to fight him for the sum proposed—namely, forty guineas—within a week of this date.

Of course this was accepted, and Tom Spring had no difficulty in getting a holiday from the hippodrome; and, as they were both fit as the proverbial fiddle, there was no necessity to delay the battle. Spring had plenty of practice, for besides his work at the circus he sparred every morning for an hour or so with such men as Cribb, Oliver, and Head. The men had but a few days to get ready. Spring went to the Horse and Groom, Hampstead, whilst Stringer remained in town. The match did not create very much excitement, so the attendance at Moulsey Hurst, the place appointed, was not particularly great, although it was very select. Lord Lonsdale

was there with General Lowthers. The Duke of
Hamilton came down driving a beautiful team of white
and steel-grays accompanied by Barclay and Berkeley;
the Marquis of Tweeddale and the Earl of Yarmouth
were there, the latter bringing down the information
that the Pugilistic Club had voted the winning man an
extra £10. Mr. John Jackson drove up in the tilbury
of Sir Charles Burckley. Bob Gregson, Jack Randall,
Tom Oliver, and Ned Painter were all there together
with the principal members of the Fancy, save Tom
Cribb.

Mr. Astley determined to make the most of an
advertisement, so he drove Tom Spring to the ground
in a magnificent gilded carriage, presented to the proprietor of the Westminster Bridge Road Circus by the
Mikado of Japan. He wanted to bring the band from
the hippodrome, but was dissuaded at the last moment.
There was one great disappointment, especially to Tom
Spring; the Champion, owing to an attack of gout,
from which he suffered terribly about this time,
was unable to leave the house. Tom Owen, however,
had been requested by the Champion to take his place
in the ring.

This not being a Championship fight, but only the
first battle proper of a coming Champion, we do not
propose to give the full details. As they faced each other,
it was observable that Spring was remarkable for his
erect attitude and thoroughly manly bearing.   They
were both as near as possible six feet in height, and
there was not more than a few pounds difference in
weight. While the figure of Stringer was rugged and ill-
shapen, that of Spring was graceful and finely-moulded.
In arms the Hereford man had the advantage in reach.
But there was a marked difference in their hands; Jack's
were of prodigious size, and looked as if one blow from
them would smash any ordinary visage out of shape
altogether. Tom Spring's hands, on the contrary, were
small, white, and apparently delicate, and, indeed, they
hardly seemed as if they could be used as weapons of
war.

In the second round 2 to 1 was offered about Spring.
They made a good fight of it, but the coming Champion's
blows were better directed, and, in spite of his "lady
hands" and " dainty blows," to quote from a comic
song written by Mr. Poet Laureate Gregson after the
fight, Stringer got the worst of it round after round.
In the fifth the betting was 3 to 1 against him, although
he fought with the greatest determination.

We will quote the final round from one of the reports :
" Twenty-ninth and last.—Spring, acting on a hint from

Tom Owen, had now evidently made up his mind to bring matters to a conclusion. Stringer was by this time completely blind of one eye, and could see but dimly with the other, and had the signs of almost complete exhaustion. Tom, having dallied a little with sparring, rushed forward and landed a succession of blows on Stringer's face, until at last he wound up with one tremendous hit between the eyes, which sent the Yorkshireman fainting to the ground. When time was called he was still in a state of stupor, and Spring was declared the winner of his first fight in the London Ring."

The criticism upon the style, coolness, grace, and determination of the young pugilist was most favourable, and when Tom Cribb learned how he had acquitted himself he was greatly elated, and declared that he would before long become Champion of England. How truly prophetic were Tom's words we shall relate in future chapters. Spring, by this victory, was certainly a made man, and now had no lack of patrons.

CHAPTER IV.

ROYALTY AND ROMANCE AT BLACKHEATH.—THE ARCTIC EXⁱ PEDITION.—STRANGE INCIDENT OF THE QUARREL BETWEEN TOM SPRING AND NED PAINTER.—THEIR FIRST GREAT BATTLE.

AFTER Spring's battle with Stringer he was so elated that he felt nothing short of the Champion's belt would satisfy his ambition, and he was all anxiety to get matched. One man on whom he fixed his attention was Ned Painter, who had had considerable experience in the ring, for he had beaten Coyne, Alexander, and the celebrated Sambo Sutton, although he had been defeated by such old warriors as Tom Oliver and Jack Shaw, whilst Sutton had defeated him once. Yet it must be admitted that with such battles Ned's experience

had been great, and when Spring spoke to Tom Cribb
about challenging Painter, the Champion opened his
eyes. Not that he thought his *protégé* unequal to the
task, but he considered, whilst admiring Tom's ambition
and confidence, it would be advisable for him to have a
little more experience before tackling a man like Painter,
who had gone through the mill, and knew as much of
ring-craft as most of the pugilists of the day.

However, accident favoured the aspiring young pugilist, and this is how it came about. In the month of
March, 1818, London was excited, for at Deptford had
been fitted out three ships forming one of those Arctic
expeditions which have furnished the brightest pages in
the brilliant and voluminous annals of our heroic naval
history. They were the *Esquimaux*, Captain Ross; the
Arctic, Captain Becker; and the *North Pole*, Captain
Farmer. These were the ships, as one writer puts it,
which "were about to set out on the ever-entrancing
enterprise of exploring the mythic regions of the Pole,
amid the mysterious continent of eternal ice."

Among the crew of the *Esquimaux* was a young fellow
named John Winter, and our readers will readily guess
that he must have been a relation of Tom Spring's, when
we inform them that he came from Fownhope, in Herefordshire. He was a younger brother. Now on the
occasion of the departure of the vessels referred to above,
there was to be held at Blackheath a gigantic fair. On
the 27th of the month, Prince George, Regent, was to
dine aboard the *Esquimaux*, and afterwards pay a visit
to Blackheath. This part of the programme having
been arranged, Lord Yarmouth (as will be remembered,
a great patron of pugilism), knowing the Prince's
penchant for the Fancy, consulted his Royal Highness as
to providing a display of sparring by the best men of
the day. George was delighted at the suggestion.
Accordingly a meeting was held at the Castle, in
Holborn, then kept by Tom Belcher, successor to Bob
Gregson, where a number of aristocratic patrons of
pugilism and the leading men of the Ring met and
arranged for a first-class entertainment. Philip Astley,
the founder of the circus and theatre that was recently
standing in the Westminster Bridge Road, was entrusted
with the fitting up of a colossal tent, in which boxes
were to be erected, and the interior to be decorated in a
most elaborate manner.

The day at length arrived. We will quote from one
description before us:—"Long before three—the hour
appointed for the banquet—Deptford was in a state of
almost painful expectancy. The little town was bedizened
with the flags of fifty nations, every puny craft on the

river was gay with bunting, business was suspended, except the public-houses, and they were flaming with loyal devices, and reeking with hot punch. Equality was the order of the day, and citizen elbowed countryman. The lass that loves a sailor was, if anything, more conspicuous than usual, the brilliancy of their plumage lending to those birds of passage and of Paradise a plumpness always pleasant to a seaman's eyes. On board the *Esquimaux* all was bustle and excitement; but it could be seen at a glance that the perfect order, which has always been a characteristic of the service, was disturbed. His Royal Highness was unusually punctual, and was accompanied by a very distinguished suite— Lord Castlereagh, fresh from his labours at Vienna; Lord Yarmouth, who was the best-dressed man of the party; Mr. Greville, with his easy smile and not unfrequent sneer; besides a number of military men, who were now enjoying a well-earned vacation after the prolonged campaigns in Belgium and France. The dinner was sumptuous, the wines were of the finest *cru*, the speeches in honour of the expedition to the point, and the toasts drunk heartily."

The scene on Blackheath as the hour approached for the Prince Regent to make his appearance, which was seven o'clock, is described as wonderful. The whole place was ablaze with naphtha lamps and Chinese lanterns. The din from the beating of drums at the various shows, the numerous bands playing, and the firing in the shooting galleries was deafening, whilst the shouts and laughter of the great crowd made the place a perfect pandemonium.

The tent that Mr. Astley had erected was capable of holding about a thousand people. The royal box had been erected at one end, whilst all around were others all covered with crimson cloth, and dazzling with gold and lacquer. In the centre was erected a platform for the competitors, whilst surrounding it was the multitude, consisting of every class, packed together like sardines in a box. At length there was a stir in the royal box, the Prince and his suite entered, and, after bowing to the cheering crowd, took their seats and the performance began. It is not our intention to describe it here; suffice it to say that it was excellent. Harry Harmer sparred with Tom Oliver, Jack Randall with Jack Scroggins, Aby Belasco with Dan M'Carthy, and the Champion put on the gloves with Ben Burn, one of the prettiest sparrers of the period. That the Prince enjoyed the show was evident from his repeated applause. At length he had had sufficient and retired, when the tent began to clear. No sooner,

however, had his Royal Highness left than on one side
of the ring there was a terrific disturbance amongst some
of the man-o'-war crews, for, strange as it may appear,
there was a bitter jealousy amongst the three crews of the
ships that were about to start on the expedition.

Now to chronicle a most curious coincidence. Ned
Painter, like Tom Spring, had a nephew named Joe
Heap, who was sailing on the *North Pole.* He was
the son of Ned's sister, and a ne'er-do-well, who had
left a good situation in the brewing business to go to
sea. The *melée,* to which we have just referred, happened
to arise from a collision between some of the crew of
the *North Pole* and those of the *Esquimaux,* and Heap and
Winter got at it hammer and tongs. Ned Painter, who
was standing near, and who had been hobnobbing with his
nephew, immediately stepped in between the two sailor
boys with, no doubt, the best intention, to part them,
as he didn't care for his relation to rejoin the ship with
a bruised and bleeding face. We presume, however, that
young Winter objected to this interference, and, not
knowing Painter, turned upon him. Anyhow, we have
it on the best authority that Ned forcibly separated them,
and gave Winter a back-hander on the cheek. To the
astonishment of Tom Spring (who at that moment came
up and saw what had happened), he recognised his young
brother, who had been away from home somewhile, nobody knew where. In an instant Tom's blood was up,
and he was about to turn on Painter then and there,
but Tom Oliver and Ben Burn pulled him aside. " By
G——, you'll pay me for this," said Spring, and
he left with his brother to enjoy a few hours with the
lad, whose spirit, so much like his own, he must have
admired. We can, in the mind's eye, see the two marching together through the fair, enjoying what was to be,
perhaps, the last conversation they were ever to hold,
for Jack Winter was determined at all costs to go with
the expedition.

But the next day Spring had not forgotten the blow
struck by Ned Painter, so early in the day he went to
the King's Arms and saw the landlord and Champion
upon this matter. He declared that his opportunity had
now come, and that he was certain he could thrash
Painter, mentioning that he could find forty guineas to
stake. Again Cribb objected to his *protégé* fighting for
so small a sum, and declared that it must be a hundred
guineas or nothing, at the same time telling Tom that
he himself would find the other sixty. So the challenge
was written and sent down by hand to the Castle, in
Holborn, the house of Tom Belcher, which Painter most
frequented. The latter did not come in until the even-

ing, however. In the meanwhile Harry Harmer called
and told Belcher all about what he had heard at the
King's Arms, for they made it no secret there. The
landlord of the Castle winked and declared that it was
all bunkum, for he never believed that Spring could hold
the slightest chance against a man like Ned Painter.
He asked Harmer, who was the "mug" who had put
the money down. The latter told him Mr. Thomas
Cribb, which, we should imagine, somewhat altered Tom
Belcher's tone.

Anyway, when Ned Painter arrived the three put

NED PAINTER.

their heads together; and Ned, being quite willing to
take up the gauntlet, and Belcher to find one fifty and
Harmer the other, the challenge was accepted and a
meeting arranged to take place at the Hole in the Wall
Tavern, Chancery Lane, on the following Thursday.
There was a deal of discussion about where and when
the fight should take place; but it was at length decided
that the date should be the 1st of April, and the *locale*
Mickleham Downs. This gave no time for training, as
the eventful day was distant but a week. But both
men were fairly fit for the fray.

We cannot find space to give a list of the fashionable sportsmen of the time who were present. Their names have frequently appeared upon these pages, as also has the journey down on such occasions. Needless to say, the fight created the greatest interest in all classes of society, and the muster on the common was one of the largest that had been for a long period. Conspicuous amongst those assembled were the officers attached to the Arctic Expedition, for they were not due to sail until the second week in April, the ships not having been victualled. The prints of the period state that there were more than 20,000 people.

Mr. John Gully was selected as referee, Tom Cribb and Ned Burns were second and bottle-holder for Tom Spring; whilst Tom Belcher and Harry Harmer did the amiable for Ned Painter. Ned's colours were the Bristol "yellowman," two of which he had tied round his waist. Spring and his friends sported the usual red and black spots. It is stated that Mendoza, the ex-Champion, went round with Painter, and he must have sold hundreds, the price being a guinea if a winner, 5s. a loser. There was no time lost in preparation. Spring was first in the ring, and was well received. He had to wait quite five minutes before his opponent entered an appearance, the cause being that his fighting clothes had been left behind in the carriage, so he had to appear in his ordinary nankeen breeches. "Time" was called, and the men immediately began to spar, when a curious and unusual incident happened. There was a loud roar from the mob, and cries of " Shake hands !" " Shake hands !" Painter at once put down his arms and turned to Mr. Gully, saying " I beg your pardon, sir," took Spring's proffered hand and shook it heartily. The crowd cheered and applauded vociferously as Spring exclaimed, " Now then, Ned !"

They then put themselves into attitude, and the battle, which was to make or mar the good fortune of the future Champion, commenced.

Ned Painter was evidently the more popular man of the pair, and the betting was considerably in his favour, for, comparatively, Ned was an old hand, Tom Spring having his laurels yet to win. There was a deal of time cut to waste in cautious sparring, for Spring evidently desired to feel his way, and Painter had no desire to lead off until he had reckoned his man up. At length, Ned let go, but was short, and Tom prettily countered upon the nasal organ. It was only a tap, but it set Painter on the move, and he went at it in a very brisk manner. Fast and furious were the blows delivered,

and those who had shown impatience at the long sparring bout at the start had no cause to complain. With
marvellous rapidity Spring put in blow after blow, to
the evident astonishment of Painter and his friends, and
Ned finished the first round by falling from a clean
knock-down blow, which brought his head in contact
with one of the stakes and very nearly settled the
contest in the first round. Harry Harmer, Ned's second,
had no little difficulty in getting him round, and thus
early in the battle the brandy bottle was brought into
requisition.

As Painter came up for the second round it was
evident that there was something very much amiss with
him, and he staggered all over the ring, but like a
good general that he was, he forght on the defensive,
and steadied himself again. Spring took the initiative,
however, and sent Painter to grass for the second time.
It was palpable to all present that Painter had caught
a tartar, and when in the sixth round Tom cleverly
avoided and lurched his left full upon Ned's nose, the
blood gushed out, and Spring claimed the first event, a
roar of excitement went up, and the old ring-goers knew
that a marvel had been unearthed.

So fiercely did they do battle that before the tenth
round both showed symptoms of fatigue, and as they
finished the eighth round the betting was 2 to 1 on
Spring. It will be needless for us to follow the
whole of the thirty-one rounds which were fought,
but we may be satisfied by quoting a few
lines from a report that appeared at the time :—
"It was now pretty clear that Spring had only to go in
and win. Cribb, in a loud voice said, ' Now Tom, finish
it up,' and the greater part of the crowd who had come
to the conclusion that poor Ned Painter had sufficiently
shown his thorough bottom, began to cry out ' Take
him away.' But Painter would come up again.
It was, though, with a very tottering gait, and
as he rushed forward, Spring was there to meet
him, stepping back a pace or two, he hit Ned such
a severe blow at the base of the throat that sent him
spinning to the ground, and the fight was over, whilst
Tom Spring became the hero of the hour."

That Ned Painter was amiss there could be little
doubt, and so his friends thought, for they were by no
means satisfied, and before the men left the ring another
battle was proposed, many of Ned's old friends offering to
find the money there and then. But of that and how far
they were right in reposing such confidence in the more
experienced gladiator we must leave for another
chapter.

CHAPTER X.

TOM SPRING.—HIS SECOND FIGHT WITH NED PAINTER, AND HIS
DESPERATE BATTLE WITH JACK CARTER.—A BRILLIANT
ASSEMBLAGE ON CRAWLEY COMMON.

AFTER the defeat of Ned Painter by Tom Spring,
described in our previous chapter, that worthy determined to give up pugilism as a profession. Indeed,
he had, after his fight with Sutton, which took
place immediately before the battle referred to,
become engaged to the daughter of a Quaker, well
known in Norwich. The wish of the old man was that
Ned should, if he married his daughter, bid farewell to
the Ring. This Painter consented to, and the marriage
was arranged to take place, everything being settled for
him to go into business as a publican at the Anchor,
then a well-known hostelry in the Norfolk capital. In the
meanwhile, however, articles appeared both in the
Weekly Dispatch and the *Morning Herald*, suggesting that
the battle with Spring was a "cross," and that Ned had
sold his backers. This was a vile calumny, said to have
emanated from no less a person than Lord Derby, who
had backed Painter very heavily, and, indeed, one of
those articles, it was alleged, came from the nobleman's
own pen.

Ned Painter at once threw up the pub. and
the girl, and, boiling over with rage, came to
London. The first place he went to was Tom Cribb's,
in the hope that he might meet Spring and challenge
him there and then as to whether he had any share in
setting this atrocious lie on foot. One chronicler
tells us that, when the men met, Tom Spring's first
remark was, "Ned, my boy, I'm glad to see you've come
up to defend yourself from the d——d vermin who are
attacking you." Cribb himself was equally warm in
his reception of Painter, and declared that if he could
only discover the scoundrel who had thus attempted to
throw discredit on the whole profession by maligning

two of its most noted members, he would chastise them at all risks, no matter who they were. Captain Barclay, Jackson, John Gully, and all the lights and patrons of the Ring were unanimous in the opinion that the best way to prove that no underhand business had taken place would be for the men to meet again. This Painter agreed to, upon one condition, and that was for them to fight for the nominal sum of £50 a-side—the men to find their own money, and not to have a single guinea put up by the backers.

And so it was agreed that they should meet on August 7, 1818. Spring went to Margate to train, and Painter returned to Norwich, and at once set up a sparring exhibition, which became one of the most popular resorts of the town, much to the disgust of the Quaker and man of peace who was to have been his father-in-law.

It is not our intention to follow out the details of this, the second battle between these two heroes, who were undoubtedly the best men of their day. Space will not permit, for there are many matters to write about in connection with the rise of Thomas Spring to the honours of the Championship. We have here to chronicle the fact that Painter vindicated his character by defeating his opponent; and once more the unanswerable question was constantly asked, "Who is to wear the Belt ?"

They fought in a field between Kingston and Thames Ditton. The weather was lovely and the attendance great, many making it an aquatic trip, whilst those who drove down by road numbered amongst them the *élite* of the sporting world. Here is a description of the last round, which must suffice, for we have to push on with our account of Tom Spring's other engagements.

"After fighting desperately until the forty-second round, the battle was altogether in Painter's hands, and nothing but Spring's great strength and pluck could have enabled him to face his man so often. He was for ten rounds completely done, and was knocked about as easily as if he were a child. He was satisfied that he could not win, but so dogged was his resolution that he could not be persuaded to strike his colours as long as he could struggle to his legs. He was punished severely. At length exhausted nature gave in, and in one hour and four minutes he was knocked out of time, and "Daddy" Cribb threw up the sponge."

It was a brilliant victory, and Ned Painter had vindicated his character. That he would have had his name enrolled upon our list of Champions is certain had he followed up the profession. As soon, however, as he had beaten Tom Spring he declared his intention of bidding farewell to the Ring, and returned to Norwich, where he made it up with his ladylove, obtained the forgiveness of the old man, and settled down after his marriage, at the Anchor Inn, Lobster Lane. We may not have occasion to deal with Ned Painter again, so it will be as well to state here that he did not keep his promise, for he met, after great provocation, his old opponent, Tom Oliver, whom he defeated for £100 a-side on July 17, 1820, when he finally retired. He died at Norwich thirty-three years afterwards, much respected, and his name will be always linked with that of Spring's, for had he but thrown his heart and soul into pugilism, he certainly would have taken that Champion's place.

But to return to Tom Spring, successor to the great Tom Cribb. After his defeat—which, by the bye, was to be his first and last—he was looked down upon by many and considered an overrated man. There was one, however, who stood staunchly by him, and that was the Champion himself. Now old Tom had held the belt since 1809, and the period to which we have brought our readers is 1819, consequently he had been Champion for ten years. There were many young aspiring pugilists who considered that Cribb should retire, for he made it next to impossible for a match to be made with him, as he refused to fight anybody for less than £1,000, which amount not one man could find, especially against such as the redoubtable Thomas. So he enjoyed the title and the belt year after year, without having to do battle to hold it. Undoubtedly this was a very unsatisfactory state of affairs, for the Champion was close on forty years of age, and had become a corpulent, prosperous Boniface, having sold the King's Arms and removed to a much better house, the Union Arms, in Panton Street, W., where he entertained all the most aristocratic sports of the period. Besides his want of condition, too, Tom was known to have periodical twinges of gout, and altogether was really physically incapable to enter the Ring.

Consequently many looked upon him as the ex-Champion, and whatever young pugilist could gain the top of the tree (leaving Cribb out of the question) would be entitled to be recognised as Champion. Amongst those who classed themselves as candidates were Bill Neat, who had defeated Oliver; "Gas" Hickman, who had defeated Peter Crawley; and Jack Carter, who was recognised as one of the cleverest and most successful pugilists of the day. It was to the latter all eyes were turned to take the place of the old Champion, especially after Tom Spring's disappointment. Certainly, Carter had a better record than anybody then before the public qualified for Championship honours, it will be well, then, to give an outline of his career.

He was born in 1789, consequently was six years older than Tom Spring. Coming to London from Manchester, he attracted the attention of our old friend, Bob Gregson,

JACK CARTER

who was then living at the Castle, in Holborn. Carter was taken in hand by that worthy, and under his patronage made his *début* at the Fives Court. Having there made himself conspicuous by defeating an Irishman named Flaherty, he was soon able to get a good engagement in the shape of a match with that fine fighter, Jack Power, who, but for his dissipated habits, would undoubtedly have risen high in his profession. Carter was defeated by Power, and again, in the following year, fell beneath the powerful arm of the great Molyneux. But after these two defeats his luck changed, and Master Carter carried all before him. Curiously enough, his antagonists in numerous cases were black men. Stevenson, the well-known dusky pugilist, met him first, and in something like forty-four minutes Carter compelled him to cry "enough." This was in the February of 1816, and in the April of the same year Jack was opposed by Robinson, another black, whom he defeated in twelve rounds, which lasted only eighteen minutes. Then followed his most important conquest. This was his battle at Gretna Green with Tom Oliver, when Jack Carter astonished everybody by winning, for Oliver had never been beaten, and had defeated such famous men as George Cooper and Ned Painter.

Little wonder, then, the Fancy looked upon him as Cribb's successor. Anyhow, Master Jack thought so himself, for the whole sporting world was astonished one morning when they took up their *Weekly Dispatch*. Carter, who spent most of his time giving sparring exhibitions around the country, had induced Dan Donnelly to come over from Ireland and join him, and publicly announced that "Carter, the Champion of England, and Donnelly, the Champion of Ireland," would favour the multitude with a display of the art of self-defence. When people read this in the above paper they asked themselves, What will Cribb say to this?

The old Champion said very little when asked what he was going to do about such a statement. He replied that they would see when Carter came to London. So the arrival of the self-termed Champion and the celebrated Irishman was looked forward to with interest. At length an announcement appeared, setting forth that on the evening of February 14, 1819, the two would give an exhibition at the Mirror Theatre, Catherine Street, Strand. It was to be an important night, for, besides the appearance of the strangers, Dan Donnelly, Jack Randall, and Jack Martin were to give a taste of their qualities. Tom Oliver intended challenging the Irish Champion, and some other business was to be transacted which would influence the future fortunes of the Ring.

To the astonishment of many and the amusement of all, Paddington Jones, who was officiating as master of the ceremonies on the memorable evening at the Mirror, introduced Jack Carter as the " Real self-elected Champion of England." Carter, though, did not look overpleased, and still less so when a yell announced the arrival of Tom Cribb, who, seeing Jack Carter upon the platform ready to box with Bob Gregson, clambered on to the stage and said, according to a report before us, " Come on, Jack, best man win ; may the devil take the hindermost." Then the stalwart landlord of the Union Arms proceeded to don the gloves, and to the joy of those assembled held his own with the man who was in perfect training. Of course it was only a short bout, for Cribb's wind was none too good, and he carried at least four stone of beef too much.

At the end of the business there was a hush, for it was observed that the Champion was about to make a speech. He, in a very good-humoured manner, told how Mr. Carter had assumed the high privilege of styling himself the Champion of England. He now begged to ask his rival by what right he had performed this act of self-consecration. Carter looked somewhat confused at first, but being an old showman soon regained his coolness, and in a neat little speech justified what he had done.

"First," he said, "I have several times during the past two years issued a challenge to all England, and no one has hitherto come forward to take it up. Next I was informed on credible authority that Oliver had challenged Cribb, and that the Champion had declined to meet him. Now I have beaten Oliver, and having thus overcome whom the Champion was afraid to meet, I consider myself justified in claiming the Championship."

" Afraid to meet !" shouted Tom Cribb. " I was never afraid to meet any man breathing." He then went on to explain that the challenge he received from Oliver was a mere flash in the pan—an affair of two days' notice, and he asked the public present if he was bound to take up a challenge made in such haphazard fashion. " However," went on the veteran, " I have no wish to take from Mr. Carter his laurels. I don't think he could afford to fight for my figure, and besides I want to give a chance to the younger men. You all know," he continued, " I've a young and promising boy, and I think he is quite capable of keeping up the reputation of his dad." At this point Cribb beckoned to a stalwart, ruddy-faced man, and Tom Spring stepped upon the stage, when Carter walked across and shook him heartily by the hand, amidst much cheering, and declared that he should be quite happy to fight so honourable an opponent.

So that's how the match was made, and Cribb must have have had still great confidence in his *protégé* to

nominate him in such a manner. A meeting took place
a few days after the exhibitition at the theatre in
Catherine Street, at which it was arranged that the
fight should take place on the 4th of May, 1819, on the
same day as the coming big battle between Randall and
Martin, and that the stakes should be £150 a-side.
Betting was two to one on Carter. Of course, the great
attraction of the day was the battle between the first
brace of pugilists, and it is stated that no less then
25,000 were on the Crawley Downs.

According to one account, the influx towards the neighbourhood was such as annually descends on the Epsom
district on the Derby day. Large numbers of the
humbler classes of pugilists had to walk the thirty odd
miles. The next scale in the social rank, *i.e.*, the
costers, went down blessed with a cart and a "moke."
Those whose means enabled them to do things in a more
leisurely and comfortable fashion went down the night
before, and there was not an inn in Godstone, Reigate,
Redhill, or any of the surrounding towns that was not
crowded to suffocation. The weather was delightful,
and the nobility included the Archduke Maximilian of
Austria, who was on a visit to the Prince Regent, and
who was entrusted to the care of the Marquis of Worcester, Prince George being laid up with gout ; there
was Prince Taxis and Thun, who came with Earl
Cassilis ; the Marquis de la Tour Massbourg ; the
French Ambassador, Lord Bessborough, the Duke of
Grafton, Earl of Donoughmore, Sir R. Wilson, and any
number of Lords and Commoners. There was the Hon.
George Lamb, M.P., who had just been returned for
Westminster, against John Cane Hobhouse, and Radical-
ism generally, after a furious poll extending over *sixteen*
days ! Only fancy an election lasting such a time now-
adays !

About one hundred yards from the outside ring the
coaches, drags, waggons, gigs, carts, and Billingsgate
"broughams," and various other forms of conveyance
were ranged ; and when day dawned Crawley Downs
was a sort of Greenwich Fair on the opening day.

Jack Randall and Jack Martin were, as we have
said, the luminaries on this occasion, and a desperate
battle resulted in victory for the former. Then came the
battle between our two heroes, which there is no necessity
to give in detail. Certain it was Spring had improved in a marvellous way, for although Jack Carter
fought in a most stubborn and desperate manner, Tom
Cribb's pupil displayed the greater amount of science,
and his hitting was tremendous. In the seventieth
round apparently the fight was all over. Carter was so

weak that when Spring got him to the ropes he actually was unable to defend himself; in the next bout Carter fell senseless, and the sponge was thrown up.

This brought Tom Spring one nearer the coveted title, and, of course, put Jack Carter out of court altogether, and his after-career was one long series of disastrous defeats, whilst his opponent made the most rapid progress.

But of Tom Spring's progress, whilst meeting some of the best men of the time, and his rapid rise to Championship honours, we must leave to future chapters.

CHAPTER XI.

BIDS FOR THE BELT.—TOM SPRING'S BATTLES WITH BEN AND BOB BURN.—THE CASTLE, HOLBORN, IN ITS PALMY AYS.

AFTER Spring's defeat of Carter he was sadly in want of work, so that he might properly qualify himself for Championship honours. There were only three other men who were likely to try conclusions with Tom, and they were Bill Neat, of Bristol, the veteran Tom Oliver, and Tom Shelton, although there were two others whose performances, in our opinion, qualified them more than all the others to make a bid for the highest position, and they were Ned Turner and Jack Randall. Yet the last two belonged to the middle-weight division, and it was not until the appearance of Tom Sayers, many years after the period of which we are writing, that any but the heavies dreamed of ranking as Champions. The high post was considered to be an appendage only of men of tall stature and heavy weight, and to the generation which knew Randall and Turner the idea of their attempting to be Champions would have appeared so presumptuous and ridiculous that we doubt whether they would have found backers.

Besides Tom Cribb, as our readers are aware, had made up his mind that Spring should be his successor

6

whenever he should retire. Just about this time Neat
had actually made a match with Cribb, but, after putting
down £20, had forfeited. As a consolation to the
Champion, it was therefore decided that a dinner
should be got up by a few friends.

This was done, and at the Union Arms quite a number
of swells, with Lord Yarmouth in the chair, sat down
with the leading pugilists of the day. In response to
the drinking of his health after dinner, the Champion
made a speech of some length. He began by scornfully
denouncing the manner in which Neat had played fast
and loose with him in the question of the Championship.
He pointed out how the Bristolian had for months been
bragging about the country that he was by far the best
man in England; and now, when the opportunity
offered, refused to put his claim to the test. Then he
went on to speak of Mr. Jack Carter, and great was the
laughter as he described how that hapless fellow had
soon yielded before the arm of Spring. This got him
to what was the most interesting feature in his speech.
He said, speaking in a cloud of tobacco smoke, and
amid uproarious clattering of glasses, stamping of feet,
and friendly cries of "No, no," that he now wished to
cease to be Champion. It was, he remarked, nearly
eight years since he had last taken off his shirt to fight
in the ring, and that time was too long gone to hold the
office without putting up his naked "forks" again. It
rejoiced him, he added, that he would have a worthy
successor ; and when he reached this point he put his
hand on the shoulder of Tom Spring, whom he had
taken care to place beside him. He recalled the fact
that Carter had assumed the title of Champion, and
that the Lancashire prize-fighter had been defeated by
Spring, and, by way of giving a clincher to the business,
he announced his readiness to back Spring himself for
£100 against any man in England, no matter who he
was or where he came from.

Tom Shelton, who was present, jumped up and stated
that he was quite ready to fight Tom Spring, or any
other man, for the Championship, but Tom Belcher
interrupted, and declared that if anybody had preference
it was Tom Oliver, who, like Spring, had fought Ned
Painter and been victorious over, and been beaten
by that worthy. Then quite a long argument ensued,
nothing being definitely settled that night.

However, the ball had been set rolling, and Oliver
was delighted with the prospect of having a go at the
coveted title, but he could find nobody to cover Cribb's
money. Shelton was more fortunate, for Lord George
Cavendish volunteered to supply the hundred guineas,

and the match was made, the first £10 being put down
on both sides with Ben Burn, at the Rising Sun, in
Windmill Street. Then, unfortunately, Shelton met
with an accident. Coming home one night the worse
for liquor he stumbled over the threshold of his door,
fell, and broke his arm and injured his ribs. So serious
was this that he had to forfeit.

Spring no doubt believed the time had come when he
might assume the title of Champion. Many of the
Fancy thought otherwise, though, and a deal of bitterness of feeling was displayed. Sutton (the black) declared
that he was a better man than Spring, and had actually
jumped into the ring when Martin and Turner fought,
and challenged Spring to fight then and there for love.
Of course Tom would do nothing of the kind, but he
gave the Black to understand that he was quite ready to
meet him in the proper manner for a respectable sum.
This Sutton could not do, so Tom Spring continued to
remain without an opponent.

One night, on the 18th of December, 1820, Spring and
a few friends called upon Ben Burn, at the Rising Sun,
to receive the money forfeited by Shelton. Now Ben, a
great raw-boned Yorkshireman, had been drinking
heavily, and "of all the men in the profession there
was none he had a greater jealousy of than Spring,
who came to get money from him. Consequently a
little breezy conversation arose between them, and
Burn used some remarkably strong language. Tom
Spring, who was always gentlemanly, took the matter
coolly, saying that if Mr. Burn desired to pick a
quarrel with him, he was quite willing to give him the
chance. Burn replied that he knew how mighty polite
Mr. Spring was, but he didn't mean to be made a fool
of like Oliver and Sutton, adding, "D—— your eyes,
if you really have the spunk to fight me, come into the
back parlour, and we'll have it out now." Spring
politely declined, except under regular conditions and
proper circumstances. As we have said, this little scene
took place on December 18, and it was decided to fight
out this impromptu battle at Wimbledon on the 21st.

Short as the notice was, it soon got buzzed about, and
excited the greatest interest, on account of Spring's pre-
tentions to the Championship. Mr. Jackson was appointed referee, and there was a very large attendance. It
is not our intention to describe the somewhat uninteresting battle, resulting in a victory for Spring, but a few
words about Ben Burn should find a place here. He was
born in Yorkshire on the 16th September, 1785, and Spring
had the advantage of him in point of weight, for he could
never, when fit, put in more than 12st. Ben's two first

appearances were very satisfactory, for he beat J.
Christie for 40 guineas, in forty minutes, at Highgate
Common, on the 1st of January, 1810, and polished off
Flannagan in the March of the same year, at the Old
Oak Common, when he pocketed 100 guineas. After this
his star of fortune was in the descendant. The first of
his series of defeats commenced by falling to the powerful arm of Dan Dogherty, which was followed on by
Ben's defeat by Silverthorne, Palmer Jones, Tom Spring
(referred to above), and Tom Oliver later on. The only
other battle he had was with Giblets in a room in Bow
Street, a year after his turn-up with Tom Spring, whom
he defeated.

Ben Burn—" Uncle Ben," as he was called in later
days when his nephew Jem came to London (and who
will in due course be introduced to our readers) was
known as a clever boxer at the Fives Court, but there
was a kind of suspicion that his courage was not
equal to his science. This idea, no doubt, was partly
grounded on the fact that Ben was then, and indeed
always was, given to bragging of what he could do in
the ring. He was no coward, though, as he proved in
his fight with Oliver, but at the same time he was no
glutton for punishment ; the moment he began to be hit
about he showed a disposition to " cut it." That he could
not stand the quick hitting of Spring's was certain, so
that worthy was left still upon another higher rung upon
the ladder leading him to the coveted title.

Six months after Spring's fight with Uncle Ben Burn,
the latter's nephew, Bob of that ilk, threw down the
gauntlet to Cribb's *protégé*. Bob Burn was smarting
under the defeat by Tom Shelton, and vexed at the
beating his uncle had received, so he thought he would
make a bid for victory over Spring, so that he might
stop that gentleman's career, which was so rapidly
approaching the portals of the Championship.

So let us to the Castle Tavern, where an appointment
had been made one evening in April for the men and
their friends to meet and make arrangements for the
battle to come off at an early date. The once popular
sporting house was at the very zenith of its fame, for
mine host was Tom Belcher at this period, and it was
under his *régime* that the house flourished at its best.

It will be remembered that big Bob Gregson, the
Lancastrian hero, the game opponent of John Gully,
Tom Cribb, and George Head, the latter never having
won a fight, but whose defeats were looked upon as more
creditable than most men's victories, took the premises
in Holborn, now known as the Napier, which he christened " Bob's Chophouse." The place at once became

a popular resort of the Fancy, and in the following year
its name was changed to the Castle Tavern (why it was
ever altered to its present title we never could understand), under which name it became and long continued to
be the most famous sporting public in the three kingdoms.
Under Gregson's management, the Castle was the great
Lancashire house of the metropolis, to which all sportsmen from that county gravitated, as a matter of course,
the moment they set oot in London, and a fine sight it

BEN BURN.

must have been to see Bob, with his imposing figure
clad in the most fashionable attire, doing the honours of
host with the air of a well-bred gentleman. Still, in
spite of the good patronage Bob received from "the
swells," he did not succeed as a Boniface. He thought
more of verse making (being dubbed the "Poet Laureate
of the Ring") and good fellowship than looking after
business matters, for which he had no head. Besides
his good nature was taken great advantage of, and he

rarely refused a loan to a brother in distress. Anyhow,
in 1814, he found himself in His Majesty's Prison, the
Fleet, and the Castle was closed for six months. Then
Tom Belcher returned from his lucrative journey from
Ireland with a purse filled with no less than 2,000
guineas (that representing considerably more wealth
than it would to-day), and through the advice of Shelton
took the hostelry in Holborn.

Our chronicler, who knew the house at the time,
writes :—" In the month of August, 1814, it was known
to all the sporting world that Tom Belcher had taken
the Castle Tavern, Holborn, and that no pains or expense
would be spared to make it attractive to all classes.
The promises which Tom Belcher made to the public
were more than redeemed, and the gallant Boniface
found himself soon doing a roaring business. His
aristocratic patrons literally mobbed the house — the
bloods, the bucks, the men of *ton*, all the cream, in
fact, of sporting rank and fashion made the jolly tavern
in Holborn their headquarters. Yes, the palmy days of
the Castle were those of Tom Belcher. In the snuggery
behind the bar the choicest spirits of the period gathered
of an evening.

" Persons of the highest consequence in the state
might be seen in Tom Belcher's parlour—royal dukes
had condescended to visit it, whilst any night you might
find yourself hobnobbing with celebrities of all kinds—
noble ' Corinthians ' seeing life, M.P.'s eager to hear
the gossip of the racecourse and the ring, poets on the
lookout for heroes, country gentlemen up by coach,
artists for subjects, boxers for customers, and young
Templars and surgeons for fresh means of killing time.
Here Jack Emery, the inimitable comedian, sang his
comic songs and told his side-splitting tales. Here too
came nightly Mr. James Soares, the founder of the famous
Daffy Club, which had its headquarters at the Castle,
and added a new feature of popularity to Tom's house.
The long gas-lit club room, with its gallery of sporting
pictures and portraits, was scarcely a less favourite spot
with the Fancy than the cosy parlour.

" The Daffy Club was the parent of innumerable
similar societies all over England, and a merrier crew
than gathered round that long table could not have been
found in any country in the world. When Pierce
Egan's, play *Life in London*, was produced in 1822, one of
the most popular of its scenic effects was a fac-simile of
the coffee-room of the Castle, carefully painted by the
celebrated Tom Greenwood. As a caterer for the Fancy,
Tom Belcher was unrivalled. No man knew better than
mine host how to keep the ball rolling. The Castle,

Holborn, under the *régime* of Thomas Belcher, was to
the sportsmen of the early portion of the ninteenth
century what the Mermaid was to the jovial poets of
Shakespeare's age, and, with a slight variation, we might
apostrophise it in the words of Keats :—

> Souls of *sportsmen* dead and gone,
> What Elysium have ye known—
> Happy field or mossy cavern—
> Choicer than the *Castle Tavern?*

And so Tom Spring, Tom Cribb, Ben Burn and his
nephew Bob met at the famous Holborn hostelry in
order to sign articles for the battle between the first and
last named professors of the art. Arrangements were
quickly completed, for Spring was one of the few
pugilists of that period who possessed a decent amount
of business-like capacity in settling the particulars of a
match. The Yorkshireman was allowed to have his
own way pretty much as he pleased, and over a bottle of
wine in the long room where the Daffy Club was held
everything was amicably settled. They agreed to fight
on May 16, 1820 on Epsom Downs, in the ring prepared
for Jack Rasher (alias Iron Face) and Charles Grantham
(alias Giblets). The stakes were to be £100, which had
been raised; and the time that the battle was to take
place was to be an early hour to allow the Giblets-Rasher
fight plenty of time to follow. Larkin and Jack Randall
were to attend to Bob Burn, and Cribb and Shelton
would look after his distinguished antagonist.

It seems that Bob Burn was favourite, although why
we fail to understand, for he had only thrown his sixteen
stone of "summat," as he called it, against Shelton
twice, both times unsuccessfully; whilst, as our readers
know, the princely Tom Spring had won five stubbornly
fought battles and lost but one. The reason that Bob
was fancied by a certain section was perhaps on account
of his brilliant display with the gloves against Larkin
but a few months before, and that Tom Spring was well
known to be a good deal off colour at that particular time.

The morning was bitterly cold for the time of year,
and the muster of spectators none too numerous. When
they entered the ring the Yorkshireman weighed 15st,
it was asserted, as against 16st when he fought Shelton,
but still was 25lb heavier than Spring. He peeled
well, for one chronicler speaks of Bob in the highest
terms. He says "his condition was as fine as the
combination of art and nature could exhibit." Besides,
he had great confidence in himself, so Spring had no
infant to contend with.

Without going into every particular of the rounds as
recorded, it will be sufficient to say that in the first

four, all of which were fiercely fought, Bob measured
his length upon the turf in every one, and of course the
odds were then betted upon Spring.   In the fifth he
again felled his man, and offers were made to bet that
Tom polished off Master Robert within half an hour.
Cribb's lad, however, as the fight progressed, became
very exhausted, and it was evident that he was in
shocking condition, for he panted, and once or twice
nearly fell, knocked out; yet he put in blows more
frequently and with greater force than his antagonist,
who, after the many falls he had received, had evidently
lost confidence.

As the fight progressed to the eighteenth round Bob
Burn became very shaky, and in that round, which was the
last, he could scarcely stand.   Spring could have slashed
him to earth had he chosen; but he behaved mercifully by
catching him round the waist and throwing him lightly
to the ground.   There he lay for a few seconds, and
then tried to rise; but Jack Randall, seeing his helpless condition, said he should fight no more and skied
the sponge.   The eighteen rounds had taken exactly thirty
minutes, and Tom Spring was one nearer the Championship, this being his sixth victory.

CHAPTER XII.

EARLY CAREER OF TOM OLIVER.—GEORGE BORROWS' DES-
CRIPTION OF A PRIZE FIGHT.— THE MATCH IS MADE BE-
TWEEN TOM SPRING AND TOM OLIVER.— PUGILISTS AS
BODY-GUARD TO KING GEORGE IV.

AND now we come to Tom Spring's fight with, in our
opinion, the best man he ever met throughout the whole
of his career. A man who, by falling beneath the superior
skill and activity of the coming Champion, proved
indisputably his qualities, and was as great a test as
it would be possible to put him to.   Tom Oliver (in
later years known as the " Commissary of the Ring ")
was one of the most conspicuous pugilists of his time,

and undoubtedly would have been Champion of England
had he been but a stone or two heavier. His battle with
Spring we shall presently relate. Before doing so we
feel it our duty to give a sketch of this fine fellow's life,
for it comes in such close contact with all the Champions,
from the time of Gully down to Tom King. What man,
like Oliver, could say that he had seen no less than
sixteen Champions of England take the title, and hob-
nob with them daily? Few, indeed, we trow.

Tom Oliver was born in Buckinghamshire in the
year 1789. He seems as a young man to have had no
inclination for pugnacity, but lived a quiet, secluded life,
following the oldest and most peaceful avocation in the
world—that of a gardener.

It is scarcely possible to conceive that a man who had
lived amongst the flowers and the fruit trees—tended
the roses and the lilac, the violets and the pansies, the
orchids and the pelargoniums, who has trained the grape
vine, and cared for the peaches and nectarines—has
looked to the apples, pears, strawberries, and raspberries
—watched the growing of the peas, cabbages, and beans—
could have any idea of becoming a gladiator by profession.

But honest Tom was destined to leave the peaceful
quietude of the garden and orchard, and spend the
remainder of his life in the bustle and turmoil of town,
and amidst the howling and bloodshed of the Ring and
its followers. Such a change, however, was in store
for him. And this is how it happened. Tom had come
to London somewhere about the year 1810, and we
believe was engaged as a gardener at Battersea. On
the 18th of January, 1811, having heard of a prize-fight
coming off at Combe Warren, near Kingston-on-Thames,
and having nothing better to do, Tom trudged over with
a pal to see the battle out of sheer curiosity, for he had
never witnessed anything of the kind before in his life.
The fight was a memorable one, and was long remembered as one of the fiercest ever fought. The combatants
were Dan Dogherty and George Silverthorne. So bad
were both men at the finish that neither could stand;
but the last-named was well looked after by his seconds
and sent up to the scratch staggering, whilst Dogherty
was almost carried to the scratch. Silverthorne had
just strength enough left to deliver one feeble blow, and
his opponent went down like a lump of lead, and the
sponge was thrown up. There was, to the surprise of
Tom Oliver, much cheering, and he was told that the
winner had to receive 100 guineas.

Tom Oliver viewed the matter in quite a different
light, however. We are told that he turned round to a

friend and said, " Whoy, if that's what ye call proize-
fightin', I'm danged if I don't think as 'ow I could do a
bit in that loin meself." His friends laughed at his
audacity, and on the Saturday night, at the Jolly
Gardeners, in Battersea Fields, a strapping labourer,
who thought he could " scrap " a bit, ridiculed Oliver's
ideas to such an extent that the latter, one of the best-
tempered of men, lost control over himself, and challenged the joker to prove his words with blows. They
agreed to meet early the following morning close by,
and fight for half a sovereign a-side.

Oliver proved himself to be a natural fighter, and
his antagonist had not the ghost of a chance with the
countryman. Tom had broken the spell of his peaceful
life. All the mad joy and ecstasy of battle was rioting
in his heart, and he fought so fiercely and resolutely
that the other man stood no chance whatever against
him, and in less than half an hour was hit senseless.

Oliver's master, the market - gardener, was present,
and being a bit of a fancier himself, asked Tom if he
would like to become a bruiser. The Bucks man thought
of the £100 that had been gained by Silverthorne, and
without hesitation declared that nothing would suit him
better. Smithers, which was Tom's master's name, the
next day took young Oliver to Caleb Baldwin and George
Maddox, the two Westminster veterans. The first-named
eyed him up and down, and after admiring his fine,
athletic figure, questioned him as to whether he would
like to go in for fighting. " Yes," said Tom, " I'll fight
anybody in Westminster, and run my chance of a
thrashing."

Caleb thought, after the exhibition of such confidence,
it was high time to give the youngster a lesson, so he
took him to the Duke's Head, in Peter Street, and there
in the big room put on the gloves with the ambitious
young aspirant. Baldwin was astounded at his quickness and ability, and pronounced him a genuine natural
fighter. He was taken in hand at once, and sparred with
old Caleb or some accomplished professor every day,
making wonderful progress. Some time afterwards
young Tom was taken to the Fives Court, St. Martin's
Street, where Mendoza took his benefit, and to which we
have already referred in an earlier chapter. This was
on the 31st of October, 1811. The Black, Molyneux,
sparred with an Israelite, named Bitton, and made
it so warm for that worthy that he took the gloves cff
and refused to continue. Whereupon Molyneux, in his
bumptious and offensive manner, offered to box any
man they could produce against him. Tom Oliver was
there to spar with Jack Power, and was awaiting his

turn. On hearing the Black's challenge, however, to the surprise of everybody he jumped upon the platform and offered himself to Molyneux. The latter turned upon him savagely, and demanded, " Who de debble are you, sah ? I nebber see you before. I don't fight wid people I don't know, sah !" and thereupon turned upon his heel. Oliver, though, stayed upon the platform until Power joined him, and they had a regular

TOM OLIVER.

good set-to, which astounded everybody present, and called for cheers and applause for the young novice.

But Tom Oliver's first ring fight was with a man named Kimber, who was a *protégé* of Maddox, there existing a friendly rivalry between the two veterans. It took place upon Tothill Fields, the Royal Aquarium now covering a part of the site of the old waste grounds which looked like a colossal rubbish heap. The fight took place upon one murky November morning, in the

presence of a very low and mixed crowd of costers,
market-gardeners, professional thieves, and nondescript
loafers.   Tom Oliver was as cool as the proverbial cucumber, and never faltered once.   One account describes
his appearance in the following glowing manner:—
" Tom was now two-and-twenty years of age ; he stood
about five feet nine and a half inches, and weighed a trifle
more than twelve stone. His skin was white as a duchess',
his arms as corded as a blacksmith's—a more beautifully symmetrical frame and more splendidly developed
muscular limbs no one could wish to see.   Indeed, Tom's
torso and arms served as models to many a sculptor and
painter in later days.   His face was a singularly pleasing
and good-natured one."   Kimber was a man of six feet,
a great hulking fellow, weighing some fourteen stone,
and had had many an impromptu fight, and was a most
formidable antagonist.   Tom was too good for him, and
with his coolness and judgment hit him away every
time, until at last, after struggling gamely for five-and-
twenty minutes—covered with blood and bruises—a
ghastly spectacle scarcely recognisable by his oldest pals
—reluctantly Kimber gave in, and Thomas Oliver, the
Battersea gardener, was hailed the winner of his first
battle in the Prize Ring, the herald of a long list of
brilliant victories to come.

We have no space to record them all here, but we may
find room for the list of battles he fought prior to that with
Tom Spring, which we shall presently briefly describe.
His second fight was with H. Lancaster, for 20 guineas
a-side, which he won in eighteen minutes, on June 2,
1812 ; the next was a victory over Ford for 25 guineas
a-side, at Greenford Common, in two hours and five
minutes, on October 6, 1812; then followed his fight
with George Cooper, whom he defeated for 25 guineas
a-side, on May 15, 1813, at Moulsey Hurst, in seventeen
minutes, after fighting thirteen rounds ; he then beat
Ned Painter, for £50, at Shepperton Range, on May 17,
1814, in eight rounds, lasting twenty-six minutes.   Then
came his first reverses.   He was defeated by Jack Carter
and Bill Neat, but succeeded in defeating Kendrick in
the May of 1819, on Epsom racecourse, fighting thirty
rounds in one hour and ten minutes.   He was then
defeated by Donnelly, and afterwards beat Shelton for
100 guineas a-side, at Sawbridgeworth, on Jan. 13, 1820,
fighting thirty-nine rounds in fifty-one minutes.

Then came his great battle with Ned Painter, in which
the tables were reversed, Tom Oliver losing the fight.   The
great George Borrows, in his wonderful book, " Lavengro," has described this contest, so Tom Oliver has the
honour of having one of his fights embalmed in English

literature, for "Lavengro" is a book that will find
readers to the end of time.

George Borrows, the great gipsy traveller and scholar,
had an intense affection for the good old English race
of bruisers, and was an accomplished boxer himself.
This fight between Painter and Oliver, which he
witnessed when a youth, at Norwich, is put before us
with such powerful vigour and realism that we are sure
a quotation from this chapter in "Lavengro" will
embellish these pages, and not be out of place.

"I have known the time," he says, writing now some
fifty years ago, "when a pugilistic encounter between
two noted champions was almost considered in the light
of a national affair, when tens of thousands of indivi-
duals, high and low, meditated and brooded upon it,
the first thing in the morning and the last thing at
night, until the great event was decided. . . . Pugilism was then at its height, and consequently near its
decline, for corruption had crept into the Ring. And
how many things, states, sects among the rest, owe
their decline to this cause? But what a bold and
vigorous aspect pugilism wore at that time! And the
great battle was just then coming off. A day had been
decided upon, and the spot, a convenient distance from
the old town (Norwich), and to the old town were
now flocking the bruisers of England, men of tremendous renown. Let no one sneer at the bruisers of
England—what were the gladiators of Rome, or the
bull-fighters of Spain, in its palmiest days compared to
England's bruisers? Pity that ever corruption should
have crept in amongst them—but of that I wish not to
talk; let us still hope that a spark of the religion, of
which they were the priests, still lingers in the breasts
of Englishmen. There they come, the bruisers, far from
London, or from wherever else they might chance to be
at the time, to the great rendezvous in the old city;
some came one way, some another; some of tip-top
reputation came with peers in their chariots, for glory
and fame are such fair things that even peers are
proud to have those invested therewith by their
sides; others came in their own gigs, driving their
own bits of blood, and I heard one say, 'I have driven
through, at a heat, the whole one hundred and eleven
miles, and only stopped to bait twice.' Oh! the blood
horses of Old England! but they, too, have had their
day, for everything beneath the sun there is a season
and a time. But the greater number come just as they
can contrive—on the tops of coaches, for example, and
amongst these are fellows with dark, sallow faces and
sharp, shining eyes; and it is these that have planted

rottenness in the core of pugilism, for they are Jews,
and, true to their kind, have only filthy lucre in view.
. . . . So the bruisers of England are come to be
present at the great fight speedily coming off; there they
are met at a fitting rendezvous, where a retired coachman, with one leg, keeps an hotel and a bowling-green.
I think I now see them upon the bowling-green—the
men of renown amidst hundreds of people of no renown
at all, who gaze upon them with timid wonder. Fame,
after all, is a glorious thing, although it lasts only for
a day.

"There's the Champion of England, and perhaps
the best man in England—there he is with his huge,
massive figure and face wonderfully like that of a lion.
There is Belcher, the younger, not the mighty one who
is gone to his peace, but Tom Belcher, the most scientific
pugilist that ever entered a ring, only wanting strength
to be—I won't say what. He seems to walk before me
now as he did that evening with his white hat, white great-
coat, thin, genteel figure, springing step, and keen, determined eye. Cross him, what a contrast! Grim, savage
Shelton, who has a civil word for nobody and a grim word
for anybody, one blow given with the proper play of his
athletic arms will unnerve a giant. Yonder individual,
who strolls about with his hands behind him, support-
ing his brown coat lappets, undersized, and who looks
anything but what he is—the king of the light-weights
so called—Randall, the terrible Randall, who has Irish
blood in his veins—not the better for that, nor the worse;
and not far from him is his last antagonist, Ned
Turner, who, though beaten by him, still thinks himself as good a man—in which he perhaps is right, for
it was a near thing—and 'a better shentleman,' in
which he is quite right, for he is a Welshman. But
how shall I name them all? There was bull-dog Hudson and fearless Scroggins, who beat the conqueror of
Sam, the Jew. There was black Richmond—no, he was
not there; but I knew him well; he was the most
dangerous of blacks, with a broken thigh. There was
Purcell, who could never conquer till all seemed over
with him. There was—what, shall I name the last?
Aye, why not? I believe that thou art the last of all
the strong family still above the sod, where mayest thou
long continue—true piece of English stuff—Tom of Bedford, sharp as 'Winter,' kind as 'Spring.' Hail to
the Tom of Bedford, or by whatever name it may
please thee to be called—'Spring' or 'Summer!' Hail
to thee, six-feet Englishman with the brown eye,
worthy to have carried a six-foot bow at Flodden, where
England's yeomen triumphed over Scotland's King, his

clans and chivalry ! Hail to thee, last of England's
bruisers ; after all, the many victories which thou hast
achieved—true English victories, unbought by yellow
gold—need I recount them? Nay, nay ! They are already
well known to fame. Sufficient that Bristol's bull
and Ireland's champion were vanquished by thee and one
mightier still—gold itself—thou didst overcome, for gold
itself strove in vain to deaden the power of thy arm,
and thus thou didst proceed till men left off challenging
thee—the unvanquishable, the incorruptible."

There, now, was the above not worth quoting? For
weird and vivid picturesqueness we know nothing in
English literature to surpass George Borrows' chapter
from "Lavengro." Of the fight never mind. It was
the last Tom Oliver fought before meeting Tom Spring,
and was exceedingly short, only lasted for twelve rounds,
when Ned Painter was proclaimed the winner, Oliver
receiving a blow upon the neck. Some said that Tom had
sold the fight, but it was not true. There was an
enormous amount of money changed hands; there were
more than 20,000 people present, and every publican in
North Walsham and its vicinity sold out every drink on
that eventful day.

But let us return to the match between Oliver and
Spring. We have already said enough about both men
for our readers to understand that, whilst the first-
named was approaching his decline as a pugilist,
Spring had not yet reached the pinnacle of his fame.
Yet nobody had a better right than Oliver to try con-
clusions with the coming Champion. They had both
been pitted against the same opponents—to wit, Tom
Oliver and Tom Spring had both fought Jack Carter.
Still more important was the fact that each had twice
met Ned Painter, with precisely the same results, the
Norwich Champion defeating both and falling to both.
This alone was a good reason why the two men should
meet.

Passing over the many interruptions which occurred
to their meeting—for the first attempt to bring them
together went as far back as 1819, and we are now
writing about the early months of 1821—we need but
mention that many important things had happened
both to Spring and Oliver since then. The former had
figured in the ring but once since his fight with Bob
Burn, described in our last chapter, and that really
only a dust-up with Josh Hudson, at Moulsey Hurst,
for £20 a-side—a stupid affair, which never should have
takes place, in which Spring knocked his man out quite
easily in five rounds. Tom had after that, seeing no
chance of getting a match on, settled down quietly at

his snug little house, the Catherine Wheel, in Little James Street.

Not so Tom Oliver, though. After his defeat by Ned Painter, in which he had invested all he possessed, he came to utter grief.   He had lost his public-house in Peter Street, in which he had prospered for so many years, and had really to depend upon friends for his livelihood. But for the kindness of Jack Hilton, who kept the once famous Magpie at Hounslow, he would have come to utter grief. There Tom looked after the skittle alley, and taught some of the officers.

One morning towards the close of 1820, Spring having just returned from a tour with Ned Painter in the Eastern Counties, where he had netted a nice little sum, was sitting in his snug little parlour at the Catherine Wheel, when Tom Owen, "the dandy pugilist," as he was called, entered. It was easy for Spring to tell that he had business on hand, so after a short conversation it came out that he was authorised to challenge Tom to fight Oliver for a purse of £50 or £25 a-side. This mine host of the Wheel laughed at as a ridiculous proposal that he should leave business for so small a sum. In vain Owen pleaded Oliver's poverty.

On his return to Hounslow, Oliver was mad at the refusal; but fortunately a few weeks after fortune favoured him. His Majesty King George IV., in the January of 1821, made up his mind to visit Drury Lane Theatre for the first time since his coronation, and Oliver was selected to help keep the door. A little accident on this particular evening secured him an excellent and useful friend. Two noblemen who were in attendance upon the King (the Duke of Montrose and Lord Cathcart) were entering the theatre, and the former was saved from a blow made by a drunken ruffian, Tom rushing forward and knocking the fellow down. A £10 note was sent to Oliver next day, and when the Royal Equerry was informed Tom's position and his desire to meet Spring, two more notes of the same value followed. So Owen once more visited the Catherine Wheel, and offered, on behalf of Oliver, that the two Toms should meet for 100 guineas. This Spring accepted, and the match was made. But of the progress of the affair, and a brief description of the battle, together with Spring's desperate encounter with Bill Neat, in which the former won the Championship and belt, we must reserve for our next chapter.

CHAPTER XIII.

OLIVER IS VANQUISHED — TOM CRIBB AS AN ORATOR — "DAD"
RETIRES FROM THE RING. — TOM SPRING AND BILL
NEAT. — MATCH FOR THE CHAMPIONSHIP.

THE January of 1821 was bitterly cold, and sport
throughout the country was at a standstill, save skating,
so when the news came that there was to be a fight
between these two of the first fistic stars of the arena,
it caused quite a little flutter in sporting circles.
February 20 was the day fixed for the fight, and Spring
who had been keeping himself pretty fit in his sparring
displays, only wanted to put the finishing touches to
make himself in tip - top condition. He, therefore,
determined to go to his native town, near Hereford, so,
to the surprise and delight of his old friends and rela-
tions, he arrived at the cathedral town by coach, and
walked over to Fownhope, intending to stay with a
younger brother, who still kept up the business of
butcher.

It is said that on his journey down to the county of
cider, that he was received at every place where the
coach stopped, as if he had been the Duke of Wellington
himself just returned from the wars, and his reception
by his old friends when he arrived at his destination
was of the warmest and heartiest; his own family
being very proud of their Tom, who in so short a time
had made such a name and position, He set to work
getting himself right by walking, riding, and occasionally
skating, although that was rather a dangerous exercise
to indulge in when the time was so short before the
fight took place.

Oliver at first thought of staying with his friend at
the Magpie, at Hounslow, and there take his breathers ;
but he found that impossible, for it was too near town,
and the officers and friends worried his life out when
they knew that the match had been made. From the
humble skittle-alley custodian he became a hero in
their eyes, and he was sorely tempted to drink. So he
went off to some friends at Chipping Wycombe, in
Bucks. Whilst there he was visited by several sporting
squires, who offered to add £25 to the stakes if he could

7

arrange that the fight should take place in their county.
He communicated with Cribb upon the subject, and
that worthy came down and accepted the gentlemen's
offer. In company with Captain James, of Beaconsfield,
and Tom Owen, who had accompanied Cribb to
Wycombe, they went in search of a suitable place to
bring off the battle, and decided upon Salt Hill.

How the Bucks magistrates issued warrants; and
how Oliver was arrested and only let off on his solemn
promise not to fight in their county, and how when, on
the day they went to a place near Arlington Corner,
where the magistrates followed them and stopped the
fight, we have no space to relate here. Never were two
prize-fighters so much harassed as Spring and Oliver
over this particular fight. At length, after journeying
from pillar to post, they found themselves at Hayes, in
Middlesex, and it was not until three o'clock on this
February afternoon that Oliver's yellow and Spring's
blue were seen waving from the stakes.

The first few rounds were fought with very little go
in them, although there was plenty of science displayed,
and were remarkable exemplifications of the coolness of
great boxers. And it was not until the fourth round that
Oliver came up after a nasty throw, looking fierce and
very determined. In the succeeding ten rounds Oliver
was grassed every time, and it was soon evident that
although he started favourite, he held not a ghost of a
chance.

In vain after the sixteenth round did his friends try
to persuade Tom Oliver to give in. His friend Clarke,
a well-known trainer, even went so far as to jump into
the ring, when the utmost confusion followed, giving
time for the beaten man to pull himself together a bit.
In spite of all they could say or do the plucky veteran
would come to the scratch, although he could scarcely
stand.

Here is a description of the last two rounds, which,
quoted in their entirety, read somewhat sickening :—
" Oliver, who had slightly recovered his senses amid the
tumult, made another attempt to retrieve his fortunes.
Spring, however, who now saw it was unsafe to prolong
the contest, went in for the finishing touch, got Oliver's
head in chancery, pummelled his already bruised face
until it was one mass of bloody jelly, and, having
punished Oliver until he had to scream with pain, threw
him a cross-buttock, which seemed to dislocate his neck.
But the game, the plucky, the indomitable Oliver even
yet was not defeated, and when he once more was able
to raise himself from the ground he insisted on being
led to the scratch. Unable to stand, he signalled to his

seconds, who took him by each arm, and they left him in the centre of the ring. But the moment their arms were withdrawn he fell down in a fainting fit, and so, after a battle of fifty-two minutes' duration, Spring, amid the tremendous cheers of his friends, was declared the victor."

Tom Winter Spring undoubtedly proved himself n this fight the scientist of the time, and immensely increased his already great reputation, which was so soon to culminate in the proud title of Champion of England.

And now let us turn to matters concerning h actual Championship in connection with our hero. In the early part of January, 1821, when Oliver and Spring were arranging their battle which we have just described, Tom Cribb, after ten years' inactivity, once more threw down the gauntlet.

One evening, during a spar between Harry Harmer and Lancaster, at the Fives Court, Cribb rushed into the place almost out of breath (he weighed just on seventeen stone at the time), pushing through the audience, he mounted the stage and tossing his hat in the air, and holding his pocket-book over his head in the greatest agitation and excitement, addressed the assembly thus: "Gentlemen,—I will fight Neat for 1,000 guineas, or for 500 a-side, or for whatever he can get. I have been just told, while I was taking a few whiffs over some cold brandy and water, that Neat had publicly challenged me. I therefore lost no time in showing myself before you. Gentlemen, I do not like this chaffing behind my back; and another thing is, I won't have it. I am an Englishman, and I will behave like one. An Englishman never refuses a challenge. Neat is my countryman, But what of that? If he refuses to fight me I will fight any man in Bristol for 1,000 guineas, and stake £100 directly. Here's the blunt! My countrymen used me ill when I was last at Bristol, and Neat behaved rude to me. Perhaps 'the old fool' may be licked, but I will give any of them some trouble before they do it, and will tell you, gentlemen, they say Neat shall fight my boy Spring, because they know he is unwell. This conduct isn't right, my boy's in a consumption, therefore I will fight Neat instead of him. My boy Spring has not got belly enough for him, but I have. I will fight and, blow my dicky, but I will give any of them that fight me pepper."

Never had the old Champion delivered himself of such oratory before, and the enthusiasm was great. Anyhow the result was a match between Neat and the Champion for £200 a-side. The date fixed was May 9, 1821. There

were two opinions as to who would win, for most looked
upon Tom Cribb as being too fat, gouty, and old.
No doubt they who took that view were perfectly
correct, and it would have been painful for the old
man to have gone into the arena again with a young,
powerful, quick man like Neat pitted against him.
However, Neat's backers failed to enter an appearance
when the second deposit was due, so the first was forfeited to the Champion, and the whole thing fell through.
Everybody in the sporting world was pleased at this
result, and at a meeting of the leading patrons of the
P.R. it was decided that Cribb should remain nominally
Champion until his death, but that he should not again
be called upon to defend the title in the roped arena.

This was all very well, but the old war-horse had been
aroused, and Tom did not care to admit that his day
had passed to do battle in the ring. So it was not until
the following year that he determined upon relinquishing the title, and to retire in company with his gentlemanly ailment, the gout, and his wife and children, into
quiet, domestic life, and give up once for all the glories
of the Prize Ring.

And then the most touching scene in all the old
Champion's career took place on May 18, 1822. It was
at the Fives Court. Every noble patron of the Ring,
who could by any possibility get from business or duty,
was there. To enumerate them would occupy too much
space. It was a representative meeting of all the true
lovers of the manly art, and they had come there to hear
a few words of farewell from the old Champion. It was
a touching scene. After the few bouts Thomas Cribb,
who had enjoyed a more lasting popularity than any
man since the Ring was an institution, stepped upon
the stage. He wore the belt with the lion's skin and
lion's head—the same which we ourselves have proudly
buckled on, and which we believe is still in the possession of Jem Mace; and he made his farewell speech.
His heart was in his throat though, and his utterances
were indistinct, for never did he feel so undone, so
grieved to have to say adieu to his sincerest friends
there present, and to tear himself from the activity of
the Ring. The spectators were as much moved as the
old Champion, and incredible as it may seem that such
could happen amongst men who had seen so much, and
had become callous to tender feelings, many an eye
glistened on that eventful evening, and not the least
conspicuous were those of old Tom himself.

When the Champion had thus positively, formally
yet regretfully retired, Tom Spring (who by the bye,
looked in quite robust condition, and had evidently

recovered his rosy cheeks and cheerful manner, after his long indisposition) mounted the platform, and in a curt, pithy speech, said :—" Gentlemen,—My old dad, as I am proud to call him, has retired from the stage and the Prize Ring altogether, and as I have stood next to him for some time past, I mean now to stand in his place until I am beaten out of it."

Now, to make matters quite explicit to our readers, it will be necessary for us to hie back a bit. It will be remembered that in 1819 we mentioned that Neat and Spring were matched, but that the former forfeited through an accident to his arm. In the early part of 1821 Tom Spring advertised that Cribb had made over the title of Champion to him, and he offered a challenge to all England, which should be open for three months. This time expired on June 25, 1821, and Spring believed that he was quite entitled to dub himself Champion until somebody defeated him. So he went down to Cheltenham, married a girl of respectable family and with money, came back, took the Weymouth Arms, Weymouth Street, Portman Square, and settled down quietly as a family man. Then, before Tom had got through his honeymoon, Master Bill Neat offered to fight him. This was rather unkind, and Spring pointed out that there had been three months open to him, and asked him why had he not responded then. Nevertheless, Tom Spring declared that he was willing to sacrifice his personal comfort, and that he would meet Neat for £50) a-side. A good deal of angry correspondence ensued, and eventually the whole thing dropped through, and Neat fought and defeated Hickman, the terrible " Gasman." This was the latter's first and last defeat, and proved what a tower of strength Bill Neat possessed.

Neat after this assumed the title of Champion of England. So there were two Richmonds in the field. And certainly we think that he had just as much right to it as Spring, for it was absurd to think that Cribb could hand the honour to his boy, or that a three months' challenge open to all England could confirm it.

But to pursue the negotiations between these two men. On the 12th of June 1822, after the fights between Jem Ward and Dick Acton (to which we shall in a future chapter have to allude) and that of Jack Scroggins and Gipsy Cooper, at a snug little dinner, for which Mr. Bob Lawrence, of the Red Lion, Hampton, was famous, Mr. Thomas Elliott backed Spring against Neat, and Randall against Martin. All went well until the 12th of November, the day for the posting of the last of the stakes to be made at the Castle, in Holborn. For some reason, however, which we have been unable to discover, Mr. Elliott never came near the place, so, at the eleventh hour, everything was knocked on the head. Neat received £150 and Martin £200. .

After this Tom Spring was determined not to leave a stone unturned to get himself matched with his rival for Championship honours, and Mr. Laurence Sant (to whom we have already referred) offered willingly to put the money down, no matter to what amount. A correspondence lasting no end of time was the result, when eventually a climax was arrived at on the 12th March, 1823, when they met, and the two men finally agreed to fight for £200 a-side on Tuesday, May 20, 1823.

The excitement which had been pent up during the numerous previous matches and disappointments now burst out, and the interest displayed in every movement of the two men was intense. There had been no such thing as a fight for the Championship for just upon twelve years, and the younger rising generation were almost too juvenile at the time Cribb and Molyneux fought to remember much about it.

Every movement of the men was watched, and the talk was of nothing else in sporting ken or club. Spring, accompanied by his former pupil, George Head (one of the finest sparrers who ever put on glove), and Tom Cribb went to Brighton to breathe the fine ozone and take their sweats over the breezy downs.

And here we must break off to tell of a little circumstance that happened, which was so serious that it very nearly spoiled the whole arrangement, and once more prevented these men from meeting.

Tom Shelton came down to London-super-Mare to conduct a merry little mill between two local pugilists, named Dan Walls and Jem Smith. Shelton persuaded Spring to go and see the fight, and Tom very foolishly, against the wish of Cribb, did. When on the ground he was persuaded to act as referee, his kind heart and delight in pugilism rendering him exceedingly tractable. All went well until, in the last round, Walls struck Smith an unlucky blow on the head, and he fell against the stakes. He was picked up insensible, never recovered consciousness, and died. Both Shelton and Spring, together with others were arrested and brought up before Sir David Scott, who ordered the two Londoners to find bail to keep the peace for twelve months. Here was a nice thing. For some days until the bail arrived, they were kept locked up in a public-house with the bailiffs, when they were liberated in a surety of £100 each, "to be of good behaviour for twelve months."

Spring was determined not to be baulked, so he went on training, meaning to sacrifice the £100 out of the £200 he was fighting for if he won. If not that, his surety must pay. However, we may state here that although the fight came off the £100 was never estreated.

It may well be imagined what the sporting public thought of this, especially those who had put their money on Tom Spring, for the trial and inquest were printed in all the London newspapers.

Mr. William Neat was at the same time not quite devoid of adventure, although scarcely of such a serious nature. Tom Belcher was looking after Neat, together with Harry Harmer, at Marlborough, and taking their breathings over the beautiful downs which surround Alec and Tom Taylor's place at Manton. One afternoon Tom was sitting in the parlour of their inn, awaiting Neat's return from changing his flannels before they took tea, when two ladies walked into the apartment. Tom, with his usual politeness, bade them be seated, and suggested that perhaps they had made a mistake in coming to the room. "Oh, no," said the elder lady. "Is not thy name Thomas Belcher?" Tom, taken aback, replied that it was. "And thou art with William Neat, of Bristol, preparing for one of those cruel and ungodly exhibitions called prize-fights?" Tom bowed assent, and the lady proceeded : "We have come to speak with William Neat, and will thank thee to tell him so." At that juncture enters Master William, with a look of astonishment. The lady visitor was no other than the famous Mrs. Fry, Quakeress, whose visits to the prisons of England made her name honoured all over the country. She implored Bill Neat to forego this engagement ; she offered to give him a cheque for £500. Bill was obdurate. He talked about his honour and all that sort of thing. Mrs. Fry persevered, but Neat won the contest at the finish, and the lady retired after facing him for nearly two hours, sparring about with him in every conceivable way, and getting through any number of rounds. Bill often said after that little entertainment that he would rather face Tom Spring for two hours than Mrs. Fry for half that time and double the money.

The final deposit was made at Mr. Jackson's on the 3rd of May, and everything went smoothly, the 20th being fixed for the fight ; but that and the other matters connected therewith we must leave for the next chapter.

CHAPTER XIV.

A ROMANTIC IRISH CAREER.—THE TWO GREAT FIGHTS BE-
TWEEN TOM SPRING AND JACK LANGAN.—SPRING'S LAST
APPEARANCE IN THE RING.

AND now that we have followed Tom Spring to the
highest rung of the ladder which has led him to the
Championship, it will be our duty to record his two last
battles in the Ring. It is curious to note that he only
fought one man whilst in possession of the title. All his
best work was done before he rose to the top of the tree
—to which we have already devoted perhaps too much
space. We shall, however, cut short his doings as
Champion, and confine ourselves in the present chapter
to dealing with the remainder of his career as a pugilist, although, of course, he will figure in these pages
in connection with many another aspirant for the great
fistic honour, for he lived prosperously and prominently
for more than a quarter of a century after he made his
exit from the Ring.

But before proceeding to narrate the two fights
referred to above, it will be well to introduce the man
with whom Tom Spring fought, Jack Langan, whose
early life and history are dealt with at some length in
"Boxiana," by Pierce Egan, who was undoubtedly on
the most intimate terms with this fistic hero.

1798 was a memorable year for Ireland. She was
lit up by the full blaze of insurrection. It was the
year of the "Great Rebellion" and also the year in
which the greatest of all Irish boxers saw the light of
day, for Jack Langan was born in that memorable year
at Clondalton, in the county Kildare, on the 19th of May.
According to the story, little Jack (but he wasn't christened then, by the bye), as soon as he was born had
his ears saluted with a volley of musketry fired at a
powder magazine by a company of "United Men"
attempting to get possession of the place, which was
within a few yards of the Langans' mud castle. His
biographer tells us that Mrs. O'Shaughnessy, his nurse,
had her own way of explaining this, as rather ominous
that little Langan was born to make a noise in the
world.

"The early years of Little Jack," continues Pierce Egan, " passed, as is usual with urchins, until his father left Clondalton and settled in the suburbs of Dublin, at a place called Ballybough Lane, adjoining that beautiful spot of freedom known as Mud Island." Then, after giving minute details of the lad's juvenile career, his biographer tells us of his early years and progress. But as it would occupy too much space here, we must abbreviate, whilst adhering closely to facts as far as possible.

It would be difficult to find a more romantic career in the P.R. than that of Jack Langan. At the age of thirteen he went to sea, and sailed for Oporto and Lisbon. At the last-named place he had a narrow escape, as for some reason a couple of ruffians drew their stilettos upon him. Jack was so quick of eye and so active, however, that he made the two olive-skinned curs run in precious quick time, landing them right and left with his mawleys, not before they had inflicted a couple of stabs upon him though ; one on the arm and another on the shoulder.

For a time Jack was happy on the billows, but the seamy side of a sailor's life soon disgusted him, and on his return to Dublin after his first voyage, he begged his father to get the captain of the ship to cancel his indentures, and then have him taught a trade. This the old dad did, and Master John was in due course apprenticed to a sawyer. Those who desire to know how he conducted himself, and of the scrimmages into which he got, must refer to " Boxiana." He fought with his fellow-apprentices like a little demon, and was always in hot water. Here is one story that may amuse. He had a fight with a man named Savage, who weighed something like 11st, and was Jack's senior by five years, Langan being at that time only seventeen. The battle came off on the banks of the Dublin canal, and only a very few friends attended to see fair play. The contest lasted so long that it began to get dark, and as neither would give in, and it was thought only honourable to fight it out, candles were introduced upon the scene. In a very short time after a light had been thrown upon the subject, Langan floored his antagonist with such a fearful blow upon the jugular vein, that Savage was carried home dead, amid the lamentations of his friends and the dread of Jack, as to what would be done to him.

Master Savage was washed and made tidy, put into his coffin in the parlour in a propped-up attitude, and the neighbours invited to come in and take some of the " crater." Fifty or sixty old men and women were wailing, drinking, and all smoking during the whole

night, in the midst of which was the interesting corpse
of Mr. Savage. During this touching solemnity, " to
the great surprise and confusion," as Langan's biographer puts it, " of the company, Mr. Savage suddenly
waked himself and tumbled out of the coffin on to the
floor, from which ignominious position he quickly rose
to his feet. At the sight of this marvellous resurrec-
tion the wakists with one accord fled, shrieking with
horror and dismay from the scene, leaving the corpse
master of the situation. But, however terrified the
ladies and gentlemen assembled for the wake may have
been at this unexpected apparition, it was an immense
relief to John Langan to hear the next day that his dead
foe was alive and kicking, and that, therefore, he might
dismiss all fears of committal on a charge of man-
slaughter.

After this victory some of his friends thought Jack
good enough to be matched against a professional bruiser
named Slanthea, and here comes another anecdote about
the boy. The fight was for £20 a-side, and the day
before, Jack hearing that the great Dan Donnelly was in
Dublin, went to him for advice. Jack timidly asked the
great pugilist what was the best mode of training. But
let us tell it in the chronicler's words:

" ' Is it training ye mane?' replied Donnelly, with a
smile upon his comical mug. ' By the hokey I niver
throubled meself about that training, d'ye see, which
the fellows in the Long-town make so much bhother
aboot. But I'll give ye may opinion of what ye ought
to do. First of all, Jack Langan, ye must take off your
shirt, then walk up and down the room briskly, and hit
out well with both hands, as if you intended giving your
man a snoozing without asking for his nightcap. Jump
backwards and forwards a hundred times at laste,
to find out if the wind is good, for being out of,
breath in fighting, my bhoy, is a terrible thing.' ' Now,
Jack,' says Dan, ' it being then about midnight before
the fight, ' you must go home directly, and drink half
a gallon of the sourest buttermilk you can get, and then
go to bed. At five o'clock—not a minute after five o'clock—
in the morning, ye must get up and run three or four
miles, and at every mile ye must swig not whisky, by
Jasus, but a quart of spring water. Mind, now, Langan,
and do as I bid ye.'

" Jack thanked Dan for his friendly advice, and
started off to procure the buttermilk, but could obtain
only three pints for love or money. At five in the
morning, though he had had barely two hours' rest, up
jumped Langan to finish his *training!* To make
up for the deficiency, he added water. The time

appointed for the fight was six o'clock, but Jack, in his eagerness to 'train,' was nearly half an hour behind his time. His antagonist was just leaving the ground when Langan mounted the brow of a hill in sight of the ring quite out of breath, and, dripping with perspiration, roared out as loud as he could, 'Don't go yet, man; I'll be wid ye in a jiffey!' The ring was again formed, and Langan, as hot as fire, stripped as cool as a cucumber.

"Slantlea began well, and took the lead as he gave

JACK LANGAN, IRISH CHAMPION.

Langan some nasty blows, and had decidedly the best of Master Jack in the first four rounds. 'You've got your masther now, Jack,' cried the exultant friends of Slanthea. 'Ah, be aisy,' retorted Langan, 'I've thrained undther Misther Dan Donnelly, and I'll bate yondther omadhaun yet, no fear; I'm just going to begin, look now,' and letting fly his left he caught Slantlea full in the forehead and dropped him like a shot. The other, however, fought thirteen rounds more, but never

had a chance, and Langan was proclaimed victor after a
fight of thirty-seven minutes."

When Jack left the ring he often told the story of Dan
Donnelly's brilliant, scientific training to his customers
in the back parlour of his pub. at Liverpool.

So much for the first ring-fight of Jack Langan, who
was to become one of the greatest pugilists of the day,
Ireland's champion, and a worthy antagonist to the
famous Tom Spring.

We must hurry through the remainder of the Irishman's career, although his biographer gives us any
number of amusing anecdotes quite worth relating. His
next engagement was with Owen McGowran, of Donny-
brook, whom he defeated in thirty-five rounds, occupying
1 hour 47min. He then issued a challenge to any man
in Ireland, and his friends dubbed him Champion of the
Emerald Isle, for none took up the gauntlet.

So Jack joined the regiment of Colonel Mead, which
was raised in Dublin for the assistance of the Indepen-
dents in South America. He was soon promoted to the
rank of sergeant. The sufferings of that regiment were
terrible, they landing at the island of St. Marguerite in
a starving condition in a fearful climate. Nothing,
however, seemed to affect the iron constitution of Jack
Langan. Colonel Mead mentioned Jack's qualities as a
fighter to Admiral Bryan, who matched his boatswain,
another celebrity named Jack Fower, against him.
Again Langan was victorious. This is a curious incident,
proving how great an interest our officers took in the
art of self-defence and attack, tending to make our
fighting men what they have proved to be to-day under
the flag that is flying at this moment in South Africa.

After countless adventures, which are most interesting
to peruse, he once more returned, and after staying at
Cork for some time made for Dublin, and set up in
business at the Irish Arms, in King Street, a house
which bore the following lines over the doors :—

> Quiet when stroked ;
> Fierce when provoked.

Here Jack had a merry time of it, and fell in love
with a pretty, blue-eyed, buxom dairymaid. They loved
not wisely, but too well, and she became a mother. The
enraged father brought an action for seduction, and the
trial is delightful reading. Jack had to pay £100
damages. This and other misfortunes compelled
Langan to leave Dublin, so he came to England. The
first place he made for was Bob Gregson's Punchbowl
Tavern, in George Street, Liverpool, for Bob had,
after leaving the Castle, migrated to the northern port.

Gregson had boxing-rooms, and Langan was invited to stay, but he said he wanted work, and took a situation as sawyer at Oldham. It so happened that Tom Reynolds, an old pal of Jack's, came that way with his boxing show, so Langan agreed to join Tom in the show, and help him to manage a " boxing academy " in Manchester.

Then came his match with Matthew Vipond, a livery-keeper's assistant in Manchester. This fight took place at Buxton, Langan beating Vipond (or " Weeping Mat," as he was called) in eight rounds. Jack fought magnificently, and those who saw the mill, and there were some good judges present, predicted a brilliant future for the Irish lad. This took place on April 30, 1823, and Langan shortly afterwards made his way to London, determined to try his fortunes in the metropolitan ring.

We are unable to follow his doings during the remainder of the year, but on January 7, 1824, we find that Tom Spring thinks the Irishman a worthy foe, for he accepts his challenge, although the gauntlet had been thrown down months before.

The stakes are the handsome sum of £300 a-side, for Jack Langan has many friends in Cottonopolis—rich men who believe in him, and feel confident that he can defeat the champion. It is finally settled that the fight shall come off upon Worcester racecourse, and as there is no fear of magisterial interference, thousands make their arrangements to be present. On the Monday coaches from Bristol, Birmingham, Manchester, and London are constantly arriving, crowded inside and out, and the old cathedral town is full of life. Every day until Wednesday noon is a ceaseless rush into the city. The Foregate is absolutely impassable, and never has Worcester held so many human beings.

On the racecourse it must have been a sight indeed. One chronicler thus describes it :—" At noon on Wednesday it was reckoned that at least three hundred thousand persons were collected, on the grand stand, on the temporary platforms, in glittering carriages and lumbering waggons, in neat and ugly traps of all sorts, on the masts and rigging of the tall ships moored in the Severn har l by, or squeezed together as undistinguishable ur i s in the mass of heaving, throbbing life that pressed r ro nd the little ring that had been formed on new-mr ce ground, covered with dry turf and thickly strewn with sawdust, on the spot that promised to be within the view of the greatest number of observers."

There was an enormous attendance of aristocratic sports, and the Fancy was represented from every part of England. We have no space to mention names; but many sports, good and true, who have been mentioned upon these pages were present. Whilst the preparations were being made at the ring-side, when the men had put in an appearance, there was a wild shriek and a crash. One of the temporary stands had broken down, and hurled some hundreds to the ground. Fortunately no lives were lost, but many bones were broken, and the accident caused much delay to the proceedings.

We do not intend to take our readers through the rounds of this magnificent contest. There were eighty-six in number, and the Irishman fought bravely and with the greatest pluck and determination. But the Champion was too good for him, and although at some period of the battle Langan gave much trouble, he never took the lead, and at the finish was so dreadfully punished that his seconds and friends insisted upon throwing up the sponge much against Jack's will.

Spring returned to London the next day, but Langan had to remain in Worcester for nearly a week. When he came to town, the first place he visited was the Castle, where he accidentally met Spring. There was the best of feeling exhibited between the two men, and they hob-nobbed over a glass of brandy and water and a cigar. And here we may mention that on the second day after the fight a challenge had appeared in the papers from Langan offering to fight Spring again for £500 a-side. During their talk Spring referred to it, and asked Langan if it was a hoax, or whether it came from him and was really genuine. Tom and everybody had their doubts that such a thing could be after the display at Worcester.

Jack Langan looked serious, and said that while he had no fault to find with his antagonist's conduct in the ring, no hostile feeling existed in his breast; but he added very significantly, and in the broadest brogue, that he was robbed out of the last fight, that his confidence was not in the least diminished, and that he was there to publicly challenge Spring to fight for £500 a-side upon a similar stage to that which Cribb and Molineux fought, and that he was, moreover, then ready to put down some money to make the match.

Everybody present, as may be imagined, was taken by surprise, and Spring answered his late opponent very quietly, telling him that he would be most happy to meet him again for the sum he mentioned, but that he would certainly not fight on a stage. Then there arose a very hot argument. Tom Reynolds, who had accompanied Langan to the Castle, spoke very warmly upon the subject. He wanted to know why Spring refused. He had taken the championship from his "dad," Tom Cribb, and *he* did not hesitate to fight Molineux on a stage, and why should his successor. But still Spring refused, so Langan and Reynolds left, neither of them in the best tempers, to go to the Surrey Theatre, where Langan was showing.

The matter, however, did not end at this. In the papers there continued a long, wordy warfare, and Langan and Reynolds declared that the crowd pressing against the ring at Worcester spoiled his man's chance, and he found fault with his seconds, the umpires, and the referee, winding up by asserting that he had been most scandalously and unfairly treated, and that had he fought on a raised platform nothing of the kind would have happened, and that he would have won the battle.

And so the large heart of Tom Spring gave way. He agreed to meet his late opponent on a twenty-four foot boarded stage, raised six feet from the ground.

On a blazing hot afternoon of the "glorious" 1st of June the Fives Court was packed to suffocation, for it was Tom Spring's benefit. The Champion had come up from his training quarters near Reigate to kill two birds with one stone. In the first place, he was to receive the aforesaid benefit; and, secondly, he was to be present at the final deposit, to be made at the Castle, making the £1,000, for which he was going to fight Langan on the following Tuesday.

The money having been duly put down, the next consideration was as to where the fight should come off. The Pugilistic Club held a meeting, and Mr. Jackson produced some score of letters from different lessees of racecourses offering parks, paddocks, &c., one from Warwick offering £250. This was decided upon, but when everything was practically settled Mr. George Allray, a county magistrate, rode into Warwick and informed the racecourse authorities that he should not permit it. So Chichester was decided upon, Mr. Pierce Egan being deputed to make all arrangements.

On the Monday (Whit Monday) Chichester was excited, bands of music paraded the streets, a battery of artillery had halted to see the fight, and an enormous concourse of people had assembled to witness the second great battle between the champion and Langan. A very large field had been selected about three miles from Chichester, and in the centre was erected the stage.

Before ten o'clock the field was crowded, and at noon the principals and aristocrats left their hotels and lodgings and proceeded to the rendezvous at Budham

Bridge. At one o'clock they approached the stage amidst the most vociferous cheering from some fifteen thousand people, and Mr. Jackson, who acted as referee, having taken his position, and the seconds and principals having gone through the form of hand-shaking, the former were ordered to their corners, and the men having both answered in the affirmative to the question "Are you ready?" "Time" was called, and they placed themselves in sparring attitude.

It will serve no purpose to describe this fight. Like the first between the two men, Spring took the lead all through, and punished his adversary a deal more than he did in the previous combat. They fought 72 rounds, and in the last Jack Langan was so done up, that the champion, instead of hitting him, pushed him down mercifully with his open palm, where he lay helpless and beaten, and Tom Spring was declared to be the victor, and still Champion of England.

It would take too much space to tell of the numerous tokens of respect and admiration showered upon the champion after this. Cups, purses, and testimonials without end were presented. He had fought three great battles in twelve months, and netted £2,000. This was his last fight, if we except a turn up with Phil Samson on Epsom Downs. We shall come across the famous fighter and gentleman again as we pursue the careers of the champions, so suffice it to say here that Tom Spring, after an unsuccessful speculation as a publican at Hereford, when he took the Booth Hall, on the retirement of Tom Belcher he took the famous Castle, in Holborn, in 1829, where we hope often to meet him, for he remained there until his death, which was not until the 20th of August, 1851.

Jack Langan abandoned the Ring and settled down as a genial Boniface of a snug little pub. in Liverpool, called the St. Patrick, Clarence Dock, and took unto himself a wife, enjoying as great a reputation there for his good fellowship, kindness, and charity as did his then sworn friend, Tom Spring, in London.

CHAPTER XV.

FOR THE BELT AT LAST.—BAULKED BY THE BEAKS. - A
MONSTER MEETING.—TOM SPRING AND BILL NEAT.—
THEIR DECISIVE BATTLE.

AND now to tell the story of one of the most exciting
combats for the Championship that can be found
throughout the annals of the Ring. As we have stated,
the day fixed for the great event was the 20th of May,
1823, and on Monday, the 3rd of that month, there was
a big meeting at Mr. John Jackson's rooms in Bond
Street, for the purpose of making the final deposit,
that gentleman being the stakeholder and leader of
the expedition, so the choice of locality was left in his
hands. Spring came up from Brighton and was present
at the jollification which took place at Tom Cribb's, after
all the money had been put down, although, of course,
he did not participate in the festivities. Neat remained
at Brighton. Tom Belcher was, however, present, and he
handed to Spring the £25 due to him from Neat over the
last forfeit, which had been outstanding so long, and
consequently the little sore was healed between the
two men, and a friendly spirit secured for the coming
battle.

As the eventful day approached the excitement rose
to fever heat, and nothing else was talked about in
sporting circles, both in town and country. The publicity given to the affair, indeed, had a very unpleasant
effect, for the magistrates of Berks, Wilts, and Somerset
united in issuing a proclamation declaring it their intention not to allow a breach of peace in either of their
counties, and it was feared that others, especially in the
home counties, would follow suit. It had, until the
proclamation was made public, been the intention to
bring the battle off upon Hungerford Downs, and the good
folks of Newbury and other towns had looked forward
to making a nice little penny out of the business, for it
was estimated that what with the provisions sold, the
drinks, lodgings, stabling, and one thing and the other,
at least £10,000 would be expended in their county.

8

This decision of the magistrates, too, woefully upset Mr. Jackson's plans, and on the 17th of the month, or three days before the date fixed for the battle, he had not decided where it should take place. However, after a council of war, it was determined that the men should meet at Weyhill, in Hampshire, near to Andover, and the commissaries of the Ring were despatched to arrange for the ground there. The name of the rendezvous soon leaked out, and the greatest activity was to be observed upon the roads from London, Bath, Bristol, Winchester, Southampton, and Exeter. Vehicles of every kind were moving to one centre on the day before. Every man with the least sporting tendency set out to witness the great fight for the Championship, which had not taken place for so many years. On the Monday the little town of Andover was besieged, and the streets packed with vehicles and pedestrians, whilst lodgings could not be had for love or money. The taverns were " filled with persons of the highest quality in the kingdom," special messengers having posted down to engage the rooms directly it became known where the fight was to take place. In an account before us we find the following amongst many others of our aristocracy had taken up their quarters at the little town :—The *Duke* of Beaufort, the Marquis of Worcester, Lord Portsmouth, the Duke of Marlborough, Lords Sefton, Yarmouth, and Grantley. The weather was delightful, and everything promised to pass off without a hitch.

Tom Spring had been driven down the day before by easy stages in Mr. Lawrence Sant's carriage and four, and put up at the White Hart, whilst Neat was conveyed to Applesham, some ten miles distant from Andover, where he found accommodation at the Old Pear Tree Inn. Mr. Jackson, who also arrived on the Monday morning, at once went with Bill Gibbons, Caleb Baldwin, and Jack Scroggins to choose the spot where the ring should be pitched. They selected a lovely, smooth bit of turf upon Hinckley Downs, just opposite the Queen Charlotte Inn, and a nice easy walk over from Andover, and there, provided with the ring paraphernalia, they took up their quarters for the night.

Then came another cause for anxiety. A rumour ran through the town like wildfire that application had been made to the mayor and corporation by some influential goody-goody persons to take steps to stop the fight. Jackson at once called a number of the noble sportsmen together, and they formed a deputation, who waited upon Mr. George Barnes, the bailiff of Andover, and earnestly solicited that a promise should be made that, so long as no outrage took place, no interference should

result. Could the worthy mayor resist such a request
when it came from two dukes, a marquis, and three
earls? Scarcely. So there was joy amongst thousands
when it was known that they need fear no molestation.

And now let us picture the imposing scene at
Hinckley Downs upon that beautiful May morning.
There is the open space covered with the soft emerald
carpet of nature, yielding to the tread, and making the
steps as elastic as the heart is light, as we walk past
the 24ft enclosure. Rising on the sides are verdure-
clad slopes, forming a natural amphitheatre, not at all
unlike the ground at the finish of the Goodwood Racecourse. It is very early, yet the ring-keepers are there,
and it is apparent that Mr. Jackson has taken every
precaution to preserve order and marshal the rapidly-
increasing crowd of pedestrians, and the numerous
carriages of all descriptions, into the places assigned to
them.

Those stalwart men, each provided with a whip, are
well known in the ring, and woe unto anybody, whoever
he may be, who refuses to abide by the regulations. Look
at them; on the right there, conversing with Mr. Jackson,
and no doubt taking final orders, is Tom Oliver; near
to him is Jack Scroggins, and forming a little group on
the far side, near the ropes, are Josh Hudson, Jack
Carter, Molineux, and Bittoon the Jew, whilst walking up
and down are Kemp, Tom Ford, and Jack Martin. But
there are others posted at different points, equally well
known to the Ring and the public, all armed with their
whips, which they will use, too, if necessary.

The vehicles are now arriving rapidly, and as they form
a semi-circle, passing to the places assigned to them, it
seems that there must have been a grand rehearsal.
Those on foot take up their positions on the rising
ground, and the reserved seats, or rather trusses of straw,
which are liberally scattered around the ring, some
few yards from the arena, are being taken possession of
by those who have put down their gold for the privilege of
the comfort of a seat. Look yonder, amongst the drags,
there are many of the fair sex, buxom dames and
damsels, with full busts and rosy cheeks. They are
wives and daughters of Hampshire farmers, who have
brought them for a day's outing. Those more stylishly
dressed on the drags belong to the fast set of Bath and
Bristol. It is only eight o'clock in the morning, but
thousands have taken up their position, and carriages
in the greatest variety continue to arrive, whilst scores
of waggons, brought there the night before, are in position, and are rapidly filling, the charges being from ten
shillings for a stand. Count the number of occupants

in one. Surely they represent as much as £20, more
than the old waggon cost when turned out of the wheel-
wright's.

But let us take a glance round with our field-glass, for
we shall see many a familiar face—faces which we have
oft times called up in fancy in these "Memoirs."
Yonder is Sir Thomas Apreece, that fine old Welsh
sportsman, with a heart as big as a bull, the patron of
Mendoza, and his backer for every fight. Over
there is Colonel Berkeley, of the Guards, who led the
23rd Light Dragoons in their glorious charge at Tala-
vera. There also is Captain Barclay, who will run his
critical eye over the men, and tell in an instant if Tom
Cribb has carried out his instructions as to the preparation of Spring. Again, you will recognise General
Barton, who has always backed Jack Randall. Yes,
the aristocratic sports are in full force to-day. But so
are the stars of the Ring. See, there is Mendoza
chatting with his old antagonist, Dick Humphries. The
latter is a prosperous coal merchant in the Adelphi, but
Dan is doing none too well at the Admiral Nelson, in
Whitechapel. Then you see he has a wife and eleven
children to provide for. There is Ned Painter, all smiles
as usual, and very fat he is getting. You would hardly
believe that it is the same who fought and beat Tom
Spring five years ago. Tom Cribb, of course, you cannot
overlook. What a size he has attained—a veritable
Falstaffian paunch has Master Tom, and it is well that
he has finally retired from the Ring.

But, there, we must cease our survey, for there are so
many celebrities present that we must be satisfied to
take them in at a glance. There is a murmur. Do
you hear it swelling to a roar, and now the cheering
leaves us in no doubt that one of the heroes at least is
driving through the crowd. Yes, look, there is Bill
Neat alighting from Squire Harrison's barouche, and he
is now walking arm-in-arm with that gentleman through
the crowd, which divides to let them pass to the ring.
They are followed by Tom Belcher and Harry Harmer,
who are to be his seconds to-day. Listen! the shouting
is greater than ever. Yes; it announces the arrival of
Tom Spring, in company with his backer, Mr. Lawrence
Sant. He is now walking most unconcernedly up and
down the outer ring, in company with his seconds, Cribb
and Ned Painter. No wonder they cheer again, as the
two men meet and shake hands heartily. There is no
bad feeling there, it is evident—no malice, no vindictive-
ness; this will be a battle of skill and survival of the
fittest—a fair, manly, stand-up display of science and
strength.

See, they commence their toilets, and it is evident no time will be wasted. The vast multitude is settling down. Betting appears to be going on everywhere. They are now dressed ready for the fray. Yes, that is Major Hare, of Holme Park, Sussex, who is comparing watches with Captain Barclay. He is the same Major Hare who distinguished himself so gallantly at Waterloo in the charges of Picton's Light Brigade.

Mr. Jackson steps forward. He is going to make a speech. Prick your ears: it must be something important. How silent the crowd has become. He says:— "Gentlemen,—I have to inform you that no persons but the umpires and referee can be stationed close to the ropes, and have, therefore, to request that every one of you will retire to some distance from the ring; and also, if necessity requires it, that you will give me your assistance to keep the ground clear to prevent confusion, and to have that fair fight which we have all come to witness. I have refused to be referee that I may walk about and attend to the ring."

What a cheer is that which goes up from those thousands of lungs! See, Tom Belcher is tying Neat's colours, orange - yellow, to the stakes; and Cribb, too, is knotting Spring's on the opposite side. It is the familiar true blue that has been the winning colour so often.

See, it is a case of hats off in front, and this silence tells the great battle is about to begin. Did you hear the Major? Yes, he called "Time!" for they have shaken hands, and the seconds have retired. Just look at them. What fine models! What specimens of the human form! Quite right. Tom Spring stands 5ft 11½in, and weighs 13st 4lb; and Neat 6ft ½in, and weighs 13st 7lb, Never were men so well matched—never did a finer pair face each other. It is worth the journey to look upon them and their surroundings.

> Oh, it is life to see a proud
> And dauntless man step full of hopes
> Up to the P.R. stakes and ropes;
> Throw in his hat, and with a spring
> Get gallantly within the ring;
> Eye the wide crowd, and walk awhile
> Taking all cheering with a smile.
> To see him strip his well-trained form,
> White, glowing, muscular and warm,
> All beautiful in conscious power,
> Relaxed and quiet till the hour.
> His glassy and transparent frame
> In radiant plight to fight for fame.
> To look upon the clean-shaped limb
> In silk and flannel clothed trim,

Whilst round his waist the kerchief tied
Makes the flesh glow in richer pride.
'Tis more than life to watch him hold
His hand forth—tremulous, yet bold—
Over his seconds, and to clasp
His rival's in a quiet grasp;
To watch the noble attitude
He takes—the crowd in breathless mood—
And then to see, with firmest start,
The muscles set, and the great heart
Hurl a courageous, splendid light
Into the eye—and then the fight.

A minute or two passed, which seemed like a quarter of an hour, during which nothing but the most cautious sparring was indulged in; then Spring let go the left, but there was no damage done. It was only a feeler. The next instant he tried with the right upon the body, but again without effect; yet he recovered so quickly that the return was quite futile. Then Bill commenced to feel his way. He lashed out the left with splendid direction and force; but Tom, in the neatest manner possible, stopped it amidst a roar of applause. Again the same thing happened, and the scientific manœuvring of Spring was a treat to look upon. Another long bout of sparring ensued, each eyeing the other closely; then Spring, pulling himself together, put in a slashing right-hander, but was cleverly stopped by Neat. "Bravo! bravo!" from the crowd, who, although getting a little impatient, could not help admiring the wonderful quickness and display of science on the part of the two gladiators. Then came the excitement. A well-intended blow of Bill's missed, going right over Tom's shoulder, giving him a splendid opening, and smack, smack, smack went in the blows with right and left, fairly staggering Neat. He quickly recovered, however, and forced the fighting with such dash and determination that Tom, who had no mind for slogging at that period of the battle, fought on the retreat —so much so that he very unwisely got into the corner of the ring. "Now's your time, Bill," shouted Belcher. Most certainly Spring had got himself into a bad position; but feeling the stakes at the back with his heel, to be exactly sure of his position, he met the vigorous attack made by Bill in a magnificent manner, stopping the blows which were raining in upon him in a manner that called forth cheer after cheer. Neat couldn't get at him, try all he knew, and, when a little tired of his furious attempts, Tom fought his way out and closed. It looked as if Tom was going down; but he cleverly twisted, got his heel at the back of his antagonist's, and brought him to the ground, throwing the whole of his weight upon Bill's prostrate form. The Londoners were delighted, for Tom had had far the best of it, and the betting was now 7 to 4 on him.

The provincials could not understand it. Here was a man like Spring, who, from the smallness and delicacy of his hands, had been dubbed "The Lady's Maid Fighter," "The China Man," "The Light Tapper," hitting a great deal harder than the tremendous slogger, Neat. Bill was a little vexed, but Tom was as cool as a cucumber, as solid as a rock. Neat struck out resolutely, and in an instant Tom had countered severely on the eye, cutting it to the bone, and drenching his face with blood, half-blinding him. Still he tried a return, but it was easy to see that he was confused, and Spring landing another beauty on the forehead, came to close quarters, fibbed his man severely, and threw Bill with the utmost ease. Everything was done so neatly that the applause was deafening at the finish of the second round.

Spring is said to have declared to Painter as he sat on Cribb's knee after the second round, " It's all right, Ned ; Bill has no chance. It's as right as the day ; I would not take £100 to £1 and stand it; he can't hit me in a week." So it seemed. Neat's only chance was to get home by hook or by crook one of his sledge-hammer blows and knock his opponent out. Everybody was on the tip-toe of expectation, expecting to see Bill pull himself together and make one of those desperate slogging charges for which he was so famous, and which none until then could withstand. But no rush came. It was Spring who took the lead. Yet Neat showed some excellent judgment, as to the surprise of all he fought on the defensive. He stopped two of Tom's very cleverly, and his friends cried out " Well done, Neat; steady does it." And Spring coolly remarked, " Very well stopped, Neat." The next minute Bill landed an awful smack upon Tom's ribs, and the Bristolians burst out with cheers of frantic delight, which, however, were cut short by Spring closing with his man, throwing him, and falling heavily upon him. The Springites were now as gay as larks, offering to back their man to any amount.

There was not the faintest doubt about it, you might have seen it in the man's expression. Neat was afraid of his man, and consequently dropped all those tactics which had won him his previous battles. He showed no signs of going in to fight. Where were his mad bull rushes—his desperate attacks, which none could withstand? Tom had broken his heart by stopping the blows and tries in such a manner as he did. Besides

the crowd began to get merry instead of serious. When
Neat tried, Tom either jumped out of distance, moved
his head, or guarded the blow. His quickness upon the
legs—his dexterity and activity were simply marvellous,
and so puzzled Neat that he hardly knew how to contain
himself. When the spectators began chaffing him,
and roaring with laughter at his every failure,
he lost his head, and then all knew that
he had lost the fight. A bet was made of £1,000 to
£100 on Spring. But at one period of the combat that
" thou " looked as if it were in the layer's pocket. It
was after the fourth round, when Tom had thrown his
man a fearful crash upon the ground. Only a few
noticed that there was something seriously amiss with
him ; but he scarcely ever moved his right—the very
arm he most depended upon. Not only was that so,
but he dropped at the least provocation, and in the
succeeding round a claim was made by the Springites
of a foul. The referee and Jackson both declared that
Neat had been struck before he fell, and so the fight
proceeded.

But Jackson noticed something more serious than
that, and when Tom Belcher spoke to him over the
ropes it was to tell him what he already surmised, that
poor Bill Neat had had his arm fractured in the last
throw. To give him his due, Spring knew nothing of
this, although he could see that the arm had partly gone.
He desired to finish as soon as possible, but was, as a
good general should be, cautious even after the enemy is
to all intents and purposes beaten, for he knew Bill Neat
might have a terrible punch left in that left of his. Bill
fought on the retreat. Spring was too quick for him, and
ping ! ping ! went in the blows upon his face until he was
smothered with blood. The extraordinary part of it was
that he seemed to make no defence, and had Tom liked
he could have cut him to ribbons. He was merciful.
Dab, dab on the nose and a rib bender now and again
satisfied Tom, who knew that now he was only fighting
to entertain the public. Just, however, when he got tired
of that, and meant bringing the entertainment to a close,
after the eighth round Bill Neat walked over to Spring's
corner, held out his left hand, and declared that as his
right arm was broken he could fight no more. Tom
accepted the proffered left and expressed his sorrow, and
Major Hare being assured by Neat's seconds that it was
impossible for their man to continue, awarded the battle
to Tom Spring, who was then and there publicly declared
Champion of England.

CHAPTER XVI.

INTRODUCING THE "BLACK DIAMOND."—HIS EARLY CAREER.— ·
HE MAKES HIS BOW BEFORE THE WEST END SWELLS.—
JEM WARD AND DICK ACTON.—FIGHT FOR FIFTY.

AND now we shall have the pleasure of introducing one
of the best and most scientific fighters of all times,
Jem Ward, nicknamed the "Black Diamond." It is a
double pleasure for us to dwell upon the career of this
Champion, not only for the purpose of recording his
brilliant ring career, but because we knew him personally,
and had many an interesting chat with the old man
during the time that he was in the Licensed Victuallers'
Asylum at Peckham, for he was upwards of eighty years
of age when he died, only a few years ago, and although
towards the last his memory failed him somewhat, we
were frequently able to draw him out, and learn from
his own lips incidents of his career as a prize-fighter.
Indeed, he was the oldest of the Champions we had met
in the flesh, and had the pleasure of a conversation with,
so that our task of recording his progress until he
attained the title of Champion will be agreeable and
authentic.

James Ward was born on the Boxing Day (very
suggestive and appropriate) of the year 1800, near Bow.
His parents were Irish, a breed which always has furnished excellent fighting material. Although, as our
readers will have noticed in the early days of the Prize
Ring, Bristol was the hot-bed of pugilism, at the period
about which we write the Emerald Isle had produced
some excellent material, and has continued to do so ever
since, for how numerous are the Anglo-Irish breed in
the ranks of our Army, and how pluckily they fight!

Young Ward was sent to school when very young, for
he was a smart lad and showed no little aptitude for
learning. At least so thought his parents, and for one
in so low a station (for his father was a ballast-heaver)
an excellent education was given to him. But Jem cared
not for books unless they were stories of battle and
adventure, and instead of sticking to his studies he was
more often found out in the fields with a pair of stuffed
stockings over his wrists, engaged in a friendly spar
with one of the lads, or having a fall at a wrestling

bout with a bigger youth than himself, although he
had many a thrashing from his parents for neglecting
his studies and following his athletic propensities
However, nothing would deter him, and he soon became
so proficient that few dared to meet him.

At the age of sixteen he was taken by his father into
the ballast business, when the hard work developed his
muscles, giving him a strength which was the envy and
admiration of all his fellow - labourers. After a hard
day's work nothing pleased him more than a walk up to
the sparring rooms at Bromley New Town, where he
would put on the mittens with all comers. Amongst other
materials that he loaded and unloaded from ships was
the carbonaceous products of the mine; in other words,
young Jem did a deal of coal-whipping, hence his cogno-
men of the " Black Diamond," which stuck to him all
through his career. At the above-mentioned sparring
rooms, where young Ward was a frequent visitor, was an
old gentleman who took a delight in watching the young
East-Ender aspiring to fistic honours, and his eye fell
favourably upon our hero, and he took him in hand and
introduced him to the then famous Charley Giblets. This
young gentleman, whose real name was Bradford, and
who acquired the nickname through working for a very
lean old poultryman, had made his mark in the ring,
having about this period made a stubborn stand against
the great Phil Sampson on July 17, 1821. The " Giblet
Pie," as he was frequently called, was one of the strongest
and most active athletes of the day. His arm was of
extraordinary length and exceptionally muscular, and as
a high jumper nobody could beat him. His science as a
fighter was not particularly great, for he depended upon
jumping away to avoid rather than dexterously stopping
the blows aimed at him, although the punishment he
dealt was tremendous when he did get a blow home.
Giblets, after his battle with Sampson, had migrated to
the East End, and was following the somewhat lucrative, if rather dirty, occupation of a coal-whipper, so
when introduced the two lads became great chums, and
frequently worked in the same gang together.

Of course Master Charley was looked upon down
East as a great gun, but he was also pretty well known in
the West, and frequently sparred before the Corinthians
of the Ring. Now, soon after his introduction to Ward,
Giblets had determined upon organising a benefit in conjunction with Harry Sutton, the Black, who had beaten
and been beaten by Ned Painter. This boxing display
was arranged to take place at the Fives Court on the
23rd January, 1822, and so pleased was he with Jem
Ward's performances at Bromley, that he determined

that the novice's name should appear upon the programme. So Jem was announced as a new Black
Diamond, and Giblets having sung his praises, no little
curiosity was displayed by the West End amateurs to
see what the youngster was made of. We have before

JAMES WARD.
From a painting by Patten, 1826.

us now an account of the evening's entertainment on
this particular occasion of Ward's *début*, and find some
very good names. There was a spirited set-to between
Eales and Tom Shelton. Tom Belcher and Isaac Bitton
sparred together. Tom Cribb and his " boy," Tom

Spring, gave a taste of their quality, and Scroggins and Harry Holt had a rattling go. So Master Jem Ward was in excellent company, and the critics were all there. This appearance, he must have felt, would decide his future success, for if he could only take the fancy of the patrons of the Ring, perhaps his fortune would be made. It was a trying moment for the young aspirant, for he was pitted against Joe Spencer, who had been twice beaten by Giblets, and once by Rasher, but who nevertheless was looked upon as an exceptionally good man with the gloves, and a very hard hitter.

At first, it would appear, the new Black Diamond did not show much to advantage, but as he warmed to his work and got blow after blow on to the nob of his opponent, the spectators began to open their eyes and ask who the stranger was. Paddington Jones, who was acting as M.C., informed them after the bout was over, that he was a novice of the name of Jem Ward, but no relation to old Joe or Peter of that ilk— only a young East Ender ; but he was ready to throw down the gauntlet to any man his own weight, with the exception of Tom Hickman, the " Gasman." Jem was the talk of the evening, and it was pretty certain that he would not be idle for long. However, the challenge was not accepted until after he had given a display a second time at the Fives Court. This was at the benefit of Harry Harmer, on March 27, and on that occasion Jem's mentor, Charley Giblets, sparred with him. There was no doubt that Jem made an excellent show, and confirmed the good opinion that was formed upon his first appearance. So it was with the greatest satisfaction that during the evening Giblets announced that young Jem Ward had been matched to fight Dick Acton. Some of the old stagers, though, thought that the novice was flying at rather high game, for Dick had had much experience in ring-craft, and had won all his fights, save that with Kendrick, and his friends declared that he lost that only by a fluke. However, the Pugilistic Club had put up £25, and had selected Acton, knowing that if Jem came through the ordeal, he would be entitled to a formidable position amongst the pugilists of his weight, which promised to be quite good enough to entitle him in due course to try for the Championship.

There was no time lost over the matter, and the match was made for the men to meet on Wednesday, the 12th of June, and the greatest curiosity existed as to how the novice would come out with such a formidable opponent. Now we could never understand why Jem Ward was at this time looked upon as a novice, for, according to " Fistiana," he had fought no less than

seven battles, and what is more, had won them all. The
following is a list, according to that authority, although
we are unable to turn up a record of a single engagement, nor were we able to elicit any particulars from
old Jem during his declining years. However, it is our
duty to record them and take them for what they are
worth. Jem Ward beat Geo. Robinson, May 6, 1816, in
forty-five minutes, for £20, in Stepney Fields ; beat Bill
Wall, £20, two hours, Limehouse Fields, June 18, 1816;
beat George Webb, £30, one round, three minutes, Limehouse Fields, July 27, 1817 ; beat Jack Murray, £30,
forty minutes, Dock Hill, Shadwell, February 12, 1819 ;
beat Mick Murphy, £20, thirty-five minutes, Barking,
Essex, July 4, 1819 ; beat Mike Hayes, £30, forty minutes,
Isle of Dogs, September 29, 1820 ; beat John Delany,
£30, thirty minutes, Bow Common, October, 1820.

If the above be correct — and, curiously, the dates
agree exactly with Ward's career—then all we have to
say is, he was no novice at the time he met Acton.

Now the latter was looked upon as a coming man,
and men like Tom Spring, Bill Eales, and Paddington
Jones had great faith in him, believing him to be capable
of acquiring the highest honours of the Ring. Still he
had done very little, beating only third-class men. Still
he had the reputation, and when William Eales took
him down to Brighton to train, his followers thought it
was all over bar the shouting. But the East Enders
thought very differently, for after Jem Ward had
appeared at a benefit of Jem Burns at the boxing saloon
attached to the Horse and Trumpeter, a noted sporting
house kept by Peter Pigeon, in Old Jury Street, Aldgate,
and set-to with Iron-face Rasher, everybody who saw
the way in which Jem stopped the two-handed fighter,
who was known to be such a glutton, and displayed
such extraordinary quickness, backed Ward to a
man. This had the effect of making the odds 6 to 4
on the "novice." But dark as the early part of
Jem's career had been kept, we imagine that his early
victories got wind, and the Fancy began to discover that
the young Black Diamond had had more experience in
the twenty-four foot ring than they had at first imagined.

Under the careful eye of Giblets, Jem went to Snaresbrook to take his breathings, making his headquarters
the Eagle. As we have said, the day fixed for the battle
was Wednesday, the 12th of June, the week after Ascot
Races. The weather had been glorious, and a rattling
good day's sport was anticipated, for all the *élite* of the
Fancy and patrons of the sport had arranged to be present, as there were three attractions on the programme,
and young Ward must have been lucky indeed to have

such an audience to witness his first appearance before West Enders and lights of the Ring. To begin with, Tom Oliver and Bill Abbott were, after months of wrangling, to meet and decide who was the better man. After this our hero and his opponent were to try for supremacy, and the performance was to finish up with a mill between James Blake and Marshall.

At length the memorable day arrived, and it turned out to be the very hottest of a most sweltering summer. The rendezvous was Moulsey Hurst, and the description we read of the journey down inspires us with a thirst well-nigh insatiable. To compare it to a journey to Epsom on a burning hot day hardly conveys the state of affairs, for the road was packed with every conceivable vehicle, and there were crowds of pedestrians kicking up such a dust that from a distance obscured all from view. The blazing sun and the state of the roads made everybody as dry as limekilns, and the rush upon the roadside inns by these parched travellers was tremendous, many selling out their whole stock of beer before the procession had passed by. The crowd looked like millers as they wended their way to the classic Hurst, and when they arrived upon the field of battle the sun was more powerful than ever. The question was asked as to how the men were to fight beneath such a tropical heat, and it was with the greatest difficulty that the stakes were driven into the hard ground, which was in a terrible state for those who were likely to suffer falls.

All being adjusted, and the outer and inner ring being cleared, the sweating, dusty, steaming crowd took their places as best they could, gasping for air, and in no happy mood. Then came a disappointment, which by no means improved the temper of the spectators. They had most of them trudged or driven down from London in order to witness the great fight between Tom Oliver and Bill Abbott, when it was announced that those two gladiators were not about to appear, the latter having paid £10 on the previous evening to be let off. The groans and hisses were terrible to listen to by all accounts, and at one time it looked very like a break into the ring and a free fight. However, Mr. John Jackson calmed down the multitude and announced the second brace of pugilists, and the curiosity still being very great about the Black Diamond, order was restored, and the men entered the ring, Acton being the first to throw in his cap. The latter was honoured with the presence of Tom Spring and Bill Eales as second and bottle-holder, whilst Paddington Jones and Josh Hudson officiated for Jem Ward.

When they both stripped, Acton appeared to be the

heavier of the two, and stood some inches taller than
the Diamond, the former standing 5ft 11in, and weighing
about 13st, whilst Jem pulled the beam down at 12st 4lb,
and stood 5ft 9in. Fine specimen of a man as Dick Acton
was, the Black Diamond showed more elegance and
symmetry of figure. One eye-witness describes his
appearance in the following manner :—" He was so beautifully proportioned that he looked slighter than he really
was. Anyone with an eye for points could see at once
how much finer made a man he was than Acton. Jem's
chest was 44in in girth (when he was thirty it was 46in).
His arms tapered from the shoulder to the wrist, with
that perfect graduation which sculptors tell us is rarely
found except in the masterpieces of old Greek sculpture.
Similarly his legs "fined down" from the thighs to the
ankle, both wrists and ankles being like the fetlocks
of a thoroughbred. Jem's face, with its straight nose
and short upper lip, was remarkable for the amiability
of its expression and mildness, mixed with firmness
which led one of his heartiest and most distinguished
admirers to say : "Jem is a man only in the ring ; he is
a child out of it !"

Yes, Jem Ward must have been a fine man in his
prime, but the perspiring crowd felt no inclination to
admire their manly beauty, and was only anxious for
the fight to commence. Such a good impression, however, did Ward make, that before "Time" was called
the swells were laying 10 to 8 on his chance. Precisely
at ten minutes past three all was in readiness, the
colours (green for Ward and blue for Acton) were tied
to the stakes, and Mr. Jackson gave the signal to commence.

Both were very cautious, Bill evidently playing a
waiting game to feel what his opponent's style was like,
whilst Jem was in no hurry to take the lead. So there
was a deal of elegant but somewhat tedious sparring,
until Jem, seeing an opening, tapped his opponent lightly
on the jaw and jumped out of range. After some more
sparring Ward succeeded in putting in a sharp one on the
jaw with his awkward left, to which he gave a peculiar
turn as he let drive. Following up with another on the
forehead, he got away without a return, and Acton was
evidently getting riled, for he followed Ward, who was
on the retreat to the ropes, and a few harmless exchanges
took place, when Jem, making use of his legs, got away
from his rather awkward position. Then as quick as
lightning he dashed in and landed Bill a smart smack on
the side of the nasal organ, which at once produced the
carmine, and Ward scored the first event. This woke
Acton up to activity, and he retaliated with a lunge at

Jem's ribs, getting well home on the right side. Ward, however, made matters even, for he jobbed him twice heavily on the unfortunate nose, and the claret flowed in rivulets. Acton got wild and rushed in, but Jem was so nimble on his legs that he made his man dance all over the ring until he got winded. Jem was far too quick for him. Letting him come to close quarters, he let go the left twice upon the right eye, cutting the flesh, but none of the blows were heavy enough for a knock-down, and the round terminated with Jem throwing his man cleverly over his knee. There was not much in it, and considering the bout had lasted eight minutes and a half with two such powerful men, very little damage had been done, and the crowd, not having got over their disappointment, did not rise to enthusiasm, some declaring that it was going to be a ginger-bread fight.

The second round was not productive of any more damage, only a few blows being exchanged, and terminating by Ward in turn being thrown. In the next turn Ward seemed somewhat distressed, for the fall had made him pipe a bit. Acton was first to the attack, and put in a smart blow upon Jem's cheek, but trying to repeat it was neatly stopped, and caught a stinging left-hander on the jaw for his pains. After this Ward landed repeatedly on the damaged nose, and Bill, completely losing his temper, bored his opponent to the ropes, where a struggle took place, when Jem threw his man a "buster" on to the hard ground. Three to one on the "novice."

Without giving the details of the three succeeding rounds, it will be sufficient to record that in the fourth round there were some heavy exchanges. Jem getting all the best of it, although he received one smasher on the nose that drew the claret. Yet they betted 5 to 1 on Jem, telling plainly that this round was the turning point of the battle. In the next bout Acton came up woefully cut about the face, and looking all over a beaten man. Hudson and Jones, seeing his condition, instructed Ward to go in and win. Jem took their advice and was soon busy with his man, getting all over his face until he drove him to the ropes, where he dashed his right in and caught him a "hot 'un" on the bridge of that unfortunate nose, "rather a slanting blow upwards." Anyhow, one report says: "That that blow was an exceedingly painful one was evident from the way in which Acton shook his head like a horse over a bin of musty corn." The heat and loss of blood were evidently telling on Acton, and Jem being comparatively fresh, his seconds assured him that he must win.

In the sixth and last round Dick seemed all abroad.
Pulling himself together, however, he went to the attack,
but the Diamond parried him with ease, and then, planting a terrific blow over the eye, knocked all the sense out
of him. A report before us describes the finish in the
following manner :—"From that moment Jem hit him
just as he pleased, landing a succession of blows here,
there, and everywhere. Ward's left arm was not still for
a second, but was rattling incessantly about his opponent's head, till at last Acton went down heavily, and
lay there with his head rolling about from side to side
like a harlequin in a fit, or a Chinese mandarin at a
tobacconist's. All the efforts of Tom Spring and Eales
to get Dick up to the scratch in time failed, so there was
nothing for it but to throw up the sponge and proclaim
Jem Ward the winner, after the fight lasting only nineteen minutes and a half."

Although the battle was of not much importance, it
served to show that Jem Ward was entitled to a place
amongst the aspirants for the Championship, and that
he was entitled to meet men of a better class than Dick
Acton. Altogether it was a most creditable *début*.
We have described this, his first fight, rather in detail ;
but until we come to his fights for the Championship we
must treat that part of his career with less minute
details, or he would occupy too much space upon our
pages, he having fought no less than fourteen battles
before finally retiring from the Ring.

CHAPTER XVII.

A MERRY MEETING AT THE GOLDEN CROSS.—AN IMPROMPTU
MATCH. - A MELANCHOLY TURN UP.—JEM WARD AND
WILLIAM ABBOTT.—A "CROSS" FOR A HUNDRED.— RE-
PENTANCE OF THE "BLACK DIAMOND."

AND now comes that blot upon the escutcheon of Jem
Ward, which all his after battles—every one of them as
straight as a gun-barrel—failed to wipe out entirely. It
was a great pity that it should have occurred just at the
moment when he had his foot upon the ladder of fame,
and could have easily mounted without fear. But in
an evil moment he gave way to the seduction and bad

advice of one who should have known better and paid
the penalty, although his open confession after the affair,
and his public expression of regret, proved that at heart
he was an honest man, and that what he did was enacted
in a weak moment.

But let us not anticipate, for it will be our duty, however painful, to chronicle the event, even if it reflects
upon one of our best and, but for this incident, most
straightforward pugilists who have ever stripped for the
purpose of winning the belt and title of Champion of
England.

Before going into the details of Jem Ward's engagement with William Abbott, we wish you to accompany us
to one of the best patronised and highest-class sporting
drums of that period. It is the Golden Cross, in Long
Acre, kept by that splendid ornament to the Prize
Ring, Harry Holt, who afterwards became reporter
to the *Era*, and attended all the principal fights and
pedestrian matches for that journal. He was known as
the Cicero of the Ring, and a more honourable, more
gentlemanly, or a more popular man amongst the
Corinthians of the metropolis could nowhere be found,
He was the friend of all the sporting swells of the period,
and his house, the Golden Cross, was patronised by the
élite of the patrons of the Ring, for Harry was one of
Nature's gentlemen, and his friends were many.

On this particular evening, Monday, July 22, 1822,
are at the Golden Cross assembled in the big room upstairs, the following galaxy of "swells":—The Marquis
of Worcester, Lord Yarmouth, Lord Alvanley, Lord
Fife, Sir John Shelley, Colonel Cooke, Major Colquitt,
Captain Ponsonby, Mr. Muter, Mr. Stewart, Hon. Tom
Duncombe, Mr. James Soars, Tom Watson, of the Turf
Coffee House, and a host of others whose names are
more or less known as good sports and true. The champagne cup is being freely ladled out and handed round,
for the Marquis of Worcester is in the chair, and
when occupying that position no empty glasses are permitted, and the smoke from the fragrant havannahs curls
about the ceiling and escapes in wreaths through the
open windows.

It is the eve of the fight between Neat and Spring,
which has been described in a previous chapter. The
party has dined wisely and well, for Harry Holt could
put on a banquet with any of them at the Golden Cross,
and now that the tables are cleared, naturally the conversation turns upon the big event which is to take place
on the morrow, and the relative chances of the two
great guns are discussed, whilst amongst other sporting
matters the conversation drifts upon the marvellous per-

formance of the famous Billy in the Westminster rat-
pit, where he had just made his first record against time,
killing one hundred in twelve minutes. Then the great
running feat by Lord Newry, from Oxford to London
in eighteen hours, is discussed, and the time passes swiftly
and pleasantly. Another champagne cup, with little
icebergs floating about in a miniature foaming sea, is
made by host Harry Holt, and there is a lull in the
conversation when Tom Watson calls over to Mr.
Stewart to ask him whether it is true that he had
expressed a willingness to match Abbott against Jem
Ward. "Halloa, what's that?" cries the Marquis of
Worcester. "Ward and Abbott matched?" "Not
quite, my lord," says Watson, "but I hope going
to be before we leave this house to-night." At this
remark there is much applause. Mr. Stewart thereupon replies that he is willing to put £50 down for
Abbott, and Watson instantly replies, "Then I'm your
man, sir." Instantly pen, ink, and paper are placed on
the table, and Mr. William Stewart on behalf of Mr.
William Abbott, and Mr. Thomas Watson on behalf of
Mr. James Ward, agree that the men shall fight within
six weeks of that date. There is quite a flutter of excitement in the Golden Cross that evening, for nowhere
could two men be found so equal to match, it is thought
by all present, and the matter meets with general
approval, whilst it is nearly the only subject discussed
during the remainder of the evening.

Now, it will be remembered that Jem Ward had
earned golden opinions as a boxer on two occasions at
the Fives Court before the noble patrons of the Ring,
and he had defeated Dick Acton at Moulsey Hurst,
although the combat was not very exciting. Yet he
proved himself to be a quick fighter and a heavy
hitter. Since then he had not been matched. But he
had appeared in public subsequently in a turn-up for a
purse, and although he won there was nothing much to
his credit. This is how it happened. The memorable
but disappointing fight between Josh Hudson and Barlow
had taken place at Harpenden Common, on September
10, in which the latter was knocked senseless in six
minutes. This was naturally very disappointing to those
who had come down from London in order to witness
what was expected to be a lively mill; so when the excitement was over the question arose, "What was to be
done?" Hudson went over to where Jem Ward was
standing, and whispered a few words into the Black
Diamond's ear. The latter nodded, and in the twinkling
of an eye Josh had taken off his white hat and was
going round to the " swells " soliciting guineas for a

purse. Twenty-three were soon subscribed, when Ward
declared that he was quite willing to take anybody on in
the ring then and there, his own weight. He had not
long to wait for an answer to his challenge, for Burke,
of Woolwich, who immediately accepted the challeng·.
So far so good, but the spectators were doomed to disappointment on that day, for both Jem Ward and his
opponent, for some reason best known to themselves,
made no fight of it. The whole affair was a pully-hauly
game of wrestling, and scarcely a blow was struck
throughout the seven rounds, which lasted only seven
minutes. At last Jem Ward threw his man, and his head
came against one of the stakes, seriously injuring his neck,
for the blood poured from his nose and ears, and it was
thought at first that his neck was broken. Happily this
was not so, for Burke came to, and they were both
hooted and hissed by the disappointed, not to say
infuriated, mob. This did Ward no good, for he was
put down as a good sparrer, but no good when it came
to the raw 'uns.

However, to return to the match between Jem and
William Abbott, which had been settled at the Golden
Cross. Although articles had been signed, no stakes
had been deposited, and it was thought in sporting
circles that the match would after all fall through.
However, on the day after Ward's turn-up with Burke,
Abbott made some disparaging remarks about Jem,
which Mr. Watson warmly resented, and the money,
£50 a-side, was posted that very night, and the men
agreed to fight in October, 1822.

William Abbott sailed for Margate in the old *Hoy*,
and was accompanied by Caleb Baldwin and Hopping
Ned. Charley Gi'blets took Jem Ward to Epping
Forest, and there ın sylvan grove and upon the banks of
the forest stream, the Roding, Jem took his breathings.
He was frequently visited by his backer, Tom Watson,
who usually came in company with a Mr. John Freshfield, who was a queer customer, who had but a short time
previously cut a ridiculous figure in Bow Street Police
Court. before Sir Robert Bernie, Freshfield having
sworn that he had lost a cheque for £300, which turned
out had been won from him by Ben Burn. This Mr.
Freshfield was by no means a total abstainer, and in the
police court he was far from sober, affording much
amusement and provoking a deal of laughter by his
eccentric behaviour. We have no space to give the
details of the case here, but let us keep our eyes on this
Mr. Freshfield, for he plays an important part in the
present chapter.

On the Monday both men came up from thei͞ training

quarters, Jem Ward in a chaise from the Forest, and William Abbott by coach from Margate, when they met at Tom Belcher's to decide the rendezvous, and to settle minor details. It was then noticed that Tom Watson and this Mr. Freshfield never left their men, and when it became known that Josh Hudson, who had helped to train Ward, was going to be second to Abbott, people wondered what the meaning of it all was. Still, when they discovered that Paddington Jones and William Eales were to wait upon Ward, they were satisfied.

Moulsey Hurst was the place fixed for the battle, and on the Tuesday morning, October 22, the company began to flock into Hampton, and the watermen had a fine harvest ferrying people over to the Hurst. Quality and quantity was the order of the day, and there was really a good sprinkling of "Corinthians," who had just come to stay in London for a short spell before the hunting season began.

At one o'clock Abbott, followed by Bill Richmond, the Black, and Josh Hudson, pitched his castor into the ring, followed five minutes later by Jem Ward, who was accompanied by Jones and Eales.

Now, when the match was made, the friends and backers of Abbott were under the impression that their man was the heavier of the two, for it had always been put forward that Ward's weight was but 11st, whilst Abbott confessed to 11st 7lb. As a matter of fact, Jem Ward at this time weighed no less than 12st 4lb, and when "Bee," the astute editor of the *Fancy Gazette*, called public attention to this fact, the backers of Master William became shy, and they would not lay a penny out unless they obtained the odds of 2 to 1. This hardly suited Messrs. Watson, Freshfield, and Co., so they determined upon another line of action.

As soon as "Time" was called, they commenced sparring very warily until two minutes had been occupied without a blow being attempted. Then a light tap upon the forehead from the Black Diamond opened the ball, which Abbott failed to return, and in quick succession Jem reached him again and again over his guard, but so light were the blows that no damage whatever was done. This made Bill very cross, and in answer to the advice of his friends, he dashed in to close quarters. But he was nowhere with Jem at wrestling, and was cross-buttocked in an instant, amidst the yells and cheers of the East Enders.

It will be useless to describe all the rounds, for they meant nothing, Jem Ward undoubtedly being capable of doing just what he pleased with his man. He was a mere plaything in his hands. Here, however, is a quotation from one report of the second round :—" With a feint at the head, he put in a body blow of such severity with his right, that Abbott went staggering back three or four yards, and would have fallen had he not backed on to the ropes. Before he could get from his awkward position, Ward had him in chancery, and was fibbing away with his left until he was red to the elbow with the blood that streamed from Abbott's nose and mouth. At last, with a desperate and supreme effort, Abbott tore himself away from that frightful grasp and fell on the grass, amid roars of frantic applause from Ward's friends, and offers of 5 to 1 on Jem.

Round after round Ward threw his man and dealt him the most fearful punishment, until at the close of the eighteenth bout the fight was apparently all over bar the shouting, and Tom Belcher left the side of the ring to get his pigeons to send off with the news of Jem's victory. Still Abbott's seconds set him up, and in the nineteenth round all should have been settled. Then, however, to the amazement of everybody, Jem in the most unaccountable manner let slip several easy opportunities. "What's up with Ward?" was the general question. Something was wrong evidently, for Bill Eales called out to Mr. Watson to come and speak to him, and Jones in a state of high indignation exclaimed, "What does this mean? Here's Ward says he means to cut it next round, and lose the fight. Do you know anything about it?" "Certainly not," said Watson, warmly. "I expect Ward to do his best to win."

Again the same farce was played. Abbott evidently could not understand Ward's game, for he had been completely outfought all through. Still he had his duty to do to his backers, and he made a feeble effort in the twenty-second round. After a little sparring he managed to get in a blow upon Jem's chin that would scarcely have knocked a fly off, and Jem Ward dropped. This is what one report says, and if it be true never was there such a barefaced robbery perpetrated in any roped arena :—" On being picked up and placed on Paddington Jones's knee, Jem raised himself erect almost without an effort, and smiled at Eales; but then, suddenly recollecting the part he was to play, he gave a quick glance over at Abbott's corner, and, seeing that Bill looked uncommonly like giving in, Jem, with a frightful contortion of the face, fell back into Jones's arms and *swooned!* In vain old Paddington cursed and swore at him, in vain Eales shook him, tweaked his ears, pulled his nose, and pinched his calves; Jem lay limp as a dead cabbage, and Mr. James Soares, the referee, having thrice called

"Time" without any response from Ward, Abbott was just able to stagger to the scratch, and was proclaimed the winner."

The spectators were paralysed, and fortunate for Ward they were, for it enabled him to slip out of the ring, get a scarf and coat on, and make a bolt for it, jumping some hurdles as he made for the river, proving indisputably that he was perfectly fresh. Never was such a bare-faced "cross" known by the oldest ring-goer. At first the crowd became frantic, but when the excitement had somewhat toned down it was determined that the most complete investigation should be made on the morrow, before a committee of the foremost sportsmen of the day to decide what should be done.

On the morrow the meeting was convened at the One Tun, Jermyn Street, with Mr. Minchin, of Turnham Green, the Nestor of sport, in the chair, and amongst those present were several noblemen and distinguished supporters of the Prize Ring. Mr. William Stewart, Abbott's backer, declined to receive a shilling of the stakes or bets, stating that in his opinion "a more flagrant cross never disgraced the P.R. (*a fact already incontestably proved*), and that, consequently, no real sporting character can expect his bets to be valid.

Jem Ward, his backers, Messrs. Watson and Freshfield, were there, and it transpired that they had that morning been with their solicitor, Mr. Edward Parlin, to the police magistrate at Hatton Garden, to swear an affidavit to the effect that Jem had fought honestly, and had done his best to win. The magistrate, however, refused to countenance such an affidavit, on the grounds that all parties concerned, by their own confession, had been guilty of a breach of the peace.

At first Jem Ward, in answer to the chairman's questions, denied the truth of the allegations made against him, but his agitation was so great that it was evident that he was telling lies. At length he broke down altogether, and, bursting into tears, confessed that Mr. Watson had promised him £100 to sell the fight. The painful scene was made humorous when Jem declared that "it was a proper fair cross; that he was ignorant of the ways of the world, not used to company, nor to drink wine; that his backers had endeavoured to make him drunk the night before fight-ing, saying, 'Never mind, Ward, you have but little work to do to-morrow, it's of no consequence how much you drink!'" The committee unanimously voted that it was a cross, Messrs. Watson and Freshfield agreeing to the vote.

Tom Cribb, who was present, came to poor Ward's

rescue, and declared that he was a poor, ignorant young man, who had been led away by artful deceivers, but was not bad at heart, and as a proof of his opinion he should give him a sovereign. No less than twenty - seven others followed suit, so he left the room with a little golden salve for his wounded heart. No proof could be brought absolutely against Freshfield and Watson, for they would admit nothing, declaring that Ward had been guilty of the basest ingratitude, so neither of them were tabooed from sporting circles, although there was little doubt as to their complicity and guilt.

Poor Jem Ward, however, was the victim. He had condemned himself by his own confession, and was formally expelled from the Pugilistic Club, and was denounced by all the sporting journals as a disgrace to the Fancy.

And there in disgrace we must leave him, deferring until next chapter an account of how he at length succeeded in getting over his difficulties.

CHAPTER XVIII.

RETURN OF THE LAMB TO THE FOLD.— THE "BLACK DIAMOND"
AS A YOKEL.— JEM WARD'S INTRODUCTIONS TO BALDWIN,
RICKENS, AND JEMMY THE BLACK - A "WEST COUNTREE"
TOUR.

IT will be remembered that we left Jem Ward in sad disgrace through the cross to which he was a party in his fight with Abbott. Although he was cut off from the Pugilistic Club and disgraced, the clumsy way in which he had managed the whole business proved conclusively that he was but the tool of others, and a lad of rare simplicity.

His confession, too, did much to mollify the feelings of the sporting world towards him, and by most he was more pitied than blamed. There was not the slightest doubt but that he sincerely regretted what had happened, and his letter to the sporting newspapers of the day showed his contrition ; so we cannot do better than quote it :—

" SIR,—I trust you will excuse my obtruding upon you in requesting the insertion of a letter from me, whom I hope the sporting world will consider sinned against as sinning. My last fight with Abbott having given rise to much, I may say much-merited, animadversion, I hope, in extenuation, some consideration may be made for my inexperience in the world, and a too great reliance on those who have seduced and deceived me. Had I taken the advice of my trainer in lieu of my backer, I should not have to deplore the commitment of an act which has caused me the most bitter regret. I should be most happy, by way of retrieving in some degree the credit I have lost, to fight Abbott again for the present stakes. If I ask too much in this, I am willing to meet him in the same ring with Hudson and Shelton, on the 19th inst., for a purse, or even for love.—I am, sir, with the greatest respect, your obliged servant,   " JAMES WARD.

" November 12, 1822."

The above letter proves that Jem was not dishonest at heart, and his friends took the matter in hand, and through the unremitting exertions of Mr. Turner, the landlord of the Mulberry Tree, Whitechapel, Jem Ward was once more made eligible to enter the arena, where it will be our pleasant duty in future chapters to record that he, throughout his long and brilliant career, gloriously retrieved his reputation, never again to be soiled or tarnished by suspicion of dishonour.

Although Jem Ward appeared on a few occasions as a second, it was not until the 4th of February, 1823, that he entered the arena as a principal. It was but for a purse of £5, and his antagonist was said to be only a " Johnny Raw." It turned out, however, that the yokel, as he was supposed to be, was no other than a pupil of the wary Bill Eales and Bill Acton, whom these artful dodgers were running as a dark horse, and who afterwards came out before the public as the celebrated Ned Baldwin (White-headed Bob), who became one of the first pugilists of the day. The battle took place on Wimbledon Common. Ned Baldwin stuck to his man bravely, but he had no chance with the Black Diamond, who had immensely improved, and with quickness in hitting and getting away astounded everybody present. Twenty rounds were fought in nineteen minutes, when Ward was declared the winner. This victory re-established Jem with his friends, for he had given the White-headed one a fearful " gruelling," his face being terribly lacerated and his head contused, proving what a hard as well as quick hitter Ward was.

Shortly after this, on the 11th of February, 1823, Josh Hudson took a benefit at the Fives Court, the whole *élite* of the Fancy being present. To Jem's delight he was selected to pair off with Tom Spring, who was still looked upon as the tip-top heavy-weight. It was a grand opportunity for Ward to show what he was capable of doing, and he made a grand display. Here is a quotation from one report :—" The bout between the two heroes was the event of the evening. The spectators—and they included all the leading patrons of the sport—were roused to an extraordinary pitch of enthusiasm by the magnificent display of science to which they were treated. Spring was in his best form. He said that he felt fit and well enough to fight anybody, but the rapidity of Ward's hitting, and his wonderful quickness in getting away, fairly bothered Tom, who had to do all he knew to hold his own, and was generally thought to have had the worst of it."

This was a great feather in the Black Diamond's cap and he felt himself so strong that he immediately issued a challenge to fight " any twelve or thirteen stone man, or to give a few pounds." To this Tom Shelton, Jack Carter, and Peter Crawley replied, but nothing came of their nibbles, and it looked as if Jem would be for a long while idle.

Just about this time Jem Ward made the acquaintance of a man who was destined to become as great a celebrity as himself. This was Nicholson, afterwards the notorious Lord Chief Baron of Judge and Jury fame, and the companion and entertainer to the whole fast sporting set of London, whose midnight orgies and mock trials were the talk of the town. At this time, however, Renton Nicholson was only a pawnbroker's assistant at Shadwell. In his " Autobiography," which is before us, he tells us that he was " able-bodied, had large, manly whiskers, and at the age of fourteen and a half might have passed for twenty."

Jem Ward had but recently left the athletic occupation of coal-whipping when he met Renton Nicholson, who describes him as the " Phenomenon," one who was young, generous, scientific, and brave. In his book the Baron leaves it on record that Jem was always the champion of the weak against the opposition of the strong; and many were the thrashings he administered to brutes who assaulted women in the streets about Shadwell, Ratcliff Highway and Wapping. Here is an incident which we may relate, and which is taken from Renton Nicholson's " Autobiography ":—" In the rear of my master's premises was a narrow roadway named Fox's Lane. The houses then standing were old in the tenancy of iniquity;

there profligacy was king;—debauchery queen, and
robbery and vice the constitution. In the middle of this
empire of infamy lived Mary Billington, associating
with one Joe Strong, a monster in human form, *but*
good looking—at least as well favoured as high cheek-
bones and a handsome bull-dog sort of head would allow
him to be. Poor Mary Billington—or Poll Billington, as
she was usually called—had been a beautiful girl before
her features had become disfigured and swollen by the
ill-treatment of the Herculean Josephus. She was rarely
without a black eye veiling her exquisite blue one; her
fair face was too often bruised and bloodshot by the adroit
blows of the inhuman wretch to whom she yet remained
devoted, despite his unparalleled brutality. A young
man who had loved her in her virtue, and continued
fondly attached to her in her degradation, sought her in
an illness, which was of more than a month's duration,
arising from one of Joe's periodical attacks upon her life,
for the protection of which she could never be prevailed
upon to seek magisterial interference. The young man,
whose notions and conduct were alike so compassionate
and platonic, was one day surprised while sitting at the side
of poor Polly's bed, engaged in serious conversation with
her, by the entrance of Joe Strong. The savage nature
of the villain wanted but little suspicion to excite him
into demoniacal ferocity. Taking up the poker, he laid
the unfortunate visitor bleeding on the floor; he then
seized the unhappy bed-ridden girl by her streaming
hair and dragged her into the street. Jem Ward was
talking with me at the shop door. ' What the deuce is
that ?' said Jem. The question was in another instant
answered by the appearance of Joe Strong, brandishing
the poker in his right hand, and with his left trailing
the half-naked invalid girl in his wake. I have never, in
all his great contests, been half so proud of Jem Ward
as I was on that terrible and momentous occasion.
' Leave go that woman,' said Jem. Mr. Strong replied
by aiming a blow at Jem with the poker, who met Mr.
Strong with one of those scientific left-handed hits—which
afterwards settled many a more important conflict—
right in the middle of the face, smashing his ignominious
nose, prostrating him on the broad of his back, and
with magical velocity forcing the poker from his grasp
into the middle of the road. Mr. Strong was knocked
out of time by the first hit. There he sprawled, deaf to
everything around. The woman, the miserable victim
to his murderous attack, sick, bleeding, with hair dis-
hevelled, and her clothes torn from her back, had no
thought for herself, and but little for the benefactor
who still lay senseless in her apartment. Her mad

tenderness was all for the sprawling coward who fell by the manly and victorious fist of the gallant Jem. Polly Billington was the ministering angel of the ruffian Strong. Humanity shuddered to assist him; but that misguided girl tried to lift him from the pavement. She could not. Entreaty and remonstrance were both had recourse to, and at last the required aid was obtained and the well-punished and inhuman scoundrel was shortly placed upon the bed from which he had so recently dragged the ill-fated Polly. The wounded lover was induced by the prayers and entreaties of the once-beloved Mary to take no steps to prosecute the vagabond who had so wantonly assailed him. He promised her he would not, and he kept his word."

We have given space to Renton Nicholson's story, which savours much of the Sykes and Nancy episode, to show what Jem Ward's character was out of the ring. This is only one instance proving how fine a fellow he was, and gained him the greatest respect and esteem of all who knew him.

But to return to his pugilistic career. Nobody in London could be induced to take up the gauntlet, so Jem, tiring of this inactive life, determined to visit the provinces, and try his luck in the " West Countree." Bath and Bristol, as our readers will remember, being hot-beds of pugilism. He took with him as companions, Maurice Delay and George Weston. According to Nicholson, the former, he says, " was one of the finest-looking ruffians I ever saw." Delay was a coal-whipper, and had fought several times, having defeated Charley Gibblets, but eventually he came to grief, joining a gang of thieves, getting caught red-handed and transported for life. At this time, however, he was an honest man. George Weston, Jem's other companion, had experienced much more in the ring, for he had fought Jack Ford, Aby Belasco, and Jem Wynes, the Bristol Sawyer. So the three knights of the fist made up a very formidable trio. The men going down to Bath on the tramp, having walked something like thirty miles a day, arriving at the opening of the races, July 1, 1823.

Bath, not the sleepy, straight-laced town of to-day, but then the Queen of the West, the liveliest, wickedest, and most fashionable resort in the kingdom, was crowded on this occasion. Belles and beaux of all ages and degrees there congregated, some to take the waters, others to enjoy the racing. It must have been a terribly naughty place in those days, for one satirist writes about it and tells us that it was "a valley of pleasure, yet a sink of iniquity, and that every vice in the metropolis was counterfeited, and sometimes improved upon, in Bath."

Both sexes used to promenade in the water with the slightest of bathing costumes, the water up to their necks, so that their heads appeared to be all floating. Then there was the Grove and the Meadows, both crowded during the day with fops and pretty women,

The ladies of Bath have so dashing an air,
So charming a smirk, and agreeable stare,
Not to say how they show all their shapes in the wind,
With nothing before, and their pockets behind.

But to return to Jem Ward and his friends, who had arrived in the midst of all this gaiety. It had been the custom during the race week always to have a purse subscribed and fought for, open to all comers ; and our trio of pugilists being aware of this, made their way to the principal sporting house, the Castle and Ball Tavern. There they discovered that the purse had been twice won by the Somerset champion, Joe Rickens, and that he was there to take it for the third time. Now few of those present in the parlour of the inn recognised our friends, especially as they were somewhat disguised, being clothed in countrymen's smocks, which articles they had purchased on the road. There were, however, a few Jews from London well known in sporting circles, and they at once recognised Jem Ward, but the word having been passed for secrecy, they took the hint, knowing that if the game were not given away they would be able to make a tidy little sum. It had been arranged that Ward should play the part of a North-country yokel, and that he should pass as a Mr. Sawney Wilson, a simple chap, who thought he could fight a bit, and had come to Bath to try for the purse. This soon got about, and one of the friends of Joe Rickens sent for that worthy, who quickly arrived on the scene. In a swaggering way he came up to Jem Ward, and looked contemptibly at our hero. One account gives a most amusing scene, and it must have been a treat for those to be present who were in the know. It appears that the West-country Champion, when he saw the simple countryman, laughed outright, and asked him if he had any money. To this Jem replied that he had not, but he wanted to have a go for the purse, and that he thought some of the gentlemen present, pointing to the " peoplesh," would back him for a few pounds, just for the sake of the sport.

At this Rickens and his friends were delighted, and arrangements were made for the fight to come off on the following day, at five o'clock in the afternoon, the Somersetshire man insisting that articles should be drawn up in case Sawney should back out, and if he did so he might claim the purse, especially as there were no other candidates. Added to the purse of 20 guineas, the

Jews had put down the sum of another twenty, which had been covered by Rickens' friends, and so cock-sure were they, that odds were laid of three and four to one, which were taken up cautiously by those in the know, to a large sum of money. The news soon spread through the town, when it was known that the battle was to take place at Lansdowne, and the talk in the Pump Room and the Tap Room was of nothing else.

Long before five o'clock the spot of ground upon which the ring had been formed, was thronged with people; all Bath, visitors and residents, having turned out to see the great Somersetshire giant thrash the presumptuous countryman.

Great was the excitement as the two men faced each other; Rickens in proper fighting costume, but "Sawney" in brown breeches and thick boots. As the latter shaped, however, there was a rumour passed round that he was a Londoner, and that Master Joe would find that he had caught a Tartar. His friends, though, laughed at such an eventuality, and offered to lay out extra money on their man, an easy enough task, for the Jews were hungering for more. Rickens towered above his man, standing 6ft 1in, and weighing 14st, certainly a very fine fellow, and it really looked as if the smaller man had very little chance with such a giant. Joe was three inches taller and 2st heavier than Jem Ward.

Of course Delay and Weston seconded "Sawney Wilson," and Pearce (brother to the Game Chicken) and Harris looked after Rickens. As they sparred together it was palpable to everybody that the supposed yokel was no novice at the game; but Jem made none too great a display, for he tried not to give the game away; and although being quite confident as to the result, he thought it would be unwise to win too soon. So he played about with his opponent for two or three minutes, when, getting too close, and not being sufficiently cautious, the big 'un swung his arm round, and to the delight of most, and to the surprise of the few, caught Jem a terrific blow on the side of the neck, which very nearly sent him sprawling. There was a tremendous shout from the followers of the Somersetshire lad, but Ward was in no way dismayed, and pulled himself together in the coolest manner; and, springing in before his opponent knew what he was doing, let go right and left with such rapidity and force that the Bath man was sent spinning away, and measured his length at the feet of his seconds. There was a dead silence, and Rickens' friends looked at each other in blank amazement.

The big man came up to the scratch for the second

round furious, and dashed in with all his brute force, evidently intent upon slaughtering the countryman right off the reel. But Jem Ward astonished the spectators, for he stopped blow after blow with the utmost coolness, and avoided the rushes in a masterly manner, until he had got his man out of breath; when he sprang in, and dealing Joseph a terrible blow on the throat, sent him to grass again upon his back. We can imagine the consternation; and one report says that a remark made was, "What do they call him? Sawney Wilson? By gum, he bean't half such a Sawney as some volk may think; why he makes Rickens spin loike a humming-top." 3 to 1 on Sawney, and no takers.

Jem at this juncture determined to give the company a taste of his abilities, and chance the result, so he commenced fighting in real earnest, hitting his man about just as he pleased. He gave him a terrific left-hander full on the nose, which flattened that organ upon his face, and once more sent him to grass. There was a dreadful uproar at this; and when, in the fourth round, he hit him on the cheek and laid it open, following up the blow with some terrible hits on the ribs, and knocking the big chap down for the fourth time, there was a general uproar; and as Ward sat upon his second's knees he had sticks flourished at him, and had it not been for some of the Bristol boys, who insisted on fair-play, no doubt he would have been roughly handled; so incensed were those who had lost their money over what they called a dodge.

Ward after this determined to finish the affair as quickly as possible, and although Rickens came up pluckily for another four rounds, he got punished so fearfully that in the end he was knocked clean out of time; the battle only having lasted fifteen minutes. Jem was without a single mark, whilst his opponent's face was so bruised and bleeding, that a wag was stated to have remarked, "one-half of his face looked like a live lobster, and the other half like a boiled one."

When the fight was over there was a dreadful scene, and it was only by the skin of their teeth that the three Londoners escaped the fury of the mob, and made their way to the Castle and Ball. Then they discovered that the stakeholder refused to part with the money, declaring that it was all a swindle, and that the Bath man had been imposed upon unfairly. So incensed did Rickens' followers become, that they threatened to lynch Ward, so the three, thinking discretion the better part of valour, made tracks from Bath (minus their money), only too glad to get out of harm's way.

How they escaped from Bath, and the details of the

incidents of their travels in the West country, we have
no space to describe now. Suffice it to say that he made
his mark wherever he went, although not much money
was netted, he only winning a purse in an engagement
with Jemmy the Black, at Southampton, and receiving
a few pounds a week at exhibition sparring. So Jem
Ward was glad to come back to London, although his
provincial trip had done him no harm. On the contrary,
it had raised him in the eyes of the Fancy, both London
and provincial, and enabled him to start fairly on to the
goal for which he was aiming—viz,, the Championship
of England.

CHAPTER XIX.

AN EVENING AT THE HOLE IN THE WALL.—JEM WARD AND
JOSH HUDSON, AND HIS FIRST FIGHT WITH PHIL SAMPSON.

At the period of which we write, when Jem Ward was
making a bid for the Championship, that is to say, in
the early twenties, there were two well-known sporting
houses in London, both of the same name—the Hole in
the Wall, Chancery Lane (now, we believe, turned into a
Bodega), and a house with the same sign in Gate Street,
Lincoln's Inn. The first-mentioned was kept by Jack
Randall, the "Nonpareil," and the other by Tom Shelton.
The tavern in Chancery Lane has been immortalised by
the great English critic, William Hazlitt, in his description of the fight between Gas and Neate, which stands
as a unique specimen of classical English literature.
But it would seem that Mr. Hazlitt was none too partial
to Randall or his house, for he writes: "I was not
fond of going into this house of call for heroes and philo-
sophers ever since the owner of it (for Jack is no
gentleman) threatened once upon a time to kick me out
of doors for wanting a mutton-chop at his hospitable
board, when the conqueror in thirteen battles was
more full of *blue ruin* (gin) than good manners. I was
the more mortified at this repulse, as I had heard Mr.
James Simpkins, hosier, in the Strand, one day when the
character of the Hole in the Wall was brought into

question, observe :—' The house is a very good house, and the company quite genteel. I have been there my-self.' "

Let us then, in fancy, look in at Jack Randall's hostelry on the evening of Wednesday, October 29, 1823. There the company is " quite genteel," for there are many of the most aristocratic supporters of the Ring, whilst the other part of the house is crowded with sports of every grade. These ruddy-faced sportsmen sit quaffing mulled wine in the snuggery, or smoking long pipes and sipping warm brandy in the long parlour. The occasion is the final deposit of £50 for the match which has been made by Josh Hudson and Jem Ward for £100 a-side. No such important an event has taken place since the battle between Spring and Neate for the Championship.

The appearance of Josh Hudson himself, accompanied by Tom Owen and his backer, Mr. Hart, a son of old Lemon Hart, the rum contractor, of Tower Hill), creates quite a sensation, but it is disappointing to learn that neither Jem Ward nor his backer, Sir Bellingham Graham, will be present, for Tom Spring has been deputed to plank down the money. This having been done, quite a jovial evening is spent, and the greatest interest is invested in the coming event, for both are " Stars from the East," and although they, so to speak, come from the same stable, both are hard up for a job, and quite willing to prove which would be the better man of the two.

It may be remembered that we stated at the time of describing Tom Johnson and Ben Brain's fight for the Championship we quoted the latter's remark, " Tommy, you and I never fell out, and that's the reason we ought to fight." Josh Hudson thought precisely the same. He detested quarrelling, but he loved fighting, and to meet his old friend Jem Ward in the ring and do battle for supremacy was to imply no breach of the warmest friendship. And so the match was made, and the last deposit put down.

Tom Owen took the " John Bull Fighter," as Josh was called, under his care to Harpenden, for he was very big, and it was necessary to take a deal of flesh off him. Ward was already in splendid condition, having just come from his West-country tour, incidents of which we described in the last chapter.

The battle was fixed to come off at Moulsey Hurst on November 11, 1823. We shall not, however, take our readers over the oft-trodden ground, but briefly describe how the Black Diamond met with his first and only reverse, or we shall be devoting too much space to the description of Jem Ward's many contests.

There were slight odds on Ward, but a great number
of the knowing ones stuck firmly to Josh Hudson, for
he had fought twenty times, won thirteen battles, and
lost seven, and they were, to some of the best men of
the day, viz., Bowen, Martin, Tom Spring, Aby Belasco
(twice), Turner, and Shelton. In any case he had had
much more experience in the ring than Jem Ward, so
little wonder he was fancied by many. That they were
justified in their fancy for Hudson events proved, for
although during the first nine or ten rounds Ward scored
heavily, and the betting was 5 to 1 on the Diamond, a
change came o'er the scene in the eleventh round, and
just as Jem seemed to be having it all his own way, by
one of those miraculous efforts noticeable in all Hudson's
hardest battles, he pulled himself together. Here is a
description of the eleventh round : " Josh came to scratch
looking as if he had taken quite a fresh lease of life.
But Jem's science and agility were too much for him.
Ward kept retreating and pinking Josh about the head
at pleasure, and with the greatest ease, as the latter
advanced. The Black Diamond appeared to be having
it all his own way, when his vigour seemed suddenly to
leave him, and he was caught napping, for Josh put in a
terrific left-hander under Jem's left eye, which closed, or
appeared to close, that optic instantly, and almost
knocked Ward's head off his shoulders. For the moment
the Diamond was all abroad--quite silly and dizzy—and
hit at random blow for blow, till Josh floored him. The
shouting for Hudson after this last exploit was awful."

By all accounts there was something wrong with Jem
Ward from this moment, and although Josh was fearfully punished and as weak as the proverbial rat, he
managed to come up for four more rounds, and gain all
the best of it, and in the fifteenth Tom Spring and Aby
Belasco, who acted as seconds for Jem, had to assist
him to the scratch, amidst shouts of " Take him away—
he's done—don't hit him, Josh." It was all over; Spring
threw up the sponge, and Mr. Gully, who was referee,
declared Josh Hudson the winner.

It was a terrible disappointment to Ward's friends,
and a bitter one for Jem himself. All kinds of reasons
were given for the break-down, but Jem Ward many
years afterwards informed a friend in the Licensed
Victuallers' Asylum that, although he looked well, he
was suffering from debility, and that his strength died
gradually away towards the close of the fight. No
doubt that was the reason, but not everybody believed it,
as was proved two days after the battle, by a most dis-
pleasing incident taking place.

There was a meeting at Peter Crawley's benefit at

the Fives Court, on November 13, 1823. During
the evening Josh Hudson, whose head was bound up,
and whose face was the colour of a rainbow, put in an
appearance, and the M.C., old Paddington Jones, informed the company that Josh had something of importance to impart to them. He ascended the platform and
delivered himself of the following :—" Gentlemen, I have
been informed by Mr. Egan that Shelton has made an

JOSH HUDSON.

assertion that Ward received £100 to lose the battle with
me. I will bet anybody £50 to £1 that he does not
prove it. (' Bravo, Josh!') I will also fight Tom
Shelton for any sum from £25 to £200, when the time he
is bound over expires. If Ward is in the Court let him
come forward and answer the charge brought against
him." Tom Shelton then ascended the stage and declared
that Ben Burn had made the statement, and that he

would have no more to do with it. At this moment
Jem Ward appeared upon the scene and said amidst
great applause : " I publicly assert that no individual
whatever offered me a single farthing to lose the battle."
Josh Hudson came forward and shook Jem heartily by
the hand, saying, "It's all a d——d lie, Jem, and
nobody but a —— fool would believe it." Then, turning
to Ben Burn, he offered to fight him any time £100 to
£60. Burn, who was in liquor, tried to speak, but the
audience would not permit him, and Jem Ward was
unanimously acquitted of the vile charge brought against
him.

Although Jem had lost much money for his backers,
Sir Bellingham Graham believed in him to such an
extent that he placed a sum of money in Pierce Egan's
hands, with instructions that Ward should have paid to
him the sum of £2 every week ; so, after all, Jem's first
and only defeat was attended by one pleasant circumstance.

And now let us take a survey over the heads of the heavy
weights, and reckon who then before the public were
entitled to aspire to the Championship. To begin with,
there was Tom Spring, who had held the honour for a
considerable time, but who, it was rumoured, was about
to give it up, and declared that he did not care again to
enter the lists. Then there were only the following to
name out of the whole army of pugilists :—Tom Shelton,
Josh Hudson, Peter Crawley, Tom Gaynor, Jack Langan,
Tom Cannon, Ned Neale, White-Headed Bob, and Phil
Sampson. Jem Ward, to be sure, was thought eligible
by some of his East End friends ; but what had he done,
to class him amongst those whose names we have just
given ? He had certainly only met third-rate men, and
his draw with Abbott and his defeat by Josh Hudson
were both affairs which told against him. Still his
magnificent display of science at the Fives Court and
his fine physique convinced the knowing ones that he
was the coming man. Why, there hadn't been such a
scientific boxer since Jem Belcher, and this even Tom
Spring was bound to admit. So there were but three
who were considered to have but a ghost of a chance
against the Black Diamond, and they were Tom Shelton,
Peter Crawley, and Jack Langan, and neither of these
seemed anxious to try conclusions with Ward.

At this period, however, Phil Sampson had been
bragging and blustering, declaring what he could do,
although he had only just got over the disgraceful business with Josh Hudson, when he did not appear at the
ring-side, and forfeited to " John Bull." The friends of
Ward heard of it, and at once threw down the gauntlet

to Sampson. And so articles were signed at Tom
Belcher's on Saturday, May 23, to the effect that
James Ward, of Bow, and Philip Sampson, of Birmingham, agreed to fight for £100 a-side, within five-and-
twenty miles of London, on June 21, 1824.

There was not a great deal of interest taken in the
match, from the fact that Phil Sampson was looked upon
as most untrustworthy, and it is marvellous to find
how the Brums stuck to him through thick and thin,
for never was there a more unreliable man to be found
in the annals of the Ring. So chequered, indeed, were
his performances, that even those who knew how good he
was at his best refrained from following him. Sometimes he fought so brilliantly that it seemed as if it
were easy for him to become Champion in Spring's place,
but at other times his performances stamped him as rogue
or cur. For instance, his displays with Hall and Abbott
were enough to condemn any man. He permitted himself to be beaten in both battles, without making the
slightest attempt to win. For ninety-nine minutes he and
Hall fought on Warwick Racecourse, and at the end, when
Sampson gave in, there was not a single bruise upon him.
Then eight months afterwards, when they met again,
Hall was polished off in two rounds. That was in-and-
out fighting with a vengeance. No wonder, then,
Master Phil Sampson was not supported to a great
extent. Then, again, his last match with Josh Hudson,
which fell through at the eleventh hour, made people
fear that if they did support him he would not turn up
at all.

Ward's friends, however, had the firmest confidence
in him, and they were determined that, if Sampson
would put in an appearance, Jem should prove himself
worthy to try for the Championship. Sampson at once
went into training at Sutton Coldfield, near Birmingham,
placing himself under the care of old Ned Holland ; but
he afterwards repaired to the Highbury Sluice House,
then a famous sporting hostelry in charge of Harry
Harmer. Jem Ward went with Tom Owen to his
favourite training quarters, Ilford, where he got himself into the primest condition.

The place selected for the battle was Colnbrook, and
the date June 21, 1824. It was to be fought in the same
ring after the battle between Arthur Matthewson and
Barney Aaron, the latter, to the dismay of everybody
present, suffering defeat. So much excitement did this
encounter produce that it was a considerable time before
Ward and Sampson could claim the attention of the
spectators.

At length the ring was cleared and they entered it

stripped, and there was at last a chance of comparing the two gladiators. One account says:—" Phil looked big and strong—twice the man he was when he fought Jack Martin in 1820. He had developed from a lanky, lean, ill-formed lad into a fine athlete. His gristle had all set into bones, his frame had grown larger, and was now plentifully clothed with muscle. He was more than a stone heavier, too, than when he met Josh Hudson, having turned the scale that morning at 12st 4lb. Phil stood 5ft 10½in, and with his long arms looked what he undoubtedly was, the picture of a slashing hard hitter. Jem showed better than he did when he fought Josh Hudson. There was a healthier appearance about his face and skin, whilst his magnificent chest and splendid limbs were as conspicuous models of muscular development as the critical student of the human frame could possibly desire. The Diamond stood 5ft 9½in, and weighed 12st 6lb, so there was little to choose between the two in these respects. But although Sampson looked the bigger man, it was evident to the eye of the connoisseur that he was nothing like so powerful and well-proportioned a man as his opponent, whose torso was the finest, with the exception of the Game Chicken, ever seen in the Prize Ring."

It is not our intention to narrate the several rounds of this, one of Jem Ward's most brilliant displays in the ring. It will be sufficient to say that Phil Sampson, although he meant business that day, was outfought at every point. He made, however, a very good stand for fifty minutes, during which twenty-six rounds were contested. Here is a specimen of some of the rounds. We will take numbers eight to thirteen: " Sampson was now furious from the punishment he had received and from his utter inability to return it. He ran at Ward, hoping to bore him down by the sheer impetus of the rush, and get home one of the terrible blows for which he was famous, and one of which might at any moment turn the tide in his favour. But Jem was ready for the rush, and choked his enemy off with fearful severe jobbing hits from his left on the ear, under the chin, on the mouth, nose, neck—anywhere and everywhere he pleased, in fact—till Sampson was all over as crimson as his colours that fluttered from the stake. Once or twice Phil got his right home on the body, but the effect was slight; whilst Ward repaid him with interest by dealing some awful punches in the ribs, which doubled him up and made him writhe with agony. Sampson tried his ducking and dropping dodge, but he couldn't tempt Jem into hitting a foul blow; and when he stood up to fight, the Diamond's fist was for ever darting into his face like a viper's tongue, till Phil's phiz was scarified all over, and looked like a juicy steak ready for the gridiron. Sampson was a mere chopping-block for Ward to show off his science upon; and the general opinion was that Jem would win the match without a scratch!"

Here is an extraordinary account of the finish of the fight, which certainly, so far as Master Phil Sampson was concerned, was nothing to be proud of:—"In the twenty-fifth round Ward hit his man a heavy blow under the chin with his left, and, as Phil was falling, knocked him up again with a half-round hit from his right, and then kept playing with him with both hands, knocking his head from one side to the other in a lively little game of battledore and shuttlecock, till he was tired, and dropped Sampson on the blood-stained grass. As soon as Phil was placed upon his second's knee, he was very sick, and some thought that this might do him good, and enable him to make some show of further fighting. But the man was past the stage when anything could do him good, or put fresh life into him. In the next round Jem knocked him down, *then sat beside him, took his hand in his two hands, looked at him commiseratingly, and finally helped him to rise to his feet.*"

After this Sampson declared he would fight no more, although his backers implored him to have another round, but he firmly declined, and Jem Ward was proclaimed the winner. Poor Phil was badly hurt, and had to be put to bed at the George Hotel, Colnbrook, but Jem was as fresh as a lark, and was driven to town by Ben Turner, and took the chair that same night at the Mulberry Tree, where they spent a jolly evening.

After this battle Jem had demonstrated that there was not a big 'un who possessed the same scientific attainments as he, and, save Tom Spring, there seemed to be none in the ranks of the heavy-weights able to hold a candle to him. The question arose, "Who is there to beat this Ward?" John Jackson expressed the general opinion when he said, "Ward may be Champion, if he only does the right thing; he is far away the best big man out as a natural fighter."

But we shall see how far the great pugilist was right in his statement as we pursue the career of the Black Diamond, which was opening in such a promising manner.

CHAPTER XX.

THE GAUNTLET THROWN DOWN.—A DISAPPOINTMENT.   THE
SECOND TIME OF ASKING. — PHIL SAMPSON AND JEM
WARD.—ANOTHER VICTORY. — THE "BLACK DIAMOND"
AND THE CHAMPIONSHIP.

AND now we come to the question of who shall be
Champion. Tom Spring still held the title and the belt,
and there was not a single man dared come forward
and question his right to it. `But Tom of Hereford—as
George Borrow dubbed him—had notified his intention of
relinquishing the title, and then came the question as to
upon whose shoulders his mantle of fame should descend.
Most people turned their eyes upon Jack Langan as the
man who had a right to challenge England for the
Championship, for he had fought two battles for the
title, and had never been beaten but by Tom Spring.
So there was a big gathering at the Fives Court on July 1,
1824—which was the occasion of the Irishman's benefit
—as it was thought that Jack would in some way make
clear what he intended to do in the matter.   Nor
were they disappointed, for after the sparring exhibition was over Langan came forward and addressed the
company in the following manner :—

"Gentlemen, the first wish nearest to my heart is to
return thanks for the kindness and attention I have
received in this country. I trust you will believe me
when I say that I do not appear here in anything like a
national point of view. There is no man loves Ireland
and her sons better than I do ; but my pretensions here
are only to show as a man among pugilists, and to contend for the Championship of England. I will contend
with honour, and that shall be my pride, or I should be
undeserving of that patronage which you have so
liberally bestowed upon me. When I met the Champion
at Manchester, my friends backed me for the sum which
was asked, £300. I would be proud to have my name
enrolled in history among those brave champions, Jem
Belcher, Pearce (the Game Chicken), John Gully, Cribb,
and Tom Spring. I am now willing to accept a challenge
to fight for that proud and enviable title for the sum
asked of me by Spring—£300."

Naturally this speech met with tremendous applause, which was renewed when Jem Ward ascended the platform and declared that he was ready to fight Jack Langan for £200. This the Irishman objected to, and the Black Diamond replied that he would make it £300 if his friends agreed.

Before, however, Jem could make arrangements with his backers, Jack Langan sailed for Ireland. Then Ward issued a challenge to the kingdom to fight for £300 a-side; but there was no response, for the likely one, Jack Hudson, was training for his second fight with Tom Cannon; Peter Crawley was laid on the shelf, and there was nobody else apparently with pretensions to championship form.

The year passed along, and still Jem Ward had no prospects of getting to work, for although it was all very well for him to feel that he inspired awe he could not live on reputation, and he began to get very disconsolate. Just when he was about to despair, however, a challenge came from a quarter whence he least expected. Phil Sampson, above all others, declared that he was ready to meet Jem again for the sum of £100. At first nobody in London would believe this to be genuine, but on inquiry of the sports in Birmingham it was found to be perfectly true.

That a man who had been so completely vanquished but four months previously should have the temerity to challenge his conqueror a second time seemed strange indeed. He was evidently infatuated with egotism, said everybody, to thus court certain defeat. Still, the greater marvel was how Phil could have persuaded the Brums to plank the money down. True, he had marvellously improved physically since his fight with Jack Martin, and even since his battle with Ward; yet the science of the latter he could never acquire, and it was a horse to a gooseberry on the Black Diamond. Yet the Birmingham division stood him, and perhaps the reason for their doing so was the appearance of another Richmond in the field, a Warwickshire man named Ben Nettle, whose strength and powers had called for great attention. A subscription had been started to back him against Jem Ward for £200, but this did not suit Phil Sampson and his followers, so they determined to be first in the field, and accordingly Ward was challenged.

Nothing could have pleased the Diamond better thus to have been aroused from his inactivity and to compete for what he was quite certain would be a mere walk-over. Not so in Birmingham, however, for in spite of Phil's "in and out running" he was looked upon as being capable when he liked, and the interest exhibited at the sporting houses was intense. At the Dog and Duck, kept by old Joe Jennings at that time, the talk was of nothing else, and at the Woodman, then in the possession of little Arthur Matthewson, who had married the pretty niece of Jennings, the excitement as the day approached was intense.

It had been arranged that Ward should receive £10 expenses to agree that the battle should come off half-way between London and Brum. So Stony Stratford was decided upon, and Tuesday, December 28, 1824, was the date fixed. That being the case, there was not a great muster from the metropolis, for few cared about making a journey of some sixty miles to witness what they felt certain would be a fiasco, for many declared that Sampson could not be in earnest about winning, or Ward had been got at to lose. So not more than fifty West Enders showed up, although a good sprinkling from the East came down to see their favourite Black Diamond gain another victory, and in the hope that the Birmingham boys would fancy their man well enough to back him.

Monday was a dreadfully cold and wet day, yet numerous squires, farmers, and residents in the vicinity of Warwick, Leamington, and Coventry came over to Stony Stratford, and at the old Cross Keys there was quite a merry time of it, for the jolly souls had not got over their Christmas festivities, and were bent upon keeping the ball rolling. The weather on the Tuesday was even worse than on the previous day, the rain falling in torrents. Yet this did not deter many from flocking in to see the fight, for it was unusual for two big prominent performers in the ring to select this spot. All the sporting gents for miles around came in, and there were also some rough members belonging to the gipsy and tramp class, and, strangest sight of all, according to one report, a number of women and girls—quite a hundred—came to witness the battle, and appeared to take as much interest as anybody.

The men entered the ring at a quarter to one. Mr. Achison, known as the Herculean squire of Kenilworth, had come over from Leamington to act as referee, and as he called "Time!" the orderly assemblage settled down quietly.

It will be impossible to describe the battle, nor would it be necessary, for we have already given a taste of Phil Sampson's style. He showed to much greater advantage, however, on the second occasion, and so well did he perform in the early part of the fight that some doubts arose as to whether Ward did not mean selling his friends. In the second round, however, he struck Sampson with such force that had it been a bit higher it would, according to Paddington Jones, have smashed his jaw and sent all his grinders down his throat. Then he delivered another blow with great force on the mouth, cutting his lip clean through. Sampson countered slightly, but Ward hit him across the ring, two fearful drives in the chest and one in the face, Phil going down, and Jem, slipping on the muddy turf, now churned up like black pudding, fell beside him.

And so they floundered about, Sampson smothered in mud and blood, and looking a pitiable object, whilst he was getting all the worst of it in every round. They fought on for thirty-seven and a half minutes, having accomplished twenty-seven rounds, when Sampson was so done up that his backers, Mr. Hudson and Mr. Butler, entered the ring and declared they should fight no more.

There was no surprise at the result in the London Ring, but the Brums were very disappointed, for they firmly believed in their man, whom they had watched improve to such an extent, and who declared he was more than a match for The Diamond.

The next day Ward returned to London, and there were lively times at the Mulberry Tree, Ben Turner liberally entertained his friends free for a couple of days, and the East Enders did not fail to take advantage of his generosity. He had won quite a pile on the battle, and was more than ever convinced that his protégé was on the fair road to claim the Championship of England.

And now it will be our pleasant duty to introduce upon the scene one of the smartest, best behaved, and cleverest pugilists of the period. His name is Tom Cannon, and he was born at Eton, near Windsor, on March 14, 1790. His experience at this time in the ring had not been very great, but all his attempts had been successful, for he had beaten D. Smith for twenty guineas a-side, and had met Josh Hudson on two occasions, defeating him both times. Now, having done this, his friends thought that he was quite good enough to aspire to the Championship, and that he had a very much better chance than Jem Ward, who had been defeated by Hudson. Shortly after Cannon's second victory over Josh in the November of 1824, he left London with his wife, and took a public-house with his winnings (£700) at Windsor, near his birthplace. So popular was Tom with the West End swells, especially with his patron, the rich Squire Hayne (Peagreen Hayne he was usually called) that they brought their united influences to bear, and succeeded in getting Cannon into the Royal Body Guard of Beefeaters to His Majesty George IV. at Windsor. There he

might have remained in clover if he had been left alone;
but the Fancy were not willing that a man who had
displayed such power, and who had twice defeated
Hudson, should vacate the ring thus abruptly, and
they did their best to woo him back to the metropolis.

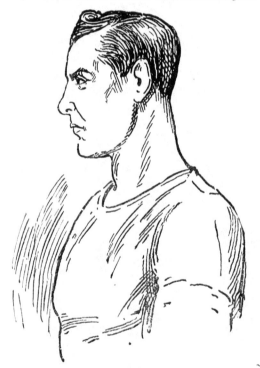

PHIL SAMPSON

So they elicited a promise that if they would take the
Fives Court for him, that he would appear and fight
over again his battle with Josh Hudson on the stage.
He having consented, the entertainment was advertised,
and Tom Cannon was described on the bills as

"Champion of England." The place was crowded to suffocation, and no less a sum than £120 was taken at the doors.

After the exhibition of boxing, Tom Cannon mounted the stage and in a very bumptious manner announced his readiness to fight any man in the world who ventured to dispute his title of Champion for the belt and 1,000 guineas. By the amateurs Cannon was much applauded, although the professionals looked upon it merely as a bit of bluster on his part, and no notice at the time was taken of it. A few days afterwards Squire Hayne and Tom Cannon went on tour together, going down to Brighton, at which place Miss Foote, the actress, was performing, and with whom the Squire had had a little affair which had cost him a considerable amount. Still he pursued her, being silly enough to flutter around the candle which had singed his wings.

On the Sunday following the benefit at Fives Court, and after Cannon and his patron had left London a challenge appeared in the sporting papers of February 26, 1825, announcing that Jem Ward was ready and anxious to fight Tom Cannon for £1,000 and the Championship. Now, in spite of Cannon's statement at the Court, Squire Hayne had elicited a promise from Tom that he would fight no more in the ring. We presume he wanted to keep Tom as his body guard, for they were always together. The consequence was Cannon took no notice whatever of the challenge, and although he was perpetually chaffed about the matter he kept silent, fearing to offend the Squire upon whom he practically depended, and who treated him most liberally. At length, however, he began to squirm under the repeated taunts and threats from Ward and his friends, for he felt that he had placed himself in a very false position by his statement at the Fives Court. Still, he made no reply to Ward, and matters for the time being remained pretty well as they were, Jem Ward still being without an opponent, and groaning under the weight of his enforced inactivity.

At length the spell was broken. On May 26, 1825, Thomas Winter Spring took a farewell benefit at the Fives Court, in order to commemorate his final retirement from the Ring. Never before had there been such a representative meeting of swells and the Fancy. Royalty, peers, officers, Members of Parliament, and the élite of the sporting world, all assembled to do honour to the famous champion, who had won the hearts of all, rich and poor, by his manly straightforwardness in the Ring and outside of it.

When Spring came forward and made his speech, in

which he thanked his patrons and the British public
generally for their kind support, and wound up with an
appeal to his brother gladiators to maintain the honour
of the Prize Ring by rigidly observing the rules of
honesty and integrity in all their dealings, both with
one another and with the sporting world outside, the
cheering was tremendous.

No doubt this speech had an effect upon Tom Cannon,
for after he had sparred with Tom Oliver, he came
forward, and formally accepted Jem Ward's challenge
to fight for £1,000 and the Championship. He explained
his silence; but informed his hearers that Squire Hayne
had not only released him from his promise, but had
most generously elected to find most of the money for
the stakes. After more cheering, there were loud cries
for Jem Ward, but he was not in the building. One of
his friends, however, a Mr. Norval, stepped on to the
platform, and stated that Ward's money was quite
ready, and that he should be pleased to meet Cannon
or his representative at Tom Cribb's on the following
day.

Two days after the great evening at the Fives
Court a select dinner party was given at Tom Cribb's
house, the Union Arms, Panton Street, and, after the
repast, the articles were drawn up and signed, whereby
Thomas Cannon and James Ward agreed to fight on
July 19, 1825, for 500 guineas a-side and the Championship of England on a 24ft square boarded stage, similar
to that on which Spring fought Langan at Colchester,
and Cannon had contended himself with Hudson at Warwick. The first deposit of £150 a-side was then and
there made good.

Both men were in attendance, and they shook hands
heartily when the usual toast, " May the best man win,"
was drunk by the whole of the company up-standing.

There was a joyous time also down the East End on
that particular night, for when Jem Ward, accompanied
by his backers, Messrs. Hinde and Norval, arrived at the
Mulberry Tree there was a tremendous ovation
awaiting them, for the wise men of the East felt confident that their Black Diamond would be sure to gain
the coveted title, and they meant having their last
shillings on him. Jem was made favourite at 5 to 4,
yet this did not deter his followers from backing him,
and immense sums were invested at this price. In the
West the argument was that on form Cannon must
win, for he had twice decisively thrashed Josh Hudson,
and the latter had defeated Jem. Still, the East Enders
stuck like a leech to their man, and declared that there
was no man in the ring (now that Spring had gone) able

to take him down if he meant business, and on this occasion his all would be at stake.

Of course Ward, was the more scientific boxer of two, but he had to reckon with the powerful, vigorous, cut-and-come again outset of such a determined and conspicuous man as Cannon. Some men went so far as to whisper that Jem had a weak spot, and that when opposed to too much force his heart gave way and he would be likely to "cut it." So divided were the opinions, indeed, that speculation was exceedingly brisk, and no such betting had taken place since the battle between Gas and Neate, when the West Country sports had all the best of it.

That nothing should be left undone to ensure Ward's success, he was sent down to Dinghouse, near York, and placed under the care of Joe Couch, then considered the finest trainer of the period. Couch had, at the time, Metcalfe, the famous runner, who was matched against Halton, of Lancashire, for £300 a-side, the first-named conceding thirty yards in a mile. Joe was known to be one who would never undertake the training of a man unless he felt sure he meant trying to win, and as he had £100 in Ward's stake-money everything looked as straight as a gun barrel. Couch gave his man plenty of pedestrian exercise, and made no attempt to reduce him to any extent, feeding him well and getting him as hard as nails. Indeed, Jem was never so fit in his life a week before the date of the battle.

Tom Cannon went in company with Squire Hayne to Henley under the care of Tom Clarke, who had trained Hudson. Now Tom was known to be very severe in his treatment, and always tried to reduce a man of every particle of fat, using much physic and plenty of sweating. What with the harsh treatment and the moist atmosphere of the river, Cannon made very bad progress at first, until Squire Hayne insisted that they should shift their quarters and go to Marlborough. They put up at the Angel, and Tom took his breathings over the beautiful downs, where he soon picked up, and came along splendidly, and both Mr. Haynes and Clarke declared that he would be fitter than ever before the day arrived.

And now we must leave the two aspirants for the Championship at their training work, and defer until our next chapter the progress and result of the great battle which was causing such a sensation.

CHAPTER XXI.

A VERY HOT TIME OF IT. — JEM WARD AND TOM CANNON
FIGHT FOR A THOUSAND. — THE BLACK DIAMOND TAKES
THE BELT IN TEN MINUTES.

THE excitement became intense over the great fight
for the £1,000 and Championship as the day drew
near. The date fixed was July 14, 1825, and on the
Wednesday preceding a meeting took place at Josh
Hudson's new house, the Half Moon Tap, Leadenhall
Market, then a favourite sporting drum. There was a
splendid muster of sports, numbering some sixty, for
whom the best in the market had been supplied, and,
according to accounts, the tables "groaned" under the
weight of poultry and sirloin, boar's head, and boiled
mutton and "trimmings," whilst wine flowed freely,
for there were some of the Corinthians present who
thought nothing of putting up a dozen at a time. Tom
Belcher, from the Castle, was there on behalf of Mr.
Hayne and Tom Cannon; whilst Mr. Norval represented Jem Ward and his backers. The meeting had
been convened to put down the last deposit, and to
finally settle the arrangements for the field-day. After
the dinner, and before the conviviality commenced,
the "blunt" was posted, and some discussion arose as
to the place to be selected. It was deemed, however,
advisable to leave that part of the business in the hands
of Mr. John Jackson, who, together with a committee of
five well-known sportsmen, undertook all the preliminaries. It was decided by them that Warwick should
be the rendezvous, although many other places had
supplied applicants. It was remembered, however, how
smoothly everything passed off at that town in the
previous November, when Cannon and Hudson fought
their battle, so Warwick was the chosen spot.

Tuesday, July 19, being the day decided upon, as
early as the previous Friday found sportsmen travelling north, and every seat was booked on the coaches,
whilst a variety of conveyances were to be seen on the
road. Birmingham, Coventry, Leamington, and, indeed,
every town or village within easy posting distance of
Warwick, was filled with sportsmen, who had come far

and near to witness the great fight for the Championship of England. Crowds came not only from London, but from Bristol, Cheltenham, Oxford, Manchester, and even places further afield. Some hundred or so East Enders had clubbed together and engaged vehicles, all starting from the King's Arms, Whitechapel, for they were determined to see their pet, Jem Ward, win the belt.

On the Sunday evening Tom Cannon arrived at Leamington, Mr. Hayne having driven him down with Clarke in his own carriage, and they intended to put up at the Regent's Hotel. Unfortunately for them, however, there were a number of Church dignitaries in the town, and they had monopolised all the best hotels. They had consequently to drive back to Warwick, but there again they found the town unpleasantly crowded, so they went to Stratford-on-Avon, where they eventually obtained lodgings at a farmhouse. Jem Ward, who had been training in Yorkshire, came down by easy stages to Stony Stratford, where he stayed on the Tuesday before the battle, and the Black Diamond ran a two hundred yards' race against Young Gas, and beat him. On the following day, accompanied by Crouch and Metcalf, they moved on to Daventry, and thence on the Sunday to Warwick, making the Hare and Hounds their headquarters. Amongst the prominent pugilists present in Warwick on the eve of the battle were Bill Richmond, Jack Randall, Ned Neale, Scroggins, Harry Holt, Josh Hudson, Peter Crawley, Tom Shelton, White Headed Bob, Young Gas, Tom Oliver, Barney Aaron, Young Dutch Sam, Phil Sampson, Arthur Matthewson, the two Belascos, and several others.

On the eve of the fight Warwick was excited, and such a crowd of strangers and queer-looking folk had never been seen in the usually quiet and sedate old town before. A most unusual place had been selected in which to pitch the ring, it being the great courtyard of a factory. On two sides of this place were houses with a great number of windows overlooking the open space, and from which a splendid view was afforded. On another side was the racecourse, separated from the yard by a very wide brook. There was only one gate to admit the public, so it was intended to charge for admission. The stage had been erected upon which the men were to do battle, and everything seemed likely to go without a hitch, when the Mayor of Warwick was waited upon by a deputation of the Society for the Suppresion of Cruelty to Animals, to point out to him that Mr. Wombwell intended exhibiting a fight between lions and dogs, and begging him to stop this barbarous display, and at the same time these

11

busybodies called attention to the coming prize-fight.
Mr. Wilmhurst (for that was the Mayor's name) was
not sure that he had power to interfere with the mena-
gerie entertainment, but he had no doubt about being
able to stop the fight. He, therefore, announced his
intention of not permitting the battle between Ward and
Cannon to take place within the precincts of his
mayoralty. This was a pretty state of affairs at the
eleventh hour, and several of the swells waited upon the
city magnate and begged him to reconsider his decision.
He stood firm, however, and it was found necessary to
erect another stage a little way outside Warwick, and
abandon that in the factory yard. A meadow on the
Birmingham road was selected, and the Mayor promised
that there he would not interfere.

The betting was very heavy overnight, the odds being
5 to 4 on Cannon; Mr. Hayne laying a thousand to
eight hundred, and everybody looked forward to a grand
day on the morrow. The weather had been painfully
hot for some time, and it was evident at sunrise that
they were in for another scorcher. Hours before
the appointed time immense numbers of people from
Warwick and the surrounding country poured towards
the meadow, where they were still at work erecting the
stage. Above all times 12.30 had been fixed for the men
to be in the ring, when the sun was at its fiercest. We
cannot discover who was answerable for this, unless it
was Mr. Jackson, but certainly it would have been better
to have selected the cool of the early morning, or even
late in the afternoon. It was not until just before noon
that Mr. Hayne brought his man in from Stratford-on-
Avon, and at the Warwick Arms he met Ward's principal backers—Messrs. Norval and Hinde—so that they
might decide upon the umpires and referee before going
into the field. This was agreeably accomplished. Sir
John Radford was selected for Cannon, and Mr. Mann,
of Warwick, for Ward; whilst Squire Osbaldistone was
to fill the onerous office of referee, so that no time was
cut to waste when the men arrived upon the ground,
which they did punctually to the hour named. Mr.
Hayne arrived with quite a party, for he was accompanied by Tom Spring, Cribb, and Jack Langan, besides
Tom Cannon and Clarke.

Surrounding the stage there were quite 15,000 people,
and as both men mounted together a tremendous cheer
rent the air. Jem Ward had a large straw hat upon his
head, which gave him the appearance of a West Indian
planter. They were soon stripped and ready for action,
and as this happens to be a battle which introduces a
fresh Champion to our readers, we purpose giving fuller

details culled from the prints of the period than is our
custom.

Cannon was trained to the hour, his white skin flashing in the sun, and the muscles of his arms and chest
standing out boldly. Yet it was remarked that he
appeared to be much older and somewhat pinched about
the face. Jem Ward was as lean and fine as any grey-

TOM CANNON.
From a Portrait by Wagsman.

hound, but as hard as nails. Both were lighter than
when they appeared before in public, for the Black
Diamond scaled 12st 5lb, and Cannon 12st 8lb, so there
was little to choose between them in respect to weight.
But in height Tom had the advantage of a good 1½in.
The Windsor man was more heavily built and looked

more powerful, but the Londoner was finer-proportioned, and a perfect model of manly symmetry. And so they stood before each other in the full blaze of the sun. Oliver and Jack Randall waited upon the Black Diamond, who had for his colours blue with white spots; whilst those two great masters of the pugilistic art, Tom Spring and Tom Cribb, looked after Tom Cannon, who sported a crimson fogel with white spots. There was a hush as the Squire called " Time," and in deep silence amongst the multitude they threw themselves into attitude and commenced the struggle for the coveted Championship.

Everybody who had seen Tom Cannon fight before knew thoroughly well his tactics—tactics which had won for him the battle with Josh Hudson, and brought him so prominently forward. These were, without troubling to spar, to walk deliberately up to his man and attempt to break down his guard, or get over it, and then dash in blow after blow at his opponent's head, regardless of the punishment he might receive in making the attempt. In other words, Tom sacrificed science for brute force, and up to this period had found it answer his purpose. But how would this style suit Jem Ward, who was not only as quick as lightning but a most punishing hitter? The audience were not kept long in suspense. Directly they came together Cannon dashed out left and right, but was neatly stopped by Jem, as he defended himself on the retreat, without attempting the return. Evidently Cannon was disappointed, for in a half-savage manner he rushed at his man and let go the left again. This time he was short, and Jem seeing his opportunity planted his right with such terrific force on Tom's eyebrow that it left a severe gash, and very nearly closed the left optic. The blood trickled down his cheek, and amidst deafening applause from the East Enders the first event was claimed for the Black Diamond. This upset Tom Cannon who, not having learned to be cautious, in spite of the blow, dashed in again. Jem Ward smiled and stepped aside nimbly, so again Tom's blow was expended in the air, and an opening left. Ward was not long in taking advantage, for he let go and landed a fearful blow just on the chin and throat, which made the Windsor man's teeth chatter, and sent him staggering back, whilst more of the crimson fluid flowed this time from the mouth. Of course, there was more cheering for Ward, which again upset Cannon, and he rushed in for a close, but Jem avoided it, and showing marvellous activity put in some useful blows with right and left on the face and head. At length Cannon forced a smart rally at half-arm distance, got hold of his man, and after a brief struggle they came down side by side and finished the round.

Ward had undoubtedly taken the lead, and even money was asked for, but little forthcoming, as Jem had shown such a much greater knowledge of science. Still on such a day it was, after all, a question of staying power, and Cannon was said to be the steadier of the two. Although they had only been at it three minutes their faces were as red as a turkey-cock, and the sweat standing in beads upon face and body, in spite of the magnificent preparation they had undergone. In the crowd, too, the heat must have been unbearable.

Here is one description of the second round, which tells conclusively who had the better chance, even at this early period of the battle. " People were fainting from the overpowering heat. Cannon evidently felt that human nature could not stand much of this sort of thing, and that if the battle was to be won at all it must be won soon ; and so he went for his man as before, hitting hard with both hands, but trying in vain for an opening, for Jem stopped his awful intention, stepped back, and as Tom followed up let him have it hot again with the right on the sore ogle, putting up the shutters, and leaving Cannon a one-eyed Cyclops. 'Go it, Jem,' yelled the Black Diamond's pals ; but Mr. Ward preferred the cautious game, and allowed his foe to rush at him again, when he popped in a warm one with his left on the cheek, which Tom tried to counter, just touching Jem's jaw. The Windsor man, undismayed, bored in and closed, but Ward cleverly twisted his leg between Cannon's stalwart props, and Tom went down heavily on the hard elm planks, whilst Ward considerately added his own weight to the severity of the fall. It was clear now that Cannon's style of fighting was of no earthly use against the Black Diamond, but either man might at any moment collapse with sunstroke, and so the odds ran no higher than 6 to 4 on Ward."

In the third round it would appear that Jem Ward, no doubt feeling confident as to the result, and being, like his opponent, desirous of finishing the combat as quickly as possible, led off, but Tom neatly stopped him. Cannon dashed in as usual, but Jem was again too quick for him, and having avoided, put a terrible hit on the cheek, which laid the flesh open. Tom got furious, for the blood was pouring from his face, and he showed signs of weakness. Pulling himself together, however, with a great effort, he made a desperate rush to do or die. This time the attack was so sudden and forcible that Ward for once was unable to stop it, and received a fearful blow on the side of the head, which sent him on to the ropes, where he came down thud upon the boards, Tom on top of him. This made Tom's friends look up a bit.

There was scarcely a mark upon Ward's face, but Tom's was painted like that of a Red Indian, and scored, like the New Zealander, whilst the daylight was completely shut out from his left eye, which, of course placed him at a great disadvantage with a man like Jem Ward, whose catlike movements were frequently too quick for two sound eyes to follow—it was apparently the same business over again. Rush by Tom Cannon, his blows stopped by Jem Ward, and then the Windsor man receiving on the face with additional decorations. Tom Cannon, too, was affected more by the heat than Ward. Yet he made desperate efforts, but the Black Diamond's fists went slap, slap, slap into his face, although the blows seemed to lack their usual force, and without a doubt the distressing heat had taken the go out of both the men. In the fifth round Jem, in dodging one of his opponent's rushes, slipped and fell heavily on the boards. There was an attempt to claim first knock-down by the Cannonites, but the Squire, amidst applause, refused to allow it.

After this Cannon was evidently beaten. As one reporter puts it : "Beaten by Ward, the weather, and his own exertions, the sun touched his brain, and he fought wildly, like a drunken man, swinging his arms about, and lashing out without attempting to judge distance." They fought on (if fighting it could be called, for some of the rounds did not last a quarter of a minute), Cannon seeming scarcely to know what he was doing, and Ward open-mouthed and scarcely able to keep his tongue from lolling out. Again Tom attempted a rush, but Jem stepped aside, and as the Windsor man passed, hit him a heavy blow on the mouth, then ran in, caught his man with both arms round the waist and threw him on the stage, adding his own weight. The exertion displayed by Ward, and the nasty fall experienced by Cannon, very nearly settled both men, and it would have been a strange finish to a Championship fight for both combatants to have been deaf to the call of "Time."

As it was, Spring and Cribb had much difficulty with their man, and Tom Oliver and Jack Randall were busy in Ward's corner. The interest in the fight had gone. The people fainting in the crowd took the attention off the doings on the stage. Besides, there was not much fun in watching two men rolling up against each other, and only now and again give a blow that would scarcely make a hole in a pound of butter. Tom was particularly abroad, for after rushing at his adversary, who retreated to the rails, he became quite exhausted and dropped into Ward's arms. The latter, however, was in such a plight that he was unable to hold him and fib, for he was scarcely able to raise his arms. "Then," one report says, "Cannon dropped almost senseless upon the boards: whilst Jem, unable to stand any longer, fell helplessly on top of him." The betting was 5 to 1 on Ward, but either might have snuffed out at any moment.

Cannon was quite stupefied and helpless when he was put on the scratch for the tenth round, and Jem's friends shouted to him to go in and finish the fight. Perhaps they thought that their man might succumb first if he did not act then and there. Here is a description of the finish :—

"By a marvellous exertion of will Jem pulled himself together, walked up to Cannon and hit him simultaneously with the left on the forehead and with the right on the nose. Then poor Tom dropped like a sack of flour, wholly inanimate and insensible. Spring lifted the helpless man on to Cribb's knee, and blew brandy up Tom's nostrils; but it was no go. Cannon's head fell on his shoulder, blood flowed copiously from his nose and mouth, but he showed no signs of life. When a minute had elapsed Squire Osbaldistone, who had thrice called "Time," stepped up to Ward and said, 'James Ward, you have won the battle.'"

The news that he was Champion of England did more than all the seconds in Christendom could have done to revive the Black Diamond. He descended from the stage amidst ringing cheers, and mounted a cob, bowing to the multitude as they flocked around him and congratulated him upon his success. Poor Cannon remained senseless for more than an hour, having been bled by a surgeon who was present, although we cannot understand why that should have been done, considering that he had lost so much during the short fight, which had lasted not much more than ten minutes, certainly a considerably less time than it has taken to write it. It was evident from the onset that Jem Ward was a better man than Tom Cannon, although it was a most unfair test under such circumstances. Still the Black Diamond had fairly won his laurels, and in the next few chapters we shall follow the hero through his career as Champion.

CHAPTER XXII.

EARLY CAREER OF THE "KILL-BULL."—AN ARISTOCRATIC
FOLLOWING.—PETER CRAWLEY AND JEM WARD.—A SUR-
PRISE FOR THE CHAMPION.

ALTHOUGH the battle for the Championship upon that
fearfully hot July afternoon, described in our last chapter,
was not altogether satisfactory, James Ward was made
much of at the East End. Three days after his victory,
at a benefit given to Harry Holt, at the Fives Court,
Jem Ward was presented with a belt, but how it could
have been prepared for him in the time it has puzzled us
to conjecture. No doubt his followers had such implicit
belief in the Black Diamond that they had it manufactured in readiness, feeling sanguine that he would one
day gain the Championship. Jem was very popular,
and met with a most cordial reception when he stood
upon the stage, and the belt was placed round his waist
by Tom Oliver. Yet there were some of the old stagers
who declared that Jem was not really entitled to call
himself Champion. They argued that Cannon had no
right to enter the lists for the purpose of competing for
the title because he had defeated Josh Hudson, and
that, consequently, Ward's victory over Tom did not
give him the right to assume the honour. The public
generally, however, were quite satisfied that the Black
Diamond had fairly earned the position, so accordingly
the belt was awarded.

We have seen the trophy many a time, and was at
one time, if not still, in the possession of Jem Mace. It
consists of the blue and crimson colours worn at the
fight with Cannon, bound with the skin of a tiger. The
clasp, or buckle, is made of highly-polished steel, and in
the middle of the clasp is a heart, worked with gold, on
which is engraved the following :—"This belt was presented to James Ward, at the Fives Court, St. Martin's
Street, Leicester Fields, on the 22nd of July, in commemo-
ration of his scientific and manly conquest of Thomas

Cannon, at Stanfield Park, Warwick, on the 19th July,
1825. This battle at the present time entitles him to the
high and distinguished appellation of the British
Champion."

After the presentation Harry Holt, the Cicero of the
Ring, made an excellent speech eulogistic of " the
prowess of the latest succession to the ranks of those
illustrious heroes who had been similarly decorated in
days past—Broughton, Tom Johnson, Big Ben Brain,
Dan Mendoza, John Jackson, Jem Belcher, the Game
Chicken, Tom Cribb, and last, but assuredly not least,
Tom Spring." No doubt Jem Ward felt himself of no
little importance after this, for he issued a challenge
to fight " any man in the world " for £200 or £300 a-side.

And now we must introduce a youth who was destined
to take the highest position in the Ring, and no doubt
would have held it for many years had he not taken a
dislike to pugilism and, like John Gully, voluntarily
retired with his honours full upon him. This is Peter
Crawley. He was a Londoner, having been born at
Newington Green on December 5, 1800. For many
years he followed the trade of a butcher. And here
we may call attention to the fact that, for some
reason or other, that profession has, perhaps, been
productive of more prize-fighters than any other. Some
of young Peter's time was passed in St. Luke's, where
his father had a butcher's shop in Whitecross Street.
At the period about which we write there were no
police, but this neighbourhood was exceedingly rough,
so Master Peter Crawley had ample opportunity of
cultivating the art of self-defence, and so powerful
was he, and so handy with his fists did he become, that he
was the terror of the neighbourhood.

Now it so happened that living in the same street.
was an Irishman named Pat Flannagan, who was also
a purveyor of meat, though of a different kind, for his
display of viands was for the feline inhabitants of St.
Luke's. In other words, he was a cats'-meat man.
Misther Pat, who had been a bit of a bruiser in his time,
resented the forward young Crawley, who dared to dispute his right to be champion of the street, a distinction
he had enjoyed for a considerable time. Of course, a
row was inevitable, and one Sunday night matters came
to a crisis. The whole street was thrown into a great
state of excitement when it became known that Peter
Crawley and Pat Flannagan were going at it hammer and
tongs. It did not last very long, for youth would be
served, and Pat found that he had caught a Tartar.
He was very much punished, and so, finding that he could
not thrash Peter, he resorted to the dastardly alternative

of summoning his opponent before the Worship Street magistrate. Peter's father, however, who was very well to do, squared the affair with Pat for a fiver, and the matter dropped.

This was the first win upon record, but Pierce Egan gives an account of his other engagements, which that gentleman informs us was gathered from Peter himself. Here is a summary. At the age of fifteen he fought and defeated Hunt, a strong and impudent blacksmith. The battle took place in the Long Fields, Somers Town. Shortly after this he migrated to Clare Market, a very hot-bed of pugilism, and where the "Kill-bulls" to a man knew how to use their "dukes." Crawley whilst there had his hands pretty full, for the Cockney market employé was the most pugnacious biped on the face of the earth. Did not Jack Randall first attract notice by his milling exploits in Covent Garden? Was it not there also that that fine Irish boxer, Tom Reynolds, learned the art which enabled him to beat the leary Belasco? Again, it was George Head, the best boxer and teacher of his time, who would go around Clare Market early morning, disguised, to seek adventures. After young Crawley fought with Hunt he was matched with Bennett, who, like himself, was a butcher in the service of Mr. Jonas Levy, a Hebrew butcher, who did business near Clare Market. This Bennett was twenty-one years of age, and weighed 10st 8lb; so he had much the advantage of the juvenile Peter. Still the youngster had all the best of it when Mr. Levy appeared on the scene and declared that if they continued they would both get the "sack."

Peter had a great weakness for cock-fighting, too, and wherever or whenever there was a main to be fought young Crawley would be sure to be there. We are informed by Pierce Egan that it was whilst watching this pastime that Peter became involved in two of the most important battles of his boyhood. One of the engagements was with a young chap named Coleman, who was, by-the-bye, a marketer, and who received a licking; the other was with Tom Price, like himself a butcher, who also fell beneath the youngster's arm. His next perform-ance was on the stones in the city, we are told, and, as all this came from Peter's own lips, we must take it as true history. Going for meat to Newgate Market in his father's cart, he was obstructed by a distiller's van in Warwick Lane. The rival Jehu was a smiling and boisterous man, a great big chap, big enough to eat young Peter by appearance. But the latter challenged him to come down and fight, and he did. Before at least five hundred people, all enthusiasts, they fought

nineteen rounds in half an hour, when, to the astonishment of all, the big 'un was completely knocked out, his
head coming in contact with the pavement, and he had
to be carried into Bartholomew's Hospital. In the Kent
Road he polished off a strong fellow in a single round,
and a month after he had the honour of an interview
with Mr. Henry Sergeant, the Worship Street magistrate.
Peter was attacked by some half-dozen ruffians in Lord

PETER CRAWLEY
At the Age of 27.
From a portrait by Wyvil.

Hill Alloy, Whitecross Street, and he inflicted some
severe punishment on several of his cowardly assailants.
A "Charley" came upon the scene and, siding with the
many, Peter was hauled off to prison by this Dogberry
and his assistants. In the morning, however, the pre-
siding magistrate at once saw the position of affairs,
and he was acquitted, and left the court, accompanied by
that highly original comment, " without a stain upon

his character." The next engagement was of more importance. It was in 1818, during the fierce election contest of that year, and it must be remembered that in the early part of the present century all kinds of rioting, intimidation, and corrupt practices were employed on both sides in order to secure votes. There being no police it was found necessary by the several candidates to employ special constables to protect the electors going to the poll, and these were mostly enlisted from the third-class pugilists or aspirants to fistic fame. Sir Samuel Romilly, who was up for election, engaged young Peter Crawley, for by this time he had done sufficient to have notice taken of him. As luck would have it, one of the other candidates had engaged the services of one Ben Sutcliffe —a stout butcher, of Clare Market, and of course well known to Crawley. There was no love lost between them, and being attached to opposing parties at the election they very naturally ran foul of each other, and a contest was about to take place then and there. By the persuasion of their friends they postponed the meeting until after the election, and the battle was arranged to take place on Friday, August 7, 1818. They met at Rusley Farm, near Kingston, amid a large attendance, when Sutcliffe was defeated after a desperate struggle, lasting fifty minutes. So much for young Peter Crawley's early career.

His next appearance was in the ring proper six months afterwards, when he met "Gas," whose real name was Tom Hickman, who eventually turned out to be one of the finest fighters of the time. It was the latter's first appearance in the London ring, although in the provinces he had made his mark, having, besides others, conquered Sudgley, Miller, Hollis, Walker, Doughty, Hollix, Thomas, and Andrews. That he was a good man may be gathered from the fact that he defeated those first-class fighters George Cooper (twice) and Tom Oliver, whilst in the battle with Peter Crawley he took down that young gentleman's colours. With Hickman we have little to do, for he never competed for the Championship. After his defeat by Neat he was killed with Mr. Rowe, returning from Hudson and Shelton's fight on December 10, 1822. It is worthy of record, though, that "Gas" defeated Peter Crawley on March 16, 1819, at Moulsey Hurst, for £50, in thirteen rounds, lasting only fourteen and a half minutes. This was a rare take-down for the ambitious young pugilist, and it was not until May 7, 1822—more than three years afterwards —that his name is mentioned as having fought again. The event was only a turn-up at Chester Races with Southern's Bully, for the not very remunerative

stakes of "nix." Anyhow, he gave his man a hiding,
and then sank into oblivion, so far as pugilism went, for
exactly another year, when he was matched to fight
Dick Acton on May 6, 1823, for £50 a-side, Peter
Crawley was successful, beating his man in thirteen
rounds, lasting sixteen minutes, at Blindlow Heath.

And now we come to his engagement with Jem Ward,
Champion, which did not take place until nearly four
years after Crawley's previous battle, he not having
entered the ring for the whole of that period. It may
have been that his business prevented him from making
matches, but we believe that the real cause was that he
suffered so much from hernia that he was advised to
lie low.

However, when Jem Ward threw down the gauntlet at
the Fives Court, after receiving the belt, to fight anybody
for £200 a-side, all eyes were turned to Peter Crawley,
for he was looked upon as the only heavy-weight likely
to lower the Black Diamond's colours. Young " Rump-
steak," as he had been dubbed on account of his calling
as a butcher, however, made no response, and it transpired that it was not because he had any disinclination
to try for the Championship, but that he could get nobody to plank down the needful for him, and was unable
to find the amount himself.

He at this time kept a butcher's shop in the Seven
Dials, and had a boxing-room upstairs. Still, notwithstanding the fact that he did a good business and had
several swell pupils, £200 was too much to take out and
risk. So matters remained until the September of 1826,
when Jem Ward issued another challenge to the world.
Then Peter communicated with Ward, and frankly told
him that he could not find so large a sum, but if he
would accommodate him for half that amount he was
his man. The Black Diamond, however, was getting
well patronised and up in the world, so he thought it
beneath the dignity of a Champion to fight for so paltry
an amount. A deal of correspondence ensued over the
matter, and at length Mr. Norval, Jem's backer, being
anxious that his man should become active, gave way
and accepted Crawley's offer, and they met on October
17, 1826, at Tom Belcher's, the Castle, in Holborn, when
articles were signed for the men to fight on January 2,
1827, the place selected to be within one hundred miles
of London.

During the festive season of 1826, in all the sporting
houses—and Christmas was kept with a deal more
jollity then than now—the principal topic was the coming
battle and the probability of where it would take place.
Several districts were mentioned, the backers of Crawley

(Mr. Carfox, Tom Crommelin, and Lord Longford) were for having it take place in Hampshire; whilst Jem Ward's supporters, Messrs. Hinck and Norval and Sir Bellingham Graham, desired that Stoney Stratford should be selected. Eventually, for a very good reason, the neighbourhood of Royston was decided upon. It was at the instigation of Sir St. Vincent Cotton, whose estates lay at Landwade and Madingley, in Cambridgeshire, for the town selected was on the borders of three counties. Sir St. Vincent sent a messenger to ask Sir Roger Palmer, an old friend and keen sportsman, whose property was in the immediate neighbourhood, to accommodate them with a large field at one of his farms. This was something to ask, but such a lover of all athletics was Sir Roger that he readily consented. Haydon Grange was the farm selected, and every detail of the arrangements seems to have been perfect.

On Monday, January 1, 1827, the old market town of Royston must have presented an exceedingly lively appearance. Vehicles of all kinds and qualities had left London on the Sunday night, and during the early hours of the Monday morning traps and postchaises continued to arrive until all the hotels were full. A guinea was charged for any kind of shakedown, even in the haylofts and corridors of the inn, whilst a bed, with two sleeping together, fetched a fiver a nob. Never had the little town made such a harvest. The Bull had been brought right over by a party of swells who had sent their agent down a week previously, and amongst the guests there were the Duke of Beaufort, Lords Yarmouth, Fife, Lyndock, and Longford, Sir Bellingham Graham, Hon. Tom Loftus, Colonel Dan Mackinnon, and the famous sporting parson of Bilsworth, Parson Ambrose. This, of course, was the headquarters of Peter Crawley. Jem Ward was located at the Red Lion with his backers, seconds, and friends, whilst the Crown was full of Cambridge University men.

But we must not dwell upon the overnight scenes and the many arrivals of illustrious men in the world of sport, as there is much to tell, but just to point out how generously the Ring was patronised at this period we must mention a few. Lord Kennedy, Lord Kelburne (better known to us as Lord Glasgow), Thomas Egerton Earl of Wilton (the celebrated gentleman jockey), Lord Yarmouth, Lord Foley, John Sydney Thorp, of Chippenham Park, and a host of other celebrities. There is John Gully, now a prosperous penciller, and in a short time about to become a great racehorse owner, Dan Mendoza, bent and broken down, Mr. Lewis Benjamin, of Howard's Coffee House, Gentleman Jackson, who looks fit to fight anybody present, Crutch Robinson, one of the most foul-mouthed men of the betting-ring, but also one of the most prominent; Jemmy Bland, another notorious bookmaker, who can neither read nor write, but enters bets with the utmost accuracy in a shorthand of hieroglyphics that he cannot explain, and nobody but himself can decipher. The above are only a few, for we could fill columns if we were to attempt a list of those who had flocked to Royston to witness the fight for the Championship between Peter Crawley and James Ward.

Let us, however, proceed with a description of the preliminaries and a short notice of the battle itself. Bill Gibbons had been deputed at a very early hour on the morning of January 2 to take with him in a cart the new ropes and stakes, together with what assistance he might require to Haydon Grange, in order to prepare the arena. Now, Master Gibbons was a very peculiar tempered sort of a fellow, and considered himself quite snubbed because he had not been asked to give his opinion upon the place selected. He felt like the district surveyor when somebody had put a structure up without first submitting the plans. So what does Master William do? He and his men drive the paraphernalia on to Royston Heath, and form the ring.

Early in the morning those who wished to be in time marched off to the Grange, and there found many already assembled, but where was the ring? Hour after hour they waited, but no ropes and stakes, no officials, were to be seen. At length, just as it was dawning upon these thousands of people that something was amiss, somebody rode up and informed them that the venue had been changed.

Helter-skelter the mob went, fearful lest they should miss the opening rounds of the battle, and the scene that met the eye, and is described as having taken place, must have been exciting. Bill Gibbons had informed Ward and Crawley of the change, but he had done nothing to notify Mr. Jackson, who had given the instructions, and it was only natural that that gentleman should be boiling over with rage at the liberty which had been taken, and he swore that Bill should suffer.

So, through the delay caused, it was ten minutes to one o'clock when the men entered the ring, Ward attended by Josh Hudson and Reuben Martin, Crawley by Tom Belcher and Harry Harmer, with Peter's stalwart old dad, the Newington butcher, bringing up the rear. Squire Osbaldiston consented to be referee, and Mr. E. N. Budd, the celebrated cricketer and all-round athlete, was appointed umpire for Ward, whilst Mr. Thomas Watson, proprietor of the Turf Coffee House, and the best amateur boxer of his day, was chosen for Crawley.

Our remarks upon the eleven rounds that were fought to decide who should be Champion must of necessity be brief. Nor is there need to describe them fully, as our readers are pretty well acquainted by this time with Jem Ward's style of fighting, and this will be the first and last time Peter Crawley will appear upon these pages as a principal.

Both looked remarkably well as they faced each other, and there certainly could not be much to choose between them so far as appearances went. Crawley stood six feet and about half an inch, his weight being 12st 12lb, and everybody who had not seen him in the "buff" before were surprised to see what a fine, athletic, well-made young fellow he was. Plenty of muscle and not an ounce of superfluous flesh. Jem weighed 12st 7lb, so there was little difference in their weights, but he stood three inches shorter than his adversary, which gave the appearance of great disparity in height. There were about two minutes spent in sparring, when Crawley came to his man and made play with the left to the face. Ward was too quick for him, though, for not only did he parry the blow, but he countered with such tremendous force under the eye that he laid the flesh open and sent Peter on the flat of his back. Never had old ring-goers seen such a terrifically severe blow delivered in like manner. The Champion's friends shrieked with delight, and the crowd, unable to control themselves, burst through the outer ropes, and drove those who had official duties to perform into the 24ft ring. For a few seconds there Peter lay, the blood pouring on to the grass. The betting was at once 3 to 1 on Ward.

In the next round, however, the tables were turned. After a brilliant display of defensive science, equal to anything that had been seen before in the Prize Ring, not excepting Jem Belcher and the Game Chicken, Jem seemed to get impatient and let go both hands, but was short. Peter saw his opportunity, and with fearful force, and as quick as lightning, sent in a thundering right-hander, which struck Jem like a sledge-hammer just below the temple. He went down as if he had been shot. Few men could have survived such a blow. There was a death-like silence. Then a tremendous shout went up for Crawley, for when it was seen that Ward was still conscious even money was betted. Crawley was exhibiting quite as much science as Ward, and that was saying a good deal. Although Jem delivered five blows to Peter's three, the latter hit with more force, and the

Champion by no means took the lead. In the fourth round Ward went staggering down with Peter on top of him, and in the fifth the Black Diamond was grassed by a heavy blow on the mouth and another on the nose.

In the sixth the exchange of blows was terrific, and when Crawley closed to throw his man he was too weak to do so, and they fell together. In the seventh, though, the spirits of the East Enders rose, for after a few exchanges Jem proved that he was by far the better wrestler, for he seized his man with an iron grip, and gave him a cross-buttock of the most dangerous kind, leaving him almost unconscious spread-eagled on the grass. Jem Bland after this offered 10 to 1 on the Champion, but found no response.

Again there came a change o'er the scene, for in a tremendous rally Ward became so weak that he could not strike another blow, and fell forward on his face. In the ninth round both were too exhausted to do anything, although Crawley was slightly the stronger, and it was quite evident that at this juncture stamina, not science, would win the fight. The tenth was productive of little interest, both men getting to the ropes and going down from sheer exhaustion. Still Crawley preserved wonderful coolness, whilst Ward was all abroad, and it was evident that the battle was drawing to a close. Here is a report of the last round, which was the eleventh :—
" Open-mouthed and hardly able to stand, Jem went in for his last supreme effort. Crawley, who still preserved his wonderful self-possession, saw that this round must terminate the battle, and collecting all his strength he struck out lightly with his left, then, drawing back a step, he came on again, and catching Jem a severe jab with his left on the mouth, dropped him—to rise no more that day. The Champion fell flat on his back, and drawing his hands up towards his stomach became to all appearance senseless. Josh lifted him from the ground and placed him on Reuben Martin's knee. But he was deaf to the call of ' Time,'—deaf to the cries of triumph which hailed Peter Crawley Champion of England.''

CHAPTER XXIII.

ARRIVAL OF A GAOL BIRD.—JEM WARD AND JACK CARTER.—
A VERY BLACK DIAMOND.—THE CHAMPION IS MATCHED
AGAIN.

THE downfall of Jem Ward created the greatest excitement and consternation. They had fought but six and
twenty minutes, but it was one of the severest battles
ever recorded, and Peter Crawley, who won the belt, was
as much punished as the late Champion. Never, we
suppose, was there such a scene as that at the finish of
a Championship battle. Jem Ward, still insensible,
was carried to a chaise and driven to the Red Lion, at
Royston, and put to bed; but it was some hours before
he regained consciousness. The amount of money that
changed hands was immense, and many of the East
Enders had lost their all.

Jem has many a time told us himself, when we have
chatted over incidents of his pugilistic career, at the
Licensed Victuallers' Asylum, that it was the blow on
the temple in the second round that settled him. That
he did not forfeit the confidence of his backers may be
inferred from the fact that they offered to back him
against Crawley or any other man in the world for
£1,000. But Peter had found out what sort of a man
Ward was, and cared not to meet him again. So, although
he had fairly won the Championship, he declined to hold
it, declaring that he would never enter the ring again.
This determination he adhered to, for he shortly afterwards took the Queen's Head and French Horn, in Duke
Street, West Smithfield, and there he remained till his
death, which took place on March 12, 1865. He rarely
busied himself with matters connected with the Prize
Ring, but followed to his favourite sport, cock-fighting,
until that pastime was prohibited by law, and even then
Peter contrived to be present at the fighting of many a
main, both in London and the provinces, unknown to,
but right under, the noses of the law officers. Peter
Crawley, as a Boniface, was much respected, and was well
patronised by the sporting butchers from the market
hard by.

Jem Ward, when he was refused a second meeting
with Crawley, naturally posed as Champion once more,

and offered to fight anybody in the world to justify the resumption of the title.

This inactivity did not suit Jem at all, so he left London and spent much of his time in Liverpool, where he had established himself as a very great favourite. Mr. Williams, the well-known actor, of Sadler's Wells, had interested himself a good deal in Ward, and had introduced him to Messrs. Whyatt and Farrell, the lessees of the Prince's Theatre, Liverpool, and of the Royal Circus, and these gentlemen had given Jem quite a nice little engagement for displays of boxing. This engagement was concluded on February 29, and Jem at once determined to return to London, as he had heard to his surprise that Jack Carter had in a most unexpected manner appeared once more upon the scene, and had thrown out a challenge to fight anybody breathing for £100 a-side.

Carter we have already introduced on the occasion of his fights with Molyneux and Tom Spring, but he had dropped out of the pugilistic ranks in rather an unpleasant manner. Travelling from Oxford by coach to the metropolis, Jack Carter was accused of stealing from a gent a five-pound note. This was in the summer of 1824, and it seems that there was evidence enough against him to get a conviction, for he was sentenced to seven years' penal servitude at the hulks. His friends to a man believed that they had got hold of the wrong individual, and declared that Jack knew perfectly well who had abstracted the note, but that he would not round on his pal, preferring himself to suffer imprisonment. Anyhow, his conduct during imprisonment was so good that he was let off when he had served but half the time, viz., three years and six months.

No wonder, then, Jem Ward was surprised to hear that Carter was in London throwing down the gauntlet, when he imagined him to be secure in prison. He had made his way to Chatham upon his release, and there, amongst a number of old friends a benefit was given him, when a few yellow-boys found their way into Jack's pocket. These did not last him very long, though, for he could not resist the temptation of a spree after his long confinement, so, being penniless, he tramped up to London, and on February 1, 1828, presented himself at the hostelry of Josh Hudson, the Half Moon, in Leadenhall Market. Now mine host of that flourishing tavern was a good-hearted fellow, and had known the Lancashire lad (for Jack Carter hailed from near Manchester) for many years. He gave him board and lodging and a rig-out of clothing, and forthwith reintroduced him to the sporting world as a man who had suffered a great

wrong, and who was ready to fight anybody breathing
for as much as he could get subscribed. Jack had
always been a favourite, for he was a most entertaining
fellow, and when Bob Gregson introduced him to London,
just fifteen years before, he made many friends. Not
only was he an excellent fighter, but he could run and
jump; he was a first-rate step-dancer, a capital clown,
and a really expert acrobat—a man, in fact, that could
get a good living in a circus. He had won his first
battle against Soldier Boone, but suffered defeat from
the hands of both Power and Molyneux. He, however,
retrieved his laurels later on by winning four battles in
succession, two against Sam Robinson, the Black, and
one each over another nigger, named Stephenson, and
the fourth over the celebrated Tom Oliver. This latter
victory placed him in the front rank of the heavy-weights,
and had he taken care of himself, and not got into
trouble, Jack Carter might have had his name enrolled
amongst the Champions.

Soon after his arrival in London Jack was fortunate
enough to meet his old friend and backer, Sir William
Maxwell, an eccentric individual, with one arm, but a
rare old sport. This was the same Scotch "Sir Wullie"
who owned Filho da Puta, winner of the St. Leger in
1815. The baronet was so excited at having secured the
classic race that he went to the Reindeer, in Doncaster,
the hotel at which he was staying, and smashed every
pier-glass he could find in the public rooms with his
walking-stick. He was guardian to young Lord Kelburne, who was afterwards Lord Glasgow.

Sir William invited Jack Carter to meet him at
Limmer's Hotel on the following day, and have a
talk about what he proposed to do in the future.
Accordingly Jack was punctual, and there, in the smoking-
room, with a magnum of champagne before them, the
Scotch Laird of Monreith and the ex-convict pugilist
fraternised. Jack, before the meeting was over, induced
the baronet to back him, and they drove off together to
Tom Belcher's, the Castle, Holborn, in the hopes of
finding the Marquis of Queensberry, who had backed
Oliver against Carter and lost his money, and who no
doubt would have liked to have had a chance of turning
the tables upon Jack by backing Jem Ward against him,
for it was the Black Diamond whom the Lancashire man
had in his mind's eye.

Unfortunately the Marquis was not there. We say
unfortunately, for the confiding Sir William Maxwell
handed the sum of £25 to Jack and told him to cover
that amount as a deposit whenever opportunity offered,
as he (the baronet) had to leave for Scotland, where he

should remain for a few weeks. This was a very impru-
dent thing to do, and, as might have been expected, the
money was squandered in a few days, and when Jem
Ward came to town (which he did during the following
week), Jack Carter did not know for the life of him what
to say when they met. Friday, the 29th, was the day
appointed for the two men to arrange for the match for
£100 a-side, and they were to enter an appearance at the
Castle.

Quite a representative gathering took place at the
celebrated sporting drum to witness the signature of
the articles. Queensberry was amongst those present,
but he was in one of the worst of moods, for on that
very morning his favourite dog, Rasper, had been killed
by Neptune in a fight; the latter belonging to Lieutenant Jolly, R N., who was in ecstasies over the victory,
and standing "fiz" to all comers. Carter was accompanied by Josh Hudson, whilst Ward was surrounded
by many old friends and supporters. The two men
shook hands cordially, and Tom Belcher, after desiring
the company to be seated, announced that they had met
for the purpose of making a match. Then Josh Hudson
got up as spokesman for Carter, and explained to the
disappointment of all that Carter found it impossible
to raise more than £50, and hoped that, under the
circumstances, Ward would consent to fight for that
amount. This Jem refused to do, and it was thought
that there would be an end to the whole business. He
declared that it was too bad to bring him all the way
from Liverpool to make a match for so paltry a sum. Jack
Carter then appealed to him so earnestly, and even
eloquently, that, influenced by the persuasion of his
friends, he at length consented to fight for the £50 a-side,
the decision being greeted with great applause. The
following articles were then drawn and signed :—

"Articles of agreement entered into this 29th day of
February, 1828, between Jem Ward and Jack Carter.
The said Jem Ward agrees to fight the said Jack Carter
a fair stand-up fight in a twenty-four foot roped ring,
half a minute time, within 100 miles of London, on
Tuesday, the 27th of May, for £50 a-side. In pursuance
of this agreement £4 a-side are now deposited; a second
deposit of £16 to be made on Tuesday, the 11th of March,
at the Marquis of Granby, Loman's Pond (Frank Redmond's), and the whole of the stakes to be completed at
the Castle Tavern, Holborn, on Tuesday, the 15th of
April. In case of magisterial interference, the stakeholder to name the place for a second meeting to decide
the match. (Signed) "J. WARD.
"J. CARTER."

Queensberry, directly the match was made, laid £200 to £100 on Jem Ward, and the odds were on offer all over the room, although there were few ready to back the Lancashire man. Twelve years' difference in their ages was considerable, and besides that the Black Diamond was acknowledged to be far away the most scientific man since the time that Jem Belcher held the Championship, and some of the old stagers declared that he was even cleverer than that brilliant ornament to the Prize Ring.

Jack Carter's troubles began immediately, and it is quite certain that had it not been for his old and staunch friend, Josh Hudson, the whole thing would have fallen through before the second deposit became due. True to his promise, the worthy host of the Half Moon organised a benefit for Carter, and so hard did Josh work that the Fives Court, where it was held, was crowded, and Jack cleared £70, which sum Hudson took care of, for it was just the amount to pay down for the stakes and defray the cost of his training. Then came an awful crushing blow for the Lancastrian. The *Times* came out with a notice of the benefit, in which the writer expressed surprise that gentlemen sports should support an ex-convict, who had only served half his time, and was, indeed, a ticket-of-leave man. Although his particular friends took no notice of this, a great number of the swells did, and poor Jack found himself considerably cold-shouldered. However, he lost no time in getting away to his training quarters, for he knew that everything depended upon the issue of the fight. It was his last and only chance to regain his position.

It is not our intention to describe the men's preparation for the battle, on which Carter had so much at stake, nor, indeed, to take our readers on to the battle-field on this occasion, for we have dwelt long enough upon the Black Diamond's ring career, and can afford but one more chapter after this to dispose of that worthy.

Briefly, then, we may state that after a series of hitches and narrow escapes from the magisterial clutches, the ring was pitched on the day appointed (Tuesday, May 27, 1828), at Shepperton Grange, around which but some 700 or 800 people gathered. It was ten minutes past one when they entered the ring, Ward looked after by Phil Sampson and Dick Curtis; Carter by Tom Oliver and Young Dutch Sam.

Both men have been described before, so it is unnecessary to repeat. In the first round Jem Ward showed his superiority by landing his man apparently where he chose, and finished up by giving him a clean throw with a back-heel. Jack Carter never had a chance. He

was overmatched, physically and scientifically, and in
the tenth round there were shouts of "Take him away;
he's licked." Carter, however, in spite of his friends'
pleading, was obstinate, and would come up round after
round only to be hit down or thrown until the seventeenth,

DICK CURTIS (The Pet).

when Tom Spring and Peter Crawley entered the ring
and declared that he should fight no more. Still the
brave fellow insisted upon facing his opponent again,
and would certainly have done so had not his seconds
both declared that they would stand by him no longer,

when he reluctantly consented to have the sponge thrown up, and Jem Ward was declared the victor, after a battle which had lasted but thirty-two minutes.

Jack Carter was so punished that he had to be taken to Staines in a gig, where he was put to bed at the Bush, and was unable to move for a day or two, whilst Jem Ward showed little or no signs of the encounter, driving back to town and attending a supper and jollification at the Castle, in Holborn, the same evening. And so Jem Ward had (Peter Crawley being out of the way) proved himself the best man amongst the heavy-weights, and it looked as if it would be difficult indeed for him to get matched again.

A long, weary year dragged on without any sign of a battle coming off with the Black Diamond, when at length the gauntlet was thrown down to Jem by one Simon Byrne, an Irish pugilist, who had done some good business in Scotland, and made quite a reputation for himself in Glasgow. He had been beaten by Mike Larkins, one of his own countrymen, whom he encountered for £50 a-side at Brassington Course, Ireland, on June 4, 1825. The men fought one hundred and thirty-eight rounds. His next attempt was with Manning, for £100 a-side, which took place on February 17, 1826, when the police interrupted. On May 3, 1827, he defeated Alexander M'Kay in five rounds, lasting forty-seven minutes, near Glasgow, for £50 a-side, and on the 30th of the following August he gained a victory over Avery for the same sum (thirty-six rounds, one hour and thirty-five minutes), at Kilmachon, near Glasgow. The brave Irish boy, having been so successful in the North, thought he would like to try his hand in the metropolitan ring, so he journeyed to London and, nothing daunted, selected the best man, by challenging Jem Ward.

And now it is our painful duty to point out the second black mark that appears upon the pages of the Champion's history. In the March of 1828 it had been arranged that Simon Byrne and Ward should meet and fight for £100 a-side. The place selected was Leicester, and the ring was to be pitched upon the cricket-field. Thousands of persons journeyed to the Midland town to witness the battle, which had created no end of interest, and an immense amount of money had been wagered upon the result. Everything seemed to be going well until the eleventh hour, when Jem Ward declared that he was taken seriously ill, and that he did not think it right for him to allow those who had backed him to lose their money. There was a dreadful row over this affair, which was named " The Leicester Hoax," and it would have gone badly with the Black Diamond had he been caught on that particular day. It was distinctly proved that there was nothing physically amiss with him, but he was selling the fight for a paltry sum of money, too ridiculously small to have warranted such an act. He had got into bad hands—a lot of unscrupulous gamblers —and he consented to act in this disgraceful manner. He had become associated with this school of blacklegs, and rather than forfeit their acquaintanceship he chose to behave in this dishonest manner. For the second time he had shown himself to be a weak fool, for there is little doubt that his want of resolution brought him to grief on both occasions. A writer, making excuses somewhat for him, does so in the following manner :—" It was his misfortune to be too thin-skinned to make a good rogue. He fell between two stools. He could not make up his mind to be either wholly false to his backers and the public, or wholly true to the gambling scoundrels who were his pals. He did not want to betray either party ; he wanted, if possible, to do the fair thing by both. It was an insane idea, and none but a very simpleminded and foolish man would have fancied such a course possible ; and, as was to be expected, James Ward came to unmitigated grief over the business. His punishment was severe ; he was expelled from the Fairplay Club, and the committee passed a resolution that any pugilist, who was a member of that club, accepting a challenge from him, or consenting to spar with him in public, should forfeit his membership at once. In fact, Ward was ostracised from all respectable sporting society, and his career in the ring was apparently blasted for ever."

Such was the position of the man who had won golden opinions as a fighter. As a scientific exponent of boxing, perhaps, up to that time none had been his equal, for he belonged to a more advanced school than that in which the clever Jem Belcher had been trained, and certainly possessed all the knowledge and quickness of that phenomenon. As we have said, this " hoax " was perpetrated on March 10, 1829, and for months poor Ward (for he really was to be pitied) sank into oblivion, deserted by his so-called pals, and shunned by nearly all his old friends. We say nearly, for there were still a few who stuck by him, being charitable enough to see that Jem had been more sinned against than sinning. There were good old sportsmen, too, who thought it a dreadful thing that such exceptional talent should be put on the shelf like this. It was, they declared, an injustice to sport. These staunch friends numbered amongst them the Marquis of Queensberry, Sir Bellingham Graham,

Messrs. Hinde and Norval, and Ben Turner, of the Mulberry Tree Inn, Commercial Road. The latter will be remembered, as the gentleman who, on the first occasion of Jem's "mistake," stuck to him through thick and thin, and saved him.

Then in the autumn of 1829 there appeared in the sporting journals a challenge from an "Unknown" to fight Simon Byrne for any sum from £200 to £500 a-side. The challenge was accepted, but on condition that Ward was barred. The "Unknown" turned out to be the Black Diamond, so, of course, the match fell through. After this, however, every sportsman, even those who had been very bitter against Jem, perceived how the Ring was suffering through the enforced absence of the Champion, and their hearts began to melt towards him. Then followed a number of letters in the sporting papers, touching lightly upon Ward's "talents" and misfortunes, and at this very moment Simon Byrne helped the fallen one's cause more than anybody else. He declared that he would under no consideration fight such a black sheep for a money stake, but to show his superiority he would thrash him for love, if he would only give him the chance. Jem's reply was that he never fought for love, but that if Simon Byrne would mention a sum he would be delighted to meet him whenever he pleased.

Just at this time, when the wordy warfare was at its highest, a letter signed "Old Patron of the Ring," appeared in the journals. The writer of this was none other than Sir Bellingham Graham, and so manly an appeal was it on behalf of Ward that it produced a most favourable impression on the disgraced one's behalf. The desire that Ward should have another chance of retrieving his lost laurels grew apace, and it was the talk at every sporting drum. That which settled the matter, though, came about quite by accident. Simon Byrne had been taking a benefit at the Tennis Court. It was St. Patrick's Day, and the Irishman was well primed with his native potheen, which had undoubtedly softened his heart, and his pockets being well lined he felt at peace with all men. It so happened that he having gone to the Castle, at Holborn, met there Jem Ward. The whole thing was done in an instant. With tears (no doubt flavoured with whisky) in his eyes, Simon grasped Jem's hand, shook it for about half a minute, insisted upon drinking with him, and declared that he would fight him (hic - cough!), wheneverhepleashed, for whateverheliked. And so a long step in the right direction had been taken. But what came of it we must leave to the next chapter.

CHAPTER XXIV.

THE RETURN TO THE FOLD.—JEM WARD AND SIMON BYRNE.
—GREAT FIGHT FOR THE BELT.—DECLINING YEARS AND
DEATH OF THE " BLACK DIAMOND."

THE reconciliation between Simon Byrne and Jem
Ward, as described in the previous chapter, altered
Jem's position entirely in the eyes of the sporting world,
and the Fairplay Club having waived their objection, he
soon rejoined the ranks of the Fancy, and appeared in
his old haunts. It took less than no time to match the
two men, and articles were drawn up for them to fight
for £200 a-side, to take place after Byrne's battle with
Sandy M'Kay on June 2, 1830. How the issue of this event
upset Ward's arrangement we need only note in
passing. The fight took place at Selcey Forest, North-
amptonshire, and was for £200 a-side. Forty-seven
rounds were fought in fifty-three minutes ; but, unfortunately, the battle terminated fatally to Sandy M'Kay.
Simon Byrne was, of course, tried for manslaughter at the
Buckinghamshire Assizes and acquitted. This sad affair
was instrumental in breaking off the match with Ward ;
but the latter, as soon as the matter had blown over,
renewed his challenge for £100 a-side. Byrne, however, who had always fought for big stakes, refused to
meet Jem unless he made it the original amount—viz.,
£200 a-side. After months of correspondence on this
point the match fell through. By a curious coincidence,
once more on St. Patrick's Day, exactly two years after
the men had made friends, they met at Tom Spring's.
Whether it was through the intervention of the patron
saint, or that the copious potations of the national
beverage had asserted themselves, we know not. Anyhow, Simon Byrne was in an excellent mood, and the
two fraternised until a late hour, and during the time
they spent together they came to terms, and it was
arranged that they should fight for £200 a-side and
the Championship of England, on Tuesday, July 12,
1831, within 100 miles of London, on the Liverpool
Road, and an agreement was signed to that effect. Tom
Cribb became stakeholder, and as all the tip-top sports
were backing the men, it was evident that this time the
match was genuine and there was no fear of a cross.

But Jem and the Irishman had been so long out of
training that they had all their work cut out to get

themselves into trim. It was said that Ward weighed
15st, and that Byrne pulled the beam at 16st. Jem went
away with Mat Robinson, and after a short boxing tour
through the Midlands made for Oxton, near Liverpool,
on the Cheshire banks of the Mersey, and there settled
steadily down to work.

The Emerald Gem, as Simon Byrne was dubbed, took
things more easily, and went first to Dublin, staying
there until May, and making not the slightest effort to
get himself into condition. Indeed, he was living a very
fast life in the capital, by all accounts, and Tom Reynolds, who kept a pub. in Abbey Street, and was supposed to look after him, must have sadly neglected his
charge. Byrne left Dublin on May 25, and came to
London. There he astonished his friends and backers,
for he was still considerably over 15st, and his proper
fighting weight was 13st. To get 28lb down in about six
weeks, without the aid of powerful physic was impossible
with a man like Byrne, so he was sent away to Ned Neale,
at Norwood, where that worthy had taken the Rose
and Crown, with instructions to put the Irishman
through a severe course of treatment. Ned gave him
plenty of work up the Norwood hills, but failed to
bring him to his proper weight, and when he came
to London on July 5, just a week before the battle
was to take place, he scaled 14st 2lb. His trainers then
resorted to the very questionable process of physicking
him, and naturally with the result that he was considerably weakened. Added to this he was exposed to a
thunderstorm whilst at exercise on the Sunday before
the fight, from which he caught a severe cold. Ward,
on the other hand, had trained himself to an ounce, and
was never better prepared or in sounder health for any
of his fights.

It had been given out that the highest bidding should
have the honour of the company, and Warwick, as
before, offered the biggest price for the men to come into
their district, the money (£60) being subscribed principally by publicans of the town. Accordingly, Tom
Spring went down on the Saturday and put up at the
George Inn, having with him Simon Byrne and Tom
Reynolds. During the day, however, the ex-Champion
had a visit from a police-magistrate, who came specially
to inform him that it had been decided not to permit
the fight to come off on the racecourse, nor, indeed, upon
any ground within the jurisdiction of the borough. This
was unfortunate; but Tom Spring was equal to the
occasion, and he prospected with the result that he
determined that the contest should take place, if possible,
in the direction of Stratford-on-Avon, the spot selected

being Willeycutt. The invasion of Warwick by those
who knew nothing about the change of venue was
enormous on the Sunday and Monday, and although
the people who had subscribed were disappointed when
they learned what the beaks had done, they had no cause
to regret having subscribed, for they did a roaring trade.

But to the ring side. Tuesday, July 12, which had
been selected as the day upon which the sporting world

SIMON BYRNE.

would know whether the honour of being Champion
should rest with the Emerald Gem of Ireland or the
Black Diamond of Old England, was about as cloudy
and moist as could well be imagined. The morning
broke with a drizzle, which was followed by a steady
downpour. Nevertheless, gathered round the ring were
quite 15,000, and amongst them were some of the
greatest sporting swells of the day. Here are a few :—
The Duke of Beaufort, the Marquis of Worcester, the
Marquis of Queensberry, Lord Kilburne, Lord Kennedy,

Lord Wilton, Lord Dewhurst, Sir Billingham Graham, Sir St. Vincent Cotton, Sir Henry Goodricke, Captain Horatio Ross, Squire Osbaldestone, Mr. E. H. Budd, John Gully, Sir Tatton Sykes, Mr. Richard Tattersall, Lord Southampton (Master of the Quorn), Fulwar Craven, " Ginger " Stubbs, " Pea-Green " Hayne, Sir William Maxwell, Tom Duncomb, Mr. Henry Temple (afterwards Lord Palmerston), and many others well known in sporting and fast circles about town.

It is half-past twelve when all have taken their places around the ring, but there is no appearance of the men as yet. But the time passes quickly, for, in spite of the rain, the audience is exceedingly lively, coarse chaff going on in the outskirts, whilst the swells hob-nob and hand the flasks around from the capacious pockets of their waterproofs. A few minutes past one o'clock there is a distant shout, which swells into a roar as an opening in the crowd allows the Irishman, Simon Byrne, to make his way towards the arena. Then there is a peal of laughter, for behind the gig, in which is seated Byrne and Spring, comes a mourning-coach, drawn by a pair of long-tailed blacks, in which is seated Ned Neale and Isaac Bitton, and two officers of the 13th Hussars, heavy backers of the Irishman. It is soon explained. All the vehicles had been bespoke, when it was found to be such a wet morning. So the funeral coach was the only available conveyance in Warwick.

In a few minutes there is another shout, even louder than the first, and Jem Ward, accompanied by Harry Holt and Peter Crawley, his seconds, appears upon the scene in a close carriage. Although last to arrive, he is first to throw his castor into the enclosure. Byrne quickly follows suit, and enters the ring with his esquires, Tom Spring and Tom Reynolds. Mr. White, of Bridgnorth, is chosen referee, and while the final touches are being put to the combatants, as if to cheer them up, the sun bursts out brightly, the rain ceases, and the men advance to the scratch. They are both formidable looking gladiators. Rarely, if ever, has there been seen a grander specimen of an athlete than Jem Ward as he stands before the vast crowd. Somebody remarks : " He is trained as fine as a stag. The skin like satin, firm of texture, and so clear that you can see the muscle moving like ivory at every motion of the body; the bright eye, the glowing face, all speak of perfect health. The deep chest, the broad shoulders, the superb limbs, tell of prodigious strength; whilst the perfect symmetry of the frame indicates no less agility than power."

Simon Byrne looks what he is, a strong, powerful

man, but not sufficiently trained. He is almost "beefy," and could have done with quite 1½st less flesh. " Time " is called, and they stand still looking at each other with scarcely a movement. Each seems waiting for the other to break the ice. Simon is the first to commence ; he lets go with the left, but is stopped with the greatest ease. After a pause Ward feints with the right; but Byrne jumps back in a nervous kind of manner, and Jem, with a smile at his timidity, follows Simon, who quickly retires to his corner, when Jem comes to close quarters, and after a little fibbing, in which Byrne receives a nasty smack in the mouth, they clinch and roll over together, the blood streaming from the Irishman's mouth.

The second round is almost a repetition of the first, only Simon goes down alone this time, and is the recipient of much chaff, in spite of which he follows the same tactics in the third bout. After this Ward takes the lead, and Byrne naps some very warm ones about the mouth and chin. Each time that Jem Ward comes to the scratch he is greeted with tremendous applause, and it is easy to tell what is the opinion of the onlookers, for it seems that the Irishman is unable to touch his man, whilst Jem keeps getting home blow after blow. Pat is in a funk, and you can see his knees tremble. There is some cruel chaff going on at the expense of the Irishman, too, and that causes him to lose his temper, and he dashes in at the Diamond with a savage expression upon his damaged "mug." Simon's reputed hard hitting is set at naught by Ward, and although the punishment he administers is not very great, Jem keeps hitting him in the same place, and his mouth and cheeks are beginning to alter the usual amiable expression of his countenance. He has already discovered that he is no match for the Diamond in the closes, and has not nearly such a knowledge of the tricks in wrestling. Indeed, it is easy to see by Byrne's style that he feels that he has caught a Tartar in the East Ender, who is his superior all round, and that the only chance he has of winning the fight is by getting one of his tremendous chance blows in.

The eighth round is remarkable for the cool and effective manner in which Jem goes to the attack. He sends a couple of heavy left-handers in quick succession, and follows them up with a third, so emphatically administered that Simon goes to grass, and the Londoner scores the first two events. Simon, after this, finds himself checkmated at every move. Round after round continues with the same result. Once only are the sinking hearts of the Irishman's party quickened with hope. At

the very time when it seems hopeless for Byrne, and the
betting is at 20 to 1, for a moment a change comes o'er
the scene. It is in the twenty-fifth round, and the Irishman has appeared dazed and groggy, when by a supreme
effort he seems to pull himself together, and with a
suddenness that takes Ward this time quite unawares,
he delivers a blow with the right on the throat, which
drives Jem back staggering and almost chokes him. His
face turns a livid purple, he gasps terribly for breath,
and the excitement is tremendous. Jem, borne back by
the impetus of Byrne's rush, before he can recover himself has his opponent upon him. It is lucky for him that
the wild Irishman does not keep his head, or it must
all have been over with the Londoner. Pat, goaded on
to madness by the cries of his party, hits away right
and left, but without precision, and scarcely a blow tells.
Simon is now dazed and nearly beaten himself, whilst
Ward is fast recovering his breath, and as Simon makes
another charge at him, he stops him with a straight hit
full on the nose, Jem gradually retreating round the
ring and fighting on the defensive, the Irishman
savagely pursuing him. The excitement amongst the
bystanders is now at the height of its intensity. But
Ward is recovering, and he is placing blows with marvellous precision and effect upon Pat's nose and mouth
until Simon, faint from loss of blood and worn out by
his own exertions, stops dead short. It is now Jem's
chance. Like the bullet from a rifle in goes a blow
straight from the shoulder into poor Simon's bleeding
face—you can hear the crack—it is the hardest Jem has
yet delivered, and Byrne reels from the effects of it,
and cannot save himself from falling. But Jem does not
intend to let him off with this, for as he falls forward
the Diamond administers a terrible upper-cut with the
right, which drenches the poor fellow with blood, and
lays him helpless on the grass with his legs under him.
It is perfectly clear that the Emerald Gem has shot his
bolt.

Yet he is game to the backbone, and insists upon
coming again to receive chastisement from his clever
foeman. But the story is told. Byrne makes rushes,
which grow feebler and feebler, till they are no more
than lurches. He is a mere chopping-block in Jem's
hands. His want of condition has been fatal to his
chance, even if his science could have compared in the
slightest degree with that of his adversary. During the
last seven rounds Jem Ward is merciful, for he refrains
from punishing him as severely as he might easily have
done. At the end of the thirty-third Tom Spring
and Reynolds have a brief consultation, when the ex-

Champion, taking the large horse-sponge with which he has been bathing the bleeding face of his man, shouts to Crawley, "There you are, Peter! We can do no more—our man's done," and the sponge spins up sky-wards.

Now there is such a scene of excitement as is rarely witnessed at a Championship or any other fight. Hats and sticks are flying in the air, and the voices of 15,000 people make the earth tremble as if peal of thunder after peal were full about the ears. Jem Ward runs across the ring and jumps the ropes ; then, turning again, leaps back again like a greyhound, just to show how fresh he is. Turning then to his fallen foe, he takes him by the hand and says : " You're a brave man, Simon, and I've had a hard job to lick you."

Such was James Ward's last battle, which placed him unquestionably Champion of England, and proved him to rank amongst the finest fighters of that or any other period, for we may safely regard Jem Ward, Jem Belcher, Tom Spring, and Jem Mace as the four greatest scientific and natural fighters that ever won the Cham-pionship Belt.

Two days later Jem Ward was presented with a belt by Tom Spring and Peter Crawley at the Tennis Court, Windmill Street, on the occasion of Reuben Martin's benefit, Thursday, July 14, 1831. The place was crowded, there being many foreigners of distinction present. So James Ward was duly invested with the Championship of England. Following the presentation, on the next evening, when the battle-money was handed to him, Jem issued a challenge to fight anybody in the world, for from £100 to £500 a-side, but there was no response, save from Young Dutch Sam, which was absurd on the face of it. Mr. Sam Evans (for that was the Dutch-man's name) accepted the challenge conditionally that Ward would bring himself to 12st and stake odds, which proved conclusively that it was only idle talk.

Just one year after, on June 25, 1832, Jem Ward wrote to the sporting papers notifying that he had taken the Belt Tavern at Liverpool, and that he should retire from the Ring and hand over the belt to the first man who proved himself worthy of it. Deaf Burke declared that he was anxious to try conclusions with the Champion, but nothing came of the matter, and Jem Ward con-tinued to hold the title until the summer of 1839, when at the Queen's Theatre, Liverpool, he bade farewell to the Ring, and handed to Bendigo a facsimile of the belt.

He made Liverpool his home for a considerable time, carrying on the business of a publican at the Belt; then at the Star, and afterwards at the York Hotel, in

13

Williamson Square. He continued in the great seaport town until 1853, when the ex-Champion came to London and became Boniface of the Rose, in Jermyn Street, the same little house that was not so long ago kept by Frank Slavin, the Australian boxer. There he did very badly for Jem was never a very good business man, and he was in very low water. His friends, however, rallied round, him and found the necessary funds to get him into the Three Tuns, in Oxford Street, which was out of compliment to him re-christened the Champion Stores.

There he was by no means successful, so he determined to try a house in the midst of the scenes of his youth, and became landlord of the George, Ratcliff Highway. Still he made no satisfactory progress, and, like a rolling stone, gathering no moss, he harked back again to the West, and took the Sir John Falstaff, Catherine Street, Strand (then called Brydges Street), immediately facing the front of Drury Lane Theatre. At this time the house was a very celebrated theatrical tavern, but somehow Jem did not get on very well, and after being there some time found himself on the rocks once more. In 1858 he determined to pay a visit to New York, where he met with a most enthusiastic reception. Here he thought he had found a home in which to settle for the remainder of his life, for, introduced by the ex-pugilist, John Morrissey (who, like John Gully, had made a pile of money, and was a member of Congress), Jem Ward became quite a lion. In the Broadway, Central Park, and at Jerome Park Races he was the observed of all observers.

He was courted by artists (Jem was by no means a bad painter himself), men of letters, politicians, and sportsmen. An enormous benefit was organised for him, and he thought that the New World was a paradise on earth, and determined to stay. But oh! the fickleness of human nature. He soon discovered that the lion of one season was not the lion of the next, and Jem Ward found that his admirers and supporters gradually melted away; so he thought "home, sweet home" was the best place after all, and back he came to the land of his birth.

We have no space to write a further biography of the celebrated Champion. He was really talented outside pugilism, and his tastes for painting and music would undoubtedly have proved profitable to him after his pugilistic career had ended, had he had but training in his early life. As an artist he certainly had talent, and we have seen some excellent seascapes in oil from his brush. His taste for music, too, was excellent. His daughter, Miss Eleanor Ward, was a pupil of Sir Julius Benedict, and it was a pity that she should have married and retired

from the profession just at the period when she was
taking a prominent position amongst the first-class piano-
forte players of the time.

And now I think we must say farewell to the Black
Diamond by just mentioning that the Licensed Victuallers' Asylum, off the Old Kent Road, that excellent
Trade charity that has given shelter and comfort to
many a good man before and since, placed its welcome
roof over the head of the veteran pugilist, and there he
died, happy and in comfort, with those dear to him
around, on April 3, 1884, in the 84th year of his age.

CHAPTER XXV.

THE STRAND SEVENTY-FIVE YEARS AGO.—THE OLD SPOTTED
DOG.—THE DEAF 'UN AS A DEBUTANT.—JEM BURKE'S
MAIDEN FIGHT WITH NED MURPHY.

AND now we come to the name of a pugilist who was
destined to figure amongst the roll of Champions, and
whose performances in the roped arena were more
numerous, perhaps, than any gladiator who aspired to
the honoured title. Deaf Burke fought no less than
twenty battles, and lost but two. It is evident, then,
that with the space at our disposal we shall have to deal
sparingly with this marvellous pugilist's engagements,
and be content to cull from the multiplicity of episodes
and adventures that surround him only those which
may prove most interesting to our readers.

Nevertheless, as a form of introduction, we will devote
this chapter to a description of his early career and first
performance in the roped arena, as it will be well for our
readers to become acquainted at the outset with the simple,
honest lad, who remained faithful to his friends and the
public throughout that brilliant career which made him
so famous in the annals of the Prize Ring—the youth
who was to grow up to be the future opponent of Tim
Crawley, Birmingham Davis, Jack Carter, Simon Byrne,
O'Rourke, Nick Ward, and Bendigo—the youth who
went to America, where he won golden honours and
defeated the two greatest Yankee gladiators of the time.

In fancy, then, let us take a stroll down the Strand
some three-quarters of a century ago. It was not so very

much altered in 1899, save here and there where space
has been cleared for new hotels and modern buildings
dotted along the south side, but the succeeding year great
changes were made by the London County Council.
Facing the Strand was an old Tavern, the Spotted Dog,
immediately facing the Strand Theatre, which has
disappeared in these improvements. To it, in fancy,
we must conduct our readers.

It is the winter time, somewhere about the middle of
the twenties, and the weather is bitterly cold. In the
tap-room of the old Spotted Dog are a few hackney
coachmen, with their coats of many capes and their
great woollen scarfs wound around their necks, regaling
themselves with bread and cheese, and some of the best
old ale that can be had in the hostelry. Standing near
the fire-place is a rough-looking lad, about sixteen years
of age. His clothes are steaming, for he has evidently
been wet through, and has looked in at the Spotted Dog
for the purpose of having a warm and to dry his gar-
ments. " Good morning, Master Parish," says the
youth as the landlord comes round to clear the plates
and glasses. " Good morning, Jem," says that gentleman, who is none other than Joe Parish, the ex-pugilist,
who is well known in the Ring and amongst every sportsman. His principal opponents have been Harry Holt,
Cabbage, Davis, and Lashbrook; all, save Cabbage,
having been defeated by mine host of the Spotted Dog.

The lad, who is privileged to make himself comfortable in the tap-room, is James Burke. Born in St.
Giles', and deaf from his infancy, he has been dragged
up in the gutter, unable to read or write. He is a "Jack-
in-the-Water" at Strand stairs, and gets his living by
minding the boats, depending entirely upon the gratuities
given him by the "fares" who hire the wherries, shallops,
or pinnaces, for the river is as much a highway for the
travelling public at this period as the streets. At this occupation he had remained for a considerable time before
we meet him, and Joe Parish has from the very first
shown him the greatest kindness, for Jem has proved on
more than one occasion a courage and determination
that have delighted the old pugilist.

Naturally the landlord of the Spotted Dog had an eye
for points, and as Jem grew up he could see in him the
makings of a fine sturdy fighter. Once he had him up
in his parlour (for Parish still taught the art of self-
defence), and made him put the gloves on, and so
delighted was he with the manner in which he performed that he took him in hand. So well did he
progress that Parish used to say, " You go straight,
Jemmy, and we'll see if you won't be a top-sawyer

among 'em yet." And Jemmy did go straight. He had
had many temptations to be dishonest, poor lad, but it
wasn't in his nature. Untutored as he was, he resisted,
and always remarked when encouraged to do what was
wrong : " No; there's a Gods aboves us what sees us,
and I won't have its." And here let it be noted Jem
Burke, from his earliest boyhood until his death, always
put things in the plural in a most comical and unaccountable manner.

So matters went on, and Jem improved marvellously
in the fistic art (much to the delight of Parish) until
1828, when he was nineteen years of age, he having been
born on December 8, 1809.

And in the year we have named we find the first mention
of the youngster in any of the sporting papers. In one of
the popular journals, dated Sunday, January 27, 1828, we
read the following :—" Jack Scroggins' benefit at the
Hope Tavern, Blackmore Street, Clare Market, was but
thinly attended on Thursday last, and Jack, if he
depended for a supply of *wittels* on the patronage thus
afforded must be placed on short commons for a day or
two. At all events he would, we fear, be unable to
procure more than sufficient to satisfy three beefeaters
and half a dozen aldermen—a supply by no means more
than adequate to his wants. The sparring was of an
inferior character; we witnessed but one set-to worth
recording, and that was between Alec Reid and a young
Patlander named Burke, a fellow who carried a nob
vastly like that of a bull-dog, only not quite so handsome. However, he was a game fellow and stood well
up to his work, but Alec nobbed him with the left hand
and bodied him with the right, until he was absolutely
hit to a standstill. He left off with the character of
being a good *taker*, but he possesses much strength, and
if he takes care to improve himself, may turn out a good
one."

After this Joe Parish determined to get him matched,
and caused the following paragraph to appear :—" Jem
Burke says he can be backed against Mike Murphy for
£5 a-side. Burke may be met with to-morrow (Monday,
February 4), and on Tuesday at Peter Crawley's ; or
Wednesday and Thursday at Jack Randall's." So on
the nights mentioned Jem, in company with his mentor,
Joe Parish, went to the Queen's Head and French
Horn, Smithfield, whereof our old friend Peter Crawley
was Boniface, but the Deaf 'Un failed to find anybody
to accommodate him, although the place was packed
with fighting men.

Now the reason for this great assemblage was the
occasion of the final arrangements for a battle which

was to be brought off between two dwarfs, both men
under 4ft in height. Their names were Peter M'Bean
and David Morgan, the first hailing from the Land o'
Cakes, and the other a Taffy, as the name would imply.

It was a silly match, and quite beneath the dignity of
the Ring, but at the time it created no end of excitement
and fun. They were both waiters, and said to be very
smart with their hands. The Scot was engaged at Mr.
Gwillim's the Weavers' Arms, Grub Street, Cripplegate,
and the Welshman was engaged by Mr, Edwards, at the
Adam and Eve, Jewin Street. Peter Crawley had the
affair in hand, so on the Tuesday evening upon which
Parish and Burke had called they heard it announced
that the "battle of the dwarfs" would take place in the
neighbourhood of Whetstone, on the Barnet Road, and
that the meeting-place would be the Two Swans, on the
Wednesday (the morrow) at twelve o'clock.

Joe Parish determined to go and to take Jem with
him, and the latter had cause to remember that visit. It
is not our intention to describe the laughable and curious
performance of these Liliputians, which must have
afforded the greatest amusement to the vast crowd.
Suffice it to say that they fought no less than twenty-
one rounds, the Welshman winning the stakes, which
consisted of £5 a-side.

After the grotesque exhibition was over, it dawned
upon all present that the thirty-seven minutes' sport of
such a kind was scarcely worth the trouble of so long a
journey to witness, so it was suggested to Peter Crawley
that a purse should be subscribed, and that a couple of
volunteers should add to the day's sport. So the host
of the Queen's Head and French Horn took round the
hat, and was successful in collecting £13, for just a few
swells had come down to witness the novelty of the
whole thing. Amongst them were Lord Suffield (one of the
greatest "flats" connected with the Turf), Lord Chesterfield, and Viscount Chetwynd.

Then Peter the Great invited two combatants to enter
the lists. The first to respond by throwing his cap into
the ring was Ned Murphy. Then, standing close to the
ropes, young Jem Burke said to Parish, "May I,
Guv'nor?" to which Joe replied, "Certainly, my lad,"
and in went Jem's castor. Now Ned Murphy was known
pretty well to the Fancy, but the question asked by
everybody was about the other Paddy, for there was no
mistaking Jem's nationality, he having the true
Hibernian forehead and cheek bones.

Peter Crawley asked him his name, when Parish told
him that he was a pupil of his, and that the gents need
have no fear about having some sport for their money ;

so the lads were ordered to peel and enter the arena.
When they faced each other, it was at once seen that
Murphy was much the lighter man, weighing not more
than 10st 7lb, whilst the Deaf 'Un must have been a
stone heavier, for he was only nineteen at this period,
and when he had fully grown and set his fighting weight
was 12st 6lb. He was, anybody could see at a glance,
as hard as nails and as tough as pin wire, very strongly

JAMES BURKE (THE DEAF 'UN).

built, with thick, muscular limbs, and he stood 5ft 8¼in.
Jem Burke was not handsome, but there was a pleasant,
humorous, good-natured expression on his honest face,
which never failed to prepossess people in his favour.

Murphy's attitude was far the more graceful of the two
for Jem was too clumsy and awkward, not having had the
training that his brother Patlander had received. Still
Joe Parish had even then taught him how to cover himself, and his guard and pose of the left were good.

We will just quote a description of the first round—
the first that Deaf Burke ever fought in the 24ft ring,
as given by an eye witness. It will serve to show what
sort of a battle his maiden one was like. Of course,
Ned Murphy thought it was a walk-over, and did not fail
to say so. He soon found out his mistake though. Here
is the description :—"Ned Murphy was evidently anxious
to finger the coin as soon as possible, so gave no time
for the spectators to study the attitudes of the men.
He went in at once to polish off ' the boy,' anticipating
the easiest of victories. But Master Ed'ard had been
counting his chickens before they were hatched, which,
as the old proverb tells us, is at all times a dangerous
forestalment of events. As he rushed gaily in the Deaf
'Un caught him a clinking straight left-hander on the
cheek, which raised a swelling instanter, for Ned's condition was none of the best, and effectually stopped his
impetuous charge, whilst almost simultaneously with
the delivery of the blow Burke fell back to avoid the
return. For a second Ned was surprised and puzzled,
but the yells of his own friends and the cheers of the
opposite side quickly restored his presence of mind, and
he went for his man again. But the Deaf 'Un steadily
retreated, drawing Murphy on till the latter gave an
opening, and then again Jem's fist went straight into his
antagonist's face. ' Bravo! Jemmy, my boy ; that's the
way to do it,' roared Joe Parish, and apparently Burke
must have heard him, for a smile played for a moment
over his countenance, while he retreated as before. The
Irishmen yelled to Murphy to go in quicker and fight
his man at the ropes. Easier said than done, for in
trying it on Master Ed'ard caught another punch on the
nose, which set that organ to flow ; but despite his warm
reception Murphy fought his way in desperately to close
quarters, where he had the best of it ; for Burke, although
far the stronger of the two, did not seem to know much
about half-arm hitting. A furious scuffle ensued at the
ropes, and both came to the ground, Murphy undermost."
    The above is a fair specimen of the succeeding rounds,
that having entirely altered the aspect of things. No
longer did the friends of Murphy offer 2 to 1 on their
man, as they had done at the onset ; even money was
the price, and there was little of that. Every time
Murphy dashed in the Deaf 'Un met him with straight
jobs in the face, then fell steadily back, drawing his
man and frequently delivering a severe uppercut when
Ned bustled his way into close quarters.
    Before a dozen rounds had been fought Ned, who had
succeeded in getting in several blows about Burke's
head and face, found that his left was going. He was,

in fact, the first to discover the "iron nut" of the
Deaf 'Un, which served him so well throughout his
career. So Harry Jones, who was a friend of Murphy's,
shouted to him to let the novice's granite nut alone, and
go for the victualling department. Ned adopted this
advice, and getting several in on the ribs, had found the
only vulnerable part of Jem's anatomy, judging from
the grimaces he is said to have made.

After fighting some twenty rounds Murphy, by the
advice of his friends, ceased to take the initiative, but
played a waiting game, trying to draw Jem on. But the
Deaf 'Un would have none of it, and stood stock-still
with his foot planted firmly on the mark. A long pause
ensued, and the spectators got very impatient, until the
uproar was tremendous. Had Burke been able to hear
all that was said, he would have by no means felt
flattered. At length Murphy, who could hear, and
began to feel anxious about the menaces of the mob,
feinted and played about the Deaf 'Un in a manner
calculated to perplex a much older hand than Jem.
Cautious as Burke had been all through the fight, he
was tempted to let out, and he suffered for his error, for
bang went Ned's right into his mouth, and his left into
the small ribs. They were a couple of scorchers and no
mistake. Then Ned closed and tried to put on the hug,
but the Deaf 'Un, with one of those telling upper-cuts,
for which he afterwards became so famous, caught him in
the mouth with such severity that every front tooth in
his head must have been loosened.

This was said to be one of the best rounds in the
fight; both men did all they knew, and came off quits,
falling side by side at the finish. After this Murphy,
who, as we have stated, was an older hand at the game,
thought he had given enough display for the money.
Besides he did not relish those upper-cuts, so he played
about all over the ring, and in spite of threats and entreaties declined to come within distance. So it went
on for nearly half an hour, and darkness was setting in.
Although the fight was protracted for fifty rounds, half
these could not be called rounds at all, for scarcely a
blow was struck, and Murphy on every available occasion got down to finish.

Somebody then suggested that, as there seemed no
possibility of the fight coming to a satisfactory end
before the daylight vanished, they should divide. Both
had shown good sport, and had knocked one another
about as much as could be expected for the money.
Peter Crawley who was heartily sick of the whole thing,
concurred readily, and put the question to the men.
Ned Murphy was quite agreeable, but Burke hesitated

and wanted to fight it out if his man would only come on. Joe Parish, however, persuaded him to agree to divide, so the lads shook hands, and had presented to them £6 6s. each.

Jem was in the seventh heaven of delight. He had never had a bit of gold in his possession in his life, and now he had seven pieces. He clutched them in his pocket, and the tears of delight came into his eyes. Five of the golden sovereigns were for his poor old mother, whom he had kept for years out of the workhouse by dint of his labours. How happy she would be, and how she would bless her dear, honest boy. Those are the thoughts which must have passed through Jem's mind as he returned with Joe Parish, Ned Murphy, and a few friends to London, where, after he had been home, he had promised to have an evening of it at the Spotted Dog with Joe Parish (who was very proud of his *protégé*), to commemorate, with song and glass, his first appearance in the Prize Ring.

Such was the Deaf 'Un as a *débutant*. In our next chapters we shall follow his honourable and, as we have already stated, brilliant career.

CHAPTER XXVI.

THREE MILLS IN THREE WEEKS.—JEM'S HEROIC DEEDS.— DEAF BURKE AND FITZMAURICE.—ONE HUNDRED AND SIXTY ROUNDS IN THREE HOURS.

THE discovery of a new star in the fistic firmament likely to become a shining light soon became known throughout the Fancy, and Jem Burke's turn-up with Ned Murphy, when he made his *début* before some of the best judges of the art, certainly created a favourable impression, and he was the talk in sporting circles, both in the West and East. In fact, Jem Burke leaped with one bound from his humble, nondescript position into that of a great favourite. For his simplicity and honest face, none the less for his grand physique and great promise, he was courted by sporting men of note, and he became, as a fellow-pug said of him, "not only a card at the Strand Lane *soirées*, but a free and accepted brother at all the sporting cribs in the kindred Drury, Wild Street, the pugnacious purlieus of Clare Market, and among the porterhood of Covent Garden."

It was not long before Jem's sudden notoriety brought him prominently before the public again ; for about a fortnight after the event related in our last chapter, the Deaf 'Un was proceeding down Clare Market, on his way to the Spotted Dog, in the Strand, when he ran against a gentleman of the marrow-bone and cleaver persuasion. His name was Thomas Hands, and he was the captain of the gang of butchers in that locality, who, known as they were as "Kill Bulls," were a very rowdy, quarrelsome lot, and numbered amongst them some fellows who could use their fists in a very smart manner. Now Deaf Burke, although a good-tempered chap enough, easily took offence if interfered with, and on this occasion Hands and his party not only made some very uncomplimentary remarks to the Deaf 'Un, which fortunately he could not hear, but jostled him into the gutter. As quick as lightning the Deaf 'Un landed Tom on the jaw, and the fun commenced. An impromtu ring was formed, and the two men went at it hammer and tongs.

As luck would have it, at that moment Joe Parish and Jack Teasdale, another well-known bruiser, came along and parted the men, declaring that they should have an opportunity of meeting each other under more convenient auspices. The time soon came, for a few days after Jem, Joe Parish, and Hands were all present at a fight which had been organised to take place on Thursday, August 6, 1828, at Old Oak Common, over a quarrel which had taken place at a dinner held at Mr. Ellis', the High House, Pimlico, between an Irish pugilist named Sweeney and Ned Stockman. A good muster of friends were present to see this impromptu battle, but to the disgust of everybody Master Ned did not enter an appearance.

Those assembled naturally did not feel disposed to draw an entire blank, and so a small purse, consisting only of £2 17s., was made up, for there were no swells present. Nobody cared about peeling for so small an amount, and in all probability those present would have gone away disappointed had not our friend been there ready to finish the misunderstanding with the butcher, who, on his part, was equally anxious. So they stripped and gave the company a taste of their qualities, Jem Burke polishing off the "Kill-Bull" in twelve rounds, having made a nice spectacle of the butcher, whose "left eye was quite closed, the right much bruised and blackened, his cheek gashed in several places, his lips cut through, and his bulky carcase seriously shaken by violent contact with mother earth," as one reporter described him after the fight.

The Deaf 'Un was particularly gratified, and when presented with the not too extravagant stakes observed in his curious lingo of plurals, "Fifty bobs wasn't bads for twenty minutes easy works." Joe Parish was getting very proud of his pupil, and took him about everywhere. So little damage had he received from the Clare Market butcher that he was off again with his mentor on the following Tuesday, to Old Oak Common to witness a turn up with Pat M'Dournell and Mike Driscoll, and to see if he could compete for another purse. Parish encouraged Jem in this, for it was capital experience, and kept Burke in pocket money.

After the fight between the two Irishmen above-named, a purse was subscribed, which only amounted to £2 14s. 4¾d. (The farthing is vouched for in the contemporary reports.) But what a crowd must have been there—the lowest of the low. All the celebrities of St. Giles's and the Dials were present, and indeed the riff-raff of London was represented, so it may be imagined that the company was neither rich nor aristocratic.

A black known as Young Sambo (no relation to he of the same name who afterwards figured prominently in the prize ring) was the first to throw in his castor, and Jem Burke was not long in slipping away from Parish, and going up to Mike Brookery, the M.C. Touching his cap politely he addressed himself somewhat after this style, saying: "As how he should be glad to fights the blacks gentlemans for whatever dere was to gives."

Again Jem resorted to his wrestling tactics, and threw Massa Sambo nearly every round, in the seventh giving him a cross buttock that brought the black upon his head, making it bounce on the turf like a great indiarubber ball. Jem never fought better, but had it not been for Joe Parish's advice he would have thrown the battle away. It was evident that he was a magnificent natural fighter, and all he required was experience. That he was getting, for this defeat of the black in fifteen rounds was his third fight in the short space of three weeks.

After these successes Jem Burke had a rest, but he constantly attended the boxing rooms, and never missed a day without having the gloves on with Joe Parish, accepting that astute gentleman's advice in every detail.

At the beginning of March, however, all London was agog with excitement over the battle, which was to take place in the Leicester Cricket Field between Jem Ward

and Simon Byrne, to which we have alluded in a previous
chapter as the "Leicester Hoax," upon which occasion
Jem Ward sold the public and disgraced himself. The
battle was supposed to take place on February 25, 1829,
and people from London, Nottingham, Birmingham,
Coventry, Warwick, Melton, Harborough, Derby, Lichfield, and even Manchester, foregathered at Leicester to
witness the great fight. But when the morning arrived
and both men were on the spot, Ward, having slept at
Whitstone, near Leicester, had told Peter Crawley
that morning that he did not intend to appear,
that he had brought up a pint of blood, and that
he could not fight for twopence. Crawley, as honest
a man as ever entered the ring, declared that, in his
opinion, Jem Ward didn't dare go in and win, and that
something wrong had taken place. Tom Spring begged
him to act honourably, and if he had been tampered
with to go and do his best to "put the 'cross' men in the
basket." But Jem was obstinate; he said he thought it
better not to put either his backers on the one hand, or
those who had taken the odds on the other in jeopardy,
and therefore he had made up his mind not to fight.
The disgrace this brought upon Ward we have already
mentioned. Anyhow the two great guns did not fight,
and the spectators had to fall back upon the second item
on the programme, which had fortunately been
provided for this entertainment, viz., the contest between
Joe Randall and Bill Atkinson, the two Nottingham
cracks.

About this fight we have nothing to say, so it will be
sufficient to state that Atkinson was victorious after a
splendid battle, lasting fifty-two minutes and extending
over forty-one rounds.

This entertainment saved the company from absolute
disappointment, but as they had come all this distance
to witness two fights, two fights they would have. So
Peter Crawley, always ready and willing on these
occasions, suggested a purse, and in a very short time
collected £10. Of course, the Deaf 'Un was one of the
first to respond, and immediately a Leicestershire lad
named Berridge chucked his greasy and battered billy-
cock into the ring, and offered to fight him for the
money. It was a painfully one-sided affair, for the poor
countryman stripped like a skeleton, and looked more
as if a "square meal" would have done him more good
than a punch in the jaw. He was, according to all
accounts, a game 'un, though, and once or twice gave
Master Jem a little trouble, and some asserted that he
would have been a match for the Londoner had he been
given a few weeks' training on rump steaks. The contest

was settled in twenty-two minutes, eleven rounds having been got through.

And now we will follow our hero's career to Epsom Downs, but before we renew our story of the champion there will be just time to have a look at the most sensational Derby that was ever contested. Thursday, June 4 (for the Derby was run on a Thursday then), a delightful day, had attracted between 100,000 and 150,000 people to the Downs—some for the big race and others who took a greater interest in matters pugilistic, for it had been arranged that Deaf Burke and Bill Fitzmaurice were to entertain the sporting public after the races, they having been matched for £25 to fight in the Epsom week.

But to recall the Derby of 1829. There was a jockey over sixty years of age piloting to victory for the Blue Riband of the Turf a horse against which 50 to 1 had been betted at the start, and second to him was another horse which had occupied a similarly forlorn position in the market when the flag fell. Frederick the winner of the Derby of 1829, was ridden by Old Forth, his trainer, and Exquisite, who took second honours (ridden by Frank Buckle), was Old Forth's own horse. Frederick, in a trial, proved 7lb better than his stable-companion, and the artful old trainer had netted £20,000 as the hay and straw stakes to keep him comfortable in his old days. Was there ever a Derby to touch that of 1829?

After the surprise there was a great gathering at Merryweather's, known as the "Fives Courts Booth," that was usually erected at most of the race meetings. It was the rendezvous of the élite of the Fancy, and the prices charged "licked all creation," as the Yankees say. How is this for a refreshment tariff:—Plate of cold meat, 3s. 6d.; bread, 1s.; cheese, 1s.; pint bottle stout, 2s. Those were the prices charged and paid. But then the swells could afford it, and Merryweather made them.

Whilst they were laughing and chatting a messenger came to Tom Spring, and called him aside. When the ex-champion returned to the company he had a look of disappointment on his countenance, and amidst silence informed his listeners that he had just received some bad intelligence. He was very sorry to say that there would be no fight that day between Deaf Burke and Fitzmaurice. Both men had been arrested the night before on a warrant from the Union Hall police magistrate, and brought up before him that morning, when they had been bound over in sureties of £50 each to keep the peace for three months in the county of Surrey.

This was a bitter disappointment to the Deaf 'Un, as well as to the sporting fraternity at Epsom on that memorable Derby Day, for it was felt that he was a rising young fellow, and this would have been a splendid chance for him to have displayed his talents to the Fancy in particular and the public in general.

Jem had certainly not up to this time made much money out of his pugilistic talents, the total amount of

BILL FITZMAURICE.

his first four battles only amounting to £14 11s. 8¾d. But he had received several presents for his heroic conduct outside the roped arena, and one way or another the Deaf 'Un managed to pull along and keep his aged mother and himself fairly well.

And now the life of our champion would be quite incomp'ete if we did not narrate the circumstance which caused him to be recognised outside the ring, and which at the time gave him more popularity with the general public than all the fights he had up till then been engaged in.

Let us quote from a report made at the time. "About half-past two o'clock on the afternoon of Wednesday, September 24 [1828], the residents in Exeter Street, Burleigh Street and Southampton Street, and all who happened to be passing along the Strand at the time, were startled by a tremendous crash, Exeter Street was filled with a cloud of dust, and in a few moments it was discovered that two houses in that street, Nos. 4 and 5, had fallen in, burying their unfortunate occupants in the ruins. The alarm was given, and a number of workmen who were engaged in making excavations for the new sewer in Catherine Street and Brydges Street hurried to the spot. The excitement was intense, for groans and screams of agony came from the mass of rubbish, too clearly indicating that there were mangled and dying—and who could tell how many dead?—human beings entombed there. But the work of exploration was a most difficult and dangerous one, for there were walls and beams, and masses of loose masonry still toppling over, and threatening every moment to descend and crush everything in the way. Whilst the men who had gathered were looking on in perplexity, not knowing exactly what to do, a figure was seen threading its way amongst the overhanging timbers and treacherous walls, keeping steadily on, though death seemed to threaten him at every step. 'Who is he?' was the question bandied among the awe-stricken crowd, and then some bystander said it was a lad named Burke from the Strand Stairs."

Yes, it was the young pugilist and Jack-in-the-Water who knew not what fear meant. When he heard the cries he dashed in and risked his own life to save those who were suffering agonies. The account goes on to say that he soon appeared carrying a child, which he brought safe and sound to the crowd, who cheered him to the echo. Never could the applause have been more welcome at the ring-side than that spontaneously accorded the Deaf 'Un on that sad and memorable occasion. Again and again he returned amongst the *débris* of the wrecked dwellings, and succeeded in bringing two more children, one of them dead.

His coolness and bravery displayed called for general admiration, and paragraphs appeared in all the newspapers praising him for his daring intrepidity. Swells came to the Spotted Dog to see him, and gave him half-crowns and even gold. The Deaf 'Un had unwittingly raised himself in the social scale by this act of heroism, and he found plenty of opportunities for engagements with the gloves after this, although he could not get anything in the way of an engagement to suit him, and until the match was made to fight at Epsom—resulting in another disappointment—his turn-up with Berridge at Leicester was the only encounter he had had since the life-saving business. So naturally Master Burke was getting somewhat impatient that his fight with Fitzmaurice should take place as speedily as possible, he only being barred Surrey by the magistrate. So on the evening of the day after the Derby there was a meeting at Tom Spring's to take into consideration what should be done in the matter. A Mr. Longey, a Liverpool gentleman, who had recently returned from Africa, was Burke's backer, and he had put down £25 for him to fight the East End Chicken, as Fitzmaurice was called. It was decided that the postponed fight should take place on the following Tuesday, June 9, in the same ring, after Ned Favrige and Davis, the Manchester black, had settled their difference, and that the battle should take place at Harpenden Common.

It is not our intention to describe this fight, which was certainly *not* the most brilliant performance throughout Deaf Burke's long career. There was some good fighting at different periods of the encounter, but take it all through it forms one of the best specimens of disinclination for business ever illustrated in the Prize Ring. It was, indeed, lengthened sweetness long drawn out. The battle lasted *three hours* less *ten minutes*, and the number of rounds contested were no less than *one hundred and sixty-six.* Is it to be wondered at that both men were thoroughly exhausted at the finish, and indeed Fitzmaurice's seconds gave in for their man, as they feared that fatal results would ensue. As it was, the East End Chicken's countenance was fearful to look upon, for he had been terribly mauled about the face and head. He was driven off to the Bull at Harpenden, where he was put to bed and there remained for forty-eight hours. The Deaf 'Un was much bruised about the body, and one eye was closed. Jem had been victorious, but it was not a very creditable performance this his really first fight for a decent stake, and *Bell's Life* said in reporting it, and commenting on Burke's display, "We can only pronounce him a good glove fighter with some knowledge of biting and scratching." How this unkind statement was confirmed by the Deaf 'Un's more brilliant performances we shall discover in future chapters.

14

CHAPTER XXVII.

AFTER Deaf Burke's victory over Fitzmaurice and a
bit of a flare-up, it would appear that he got into very
low water, and although there were two or three challenges from fairly good men, Jem, for the want of the
" ready " was unable to take them up. He managed,
however, to jog along somehow by giving sparring
lessons and exhibitions with the gloves. In fact, he had
by this time shown such ability that he gained for
himself the nickname of the " Glove Phenomenon,"
and deserved it ; for few could touch him. One
gentleman, however, who had just been introduced to
the London Fancy by Mr. Preece, from Chichester,
had shown very high-class form with the mittens. His
name was Bill Cousens, and Preece, who had just taken
the Hole in the Wall Tavern, in Chancery Lane, from
Randall, was so confident in his ability that he
offered to put down anything up to a hundred. The
Deaf 'Un had on several occasions met Cousens on
the sparring platforms, and never had much the best
of it, which sadly galled Master Jem, and one evening,
at the Fives Court, they went at it hammer and tongs,
and Burke was accused of having slung the glove and
boxed unfairly. Had they not been stopped, off would
have come the mittens, and there would have been
a set-to with the genuine articles. Our hero, who
was one of the straightest men who ever stripped,
and would take advantage of no man, couldn't
forgive the Chichester lad for the accusation, and
offered to fight him when and where he liked for a
fiver. Now Mr. William Cousens looked with contempt
upon such a small amount, and drew the line at £25.
To the Deaf 'Un's mortification, he could find nobody to
put this amount down for him, so he humbly begged his
rival of the boxing stage to give him a chance. Mr.
Preece, anxious to trot out his *protégé*, at length gave
way, and they were matched for the small stakes, the
Boniface of the Hole in the Wall offering to lay 2 to 1
to hundreds on his man. This was taken up in small
amounts by those who were too mean to find money for
Burke's stakes or training expenses.

The fight was fixed for Tuesday, August 25, 1829, giving

only a week to get ready after the fiver a-side was put down. Burke declared that when this amount was in the hands of the stakeholder all he had was 30s. in the world. So he borrowed a skiff from the Strand Stairs, and trained himself by taking a twelve-mile spin upon the river daily, and some long walks morning and evening out of London, and back to his lodgings off Clare Market. This was poor work for a man to train for a fight, the result of which would control hundreds and, without doubt, had the Deaf 'Un made his circumstances known in the right quarters somebody would have come to the rescue and looked after him. But he was, as we have described, a modest, retiring fellow, who at this period had not learned the art of pushing himself forward.

Bill Cousens, on the other hand, was excellently well looked after, for, besides his fellow-townsman, Mr. Preece, Tom Owen was one of his backers. Now Tom just at this period had come into a considerable legacy, which really amounted to a fortune, so he had advertised his well-known shop at 80, Cable Street, London Docks (in which for so many years he had carried on a dining business) and had migrated to the West, where in fashionably cut clothes he played the *role* of a sporting gent, a character for which the Sage of the East, as he was called, by all accounts was particularly well adapted, for Tom Owen had a good address, a fair education, and a natural and exceptional turn of wit. Cousens had fought twice before, being victorious over both Sweeney and the Cheshire Hero, whilst, as we have described in previous chapters, Deaf Burke had won all his fights—six in number.

There was not a single contest down for decision in the Prize Ring during this month of August, so the followers of the fistic art mustered strongly, no less than 10,000 having assembled in that meadow near Whetstone upon the day fixed. The weather was glorious, and although the company were not too select they were fairly orderly. Nobody noticed the Deaf 'Un's arrival until he was observed at the side of the ring quietly dropping his cap over the ropes, and it was stated that, for the want of the means to hire a vehicle, or because of his reticence, he had actually walked every step of the way from London. Not the sort of preparation certainly for a severe battle. Cousens, on the other hand, drove up in style with a chaise and a pair of horses. in company with Tom Owen and Mr. Preece. Burke was looked after by Ned Stockman and Mike Kennedy, the two wrestlers, whilst Cousens had Tom Oliver and a young amateur, named Bourchier, for his seconds.

It is not our intention to describe this battle. 'We

shall be content to cull from one report the finishing round, which had so much to do with checking our hero's career. They both fought fiercely, but the Chichester man was stronger, and palpably in better condition than the poor Deaf 'Un. In the seventy-fifth round he gave Burke a tremendous fall, and came down with his thirteen stone upon the prostrate Irishman. This tumble had a curious effect on Burke—it seemed to stupefy and paralyse him. When he came up to the call of " Time," he rolled about unsteadily, his energy had apparently deserted him. He made scarcely any attempt at resistance, and Bill threw him again as if he had been a child. Once down it was no easy matter to get the Deaf 'Un up again. He shut his eyes, his head drooped upon his shoulders, he looked dead beat. A minute elapsed, the referee got impatient, and was about to call Cousens the victor when Reuben Martin jumped over the ropes and smacked Jem in the middle of the back, and he seemed to revive, for he came to the scratch, but instead of renewing the combat at once walked over to where Mr. George Smith, of the *Weekly Dispatch*, sat, note-book in hand, saying in his curious jargon of plurals : " I says, sirs, how the devils can I fights whiles they're alls slappings me about the backs, and I haven't a drops of anythings to drinks." Mr. Smith took the hint, and laughingly handed Jem his flask, from which he took a long pull. If this incident be true we wonder what Bill Cousens was doing to permit his man to do such a thing after " Time " was called. But in those days it seemed not to matter what they did in the arena, and greater irregularities than that were indulged in. The account goes on to state that after this he seemed to wake up a bit. To the amusement of all, the resuscitated Burke fought with uncommon fury, tackled his man in rare style, and threw him at the ropes, whilst the air rang with the wild hooroos of the Irishmen and friends of Burke. Three times Cousens was floored, and the excitement was tremendous, 5 to 1 being offered on the Deaf 'Un. Then, just as victory seemed in his grasp, he went off into a stupor again, from which nothing could rouse him. So at the close of the one hundred and eleventh round, Mr. Manvers, the referee, pronounced the Chichester man the winner, the men having fought two hours and five minutes.

Bad as Jem's position was before the fight, it was worse afterwards, for few would stand by him, and he seemed to have lost heart. Joe Parish, his old friend and mentor, was sadly disappointed after the promise he had at first shown. Still the Boniface never deserted

him, and there was always a "square meal" for him at
the Spotted Dog. But Jem cared not to sponge, so he
did odd jobs, acted as porter in Covent Garden Market,
knocked around the Haymarket in the evening, and held
gentlemen's horses and picked up a shilling, and even

BILL COUSENS

went so low down again as to hang about his old haunt
at the Strand Stairs to get a few coppers as a " Jack-in-
the-Water."

Nobody thought the Deaf 'Un was destined to become

an ornament to the Prize Ring at this period, and one day become Champion of England. And perhaps poor Jem himself never dreamed of such a thing. He seemed satisfied if he could only get an honest living.

And so matters went on until the end of the year 1829. On December 1, at a little village in the centre of Sussex, called North Chapel, between Milford Bay and Lynn, there was tremendous excitement. The drowsy place was invaded at a very early hour by "military and naval officers from Portsmouth and Winchester and Southampton, country squires and farmers from all the neighbourhood around, swell sportsmen from London, who had run down from town and slept the night at Chichester or Godalming—all had gathered at this little Sussex village," says the account before us, " in the expectation of witnessing one of the most interesting battles which had taken place since Tom Spring thrashed John Langan." Young Dutch Sam and Ned Neale were to bring to an issue their second great match for four hundred and twenty sovereigns.

The ropes and stakes had been fixed in a meadow, which had been hired for the day, and all was in readiness. Sam was there, but Neale failed to put in an appearance, and when the patience of all became nearly exhausted it was said that Ned had been arrested in London the previous night. This rumour only proved to be too true, for Will Scarlett, the dragsman of the Portsmouth coach, and who was a backer of Neale, brought the news direct from London that morning. It transpired afterwards that a number of scoundrels had made p.p. bets to the extent of thousands, and had taken good care that Ned should not appear upon the scene. The wrath and indignation when it became generally known may be better imagined than described. To travel such a distance, some forty-five miles from London, and have no fun for the trouble and expense, was naturally exasperating, and the question arose as to what could be done. Harry Holt, the Cicero of the Ring; decided to have a fight of some kind, so hat in hand he went amongst the swells, and with his eloquence talked them out of their sovereigns and half sovereigns until he had a purse of £15. So Harry Holt announced that £12 would be given to the winner, and a consolation of £3 to the loser.

Now amongst those present was Deaf Burke, who had come down by easy stages on foot to witness the big fight, and this just suited him, so he made his way as quickly as he could to the arena, pushing the crowd aside and calling forth some exceedingly strong language from those who were not acquainted with the comical

" mug " of the Deaf 'Un. There was somebody before
him, though, who had entered the ring, and was challenging anybody to single combat with him. He was a
great big, brawny fellow, a native of Sussex, named
Girdler. He was said to have proved himself a tough
handful, too. He was big enough for anything, standing
six feet, with broad shoulders, deep chest, and remarkably long arms. He was, in fact, a very ugly customer
to tackle. But when the Deaf 'Un came to the ropes and
pitched his greasy hat into the ring there was a tremendous cheer, for Jem was a great favourite. Mr. Girdler
was informed who the gentleman was who had responded
to his challenge, and he replied that he didn't care for
fifty Mr. Burkes, if they'd only come on one at a time.
Jem smiled, hopped over into the ropes, and extended his
hand to the yokel. The latter looked vacantly at him
for a moment, when the chawbacon placed his great
shoulder of mutton fist into Jem's paw. Harry Holt,
who had the management of the affair, made up his
mind to do the business properly, so he managed to secure
the services of Young Dutch Sam to look after Girdler,
and Jem Ward for Burke, the first-named being assisted
by Holt himself, and the last-named by Frosty-faced
Fogo.

Directly they started, anybody with half an eye could
see that, bar accident, it was a horse to a gooseberry on
one, and that one wasn't the chawbacon. It was the
same thing every round—a rush from the countryman
—a sweeping blow, averted by a quick dodge from Burke,
then both the Deaf 'Un's fists, hard and straight in the
face. In fact, Girdler never had the ghost of a chance—
he was hit to pieces all over the ring; but he was game
to the backbone, wouldn't give in—not he—said he'd
die first. But, after the seventeenth round, Jem had
punished him so severely that Holt called Burke over to
shake hands with his man, and skied the sponge.

This unexpected turn-up was a rare bit of luck for the
poor Deaf 'Un, and he made good use of his £12, which
lasted him until he could settle another little match.
This he found very difficult, though, for he had proved
himself a bit too good for commoners to tackle, and his
modest offer to take any 12st or 12½st man for £25
a-side (that being all his backers could find) was treated
with scorn. Nothing less than a hundred a-side would
suit the top-sawyers, which was far too high a figure for
poor Jem to aspire to. And so nearly a year passed by
and nothing came in his way. Yet he managed to jog
along pretty well, for his services were more and more
in demand at the boxing exhibitions, where he had a fine
opportunity to practise and improve. But in September,

1833, the Deaf 'Un had another slice of luck. A young carpenter from Liverpool came to London, and putting up at Tom Spring's house, in Holborn, issued a challenge to fight any man not exceeding 11½st for £25 a-side. This, as we have already stated, was not sufficient to tempt the big pots, but it was just the amount Jem could manage, so the match was duly made, and they signed articles to fight in a month from that date, *i.e.*, Tuesday, October 26.

They say it never rains but it pours, so far as good fortune is concerned, and poor Jem was in the seventh heaven of delight when, on the occasion of paying the first deposit at Spring's, he met there a man named Gow, a great big, raw-boned Scotchman, with whom he had boxed at the Fives Court upon the occasion of Reuben's benefit. Gow had lost his temper, and made up his mind to fight Burke with the "raw 'uns" for a fiver a-side. They soon came to terms, and arranged that the battle should take place on October 4, and as this would be about three weeks before what Jem called his big fight, the fiver won would come in nicely to help training expenses, for Master James Burke never dreamed of losing a battle, and looked upon that £5 as already in his pocket.

Perhaps never was there so much trouble taken of a fight for so small a stake. They had arranged to bring it off at Woolwich, but the river police were guarding the banks, and threatened to land if they attempted to form a ring. So they tried further inland, but with the same result, the myrmidons of the law were on the alert wherever they went. Then they crossed the river and made for Snaresbrook, where they thought they were safe. But no, there also were they interrupted, and they made for Temple Mills, where the coast was clear. We need not give details of this little battle, which enabled Burke to climb one more rung of the ladder to fame and the Championship. It is remarkable for one curious eccentricity of the Deaf 'Un's. To the amusement of everybody, he turned up in a most extraordinary fighting costume, which he affected afterwards in all his fights. He wore green baize drawers, profusely trimmed with yellow braid, and decorated with flying knots of yellow ribbon at the knees, whilst his calves were cased in a pair of bright striped worsted stockings, and his feet in laced high-lows. It appears that somebody had informed him that such was the costume of the early great masters of pugilism, and that Slack, Broughton, and other great pugilists always appeared in the ring attired like that, and so he desired to imitate as near as possible those heroes of the Ring.

Gow stood no chance with him, for, as in his previous two fights, he showed a marvellous quickness in getting his head out of the way, and returning with precision and force that told at the very commencement of the battle. Here is an account of the latter part of the battle :—" The Deaf 'Un welted his man dreadfully about the head, till the blood ran from poor Andrew Gow's nose, mouth, ears, and eyes, while his body was fearfully bruised by Burke's tremendous rib-benders. After two-and-twenty heavy rounds had been got through in twenty-five minutes, Teesdale, the Scotchman's second gave in, as his man was in a lamentable condition."

So Master Burke added another to his victories, making a total of seven wins, and but one loss. After this merry little mill for a fiver, he continued his training for his big fight with Bob Hampson, which was to take place three weeks after his defeat of Gow, and about which, together with other victories, we shall relate in the next chapter.

CHAPTER XXVIII.

A BATCH OF BATTLES.—JAMES BURKE (THE DEAF 'UN) VERSUS TIM CRAWLEY, BLISSETT, CARTER, AND MACONE.

AFTER his defeat of Gow, Jem Burke, with the fiver he had won, was enabled to pursue his three weeks' training for his match with Bob Hampson with more comfort, for he had been desperately hard-up prior to this. Still £5 does not go far, his allowance being less than 5s. per diem. So he contented himself with a tramp from Soho, where he was staying with Reuben Martin, to Hampstead Heath and back, and whenever he could borrow a skiff he would take a long, steady pull on the river. Hampson was well looked after by Tom Spring, who had tried him on several occasions with the gloves, and had unhesitatingly pronounced him an accomplished fighter, declaring that if he could stay as well when using the "raw 'uns," as he did with the mittens, he predicted a brilliant future for Bob of Liverpool. So it got rumoured about that Burke this time had found more than his match, and that he would be vanquished for a second time, and 6 to 4 was laid on Hampson.

Hampden Common, some four miles from St. Albans, was the spot fixed to bring off the mill, and on a glorious morning, that of Thursday, October 26, 1830, a considerable crowd made their way to the battle-field, both in vehicle and upon foot, for there was another event down on the programme, a merry little mill between Sam Hutton, a promising young pugilist from the East, and Mike Davis, of Bristol.

Bob Wilbore, of the Blue Boar, did the best business, he being a great favourite amongst the Fancy, and Lord Crofton, Lord Longford, and several of the officers belonging to the Guards made this hostelry their head-quarters, and took luncheon there before going to the battle-field. It was just one o'clock when Burke and Hampson threw their caps into the arena. Tom Oliver and Harry Jones looked after the Liverpudlian, whilst Jem's old opponent, Fitzmaurice, and Ned Stockman (the Lively Kid) did the amiable for the Deaf 'Un. Tom Spring held the watch and filled the post of referee. Without going into details of this battle, it will be necessary to state only that Hampson was woefully overmatched, being a much weaker and lighter man than Burke, who took the lead, and after forty-five minutes he beat his man to a standstill.

Although nobody believed in the Deaf 'Un's science, (for he gave his head away too much), this victory made him many friends, and as a proof of his growing popularity, on the very next Tuesday no less than three deposits were made for Burke for three different matches, all to come off within two months. The first was one with the notorious Ned Neale to stake £200 against the Deaf 'Un's £100; the second was for £25 a-side, with Jack Nicholls, the butcher; and the third was with a new man named Timothy Crawley. The first two fell through before the articles were signed, and in each case a small amount was forfeited, but the third proved to be serious business, for the novice was under the care of our old friend, General Barton, that fine sportsman, who had so often stood by Jack Randall. Here is an account of how it all came about, which we cannot do better than repeat. On Thursday evening, November 2, 1830, General Barton entered the Castle, Holborn, accompanied by a strapping young chap, and, everybody being pleased to see the fine old officer, who had been away from London for a considerable time, he was very cordially greeted. "Now, Tom," said the General, after he had sat down and ordered a glass of Irish whisky hot for himself, and another for his *protégé*, addressing himself to Spring: "Now, Tom, I've brought a lad with me that I want to introduce to you and all these gentle-

men here. He's a countryman of my own, and, bedad,
I'll go bail for him that he'll make his mark with the
pair of fists he's got on him before he's a year older;
ay, and do credit to the ould country that reared him."
During this speech of the General's the young man's face
at his side got very red at being thus eulogised and
having all eyes turned upon him. Spring nodded
acquiescence in the old soldier's remarks, while he eyed
the young 'un critically. The youngster was Tim
Crawley, whose portrait we give, taken during the latter
part of his career. Tom considered for a moment, and
then, jerking his thumb over his shoulder in the direction of the fire-place, said: "There's the Deaf 'Un—how
would he suit you?" The General looked at young
Crawley inquiringly. "The very man, sor, I'd like
to fight," said Tim, so Spring walked up to Burke and
speaking into his ear, asked when he would be ready to
fight if a match could be made for him. The Deaf 'Un
rose to his feet, pulled off his hat, made a polite bow,
which was intended to include all gentlemen present,
then scratched his head and said: "Well, you see,
misters, I'se ready at any times—the sooner the betters;
but where's the moneys to come from? I'll put down
five of my own, buts—" Here he paused. Then a cheery
voice from the other end of the room sang out, "And
I'll find the second five, and perhaps some more if it's
wanted." The speaker was Mr. Fred Soden, a well-
known member of the Stock Exchange, and a keen
sportsman to boot. The Deaf 'Un's face brightened
with a radiant smile as this generous offer was repeated
with a roar into his ear, "Is it hims as I've got to
fights?" then asked Burke, pointing to Crawley. He
was told that it was; then he rubbed his hands with
glee. "The sooners the betters," said he, and in the
exuberance of his joys came forward and insisted upon
shaking hands with his future opponent. Pen, ink, and
paper were then called for, and articles were at once
drawn up, binding the men to fight for £25 a-side, within
thirty miles of London, on Tuesday, November 16, 1830,
thus allowing the lads a clear fortnight to get fit for
the fray. The above is pretty nearly in the words of
one who was present at the Castle when the match with
Tim Crawley and our hero was made, and gives a very
good picture of how and by whom these little affairs
were arranged.

The Deaf 'Un went into training at Tom Callas', at
the Black Horse, Greenford Green, on the Harrow Road,
where he had the advantage of some practice with the
gloves with that accomplished boxer, Young Dutch Sam.
Tim Crawley went to the Fox under the Hill, at High-

gate, a house that was then kept by Sam Tebbutts, who
looked after the Irishman; and the same hostelry at
which Her Most Gracious Majesty once rested in the
coffee-room when the horses dashed down the hill, and
nearly caused the death of the greatest woman at
present existing.

The p'ace selected was Whetstone, close to the borders
of Hertfordshire, and such interest was taken in the
affair that a very large muster of swells was the result.
But the day was simply awful. Here is a description
of the weather. "Across the grey, sullen sky black
rain clouds scudded at railway speed, driven before a
furious blast, which at intervals sent showers of rain
and sleet full into the faces of those who journeyed along
the Great North Road to Barnet." This inclement
weather, however, apparently did not deter the lovers of
a prize-fight from making the short journey, and before
noon there was a big crowd awaiting the arrival of the
men. At length Crawley appeared, but a considerable
time elapsed and there was no sign of the Deaf 'Un. It
was close upon one o'clock and still he did not come, and
most began to fear that there would be no fight, whilst
the wind blew as if it would really tear the stakes out
of the ground, and the rain whipped the faces of the
shivering crowd until many wished themselves at home
by the cheerful fire. At length Reuben Martin appeared
on the scene, and explained that Burke had met with an
accident, but that it was all right, he would be on in a
few minutes. It appears that the horse had bolted with
the gig in which the Deaf 'Un was coming to the fight,
had galloped up the Finchley Road and taken a bye
lane, when the wheel, coming in contact with a post,
smashed the trap and threw the two occupants out, fortunately into a soft, muddy ditch. The Deaf 'Un, when
he appeared, was seen to have a nasty cut on his head,
but in answer to inquiries declared that he was "All
rights."

It is not our intention to describe this fight. The Irishman was overmatched, for in the sixth round, although
he landed Burke heavily on the nose and made the claret
flow, the latter countered with tremendous force on the
mouth, closed, and threw his man a burster on the
sodden turf that was assuming a consistency of peas
pudding, splashing the mud into the faces of the bystanders. After this it went all one way, and the Deaf
'Un gave for the first time a demonstration of that
wonderful judgment in fighting, that coolness of temperament, and marvellous gluttony, which was shortly to
prove him to be the finest heavy-weight of his time.

It was not until three months after Jem Burke

defeated the Irishman, that he appeared again in the
ring, when he was victorious over Davis, of Birmingham, fighting him for £50 a-side at Shepperton Range,
on February 22, 1831. The Deaf 'Un polished his man
off in the short space of twenty-seven minutes, during
which twelve rounds were fought. The details of this
battle we must omit, for we are already devoting enough

TIM CRAWLEY.

space to our hero, and there is much more to tell of his
long and prosperous career. His defeat of the Brum sent
him up two or three rungs of the ladder of Fame, and
the Deaf 'Un was recognised as the man who was likely
to prove himself entitled to wear the Championship
Belt.

His next appearance before the public was in a short

and merry mill with James Blissett, who had been backed by our old friend Squire Hayne, better known as "Peagreen." It will be remembered that this enthusiastic sportsman had been the backer of Tom Cannon, who at this time kept the Castle, in Jermyn Street. The Squire had seen some ups and downs since last we met him, for he had gone the devil of a pace, what with the Ring, the Turf, the dice-box, and the Drama, in the shape of extravagant ladies of the ballet. After the Derby of 1826, "Peagreen" Hayne, Esq., found himself such a loser over the victory of Lapdog that he was absolutely "broke," and his magnificent mansion in Upper Brook Street, Grosvenor Square, was sold up with its contents under the hammer. The things disposed of were most costly, as may be judged when it is known that a dressing-case fetched 500 guineas, and was purchased for George IV. Fortunately his estate, Bendrop Park, was entailed; but so far down did he fall that before long he found himself in the King's Bench Prison. He was soon relieved, however, and went to Scotland to live.

Returning to London, his attention was called to a strapping chap, named James Blissett, whose trade was that of a stonemason, and who was a native of Somersetshire, who came to London and joined the "Kill-bulls" of Clare Market. Now, the Squire had heard a great deal about Deaf Burke, but owing to his absence for some years had never seen him perform, and discovering that Blissett was eager for a match, and having it from Tom Cannon that the Somerset lad was a long way above the average, he determined that the Deaf 'Un should have a shy, and posted the money for him to the extent of fifty pounds, whilst a similar amount was found by the Knights of the Cleaver in Clare Market for Blissett. Articles were signed for them to fight within twenty-eight miles from London on Tuesday, May 28, 1831. Reuben Martin took charge of Burke, and they made the Crown, Holloway (then kept by that good old sport, Joe Ennis) their training headquarters. There "Peagreen" Hayne and a number of his fast-going pals would be found very frequently, and the empty bottles of "fiz" testified to the trade that mine host of the Crown was doing. This was none too good for Master Burke, and it was a mistake to have trained so near to town, for besides the tip-top swells, ladies whose gaiety surpassed their morals became frequent visitors, and we are afraid led him from the path of virtue.

What a difference a few years had made in the Deaf 'Un. From the poor Strand Stairs "water-jack" Jem

Burke had developed into the fashionably-attired man about town. Where he used to be glad of 'arf-o'-four-'arf, a screw o' baccy, and thought them luxuries, he now sipped the sparkling and puffed at the expensive Havanah. Still, "in spite of all temptation," Jem, we must say, stuck to work and conscientiously regarded his backer's money.

Blissett went to train at the Black Horse, Greenford, and placed himself under the care of Tom Callas, who was landlord of that house, and than whom a better trainer never lived. Colney Heath, in Hertfordshire, was the place selected for the battle. The weather was fine, and as another pair (Jack Adams and Young Richmond, the Black) having arranged to mill in the same ring, an excellent day's sport was provided.

Without describing the nineteen rounds fully, it will be sufficient to say that the Deaf 'Un added one more victory to his long list, and the West-countryman was hopelessly beaten after the first few bouts.

Jem Burke's next encounter was with the veteran Jack Carter, whose name has appeared upon these pages several times before, he having been introduced to the London Ring as far back as 1812 by Bob Gregson, Gully's old opponent. Jack's last performance, it will be remembered, was with Jem Ward, by whom he was defeated. That was in 1828, four years before the match was made with Burke. Although Carter was forty-three years old, many thought him still good enough to conquer a man like Jem Burke, but they little knew how the Deaf 'Un had steadily, if slowly, improved. The battle took place on May 8, 1832, just twelve months after he had thrashed Blissett. During that period, however, things had gone by no means well with Burke, for he had, whilst rowing, in some way injured his knee-cap, and was compelled to remain in hospital for many weeks, the surgeons at one time thinking that an amputation would be necessary. He is reported to have said in later days, "Though you can't see nothings, masters, I often feels my leg goes all of a suddents." However, he got well enough to meet Carter on the above date, and they fought it out at the Old Barge House, Woolwich, before a select audience of about two hundred. The stakes were only £10 a-side, which the Deaf 'Un secured in the eleventh round, Carter breaking his arm. This was Jack Carter's last battle. He died at Thomas Street, Manchester, on May 27, 1844, in the fifty-sixth year of his age.

The Deaf 'Un's next performance was with a Hull man, named Harry Macone, who worked upon a farm as thrasher, belonging to a Mr. Slingsby, of Hessle, a

village near Hull. He had distinguished himself by
beating several stalwart yokels, and had earned for himself the sobriquet of the "Yorkshire Hero." It so
happened that Jack Carter was conducting a number of
London boxers on a provincial tour through Lancashire and Yorkshire. After successful visits to Liverpool, Manchester, Sheffield, Bradford, and Leeds, the
party found themselves at the beginning of January,
1833, in Hull. Besides Carter, there were in the company Jones (the Welch Champion), Deaf Burke, Alec
Reid, Harry Jones, Anthony Noon, and Jem Stockman
(the "Lively Kid's" brother). The Assembly Rooms,
the George, Whitefriargate, were hired for this exhibition of the fistic art, and it was there that Mr. Harry
Macone went to criticise the Londoners. The Yorkshireman was no morsel, for he stood 6ft 2in and weighed
15st. So when he persisted in having the gloves on
with Deaf Burke, although he was nowhere on points,
by dint of rushing and lashing out he managed to force
Jem out of the limited sized ring in amongst the spectators. When the bout was over, so cocky did Macone
become that he declared that he would take on any one
of them with the raw 'uns. His challenge was, as might
be expected, quickly taken up by the Deaf 'Un, and the
Yorkshireman's master, Mr. Slingsby, offering to put
£20 down, that amount was soon covered, and the men
arranged to fight on the following Tuesday in the neighbourhood of Hull. Lockington Bottom, near the village
of Lund, was fixed upon, and there the men met, surrounded by as enthusiastic an audience as could well be
imagined, for the Tykes had turned out in their hundreds
to see their champion lick the Londoner.

It was indeed a terrific battle, consisting of fifty-nine
rounds, and the Deaf 'Un had a rough time of it, for he
was thrown many times. Science, however, triumphed
in the end, and Burke won. The report of this battle
says that after the fortieth round it was melancholy to
see the great half-blind giant groping his way about the
ring, stumbling and reeling, hardly knowing where his
foe was, till a tremendous slap in the face told him too
surely of the presence of the Deaf 'Un's fist. In the
middle of the fiftieth round the Yorkshire giant stopped
short in the centre of the ring, held up his hand and
shouted, " I can't see thee no longer, laad; au must gie
it oop; gie us tha fist, laad, and a'll own thou'st done me
this toime." And so Jem Burke scored another victory
for what it was worth. But his next battle was to give
him greater fame, although the result was well-nigh
putting an end to his fistic career. But of that in the
next chapter.

CHAPTER XXIX.

WHO SHALL BE CHAMPION ?—DEAF BURKE AND SIMON BYRNE.
A DESPERATE BATTLE.—ENDS IN A TRAGEDY.

AFTER Jem Burke's fight with Macone he had established himself in the Prize Ring as a man of tremendous hitting power and possessed of no small amount of
science, whilst his generalship was undoubtedly good. It
will, perhaps, be remembered that we stated in a former
chapter that on June 25, 1832, Jem Ward had announced his retirement from the Ring, and expressed
his willingness to hand over the belt to the first man who
proved himself worthy of it. Now at this particular
time there were few good ones amongst the heavy-
weights, and although some of the ten or eleven stoners
were first-class, nobody ever dreamed in those days of
competing for the Championship under 12st. To be
sure, Dan Mendoza was an exception, and carried nearly
all before him until he met a big 'un of quality, when
he was nowhere, John Jackson defeating him easily.
But there was nobody willing to set-to with Deaf Burke
after his many victories, so for six months nothing was
done. In the meanwhile the Ring was going all to pieces,
so a great meeting was called in the January of 1833 to
see what could be done to recover its scattered fortunes.
It was called the "Great Pugilistic Congress," and was
held at Tom Spring's, the Castle, in Holborn. Every
leading pugilist and every patron of the Ring was
present, and much was done to bring back the sport to
public favour, so far as suggestions were concerned.
But with that we have nothing to do here. After the
formal business was got through, Jem Burke, to the
satisfaction of all, arose and expressed himself in his
comical and peculiar manner, offering himself to fight
Young Dutch Sam or Simon Byrne, the first-named,
"becos he was so clevers," or the latter "becos he was bigs
enoughs for anythings," or he would fight " anybodys
who toughts himselfs Champions."

Young Dutch Sam, who was present, immediately
accepted, and a sovereign by each of the men was handed
to Tom Spring, and an arrangement made to meet on
the Friday following to enter into proper arrangements.
When the day came, however, much to the disappoint-

15

ment of Burke, Sam had thought better of it, his friends persuading him that to give away a stone and a half was madness to a fighter like the Deaf 'Un, clever as the Dutchman was. Now during Jem's lamentations, who should enter the parlour of the Castle but those two good old Irish sportsmen, General Barton and Colonel O'Neil, of Salt Hill, who had backed Jack Langan through all his battles. Hearing of Burke's disappointment, and that he was desirous of taking on Simon Byrne, the old officer immediately volunteered to back him against Burke for a hundred, supposing that Byrne was willing, of course. But as that worthy was upon his native heath in the Emerald Isle, the affair was postponed for a couple of weeks or so to enable the General to communicate with him. Anyhow, to bind the match, a fiver was placed by each side in Tom Spring's hands, and this time, always providing that Jem could find backers, the affair looked like being settled.

On Thursday, February 21, they met again at the Castle, and General Barton having heard from Simon Byrne that he was ready and willing, and the Deaf 'Un, after much trouble and anxiety, having found a backer, another £10 was staked by each party, and articles prepared for signature, agreeing upon May 28 (the week between Epsom and Ascot), the place to be within forty miles of London, the amount to be £100 a-side. Simon Byrne was sent for by a special messenger, who travelled to Ireland (no trifling journey in those days), to bring the bruiser home. It was soon seen upon his arrival that he had been indulging pretty freely in his country's product of the still, and we have an extract from a letter before us, in which a gentleman who travelled across upon the same ship with Byrne, states that he was "a proper blackguard, and drank all the while he was aboard." Undoubtedly this was Simon's great weakness, and had much to do with his defeat by Jem Ward the last time that Byrne had appeared in the ring, for he went to his native country, determined to settle down and give up all idea of ever fighting again. This resolution he would no doubt have kept had it not been for General Barton and Colonel O'Neil, who so generously offered to pay all expenses and find the stake money. Better would it have been for the Irishman, however, had he stuck to his resolution and remained in Ould Ireland, as will be proved as we pursue the course of our narrative.

Directly Byrne arrived in Liverpool he was taken in hand by his old opponent, Jem Ward, who placed a room in the Belt Tavern, where the Black Diamond was Boniface, at his disposal. Jem was very kind to him, as

indeed were many of the sporting fraternity in Liverpool, amongst them Mat Robinson (Yorkshire Mat), who
kept a tavern in the town. So cordial a reception did
he get, indeed, that he prolonged his stay until the end
of March, when imperative orders came for him to
journey to London, where he arrived on April 3, and
at once proceeded to the Castle. There he met Jem
Burke on the most friendly terms, and the seventh
deposit was staked. The General and the Colonel were
also both present, and were horrified to see the size of
their man. The good living and air of his native land,
together with the feasting he had enjoyed during his
sojourn in Liverpool, had put such a paunch on him that
he weighed at least sixteen stone. Ned Neale, who then
kept the Rose and Crown at Norwood, and who had
trained Simon for his fight with Ward, was entrusted
with the task of reducing him—no easy matter when
there were but two months to accomplish the pulling
down of 3st, as he was thought to have no chance with
the Deaf 'Un if he fought over 13st, the latter being as
hard as nails and always in condition. However, Ned
seems to have set about his job in real earnest, and
pound by pound came off the Irishman's carcase until,
ten days before the fight, when Colonel O'Neil went to
Norwood to see how he was progressing, he was found to
scale 13st 7lb.

Jem Burke needed very little attention. At that
time he was very abstemious, and, his preparation being
entrusted to Tom Owen, "The Sage of the East," who
then kept the Shipwrights' Arms, Northfleet, he got into
the most perfect condition. As usual, though, the
Deaf 'Un was woefully short of cash, and but for a little
incident that happened before he went into training, it
is hard to tell how he would have managed, although no
doubt his friend Tom Gaynor would have stood by him.

This is what happened. On the very night upon
which the match was made, as Burke was going home,
having stayed somewhat late at the Castle Tavern, he
was passing down Long Acre. At a wax and tallow-
chandler's shop, kept by a Mr. Matthews, a fierce fire
had broken out. It was the Deaf 'Un who was the first
to rush in and rescue lives and property, regardless of
danger to himself. Indeed, he knew not what fear was,
either in or out of the Ring. It will be remembered
how he once before distinguished himself by saving life
in the Strand, when some houses fell down; so when it
became known what he had done at the scene of the
fire, the journals of the day praised the heroism of the
bruiser, and James Burke had a subscription made for
him, and amongst his pals a couple of benefits were

successfully arranged, so that he was really in clover.

The date of the fight, as we have already stated, was May 28, but this day having been fixed for settling day at Tattersall's, the fight was postponed until Thursday, the 30th, to enable those sports whose business was on the Turf to attend. The Derby and Oaks of the year 1833 must have been heavy settling races, and much money changed hands, a few bookmakers being hit very hard, although backers, amongst whom were the principal supporters of the Ring, had a very bad time. The favourite, Glaucus, was nowhere, the winner, Dangerous, being 30 to 1, 100 to 1 against Connoisseur, the second, and 18 to 1 against Revenge, who finished third. The Oaks, too, was even worse, for 50 to 1 was laid against Vespa, the winner.

Mr. Coleman, the host of the Turf Tavern, St. Albans, having offered £25, which he had collected in the town, for the fight to come off near that place, it was determined to accept his generosity, and No Man's Land, some five miles from the cathedral town, was decided upon. Jem Burke took up his residence at the Turf Tavern, and the "Emerald Gem," as Simon was called, at the Woolpack. There was, as may be imagined, a tremendous gathering, and at the above - mentioned taverns, the Pea-Hen, and other hostelries in St. Albans, there wasn't a bed to be had for love or money, many paying five shillings to be allowed to lie upon the floors of the billiard-rooms, or anywhere that provided shelter. The morning of the fight, too, brought down thousands in every conceivable kind of vehicle, and the pubs and eating-houses did a roaring trade.

The men were on view at their respective inns from ten o'clock to twelve, and the crush to get a look at them was tremendous, and Mr. Coleman and his brother-bungs had no cause to regret having paid the £25. Soon after twelve both drove off to the scene of action in open carriages, the Deaf 'Un creating the greatest amusement and laughter, for he had daubed his face with white and red paint, like a circus clown, and all along the road displayed the most comical grimaces, much to the enjoyment of the yokels. Jem was a funny fellow, and took nothing seriously. Both arrived at the ring-side, Byrne accompanied by those two famous gladiators, Tom Spring and Jem Ward, who had consented to look after him during the fight, and the Deaf 'Un by Tom Gaynor and Dick Curtis. Preparations were at once commenced. Whilst Jem's seconds were arranging his toilet and removing the colour from his face, to send him up decent, Curtis was seen to be rubbing something round his man's neck: but the eagle eye of Tom Spring

was upon him, and crossing over he found Dick to have
smeared his man's neck and shoulders with grease, a
dodge sometimes introduced to prevent the opponent
from getting a grip when wrestling for the fall. Spring
at once lodged an objection, and the referee upheld it,
so another cleaning process had to be reverted to, and
Master Jem indulged in such idiotic antics, that

TOM GAYNOR, DEAF BURKE'S SECOND.

many thought that he had entirely taken leave of his
senses. Here is a description of how he conducted himself whilst the final preparations were being made:—
" When the money was being collected to make up the
£25 promised by Mr. Coleman, the seconds refusing to
go into the ring until that had been paid, the Deaf 'Un
went through a series of most extraordinary freaks. At

one moment, to the horror of his backers, he was discovered puffing away at an enormous Havannah cigar; but it turned out to be only an imitation 'weed.' Then the irrepressible person locked his arm in that of Simon Byrne, and walked round and round the ring with him, going through all sorts of mimetic contortions, as if he were engaged in some very serious but quite friendly conversation with his opponent. Simon was rather perplexed by the humorous antics of Mr. Burke. He couldn't quite see the drift of all this tomfoolery; and, though he laughed and put as good a face as possible on it, because he saw the spectators were intensely amused, yet, when he had released himself from Jem's friendly but embarrassing grasp, the Irishman went up to Spring and Ward, his seconds, and said he thought it a great liberty of the Deaf 'Un to take, adding 'Pon my sowl, I think the Deaf 'Un ain't in his right senses. He's ravin' about Harry Jones havin' tould his mother he was to be licked, and promises to towel Harry well the next time he sees him.' Certainly, no one who saw the Deaf 'Un playing his mountebank tricks that day would ever have believed that he had come there to fight a desperate battle against a most formidable foe. But then Master James was a natural comedian, and had he received the education, and been brought up differently, his ready wit, his pliable mug, and his extraordinary gait would have well fitted him to take a place upon the stage that in years afterwards was occupied by J. L. Toole and Lionel Brough."

But to the fight, for we shall presently have to change the scene from light to shade, from comedy to tragedy. Although we do not wish to weary our readers with too many details of the actual fight, we, as historians of the Champions, must place on record this, for it was perhaps the most memorable fight in which James Burke was ever engaged. Certain it is that it had a more staggering effect upon him than any of the few defeats he suffered, and was of greater moment to him than all his other victories, not excepting his fights to win and hold the Championship.

It could be seen when they faced each other that Burke was trained to the hour. His weight was 12st 4lb, two or three pounds less than he usually fought at, but his condition was perfect. As one reporter put it: "The man was in the rudest health, brimful of spirits and confidence, without a morsel of superfluous beef anywhere about him, his skin clear, his flesh firm and hard, every muscle on his square, powerful frame and massive limbs standing out like whipcord. Never in his life had

James Burke been anything like so fit. His rugged,
Dutch-built figure looked as strong as a tower." Simon
Byrne, too, was in better fettle than perhaps he had
ever been before when facing an opponent. He weighed
13st 4lb, but he stood at least an inch and a half taller
than the Deaf 'Un, although when sparring there seemed
to be very little difference, especially in the reach, for
Jem's broad shoulders and long arms gave him an
advantage over men even much taller than himself.

Burke started in a comic mood, making many obser-
vations to his opponent as they opened the ball with a
farce, little dreaming then that the programme would a
short time later wind up the entertainment with a
tragedy. Both men warmed to their work, and Jem,
getting several nasty punches, changed the comical
expression of his face and dropped his chaff. He
evidently discovered that in the Irishman he had a
pretty stiff customer to deal with, and that it was by no
means a walk-over. Indeed, as we read the full account,
round by round, it is quite obvious that after the seventeenth round Byrne was having the best of it, and they
were laying 6 to 4 on Byrne, and with a few exceptions
Simon took the lead, and looked like keeping it. It was
surprising to find that, after they had been at it for
nearly two hours and had by no means been idle, the
"lushington," Simon Byrne, whose condition did not
appear to be comparable to that of his powerful opponent, was stronger and more active. Two or three times
the Deaf 'Un had been sick, and in the forty-fifth round
he was exceedingly bad; but in the forty-ninth a change
came o'er the scene, and Burke pulled himself together.
Making a rush at Simon, he attacked him with such
fury with both hands that Pat fell exhausted. Then
Burke gave way, and both men seemed as if incapable
of fighting another round. Yet they were carried or
supported to the scratch, and no doubt here the battle
should have been called a draw, for neither man had the
power to hit. One writer, speaking of it in not very
flattering terms to the noble art, declared that " Humanity demanded that at this point the combat should
have been stopped. But cupidity was stronger than
humanity, and so these two wretched, bruised, battered
and bleeding creatures were sent up to hug and pull
and feebly punch at one another till one should succumb.
For round after round the men were carried to the
scratch by their seconds, and stood up surrounded by a
mob of their partisans, who crowded the arena, sprinkling water on the combatants, fanning them with their
hats, and doing all they knew to keep their respective
champions from collapsing. The uproar was fearful, and

a more disorderly and disgraceful scene had probably never been witnessed at the ring-side before."

It appears that as the apology for rounds went on Byrne recovered somewhat, and although his hands were too swollen to hit, and he could hardly raise his arms, he was able to clutch at his opponent, and once succeeded in throwing him and falling heavily upon the prostrate form. Everybody thought, and many hoped, that this was the finishing touch, and that Simon would be proclaimed winner. Yet Dick Curtis persevered with brandy bottle, cold water and sponge, &c., and, resorting to all the *dernier ressort* known to the accomplished second, succeeded in getting Jem round and on to the scratch just as time was being counted out.

Then it was the Deaf 'Un's turn. Plied with brandy, he seemed to recover some of his strength, whilst his opponent tottered and seemed all abroad. Jem astonished everybody by the force with which he hit out and brought his man to grass. Simon had shot his bolt in the ninety-ninth round and fell insensible, when, more than the time being allowed, the Deaf 'Un was proclaimed the winner, after the two men had been in the ring for *three hours and sixteen minutes.*

Jem was fearfully punished, and his arms were black and blue from stopping the fearful blows aimed at him by the powerful Irishman. But Simon Byrne had suffered greater damage. "The left side of his head and body were fearfully damaged, the left eye was completely closed, the mouth terribly swollen, and the whole visage wofully disfigured," said one account. He was taken to the Woolpack still unconscious, where he received the best attention. On the following Saturday he appeared better. But he seemed to have no heart left, and more than once said he would never get up again. "If I die," he remarked, "it won't be the Deaf 'Un's fault. It will be through the life I led before going into training." On the Sunday he got much worse, and Tom Spring was fetched by special messenger sent to him on horseback. The landlord of the Castle, feeling how serious was the situation, went for the eminent surgeon, Sir Astley Cooper, and drove him to St. Albans. After seeing the man he declared there was no hope, and at half-past eight in the evening Simon Byrne died.

Of course, an inquest was held and a verdict of manslaughter returned against Deaf Burke, Tom Spring, Jem Ward, Tom Gaynor, and Dick Curtis. The trial took place at the Hertford Assizes, on Thursday, July 11, 1833. Mr. Justice Parker was the judge, and having taken the evidence of Mr. Kingston, the surgeon who had attended the deceased, and made the *post-mortem*, in which he (the surgeon) could not say that the blows received were the cause of death, either in whole or part, his lordship turned to the jury and said, " Gentlemen, that makes an end of the case. The indictment charges that death was occasioned by blows and violence, whereas it appears that deceased died from other causes. The prisoners, therefore, must be acquitted." And to the great relief of everybody they were discharged.

CHAPTER XXX.

A CLAIMANT FOR THE BELT.—FIELDS AND PASTURES NEW.— DEAF BURKE IN AMERICA.—HIS FIGHTS WITH O'ROURKE AND O'CONNELL.

AND now in order to follow the fortunes of our Champion we shall have to take our readers across the Atlantic. But before doing so we will just record his doings after his defeat of poor Simon Byrne. That victory undoubtedly placed him at the top of the tree amongst the heavy-weights, always excepting, of course, Jem Ward, who still held on to the title.

The Black Diamond, however, had on June 25, 1832, about a year from the date of his defeat of Simon Byrne, announced by speech and pen his formal retirement from the Ring, and, as we have stated in a former chapter, expressed his readiness to hand over the belt to the man who proved himself worthy of the same. So the Deaf 'Un having beaten Byrne, who was admitted to be second to Jem Ward, thought himself justified in claiming the championship. But Jem Ward, in a dog-in-the manger kind of manner, felt no disposition to part with the title when it came to the finish, so when Burke challenged him, he replied that he would fight no man unless it were for £500 a-side. This amount the Deaf 'Un could by no possibility find, for even his staunchest friends thought that the Black Diamond would be too good for him. Then, after much palaver, Ward condescended to go into the Ring with Burke, and lay him the odds of £300 to £200.

Even that amount was not forthcoming; but Jem, anxious not to be done, started off on tour through the country, with a determination to find the money by hook or by crook. He travelled from town to town, giving exhibitions of boxing, and saved every sovereign he could lay his hands upon. He even accepted an engagement at Sheffield to play in the pantomime of *Valentine and Orson,* impersonating—and very well too —the latter character.

At length he found himself possessed of the £200, and, returning to London, accepted Ward's challenge. But that worthy had in the meantime settled down, and had no disposition to fight, so he raised his price once more to £500, much to the disgust of Jem and all well-wishers of the fistic art. On account of this a resolution was come to at a meeting held at the Castle, it being the anniversary of Tom Spring's occupancy of the tavern—that in future £200 should be the maximum for the championship stakes, and it was further proposed and unanimously carried that, "If Ward refuses to fight Burke for £200 a-side he shall no longer be considered the Champion of England; but that Burke shall assume the title till compelled to yield it to a man of greater merit." Those present who voted were, amongst many other distinguished sportsmen, Mr. Laurence Sant, Colonel Neil, General Barton, Fulwar Craven, Lord Longford, Sir Bellingham Graham, Major Revell, Tom Duncombe, Tom Belcher, Ned Painter, and Harry Harmer.

The Deaf 'Un complained bitterly of Jem Ward's treatment, and on this particular evening declared his intention of going over to America to fight their champion, O'Rourke, if the Britisher would not give him a chance. He also announced that he would take a benefit at the Coach and Horses, St. Martin's Lane, in a month's time. This he did, and it turned out very successful, thanks to Lord Ward, the Earl of Wilton, and other good sports, the Deaf 'Un clearing some £80. He then visited Birmingham, and endeavoured to get a match on with Harry Preston, a heavy-weight. That worthy, however, considered the Londoner too good for him, so Jem made his way to Liverpool, and signed articles to fight young Langan. Unfortunately, though, the latter was arrested on the eve of the fight, and the disconsolate Burke was again stranded.

So in the month of January, 1836, the Deaf 'Un sailed for the States in the good ship *Oregon,* with plenty of good wishes and a moderately heavy purse; anyway enough to last him until he should get something on. With him he took letters of introduction to

William Fuller, who was looked upon there as
the John Jackson of the American Ring, a man
who had won some good battles and who was much
respected. Fuller received Burke cordially, and he was
at once attached to Fuller's Gymnasium, and described
as "the Great English Champion and Professor of
Boxing."

This was all very well, but Jem had not obtained the
object of his visit. He wanted to get a match on, but
was unsuccessful. The glowing accounts of the
American Prize Ring had misled him, and he found that
in reality there was very little of it. Hearing that he
might stand a better chance in Philadelphia, he
journeyed there and saw Andrew Maclean, a native of
that town, and a well-known bruiser. He was unable,
however, to find him a man, for the Deaf 'Un's reputation had gone before him, and it seemed that nobody
cared to try conclusions with the British boxer. He
left Pennsylvania and returned to the "Empire City,"
and there we find him in quite a different character,
Flaming posters on the walls of New York announced
"The Champion Boxer of England, the Celebrated and
Herculean Deaf Burke," had been engaged to perform at Conklin's Hall. Then the bill went on
to say: "Mr. Burke will make his first appearance as
the Venetian Statue, which he will exhibit on
a pedestal, with appropriate change of figure,
attitude, and expression. The arrangement is made
in order to convey to the classical taste of artists, in an
efficient manner, a series of beautiful compositions of
ancient sculpture. The following is the order of the
portraitures:—(1) Hercules struggling with the Nemean
lion, in five attitudes. (2) Achilles throwing the discus
or quoit, in two attitudes. (3) The slave, Emoleur, the
grinder, sharpening his knife whilst overhearing the
conspirators. (4) Two positions of the Athletic Combatants, as Fighting Gladiators. (5) Samson slaying the
Philistines with a jaw-bone. (6) The African alarmed
at the Thunder. (7) Ajax defying the Lightning.
(8) Romulus, from David's picture of the Sabines.
(9) Remus's defence, from the same. (10) Cain slaying
his brother Abel. (11) Samson lifting the gates of Gaza.
(12) The whole to conclude with the five celebrated
positions of the Dying Gladiator.

So by the above it will be seen that the Deaf 'Un
appeared in a new role. By all accounts the show "took
on" very well, and Jem made plenty of dollars. After
the novelty wore off, though, business became bad, and
he not being able to make a match had serious thoughts
of returning to England. Just at this time, however,

he was shown a New Orleans paper in which was a very high falutin challenge from a Mr. Samuel O'Rourke to fight, according to the rules of the British Prize Ring, any man, for any sum up to a thousand dollars. This was good news for the Deaf 'Un, for O'Rourke was the very man he had come over to fight, but had until then failed to discover his whereabouts.

And now it will be necessary to tell why Burke had been so anxious to find this gentleman. After his fight with Simon Byrne, which was described in the previous chapter and which ended fatally to the poor fellow, a challenge appeared in *Stewart's Despatch* published in Dublin to the following effect:— "Mr. Samuel O'Rourke, Champion of Ireland, has returned from America and is ready to fight Deaf Burke for £200 or £500 a-side in a twenty-four foot ring on the Curragh of Kildare in one or two months from this date. His money is ready at No. 9, Eden Quay. His challenge would have appeared earlier but for the fact that it might have injured Burke in the late trial for the man-slaughter of Byrne."

This challenge and allusion to the man whose death he had caused upset Jem, and he was for setting off to Ireland at once, only his backers and friends pointed out the advisability of not going to the Emerald Isle so soon after the death of their favourite. So O'Rourke was invited to come over here. But this did not suit him, so the whole thing fell through. The Irish papers were full of his exploits. He was said to have fought and won no less than fourteen battles in America, and these wild Irish organs "commended him for that patriotic spirit he displayed in recording a solemn oath that he would never rest until he had avenged the death of Erin's brave son, Simon Byrne."

No wonder the Deaf 'Un wanted to meet the O'Rourke, so he made the long and tedious journey down to the "Crescent City" with a decent amount of dollars in his belt, and a promise from Mr. William Fuller that if he could make a match 500dols. were at his disposal. New Orleans at this time was a shocking place, the centre of the slave trade, and the haunt of all the worst ruffians, desperadoes, and murderers in the States. Had the Deaf 'Un known this, he never would have gone down there. But he was ignorant of the whole thing, and went like a lamb to the slaughter.

His arrival in New Orleans was a considerable surprise to Mr. O'Rourke, for Jem was the last man to expect. Even although he may have heard of his arrival in New York, he little dreamed that he would have the audacity to come all that distance and to such a place. He

evidently was not pleased, although he liquored the Deaf
'Un up and appeared very cordial, asking him whether
it was business or pleasure that brought him there.
Burke, not mincing matters, told him that he had seen
the challenge to the world, and he had just come down to
accept it. O'Rourke, in a blustering manner, said that
now that he was doing such good business he should not
think of fighting for less than 1,000dols. This was a
knock-down blow to Jem, and he plainly told the Irishman that he could not find the money. Now, it so hap-

SAMUEL O'ROURKE.

pened that in O'Rourke's saloon where the conversation
took place were two gentlemen, one Mr. James H.
Caldwell, proprietor and manager of the St. Charles'
Theatre, Camp Street, and the other Mr. William
Brandram, an Englishman, a cotton-buyer for a Man-
chester firm. They were both enthusiastic sportsmen,
and at once offered to put down 250dols each to help
Burke out of the difficulty.

This done, O'Rourke of course, could not shuffle out of
it. So the articles were drawn and signed, the fight to
take place in a fortnight from that date, viz., May 6.

We have no space to relate the many little incidents
relating to his training, how the O'Rourke party tried to
get at him, and how, had it not been for Williamson
and Phelan, who were looking after Jem, that individual would never have lived to fight and win the
championship. It was evident that one section in New
Orleans, the Irish, which were very strong at the time,
meant their man to win by fair means or foul, and the
Deaf 'Un only too sincerely wished that he had never
gone amongst so many blackguards.

The excitement in the Cresent City was intense as
the day approached. Posters and handbills announced
the great fight to take place between the celebrated
O'Rourke, the Champion of Ireland and America, and
Deaf Burke, Champion of Great Britain, and all the scum
of New Orleans, the rowdies, the roughs, the bullies, and
the loafers looked forward to a regular gala day. We do
not purpose describing fully the scene before and during
the battle, nor the contest itself, but there is a quotation from one account which will give a pretty good idea
of what it was like:—" From an early hour swarms of
men—Creoles, half-breeds, French gamblers, Yankee
sharps, Irish roughs, and rowdies of every nationality
under the sun—began to leave New Orleans for the field
of battle. A place called Forks of Bayon, not far from
the City and on the banks of the Mississippi, was fixed
upon as the rendezvous, and there a proper twenty-four-
foot ring, with ropes and stakes in true English style,
was erected. But the crowd gathered around the arena
was very different from anything ever to be seen in
England. There was hardly a man there who had not
ruffian stamped on his face, and not one but was armed
—some with pistols and bowie knives, others with
bludgeons and slung-shot. A worse looking or more
menacing crowd it would be impossible to picture.

There were only three rounds fought. In the second
Mickey Carson, who was seconding O'Rourke, slipped
behind the Deaf 'Un whilst he was fighting and pushed
him into the arms of his opponent, who threw him. The
Deaf 'Un was indignant, and swore that if he did it again
he'd knock him down. At this Mickey, producing a
bowie knife from his belt, declared with an oath that if
Burke came near to him he'd rip him up from his navel
to his chin.

In the third round the Deaf 'Un caught O'Rourke one
or two smashing blows in the mouth, and there is little
doubt that he would have very soon knocked the
great, blustering, half-trained bully out had not Mickey
Carson again got in the way. Jem could keep his
temper no longer, with a straight hit with the left he

caught the second full on the nose, and down he went like a ninepin. Then the fat was in the fire. The wild Irish mob cut the ropes in a dozen places and entered the ring. The Deaf 'Un stood his ground for a minute, knocking over two or three, including O'Rourke's other second, MacSweeney, when Jem Phelan cried, "Run, Burke, run; they mean to have your life." Jem took to his heels and dashed through where the crowd was thinnest, with a howling mob at his heels. They would have caught and killed him if a friendly sportsman had not given him his horse and another put a bowie knife into his hand. Mr. Caldwell just had time to whisper, " To the theatre; hide there," and Jem dashed away for Orleans as fast as his nag could gallop, an odd-looking being on horseback in his fighting toggery and naked to the waist. However, he got there, and frightened the stage door keeper as he rushed past on to the theatre. There he found shelter until they got him through a private door, and ultimately through a back way into the quarters of the chief of the gendarmes.

Dan Williamson, Jem Phelan, Messrs. Caldwell and Brandram had to use their pistols, and only escaped by the skin of their teeth, all being more or less wounded. There was a free fight and any quantity of bloodshed, whilst the Deaf 'Un and his seconds had to remain *perdu* in the police station until in the night three days after the so-called fight they were smuggled away on a Mississippi steamboat going north, and escaped from their assailants. Burke had lost his 500dols, and but for the generosity of Mr. Caldwell would have had no money for travelling expenses. He was only too glad to find himself back amongst his friends in New York, and never forgot that visit to New Orleans.

O'Rourke came to a violent end, being murdered on the Ottawa by a man named Brady, with whom he had quarrelled. The tragic event took place on September 8, 1845.

On Jem Burke's return to New York he had a gay old time of it, for he was much liked by all the sportsmen, and Fuller thought a great deal of him. So he soon became initiated into the mysteries of gin-sling brandy cocktails, sangarees, mint juleps, sherry-cobblers, tuber-doodles, and other drinks, whilst his face was quite familiar to the ladies and dudes of Niblo's Gardens, then as much to the Yankees as were Vauxhall Gardens to us.

Some time after his return to the Empire City, Burke got into a quarrel about a mulatto woman at a dance in

the low quarter of New York, and was attacked by an
Irishman known as Larry. The Deaf 'Un made very
short work of him, knocking him over two or three
times, when another Hibernian, tall, muscular, and
well-built, interfered, observing that Mister Burke
should keep his fists to use on those who
know something about the game, and not knock
novices about like that. He introduced himself as
Tom O'Connell, and the Deaf 'Un, half seas over,
wanted to fight him then and there. But the Irishman,
who was brother to the youngster who had been
thrashed by Burke, positively declined to put up his
hands, offering to make an appointment for the morrow,
when perhaps they might come to business. This was
accepted by the Deaf 'Un, and they met in Mr. Fuller's
office and signed articles to fight on August 21, 1837, for
500dols. a-side. Those well-known sportsmen, Messrs.
O'Hara and Straubenzee, found the money for O'Connell,
and Fuller for Burke, so there was no doubt about the
affair being perfectly genuine.

Hart Island, near New York, was selected for the
battlefield, and everything was arranged in the most
orderly manner. O'Connell was practically beaten in the
fifth round, although ten were fought in all, the Irishman at length sinking from sheer exhaustion, being
dreadfully punished. To his dying day, Burke asserted
that this was the most orderly conducted prize fight he
had ever attended. What a contrast to the Orleans
battle !

This was the Deaf 'Un's last appearance in the
American Ring. After his defeat of O'Connell they could
not get another man to face him, and although Fuller
did all he knew to persuade Burke to stay in New York,
he declined. A farewell benefit was given to him at
Conklin's Hall, prior to his departure; and he
acknowledged years afterwards that never before or
since that time did he receive such an ovation. He
cleared about 500dols. He had been in America eighteen
months, and, with the exception of the little Orleans
episode, had received the greatest kindness and courtesy
from all with whom he had been brought in contact.

CHAPTER XXXI.

IN THE REALMS OF DISSIPATION. — AMONGST THE LAMBS.—
DEAF BURKE AND BENDIGO.—DESPERATE BATTLE FOR
THE BELT.

NEVER was Jem Burke in better form and condition than when he returned to England from his sojourn in America. He at once issued a challenge to fight any man in the three kingdoms for any sum from £100 to £500 a-side, and for the Championship. The challenge was accepted by William Thompson, better known as Bendigo, whose extraordinary career it will shortly be our duty to chronicle, for he became Champion twice. Jem Burke, however, had contracted the acquaintance —through the introduction of Young Dutch Sam—of a very fast-going set—young swells of the Tom and Jerry school, who were trying to revive the rowdiness and blackguardism that had existed some time before. The leaders of these were the Marquis of Waterford, the Earl of Waldegrave, and Lord Longford. These noblemen led the Deaf 'Un to adopt late hours, associate with bad women, drink bad wine, and appear upon scenes of disorder, ruffianism, and profligacy. Every morning at daybreak found him at one of the notorious nighthouses half drunk, sometimes wholly so. These so-called friends took him to France, where in Paris they led a life of the wildest dissipation, until the simple-hearted, once robust, Deaf 'Un descended into a debauched associate of dissipated night-birds. It took a long time to tell upon his marvellous constitution, but it did at length, and the Deaf 'Un was nothing near the man he was when he left for the States.

During his absence two heavy-weights had been unearthed, who claimed to be entitled to fight for the Championship—Bendigo and Ben Caunt—and in spite of the Deaf 'Un's dissipation the following appeared in the sporting newspapers :—

" Sir,—When I was in Yorkshire I heard a good deal about ' would-be Champions ' challenging any man in England. ' While the cat's away the mice will play,' and then the little fry took advantage of my absence to bounce and crow like cocks in a gutter. I hastened back to take the shine out of these braggadocios, and to

16

put their pretensions to the test. I beg to state that I
am now ready to fight any man in England for from
£100 to £500, and as my old friend Jem Ward has
retired from the Ring, if he will add his Champion's
belt to the prize, and let the best man wear it, he will
give new energies to the ring, and I trust afford an
opportunity for deciding the long-contested question,
' Who is Champion of England ?' I bar neither country
nor colour, age nor dimensions; and whether it be
the Goliath Caunt, or his hardy antagonist, Bendigo,
or any other man who ever wore a head, I am his
customer, and no mistake. My money is ready at Jem
Burn's, the Queen's Head, Queen's Head Court, Windmill Street, Haymarket, at a moment's notice; but I will
not consent to a less deposit than £25 at starting. If I
find the race of old English boxers of the right kidney
is extinct, I shall go back to America, where an honest
man need never want a friend or a battle.

" Windmill Street, Haymarket,   " DEAF BURKE."
        July 29, 1838."

This was the challenge that had been taken up by
Bendigo, who had just previously met and defeated Ben
Caunt, all about which we shall describe in a future
chapter when we introduce him as Champion and
record his career. But the Deaf 'Un's dissipation
affected him so much that he was compelled to forfeit
the money down, thereby getting himself into very bad
odour amongst the first-class sportsmen. He did not
return from his Parisian trip until September of 1838,
and then he renewed his challenge to Bendigo, the
Deaf 'Un's friends putting down £100 to £80, the fight
to come off within thirty miles of Nottingham on
February 12, 1839, under the new rules of the Prize
Ring, which strictly prohibited butting.

Here it will only be necessary to give a list of those with
whom Bendigo fought prior to this battle with Burke,
for we shall treat him more exhaustively in describing his
several battles. He had fought and beaten Bill Faulkes,
October, 1832; Ned Smith, March, 1833; Charley Martin,
April, 1833; Lin Jackson, May, 1833: Tom Cox, June,
1833; Charles Skelton, August, 1833; Tom Burton,
August, 1833; Bill Mason, September, 1833; Bill Winterflood, October, 1833; Bingham Champion, January, 1834;
and Ben Caunt, July 21, 1835. Not a bad record, considering Bendigo, when he accepted Burke's challenge,
was only twenty-eight years of age, and his weight was
only 11st 10lb.

After the articles were signed a second time Bendigo
(who, by-the-bye, was born at Nottingham) went into
strict training under Peter Taylor, at Crosby, near Liver-

pool. Whilst there it seems he very nearly lost his life, according to the following paragraph that appeared in one of the Lancashire papers:—"During the storm on Sunday night Bendigo, who is training at Crosby, near Liverpool, narrowly escaped being 'gathered unto his fathers.' It appears that Peter Taylor went to meet Bendigo on Monday morning, but not finding him at the appointed place, proceeded at once to Crosby, where he discovered that the house in which he had left his friend on the previous evening was almost in ruins, the roof having been blown in and nearly every window broken. Peter's fears, however, were soon allayed by ascertaining that Bendigo was at a neighbouring cottage, where he found him between a pair of blankets, and looking quite chapfallen. Bendigo said he would rather face three Burkes than pass such another night. He went to bed about nine o'clock, but was awoke about eleven by his bed rocking under him, the wind whistling around him, and the bricks tumbling down the chimney. Every minute he expected the house to fall in upon him, and at three o'clock the hurricane increased so much in violence that he got out of bed, put on his clothes, and made his escape out of the window. He had not left the house ten minutes before the roof was blown in. A knight of the awl kindly gave him shelter, and he has since obtained fresh quarters in the same village."

Bendigo stuck conscientiously to work, and Jem Ward, who was living at Liverpool, frequently went over and gave him the finishing touches, for the ex-Champion was anxious to see the Deaf 'Un beaten. The latter went into training under the mentorship of Tommy Roundhead, his faithful red-nosed secretary and esquire, at Finchley. This eccentric gent declared that Burke was getting on splendidly, and that he "was as strong as a rhinoceros and as bold as a lion." But this was far from the truth, as the Deaf 'Un could not keep away from his swell pals, and on several occasions he slipped up to town and visited his West End haunts of dissipation. Still his friends thought so much of him that they laid 6 to 4 on his chance, odds which were eagerly snapped up by the Nottingham, Sheffield, and Liverpool sports, who knew what the Bold Bendigo could do.

The greatest excitement pervaded the whole of the country as the time for the fight for the Championship drew near, and on the Monday at the Red Lion, Appleby, in Leicestershire, there was a great gathering of the clans, for thither both men came from their training quarters to settle with their backers and friends the final arrangements. The Deaf 'Un was accompanied

by Jem Burn, Dick Curtis, and Tommy Roundhead,
and they put up at Atherstone, where Young Dutch
Sam brought some of the "toffs" upon the scene. There
were Lord Waldegrave, Lord Chetwynd, Captain Buber,
Robert Grimston, and a number of others belonging to
the fast set. At Appleby itself Bold Bendigo pitched
his tent, in company with Jem Ward, Peter Taylor,
and Izzy Lazarus. On the Monday evening the friends
and backers of both met at the Red Lion, where after
much discussion it was decided that the arena should be
formed as near to Appleby as possible, and that the men
should be in the ring by two o'clock.

On the following morning, at a very early hour,
vehicles and pedestrians arrived from all parts, and the
roads from the different towns leading to Appleby presented an animated appearance, and there was no little
grumbling on the part of the visitors when it became
known that the trysting place was some seven miles
from the village. It was, as a matter of fact, a hill in
the parish of Heather, just outside the borders of Leicestershire.

In spite of the time mentioned it was half-past eleven
when the Deaf 'Un arrived, and crowds had been in
position since 9.30, so the reception was scarcely so
hearty as it might have been, for the patience of those
assembled was well-nigh exhausted. Still, late as Burke
was, he arrived first in the field, and it was not until
an hour later that Bendigo entered an appearance. By
that time quite 15,000 people were on the spot, amongst
them a vast number of aristocrats from London and the
surrounding country. The Nottingham Lambs were in
the majority amongst the rougher classes, and the Londoners had to take a back seat.

And here we may be permitted to retell a little incident which, according to one reporter, actually occurred.
Whilst the Deaf 'Un was in the ring, attended by Dick
Curtis and Jackson, of Sheffield, and awaiting the
arrival of his adversary, an exceedingly well-dressed,
buxom, and good-looking woman forced her way
through the packed mass of spectators, and, rushing
up to the arena, seized Jem by the hand and
heartily wished him success, and but for the inter-
vening ropes would no doubt have given him an embrace.
Naturally this brought forth a deal of chaff upon the
Deaf 'Un, but his imperfect hearing stood him in good
stead, for he affected not to hear a word.

Then there was a tremendous roar from two-thirds of
the multitude, and the volume of sound coming from
10,000 throats can be better imagined than described, as
Bendigo made his appearance. He was attended by Peter

Taylor and Nick Ward, and immediately walked over to Burke, shook him heartily by the hand, and anxiously inquired after his health. They were quickly prepared for the combat by their seconds, when a very unpleasant incident occurred. Having been disrobed Bendigo walked over to Burke's corner and demanded to examine the Deaf 'Un's drawers. There he found a belt, which he insisted upon having removed. In vain did Jem and

BENDIGO.

his seconds plead that it was only there to keep up a truss he was compelled to wear for a rupture sustained in America. Bendigo was obdurate; he declared that he should wear nothing more than he did; so, reluctantly, the belt was removed, the truss tied up with tape, but not before the article objected to had been handed round the ring for the swells to look at and pronounce it quite harmless. Bendigo's selfishness over this little matter did him no good, and the sympathies were with the

Deaf 'Un, especially with those in between the two rings, and there were some big swells there, too, for never since the battle between Spring and Langan had there been such a representative company. Here are a few names of those who were actually present :—The Marquis of Waterford, the Marquis of Worcester, Lord Downshire, the Earls of Wilton, Waldegrave, Longford, Chetwynd, Jersey, and Southampton ; the Hon. Robert Grimston, Captain Ross, Captain White, Captain Beecher, Squire Osbaldestone, Mr. John Gully, Gentleman Jackson, Tom Crommelin, "The Bishop of Bond Street," Squire Giffard, of Chillingham, the veteran Sir Bellingham Graham, and "Ginger" Stubbs.

Amidst the most deafening noises, offers to lay or take odds, the cries of itinerants selling their wares, the laughter of half-inebriated young swells, and the shouting and chaffing, the signal was given, and the men were divested of their overcoats and stood up in fighting "fig."

The Deaf 'Un's appearance we have already described, and we shall have more to say about Bendigo when we tell of his first big fight with Caunt, so we will get on with a few brief details of this important contest, which was to decide which man should hold the proud title of Champion of England.

Burke did not appear to be in his usual condition, for his skin was pale and inclined to be flabby ; but the Nottingham man was a picture of health. Both men were very cautious at the commencement, changing ground and manœuvring—Burke acting on the defensive, Bendy searching for a chance of getting in a blow. This lasted a few minutes amidst breathless silence, when Bendigo, seeing an opening, let go his right, and smack it came on the Deaf 'Un's ribs, leaving an impression in red thereon. Burke made no attempt to counter, but remained as stolid and as still as he did when impersonating those statues in America. Presently, however, his turn came. He hit out well with the right and caught his man a severe blow upon his favourite spot, the ear ; but instantly had a stinger in return from Bendigo's right, as straight as an arrow, under the eye. The cheers from the "Lambs" were tremendous as their man showed this smartness. The Deaf 'Un, however, never moved a muscle, and stood still awaiting an attack. In vain Bendy feinted with his left, in the hope of getting in another smasher with his right. Closer and closer the men got together, each with mischief brewing in his wicked eye. They let out simultaneously with the left, and sharp counters on both sides followed, ending in a rally, when both sent in some very warm ones right and left on the body. They closed, and there was a struggle for the throw. Neither of them was successful, though, for they fell together, side by side. As they came up for the second bout they were both very much flushed about the face. The Deaf 'Un, as before, stuck to the defensive, Bendy, as before, trying to draw him with the left, but the old 'un was not to be had. After a long spell of sparring and shifting Bendy shot in his left, which was prettily parried; but he was more fortunate with the right, nailing his man under the eye again. Then with the same hand he shot one in as straight as a dart from the shoulder, catching Jem on the cheek. The Nottingham man was making most of the points, and the straight right-hand deliveries of Bendigo's began to puzzle the Deaf 'Un. His friends began to call upon him to wake up, which he immediately did, going for his man in a fearless manner. Bendy stood his ground, though, and at it they went, hammer and tongs, ding-dong, give and take, stopping, returning, and hitting in a style that excited the greatest enthusiasm amongst the spectators. Here is an extract from a report of this fiercely-fought second round that reads very interesting:—" Neither man flinched or budged a step, though the deliveries on both sides were uncommonly severe. The Deaf 'Un hit very hard, but was slow, and was frequently fore-stalled in the counters by the superior quickness of his young adversary. Nevertheless, it was Bendy who tired soonest of this slogging business. He suddenly wheeled round and tried to break away; but the Deaf 'Un followed him in the most determined manner, and forced him to renew the rally. Bendy fought desperately, but his nerve did not appear to be equal to that of Burke, one fearful stinger from the Deaf 'Un right on the jaw, seemed to send the Nottingham man for the moment all abroad; he hit out wildly, missed twice with his right, then rushed to a close, and after a sharp struggle both came down together."

When they came up for the third bout, Bendigo's jaw was swollen and his face much flushed; but Burke showed more signs of punishment. His left eye was puffed and discoloured, and the whole of that side of his physiognomy was bruised by Bendy's right-handers. Bendigo was very busy in this round, and everybody could see that the Deaf 'Un was not fighting in his old form, and that the Nottingham man was much too lively for him. They fought desperately; but Bendy took the lead and jobbed Burke as he came on time after time in the face with awful severity, the Deaf 'Un all the while scarcely offering to return. Then Bendy went in, repeated his right-handed jobs again and again, then closed, gave his man the crook, threw him, and fell upon him with all his weight. Burke was now far away the more distressed, and vomited badly. Everybody was inquiring what had come over the Deaf 'Un. He was certainly not fighting like the man who had vanquished Simon Byrne. He appeared to have lost his head entirely, and all his judgment, self-possession, and knowledge of ring-craft seemed to have deserted him. The battle had only lasted sixteen minutes, but so well had the Nottingham man done that they were laying 6 to 4 on him.

In the next two rounds there was little to choose between them; but both were very actively engaged in dealing out damage, and in the sixth so exhausted was Burke that the brandy bottle was produced, and a long pull of the *eau de vie* seemed to put new life in Jem for the time being. Still his clever adversary pinked him over and over again on the sore spot upon the eye until that organ was on the eve of putting up its shutters, and Jem Burke looked all over a beaten man, and by the tenth round, which proved to be the last, it was evident to his warmest partisans that he was, bar accidents, hopelessly over matched; but he would not, could not admit it. Savage to a degree, he dashed in at Bendigo, and failing to get his wild blows home, with teeth grinding and eyes flashing he twice butted him in the face with that thick skull of his; but Bendy wrenched himself free, and they went down after a struggle. Jem Ward at once called "foul," and without any hesitation both the umpires and the referee agreed that such it was; so the Nottingham man was awarded the fight and claimed the championship.

Such was the downfall of Deaf Burke. Of his further adventures and engagements we shall treat in our next chapter, when, with an account of his death, we shall dismiss him as one of the best, most straightforward, and most powerful bruisers of his day, a fool to himself and a toy in the hands of his so-called friends.

CHAPTER XXXII.

JEM BURKE AND NICK WARD.—DEATH OF THE DEAF 'UN.—
ENTER ANOTHER CHAMPION.

WHEN Deaf Burke was defeated by Bendigo for the
Championship, it was one of the greatest surprises that
had fallen upon the sporting world for many a long
day. Not a member of the Fancy believed that there
was a man in the United Kingdom who could (save
Jem Ward) have taken down the colours of the Deaf
'Un, and we believe to this day that had he not fallen
into the company of that dissipated set he would have
continued to enjoy a brilliant career. He had distinguished himself both in the Old World and the New,
and met some of the best men of his time, defeating
them all very easily; the only time before that he had
lost a battle was when he had a fit of the sulks whilst
fighting Bill Cousins, and practically gave in.

That he knew well enough his condition is certain, for
he repeatedly challenged Bendy to fight him for £100; but
the Nottingham man would not enter the arena again with
him for less than £200, and Jem, after the exhibition
he had made, was unable to raise that sum. Certainly,
he made a good deal of money on his sparring tours; but
his tastes, acquired by mixing amongst the young swells,
had become extravagant, and he spent his money as
fast as he got it. Still, he believed that he would ultimately get the £200, and be able to lick the Bold Bendigo at the finish. Just when he thought that this could
be accomplished, however, Bendigo met with an accident, and the consequence was that he could not accommodate the Deaf 'Un, even if that worthy had succeeded
in raising the wind. The Nottingham man was always
up to his larks, and on one occasion as he was returning
from the Officers' Military Steeplechase, near the town
of his birth, he did a very foolish thing. Here is the
report of it as it appeared in the Notts papers at the
time :—" On Bendigo's return from the races on Monday last, he and his companions were cracking jokes
about having a steeplechase among themselves. Having
duly arrived opposite the Pinder's House, on the London
Road, about a mile from Nottingham, Bendigo exclaimed,
' Now, boys, I'll show you how to run a steeplechase in

a new style, without falling!' and immediately threw a
somersault; he felt, whilst throwing it, that he had
hurt his knee, and on alighting he attempted in vain
three times to rise from the ground. His companions,
thinking for the moment he was joking, laughed heartily,
but discovering it was serious, went to his assistance
and raised him up; but the poor fellow had no use of
his left leg. A gig was sent for immediately, in which
he was conveyed to the house of his brother, and Messrs.
Wright and Thomson, surgeons, were immediately
called in. On examination of the knee, we understand
they pronounced the injury to the cap of the knee to
be of so serious a nature that he is likely to be lame for
life."

Fortunately, however, things were not so bad as all
that, for Bendigo fought Ben Caunt after the accident,
as we shall shortly see when we come to the description
of his career. Now, through Bendigo being out of the
way and the Deaf 'Un unable to raise much money, his
inactivity was enforced, although he had the audacity
to throw out a challenge to fight anybody in the world
for £200 and the Championship. Of course, everybody
knew that Burke could not find half that sum; so when
Nicholas Ward, brother to the ex-Champion James of
that ilk, threw down the gauntlet to fight the Deaf 'Un
for £50 a-side, there was a considerable amount of
surprise in sporting circles.

Nick's antecedents were of the shadiest description,
and the only notoriety he possessed was that of showing
the white feather. His only solitary victory had been
over a countryman named Harry Lockyer, of Kent,
whilst he had sneaked out of a match with Young Molineux, procuring his own arrest on the eve of the battle,
and had been easily defeated by Master Sambo Sutton.
Besides which, Nick had lost a fight with Jem Bailey by
striking a foul blow, and had declared himself too unwell
to enter the ring on a second match being made. Certainly
this was not a very brilliant career, and it made people
smile when they learnt that he was about to meet the
Deaf 'Un, and thereby aspire to the Championship of
England. The idea was too ridiculous that he should
have the impudence to challenge the redoubtable Deaf
Burke, the game, scientific, hard-hitting fighter who
for years had been held to be invincible. The match
was, however, made and the fight came off on Tuesday,
September 22, 1840, and by all accounts a more disgraceful affair never took place in the P.R. There were
only seventeen rounds fought, and they took two hours,
Nick playing a waiting game and tiring the old warrior
out. The weather was simply dreadful, the cold rain

that was falling throughout the battle affecting the elder man in a fatal manner.

Here is a description by an eye-witness :—" To add to the old 'un's discomfiture when he came up for the fourteenth round he was met straight in the face by a terrific storm of hail and rain, which burst like a tornado upon the ring. Nick Ward had his back to it and, of course, suffered less, but poor Burke had the full benefit of it in his eyes. For a moment he was blinded, and the stinging sleet seemed to affect him in an extraordinary manner. The Deaf 'Un was all abroad, made no attempt to counter, and staggered back as if to fall—in fact, the storm helped to lick him quite as much as did Nick Ward's fists. At times the downpour was so tremendous that it was difficult to see across the ring. Still the men fought on, Nick craftily keeping the Deaf 'Un with his face to the storm, and taking advantage of the poor old chap's difficulties to dash in and nail him heavily about the nose, mouth, and eyes till Burke's visage was streaming with blood and water."

Then the account goes on to say that Nick Ward got his man on the ropes and punished him unmercifully until he dropped. Not satisfied with that, Ward went to the Deaf 'Un's corner and struck him whilst on his second's knee. There were cries of " Foul !" But the crush and confusion were so great that it was impossible for the umpires and referee to see what was really going on. It appears that there was a general free fight between seconds and principals. The referee, Mr. Dowling, of *Bell's Life*, would not give his decision at the time ; and Burke wrote to the papers claiming the stakes. The following is a copy of the letter :—

" I do hereby give you notice not to deliver up the stakes to the opposite party in the fight between me and Nick Ward, as I hereby claim the same from having received foul blows from my opponent, Nick Ward, whilst on my second's knee and before ' Time ' was called. One of the umpires bears evidence that the last statement is correct, as a friend of the other umpire (Nick Ward's) had taken away the only watch used for timekeeping while he and my second, Harry Preston, were appealing to the referee with respect to a prior foul blow. My reason for entering the protest is in order that a meeting may be obtained with the referee and an appointed number of friends of each party, so that a proper and just arbitration may be obtained. I shall be prepared at that meeting to produce affidavits in confirmation of what I assert. My backers hold you liable for the amount of the stakes.

" Sept. 23, 1840." (Signed) " JAMES BURKE.

To this was added the following certificate from Burke's umpire:—"Nick Ward *v.* Burke. I hereby declare that no 'Time' was called after the appeal to the referee."

Accordingly the meeting was held, and after all the evidence was heard Mr. Dowling decided in favour of Ward, to whom the stakes were handed. This was the poor old Deaf 'Un's downfall, and as he has occupied these pages for a considerable time, we will despatch him as quickly as possible, and pass on to our next Champion. A fortnight after the disgraceful fight with Nick Ward, Burke took a benefit at the Bloomsbury Assembly Rooms, and after a set-to with a youngster known as the "Cumberland Youth," who had taken the place of Ben Caunt, the latter not having put in an appearance, James Burke delivered himself of the following characteristic bit of oratory:—

" Gemmens,—I have dis here to say. I'm werry sorry as Caunt has not come to sets-to wid me accordin' to his promises, for he gave me his words of honours as he would attend ; but dat's de way with dese 'ere mens when dey gets to the top of de trees dey do nothings to help a poor fellows as is downs ; but dey had better minds what dey are abouts, or dey'll be as bads as Jack Scroggins, and look for a *tanners* when dey can't find it. Gemmens, I mean to say as I do not tinks as I was fairly beat by Bendigo, and I am prouds to say as I am not widout friends what tink the same, and as are ready to back me for a level hundreds against him or Nick Wards, or Jem Bailey. Bendigo is werry bounce-able now, as he says he has licked me ; but I says he took an unfair advantage in regards of my belts ; but dat's neither one ting nor toder, and if he has friends, if he's a man he'll give me anoder chance, and till he does I shall always thinks as he has won the belts without any rights to it. I went to Sheffields and Nottinghams to make a match wid 'im, and now let him show equal pluck and come to London to make a match wid me ; my pewters is always ready. (Hear, hear. Bravo, Deaf 'Un.) Dat's all I've got to says, Gemmen. I thanks my friends for coming here to-nights, but I've got something 'ere (pointing to his throat, and the poor fellow seemed overflowing with gratitude) which won't let me say no more."

But for all his boasting and complaints about Bendigo, the poor old Deaf 'Un could find no friends who retained sufficient belief in him to put down the money to fight the Nottingham man. Jem Burke's star had set. He made a match with the Tipton Slasher two years later, but it came to nothing, and he received £15 forfeit on

July 7, 1842. Only once after that he appeared in the ring, and that was on June 13, 1843, when he fought a man named Bob Castles for £25 a-side, at Rainham Ferry, in Essex, defeating his man in thirty-seven rounds, lasting one hour and ten minutes.

After this the poor old Deaf 'Un came from bad to worse. The seeds of consumption, which had no doubt

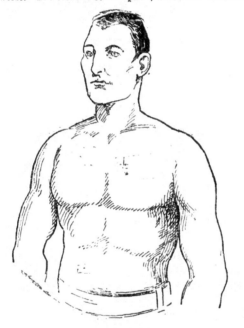

NICK WARD.

been set when he was a miserable, half-starved urchin getting his living as a Jack-in-the-Water, developed apace. His dissipated habits had wrecked his constitution, and he died penniless, deserted by all his swell acquaintances, but with Joe Parish still looking after him, at No. 7, Francis Street, Waterloo Road. He was a rough diamond, was the Deaf 'Un, and his quaint figure, comical face, and peculiar style of conversation made him one of the most original characters of the Ring. He was brave, honest, but weak-minded, yet there were many worse than he who had worn the Champion's belt, and held the proud position of premier pugilist of the world.

And now it will be necessary, in order to chronicle the careers of our Champions, to hark back a bit and revert to the doings of the Bold Bendigo, to whom our readers have already been introduced in a previous chapter, when we were compelled to bring him on the scene somewhat prematurely in our account of his fight with James Burke.

We will now take the opportunity of sketching the early part of his career, before he figures again upon our pages as a gladiator. William Thompson, better known to fame in the Ring as Bendigo, was born in New Yard, Parliament Street, Nottingham, on October 11, 1811. He was said to have been the youngest son of twenty-one, and that he was one of a triplet. He came of very respectable parents, and it is stated that amongst his ancestors were an eminent Quaker and a popular Methodist preacher.

In an account of his career which has been published, and said to have been dictated by himself, although we find it full of inaccuracies and contradictions, Bendigo tells us that his father died when he was about fifteen years of age, and that in consequence of that event he was obliged to go into the Nottingham Workhouse, where he stayed twenty-one weeks. On leaving the Union he went about the town selling oysters, but soon abandoned that and apprenticed himself to his brother, John Thompson, to learn iron-turning, and having mastered this trade obtained employment at Messrs. Smith's, machinists, of Bloomgrove, Radford, Notts. According to this supposed autobiography, Bendigo was as a youth a first-class all-round athlete, and lover of all kinds of sport. He says: "I was also passionately fond of fishing, at which I was considered a first-rate hand. I have also been noted for cock-fighting, badger-baiting, running, somersaulting, stone-throwing, cricketing, &c. I have lobbed a stone 200yds, and a cricket ball (5¾oz) 115yds. I was also matched, for a small wager, to throw half a brick over the Nottingham Trent, near the Trent Bridge, which I did (left hand), the distance being about 76yds. I have also played and beaten at cricket Gerland (?) of Leeds, one of the great All-England players at that time; also Thomas Burton, the tutor of Burton Cricket Club, Burton-on-Trent; we played at Aldres, near Lichfield. I was matched to throw a cricket-ball and play at cricket with George Parr, the then All-England cricketer; the match did not take place on account of my being seized with the gout; we met together, but I was unable to play. I have also run second in a mile handicap at Sheffield, being beaten by Cruel. I have also succeeded in carrying off the second, third, fourth, and fifth prizes at York Great All-England Fishing Match."

These are a few of Bendigo's achievements, as told by himself. And now we come to the vexed question of why Mr. Thompson should have been called Bendigo, which name he made celebrated in both the Old and New Worlds, for Bendigo, in Australia, is one of the richest gold fields in the universe, and the horse of that name, in England, was one of the fastest that ever looked through a bridle, and they both took their name from the celebrated Nottingham bruiser under notice. According to his supposed autobiography, which is now before us, Bendy is made to state: "The reason of my going by the name of Bendigo was when I was a boy, and was sent on errands by my parents, I used to stay out for hours, and sometimes all day and night, and when my father came to find me, he would see me either fighting or playing in the streets, and when my pals used to see my father coming to fetch me, they would say, ' Bendy, go, your father is coming;' thus my name Bendigo originated from these circumstances." We can hardly believe that this statement could ever have emanated from Mr. William Thompson himself. The true source of his sobriquet is, we have been able to discover in running through the chronicles of his career, due to different circumstances altogether. In a paper dated September. 29, 1833, we find Wiliam Thompson first mentioned as Abendego, and later on we find it in the same print. abbreviated to Bendigo. We then on investigation discovered that he, being one of a triplet and the last born of three boys, they were nicknamed by some friend of the family—who had a knowledge of Scripture—Shadrach, Meshach, and Abednego.

But to his Prize Ring career, as we shall have occasion to tell some strange stories about this extraordinary individual as we chronicle his doings—for he was one of the most eccentric and curious fellows that ever wore the Champion's belt. According to his own account his first prize-fight was in the year 1832, when he met one Bill Faulkes, but we are unable to find anything about this worthy. In the following year he asserts that he fought no less than nine battles, being victorious in every one; but in " Fistiana " we are able only to find the names of two of his opponents—Tom Cox, of Nottingham, who had beaten Merryman. in

1831; and Bill Winterflood, who termed himself the Bath Champion, who fought Luke Rogers and Dick Hill. In 1834 he fought and beat the Bingham Champion, whoever he was, so as a youngster, only twenty-four years of age, Master Bendigo had a very fair record, although none of these battles are recorded, and we are unable to say how scientifically he acquitted himself. It was in 1835 that Bendigo's name came prominently before the London Fancy, for he made a match with the great Ben Caunt, and it was upon the occasion of that battle that the Nottingham man entered the Ring proper, and gave the sporting world a taste of his extraordinary talent. But this *début*, and the introduction of his opponent, we must leave for the next chapter.

CHAPTER XXXIII.

BOLD BENDIGO (W. THOMPSON).—HIS FIRST FIGHT WITH BEN CAUNT.—BENDY'S BATTLE WITH BRASSEY.—TWO VICTORIES ON " FOULS."

AND now it will be our pleasure to introduce another Champion which, with Bendigo, with whom we parted in the last chapter, will make two occupying the stage at the same time, both destined to become great actors and playing leading parts in the Prize Ring. During the time that Master William Thompson, alias Bendigo, was fighting his way to notoriety in his native county, another youth, also a Nottinghamshire man, was making a name. He was an immense young chap, gigantic of stature, and mighty in thews and sinews, with a stout heart and a jolly countenance. He was a native of Hucknall Torkard, and his name was Benjamin Caunt. On the village green, at wrestling, there was not a lad could throw him, and with the gloves he held his own against all comers. With the fists, too, he had proved himself no mean performer, and had started by thrashing two big fellows, older than himself, who had ventured to tackle the young giant.

Ben Caunt was born at the above village on March 22, 1815, where his parents had been tenants of Lord

Byron, and many a story would the pugilist tell of
his recollections of his lordship at Newstead Abbey,
Byron's ancestral estate, when he settled down in
London at the Coach and Horses, in St. Martin's
Lane, where we shall meet him frequently as we
proceed with our history of the Champions. Caunt
always said that he commenced life as a young man as
a gamekeeper to a Nottinghamshire gentleman, but his
acquaintances down in the country always declared that
he was nothing more than a farm labourer. Be that as
it may, Caunt had been well used to a gun, and was in
after years considered an excellent pigeon shot.

About the time that Bendigo was being taken great
notice of at Nottingham, in 1834, young Caunt was but
nineteen years of age, and very little known outside his
native village. But there was one Jack Ridsdale, a
brother to John Gully's well-known partner, who lived
at Hucknall Torkard, and took great notice of the young
giant, predicting that he would, if properly taken in
hand, turn out a top-sawyer. A great friend of Mr.
Ridsdale was Mr. Joseph Whitaker, of Ramsdale
House, on Nottingham Forest, and one of the most
eccentric gentlemen throughout the Midlands. He was
known as "The Duke of Limbs." One who was
well acquainted with him thus describes him:—"Joe
Whitaker was one of the finest specimens of the old breed
of English yeomen we have ever come across. A giant
in strength and constitution was Joe, with a fine, open
handsome English face, adorned with a pair of huge
whiskers, clipped till they looked like a great hair brush
on each cheek. But the limbs of the man were the most
astonishing part of him ; none of your blubber and
truffles, but literally all muscle and bone, with a figure-
head and a cut-water in happy keeping with the goodly
hull. Hence Joe's sobriquet, 'His Grace of Limbs.'
No better sportsman or more convivial *bon vivant* ever
breathed—the prince of hosts, his home was the model of
a hospitable English homestead. But he was eccentric
—too fond of practical jokes of the Jack Mytton stamp,
to be altogether an agreeable acquaintance to common-
place folks. He was a keen and passionate lover of the
Ring. It was only natural, then, that a man of this
class should recognise the talents of the Bold Bendigo,
and indeed, from the very first he took a fancy to the
young Nottingham pugilist, who was as eccentric as
himself, and determined to match him as soon as
the opportunity occurred.

He had not long to wait, for, being on a visit to his
friend Ridsdale, Joe Whitaker was taken to see a
wrestling match in the village, one of the competitors

17

being young Caunt, and the other a man from Lincolnshire, named Potter. Ben came off an easy winner, and
Mr. Whitaker was struck with the youngster's mighty
limbs.   So when his friend launched out into
praises of Caunt's courage and skill as a boxer,
he thought to himself there would be a fine opportunity of matching Master Bendigo. A few weeks
after the wrestling match, Joe Whitaker once more paid
a visit to Hucknall Torkard, but this time accompanied
by Bendigo and a set of gloves, suggesting to Mr. Ridsdale that the two lads should have the gloves on. This
was readily agreed to, and young Caunt was sent for,
and in the garden the two men, who were destined to
make such names, and climb to the top of the tree, met
for the first time in their lives. It is very doubtful
whether Bendigo exhibited all his skill on this particular
occasion, for both Caunt and his backer were exceedingly pleased at the trial, and readily took up the
challenge thrown down by Bendigo to fight in the
twenty-four foot ring for £25 a-side.

The date fixed for the battle was Tuesday, July 21,
1835, and the place selected, Appleby House, on the
Ashbourne Road, thirty miles from Nottingham, and
twenty-two from Birmingham. Sam Turner took Bendigo under his wing and trained him at the Green
Dragon, Chilwell, just outside Nottingham, whilst Ben
Butler, Caunt's uncle, looked after his nephew.
Although neither of the men was much known to fame,
there was by all accounts a fair muster at Appleby
House which, by-the-bye, we may mention was a well-
known roadside inn, where cocking and other sports went
on, and where in the large meadow at the back many
a fight had been brought off. It was in this field that,
five years previous to the battle we are about to describe,
Harry Preston, of Birmingham, beat Dick Hill, of
Nottingham, and old Jack Powell—" Sir John," as he
was dubbed—the landlord of the house, declared that he
never taken so much money in the house in his life. It
was upon that occasion even Mr. Dowson, the lord of the
manor and a magistrate, witnessed the contest seated on
his cob, and made not the slightest attempt to interfere.

Many came from Birmingham and the Nottingham

district, and we read amongst those present were : Mr.
Beardsworth, Mr. Ridsdale and, of course, Joe Whitaker,
Arthur Matthewson (who was selected as referee), Jack
Mathews, Philip Bryant Sampson, and Harry Potter,
the stylish commissary of the Midlands. Many, no
doubt, will remember Harry for his marvellous get-up

BEN CAUNT.

—white hat cocked on one side, extraordinary waist-
coats, and enormous seals hanging from his watch-chain.
Caunt was waited upon by his uncle, Ben Butler, and
Harry Bamford, whilst his father was also close to his
corner, anxious no doubt as to the result of the young
hopeful's first important appearance in the ring. Ben-

digo had as his seconds Sam Turner (his trainer) and
Sam Merryman, the well-known light weight. Caunt
was in his twenty-first year, and he was certainly the
biggest man who had thrown his castor into the arena
since Tom Brown, of Bridgnorth. Young Ben stood
6ft 2½in in his stockings, and Bendigo's friends declared
that he weighed quite 15st, although we should think
that an exaggeration, for his fighting weight in later years
was never over 14st 7lb. Bendigo was 5ft 9¾in, without his shoes, and his best fighting weight was 11st 10lb.

There was, of course, a great disparity in their sizes,
and Bendy must have looked quite a David beside
this Goliath, yet the smaller man was a better figure for
an athlete, as Caunt had no symmetry or grace about
his figure—big bones, prominent muscles, and tremendous limbs. His opponent was a powerfully built man
and possessed of great strength, well-proportioned,
springy, sinewy, and muscular, with a combination of
power and agility, which caused him to enjoy such a
successful career.

Bendigo fought with his right foot foremost, a puzzling
attitude for a man who has been accustomed to spar in
the usual left-legged manner, but he could change quickly
when necessary. Caunt stood in a clumsy attitude, and,
indeed, never through his fighting career could ever be
taught to stand otherwise. The Bold One eyed his
adversary quite coolly, and no doubt he had felt his way
at that little boxing bout they had had together in the
garden, although Caunt was under the impression that
he had the advantage in science, as well as strength.
He was, however, destined to be quickly undeceived.
Here is an account of the start of the battle :—"Erect
and square towered the massive figure of Big Ben,
but Bendy dropped his right shoulder and stooped
a little, as if meditating a spring. The question
was, which should begin? This Ben speedily settled
by bearing down like a huge three - decker, with all
sails set, on his foe. Bendy drew back, Ben pressed
on anxious to get his sledge-hammer fist home somewhere on the other's carcase. Smack at last went his
right half-round at the head. Bendy ducked, and before
the big 'un could realise what he was about, the lithe
Nottingham man sprang in and nailed Caunt a tremendous blow on the nose. Ben stopped short, and put up
his hand to the wounded organ, amid mingled cheers
from the crowd. A second later the blood came slowly
trickling from the giant's nostrils and a roar of 'First
blood to Bendy' proclaimed that the premier event had
been booked to Mr. William Thompson. Caunt shook
his head, and went gamely for his man again—another

sweeping right-hander; missed clean, and, quick as lightning, Bendy nailed him again on the nose, and was away before the big 'un could touch him."

This was not at all whatCaunt had expected—nothing of that sort had happened in the garden with the gloves, and he was puzzled. Our informant then goes on to describe how Caunt, losing his temper, dashes after Bendy, in order to give him one of his hugs, but the wily one slips down just as Ben is about to grip, and sits on the turf grinning at his opponent, much to the disgust of Ben, who walks angrily to his corner.

And so the fight proceeds; round after round there is a repetition, Bendigo being too quick for his man, and planting blow after blow upon the bruised and bleeding face of the countryman. Bendy always avoided the clumsy and slow returns by dropping. Our account goes on to say :—" Maddened with pain, and still more by the exasperating tactics of his adversary, who escaped a hiding every time by going down, at the close of the twenty-second round Caunt lost all control over himself. In a blind fury he rushed across the ring to Bendy's corner before the watch-holder had called 'Time!' and whilst his opponent was still sitting on Ned Turner's knee. " Wilt thou stand up and foight fair, thou d——d hound ? " spluttered out Ben in his passion ; but before Bendy could answer, the giant lifted his arm, and with a tremendous back-hander sent both Bendy and Sam Turner rolling on the turf. 'Foul! foul!' was the cry from Bendigo's friends; and as the blow had been deliberately struck, the two umpires and referee were unanimously of opinion that Caunt had by this outrageous act of folly lost the fight."

It was a very unsatisfactory affair, but it showed Bendigo to advantage as an exceedingly artful tactician, and when it became known that the little one had stood up to their giant and given him dreadful punishment, the Nottingham man become at once celebrated, whilst Caunt had proved himself to be as brave as a lion, and ready and willing to go on receiving any amount of punishment.

And now we must for the time being leave the giant, who was later on destined to hold the Championship, and trace the further career of Mr. William Thompson, who comes next on the list as possessor of the belt.

The result of this battle with Caunt was to bring Bendigo no end of challenges from the 12st men all over the country. Amongst those who desired to try conclusions with the Nottingham man were Mr. John Leechman (better known as Brassey, of Bradford), Young Charley Langan, Bill Looney, and Bob Hampson, of

Liverpool. But Bendigo had started off on a tour through England, giving exhibitions of sparring with Peter Taylor, Sam Pixton, and Levi Eckersley, and took little notice of the papers, which were scarce and costly in those days. He was furthermore making plenty of money, [for Bendigo was an excellent showman, and knew exactly how to entertain an audience. He would, indeed, have made an excellent circus clown, for he had a ready wit, and was a first-rate tumbler. After the tour was over, though, he thought it time to look round for someone whom he could polish off without much trouble, so he sent a letter to the leading Midland journals, couched in pompous terms, to fight any 12st man in the counties of Notts, Leicester, Derby, or Lincoln. Now this, of course, excluded the Liverpool men, Bill Looney, Bob Hampson, and Young Langan, also Brassey, of Bradford. Consequently Bendigo was unmercifully chaffed, and told plainly that he was afraid to try conclusions with any good man. At length, in response to a challenge issued by Brassey to fight any man within a hundred miles of Bradford, for £25 to £50 a-side, Bendigo, when he saw it, went down to the Lion and Unicorn, and said that he was ready to meet Brassey for any sum his friends were willing to put down for him.

So it was arranged that the sum should be £25 a-side, and that the fight should come off on May 24, 1836. Mr. Jephson, of the Lion and Unicorn, together with Mr. Joe Whitaker and Bendigo, went over to Sheffield, and there, at the Stag's Head, then kept by Jem Mapping, met Brassey and his backers, and made all the arrangements in a satisfactory manner.

And now just a word about John Leechman, *alias* Brassey. He was only in his twenty-second year, but he had fought up to that time five battles, all of which he had won—having defeated Thomas Hartley, Ned Batterson, George Ireson, Jem Bailey (the Irishman), and Tom Scrutton. So it will be seen that Bendigo had a very different sort of man to the green and inexperienced Caunt to meet. The final deposit for the match was made at the Druid's Arms, Bradford, a house kept by Brassey's uncle, Mr. Simeon Smurthwaite. The articles stipulated that they should fight half way between Nottingham and Bradford; so Sheffield was selected as the rendezvous, and the men were to meet with their backers at the Stag's Head, Preston Street, on the morning of the fight, when the exact spot would be agreed upon. Accordingly they met, and, after a consultation with Harry Potter, it was decided that the ring should be formed at Deepcar, on the old Manchester

Road, where there was an excellent bit of common ground just suited for the purpose.

The accounts say there were quite 3,000 people present. Mat Robinson, who was looked upon as the Tom Spring of the Midlands, had brought under his wing some of the aristocratic sports of the Yorkshire Ridings, and a most respectable assemblage it turned out to be, although the Sheffield "blades" and grinders were well represented. Fortunately, the Nottingham Lambs were conspicuous by their absence, so the small body of "specials" which had been provided by Mat Robinson to keep order and protect the occupants of the outer ring were found sufficient for the occasion.

As the village church was striking the hour of noon Mr. James Hutchins, editor of the *Newark Times*, an enthusiastic sportsman, and who undertook the office of referee, called "Time," and the two young pugilists stepped to the scratch. Brassey was waited upon by Jem Mapping and George Thorp, whilst Sam Merryman and Turner were again esquires for the Bold Bendigo.

Before they had hardly parted after shaking hands, Brassey let fly at his antagonist, even before Bendigo's guard was up. But, showing marvellous quickness, the Nottingham man stopped it, and then like lightning went the return with his right full on the Bradford man's mouth, such a crack that it cut his lips and the blood streamed down his chin. A tremendous cheer went up for Bendigo, which apparently made Brassey very riled, for he dashed in to gain the fall, but the other man got a better grip, and in a very clever manner gave his opponent a neat back heel. The Bradford men were astonished. Here was their Champion, one of the best wrestlers in all Yorkshire, thrown as if he had been a mere child. If the Tykes were astonished at the first round, they must have been more so with the second, for one account reads as follows :—" Jem Mapping had advised his man to ' try for the goots,' and Brassey accordingly sent in a furious pile-driver in that direction, but Bendy dropped his elbow, stopped the blow, and let Leechman have his left instantaneously smack between the eyes. So severe was the blow that the Bradford man fell back a step. Bendigo, with astonishing rapidity, followed up with a blow in the face and a tremendous right-hander on the side of the head, which drove Brassey back, though it did not knock him down. But the Yorkshireman pulled himself together, roused by the exultant shouts of the Sheffielders and the Nottingham men, who were both jubilant over Bendigo's success, and with a rush Brassey was at close quarters once more. Each caught the other with the right hand and fibbed away with the left, till the Bradford man, who apparently was no better at this game than at outfighting, clutched Bendy with both hands and tried desperately hard to throw him; but though awkwardly situated, Bendigo kept his legs, foiled every attempt to get him down, and when at last they fell together, Brassey was undermost."

It will be unnecessary to dwell upon this battle at any length. Bendigo proved once more that he was a marvel in the ring, for, as one writer says : " He twisted like an eel and skipped about like a monkey, ducking and dodging, and springing back to avoid being hit." That as in the first fight, it is true that Bendigo on several occasions dropped to avoid punishment; but that was a part of his tactics, and he never did so unless there was excellent reason for it. Bendigo was too clever for him. He fought with his brains as well as with his fists. They went on until the fifty-second round, and Brassey was fearfully punished, and like Caunt at length lost his temper, for his adversary foiled him at all points.

Exasperated at not being able to get at his man, Leechman completely lost control of himself, and, growing desperate, rushed at his man regardless of the blows that were showered on to his face, and half-blinding him with the blood that was running into his eyes. He stooped down and butted Bendigo in the stomach, and catching him by the thighs, tried to turn him a complete somersault. There were, of course, loud shouts of "Foul! foul!" It was too obvious, and the referee at once awarded the fight to Bendigo, who had thus curiously enough again secured a verdict through his adversary losing his head. Bendigo was so little distressed that he leaped clean over the ropes and back into the ring again, where he cut all kinds of absurd capers.

By this battle he had proved himself to be worthy of a top place amongst the twelve-stoners, for he had defeated Brassey long before the foul was committed, and the Bradford man had shown himself in all his previous fights as a fine natural fighter. But the continuation of Mr. William Thompson's career towards the goal to which he now turned his attention—that of the Championship—we must defer for another chapter.

CHAPTER XXXIV.

INTRODUCING MR. JOHN LEECHMAN.—HIS EARLY FIGHTS,—
BENDIGO AND "BRASSEY."— BRILLIANT PERFORMANCE
OF THE COMING CHAMPION.—A DISGRACEFUL "FOUL."

AFTER Bendigo's defeat of Ben Caunt he came suddenly into provincial notoriety, and no end of the Midland
pugilists challenged him to fight for various sums.
Amongst them was Mr. John Leechman, who was better
known as Brassey. He was born at Bradford, and on
January 1, 1815, in the same year that witnessed the birth
of his future antagonist, Ben Caunt. When quite young
he was apprenticed to a blacksmith, and afterwards
obtained employment in a brass foundry, whence he
obtained the nickname "Brassey." There can be
little doubt that as a lad he was exceedingly pugnacious,
for by the time he was fifteen he had won for himself
a name as a boxer, and was but sixteen when he first
entered the Ring. His first battle was for the small
stakes of £2 a-side, with Thomas Hartley, whom he
defeated on Eccles Moor. This was in 1831, and a little
later in the same year the young Tyke gained another
victory, defeating a Sheffield lad named Ned Batterson.
Again the stakes were insignificant, being only £3 5s.
a-side, but the battle was long and stubborn, no less
than seventy-two rounds being fought in about as many
minutes. This proved that Young Leechman must have
had marvellous staying powers for his age. We hear
nothing about him for a couple of years, when he found
an opponent at Salford, named George Ireson. They
fought near Manchester, in the month of May, 1833,
and Ireson was defeated in twenty minutes. Then, only
three weeks after this contest, we find him in the ring at
Harpurhey, near Manchester, with Young Winterflood,
of Nottingham, doing battle for a fiver a-side. For
more than an hour they went at it hammer and tongs,
and such a thrashing did Brassey give his opponent that
Winterflood's friends broke into the ring and stopped
the fight, so robbing the Bradford lad of the stakes.
After this he fought one of his own townsmen named
Jem Bailey for £10 a-side, and was again victorious,
after getting through seventy-four rounds, lasting two
hours, fifteen minutes. The battle took place on Baildon
Moor, on April 24, 1835, and Bailey having proved him-

self a clever boxer and a hard hitter, Brassey's success made him locally notorious, and he was pronounced by the Midland Fancy to be a coming lad. That he had a good man to tackle was subsequently proved, for this Jem Bailey afterwards was taken in hand by the great Ned Painter, was formerly a pupil of Levi Eckersley, and had gained considerable notoriety in the Ring as opponent to Nick Ward, Con Parker, and McDonald, of Derby. He also met Tom Scrutton, according to "Fistiana," the "Yorkshire Champion," and fought for £20 a-side, on January 11, 1836.

Anyhow, Brassey's record was not so bad, although it could not compare with that of Bendigo, who had won nine battles before he met Caunt, which brought him into notoriety, as we described in some chapter or so back. Neither Brassey nor Bendigo was a novice, yet neither had fought first-class men. Still they were fine young fellows, as strong as lions, and had learnt the use of their fists in very good schools. Betting was at evens, and as each side was very sweet upon their man there was a deal of money invested. The final deposit was made at the Druids' Arms, Bradford, which house was at the time kept by an uncle of Brassey's, who tossed Mr. Jephson, Bendigo's backer, for choice of place, and won. The articles had distinctly stated that the fight was to take place between Nottingham and Bradford, so he thought the best place to select would be Sheffield, which is as near as possible midway between the two towns. So the city of knives and forks was named for the rendezvous, and the managers of the entertainment decided to meet at the Stag's Head, Preston Street, on the morning of the fight, when they were to decide the exact spot where the ring was to be formed.

It was to take place upon May 24, 1836, and the neighbourhood of the Stag's Head and the house itself were crowded with the Sheffield "blades," who were anxious to find out which way they were to go in the morning. They learnt but little, however, as the secret was not revealed to anybody until the day of the battle. Bendigo and Brassey both came over on the previous afternoon, the first-named putting up at the Golden Lion, and Brassey, of course, going to his uncle's house in Preston Street. In the morning a meeting was held at the Stag, and it was then decided that the ring should be pitched at Deepcar, upon the Manchester Road, where there was excellent common land, with capital turf. The commissary of the Midlands drove over with Jem Mapping shortly after nine o'clock, and with their assistants soon had the ring fixed up and ready for the combatants.

The number of spectators who assembled did not amount to more than 3,000, but amongst them were many Corinthian sports, as Mat Robinson (who was regarded as the Tom Spring of the Midlands) had looked up the swells and told them that so far as a straightforward, slashing mill was concerned, they were certain to have a splendid entertainment. Besides, every precaution had been taken to keep the Nottingham Lambs, Bradfordians, and the Sheffield Blades in order. The representatives of the two latter places were indeed exceedingly numerous, and it was stated that Sheffield and Nottingham had gone halves with Bendigo on this occasion, for he was certainly the favourite, although nobody imagined at this period of his career that he was destined to become Champion of England and defeat the men he did, losing the title and winning it back again. We should imagine that Bendy's popularity arose from his extraordinary flow of spirits, as well as from the fact that he was one of the trickiest, if not one of the most scientific boxers of the day, or at any rate in the provinces. Of course, Bendigo had many friends and supporters in Nottingham, as we have mentioned in a former chapter, but that he was so popular in Sheffield is somewhat surprising. In his autobiography, to which we have frequently alluded when we introduced him to our readers, he says:—"About 1836, I went to reside in Sheffield, where I kept a tap. I was backed by the Sheffielders to fight John Leechman, *alias* ' Brassey', of Bradford." We cannot find out where that tap was, though, and possibly, like many other statements in this particular autobiography, they should be taken with several grains of salt. In all probability, he resided in Sheffield for a period, and that the tap was a tavern he frequented, and he helped to keep it by bringing numerous customers to the house. The assertion, however, that he was backed from Sheffield is perfectly correct, for several gentlemen from that town supported him, and he trained at their expense for the fight at Woodhouse Mill, between Sheffield and Rotherham.

But enough of the men's associations with the towns. It was quite clear that they had plenty of friends and supporters, judging from the number that sallied forth to Deepcar to see the lads mill. They both met with a most cordial reception when they drove up nearly simultaneously, and the choice of umpires and other preliminaries were soon over. Mr. Richard Shaw, of Nottingham, acted for Bendigo, and Mr. Bradlaugh for Brassey; whilst Mr. James Hutchins, editor and proprietor of the *Newark Times*, a very well-known sportsman, officiated as referee,

Brassey was waited on by Jem Mapping and George Thorp, and Sam Merryman and Turner acted for Bendigo. Having peeled and girded on their colours— bright yellow for Bendigo, and scarlet for Brassey—they stepped to the centre of the ring as fine a brace of pugilists ever destined to bid for the Championship.

And now it is our intention to describe this particular battle rather more fully than usual, for we shall meet Bendigo on several occasions again, when a repetition of

"BRASSEY" (JOHN LEECHMAN).

his style will be less necessary. They were both in splendid condition, and had undoubtedly taken the greatest pains with their training. Brassey had never looked so well. It was not to be wondered at, for he had ample time, and no expense had been spared, whilst Jem Mapping had given him his greatest attention, and there was no better man in the Midlands to prepare a youngster for the lists. There could be no denying it, he was a fine, strapping specimen of manhood by all accounts, was John Leechman, and as hard as nails, for his work in the foundry kept his muscles in perfect trim. His limbs were not of the heavy order, and although he weighed just 12st he was of that clean build, well shaped, and with the perfect form of an athlete. He was of that make which indicated agility and looseness about the shoulders. His open face and clear complexion were, too, the index of perfect health, and, altogether he must have been a very fine fellow to look upon.

Bendigo was a shorter man than his opponent, being only 5ft 9¾in, but he weighed within half a pound of Brassey, scaling 11st 12lb; but he had the advantage in age, being six-and-twenty, his opponent being only twenty-two, and he looked a more powerful man. Bendigo's attitude was somewhat peculiar, for he stood slightly square, like the early school of boxers whose fighting attitudes have been illustrated in these pages. He kept, in sparring, his right foot foremost, and both arms close to the body. His head was usually on one side, and he stooped or crouched a little, which made him look shorter than he really was.

Immediately they had shaken hands for the last time over the scratch, Brassey was at it in an instant, for he let go full in Bendigo's face. But the latter was too quick for him, and neatly stopping the blow, let fly with the left and caught the Yorkshireman flush on the nose, drawing blood with the first blow. There was a tremendous cheer from more than two-thirds of the spectators, for Bendigo's friends were greatly in the majority. Now it must be known that Brassey was supposed to be a very fine wrestler, and his supporters felt that he had a trump card to play if he were outmatched at quickness in the sparring, for they knew what a tricky, clever fellow the Nottingham man was, and they had not long to wait to see how the Yorkshireman could tackle his foe at close quarters; for directly they faced each other, Brassey rushed in to catch his man, regardless of a smart half-arm hit from his opponent. They both held, and it was expected, by those who knew the Yorkshireman's qualities, that Bendigo would get a shaking-up with a cross-buttock. Their surprise, therefore, can be imagined when they saw Mr. Bendigo, after a short struggle, give their man one of the neatest back-falls possible. The enthusiasm was intense, and one report states that the general cry was, "Bendy wins! Bendy wins!" although the battle had only lasted just over two minutes.

Those who were near the ring stated that as Brassey went up next time his second, Jem Mapping, said: "Try for the goots," and the Yorkshireman did, and this

is what happened in the words of the reporter:—
"Leechman sent in a pile-driver, but Bendy dropped
his elbow, stopped the blow and let Brassey have his
left instantaneously smack between the eyes. So severe
was the blow that the Bradford man fell back a step.
Bendy, with astonishing rapidity, followed up with a
blow in the face and a tremendous right-hander on the
side of the head, which drove Brassey back, though it
did not knock him down. But the Yorkshireman pulled
himself together, roused by the exultant shouts of the
Sheffielders and Nottingham men, who were both jubilant over Bendy's success, and with a rush Brassey was
at close quarters once more. Each caught the other with
the right hand and fibbed away with the left, till the
Bradford man, who apparently was no better at this
game than at out-fighting, clutched Bendy with both
hands, and tried desperately hard to throw him: but
though awkwardly situated, Bendigo kept his legs, foiled
every attempt to get him down, and when at last they
fell together, it was Brassey who was undermost."

The above description is sufficient to illustrate the
difference in the quality of the two men, and to prove
conclusively that Bendigo, as he afterwards proved in
his fights for the Championship, was a magnificent
natural fighter, and had profited greatly by the scientific
tuition he had received.

It must not be supposed, however, that in the battle
under notice Bendigo had it all his own way, for in
the third round he was taken unawares and received
Brassey's great, powerful fist full in the stomach, which
sent him staggering back, and the Tykes yelled themselves hoarse. Their delight, however, was short-lived
for the Bradford man. Before Brassey could follow up
his success Bendy pulled himself together, and rushing
in they both clinched, and before anybody could say
Jack Robinson they saw the Yorkshireman's heels go up
in the air and his head come down thud on the turf. It
was one of the cleanest cross-buttocks ever witnessed.
The Lambs and the Blades knew not how to express
their delight, and everybody declared that it was the
proverbial horse to a hen on the Nottingham man, for
he was not only far superior as a fighter, but he could
beat the Tyke at his own game—wrestling.

The marvellous part of it all was, that Bendigo on
this occasion never attempted to go down to avoid, as
he did when in the ring with the gigantic Ben Caunt.
In all probability he felt that he was more than a match
for his opponent, although he took no liberties and gave
no chances away. It was quite certain that Brassey
was no match for his foe in generalship, and before the

fifth round was over the Yorkshireman was so knocked about the head that he went down in his corner and was very sick. Two to one was offered on Bendigo; but there were no takers, and his friends believed that it was all over bar the shouting. To be sure, Bendy was on several occasions, according to all accounts, very hard pressed, and he played the artful when on the ropes, and, having no room to defend himself, by going down to finish the round, and although the Tykes called "Foul," Brassey's own umpire agreed that nothing unfair had taken place. One writer upon this particular battle says:—"No doubt the Bradford man stood up in the good old-fashioned style, took his gruel without flinching, trusting only to his guard to keep off his adversary's blows, and having no recourse to tricks or dodges, in which respect his conduct was in marked contrast to that of his opponent, who twisted like an eel and skipped like a monkey about the ring, ducking and dodging and springing back to avoid being hit. But it does not therefore follow that Bendy's system of fighting was unfair or unmanly. Why should a man let himself be struck, if he can by any means avoid it? The object of a good boxer is to beat his adversary with as little damage to himself as possible, and the true test of science is the ability to thrash another man without getting mauled oneself. Bendigo fought just as old William Clarke used to bowl, with his head. He was no coward; but he had the sense to take care of himself, and the wit to devise all sorts of dodges to thwart the designs of his adversary."

We quite agree with these remarks, and that was the style of fighting which caused Bendigo to win so many battles, to climb to the highest rung of the pugilistic ladder, and to hold the Champion's belt upon two occasions.

It will serve no purpose to follow the remainder of the fight. Sufficient has been given to show how unequally the men were matched, and to give an idea of Mr. William Thompson's style of fighting, so that in the several engagements in which he will appear in order to obtain the Championship our readers will be able to follow his method in the ring without desiring a repetition and detailed accounts.

Brassey proved to have less and less chance every round they fought, and the punishment he received was terrible. He tried everything he could, and took all the advice of his seconds. He tried the rush, the waiting game, and the retiring tactics. But it was no use. He had found his master all round at the game and at

length he lost his temper, which was the worst possible
thing he could have done for himself and the best for
Bendigo. In the fifty-second round, getting exasperated
at the punishment he had received, being unable to
return, and half-blind, with face bleeding, he rushed in
and deliberately butted Bendigo with his head, and then,
grasping him by the thighs, tried to throw him a somersault. This outrageous act, of course, could not be
permitted, and as Bendigo dropped on his knees and
was taken by his seconds to his corner, cries from every
direction of "Foul" were heard. Merryman rushed to
the umpires and claimed the fight. There could be no
two opinions about it. It was the most deliberate foul
ever perpetrated in a twenty-four foot ring, and even Mr.
Bradlaugh, Brassey's umpire, admitted it readily, so the
verdict was given by Mr. James Hutchins, the referee,
in favour of Bendigo. There was a tremendous cheer,
and Sam Merryman threw up the towel and sponge in
the air, and went to his man and congratulated him.
Bendigo, immediately he heard it, jumped over the ropes
and back again, and played several antics, just to show
how fresh he felt, and was praised all round for his
brilliant performance, which brought him one step nearer
the Championship.

CHAPTER XXXV.

MRS. THOMPSON AS AN AMAZON.—BENDIGO'S DESPERATE
BATTLES WITH YOUNG LANGAN AND BILL LOONEY.—HIS
MARCH TO THE FRONT.

AFTER Bendigo had beaten Brassey, as described in
our previous chapter, he left Nottingham, and with the
money he had won, and with what he was able to borrow,
he took a small pub. at Sheffield, a town at which he
became as great a favourite as in that of his birth. The
Nottingham boys were very sorry to lose him, and his
mother must have felt it very much, for she was a queer
sort of a dame, and had the greatest affection in her
kind of way for Master William. Indeed, his fighting
proclivities were undoubtedly inherited from the mater's
side, for his father was a respectable member of society

iu Nottingham, and one of the cleverest fancy turners in the Midlands. It used to be Mrs. Thompson's boast that she, referring to her triplets, had suckled three of the greatest men living—the best fighter, the best mechanic, and the biggest fool in England. The "mechanic" was John Thompson, to whom we have already referred. He commenced business in an optician's shop, and became one of the finest surgical instrument makers in the town, whilst his fancy lathes, &c., were the admiration of the trade. He became very rich, and was admitted into the best society of Nottingham. But Mrs. Thompson's favourite was Bendy. At various times correspondents have sent to us extraordinary stories about this lady, who lived to be a great age. One of our informants told us that he met her at the Three Crowns, in Parliament Street, Nottingham, on the night of the final deposit for the match between Tom Paddock and her son, when she said to Bendigo, shaking her fist in his face, "If you don't lick him, I'll slap your chops for you when you come home." "She was," our same informant tells us, "full of fight, and you may guess what sort of a woman she was, when I tell you that she remarked to me that she could always tell how the fight was going, when her son was doing battle with some doughty rival, by the tick of the clock. 'When Bill fought the Deaf 'Un,' she continued, 'it said, "Ben-dy, Ben-dy, by G—d!" If it had said, "Deaf 'Un," I'd have up and smashed its —— face.'"

She must, indeed, have been a dear old lady, and Master William must have missed her very much when he left his native town and went to Sheffield. Although he did very well at his little tap, Bendy could never settle down in one place, so he was soon on the road again, giving sparring exhibitions, during which he came to London. There he became a nightly visitor at Jem Burn's house in Air Street, and to the delight of the members of the "Gentleman's Sparring Club" he would give exhibitions with the gloves and crack his comical "wheezes." He soon became a great favourite at the King's Arms, and Jem Burn offered to back him against Fitzmaurice, who had fought Deaf Burke. The friends of Fitz, however, shied at the proposal. It was a very jolly life Bendigo was leading in town, but it was by no means profitable, so in September of 1836 he once more found himself in Nottingham with, it is stated, only one solitary sovereign in his pocket.

But Bendigo had some good patrons there, especially Mr. Jepherson and his friend, Joe Whitaker, of Ramsdale House, and when he told them that he would like to have

another cut at it in the roped arena, they promised to find
him somebody and to plank down the necessary money.
There had been several challenges for Bendy after his
battle with Brassey ; but as Master William had plenty
of money he preferred travelling around, so he took no
heed of the offers made to him. On his return, how:
ever, he was glad to accept the first presented, which
was from Jack Flint, of Coventry. After two deposits,
though, it fell through, Flint preferring to pay instead
of fighting. Then our hero was informed that there were
three candidates waiting for him at Liverpool, so he
thought the best thing to do would be to visit that town.
On December 1, 1836, he journeyed by the Liverpool
coach, the " Regulator," with Mr. Brandreth, one of his
backers, and arriving in that city, put up at Jem Ward's
new hotel in Williamson Square. No little curiosity was
displayed to see the Nottingham man, and on the same
evening of his arrival Bill Looney, Tom Bitton, Bob
Hampson, Charley Langan, and Massa Molyneaux were
all down at Jem Ward's to run their critical eyes over
Bendigo. The latter gave the preference to the Black,
and it was thought that a match might be arranged ; but
Massa wanted Bendy to reduce to 11st 7lb, Molyneaux's
weight being only 11st 2lb. This was refused, and
although the Black's backers offered to waive the question
of weight if Bendy would stake £100 to £50, or £75 to
£50, nothing came of it, for Mr. William Thompson was
pretty artful, and did not see the force of laying the
odds when he could get an easier job at evens.

When it was discovered that it was all off with Massa,
Mr. Ford, of the Bell Tavern, Liverpool, came forward
and offered to back Young Langan against Bendigo, the
stake to be £25 or £50 a-side. This was at once accepted,
and on December 6 a meeting was held at Mr. Ford's, the
articles were drawn, and the men agreed to fight on Tuesday, January 24, 1837, within fifty miles from Liverpool.

Charles Langan was a Dublin boy (no relation, we
believe, to Jack Langan, who had fought Tom Spring),
and had been brought over to Liverpool by Mr. M'Ardle,
a well-known Irish sportsman. Langan had flown at
rather high game, for he had induced his backers to
match him with Deaf Burke, and he had been put under
Peter Taylor for preparation. The Deaf 'Un having
failed to bring Jem Ward to the scratch, was ready to
take on anybody, it will be remembered, before he left
for America, so he was quite willing to oblige the young
Irishman for even so low a sum as £25 a-side. But on
the eve of the fight Young Langan was run in for assault-
ing the police, and bound over to keep the peace. There
were not a few who declared that this was done inten-

tionally, as he funked it at the finish. This was the only match Langan had had in England, so he was comparatively a dark horse, although the manner in which he performed with the mittens found him plenty of friends, and Mr. M'Ardle had great confidence in his abilities. He certainly had made vast strides since his arrival in Liverpool, under the tuition of Matt Robinson.

Through a little coldness which had sprung up between Peter Taylor and Langan, the former refused to train him, so was engaged by Jem Ward to look after Bendigo, whilst Dan Donovan had charge of the Irishman. Bendy trained at Runcorn, then only a small place. Although Bendy at first showed no disposition to settle down, and on one occasion gave his trainer the slip and made his way to Chester and had a rare spree, he was ultimately checked in his wild career, and went into a course of preparation which was most satisfactory to all concerned.

Jem Ward won the toss for choice of place, and as both men had expressed a wish to fight near Newcastle-under-Lyme, that Staffordshire town was selected as the rendezvous, the actual battlefield to be decided upon on the morning of the fight. On the Monday both men arrived at Newcastle, Bendigo, with his several friends, making the Albion, then kept by the veteran ex-pugilist, Turner, their headquarters; whilst Langan in company with his illustrious namesake, Jack Langan, Matt Robinson, and Dan Donovan put up at the Three Swans, just opposite. A council of war was held at Sam Turner's house, when it was decided to pitch the ring at the little village of Woore, about eight miles from Newcastle.

Unfortunately the Tuesday morning was a soaker, the rain falling in torrents and the wind blowing with great violence. The men were conveyed to Woore in covered carts, and they took refuge in the two inns of the village —Bendy in the Falcon, and Langan in the Horse and Jockey. Still the storm raged, and it was thought at one time that it would be impossible to bring the fight off. However, at noon the wind dropped and the rain ceased, so it was determined to lose no time. The number of people gathered round the ring amounted to less than 500, for the fearful weather, combined with the secrecy as to the whereabouts, had choked off all but the most enthusiastic sportsmen. The company was not kept waiting long, for the men were soon in the ring, Bendigo sporting his favourite blue colours and the Irishman his green. The betting was 6 to 4 on Bendigo, and a deal of money was on the issue of the fight, the Nottingham lads, who were present, standing their townsman to a man. The ground was little better than a quagmire, and it was evident that the combatants would have all their work cut out to keep upon their legs.

Bendigo opened the ball in a very lively manner, for Langan, after a little sparring, shot out his left, but failed to get home well, and the Nottingham man instantly countered with a tremendous smack on the Irishman's cheek with his right. Langan hit back, but only grazed Bendigo's chin, and caught another slap in the face from the right. The Notts man then gave one of his peculiar ducks, and planted his right with a terrific spank on Langan's ribs, and followed the blow up instantly with a slasher from the left upon the nose. Then, amidst the cheers of the Nottingham men, Bendigo went to work in fine style, slogging away with both hands, hard and fast, twice landing his left heavily on Charley's nose, from which the crimson fluid began to ooze, and was hailed with frantic shouts of " First blood to Bendy."

Such is the account of the opening of the battle. It goes on to state that the Notts man did not have it all his own way though, and once or twice it was a near thing for him, for he felt the wet and cold, and shivered from head to foot, and it was only by resorting to the dropping business that he saved himself. Once recovered from the chill, however, he became too much for his antagonist. It is needless to follow the details of the fight. In the thirty-first round Bendigo, to the amazement of even his friends, knocked Langan clean off his pins, stretching him on the broad of his back. From that moment the future Champion never gave his adversary a chance ; he rained blows upon him like hail, thrashed him all over the ring, and, though he never fairly knocked Langan off his pins again, yet he forced him to go down every time. One account says : ' Bendy's hitting at this point was terrific—every blow came straight from the shoulder, and flew to its mark like a bullet. Langan's left eye was speedily closed, and the right was soon following suit, whilst the blood streamed from half a dozen cuts on his lacerated face. In the thirty-second round Bendy landed his left with fearful severity on Langan's right eye, closed, and threw him. This blow practically settled the fight. When Charley was lifted on his second's knee, it was evident that he was perfectly blind ; both peepers were shut beyond all power of lancet to open. It was useless sending the helpless and sightless man up to fight any more, and Matt Robinson stepped forward and said he should take his man away, and the battle was awarded to the Bold Bendigo.

This decisive victory of the Nottingham man made him very many friends, and as he was so well received in Liverpool he took Jem Ward's advice and remained, there, taking some boxing rooms and teaching the manly art. A fortnight after the battle Bendy took a benefit at the Gothic Rooms, when Jem Ward publicly announced that he was prepared on behalf of Bendigo to make a match with any 12st man in England for £50 or £100 a-side, or give Langan another chance for the same amount. But the friends of the Irishman did not respond, and it was clear that they considered Master Bendigo a wee bit too good for their " bhoy."

Meanwhile Bendigo began to ask himself the question as to the possibility of making a bid for the Championship. In 1836-7, Jem Ward still claimed it, although he had refused to fight Deaf Burke, as our readers will remember, for a less sum than £500, and the Deaf 'Un had gone to America in disgust. Now just about this time, in the spring of 1837, there appeared a challenge full of bounce and brag from Will Looney, of Liverpool, offering to fight any man in the world for from £100 to £200 a-side. This Jem Ward could not pass over, so he replied as follows :—" Perceiving a challenge from a person of the name of Looney (although I have practically retired from the Ring for some time), I cannot refuse so tempting an offer ; and as there are no big ones in the Ring, I will accommodate this great and mighty hero for his own sum of £200 a-side."

Then came a letter from the Liverpool man, stating that he, of course, thought Jem Ward had retired from the Ring, and that he did not mean to include him ; but barring him, Bill Looney would fight any man in the world. So on Tuesday, April 11, 1837, a meeting was held at Matt Robinson's, the Molly Maloney Tavern, Liverpool, at which Looney, Ward, and several sportsmen were present. Bill had been so much chaffed about the Championship business, that he declared that he was not afraid of Ward, and if he liked he would fight him for £100 . But £200 being his original offer, the Champion positively refused to fight for less, so the whole matter fell through. Then Mr. Brandreth, who was present, asked Looney if his challenge still held good to fight anybody in the world bar the Champion. On receiving a reply in the affirmative, he said that Bendigo could be backed to fight him for £50 a-side. This Looney at once agreed to, for he had been anxious for a meeting with the Nottingham man ever since that worthy defeated Young Langan. William Looney, who was looked upon by many as a worthy successor to Jack Carter, the Lancashire Champion, was twenty - nine years of age, and had entered the Ring in February, 1831, when he beat George Hughes, the brickmaker, a much heavier, more experienced, and stronger man than himself. He next defeated Will Fisher twice, in the October of 1832 and March of 1833. Both battles were well contested, one lasting nearly four hours, and the other just upon three. Looney had also beaten on three occasions Bill Hampson, who in his turn had defeated both Fisher and Tom Bitton. The match with which we are dealing was just to Bill's liking, for he had tried on several occasions to meet Bendigo, but the Notts man seemed rather shy of the job, so Looney had been idle for a considerable time ; in the meanwhile he had taken a pub. in Hood Street, Liverpool, and was doing fairly well.

Tuesday, June 13, 1837, was the day fixed, and the place selected was Chapel-en-le-Frith, Derbyshire, a pretty village some twenty miles south-east of Manchester. There had not been so much excitement over a fight in Derbyshire for many a long day, and we are told that " Drags, chaises, tilburys, barouches, dog-carts, shandrydans, gigs, and tax-carts crowded the road, whilst the foot people were to be numbered by hundreds." The " Lambs " from Nottingham were pretty numerous, and altogether the spectators must have mustered some 2,000. Amongst the sportsmen we read the following were present :—From Liverpool came Matt Robinson, Jem Ward, Will Fisher, Tom Bitton, Bob Hampson, and the great Jack Langan, at the time one of the most successful publicans in the Mersey port. From Manchester came Sam Pixton, Levi Eckersley, Sam Rutter, Charley Jones, and old Jack Carter. Birmingham sent Harry Preston, Arthur Matthewson, Tass Parker, Hammer Lane, and Young Johnny Broome ; whilst Nottinghamshire was answerable for the appearance of Sam Turner, Bill and George Atkinson, Sam Merryman, Bill Winterflood, and huge Ben Caunt.

The weather was delightful, and the spot as pretty as could be found in all England. Mr. Richard Bethell was appointed referee, and all was quickly in readiness, 5 to 4 being laid on Looney. Without going into the particulars of this prolonged battle, we are safe in saying that it was certainly the hardest nut the bold Bendigo had been called upon to crack. One account says:—"It was an extraordinary battle, and a grander one it would be impossible to see. The interest of the spectators was never allowed for a moment to flag, for just as Bendy seemed to have made the fight safe for himself, Looney would make a wonderful effort, bringing one of his terrific right-handers to bear or throw his man in a manner which amazed his friends and foes alike, and caused Bendy's backers to tremble for their money. Once or twice the Nottingham man showed something uncommonly like a disposition to

cut it, and resorted to the unmanly practice of deliberately
throwing himself down to avoid being hit. Shouts of
disapprobation greeted every one of these suspicious
tricks of Bendy, and the storm of disapproval which
they raised appeared to shame him into abandoning
them. Slowly the fight went on. They had been at it
for two hours. Bendy retained his strength the longest.
Poor Bill was very nearly blind; he had lost a lot of

BILL LOONEY.

blood too, and the fearful battering he had received
about the head must have knocked him pretty well silly.
At length so exhausted were the two men that there was
no real fighting at all, it was but a pulley-hauley match,
and it was only a question of who would be the first to
collapse. At length Bill became totally blind, for he
rushed past Bendigo, and was carried on by his own
impetus to the ropes, where he caught hold of one of the

stakes. Clinching his right hand fiercely, and holding it level with his head, as if determined to make one final effort, Looney dashed in the direction of his foe, but Bendigo received him with open arms, and catching him by the waistband with one hand, and under the chin with the other, hoisted him up with his last ounce of strength and canted him on to his head. This was the finisher. Looney remained insensible, deaf to the call of time."

Bendy was declared the winner, having won the battle in two hours and twenty-two minutes, going hammer and tongs throughout the whole of that time. Many declared that this was the finest battle Bendigo ever fought. Further than a black eye and sore ribs, he was little hurt, and he walked half a mile to his carriage, and went to Newton Races the next day with some swells on a coach; whilst Looney was so punished that he was compelled to remain at Chapel-en-le-Frith until the following Thursday in a sad plight. He was fearfully hurt and wounded, three of his teeth being knocked out, whilst the loss of blood had really been serious.

Yet Bill Looney would not give Bendigo best, and he challenged the Nottingham man to fight him again for the same amount. This Bendigo refused, declaring that for nothing less than £100 would he enter the ring again with him. So the affair dropped through, and Bendigo became more popular than ever, for he had now fought his way well nigh to the pinnacle of his success, and was within measurable distance of the Championship, of which we shall speak in the next chapter.

<hr />

CHAPTER XXXVI.

BENDIGO'S SECOND BATTLE WITH BEN CAUNT.—A DISGRACEFUL RING SCENE.

AND now we come to the second battle between Ben Caunt and Bendigo, which was arranged to take place at Skipworth Common, Yorkshire, on April 3, 1838. Both these men had practically entered the Prize Ring together, they were destined to tread the ladder of fame side by side, and to meet half way, and again at the top. Their first battle, which we have recorded in a former chapter, proved two things distinctly, that Bendigo was

one of the trickiest, most artful, and quickest pugilists
in the Ring, and that Caunt, if a bit slow, had enormous
strength and unflinching pluck. After the latter's fight
with Bendigo he rested for two years, not finding anybody who would care to take such a mountain of flesh
on. But in 1837 Ben Caunt fought and thrashed in
quick succession two big countrymen, Boneford and
Butler, defeating the first-named in fourteen rounds and
the latter in six. Neither of these men had done anything of importance in the Ring, yet they were fine
fellows and very formidable antagonists, consequently
Benjamin made many adherents over the affair. His
friends, indeed, thought he had improved to such an
extent that they might let him tackle his old original
opponent once more. The only difficulty in the way was
that Bendy had raised his price and would not look
at a match for less than £100 a-side. He was certainly
entitled to stand out for this amount, for, having no
income, and depending entirely upon his Ring performances, his exhibition boxing, and his teaching, he
had earned sufficient fame to warrant him putting up
his price. He had won brilliant victories over Brassey,
Young Langan, and Bill Looney, and what is more he
had been taken in hand by Jem Ward, who made no
secret about his intention to match Bendigo against
poor old Deaf Burke immediately upon his return from
America. As we have before stated, his old opponent,
Looney, did all he knew to induce the Nottingham man
to fight him for less than £100, but Bendigo would not
reduce it. Equally so did Tom Bitton, of Liverpool,
try his hardest to get on for the stake of fifty. No, the
Bold One had quite made up his mind that he would
not enter the lists for a less sum than a century, and
he publicly announced that it was sheer waste of time
for anybody to challenge him for less. So Caunt's
friends, Mr. Braithwaite and Captain Hemyng, who
believed implicitly in the powers of the Hucknall Torkard
giant, resolved to back Big Ben, and see if he could not
turn the tables upon the Bold One.

Caunt himself had never been satisfied with the
result, declaring that but for the shifty tactics of his
opponent he could have won easily, and openly stated
and firmly believed that he could, given the opportunity, easily thrash Mr. William Thompson on their
second meeting. So the £100 being found for him by
his two patrons, the match was made to come off in the
neighbourhood of Doncaster, and the date fixed was
April 3, 1838.

Bendigo was principally backed from Liverpool, where
he had become a great favourite, and found a valued friend

in Jem Ward. He went into training again with his old mentor, Peter Taylor, near the Mersey, and made splendid progress. Caunt was vigorously put through the mill by his uncle, Ben Butler, at Appleby, in Leicestershire, and afterwards under Young Molyneaux, the Black, who came to put a polish on the Big 'Un.

Nothing of any interest happened during the time that the men were preparing, but as the day drew near the greatest excitement prevailed, for the office was sent to London, Liverpool, Manchester, Sheffield, and Nottingham that if they made their way to Doncaster they would find themselves "on the spot" for the important business on hand. Many took the Glasgow Mail from town, starting from the Bull and Mouth, Aldersgate Street, on the morning of April 2, and after a long cold drive, for the weather was singularly cheerless for the season, and arriving in Doncaster put up at the Salutation or Angel, then famous coaching and sporting houses in the town of gee-gees. The town by Monday evening was quite lively, and so many arrivals had taken place that it was with difficulty that sleeping accommodation could be procured. From Liverpool, Sheffield, and Birmingham conveyances of every description arrived, and all the inns of the town and upon the roads were besieged.

Bendigo was favourite over night at 6 to 4, but there were not so many takers. In the morning all were up betimes (that is to say, those who had gone to bed), the greatest bustle and excitement being apparent, everybody desiring to know the spot fixed upon to bring off the battle. At the White Swan, at Askerne—a pretty little village about seven miles out of Doncaster on the Selby Road—Bendigo had taken up his abode, in order to be out of the turmoil of the town. He had arrived on the Sunday before, and many of his personal friends had been over to see him ; and on the morning of the fight Bendy held quite a levée. All who knew him and witnessed his first fight with Caunt, pronounced him the very picture of health and condition, and he declared that he should give that "great chuckle-headed navvy," as he called Ben, an easy licking, and that he felt that the money was already in his pocket.

Ben Caunt was at the same time receiving visitors at the Hawke Arms, some two miles distant, attended by his father, Uncle Butler, and Young Molyneaux. At eleven o'clock in the morning the word is passed to take the Selby Road, and the news flies like wildfire, for away go drags, chaises, gigs, horsemen, and pedestrians helter-skelter after Jem Crutchley and Bill Fisher, who have charge of the ring paraphernalia. They make a halt, but before the stakes are driven in and the crowd

is got into order, a magistrate rides up, attended by a
posse of police, and declares that he will allow nothing
of the kind to take place where he has jurisdiction. This
is dreadfully annoying, but there is nothing for it but
to clear off. Jem Ward then takes charge of the expe-

YOUNG LANGAN.

dition, and after a consultation it is determined to make
for Hatfield, a few miles to the south of the spot origi-
nally selected.

After much difficulty, and not without several interruptions by the mounted police, they finally cross a
bridge over the Ouse, which divides the East from the

West Riding of Yorkshire, and find themselves in Selby.
Here the crowd halts for a short time, when they are
conducted for some five or six miles and turn down a
quiet lane, and in a hay-field the ring is pitched. Just
then a number of the members of the Badsworth Hunt
arrive on the scene, and in their scarlet coats and
mounted on their nags they stop to see the fun.

So great is the delay through the provoking interference of the police, that it is half-past five before the
men are ready to enter the ring. Bendigo is the first to
throw in his castor, but his toilet cannot be properly
completed, as Young Langan, who is looking after his
spiked shoes and some of his fighting toggery, has got
separated from the party, and is hopelessly lost. Bendigo
does not trouble himself much about the absence of his
shoes, and Caunt having entered the ring and completed his preparations, they stand before each other for
the second time to see who shall reign supreme.

It will be unnecessary for us to describe the appearances of the two gladiators, as they have appeared before
our readers on a previous occasion. Caunt, if anything,
looked bigger than he had done when we met him on the
first occasion, but Bendigo was in magnificent condition. As usual, the Nottingham man commenced his
manœuvring tactics, dodging backwards and forwards
to draw his man. But Ben had had experience of that
kind of business before, and was not going to be caught.
He would not move a step. In vain Bendigo tantalised
him, but Caunt kept his temper and his ground. At
length the Bold One, having exhausted his wiles, came
closer, made a feint with his right and drove his left into
Ben's face, just over the left eye. Without trying to return,
Caunt at once closed and threw his arms around Bendigo, and with a tremendous hug nearly squeezed the
breath out of him. But Bendy wriggled about like an
eel, and although Caunt tried to throw him, he managed
to slip from his grasp and take refuge on Mother Earth.

Caunt's face (according to the best account we have
read of this interesting mill) was very flushed when he
came up for the second round, and the slap over the
eye had caused him to feel riled by the frown on his
face. On the instant they came together, Ben rushed
in and went at it in a most determined manner, hitting
out right and left. So long were his arms that Bendigo
found it difficult to counter, and he therefore beat a
retreat. Caunt followed briskly, and the Bold One
received one or two heavy blows on the side of the head.
Then he steadied himself, and as his ponderous foe
came at him with a tremendous blow aimed at the head,
he ducked and avoided it, at the same time, getting under

Ben's guard, gave him such a terrific pelt in the mouth
that at once set the crimson flowing, and amidst cheers
the first event was scored to Bendigo. Eventually the
Big 'Un closed and threw his man.

In the third bout Bendigo played the artful dodger
again, worried his opponent until he nearly lost his
temper, when he feinted and dashed in with the left,
catching him full in the mouth. Ben rushed at his
man and got another grip of him, then, swinging him
round, threw him to the ground and placed h·s ponderous figure upon him. Caunt was hooted and hissed
for this; but it was perfectly fair and quite in accordance
with the rules of the Ring. But it didn't suit Bendy,
and he was in no mood to come within distance
of those terrible arms again, so he kept a respectful
distance. For quite five minutes not a blow was struck
on either side, and the spectators became very impatient,
calling out to the men to "Get to work; don't keep us
here all night." At length they got at it again, and
Bendigo received another embrace and a fearful throw.

To go through the incidents of this fight would be
impossible with the space at our command. We will
pass over the many rounds, all of which served to prove
that Bendigo was by far the better fighter; but Caunt's
strength held him in such good stead that, had not
Bendy gone down to avoid, and showed that marvellous
agility in getting out of danger, he must have lost the
battle before the twelfth round. After that the excitement was intense and the scene around the ring disgraceful. Bendigo, becoming more daring, got to closer
quarters, and time after time landed his sharp, bony
fists on Caunt's face, cutting him to ribbons, until the
Big 'Un bore down upon him like a three-decker under
full press of canvas, firing broadsides right and left,
and then grappling with his foe. Bendigo was unable to
avoid his antagonist on this occasion, and before he could
drop Caunt had him up in his arms and carried him to
the ropes, when he squeezed him against the centre
stake in a most brutal manner. Here is a description
of the scene that occurred, written by one who was
there:—"So terrible was the force brought to bear
upon his antagonist, that Bendigo was almost deprived
of sense and motion. Caunt's fingers were round
his throat, and the whole of his massive frame was
pressing Bendy against the stake. The spectators, disgusted at this mode of fighting, which was certainly
more unmanly and objectionable than Bendy's dropping
tactics, grew furious, and yelled out to Caunt, 'Thou
big, ugly tooad: dost thou call that foightin'? Whoy,
the little 'un would lick thee and two or three more

such if thee'd nobbut foight fair.' Ben's savage blo d was up, however, and he cared not a jot for their remonstrances. He had got the man who had been hitting him such stinging blows for the last six rounds in his power, and he didn't mean to let him go till he had squelched the life out of him. That, at least, seemed to be his object, for he was mad with cruel fury, and was gloating fiendishly over poor Bendy's livid features, which were absolutely purple from the awful pressure on his windpipe. In vain the people shouted ' Let him go; he'll be killed !' Bendigo's neck was over the ropes, and no doubt there would have been an end to Mr. William Thompson's career had not a rush been made by some of his friends, who with their clasped knives cut the ropes. One account says that be was nearly dead, and that when carried to his corner the blood was oozing from his ears. The mob made a rush for the ring, and it was evident that they meant mischief, and that Caunt would have been very roughly handled had not the ringkeepers surrounded him and beaten them off, for the Nottingham ' Lambs' were mustered in great force, and were furious at the manner in which their Bold Bendigo had been handled. As it was, the confusion can be better imagined than described. Referee and umpires were swept away from the ring, and a free fight ensued in which fists, sticks, and whips were freely used. Fortunately the ringkeepers were numerous and worked together, and ultimately beat the crowd back, when an attempt was made to repair the ring. This was found to be impossible, so the men had to continue the battle with one side open. Of course, the time occupied in the *mélée* was an advantage to Bendigo, who, having been attended to by his seconds, had somewhat recovered, although still very shaky when the men toed the scratch once more and commenced the thirty-ninth round."

The disorder still continued, and it was impossible to see really what the men were doing, the crowd pressing on the ropes. So we have but a very meagre account of the remainder of the fight. It would appear, though, that Bendy pulled himself together in a marvellous manner, and that his hitting was terrific, he getting all the best of it. In the fiftieth round Caunt claimed the battle on a foul, declaring that his opponent had kicked him whilst he was down, and appealed to referee and umpires to award him the fight. But the officials declared that they had observed nothing that was unfair, so the referee ordered them to continue. So great was the disturbance around the ring that it was a wonder the men were able to fight at all, and every moment it

was expected that ropes, stakes, seconds, and principals
would be swept away. Still they came up time after
time, and fought as many as seventy-five rounds, and all
was in favour of Bendigo, who literally cut his antagonist's face to pieces, avoiding punishment himself in a
marvellous manner. But during the last-mentioned
round a change came over the scene. Bendigo, whose
shoes were not spiked, slipped, his friends declared, and
went down without a blow being struck. He was up in
an instant, but Young Molyneaux saw his opportunity of
saving the fight for his man, and claimed the act as
intentional, appealing to the referee. That worthy, it
would seem, knew very little about his duties, for he
permitted everybody, right and left, to give him advice,
and, in spite of the protests and threats of Bendigo's
supporters, decided that, as the Nottingham man had
gone down without a blow, it was a foul act, and that the
fight would go to Caunt.

With a tremendous shout Molyneaux threw his hat in
the air, and nobody was more surprised than Caunt at
the decision. There was a fearful row about the matter,
and needless to say more fighting amongst the crowd.
Bendigo was mad with rage, and shouted, "By G——
he shan't have the colours though," and seizing them
he untied them from the stake and fastened them
round his throat. Caunt was pushed into a carriage,
but the crowd surrounded it and attempted to drag
him out to renew the fight. Of course, this he refused
to do, and it was only when his friends, aided by
the ring-keepers, beat off the ruffians that he was able
to leave the battle-field and make his way to the Hawke
Arms, Selby, where his wounds were dressed. Bendigo
gave notice that, as the umpires had not been consulted,
the stakes were not to be paid over to Caunt, or he
would commence an action. However, a meeting took
place, and the umpires having upheld the referee's decision, the money was paid and another match made
between the men to play off the rubber, for £200 and
the Championship of England, all about which we shall
describe in a future chapter.

CHAPTER XXXVIII.

To thee I send these lines, illustrious Caunt !
Of courage tried and huge as John of Gaunt,
To thee my foolscap with black ink I blot
To tell the Big 'Un Brassey fears him not,
And that in battle, should the fates allow,
He means to snatch the laurel from his brow,
At all his boasted pluck and prowess smile,
And give him pepper in superior style.

Yes ! Gallant Caunt, next Tuesday will declare
If you or I the Champion's belt shall wear,
And be assured, regardless of the tin,
I'll go to work and do my best to win,
Prove that in fight *one* Briton can surpass ye,
And if you ask his name, I thunder *Brassey.*

It is not often that we find a challenge for a fight
couched in heroic verse, but the above lines were sent
to Ben Caunt from the stalwart Yorkshireman, Brassey,
and were printed in the sporting journals of the day,
under the heading, " An Heroic Epistle from Brassey to
Ben Caunt."

It was on the evening of September 22, 1840, that an
unusual foregathering took place at the Castle Tavern,
Holborn. There was evidently something unusual on
the *tapis*, for we read that the old parlour, beloved by
sportsmen, was crowded with the cream of the London
Fancy, both professional and amateur. There were
veteran ring-goers present, who had seen Mendoza fight
Jackson for the Championship, and had been present at
all the great battles which have been described in these
pages since that event. There were there young bloods
having their first introduction to London life. There were
well-known bookmakers, fashionable jockeys, and pugilistic celebrities of all weights and ages. This representative company had assembled to give a hearty welcome to
our old friend, Ned Painter, the only man who had ever
beaten Tom Spring, and who had come up from Norwich,
and who had brought with him his young *protégé,*
Brassey, of Bradford, who had accepted the challenge
thrown down by big Ben Caunt.

The occasion of the meeting was the third deposit in
the match which had been made for £200. It must

have been a jolly evening, according to one account
before us, for we read that the greeting Ned Painter
received was tremendous as he entered and took his seat
on the right of his old antagonist, Tom Spring, who was
in the chair, whilst Brassey sat on the worthy host's
left. Mr. Vincent Dowling, editor of *Bell's Life*, proposed the health of Ned Painter ("Flat-nose," as he was
called in Norwich), which was given with three
times three, and with musical honours. Then Painter
got on his pedestals and asked the company to drink to
his dear old friend, Tom Spring, after thanking them
for the warm welcome he had received. Passers-by in
Holborn must have been startled by the cheering which
followed Ned's speech and continued until Tom got on
his feet to return thanks. We read : " With beaming
face he told us how delighted he was to see an old opponent under his roof, the only man that had ever plucked
the laurel from his brow, a reflection, however, that in
no respect diminished the pleasure of the interview, for
he thought the true character of the British pugilist was
founded on the fact that the moment a battle was decided
all animosity ceased between the combatants, and their
friendship was riveted the tighter. This manly sentiment
was received with loud cheers, emphasised as it was by
the two old antagonists standing up and shaking hands
cordially with one another."

Then the business of the evening was attended to ;
Ned Painter putting down the money for Brassey, and
Peter Crawley doing ditto for Caunt. An announcement was made by Tom Spring, that Brassey would
take his benefit on the following Monday at the Bloomsbury Assembly Rooms, and give the Fancy a taste of
his quality with the gloves. After that the remainder
of the evening was given up to harmony, and when we
glance at a list of the songs chanted, and learn that the
meeting continued until after 2 a.m., on the following
morning, we can imagine that they had a very jolly
time of it.

At the benefit on the following Monday, too, there was
a tremendous muster, and certainly Brassey must have
been more than satisfied with the enthusiastic reception
accorded him. Earls, right honourables, and baronets
assembled to see what the big Yorkshireman could do, and
his set-to with the gloves—Tom Spring being his antagonist—was watched with no end of interest. Of course,
Brassey's style was coarse and rough, as compared with
that of the scientific, graceful master of the art. Yet
he impressed the company with the idea that he could
hit hard, and that he was quick enough to give a lot of
trouble to any man who stood up to him.

19

And now, perhaps, it will be right only to say a few words about the previous career of Brassey, who was an aspirant for the Championship. His real name was John Leechman, and he was born at Bradford on January 1, 1815, his average weight during his Ring career being 12st, and his first battle recorded was with Thomas Hartley, for £2 a-side, and took place at Eccles Moor, in 1831, Brassey winning in one hour and fifteen minutes. He next met and defeated Ned Batterson for the extraordinary sum of £3 5s. a-side, the men fighting seventy-two rounds in one hour and fifty-two minutes. He afterwards fought and beat George Ireson, of Salford, near Manchester, for £5 a-side, in the May of 1833. In the same month he fought Young Winterflood, of Nottingham, a well-known clever pugilist, but after doing battle for upwards of an hour they ended with a wrangle, and a draw was the result. On April 24, 1835, he defeated Jem Bailey for £10 a-side, and in the January of the following year beat Tom Scrutton for £20 a-side, in seventeen rounds. Then came his defeat by Bendigo, which we have already described. This took place near Sheffield on May 24, 1836, and was for £25 a-side. He fought Jem Bailey for £25 a-side, at Hales Green, near Pulham, Norfolk, and beat him; Bailey, however, sued the stakeholder and recovered the money. Then came his battle for £50 a-side, with Young Langan, whom he defeated in seventy-five rounds at Woodhead, Cheshire, on October 8, 1839. This was Brassey's last encounter prior to the match with Ben Caunt, which we are about to describe. Certainly, he had not fought many first-rate men, yet his encounter with Young Langan was looked upon as a great performance, and brought his name prominently before the public. Accompanied by his guide, mentor, and friend, Mat Robinson, he visited Liverpool, Manchester, Leeds, Sheffield, Bradford, Hull, and Nottingham, taking benefits everywhere, and pulling in large sums of money, for he declared that he intended to throw down the gauntlet for the Championship as soon as he could raise the necessary £200. And so the match was made with the great Ben Caunt, and the deposits paid down punctually to Tom Spring, at the Castle, who acted as stakeholder.

Brassey took his breathings with Ned Painter, at Norwich, whilst Caunt trained in company with Peter Crawley, near Hatfield. The mere fact that these two men, Painter and Crawley, were retained to look after the warriors was sufficient guarantee that all was fair and above board, and proof that the contest would be fought out on its merits. So the interest taken in this contest for the Championship was much keener than usual.

Old stagers raked up their recollections of Gully and
Gregson, of Cribb and Molineaux, of Harry Pearce and
Jem Belcher, of Spring and Langan, and of Jem Ward
and Simon Byrne, and, after the fashion of old stagers,
of course, were unanimous in declaring that these two
new big 'uns were far inferior to the giants of a previous
generation, about whom we have written so much. But
still Brassey and Caunt were giants, and nobody could
deny that they were exceptionally big and powerful men,
and in those days size counted for very much.

The place chosen for the battle was a classic one in the
annals of the Prize Ring. It was the valley of Six Mile
Bottom, between Cambridge and Newmarket, where John
Gully had thrashed Bob Gregson in the autumn of 1807.

The date selected was that of the Newmarket Houghton
Meeting, and the time fixed was between eight and nine
o'clock in the morning of the 26th, so that it should not
interfere with those who desired to kill two birds with
one stone, and be in time for the racing. So on the
Monday both men left their training quarters, Brassey
journeying with Ned Painter to Newmarket, and putting
up at the Queen Victoria, whilst Caunt went to Little-
bury, in Essex, only a few miles from the Metropolis of
the Turf. Not much secrecy was observed, for it was
thought that, the racing being on, very little notice would
be taken of a large assemblage of sportsmen. Unfortunately, however, the news that the fight was to take
place on the Tuesday reached the ears of a gentleman
who had a fanatical aversion to the Prize Ring and all
its followers. This was the Rector of Cheveley, who
was also a Justice of the Peace. He declared that the
fight should not take place if he could help it. But in
the parlour of the Queen Victoria a secret conclave was
held, at which Jem Burn, Peter Crawley, Ned Painter,
Tom Spring, Young Molineaux, Johnny Broome, Dick
Curtis, and Old Tom Oliver were present, and at which
a scheme was devised to throw the reverend gentleman
off the scent.

Monday had been fine but cold, but on the Tuesday
morning the rain came down in torrents. This, however, does not appear to have damped the ardour of the
sportsmen, who had flocked to Newmarket, attracted by
the racing, the fight, or both, and rarely had the capital
of gee-gees been so full. Perhaps the presence of the
Queen and Prince Albert had caused many to arrive,
although, of course, none of that class knew or cared much
about the battle. They were there to support a fancy
bazaar which had been opened in aid of the medical
charities of the place. According to report, in spite of the
inclement weather, the streets were full of vehicles and

pedestrians soon after daybreak, and the greatest bustle
and excitement prevailed. The only dread was that
the police and the magistrates would appear upon the
scene. But the little ruse decided upon on the previous
evening worked exceedingly well. A messenger was sent
to the Rector of Cheveley, who declared that he had
come from the Chief Constable of Newmarket, and that
he was instructed to inform the reverend gentleman that
the fight was to take place at Mildenhall, in Suffolk.
His reverence, it would appear, fell into the trap readily
enough, for he arose immediately, although it was only
about six in the morning, and having sworn in a posse
of special constables, proceeded at once in the direction
of Mildenhall, where he patiently awaited the arrival of
the " breakers of the peace," whom he was resolved to
" prosecute with the utmost rigour of the law." For
hours did that unfortunate parson and his myrmidons
keep vigilant watch in the pelting rain, scouring the
lanes in every direction, and maintaining a perfect
cordon of outposts all round the village of Mildenhall.
Yet no sight of the approaching enemy rewarded their
patient vigil, and the credulous " beak " did not return
to Newmarket until the fight was over, a victim to the
clever hoax that had been perpetrated.

It had been settled that the men should be in the ring
as early as eight o'clock, and long before then Tom Oliver,
assisted by Clarke and others, had the roped arena fixed
up. On this occasion the ropes were new and the stakes
of extra thickness, in consideration of the brace of heavy-
weights who were to perform within the magic circle.
There was a very large muster of spectators, amongst
them a number of foreigners, who had come down to the
races, but who had never before witnessed a real genuine
British prize-fight. Amongst those present, too, were a
number of undergraduates from Cambridge University,
and a most distinguished audience of sportsmen. The
following is a list of a few present :—The Duke of Beaufort, with his son, the Marquis of Worcester; the Marquis of Exeter, the Earls of Chesterfield and Jersey,
Lord George Bentinck, and Lord Henry Fitzroy, Sir
John Shelley, the Hon. General Grosvenor, the Hon.
Captain Rous (so well known as the Admiral), Charles
Greville, George Payne, " Fullar " Craven, Delmé
Radcliffe, Tom Crommelin, Colonel Peel, Will Ridsdale,
and Mr. John Gully. It was the day of the Cambridgeshire, which in itself had attracted all these thorough
sportsmen, who could not resist a good mill in whatever
weather. Then there was a great muster of fighting
men present—Jem Burn, Johnny Hannan, Johnny
Broome, Dan Dismore, Johnny Walker, Young Dutch

Sam, and a host of others, all with their circles of admirers. There was Bendigo there, too, limping about on crutches, but still as light-hearted and comical as ^ver.

Brassey was the first to arrive, and it was not until nearly nine o'clock that Ben Caunt appeared on the

JEM HALL (BRASSEY'S SECOND).

scene, and at one time it was thought the Nottingham man would be too late, and that Brassey would claim forfeit, which would have been a terrible disappointment to the thousands who had assembled. Without waste of time the men were got into the ring; Caunt attended by Dick Curtis and Young Molineaux, and Brassey esquired by Jem Hall and Johnny Broome, which

created no end of amusement to see two such big men
seconded by such comparatively little ones. On entering the ring Caunt went up to Brassey and offered to lay
him a private bet on the result of the battle, but the
Yorkshireman, who at the best of times was none too
good tempered, took it as an offensive bit of bounce,
and turned from him with a scowl. Mr. Vincent
Dowling accepted the post of referee, and at five-and-
twenty minutes past nine the men stepped to the scratch
with the rain steadily falling upon their naked torsos.

Caunt looked by far the more formidable of the two,
for he stood 6ft 2½in, and scaled 14st 7lb; whilst Peter
Crawley had got him into such perfect condition, that
there did not seem to be a pound of superfluous flesh
upon his enormous figure. He wore a great Welsh wig
which, when removed, disclosed his closely-cropped
hair, and with his tremendous ears and high cheek-bones
he looked by no means a prepossessing person. Brassey's
visage was by no means inviting, and his fierce scowls
when fighting were said to be hideous. Immediately
" Time " was called Caunt rushed at his man, lashing
out his long arms like the sails of a windmill, but Brassey
managed to avoid these clumsy blows, and getting one in
on the giant's ribs, went to grass and finished the round.

As they came up for the second bout it was evident
that the Nottingham man meant playing a forcing
game, and Brassey seemed to have no desire to meet
him at too close quarters. In fact, at the commencement he seemed to be afraid of getting near to the
Herculean frame, and went down for the second time
without much provocation, being hissed by some of the
spectators. In the third round, however, Brassey nailed
his man on the nose and cheek with such slashing hits,
that the blood spurted from the big un's nostrils, and
Brassey went down.

Just as the men came up for the fourth round John
Gully, who was standing close to the ropes, turned round
to a knot of noblemen and gentlemen who were wagering
on the fight, and said, " I will back Brassey for any part
of a thousand." The words were scarcely out of his
mouth before old Ben Butler, Caunt's uncle and principal
backer, held up his hand and shouted " I'll gi' 'ee a
hundred, Muster Gully." " All right," said the veteran
gladiator, " you're on." But no one else for the moment
seemed inclined to back the big 'un. And when Caunt
appeared at the scratch, the state of his features was
not such as to inspire his friends with confidence. The
blood was still welling from his nose and from a deep
gash in his cheek, and the severity of Brassey's hitting
was thus palpably proved. Ben, too, was very un-

steady; he led off wildly with right and left, and seemed
to let fly at random. Brassey was not much better, and
the blows of both fell on one another's arms and shoulders,
doing no mischief whatever. When the Yorkshireman,
however, found Ben pressing him too close he went down
" grinning horribly a ghastly smile " as he did so. The
next eight rounds were a very poor exhibition of fighting,
and old stagers present drew very uncomplimentary
comparisons between the performances of these two
hulking pretenders and that of such men as Spring, or
Gully, or Cribb, or Bill Neate, or Big Brown of Bridgnorth. Caunt sent in some fearful blows, no doubt, any
one of which had it gone home would have been sufficient
to knock his man out of time ; but then he invariably
missed—his great shoulder of mutton fist time after
time flew harmlessly over Brassey's shoulder. The
Yorkshireman, however, was not much more successful ;
now and then he popped in a straight one with his left,
but with none of the stinging severity of the two
scorchers he had landed in the third round, and whenever Caunt rushed at him he dropped, whereupon Ben
would stand astride over him, pointing at him with
derision and contempt. Once or twice Brassey went
down so quickly that Ben had the greatest difficulty to
avoid treading on his prostrate foe. Many men would
have lost their temper at such shifty and unmanly
tactics, but Ben was not easily put out, and bore the
trying conduct of his adversary with imperturbable
phlegm. What astonished the spectators most, however, was the fact that when this Herculean giant did
get home a blow it appeared to have very little effect
upon Brassey. Ben's heaviest blows all missed their
mark, and at the close of the twelfth round neither
man was any more punished than at the end of the third.

It will be impossible for us, with the space at our
disposal, to describe all the rounds, for they were no less
than one hundred in number. At times the battle was
fearful. In the fifty-sixth Caunt planted his left
heavily on the right eye, but Brassey in return hit him
on the jaw with his right, and making up his mind for
further mischief, repeated the blow with terrific effect a
little below the same spot, Caunt countering at the same
time with the right. The collision is described as being
like that of two railway engines meeting at full speed.
Both men fell in opposite directions. Caunt lay prostrate,
apparently senseless, and Brassey was little better.
They both managed to come to time, however, and
Caunt as the fight progressed seemed to pull himself
together, Brassey only grew weaker. The remaining
rounds are not worth describing ; there was no real

fighting, neither man could do more than push the
other. Caunt pushed hardest and sent Brassey down
heavily every time, Ben as often as not falling over him,
unable to stop himself, so weak was he. For forty so-
called rounds this sort of thing went on ; Caunt retained
the strength of his legs, but could hardly do anything
with his arms, both hands being so terribly swollen that
he could not keep them closed, whilst Brassey lost the
use of both arms and legs, could neither stand nor hit,
and at last, at the close of the one-hundredth round,
when the battle had lasted an hour and a half, Johnny
Broome said his man should fight no more, and as
Brassey was too feeble to raise a protest Caunt was
awarded the battle.

CHAPTER XXXVIII.

TROUBLES ON THE ROAD.—BEN CAUNT AND NICK WARD.—
GREAT BATTLE FOR THE BELT.—ENDS IN A FIASCO.

IN the year 1840, towards the close, it was by no
means easy to decide who was entitled to call himself
Champion of England. It will be remembered that Jem
Ward had presented a belt, and appointed Bendigo his
successor to the title, which he had held for some fourteen years. It is very doubtful, though, that he had any
right to do this. The presentation took place on February
12, 1839. To be sure, Deaf Burke had challenged Ward,
and Bendigo had beaten the Deaf 'Un, so that, perhaps,
he had as much right or more to the title than anybody
at the time. It was about a year after this—to be particular, the March of 1840—that Bendigo met with the
serious accident which placed him completely *hors de
combat*, and left the Championship open once more. The
Fancy looked around for the coming man, and the most
likely one they found in the gigantic Ben Caunt, who
had, as we described in our previous chapter, just
managed to defeat Brassey by the skin of his teeth.
Indeed, Ben himself always said that it was the toughest
bit of work he ever accomplished, and it was just touch
and go.

Following this victory Ben Caunt had the stakes presented to him at Peter Crawley's house, the Queen's Head and French Horn, in Duke Street, Smithfield, at which a tremendous muster of the Fancy attended. In returning thanks to his friends, Caunt stated that he claimed the Championship, and although Nick Ward (who, it will be remembered, beat Deaf Burke) had challenged him to contest the title, he was afraid that it was all bounce, and that the brother of the ex-Champion was not inclined to meet him. This came to Jem's ears, and he at once wrote the following letter to the leading sporting journals of the day:—" The friends of Nick Ward have consulted, and consider (as his efforts in the Ring have been few, and as you, whose judgment, from long experience, is entitled to great weight, have expressed an opinion that Nick Ward never would be a first-rate man), that Caunt, who lays claim to the Championship, should, as a set-off to his superiority of weight and position, give odds to make a match. Nick Ward, without bouncing, is willing to fight Caunt if he will deposit £150 to Ward's £100.—Jem Ward."

This letter was written from the Star Hotel, Williamson Square, Liverpool, and created no small comment in sporting circles. Caunt made no direct reply, but on the Thursday following the publication of the letter he took a benefit at the Bloomsbury Assembly Rooms, and after the boxing was over there were two important matters to announce. One was that our Most Gracious Majesty the Queen had been safely delivered of a daughter, and three hearty cheers were given by those who were in the crowded house. Then came a statement by Young Dutch Sam, who said that he was empowered to post a fiver on behalf of Nick Ward, towards a match for £100 with Caunt. This was then and there accepted and covered by Big Ben, the money being handed over to Tom Spring, on the understanding that the men were to meet on Tuesday, December 8, and sign articles to fight.

The appointment was kept; Peter Crawley signed for Caunt, and Young Sam for Ward, agreeing " to fight a fair stand-up fight in a twenty-four foot ring, half-minute time, within sixty miles of London, on Tuesday, February 2, 1841, for £100 a-side, according to the provisions of the rules. The men to be in the ring between the hours of twelve and one o'clock, or the party absent to forfeit the battle-money unless an earlier hour shall be mutually agreed upon at the last deposit, to which hour the same forfeiture shall be applicable. Two umpires and a referee to be chosen on the ground; in case of dispute the decision of the latter to be conclusive. Should magisterial interference take place,

the stakeholder to name the next time and place
of meeting, if possible, on the same day. The use of
resin or other powder to the hands to be considered foul,
and the money not to be given up till fairly won or lost
by a fight." We have quoted the above from the articles
to show how strangely and minutely they entered into
every little detail. And now a word about Mr. Nicholas
Ward, the brother to the ex-Champion, and an aspirant
to the highest pugilistic honours.

He was born on April 1, 1813, at St. George's-in-the
East, and, like his two brothers and father, followed the
occupation of a coal-whipper, and undoubtedly that had
much to do with the development of the muscles of the
brothers Ward—John, James, and Nick—and that they
inherited their fighting proclivities, like Bendigo, from
their mother, there is little doubt, for by all accounts
she was a perfect Amazon, and was very smart with
her fists. Nick was some thirteen years younger than his
brother Jem, but was quite as powerful as that phenomenon, even when the latter was at his best. Furthermore,
he was, in many people's opinion, quite as clever and
as quick as lightning, besides being a tremendously hard
hitter. There was one fault, however, he possessed, and
that was the lack of that quality which is more essential
than anything else in the making of a pugilist. Nick
Ward had a heart no bigger than a chicken's, and could not
stand being hit. Unlike his brother Jem, directly he
received punishment it was all over. Yet he could
summon courage enough to engage in battle with the
best of them. And then, as the following performances
will show, he proved on several occasions to be a most
arrant coward, and his career was by no means a brilliant
one. He commenced by defeating Harry Lockyer, of
Kent, on February 24, 1835; and then he came out in
his true colours, by sneaking out of a match with Young
Molineaux, he having procured his own arrest on the
day before the fight was arranged to come off. Then after
that he showed the white feather again, when he met
Sambo Sutton during the Derby week of 1836, surren-
dering to the Black in the most ignominious and dastardly manner, when all thought he was winning in the
easiest possible manner, simply because Sam struck him a
violent blow on the nose. One writer at the time declared
that the sight and smell of his own blood turned him
sick, for nothing would induce him to stand up before
Massa Sutton after the receipt of that blow. In fact, he
openly declared that he was not cut out for a fighting
man. Still his brother and friends were still able to
persuade him to enter the lists. Sambo Sutton was for
ever chaffing Nick Ward, and at length Nick could stand

it no longer, and they were matched to fight a second
time for £50 a-side on March 27, 1838. But this came
to nothing, for Sam was captured by the police on the
morning of the battle, and Ward was chased for thirty
miles by the constables, who, however, did not succeed
in arresting him. His next attempt was in his long and
shifty fight with Jem Bailey, which took place on
October 18, 1839, when Nick Ward had the battle given
to him through his adversary striking a foul blow. Then
a second match was made, but Nick funked it again,
and declared that he was " too unwell " to enter the
arena, and so he forfeited.

We should certainly not reckon this a brilliant career,
and yet his supporters thought him good enough to
warrant him wearing the belt which had been buckled
around his brother's waist. That he must have been a
good man is proved by the fact that he defeated Deaf
Burke—that game, scientific, and hard-hitting fighter,
who had carried everything before him until defeated by
Bendigo. It is true that Burke's days were over when
he met Nick, and he was suffering from lameness, which
prevented him from following his lively antagonist about
the ring. Nobody could fight better than Ward if he
found it all going the right way with him, and in this
battle the poor old Deaf 'Un was soon winded and
exhausted, when Nick went for him in a most unmerciful
manner, the Deaf 'Un being quite overmatched. This was
the most creditable of all Ward's performances, and he
was so elated that he determined to make a bid for the
Championship. That he had a good claim to it there
could be no doubt, for he had beaten Burke, who stood
next to Bendigo for the coveted honours. There was
only Caunt to defeat, who had beaten Bendigo. That
however, it must be remembered, was before the latter
fought the Deaf 'Un and became Champion.

Ben Caunt, as we have already related, had fought but
five battles, and only two out of those with good men,
viz., Bendigo and Brassey, so it was not much of a record
for a Champion. Still the Nottingham man had won all
his engagements, and appeared always willing to fight.
Nick Ward, on the contrary, was just as likely not to
enter the ring as to face the giant, and many believed
that at the last moment he would never dare do so, for
his cowardice was at this period notorious.

Nick had been staying with his brother Jem at Liverpool, and there remained until the second week in
December, when he went off to the Hare and Hounds,
West Derby, with Peter Taylor to look after him. There
he was joined by an American bruiser of some
notoriety who had just come to this country, known as

Yankee Sullivan, and who was engaged to fight Hammer Lane, of Birmingham, in the same ring in which Nick Ward and Ben Caunt were to figure. Peter Taylor had both men in hand, turning them out in splendid condition, for there wasn't a better trainer living than Peter.

Ben Caunt, in company with that magnificent, scientific fighter, Johnny Broome, who was matched to fight Johnny Hannan, went off immediately the articles were signed, on tour, visiting Manchester, Bolton, Warrington, and other northern towns, returning to London on December 17, when Peter Crawley took Ben to Hatfield, where he went into strict training.

The last deposit for the match was duly made at Peter Crawley's, and on that occasion, Thursday, January 28, Mr. Gervase Harker, of Stoneyford, who was Caunt's principal backer, won the toss for choice of battle-ground. He selected Andover Road Station, on the South-Western (then known as the Southampton Railway). This necessitated a journey of no less a distance than two hundred and fifty miles for Nick Ward and his friends, and was most inconsiderate on the part of Mr. Harker, for the decision did not reach them until the Saturday morning, leaving them none too much time to make their arrangements for so long a journey, and get comfortably to the far-off Hampshire. On the Sunday morning Nick Ward, accompanied by his brother Jem, Peter Taylor, Young Molineaux, Mat Robinson, Yankee Sullivan, and a limited number of friends and backers, set off from Liverpool, and did not arrive at their destination until the Monday morning, when they put up at the Catherine Wheel, Andover, a well-known sporting house, that had many a time been patronised by celebrated bruisers, amongst them Neate, when he fought Tom Spring, and Dick Curtis when he fought Barney Aaron.

Ben Caunt had journeyed down comfortably from his training quarters with Hammer Lane, on the Sunday, arriving the same evening, and putting up at the Vine at Stockbridge. On the following day sportsmen arrived at Andover in hundreds, and so great was the run upon the inns that many found it necessary to go on to Winchester, finding accommodation at the Royal, the Swan, the Crown, and other hostelries. When the two parties met there was a deal of ill-feeling on the part of the Wardites, who had been brought such a distance, and when it became known that the Hampshire constabulary were on the scent their rage knew no bounds.

The principal parties engaged met on the Monday evening at the Catherine Wheel to discuss what was to be done. Caunt's backers declared that it was for no purpose of

inconveniencing Ward and Co. that they had selected
Hampshire, but for the purpose of giving the sports there
a treat, the latter having promised to pay handsomely
towards the men's expenses. Still it seemed that there
was no possibility of bringing the battle off there, and
they suggested a move into Wiltshire. This Ward
objected to, as it would have brought the place outside
the distance fixed upon by the articles. At length it was

HAMMER LANE, CAUNT'S TRAINER.

decided to journey into Berkshire, and Cookham Common
was fixed upon. This meant a journey of some fourteen
miles, and so every available vehicle from Andover,
Winchester, Stockbridge, and Odiham was secured,
whilst those who had to travel on foot had a nice journey
before them. Fortunately the Tuesday morning was
fine and frosty, but the journey was up hill and down

dale and a very tiresome route. We have no space to
relate the incidents and accidents on the road, but they
were very numerous, amongst others the break down of
the gig chartered by Johnny Hannan, who had to be
transferred to the drag upon which Ben Caunt was being
conveyed to the battle-field.

There were some swell sportsmen present, amongst
them the Earl of Portsmouth, who had driven with
some friends from his beautiful seat of Hurstbourne
Park; Mr. John Portal Brydges had come from the
Freefolk Paper Mills, near Whitchurch, where the
paper for bank notes has been manufactured since the
time of George I.; Mr. William Portal, of Laverstock,
was there, and a host of Hampshire squires, gentlemen,
and farmers.

When the party, which had dwindled down to some
four or five hundred, reached the banks of the River
Enbourne, the police, who had stuck to the skirts of the
cavalcade, left them to journey into Berkshire unmolested, and it was not until half-past three in the afternoon that they made a final halt, and Tom Oliver
pitched the ring. It is not our intention to dwell upon
the preliminaries, but only to briefly describe the
battle which was to decide who should be entitled to
call himself Champion, for it was a most disappointing
affair all through. It is not necessary either to again
picture Caunt as he stood in the ring, his colossal figure,
great, clumsy limbs, being in strange contrast to Nick
Ward's beautifully symmetrical frame, with its grand,
deep chest and finely shaped arms. He was a fine man,
standing 6ft and weighing 12st 10lb. But at the onset
Nick showed that he was afraid of his opponent. In the
opening round he flinched and drew back step by step as
the bigger man advanced. The latter at length lashed
out, but was cleverly stopped by Nick, who returned
one, two on the face. But there was little power in the
blows, and Ben grinned at his opponent, and made
another dash, when a smart rally ensued. But both
men were flurried—Caunt too eager to get home, Ward
too anxious to get away—so the blows were dealt at
random and ill-aimed. The big 'un then tried to close,
just managing to hold his opponent for a few seconds,
but the latter cleverly slipped from his grasp and went
down.

In the succeeding round Nick Ward dodged his adversary splendidly all over the ring, now and again getting
in a stinging blow, but doing little damage. Caunt,
though, got wild at not being able to hit or grapple his
foe; it seemed that his temper was getting beyond his
control, as it did in his battle with Bendigo. Ward's

tricky tactics did not suit him, and he showed unmistakable signs of rising wrath. Ward had the office
from Dick Curtis to continue to irritate Ben, who, mad
with himself for missing, rushed in to close, but Nick,
as before, eluded his grasp and dropped. Then Caunt,
when in his corner, was mercilessly chaffed by Ward's
friends. All this was done for a purpose.

In the fourth round Ben got more and more savage, and
lost control over himself. Had the other man been real
grit he could have done considerable damage to his
colossal opponent. But he was not, and took more care
to keep himself out of harm's way than to administer
punishment. And this sort of business continued until
the seventh round ; Caunt tried for a close but was
warmly peppered on the eyes and nose, and then, trying
again and getting Nick in his grasp, the latter frustrated
his intention by dropping on his knees. Mad at finding
his foe slipping from his grasp, Ben let go his hold, and
raising his ponderous fist, let drive at Nick's head,
catching him on the ear, after his knees had touched
the ground. "Foul! foul!" was the cry, and according
to the accounts the confusion beggars description. The
tumult which ensued was appalling, and Ward's friends
threatened to lynch Mr. Bailey, the referee, if that
gentleman did not award the fight to their man. But
the official was a man of nerve and courage, and when
he found that the umpires disagreed, he said in reply
to this question, "Was it fair or foul, sir?" "I believe
the blow was unintentional, and I order the men to
continue the fight."

Caunt was in a worse temper than ever when they
renewed the battle, and his friends saw it, and trembled
for the result. They had not long to wait. Ben's first
rush was met by a straight smack in the face from Nick's
left. This blow was the last to break the camel's back ;
it so riled Caunt that he completely lost all control over
himself, dashed in, lashing about wildly and frantically,
regardless of jabs in the face, and then he closed with
his man. "Just as his huge arms were tightening
round Ward," says one account, " the latter craftily
slipped as before, on his knees, with his hands up,
Whilst in this position, and evidently 'down,' according
to the rules of the Ring, Caunt drew back his arm and
twice struck Nick on the side of the head ; the second
blow rolling him over."

Of course there was a wild shriek of "Foul," and
Mr. Bailey, when the umpire had been appealed to,
gave his decision, which was to the effect that the blows
struck by Caunt were unquestionably "foul," and he
should therefore award the battle to Nicholas Ward.

CHAPTER XXXIX.

BEN CAUNT AND NICK WARD.—SECOND BATTLE FOR THE BELT.

AT the side of Drury Lane Theatre, before the removal of the buildings for the improvements which are now in progress, there was an old tavern some half century ago, known as the Black Lion. It was a celebrated house in the forties, at which many of the Fancy spent their time, and a favourite haunt for the pugilists of the day. It stood in Vinegar Yard, not far from where the once-renowned Whistling Oyster was situated, and which no doubt many of our readers will well remember. The extraordinary story told as to the origin of the latter house we may be permitted to tell briefly here, for it was at the Whistling Oyster where the merry sports of the Black Lion would consume the bivalves, and wash them down with the beer of the Lion.

It was in the year 1840, just twelve months prior to the period about which we write, that the first-mentioned house burst into notoriety and gained its curious sign. Mr. Pearkes was the proprietor, and one morning he discovered an oyster, as it lay fattening on oatmeal in one of the tubs, that was really whistling. Anyhow, it produced some sound very like whistling, beyond all question. It might have been that there was some hole in the shell through which this peculiar bivalve made the noise. Hundreds of people came to listen to the remarkable creature, and Mr. Pearkes made quite a little fortune, whilst the trade at the Black Lion increased enormously. *Punch* had jokes about it. Douglas Jerrold wrote that the oyster had been crossed in love, and that it whistled to keep up appearances, just to show that it didn't care; whilst Thackeray declared that he was once in this shop listening to the whistling shellfish, when an American came in out of curiosity, and after hearing the talented "native" go through his musical performance, said it was nothing to an oyster he knew down in Massachusetts, which whistled "Yankee Doodle" right through, and followed his master about the house like a dog. Mr. Pearkes at once re-christened his shop the "Whistling Oyster," and Vinegar Yard became quite a popular place, with a renown that it had never before acquired.

It was one evening about twelve months after the *début* of this marvellous oyster—to be particular, Thursday night, February 11, 1841—that some scores of sportsmen passed the Whistling Oyster on their way to the Black Lion. It was a nasty, foggy night, and evidently some great attraction on the *tapis* must have called them out. The Boniface of the Black Lion was then our old friend Young Dutch Sam, one of the finest middle-weight boxers of his time, for he had won a dozen battles and never once suffered defeat. The parlour of the Black Lion was filled with sports quite early in the evening, and what with the fog, the tobacco smoke, and the steaming grogs, it must have been difficult to recognise one's friend on the opposite side of the table.

The occasion of this meeting was the presentation of the £200 which was won by Nick Ward in his encounter with Ben Caunt, just nine days previously, the stakes which, as we described in our last chapter, he had gained on February 2, at Cookham Common, when Nick, by his shifty tactics and unmanly behaviour, had provoked the Big Ben to deal him a foul blow. It was, of course, quite natural that Caunt and his backers were dissatisfied with the issue of this battle, and the Nottingham man had challenged his opponent to try conclusions again in three months' time, but Ward had not given any reply. When, however, the money was paid over at the Black Lion, and Mr. Nicholas rose to return thanks for the unexpected windfall, he took the opportunity of informing those present that he expected upon that very evening, at his brother's house in Liverpool, arrangements were being made for him to fight Brassey for £100 a-side, but that if the negotiations fell through he was quite ready and willing to meet Caunt again.

At the moment that Nick Ward was upon his legs talking in rather a bouncing manner, there was nobody there to represent Caunt, but shortly afterwards Ben, accompanied by Peter Crawley, entered the room. With them was Ben's principal backer, Mr. Swaine, of the Greyhound, Hatfield, where Ben had trained, and where he had been staying since the fight. It appears that Caunt was anything but sober, and walking straight up to Nick Ward, he said: "Coom, I mean to feight thee again, and lick thee; my brass is ready, a hundred pounds." Now Nick, coward as he was, had good manners, and, indeed, was a gentlemanly, civil young fellow, with a manner in strange contrast to the blustering Caunt, so he politely informed the Nottingham man, as he had already informed the company, that if

20

Brassey did not decide to meet him he should be happy
to accommodate Caunt once more.

Ben in an exceedingly coarse manner laughed rudely
and snapped his fingers in Nick's face, and expressed an
opinion that Ward was a cur and a coward. Those who
were present say that Nick Ward's pale countenance
flushed crimson, and to the surprise of everybody, particularly Caunt, he said with no little expression of
spirit and determination, "Look here, Mr. Caunt, I
spoke to you fair and civilly, and you've answered me
like a blackguard. I'll let you see whether I'm a cur,
a coward or not. Off with your coat, and I'll fight
you here in the room for love, just to see which is the
better man."

Nobody was taken more aback than Ben Caunt at
this. He could hardly believe his ears. Then they
both peeled off their coats, and it looked very much
like business then and there, and no doubt there would
have been a savage set-to had not Tom Spring been
present. He declared that if they attempted that sort
of thing in Sam's house they would lose Sam his licence,
and the Dutchman, who had been absent when the
quarrel took place, came into the room and soon put
his veto on the matter. Then Tom Spring insisted
upon them shaking hands, which they did reluctantly,
advising them to keep their fisticuffs until they again
entered the ring. Then it was arranged that they should
meet on the following Thursday at the same house,
and if Nick Ward was found to be free, they were to
sign articles and deposit £20 each. Accordingly, the
men with their backers met, and both seemed in a very
amiable mood, and were well attended. Tom Spring,
Mr. Swaine, and Peter Crawley were there for Caunt;
and Nick Ward had two friends of his brother Jem—
Mr. Munro and Mr. Coleman—and a Liverpool friend,
named Aspinall. The agreeable announcement was
made that the match between Ward and Brassey had
fallen through, and that Nick was therefore at liberty to
fight Caunt.

So the coast was clear, and the £20 deposit made on
each side, and the articles drawn up and placed in Mr.
Dowling's hands after being duly signed and witnessed.
The document contained the usual clauses, in which
the parties " agreed to fight a fair stand-up fight in a
twenty-four foot ring, half-minute time according to the
new rules, for £100 a-side, half way between London
and Liverpool, the place not to be distant more than
twenty miles from the direct line of road, unless mutually
agreed upon to the contrary. The fight to take place on
Tuesday, May 11, 1841. The ropes and stakes to be paid

for by the men, share and share alike. Neither man to
use resin or other powder to his hands during the combat. The party winning the toss for choice of place to
name the ground seven days before fighting to the
backers of the party losing the toss."

The deposits were to be made at the following houses:—
Two at Hatfield, at the houses of Ben Caunt's backers, Mr.
Swaine of the Greyhound, and Mr. Adcock of the Bell;
one at Liverpool, at Jem Ward's, The Star, Williamson
Square; and four in London, viz., two at Young Dutch
Sam's, the Black Lion, in Vinegar Yard; one at Tom
Spring's, The Castle, in Holborn; and one at Mr.
Coleman's, The Cherry Tree, Kingsland Road. Peter
Crawley's house was not mentioned, for he had had a
tiff with Ben Caunt, feeling rather jealous of the Hat-
field publican.

Although there was a good deal of interest displayed
in the coming fight, very little betting took place, the
market price being 5 to 4 on Ward, which was strange
when one considers that the fight was for the Championship and belt, a new one specially manufactured for the
occasion.. It was of purple velvet lined with leather; in
the centre were a pair of clasped hands, surrounded by
a wreath of the Rose, the Thistle, and the Shamrock
entwined in embossed silver; on each side of this were
three shields of bright silver, on which were to be
engraved the names of all the preceding Champions of
England. The clasps in front were formed of two
hands encased in boxing gloves.

Both men went to their former training quarters;
Caunt to Hatfield, Ward to West Derby, and progressed
in first-rate style until a fortnight before the fight, when
Ben met with a mishap. He was taking one of his
long walks, when he accidentally trod on a rolling stone
which twisted his ankle with such force that it strained
the muscles very severely, so that he was compelled to
lay up. Not being able to put his feet to the ground for
nearly a week was scarcely the kind of thing for a man
training for a fight for the Championship, but Caunt had
to grin and bear it. Fortunately, he had excellent
surgical advice, so that he was sufficiently recovered to
resume his exercise for the last week before the fight.

Nick Ward won the toss for choice of place, and after
a consultation with Young Dutch Sam, named the classic
town of Stratford-on-Avon. Without doubt this selection
really came from Jem, for it was close to the birthplace
of Shakespeare that the Black Diamond won his last
battle as Champion. He fought Simon Byrne, it will be
remembered, at Willeycuts, on July 12, 1831, just ten
years before his brother Nick had arranged to meet

Caunt for this their second battle. So on the Monday
afternoon both claimants for the Championship arrived

OLD BEN BUTLER (CAUNT'S FATHER-IN-
LAW.)

at Stratford-on-Avon. Tom Spring journeyed to the
Warwickshire town with Ben Caunt, and they put up at

the Red Lion. Nick Ward, with his brother Jem, made
the White Lion his headquarters. Besides these there
arrived a couple of brace of other gladiators, who were
to do battle in the same ring as the two big 'uns. These
were Peter Taylor and Levi Eckersley paired off
together, and Fred Mason (the Bull Dog) and Stephen
Puttock, who were expected to give a fine display. So
there was an excellent programme, sufficient to draw
the sports down in their hundreds. Indeed, so great was
the influx of visitors on the evening before the fights,
that every hostelry was full to overflowing, and sleeping
accommodation could not be had for love or money, and
many had to make their way to Leamington, Warwick,
and to Coventry.

The hunting season had not been long over, and many
sportsmen delayed their departure from the shires so
that they might be present at such a field day, for it was
rarely that one could witness a fight for the Championship, and a couple of first class mills thrown in on the
same day.

In a report before us, we read that from Melton,
Loughborough, Market Harborough, Rugby, and Leam-
ington the hunting men came on their way south.
They included such distinguished sportsmen as the
Earl of Wilton, Lord Kennedy, Lord Deerhurst, Lord
Chetwynd, the veteran Sir Bellingham Graham, Squire
Osbaldeston, Captain Horatio Ross, Lord Southamp-
ton, Sir William Maxwell, Captain John White, and
many other well-known followers of the chase ; whilst
from London had come Fulwar Craven, "Ginger"
Stubbs, Lord William Lennox, Mr. Richard Tattersall,
the Duke of Beaufort, the Marquis of Queensberry,
Lord Longford, Lord Wharncliffe, Sir St. Vincent
Cotton, Tom Crommelin, the Bishop of Bond Street,
Baron Renton Nicholson, Jem Burn, and many other
notable stars of the Fancy.

The morning of the fight was beautiful, and the place
was literally besieged. We wonder what "The Swan of
Avon" would have thought could he have risen from his
tomb and strolled down the High Street. The spot
chosen for the battle was Long Marsden, about five
miles from Stratford, where a farmer named Pratt, who
was an enthusiastic sportsman, offered a large meadow
for the purpose of pitching the ring. Tom Oliver and
his assistant, Tom Callas, were early on the spot with
stakes and tackle. Tom Spring had some days before
collected from the swells about £20 for the purpose of
engaging a score of pugilists from London and Birmingham to keep order, and these special constables
were augmented by about a dozen of Mr. Pratt's

labourers, who each received half a crown, and were provided with stiff ash sticks in case of a disturbance.

It must have been a capital spot to bring off the fight, for on one side the ground sloped and formed a "rake," which enabled everybody to get a splendid view of the ring.

At half-past twelve Ward and Caunt made their appearance amidst a burst of cheering, the first-named escorted by his seconds, Harry Holt, the Cicero of the Ring, and Dick Curtis; the Nottingham man by old Ben Butler and Bill Atkinson. Before the men entered the ring Harry Holt, with the new belt, which he exhibited and handed round to the swells in the outer ring to look at, making quite an eloquent speech prepared for the occasion, for Harry was a great orator.

It was just twenty minutes to one when the referee called "Time," and the two men having once more shaken hands, they put up their fists and commenced to fight for the handsome trophy and the Championship of England. It will be unnecessary for us to describe the gladiators again, as we called attention to their points and different styles in the previous chapter. There was less difference in weight between them than on the last occasion. After one or two attempts Ward got in a slight jabbing hit, and as his opponent tried to counter he went down upon his knees, amidst hisses and loud cries of disapprobation. It was thought that he intended playing his old game in the evasive, tricky style adopted in the previous fight. This time, however, Caunt did not lose his temper, and it was evident that he did not intend to throw away the fight as he did the other, for he came up wreathed in smiles for the second bout.

The next few rounds ended precisely the same as the first, Nick Ward after a few exchanges going down on his knees and woefully tempting his opponent to hit him foul. But Ben threw up his arms each time, amidst bursts of cheers from his friends, who appreciated his coolness and tact. Ward, although a splendid counter-hitter, would not venture near enough to Ben's shoulder-of-mutton fist, and therefore he rarely reached his adversary, and brother Jem came several times to the ring-side to remonstrate with Nick, who plucked up a bit, went in and caught the big 'un a slashing blow over the eye, cutting it to the bone. Ben dashed in wildly, striking out right and left, but Nick went down again and Caunt fell over him.

Right away from the tenth round to the twenty-fourth the same wearisome fighting continued, when in that Ben nailed his man a frightful blow on the nose and another upon the side of the head, and, of course, Nick dropped. In the succeeding three rounds nearly the same thing happened, and Ward was undoubtedly showing the white feather, and would have given in had it not been for his brother and his seconds, who urged him to make one bold bid for victory.

In the thirty-fourth round Nick went down without a blow, and there were loud cries of " Take him away— take the —— cur out of the ring." But Harry Holt and Curtis persuaded him to go up for one more. Then Ben went for him with right and left in the face, and down Nicholas dropped for the last time. His brother Jem ducked under the ropes and implored him to fight one plucky round for the credit of the family, but Nick had had enough, and lay groaning, declaring that Caunt had broken his ribs. This excuse didn't impose upon brother Jem. He turned away disdainfully, and holding up his hand, said, " You've won, Ben !" There was a wild cheer from Caunt's friends as they realised the fact that Big Ben was Champion of England.

CHAPTER XL.

THEY PLAY OFF THE RUBBER.—A LONG MARCH BY TEN THOUSAND SPECTATORS TO SEE BEN CAUNT AND BENDIGO. —BATTLE FOR £400 AND THE BELT.

AFTER the most unsatisfactory second meeting between Caunt and Bendigo, which we have already described, and in which it will be remembered the latter went down without a blow being delivered, the latter was mad with rage. He declared that he had gone down accidentally, through having no spikes in his shoes, and that the referee had no right to have given the fight to his colossal opponent. He swore he would meet Caunt " anywhere, anyhow, on any terms—to-morrow, next week, or next month—anything to accommodate the big chucklehead." The latter epithet was a favourite with Bendy, not only when speaking of, but when speaking to, his gigantic antagonist. Yet, desirous as Bendigo appeared to be to

meet the Nottingham man, time flew on and still they
were not matched, although a paper warfare was persistently carried on, during which period Bendigo met
and defeated Deaf Burke, as we have already narrated, on
February 12, 1839. First one, then the other, gave notice
that the money could be covered, and at last, in 1840,
the public were informed that " Caunt's money, to be
made into a stake, was lying at Tom Spring's, but
nothing had been heard of Bendigo." In the same
week a paragraph appeared in the Nottingham papers
announcing a serious accident which had happened to
the Nottingham man.

Bendigo, who was, as our readers will remember, a
careless, devil-may-care sort of a fellow, fond of practical joking and clowning of all kinds, or any caper
which would provoke a laugh from his comrades, was
returning from the military steeplechases held near
Nottingham. When they arrived close to the Pender's
House, on the London Road, Bendy exclaimed, " Now,
boys, I'll show you how to run a steeplechase without
falling." He at once threw a somersault, and, on alighting, fell down. In vain he attempted to rise, and his
friends, thinking he was still keeping up the game,
laughed heartily. They discovered, however, it was no
laughing matter, for he had received a serious injury to
his knee-cap, and he had to be at once conveyed to the
surgeon's.

This accident put Master Bendy on the shelf for some
time, and it was not until 1843 that he was sufficiently
recovered to feel justified in disputing the claim of
Caunt to the Championship of England. Brassey at
this time had offered himself to Bendigo's notice, but
the money was not forthcoming, and in the early part of
1844 the Notts man published some capital verses in
Bell's Life, two of which we reprint :—

" May I never again take a sip of ' blue ruin,'
  If I love to see fair English fighting take wing ;
  'Tis time for the ' Big 'Un ' to be up and doing,
  For bantam cocks only show now in the Ring.

Then again for the laurel crown let us be tugging,
  May fair play be always our motto and plan ;
But Caunt I denounce, and his system of hugging—
  A practice more fit for a bear than a man."

Bendigo was now only too anxious to meet his old
adversary, and after much correspondence the match
was made on April 17, Bendy, shortly after taking himself to his old training quarters at Crosby, near Liverpool, under the care of Jem Ward.

Ben Caunt also hailed from Nottingham, and was at
the time of the match being made just turned thirty, or

three and a half years junior to his antagonist. After his victory over Brassey he fought Nick Ward twice, as described in the two previous chapters. After this Caunt determined upon a trip to New York, where he discovered the American giant, Freeman, and brought him over to England in the March of 1842. They went on a sparring tour through the provinces. Caunt was at this time landlord of the Coach and Horses (now the Salisbury), St. Martin's Lane, and many will remember the genial great Boniface. After his defeat of Nick Ward, and Bendigo having been heard of but little since his accident, it was thought that Ben Caunt would hold the Championship against all comers, for there were few able to try conclusions with him. But at a sporting dinner attended by many of the P.R. and a big muster of Corinthians, it was announced that Bendigo was willing for the third time to take up the gauntlet, and the match was made to fight in the September of 1845 for £200 a-side, and the Championship belt. Caunt, whose weight was then something over 17st, went into training at Hatfield, under the care of his uncle, Ben Butler, and Jem Turner, and did such good work that he reduced his mountain of flesh quite 3st.

The day before the battle was to come off, September 9, so great was the interest centred in the affair, hundreds of people journeyed to Wolverton, in the neighbourhood of which the fight was supposed to come off. The weather was fearfully hot, and every tavern and lodging that could be had was occupied. Bendigo, accompanied by Jem Ward and Merryman, arrived on the eve of the battle and put up at Tom Westley's house, the Swan. Jem Ward immediately sought a convenient spot to form the arena, and selected the banks of the Ouse, near where the poet Cowper once resided, some four miles from the town. The excitement was intense in Wolverton, for amongst the latest arrivals was the High Constable, who had instructions to arrest the principals; but Bendigo had timely warning, and was smuggled from the Swan and taken to a farmhouse.

Meanwhile Ben Caunt had arrived in London from his training quarters, accompanied by his uncle and Turner, when they went to the Castle, in Holborn. After dinner there, at which Tom Spring and the *élite* of the Fancy were present, and at which Ben Butler disposed of some two hundred colours on the usual terms—£1 for a win, nothing if a loss—the party caught the four o'clock train to Stoney Stratford, putting up at the Cock, which was selected as Caunt's headquarters. The same evening Tom Spring went over to Jem Ward for a council of war, and when he heard which place had been selected, he pointed out that the fight would never be permitted in Buckinghamshire. He suggested, therefore, that they should change the venue to Lillingstone Level, Oxfordshire, where Nick Ward and Deaf Burke had fought five years before. Bendigo and his party, however, were very obstinate, so it was ultimately decided to settle it by tossing. Jem Ward, for Bendigo, won, and insisted upon Bedfordshire; so it was arranged that the ropes and stakes should come on to Newport Pagnell in the morning early, and a journey made thence to the battlefield. When Jem Ward's party arrived, followed by the crowd which had been at Wolverton, it was decided that Whaddon must be the place, which was at least ten miles away. Tom Oliver journeyed off with the ropes and stakes in a cart, and the cavalcade that followed must have been something to have remembered. It was very early when they started, but the sun was beginning to throw down an unusual amount of heat, whilst the majority had to " toddle " it, and did not forget to make public their feelings of annoyance at the selection of a spot so far away, in terms more expressive than polite. After a trudge of about three hours a suitable piece of ground was selected and the arena formed, whilst a brisk business was done in the sale of tickets at from one shilling to five shillings each.

Altogether there were quite five thousand people, and the cry was " still they come." During the time all these arrangements were being made, it appeared that whilst Tom Spring, with Caunt and his supporters, were leaving Stoney Stratford, the High Constable again appeared on the scene, and warned Tom that Whaddon was in Bucks, and that it was positively determined that no breach of the peace should be allowed in that county. This was a pretty pickle to have been in. Spring, however, was equal to the emergency, and despatched a mounted messenger, explaining the position, and saying that they must meet at Lillingstone Level, as at first suggested. When the messenger arrived and the situation became known to the crowd, the roughs swore that they would move no further, and declared that the stakes and ropes should not be shifted. But when it was pointed out that the men would not arrive, they reluctantly permitted Oliver and his assistants to strike the stakes, and once more started on the road. The cursing and swearing is said to have been fearful, for the journey was some eight miles, the sun broiling hot, and no refreshments to be had on the road. The irritated mass moved forward to Oxfordshire, some—the majority, in fact—across country to save distance, and the remainder in vehicles along the dusty road. Whilst the exasperated crowd was making its second pilgrimage, Bendigo, Merriman, and his patrons arrived at Stoney Stratford, having left Newport Pagnell at 9 a.m. At the Cock there was quite a scene between the two combatants. Bendigo, seeing Caunt at the window, swore he would pay him for all the the trouble that had been given when they got into the ring.

Although this journeying about was exceedingly mortifying to many, it was a piece of good fortune to thou-

SQUIRE OSBALDESTON.

sands who came down by the later morning trains to Stoney Stratford, for had not the delay occurred many would have had this journey for nothing. When the string of carriages, horsemen, and pedestrians arrived at the final rendezvous the numbers had swollen to quite ten thousand—all ranks, from the blasphemous Midland rough to the fashionably attired London Corinthian. As much as a sovereign was paid for a lift on the road, and many from sheer exhaustion had to fall out.

It was not until 2.30 that the ring was formed finally, and in order to save as much confusion as possible, a large outer circle was arranged. The ticket system commenced once more, but the disorder was terrific. A number of roughs, armed with sticks, dashed into the ring and demanded money from all those who had already paid for a front seat, whilst the half-drunken, infuriated crowd were cursing, fighting, thieving, and yelling.

At precisely 3.20, amidst deafening cheers from the 10,000 spectators, the men arrived. Caunt attended by Molineaux, the Black, and Jem Turner, entered the ring first with his uncle, Ben Butler, as his bottleholder. Bendigo immediately followed, and was waited on by Nick Ward, Jack Hannan, Jem Ward, and John Burn. After cordially shaking hands, they tossed for corners, Bendigo losing ; and Caunt, of course, took the ground with his back to the sun. Tom Spring produced the belt, and handed it to Bendigo, who laughingly buckled it round his waist, as much as to intimate that it would have a right to remain there after the fight was over. He chaffed Ben, and offered to bet him £50 on the result. Names were suggested and rejected for the post of referee, for it certainly required an amount of pluck to undertake so delicate an office to the satisfaction of so questionable a mob. At length George Osbaldeston ("t'Auld Squire") was named. He had, to avoid the crush, gone to his carriage; but when he was told that without he came forward there would be no fight, he generously returned and accepted office.

The men having completed their toilets, the colours were tied to the stakes; Caunt's consisted of bright orange, with blue border, and had the following inscription upon it : "Caunt and Bendigo, for £200 and the Championship of England, 9th September, 1845," surrounded by the words, "May the best man win." All was in readiness, "Time" was called amidst breathless silence, and the two veterans toed the scratch.

Caunt smiled pleasantly as he put himself into sparring attitude, and looked very confident. Bendigo, who appeared to be as light as a cork, danced round Ben in an acrobatic manner, and had a grim look of satisfaction upon his grinning "mug." No time was lost, and Bendy, dodging about and shifting ground in the old familiar style, at length came to close quarters, and seeing an opening, as quick as thought dashed in his left, catching Ben a resounding crack on the eye. A little more capering, while Caunt firmly stood his ground, afforded another chance, and in went the left again, landing a stinger on Ben's cheek, and opening an old wound left by Brassey, from which the blood flowed copiously. Yells of delight went up from the Midland division. Caunt got close for a try but missed an intended crusher, and the men coming together Caunt, got his opponent down in his corner.

A few insignificant exchanges were then made, when Bendigo, retreating from a vicious blow, slipped down, but was up again in an instant. In the third round Bendy played round his man, but as he dashed in Ben caught him in his arms, threw him across the ropes, and fell over him. During the next few bouts nothing of interest was worth recording, save in the eighth Caunt again gave his opponent the hug and bent his man over the ropes. In the twelfth Caunt made a vigorous charge, hitting out with right and left. Bendigo whilst retreating again slipped down, but was up again to renew, and after some wild hitting Bendy fell suspiciously in his corner, and cries of "Foul" were raised.

The succeeding rounds to the twenty-fourth were all characterised by the same artful manœuvring and questionable manner of getting down adopted by Bendigo, whilst Caunt, who rarely had a chance of getting a blow home, stood up fairly, but had to depend principally upon his wrestling qualities. In the twenty-fourth the excitement round the ring was so great when the referee was appealed to by Caunt's seconds, that some of the Nottingham roughs broke into the enclosure for the purpose of enforcing their arguments in favour of Bendigo. So often had he gone down that Nick Ward became exhausted at having to pick him up, and Nobby Clarke had to take his place.

Order having been somewhat restored, they continued the fight. It would, however, be impossible, even if interesting to our readers, to record all the incidents of these rounds; to describe how Spring, indignant at the unfair manner in which Bendigo was continuing the fight, appealed to the referee, and received a blow from a bludgeon on the shoulder, which was intended undoubtedly for his head. Squire Osbaldeston must have possessed no small amount of nerve to have stood there calmly doing what he considered justice. In one of the rounds, as Bendy fell, Caunt jumped over his prostrate body, and nobody would have been surprised if he had jumped *on* him, for the style of Bendy's tactics was enough to make Job himself hit out vigorously.

At length, through his constant falling, the smaller man showed palpable signs of fatigue, whilst Caunt showed severe wounds about the face, his lower lip was split, and the ugly gaping gash across his cheek gave a warlike appearance to his visage. About the fiftieth round the confusion became fearful, and it was with difficulty the ropes and stakes were preserved. Many of the spectators, from the pressure of the crowd, beat a retreat where it was possible, whilst the ring-keepers remained quite passive, apparently considering discretion the better part of valour when opposed by some hundreds of roughs armed with bludgeons.

The fight at the sixtieth round had lasted one hour and twenty-four minutes, and was further continued until it occupied two hours and ten minutes, ninety-three rounds being fought. Without going fully into details, however, it will be necessary only to relate the most important incidents. They were both very much fatigued owing to the fearful heat of the sun, and Bendigo continued to go down on every available occasion. In the eighty-second round Bendigo fell; but as Caunt was retiring to his corner, he jumped up and renewed the attack, fighting his opponent from the back, and administering severe punishment to his neck. The big 'un threw his man, and only just avoided doing him a serious injury with his knee in a vital part.

Scarcely a round passed without claims and counter-claims. Scrambling rounds were fought, and the yells of the multitude were fearful. In the ninety-second round Bendy, stooping to avoid a blow from Caunt, fell, and in doing so struck out, catching his opponent on the lower part of the abdomen, when Caunt dropped his hands upon the place and rolled over in great pain. An appeal was made, but the Squire justly declared that it was unintentional, so he ordered them to fight on. In the next round Caunt opened in a determined manner. Bendigo was forced back upon the ropes, but managed to extricate himself. He was immediately knocked down by Caunt, who turned from him, evidently considering the round at an end. Bendigo, as he had done before, jumped up and attempted to recommence, but Caunt—whether from accident or design—dropped on his nether end. An appeal was now made amidst the most fearful turmoil, and the referee pronounced the fatal word "Foul," amidst the cheers, yells, shrieks, groans, and hisses of thousands of voices.

Naturally there was great dissatisfaction at this verdict, and Squire Osbaldeston was unjustly accused of having been intimidated by the Nottingham Lambs. But the Squire wrote the following to *Bell's Life:*—" I saw every round distinctly, and when Caunt came up for the last round he had evidently not recovered from the ninety-second. After the men were in position Bendigo very soon commenced operations, and Caunt

turned round directly and skulked away with his back to
Bendigo, and sat down on his nether end. He never
knocked Bendigo down once in the fight, and never got
him against the ropes in the last round. In my opinion
Caunt got away as soon as he could from Bendigo, fell
without a blow to avoid being hit out of time, and fairly
lost the fight."

So William Thompson, better known as Bendigo
became for the second time Champion of England.

CHAPTER XLI.

FIERCE BATTLE FOR THE BELT.— BENDIGO AND TOM PADDOCK.
—ANECDOTES OF THE ECCENTRIC BENDY.—HIS CONVER-
SION AND DEATH.

AFTER Bendigo's third battle with Ben Caunt, there
was no end of quarrelling between the partisans of the
men. Those who had backed Caunt declared that
Squire Osbaldeston, the referee, had made a great error,
and that he had not awarded the fight to Ben because
he was afraid of the Nottingham roughs, who had
mustered in such large numbers. But those who knew
the "Squire" were able to contradict such a statement,
for there was never a more fearless man or fair sport to
be found in the kingdom, and it is certain that he gave
his verdict according to his belief most conscientiously.

Ben Caunt declared that he would have another try,
and, indeed, challenged Bendigo to fight him for £500,
or even £1,000, but they never met again in the ring.
Indeed, not for five years did they speak, when at the
expiration of that period they were induced to shake
hands, bury the hatchet, and commemorate the occasion
by taking a joint benefit. This was early in 1850, and
the benefit was arranged to come off at the National
Baths, Westminster, on January 4. There was a monster
meeting, all the London members of the Fancy, and a
good sprinkling of Corinthians attending to see the two
former rivals have a friendly spar. This, of course, was
the event of the evening, and when the applause which
followed subsided the Bold Bendigo came to the front
of the stage and announced that he was ready to fight

any man in the world for £200 and the belt. Nobody believed that there would be any response, for Caunt was not likely to take it up, having at this time settled down in business, and there seemed nobody else qualified to tackle the clever Champion. Imagine the surprise of all, no less Bendigo himself, when a fine, stiff-built, fresh-coloured young fellow pushed through the crowd and made his way to the platform. Confronting Bendigo, he pulled out a handful of notes and declared that he was ready to make the match, and planked down the money. At the same time he declared that he was Tom Paddock, of Redditch, and identified himself with the mysterious " Unknown," whom Johnny Broome was anxious to bring out in the London Ring.

Paddock was fairly well-known in the provinces, and everybody present felt pleased when Bendigo, with his usual hankey-pankey style, caught hold of Tom's hand, and to that worthy's astonishment waltzed him round the platform, and then made the following little speech — " Gentlemen,—This is the happiest moment of my life. This is just what I wanted. You'll have a fight for the belt and you'll see what old Bendy can do when he tries."

There was, however, a good deal of time wasted before the match was made, and the date was not fixed for a couple of months after the benefit, when June 5 was decided upon, the stakes being £200 a-side with the belt and the Championship included.

This Bendigo determined should be his last fight, for he was then just forty years of age, too old for a pugilist to think of keeping the Championship. He made up his mind, though, to do his very best to hold the position to the finish, and so took the greatest pains with his training, and his backers had such confidence in him that they laid freely 2 to 1 on his chance. Paddock also was well supported by his Midland friends, who believed that youth would triumph, and his grand physique prove too much for the veteran Champion. Tom Paddock had, as we have said, done fairly well, for he appeared first in the ring upon December 4, 1844, beating Elijah Parsons, good man in his time, standing 6ft and weighing 13st, whilst Paddock was but 5ft 10½in, and scaled 11st 12lb. A few weeks after this he defeated a man from Redditch named Sam Hurst, and then won two fights with Nobby Clarke, who would have been a first-rate man had he had a little more heart. The second battle was on April 6, 1847, and from that date Paddock was not seen in the ring.

Bendigo had as usual taken up his quarters near Nottingham, and there he had some very unpleasant experiences, which nearly prevented the fight from coming off. A number of the Nottingham Lambs came over to see him the week before the date fixed for the battle, and kicked up such a disturbance that the inhabitants made complaints, and a warrant was issued for Bendigo's arrest. He managed, however, to get away, but a few days afterwards was recognised by a constable upon a railway station. The officious minion of the law attempted to arrest him, but Bendy made a rush for it and broke away from the policeman, who, however, gave chase and was joined by several other officers. It will be remembered that the Champion had some time prior to this hurt his knee, so that he was not quite so fleet as he formerly was. But his quick wit saved him. After running some distance he saw the door of a house open, so he darted in and locked it behind him, and then made his way out of the back and through some piggeries unobserved. When he got into the open, however, he was seen, and the chase commenced again. Fortunately, someone whom he knew came along with a gig, and took him along the road at racing speed to Newark. Thence he posted to Stamford, staying there for the night, and going on to Mildenhall (the spot chosen for the battle) in the morning, and put up at the Railway Hotel.

There was a good attendance, a large crowd coming down by the special on the morning of the fight, and both the outer and inner rings were admirably placed. The weather was fearfully hot, and whilst the company awaited the arrival of the men upon the field of battle, umbrellas were very much in evidence to keep off the powerful rays of the sun. Paddock was the first to appear, but there was no sign of Bendigo until more than an hour after Tom's arrival, so the latter stretched himself full length under the shade of a tree, whilst the company, sweltering in the tropical sun, waited as patiently as they could under the circumstances. The rings had been formed, and the spectators had taken their places long before noon, but it was not until just upon one o'clock that Bendigo came gently sauntering down towards the arena, accompanied by several friends. Paddock came to meet him, and they shook hands cordially, Bendy producing a bunch of notes—it was said ten £5—and offered to back himself to that amount. Tom, however, was not prepared, so they at once got to business.

Some delay was caused in the difficulty in appointing a referee, until Mr. Vincent Dowling, editor of *Bell's Life*, consented to take the post. Young Molyneux (known as the Morocco Prince) and Johnny Hannan were Bendigo's seconds, whilst Tom Paddock was esquired by Solid Coates and Jack Macdonald. An extraordinary thing

21

occurred when they tossed for positions in the ring. Bendigo selected that facing the sun, for what reason it would be difficult to surmise, unless he preferred that his opponent should have his back to the fierce heat, and run a chance of getting sunstroke.

Bendigo appeared somewhat stale but was trained to a day, and only weighed two pounds less than when he fought Caunt. "Paddock," one account says, "with his red face and lusty limbs, looked the picture of health and strength."

It is not our intention to describe the rounds of this, Bendigo's last appearance in the ring, for we have already had him in fighting attitude before our readers in several battles, and Tom Paddock will appear again in due course. Suffice it to state that the veteran still showed his old craftiness and judgment. He fought like an able general, with his head as well as his arms, and puzzled Paddock all through the battle. The latter had received orders from the brothers Broome to fight on the rush and try to confuse Bendigo, but the Nottingham man, old as he was, showed sufficient activity to avoid, and so worried Paddock that he lost his temper over and over again. Paddock was in such a hurry to force the fighting, that frequently before "Time" was called he had left his corner and seldom gave Bendigo the opportunity to reach the scratch. In vain Bendy's seconds appealed and claimed these acts as "foul," but Mr. Dowling always said, "Fight on." .

Then in the thirty-seventh round an incident occurred that certainly was most favourable to the Nottingham man, for Bendy's wind was not so good as it was formerly, and the previous round had been a regular pumper. Johnny Hannan called attention to Paddock's hands, and declared that he had been using resin and turpentine on them, and that it was a breach of Rule 27 of the laws of the Prize Ring. The referee discovered that resin had been used, and could, of course, have disqualified him. In spite of this appeal though by Bendigo's seconds, Mr. Dowling ordered them to resume, after Paddock had washed his hands. This three or four minutes' pause gave Bendy time to recover, and when he came up for the next bout he was as fresh as ever.

After this Bendigo waited for his man, and as he came in with his accustomed rush met him with a terrific blow on the bridge of the nose, which quite staggered the Redditch man and caused the nasal organ to pour with torrents of blood. Then as one account tells us, "he stopped Paddock's slashing one-two cleverly, and gave him three sounding punches in the ribs, which resounded over the ring."

Paddock after this got angrier than ever, he was so wild with passion that he scarcely knew what he was about, and "Foul" was being called during every round. At length the indulgent Mr. Dowling could not cease to take notice of his extraordinary behaviour. In the forty-ninth round, when the fight had lasted just over an hour, Tom Paddock forced Bendigo back on to the lower rope, where he fell seated upon the ground. When in that attitude he struck him two blows deliberately on the

VINCENT DOWLING (EDITOR OF *BELL'S LIFE*).

head. There could be no doubt about the "foul" then, and the referee without hesitation awarded the battle to Bendigo.

Then Paddock, mad with rage and quite losing his head with passion, immediately Bendigo got to his feet, and was standing with his hands beside him, naturally thinking that the fight was at an end, struck the Nottingham man two fearful blows in the face, knocking him down at the referee's feet.

And then one of the most disgraceful scenes ever witnessed at a prize-fight was enacted. Tom Paddock's friends, many of them hailing from Birmingham, and coming from the lowest of the roughs of the hardware town, got round Mr. Vincent Dowling and bustled him for having given the just verdict against Paddock. One of their number, Long Charley Smith, a notorious character, stole up behind the editor of *Bell's Life*, and with a bludgeon he carried struck him across the back of the head a blow, which for the time being stunned him. Tom Spring, who was standing near, let go at the Long Charley, one, two, and sent him sprawling, when the crowd attacked Spring with their sticks, and if Ben Caunt, Peter Crawley, and others had not come to the rescue it would have gone hard with Tom. Such a pasting did the roughs get that in a few minutes they were making off as quick as their legs could carry them.

Paddock went back to London in the special. He was very much mauled, and when he appeared at Jem Burn's house on the following evening he had his arm in a sling, and his face was considerably bruised, his eyes and nose particularly damaged. Bendigo, too, was severely punished. Until then it had been his proud boast that he had never had a black eye given to him in the ring. But this time the right side of his face was very much discoloured and damaged, whilst the eye was nearly closed. The veteran went to Nottingham on the following day, and was received at the station by a tremendous crowd of friends and a brass band, which played "See the Conquering Hero comes." He certainly deserved the greatest praise for having at forty years of age defeated a young, lusty fellow of twenty-six, particularly as he was queer about the leg through the accident we have already referred to, and suffered fearfully from rheumatism. It was Bendigo's last appearance in the Ring. But he remained a conspicuous character in Nottingham for many years, living until August, 1880, when he fell down stairs at his own house, and fractured his ribs, a splinter penetrating his lungs. He was then in his seventieth year, and the accident was fatal. He was buried in St. Mary's Cemetery, St. Ann's Well Road, better known as Fox's Close.

We could write pages about the ex-pugilist's career after he left the Ring, for he made himself a very prominent character in his native town, and the stories told about his eccentricities would fill a volume. When sober, Bendigo was one of the pleasantest and most entertaining fellows possible. He was a born comedian, and would have made a fine court jester or circus clown. But when in his cups he was really a dangerous imbecile, and the unfortunate part of it was, very little made him intoxicated. Consequently he was always in trouble. His brother allowed him £1 per week, and he possessed a little property of his own, so he could afford to go merrymaking in the taverns of his native city, in many of which he was looked upon as a terror. One of his pranks was to enter the bar when he was getting a bit on, and take up anybody's drink that might be upon the counter, finishing the glasses or tankards off one after the other, and he rarely got stopped, for everybody knew Bendy and his pugilistic proclivities when in that particular state. We remember being told of an incident which happened upon one of these occasions. Bendy walked into a bar where a soldier and his friends were drinking, and commenced his old game. The soldier, a stranger to the town, at once turned round, and, with an oath, let go at Bendigo, catching him full in the face and knocking him all of a heap into the corner, where he lay half drunk and helpless. Then somebody said to the warrior bold, "Good G——, do you know who you have knocked down? Why, that's Bendigo, the ex-Champion." Whereupon the soldier, no doubt, thinking discretion the better part of valour, opened the door and shot down the street in double-quick time.

Bendigo, when in that state, would draw the line at nothing, and he has been known to clear a butcher's shop by pelting the crowd outside with joints of meat. Of course he was constantly before the magistrates, and frequently fined or imprisoned. One of his eccentric acts was to take a beautiful bouquet of rare and valuable flowers, and when appearing before the "beak" after a remand, present it to the bench. Sometimes (particularly if there had been no assault), when only drunkenness was the charge, this would have some weight with the sitting magistrate, who would let him off with a small fine.

Yet there were some good points about this, the most extraordinary of all our Champions. He was fondly devoted to his mother—terrible old lady that she was, and from whom there is little doubt he inherited all his ferocity —and his affection for children were both redeeming traits in his character. He saved no less than three lives from drowning, too, in the Trent, upon whose banks he would spend hours fishing, which was his favourite pastime. On one occasion he saw a young woman struggling in the water, and laying down his fishing tackle, he jumped in with all his clothes and boots on, and succeeded in bringing her to shore. For this a considerable sum of money was offered to him, but he declined to take a penny.

Ten years before his death, Richard Weaver, the Revivalist, paid a visit to Nottingham, and found Bendigo willing to listen to him. The palm-smiting gentleman succeeded in persuading the ex-Champion to join their ranks, and Bendy donning the black frock-coat, tall hat, and black kid gloves, with his hair long and plastered down, *à la* Mr. Stiggins, was taken through the provinces, and put up as an example and specimen of a converted character. When he came to London on one occasion, he was walking down Oxford Street, when Lord Longford, who had backed him for many a fight, recognised him, and this is the conversation that passed between them, as the story goes. My Lord, looking at his get-up in amazement, exclaimed, " Hulloa, Bendy ! What's your little game now ?" " I am fighting Satan, and, behold, Scripture says the victory shall be mine." " Hope, so, Bendy," rejoined his lordship, dryly, " but pray fight Beelzebub more fairly than you fought Ben Caunt, or else I shall change sides, and all my sympathies will go with Old Nick." " My lord," answered Bendy, " you backed me against Ben Caunt, and I won your money, so *you've* no cause to complain. I beat Caunt, and I mean to beat the Devil ; you'd better back me again." But his lordship shook his head and went away laughing.

On several occasions Bendy broke out in a fresh place, and once he went to a pigeon match, backed the birds, and got drunk, but he always came back like a lamb to the fold.

One more anecdote, and then we must leave the Bold Bendigo and get on with the biographies of the few other Champions it will be our province to write, in order to bring our task to a close. He had joined the Good Templars, and for a considerable time proved a great attraction, causing their meetings to be crowded, and inducing many converts. On one occasion, in the Goose Market, Nottingham, whilst in company of one of the G.T.'s, he was stopped by a very old friend he had not met for years. His pal asked him to come and just have one drink for the sake of old times. Bendy, with his eyes turned towards heaven, however, steadfastly refused, and declared that he would not break the pledge for untold wealth. The friend protested, and at last Bendigo consented to enter one of their old haunts, where he would continue their conversation whilst the friend refreshed himself. Bendy would look on ; not a drop of intoxicating liquor would he touch. In vain the Good Templar persuaded him not to go, but Bendigo was obdurate, and accompanied his friend. The G.T. remained outside for a considerable time, until at last he heard laughter and sounds of convivial merriment

from within. He could wait no longer; opening the
door he peeped in, and there was the Bold One with a
pint mug of old Nottingham ale in his hand, relating
anecdotes of his fights with Caunt and Paddock. Deeply
shocked, the Good Templar exclaimed: " Oh, Mr.
Thompson, this is indeed sad! I see Satan has again
entrapped you." To which the hilarious convert pro-
fanely replied: " Bother owd Satan. He may go to
Hell and take you with him." The Good Templar fled.
But Bendigo always went back penitent, and died, as
we have already said, in 1880, with his friends around
him praying, with whom this extraordinary pugilist
.ervently joined.

CHAPTER XVII.

A TERRIBLE CATASTROPHE.—FAMILY JARS.— BEN CAUNT AND NAT LANGHAM.— A BRACE OF VETERANS. — BATTLE FOR FOUR HUNDRED POUNDS.

AND now we must skip over a number of years to
bring Ben Caunt's fistic career to a close, for it was, as
described in the previous chapter, in the year 1845 that
he lost the Championship, and it was not until 1857
that he again figured in the Ring. This was not for
the Championship, yet it must be recorded here, for it
was with the only man who succeeded in defeating the
notorious Tom Sayers; he was one of the middle-
weights, and his name was Nat Langham.

Before, however, describing the origin of the match
and giving a description of the battle, it may be interesting to sketch the life of Ben Caunt during those
twelve years. After his defeat by Bendigo, he declared
that he should like to meet him a fourth time, and that
he was willing to put down from £500 to £1,000, on the
condition that they should fight upon a raised platform,
so that the ruffians could not get at the combatants, and
that the battle should take place a sufficient distance
from the Nottingham Lambs to preclude their presence.
But it all fell through, and as time passed by he was
looked upon as being on the shelf, for he was thirty-five
years of age, considered quite old for a member of the
P.R. He still talked about fighting, however, and would

not admit that he was on the retired list. But as he
was doing excellent business at his pub., the Coach and
Horses, St. Martin's Lane, he would, we should think,
have thought twice before meeting his old antagonist
again.

Ben was no fool. Although but a simple countryman,
he was as sharp as a needle in looking after business, and was a most genial host, until a misfortune
happened to him that all but turned his brain, and
altered his disposition entirely, transforming him from
a jovial host to an irritable man, who easily lost his
temper, and was not always answerable for what he said
and did. It was in the year 1851, or six years after he
had fought Bendigo, during which period he had been
very prosperous, that he paid a visit to some friends in
Herefordshire. On the eve of his return the Coach
and Horses had been closed some hours when the cellar-
man, who slept upstairs, smelt smoke, and on going to
the landing discovered that the place was on fire. First
rousing the barmaid, Sarah Martin, and then Mrs.
Caunt, who was sleeping with her cousin, Susannah
Thorpe, he made for the street to give the alarm. So
rapidly did the flames spread that the three women, but
partly dressed, had some difficulty in escaping down
stairs, and all of them lost their presence of mind, and
forgot (or believed that they had been called) all about
the two children, who, together with the maid, were sleeping in an attic. Nobody even seemed to think of them
when they got into the street, too, and the firemen
declared that when the escape arrived they were not
informed at first that any people were in the house.
When they did know of it and tried to get into the top
room over the parapet it was too late, for the flames burst
through the window and made it impossible to enter.
So the two children—a girl and a boy—aged respectively
nine years and six, together with the girl of eighteen,
Ruth Lowe, a cousin of Mrs. Caunt's, perished in the
flames. The tragedy sent a thrill throughout the sporting world and the most touching part of the unfortunate catastrophe was that not only was Ben away when
he could have saved the children had he been at home,
but he arrived next morning, without the slightest
knowledge of the occurrence, to find when he got to St,
Martin's Lane that his house was in ruins, and the little
children whom he loved dead.

One who was present at the funeral describes the
pathetic scene. He says: "At the inquest and at the
funeral the grief displayed by the unhappy father excited
general commiseration. No one could have suspected
that the big, rough prize-fighter had so tender a heart

and so emotional a nature. Never was witnessed a more
pathetic and a more distressing spectacle than that of
Ben Caunt, with the tears running down his rugged
cheeks, and the sobs shaking his huge frame as he stood
by the grave-side when the charred remains of the two
children whom he loved so dearly were committed to
the earth."

Ben was never the same man afterwards, and it
was this misfortune that undoubtedly led him to
enter the lists again, for the irritability of his temper
brought about the quarrel with Nat Langham. Nat was
related by marriage to the Caunts, the wives of the two
men being cousins. But there was very little affection
between the two ladies, who were always giving vent to
ill-temper and sarcastic remarks about each other's
husband, for there were petty jealousies founded on
Caunt's greater success in business. It proved the fact
that a woman is always at the bottom of a quarrel, for
the unfriendliness of the two women soon turned to
hatred, and Mrs. Caunt particularly did all she knew to
quarrel and induce her husband to do the same to
Langham. If Ben had been left to himself no doubt
they would have made it up; but his wife was always
calling attention to the way that Nat was carrying on
the Cambrian Stores close by, and declared that he was
doing all he could to take the custom away from the
Coach and Horses. Again, Nat Langham was a most
provoking fellow, with a sarcastic tongue and a wit that
brought him many admirers. He would to Ben Caunt's
face tell him that he never could fight, and that should
they ever stand up together he could not hit him in a
month of Sundays.

All this rankled in Caunt's bosom, but what put the
finishing touch to the whole affair was the presence of
old Ben Butler, to whom we have already referred as
Ben's uncle, and who resided with them. He had become
a disagreeable, sour old man, sitting in the bar parlour
drinking his " blue ruin " and grumbling and swearing
all day long, boasting that it was he who had brought
out his nephew, and that it was all through him that
Ben had made his pugilistic successes, and had been
enabled to take the tavern in which he was doing such
good business. Be that as it may, it is certain that old
Ben Butler helped him a great deal, and never missed
one of his fights, whilst he always trained him, and
gave him the best advice. So Caunt had a great deal of
faith in the old man. What wonder, then, that with
Butler and the wife always nagging him, and declaring
that Nat Langham was his worst enemy, he should form
a dislike to the celebrated middle-weight? Langham went

to the Coach and Horses one morning and commenced
in his usual style to chaff Big Ben. The latter turned
round and exclaimed, " Sitha, laad, th' art allus sayin'
as tha can lick me, and as I can't hit thee in a month o'
Sundays. Well, naw I'll give thee a chance o' showin'
whether tha can do what tha says. Coover these ten
pun'—" and he slapped down upon the counter two five-
pound notes—" coover yon, and I'll fight thee for as
much as thou loikes ; for nowt but a feight will work
my ill blood off."

Everybody was surprised when they heard that it
looked like serious business, for here was Nat Langham,
who, as we have said, belonged to the middle-weights,
accepting the challenge of an ex-Champion, and one of
the biggest men who had ever won the Champion's belt.
True, at this time the Tipton Slasher had been defeated
by Tom Sayers (all about which in due course we shall
have something to say), which was very astonishing to
the sporting world, for until then nobody dreamed of
matching an 11st man of medium height against a
14st man, standing over six feet. This upset of the
weights had an effect on Ben Caunt, and he caused the
following to appear in *Bell's Life* :—

SIR,—Unaccustomed as I am to public challenging, long
laid upon the shelf as I have been, it may perchance startle
the sporting world to hear that Ben Caunt is once more a
candidate for the Championship. Win or lose with Langham, I challenge Tom Sayers for £200 a-side and the Championship, the contest to take place within six months of
my forthcoming fight. My money is ready at your office,
and I trust that this offer will be accepted, in order that the
world may be as speedily as possible undeceived with regard
to the merits of the much-vaunted new school of British
boxing.—Yours obediently,   BENJAMIN CAUNT.
June 18, 1857.

With this letter was left the sum of £10 with the
editor, so there was no doubt about Ben being actually
in earnest. Tom Sayers was away on tour, making a
lot of money in the provinces after beating the Slasher ;
so when Caunt wanted to have the articles signed at the
Coach and Horses (of course the host looking at the
custom this would bring him), Sayers declined, but said
that he would send the deposit and sign, if the articles
were sent to him. This did not suit Ben, who, we
think, regretted having embarked on the match at all,
so after a deal of letter writing the whole thing fell
through.

Not so the matter with Langham, though. But Ben
Butler very nearly made a mess of it for his nephew, whilst
the latter was away at Brighton. On May 11, 1857, the
men had affixed their signatures to the articles, which

provided that they should fight for £200 a-side, on September 23. Langham happened to be going out of town before the second deposit fell due, so he sent the tenner before the date that it was due, and old Ben Butler protested that it was not in accordance with the strict wording of the articles, and claimed on behalf of his nephew the first deposit put down. This was a paltry

NAT LANGHAM.

bit of business, and directly Caunt heard of it he wrote to *Bell's Life* the following letter:—

MR. EDITOR,—I respectfully ask that you will admit into your columns this declaration on my part:—That my match with Langham is the result of a dispute that can only be settled, so far as I am concerned, by an appeal to the fists. That the articles will be strictly abided by on my part; but so far from throwing any impediment in the way of the match it is my anxious desire to bring it to an issue in the ring. Thus far I beg my friends will accept my assurance of "honourable intentions." Were they but

aware of the personal nature of the affair, such assurances
would not be needed ; but as many must necessarily be
unacquainted with the cause of the origin, it is due to my
character to take the course I have now done, in writing to
you an emphatic statement of my intentions, which I
solemnly assert are unalterable until that result comes to
pass, which shall prove either me or my antagonist the
better man.—Yours, &c.,   BENJAMIN CAUNT.
Coach and Horses, St. Martin's Lane, May 27, 1857.

Not only was the letter published, but Ben paid the
editor a visit and repeated his determination, and
entered more fully into the origin of the match.

Nat Langham, whose fight with Sayers we shall have
to refer to in due course, was much concerned about
that worthy's defeat of the Tipton. For the life of him
he could not understand why he had not aspired to the
Championship when he was in his prime. But he never
thought of it, and his time had gone by, for he was
getting on in years, like Caunt, and furthermore he was
suffering from weak lungs, having been attending the
Hospital for Consumptives at Brompton. Yet after little
Tom's performance with the Tipton, many good judges,
who knew Nat Langham's superior science, believed
that he would be more than a match for Big Ben, in
spite of the disparity in their heights and weights. So
when it was discovered that both men were serious, not
a little excitement and interest were invested in the
affair. Deposit after deposit was punctually put
down, and the bitterness between them increased apace.

Caunt had, during the twelve years he had been idle,
naturally put on a good deal of superfluous flesh, and
weighed considerably over seventeen stone, so it was
necessary for him to get into training in ample time, for
to fight Langham it was considered that he should be
as near 14st as possible. So, four months before the
date set down for the battle he commenced gentle exercise
by going down every day to the White Bear, Kenning-
ton, and there played quoits for hours. Then he
went to Ramsgate with Job Cobley, who was at the
time matched to fight Bob Brettle. Caunt was a fine
swimmer, so he took plenty of exercise in the sea and
long walks in the bracing fresh air, whilst he did daily
practice with the gloves. After being at Ramsgate, old
Ben Butler appeared upon the scene, and it was thought
better to go to the quieter and more secluded Saltpan,
Sandwich ; so they took a place for a month, and did
much about the same exercise. At the expiration of
this period they came nearer to town, putting up at the
Greyhound Inn, at Hadfield, near Woodside, in Surrey,
and Ben made wonderful progress for an old 'un.

Nat Langham, who really wanted to pick up strength

rather than waste, went to Dover, in company with Frank Widdows, who came from Norwich, a comical character, and just the sort of companion to have on such an excursion, for he was the life and soul of every convivial party, and a favourite with all. Langham declared that Widdows was worth a dozen other trainers, for he could keep his man in the highest spirits with his inexhaustible fund of anecdote, songs, and jokes. From Dover Nat took up his quarters at Stockbridge, near Tom Cannon's training stables and residence.

Although many people thought that really there would be no fight, knowing what a tricky fellow Langham was, and believed that it would all turn out a " barney," when Dan Dismore, Jemmy Shaw, and Uncle Ben were found to be acting in concert, and two steamers had been chartered, the disbelievers changed their minds. The steamboats were to have laid off Tilbury, but that was thought to be unsafe, and so Nat's friends telegraphed to the owners for the boats to proceed to Southend. By some oversight this was not communicated to Caunt. Perhaps they felt sure of seeing him at Fenchurch Street Station, whence the party started, but he, to the disappointment of everybody, was not there. But there was nothing for it but to proceed at any rate to Tilbury, where they hoped to pick him up. On arriving there, however, there was no sign of Ben or Fred Oliver, who was to have accompanied him, so they proceeded to Southend, with a feeling that after all there would be no fight. At that place, again, there were no tidings, and the only alternative was to wait patiently, for word had been left at Tilbury for him to come on by the next train. Two hours passed; and no Ben Caunt by the next train, but when misgiving was almost turned to despair a message came that the ex-Champion, finding that the party had gone on, had chartered the tug, *Ben Bolt* (ominous name for him), and that he was steaming on to Southend, where he arrived after two o'clock, and the boats steamed away for the Standing Creek, on the Medway, where the party was landed, immediately opposite to the spot where Sayers and Aaron Jones had fought their battle.

The ring was soon pitched and the men entered, Caunt being looked after by two extraordinary seconds —little Jemmy Shaw and Jack Gill, of Nottingham, who was not much bigger. A nice pair to lift about a giant like Caunt. Nat Langham had Jack Macdonald and Tom Sayers, who was then Champion of England. Now it is not our intention to describe this fight, that should never have been allowed to take place. Ben Caunt was forty-two years old, and Nat Langham thirty-seven. The former stood 6ft 2½in, and weighed 14½st. He never stripped better in his life, and it must have looked any odds on him as he stood towering above his slight adversary. Still, Nat was in splendid condition, but his height was only 5ft 10in, and he scaled exactly 11st. It was soon evident, though, who was the quicker and more scientific man. Caunt from the first made rushes at Langham, as if he were going to knock him out then and there, and no doubt if his blows had reached where they were intended the battle would have been very soon over. But the wary Nat avoided with marvellous quickness, and got down cleverly every time to avoid, and only when he had a certain opening did he let go. When he did it was always there, and during the first few rounds Caunt's face was cut and bleeding. Caunt always came in too much of a hurry, and threw away his chances with a wooden-headed obstinacy. Although he was fearfully mauled by Langham he never lost his temper, and appeared to be anticipating that he would wear Nat out, when he would polish him off in double-quick time. He did manage to get one blow on the forehead, which gave him the first knock-down, but followed this up with too much impetuosity, so consequently suffered again.

One very exciting round was fought, and here is an account of it:—"Ben for once was rather slow to begin, and seemed inclined to stand his ground and let his foe come to him. Nat did not baulk him, but crept in cunningly, and, quick as thought, popped his left on Caunt's nose. Then came two most terrific counters. Simultaneously the men let out, Caunt landing on the cheek, Nat on the jaw, both blows as hard as the men could hit. Nat fell instantly head foremost, knocked clean off his legs. Ben stood for a moment, dazed, with the blood running from his mouth, then reeled and went staggering to his corner. It took his seconds all their time to get Ben up to the scratch. But Langham was no better. He was nearly done for, and it was evident that that tremendous exchange of counters had severely shaken both of them."

There is nothing to describe after that. Darkness was setting in, and although Caunt in his terrific lunges nearly succeeded in knocking Langham out, the latter was too quick. At length both seemed to have had enough of it, and they stood for many minutes rubbing their chests, and looking at each other, and it was evident that they were waiting for darkness to make it a draw. Dan Dismore then went to Mr. Frank Dowling, editor of *Bell's Life*, and had an earnest conversation with him, for he was referee. Dan then stepped into

the ring and asked the men to shake hands. Ben said
he was willing to do so if Nat was. The latter, after
slight hesitation, extended his hand, which was shaken
heartily, and the men dressed.

On the way home, though, Langham wanted to say that
he had had no intention of finishing the battle, that he
only considered it an adjournment, and that the referee
must name another day in the same week. This Mr.
Dowling refused to do, so there was a tremendous row,
and they were as bad friends as ever, but after a wordy
warfare in the sporting papers they met and drew the
stakes, shaking hands and making it up, remaining
friends until Caunt's death, which took place in 1861. He
caught cold at a pigeon match, which settled on his
lungs.

Nat Langham never entered the ring again, but continued as a sporting Boniface until 1871, in which year
he died at the Cambrian Stores, Castle Street, Leicester
Square, on September 1, and his death may be regarded
as the snapping of the link which divided the old school
from the new.

CHAPTER XLIII.

EARLY CAREER OF THE TIPTON SLASHER (WILLIAM PERRY) —
HIS MATCH WITH TOM PADDOCK.—£100 A-SIDE AND THE
BELT.

AND now we come to perhaps the most interesting
period of the Championship, for it was William Perry,
alias the Tipton Slasher, who lost the belt to Tom
Sayers, and for the first time in the annals of pugilism
it was proved that a man, little and good, was better
than the average big 'un. In other words, it was
feasible that a middle-weight could tackle a heavy and
gain the Championship.

But let us introduce the Tipton Slasher, who comes
next upon our list of warriors who have fought bravely
and won the belt. William Perry was born at Tipton,
in the Black Country, in the same year as our Most
Gracious Majesty the Queen—1819, and when he was

only sixteen he came to London, where he made, in 1835, his first appearance in the Ring. He fought, according to the " Oracle of the Ring," one Dogherty, at Chelsea, beating him in seven rounds. This, however, appears to have been but an off-hand fight, and his *début* in the Ring proper may be said to have taken place on December 27, 1836, when he defeated Ben Spilsbury, at Oldbury, for £10 a-side. His terrific hitting caused him to be christened the Tipton Slasher, and the nick-name stuck to him throughout his long and somewhat brilliant career. After defeating the Birmingham man he tried conclusions with Jem Scunner, the Gornal champion, whom he fought near Wolverhampton, on November 22, 1837, for £25 a-side. The battle lasted an hour, during which thirty-one rounds were got through, and the Slasher again proved victorious. So decisive were his victories that, amongst others, he attracted the attention of Johnny Broome, who was then just commencing his fistic career.

After his fight with Scunner, Johnny, who had witnessed the battle at Wolverhampton, brought the Slasher to London, determined to run him for all he was worth, and make capital out of the uncommon youngster. There was a story going about, which, of course, must not be accepted, that Johnny Broome took his *protégé* about town with a chain round his neck, pretending that he was a sort of wild man of the woods. Perry certainly had rather a savage appearance when he first came to London, and no doubt that gave rise to the invention. Ben Burn, of the Queen's Head, Windmill Street, though, always declared the chain business to be a fact, and he used to add, " Yes, and I am not quite sure whether he wasn't muzzled, too." In the first place, Broome tried to get the Slasher matched with a Devonshire man named Randall, whom Burn had in hand, but the latter did not like the look of the " wild man," so the match was never made. Then there was an attempt made to match him against Deaf Burke, who had only just arrived from America, but that, too, proved futile, although no fault of the Slasher's. The match was, indeed, made for £100 a-side, and the date was fixed for August, 1842, and £15 had actually been put down. Johnny Broome, however, then, for some reason best known to himself, failed to put in an appearance when the next deposit was due, and the Deaf 'Un claimed forfeit, and the Slasher was left in the lurch, although several gentlemen had promised to find the money through Broome. Johnny tried to make the public believe that the fault was with the other side, and perhaps there may have been some truth in

it, for we find the following editorial in *Bell's Life*:—
"Though Broome was certainly late, their insistence on
forfeit seems very sharp practice; the more so as the

WILLIAM PERRY (THE TIPTON SLASHER.)
(From a drawing by Read.)

same gentleman who backs Perry actually assisted
Burke with his first deposit. The forfeit, however, has
yet to be taken by Burke's backers, as he had nothing

22

to do with it, beyond their approval, and we may yet find
that the last and remaining deposits will be deposited,
and the ' ball go on.' We have since received a letter
from the gentleman who put down £4 of the first
deposit, stating that he will not consent to the forfeit
being received, and expresses his desire that the match
should proceed, as his only desire is to encourage the
manly sports of the Ring."

However, the match did not go on, and the Deaf 'Un
received his £15. No doubt Johnny Broome was not
ready to spring his man upon the public with first-class
men, but preferred for the time being to keep him
" dark." This might have been all right from his point
of view, but it certainly did the Slasher's reputation no
good.

Shortly after this, Ben Caunt who it will be remembered, paid a visit to New York, after his defeat of Nick
Ward, again visited the States. On his return to this
country he brought with him a man called Freeman, a
giant who stood 6ft 10½in, and weighed 18st. He was a
fine man, and exceedingly powerful. Caunt had no idea
of introducing him to the P.R., nor, indeed, had this
colossal Hercules any proclivities for milling. He and
Caunt were to go about the country exhibiting his
feats of strength and horsemanship in the circus, Ben
to do a turn with the gloves, and they were to be
partners. However, not long after his arrival, somebody
sent paragraphs to the sporting papers, eulogising
Freeman as a scientific boxer, and declaring that his
strength and ability as a fighting man had frightened
the British boxers.

Whether this really made Johnny Broome wild from
a patriotic point of view, or whether he saw a fine
opportunity to get the Slasher matched with one who
would bring grist to the mill, we know not, but he called
a meeting of noble patrons at his house, the Rising Sun,
in Air Street, Piccadilly, and then protested against the
statement that the English prize-fighters had received a
scare from the presence of the big American. He declared
that he had a " novice " whom he would back for £100.
So it was unanimously agreed that a challenge should
formally be issued for " Broome's Unknown " to fight
the American giant. To their delight there came a
prompt reply. It was couched in the most polite
language, and stated that Freeman had not come to this
country with any desire or intention of fighting; that
his pursuits were purely peaceful, and that he had
challenged no man, and was not responsible for the
paragraphs that had appeared. He felt, however, that
Broome's manifesto was a slur upon his own courage

and an insult to his country, so he had determined to accept the challenge.

The two fights the Slasher had with Freeman, the giant, need not be given in detail here, as they were by no means feathers in the cap of Mr. Perry, nor a test as to his quality as a prize-fighter. He certainly was not prepared to run the risk of having the shoulder-of-mutton fists of this great Herculean warrior placed about any part of his person, and resorted to the dropping tactics. The first battle took place on December 14, 1842, after an interruption by the authorities, in a field near Sawbridgeworth. No less than seventy rounds, which only lasted one hour and twenty-four minutes, were gone through without any damage being done, so it may well be imagined what sort of a battle it was. Darkness came on and stopped the farce. They met again the same week at Taplow Heath, but the police interfered and the fight was declared a draw. The next battle the Slasher lost on a foul, dropping before the giant without a blow being struck. It took place in Cliffe Marshes, below Gravesend, on December 20, 1842, when only thirty-eight rounds had been fought in thirty-nine minutes. Thus ended the two farces, and Charles Freeman never entered the ring again, for he died at the early age of twenty-eight, of consumption, at Winchester Hospital.

Next on the Slasher's list was Tass Parker, the West Bromwich champion, but this was also a fiasco, although no blame could be accorded the Slasher, for Tass Parker positively declined to stand up for a fair fight, although he should not have been afraid of the ungainly K-legged Slasher, for Tass was heavier, and was certainly more scientific. Parker was attached to Mr. Merry's stables in the capacity of servant and guardian, and fulfilled his post to the greatest satisfaction. But he was never cut out for the Ring, his honesty there being very questionable, and his courage found greatly wanting. The men met three times. The Tipton fought Parker first for £100 a-side, on Dartford Marshes, December 19, 1843, and when they had accomplished sixty-seven rounds in one hour and thirty-five minutes the police interfered. In the February of 1844 they met again for the same amount, at Horley, one hundred and thirty-three rounds in two hours and thirty-two minutes, when Parker went down without a blow, and the Slasher received the stakes. The third fight, though, was the best; Parker made a good show, and the Tipton never fought better in his life. One account of this meeting says :—" He displayed an amount of judgment, coolness, science, and generalship which no one, not even those

who knew him best, had previously credited him with,
and these qualities, added to his immense bulk and
strength, rendered him irresistible. Tass, too, faced his
man with more spirit and determination than he had
ever shown before. But his undoubted skill was not so
apparent. His friends attributed his defeat to the fact
that two of his ribs had been broken in the terrific fall
which the Slasher gave him in the seventh round. Be
this as it may, Tass was decisively licked in twenty-
three rounds, twenty-seven minutes, and the Slasher
added greatly to his reputation by his victory. The
battle took place upon Lindrick Common, August 4, 1846.

Three years elapsed before the Slasher made another
match, which he forfeited to Con Parker, September,
1849 ; and he drew his money over a match with Tom
Paddock on August 22, 1850, neither being ready with
the deposits. However, the match was made again for
£100 a-side, which also carried the Championship.

Tom Paddock has already been introduced to our
readers when we described his fight with Bendigo, and
since then he had not appeared in the ring. The original
stakes had been fixed at £150, but by some mismanage-
ment or negligence of Broome's the third deposit was
not forthcoming, although the Slasher declared he
had sent it to London. Anyhow, the match fell through,
and it was not until the first week in October, 1850, that
a meeting was held at Tom Spring's, when the contest
was fixed to take place on the 17th of the following
December, at a place thereafter to be named, not
more than eighty nor less than thirty miles from the
metropolis. So disgracefully had the dropping system
been carried on, that it was determined that Rule 19
should be revived. This was done by Mr. Pierce Egan,
who more clearly defined it, and added further instructions to referees to observe it more strictly.

Tom Spring and Jem Burn had the entire management of the fight, so matters looked rosy enough.
On Friday, December 15, the last deposits were posted
at Jem Burn's, and he and Spring met to consider final
arrangements. Twenty ring-keepers were engaged, and
a land excursion was determined upon, whilst every
precaution was taken that all rowdyism should be
excluded, both Jem and Tom declaring that should this
not be a model mill to help resuscitate the fallen
fortunes of the Ring, they would quit the ranks for ever.
On the Monday the men came from their training
quarters, the Slasher putting up at Spring's, and Paddock at Burn's. The day before the fight the betting
in town was particularly heavy, the Tipton being
favourite at 6 to 4 on.

Waterloo Station was the rendezvous, and tickets could be had for 30s. first class, and 15s. second, the train being packed at these prices. Nobody knew, save the managers, anything about the destination until they arrived at Basingstoke, and it there leaked out that Dean had been selected. However, at the first-named place it was discovered that the Wiltshire and Hampshire constabulary were out with four magistrates, so it was determined to return towards London. Another unsuccessful attempt was made near Andover, so a council of war was held, when it was determined to make for Woking Common.

There the lists were quickly formed, for it was three o'clock, and there was not much daylight left, so the men were quickly in the ring, the seconds, umpires, and referee having been selected *en route*. Still the men were not in the arena until ten minutes past four, and it must be remembered that it was December, and the sun was just dipping behind the horizon. Fortunately, the evening was beautifully clear, and the moon had risen, and was shining brightly. A mill by moonlight was something of a novelty. The Slasher had won the toss for corners, so naturally placed his back to the moon.

The Slasher appeared easy and comfortable, and, save the crooked leg, was a fine specimen of an athlete, whilst Paddock looked quite diminutive before him; but when the fists were put up the disparity in reach was evident—the Tipton had abnormally long arms. Perry opened the ball but was, even with his length, out of distance, and Paddock jumped in and caught the Slasher on the side of the head. Then the Tipton got a light one in, and, Tom fighting on the retreat, some heavy exchanges took place, until Paddock went down.

Tom seemed in a desperate hurry to begin each round, and was evidently very excited and anxious, whilst the Slasher was taking things as quietly as if he were out for a holiday and strolling about in the fields. Jumping from his second's knee immediately "Time" was called, Tom rushed at his man like a bull at a gate, but was cleverly countered, and the Slasher had all the best of the exchanges. Still Paddock blazed away, but the Tipton was evidently quicker, longer, and cleverer than his opponent, and following his man up after a rally, caught hold of him and threw him heavily, adding his own weight.

There was a commotion in Paddock's corner, and it was palpable that something had happened that was serious, although nobody but the seconds could tell what it really was. But Tom was very slow to time, and he looked pale. Yet he rushed in as usual, but Perry met him determinedly and beat him off, following him up with some crushing blows, which caused him to sit down in his corner. Again he slipped down to avoid, and from this period evinced the greatest disinclination to fight. In the next round, indeed, he dropped in such a suspicious manner that an appeal was made. The referee, whilst ordering them to continue the fight, administered a caution to Tom.

But it was obvious that Paddock for some reason did not intend to prolong the battle, and in the eleventh round he had less desire still, for although he planted his left lightly on the Slasher's face, the latter let go with terrific force on the left eye, gashing it and causing it to bleed profusely. After this Paddock continued to drop in a most unfair manner. Ned Donnelly was referee, and he curiously stated that he was lenient to Tom Paddock, because he believed that he had injured his arm. Was there ever such an absurd argument? One report says that in the twentieth round Paddock dropped palpably without a blow of any kind being struck, yet the referee when appealed to, said "Fight on." It would seem that Tom Paddock must have been trying to lose the fight, and Donnelly would not let him have his way. At length, in the twenty-second round, Paddock plucked up a bit and managed to force some exchanges, but had none the best of it, and looked exceedingly savage, and when the Slasher pressed him hard, down he went as usual. Then came an episode which is unheard-of before or since in the annals of the Ring. The Tipton, naturally believing the round to be ended, turned to walk to his corner, when Paddock as quick as lightning jumped up and hit him a heavy blow on the back of the neck. This flagrant breach of the rules was too much even for Ned Donnelly, and he immediately awarded the fight to the Tipton Slasher.

So finished this burlesque of a battle for the Championship. No doubt Paddock had hurt his shoulder badly, but it was not broken, and he might have shown a little more bulldog British pluck. However, we shall meet him again, for he had ten years more in the Ring, and to an extent retrieved his reputation. The old Tipton, who was now Champion of England, we shall also have something further to say about, for if not of the same class as Cribb, Spring, Belcher, and others, he was a good plucked 'un, and deserves to figure amongst the illustrious line of Champions.

CHAPTER XLIV.

A LIVELY NIGHT AT THE RISING SUN. — THE "GREAT
UNKNOWN."—TIPTON SLASHER AND HARRY BROOME.—
A DESPERATE SCENE IN THE RING.

WHEN the Tipton had the right to dub himself Champion of England, after defeating Paddock (Bendigo having
retired), he had gained the object of his ambition. Yet
the Slasher was anxious for a fight, and kept inserting
his challenges in the sporting papers, but without
response. He had been offering to fight anybody for the
belt and £200. Finding, however, that he received no
response, he came down with his price, and mentioned
the figure as £100. Yet nobody accepted for months, and
the Tipton was getting impatient, when one morning a
letter appeared from Johnny Broome offering to match
an " Unknown " against the Champion.

Owing to Tom Spring's illness, however, the meeting
to sign articles was postponed for several weeks, when it
was decided that a meeting should take place at Johnny
Broome's house, the Rising Sun, in Air Street, Piccadilly, when the men could come to terms. To read some
of the names of those who were present takes us back
to the jolly old days when sportsmen, friends, and comrades met and enjoyed each other's society merrily.
Here is a description which is before us, referring to this
very meeting, and written by one who was present :—

" Archibald Henning (who drew the first cartoons and
first title page for *Punch*) was there, merely to look at whose
jovial phiz was a cure for melancholy, and as the Scotch
say, ' a sight to cure sair een.' Harry Hill, the bookmaker
--big, burly, loud-voiced, uneducated, never ashamed to
own that he had been ' boots ' at a country inn, but great-
hearted and generous—was conspicuous, with a cigar
in his mouth as big as a torpedo. Baron Renton Nicholson, who had just closed his Judge and Jury Show, as he
facetiously told us, ' for internal repairs,' which Jem
Wellesley, the 'Facer,' interpreted as meaning that all
the leading ladies were in the family way, a condition
which, however gratifying to matrons who ' love their
lords,' is not quite compatible with graceful and effective posturing in the *poses plastiques.* Were there ever
whiskers bushier or blacker than those of the Chief

Baron? Owen Swift and Jem Burn gave the light of their countenances to the festive scene; and ponderous Peter Crawley, nineteen stone of unadulterated good humour, beamed upon the assembly with a face round and red as the harvest moon; the manly figure and handsome features of Lord Drumlanrig, with the grave, clerical frontispiece of his friend, Maurice Vincent, beside him; the well-dressed person and famous blue umbrella of D'Orsay Clarke; the natty, groom-like get-up of Wyndham Smith, son of the witty canon of St. Paul's; the close - cropped grey head and quiet demeanour of Tom Crommelin; the tremendous shirt-front and blazing diamond studs of young Jack Mytton, the knowing physiognomy of Sir Vincent Cotton, the martial aspect of stalwart Major William Peel—all combine to give a touch of aristocratic dignity to the scene."

Such was the company assembled at Broome's tavern on the evening of June 16 of the great Exhibition year of 1851. Besides the above-mentioned, too, were Tom Spring, the Tipton, Johnny Broome (the host), and several other shining lights of the Fancy, and supporters of the Ring. The first-named, poor Tom Spring, was but the shadow of himself. As we have stated, he he had been for some time seriously ill, and the Boniface of the Castle, in Holborn, had been sadly missed. Indeed, the hand of death was upon him, and he died two months after that meeting at the Rising Sun, to which we invite our readers to attend.

Directly Spring was well enough he took up the Tipton's and the "Unknown" match, and on the evening in question the latter was to be presented. Much speculation had been rife as to who this mysterious personage could be, for Johnny Broome had kept it a profound secret. When the waiter had gone round and the glasses were charged and cigars lit, Tom Spring called upon Broome to produce his "Unknown," and Johnny left the room, returning in a few minutes arm-in-arm with his brother Harry.

"Could it be possible?" exclaimed half a dozen all at once. The surprise was universal. Here was a youngster who had first of all been known as a lightweight, having fought Fred Mason (the Bull Dog), and afterwards in the middle-weights, doing battle with Joe Rowe and Ben Terry. The idea was preposterous that Harry, whose heaviest weight in the ring had been 11st, should be pitted against the Tipton, who scaled 13st. But the brothers Broome were quite in earnest, for Johnny, who had a wonderful "gift of the gab," explained that his brother Harry had not been in the ring for five years, and was now twenty-five years old, and had always had a bid for the Championship in view, and now, having filled out and being at his prime, was determined to have a cut at it. Then the landlord of the Rising Sun placed upon the table before Spring £50 in notes, and asked him to cover it on behalf of the Slasher. This having been promptly done, to show how ready he was, Johnny produced a draft of the articles. Then everybody knew that they meant serious business. Mr. Vincent Dowling, editor of *Bell's Life*, who was present, was requested to hold the stakes, and the £100 was handed to him. The draft of the articles was approved, that the men should fight for £200 a-side and the Championship of England three months from that date, at a spot to be selected by the stakeholder, as near as possible half-way between Birmingham and London. Eventually Michaelmas Day, September 29, 1851, was decided upon, and some of the " toffs " ordering up a couple of cases of " fiz," the business having been so satisfactorily arranged, the remainder of the evening was spent in music and conviviality.

And now we will introduce Mr. Harry Broome, and give a slight sketch of his career, for he was destined to become Champion of England, although his reign was but short-lived,and he does not figure amongst the most illustrious.

It was in the autumn of 1842 that Johnny Broome invited a small but select party to his house, the Rising Sun, to judge of the qualities of a youngster he wished to introduce to the P.R. This youth was his own brother Harry. He had arranged for the veteran and clever Byng Stocks to be the trial horse, an experienced bruiser of many battles, who was taller than the youngster, and some 2st heavier. Stocks was a pretty good test for a novice, but young Harry, who had been educated by brother John, was so quick and active that Byng could scarcely get in a blow, and Broome senior chaffed the old 'un all the time they were at it, for the bout went quite in favour of the youngster. "Don't spare him," advised Johnny, " because he's my brother; just you treat him as you would *me*." Now as Broome was the cleverest boxer of his day for the weight, it is easy to understand that there was a certain amount of irony in his remark. The trial proved very satisfactory, so far as the young 'un was concerned, and from that time Master Harry became a constant exhibitor at his brother's Thursday evening sparring displays, and the general opinion of those supposed to be good judges, was that the lad had great promise. The next step forward he made was in a fight to a finish with the gloves, for the entertainment of Lord Drumlanrig and his friends, when he met a

man named Mitchell, known as the "West End Tailor."
He was no professional pugilist, but clever with his
"dukes," and really got his living as a "minder" of
"toffs." Five pounds was the sum put down by my lord
for the friendly spar, and young Harry gave such a good
account of himself that all were of opinion that there
was a big future in store for him. Many wished to meet
him in the roped arena, but the sums they offered to
fight him for did not suit brother Johnny, who had
decided that £50 a-side should be the minimum sum the
lad should do battle for.

His first opponent to accept for that amount was Fred
Mason. And here we may mention that this bruiser
was a brother to Harry Boleno, the celebrated Drury
Lane clown, who at one time was mine host of the Old
Drury Tavern, at the corner of Vinegar Yard, Catherine
Street, now swept away for the improvements of the
neighbourhood. Mason hailed from the East End, and
they fought down the river on December 11, 1843. After
a fierce contest, lasting one hour and twenty minutes,
Mason gave in. The East Enders were greatly disappointed, for they detested Johnny Broome, and felt sure
that the Bull Dog would have accomplished his task, he
never having been beaten but by the all-powerful arm of
the celebrated Johnny Walker. It was not until a year
had elapsed that Johnny Broome would allow his brother
to enter the lists again, and this time it was with another
representative from the East End, one Joe Rowe. After
a stubborn battle, in which the latter's supporters behaved in a most disgraceful manner at the ring-side,
Tom Spring, who was referee, resigned and left the
ground, so the match had to be declared a draw. Harry
had badly injured his thumb, so the battle could not be
renewed until the following May, when Broome vanquished his foe easily within an hour.

Again Johnny kept his brother out of the Ring for
twelve months, when he matched him against Ben
Terry, of Birmingham, for £100 a-side, and they met
on February 3, 1846. This was a most unsatisfactory
meeting, for Harry, who always afterwards declared that
he had been drugged, fought shockingly in the first
dozen or so rounds. He, however, pulled himself together after they had been fighting some time, and was
undoubtedly winning fast, when "foul" was claimed for
Ben Terry, as Harry, it was alleged, had struck him a
blow upon a plaister which he wore round his loins,
whilst he was going down. So great was the wrangle
over the affair at the ring-side, that the referee fled from
the place and, of course, the fight had to be declared a
draw; Harry receiving £5 out of the stake money.

This was Harry Broome's last appearance in the ring prior to the match to which we have called attention at the opening of this chapter.

Of the Tipton Slasher we have already said sufficient of his opening career, and of his match with Tom Paddock and fight in the moonlight, so it will be unnecessary for us to recapitulate. He went into training at Hoylake, in Cheshire, where Jem Ward looked after

HARRY BROOME.

him, whilst Young Molineux put him through his daily work. Ward was then a publican in Liverpool, so it was an easy run for him, and he rarely missed a day without visiting his *protégé*.

Harry Broome was not so fortunate, however. He had just made a mess of things at the Opera Tavern, Haymarket, where he had failed, and that was the reason, undoubtedly, why brother Johnny had been so anxious

to get him matched for the Championship, feeling that
should he win or lose, his popularity would increase.
and his altered position enable him to pull through,
His creditors, though, would allow him no peace, and he
was followed with writs and judgment summonses
wherever he went, and it was only through the astuteness of the tricky Johnny that he was able to avoid
arrest. Harry's brother superintended the lad's training and in a very short time got him into splendid
condition.

Mildenhall was the place selected, for it was thought
that it would afford an opportunity for the numerous
sports attending the Newmarket First October Meeting
of being present. So on the morning of September 29,
1851, the special train started from Shoreditch. But
strange to say, although the battle was for the Championship, there was a very poor attendance, for it was
believed that the whole affair would end in a fiasco,
and many doubted the Broomes' earnestness, especially as Harry was moving about so mysteriously.
This doubt was strengthened when the train left London
with only about one hundred people who had taken
tickets, and neither of the Broomes appeared upon the
platform. At Bishop's Stortford, however, the familiar
figures of the two brothers were discerned, and all
appeared to be well as they boarded the train.

At Mildenhall no time was lost, and the arena having
been fixed up and the company being augmented
by some two or three hundred from Newmarket and
neighbourhood, soon after one o'clock the Tipton Slasher
stepped up to the ring, accompanied by his seconds,
Nobby Clarke and Young Molineux, and Jem Ward,
who was present to look after the interests of his
protégé. The Tipton was quickly followed by Harry
Broome, with his brother and two seconds, Callaghan
and Bob Castles. Then came a difficulty about a referee.
Peter Crawley was mentioned, but the Slasher objected to
every name mentioned by the Broomes, and it looked
after all that there would be no fight. At length Harry
Broome said he would not mind fighting without a
referee if his opponent did not mind. Then the Slasher
consented to Peter Crawley, when everything was
arranged, and the men entering the ring, "Time" was
called at a quarter to three o'clock.

When Harry Broome stood up everybody was
astonished at his magnificent development and beautiful
symmetry. He stood 5ft 10½in, and weighed 12st 10½lb,
and all judges pronounced him one of the finest specimens of an athlete they had ever seen stripped. What
a contrast he must have been to the big, burly, ungainly

Slasher, whose figure and attitude we have already described. On this occasion he weighed 13st 7lb, his height being 6ft 0½in. As they sparred together it was evident that the young 'un had no fear of his great opponent, and although he led him a nice dance all over the ring, when they got to the ropes he stood his ground, and getting aside from a nasty blow aimed at his ribs, Harry caught his opponent a stinging cross-counter on the face with the left.

In the next round Broome got a smasher into the Tipton's mouth, and, closing, they came down side by side. The third bout reads as if there must have been great excitement, for we learn that the Slasher, following up his retreating foe, got in his left on the right cheek, but Harry gave him a receipt in full in the shape of a tremendous smash on the nose. The Slasher hit out wildly, right and left; Harry saw his chance, and closed. Then he got an unmistakable lock with his right leg over the crooked knee of the Tipton. In a few seconds there was a desperate struggle, but at last Broome having fixed his hold, with a grand effort of mingled strength and skill brought the Slasher over on his back. Down came the huge form, shaking the earth with the concussion, while Harry rolled over him. There lay the prostrate giant apparently stunned, till his active seconds, seizing him by the legs and arms, bore him to his corner.

Then our report goes on to inform us that the Slasher tried to strangle his man on the ropes. Johnny Broome, however, sat on them, and Harry was let down. In the tenth round Harry seems to have had all the best of it, for after unmercifully punching the Tipton about the face, he got his favourite grip and brought the Tipton once more down with a thud. But the effort cost Harry dearly, for he lay on the ground afterwards, panting and blowing like a grampus. But he showed himself to be a good general, and with brother Johnny to advise him, kept out of harm's way until he recovered his wind. The Tipton's only chance was to exhaust his man ; he was no match for him in quickness of hitting, activity, nor wrestling, and the youngster certainly proved himself to be a better man. How the battle would have ended it is hard to say, but the Slasher finished the fight on a " foul," by striking Harry Broome deliberately when he was on both knees.

Then all the fat was in the fire, for the partisans of each man were yelling at the top of their voices, " Foul, foul, fair, fair," and the two umpires being mobbed and pulled about by the crowd could not agree, whilst Peter Crawley refused to listen to any appeal unless it very properly came through them. At length the two umpires admitted that they could not agree, and Peter Crawley said "It was a most deliberate foul, and I award the battle to Broome."

The language after this must have been frightful, and loudest and strongest was that of the Tipton Slasher himself. He swore that Peter Crawley was a sanguinary rogue and swindler; that he had backed Broome himself, and had acted unfairly and dishonestly in order to win his own bets.

"You're uttering a d——d lie, and you know it," thundered Peter Crawley. "No one ever breathed a word against my honesty and fairness before, and I'm ready to maintain my honesty against any living man. Come on and fight me, if you dare." With this the ponderous Peter, to the astonishment of everybody, commenced taking his coat and waistcoat off, really meaning what he said. What would have happened to the good old host of the Queen's Head and French Horn, with his tremendous paunch, if he really had tried conclusions with the Slasher, we dread to think. At that juncture, however, Lord Drumlanrig went to Crawley and remonstrated with him, and at the same time Jem Ward and the respectable friends of the Slasher took that worthy away.

And that is how this particular fight for the Championship ended, which had only lasted thirty-three minutes, but enabled Harry Broome's name to be inscribed amongst the list of Champions.

CHAPTER XLV.

RECOLLECTIONS OF OLD "BELL'S LIFE" TAVERN. — HARRY BROOME AND TOM PADDOCK. — BATTLE FOR THE NEW BELT.

IN our last chapter we called attention to the letter which was written by Harry Broome to the editor of *Bell's Life*, and we quoted the epistle. It was dated November 28, 1855, and here we may perhaps be permitted to deal with reminiscences.

Many of our readers, no doubt, will be able to accompany us in our rambles, and there are surely those who when the manly art was waning in the early fifties, can recall scenes of the times.

Sunday, December 2, 1855, in London, was one of those cheerless, wintry days that are to be found in no other city in the world. The metropolis on the Sunday is never particularly cheerful, even if the air is tempered with soft summer breezes, and the sun is pouring down upon a deserted pavement. But in the depth of winter, when the few vehicles which are to be met with in the main streets, roll along at a slow pace, silently through the snow which is fast being churned into a dirty, sloppy mass, London is anything but inviting.

" The snow, the snow, the beautiful snow," had been falling in a monotonous manner, like a coarse white gauze throughout the whole of the day, and, where undisturbed, lay in a pure white mass over pavement and road. It was certainly an evening to remain indoors before a blazing fire, in company with grog and pipe, and the untrodden waste of snow as we walked up Norfolk Street suggested to us how home comforts could be appreciated out. Ours were the only footprints making a track along the silent street, and as we turned into the Strand we met a snow-covered " bobby " and a cabby, who was muffled up with the old - fashioned coat of many capes. They were the only signs of life. Having vacated a warm, comfortable room to embrace the cold atmosphere, a tingling at the ears, and a bright light, suggested a hot drink, which was to be had at a little " pub." over the way.

The hostelry at this period was known as *Bell's Life* Tavern, afterwards re-christened the Norfolk Arms, and now swept away by the hand of Improvement, which has been doing wonders for the metropolis under the County Council, and for the Strand in particular.

So we made for the little beacon light, and pushing open the swing door, entered the tavern. There was only a small dingy bar; but there was a cheerful fire blazing up the chimney, with a bright copper kettle singing merrily on the hob. Behind the counter were some silver cups, and the sole decorations consisted of pewter pots, piled up pyramid fashion upon a shelf, or suspended from nails along the beams of the ceiling, whilst their polished surfaces reflected the flames from the fire, giving to the place a warm, cosy appearance, in pleasant contrast to the cheerless surroundings of the outside.

" Good evening, sir ! We've got some winter at last, then !" The remark came from a fine, stiff-built young fellow behind the bar. His white shirt-sleeves rolled up, disclosed a great, muscular arm, and as he stood mixing

a glass of hot brandy and water for us, with his clean-
shaven face and little square white apron, he looked a
veritable picture for a Boniface of the period. His height
was about 5ft 11in, and he was as fine a specimen of
manhood as you could meet in a day's march. His great
bull neck and broad shoulders made him appear very
formidable, and it required little else to suggest that he
was cut out by nature for a gladiator.

The landlord of the *Bell's Life* Tavern was none other
than our old friend Harry Broome, who had thrown
down the gauntlet once again, and who had sent the
letter to *Bell's Life*, offering to fight Tom Paddock for
£200, which we quoted in our previous chapter.

We had some reason to conjecture whether Harry
Broome was really serious over this affair, and we spoke
plainly to him upon the subject, but he assured us that
he was absolutely in earnest. We had, as a matter of
fact, good cause for these doubts, for the year 1855 had
been so fraught with disappointments occasioned by the
extraordinary behaviour of the top-sawyers of the P.R.
that challenges and deposits counted for little, the former
ending in paper warfare, and the latter terminating nine
times out of ten in forfeits.

And now it will be as well to just review Master
Harry Broome's performances before describing this
his last battle in the Ring, for he lived but for ten years
after our meeting with him on that quiet Sunday evening, shuffling off this mortal coil on November 2, 1865.

After his defeat of Rowe, to which we have already
referred, he scored that questionable victory over the
Tipton Slasher, it will be remembered, and then defeated
the powerful natural fighter, Harry Orme. By these
performances he became Champion. But the old Tipton
was not at all satisfied, declaring that the " foul " on
that occasion, which had deprived him of the honour of
wearing the belt, was not a just decision. So he challenged Harry, and articles were entered into for the men
to try conclusions once again. But, after £25 had been
deposited, Broome forfeited, his plea being that he had
a more important engagement with Aaron Jones. This,
however, also fell through. On February 20, 1855, the
Champion again forfeited to Tom Paddock, and once more
did this unsatisfactory business occur, upon March 12 of
the same year. That was the period at which Broome announced that he would retire from the Ring, as referred
to in the previous chapter.

Tom Paddock had also been busy. Immediately after
a brilliant fight he had with Paulson, of Nottingham, he
had little time to rest, and received a challenge from Tom
Sayers, then making his mark as a Champion Middle-

weight, to fight for £200, at catch-weights; but, owing to Sayers' backers having negotiated with Harry Paulson for their man, this fell through. Paddock then turned his attention to the Tipton Slasher, asking him if he intended to maintain his claim to the Champion, and as Harry Broome had, as we have already stated, signified his intention of retiring, Paddock declared that if neither Harry or the Tipton responded to his call, he should be justified in terming himself Champion of England. Harry Broome's retirement and forfeiture quite entitled Paddock to the assumption, and there appeared an editorial in *Bell's Life* asserting, " Tom Paddock is now Champion of England until the position is wrested from him by the Tipton Slasher or Aaron Jones, or confirmed to him by their defeat."

Tom Paddock then took on Jones for choice, and the match was made on April 3, the fight to come off on June 5, 1855, for £100 a-side. The Redditch man proved victorious once more over his old opponent, and the Slasher being matched to fight Jones, Paddock was compelled to take a rest, for he could find nobody to come forward and do battle with him. Consequently there were great rejoicings when the letter of challenge appeared from Harry Broome. Everything was settled before the end of the year, and the coming combat was looked forward to with a deal of interest in sporting circles. The anxiously-waited-for period at length arrived, and the two men who had been in strict training for several months came to London on the eve of the fight, showing themselves at their respective quarters. Harry Broome was, of course, on view at his own house in the Strand, where we had often visited him, and Tom Paddock at that of his great friend, Alec Keene's, the Three Tuns, in Moor Street, Soho.

The original intention was to have brought the mill off in Kent or Sussex, but on account of the squeamishness of one or two of the South-Coast Railway directors, who considered it highly improper to be parties to the encouragement of the noble art of self-defence, at the eleventh hour it was considered necessary to change the *venue.* The management, which consisted of Dan Dismores, Fred Broome, and Alec Keene, then made an appeal to the Eastern Counties Company, who were always ready and ever obliging, and now agreed to make up a " special."

At Shoreditch Station (now devoted to the despatch and receipt of goods, but formerly the terminus of the G.E.R.) on the morning of the fight great excitement prevailed, the entrance being literally thronged by an anxious crowd struggling to get a glimpse at the warriors.

As far as Broome was concerned they were doomed to disappointment, for he had got up with the lark, and travelled by an earlier train to Stratford, where it was arranged they should stop and pick him up. Tom Paddock was, however, recognised as he stepped out of his cab, and received a tremendous ovation.

The train rattled along through the fields—now past an orchard, now white and pink with the blossoms of the fruit trees, for it was a lovely June morning, and we and all nature were glad.

> The garden glows and fills the liberal air
> With lavished fragrance, while the promised fruit
> Lies yet a little embryo unperceived,
> Within its crimson folds.

Away we sped until we reached Manningtree, where we learned to our annoyance that the police were upon our track, and that telegrams had been despatched to the constabulary at Diss, in Norfolk, and all down the line to be on the alert. A consultation then took place, and it was decided to bring the battle off, if possible, in the vicinity of Ipswich, where it was least expected. After a short run from Manningtree we came to a halt at a likely-looking place, with meadows on each side, and the crowd, streaming from the carriages, climbed down the embankment. Shortly afterwards the other "special" drew up, and the occupants of the second train having alighted, the spectators assembled numbered over six hundred. Amongst them were many of the "nobs," including an Indian Prince and suite, besides numerous Corinthians.

The arena was formed without delay, and the outer ring was productive of no less than £47. This allowed a good margin for the Pugilistic Benevolent Association, after paying the ring-minders a sovereign a-piece, who were headed by Mike Madden, Fred Mason, and Bill Barry.

At a quarter to one everything was in readiness, and the audience was impatiently waiting for the "ring-up."

Harry Broome was waited upon by Tass Parker and Tom Sayers, and Tom Paddock was esquired by Alec Keene and Jemmy Massey. They shook hands in a pleasant, friendly manner, and the colours were tied to the stakes. There was quite a lively time over the betting, £35 to £20 being one of the wagers laid upon Broome.

At precisely one o'clock the men stepped to the scratch at the call of "Time," both stripped to the "buff." The initial round was exceedingly lively. Harry feinted with his left, ducked his head, and then landed heavily upon Tom's chest, when several quick exchanges were made, Paddock appearing to get somewhat bewildered, but he dashed in and caught Broome upon the side of the head, and in attempting to follow up slipped down. Everybody was looking for Harry's old smart form, but he made a poor display, and in the next few rounds Paddock led, letting his left go with great quickness, landing Master Harry a smart tap upon the nasal organ, in response to which the claret flowed, and first blood was awarded to Paddock.

ALEC KEENE.

At the fifth round Broome came up puffing, and not looking at all cheerful, whilst Tom was as fresh as paint, and wore a nasty grin, which made him look very dangerous. Harry tried his left, but Tom countered and caught him another severe one on the proboscis. On again facing his antagonist Harry received some severe whacks about the body. In the ninth, Tom let go his left, but was prettily stopped, and Harry countered him on the jaw with his right, so heavily that it made Tom stagger. Then, as he tried to steady himself, he slipped and fell.

After this the rounds were got through in an unusually short space of time, none lasting more than a minute. In the twentieth bout Paddock took the lead, and rattled away in a lively manner, and caught Broome a crack between the eyes, removing the "bark." Harry returned it with a slight amount of interest on the nose, when they closed and both went down. The battle had then lasted twenty-eight minutes, and the pace they had been going was sending them all to pieces. Broome came up panting like a thirsty poodle. Paddock dashed in with his left and inflicted a severe cut on the lips. Harry, too, missed his return, and Tom again caught him a stinger in the same place, which increased the length and depth of the wound, sending Master Harry once again to Mother Earth.

On entering the thirtieth round they both went in with an intense amount of ardour, but Paddock proved himself to be the stronger of the two, although he occasionally exhibited great lack of judgment. But Harry's face was most severely punished, and after a rally in the thirty-third round they both of them rolled over, and Broome's seconds made a claim, declaring that he had kicked their man. This was, however, justly overruled by the referee, and the fight continued.

In the thirty-eighth, after some sharp exchanges, Tom slipped down on his knees, and Broome hit him a fearful blow on the nasal organ. In reply to another claim the referee decided that Harry's hand had started on its journey before Tom came to ground, so it was disallowed. From the fortieth to the fifty-first and last, they stuck to it with marvellous pertinacity, Paddock getting the best of it. In the forty-eighth, Broome's left eye was closed, and he presented a sorry spectacle. He was getting so weary that it was obvious that nothing short of a miracle would prevent him from losing the battle. On coming to the scratch for the last round, Harry was very slow, weak, and tottering; he made a blow at Paddock, but missed, and Tom then aimed a vicious right-hander at the side of the head. It, however, missed the place it was intended for, and landed with a heavy thud upon Harry's chest. This blow floored the plucky gladiator, and, although at the call of " Time " he once more gained his legs, if the will was good the body was weak, and he immediately sank back, exhausted upon his second's knee, and Tass Parker threw up the sponge in token of Broome's defeat, after as determined a mill, lasting one hour and three minutes, as was ever fought within the ropes.

It was indeed a wonder that Harry, being so much of a wreck, should have made such a long fight of it. One account tells us that even at the expiration of the first half hour he did not look like lasting a quarter of an hour longer, yet he protracted the battle beyond the hour before at last he received his quietus from Tom Paddock's right. For some time before Broome's case appeared so hopeless that there were loud cries of "Take him away," and his brother Fred begged him to give in, for he was exceedingly weak. But Harry shook his head and insisted upon going on with the fight, although he could scarcely totter. But the fluky blow delivered by Tom Paddock, and to which we have alluded, settled the plucky Harry, for after a vain attempt to rise he sank back into his second's arms, and the desperate fight was over.

CHAPTER XLVI.

DEATH OF AN OLD FRIEND.—REMINISCENCE OF THE OLD
CASTLE, HOLBORN.—HARRY BROOME AND HARRY ORME.
—MATCHED FOR THE CHAMPIONSHIP.

AFTER the defeat of the Tipton Slasher, Harry
Broome became Champion of England. It was
a period of melancholy in the ranks of the P. R., for
a sad event occurred at this time, an event which we
have already recorded in the history of our fights for
the championship, but which we may be permitted to
recall here. The death of Tom Spring took place just
before Harry Broome won his laurels. It was a fearful loss to the Fancy and its supporters, for never
could the fine old Englishman be replaced. He, the
idol of the sporting world, was Tom, and although we
have had occasion to dismiss him when we recorded
his death, we think perhaps this would be a fitting
opportunity of giving a word picture of the hero as he
was described by one who knew him well, a few months
before his decease.

Let us to the "Castle," in Holborn, once more then,
the hostelry nearly facing Chancery Lane, which for
some inexplicable reason has for some years been
re-christened the "Napier." It is evening, and the
parlour of the first sporting "Ken" in the world is
filled with the cream of the Fancy and their Corinthian
supporters. Upon the walls are pictures of the champions: Broughton, Slack, Big Ben Brain, and a host of
others. Tom Spring sits in the chair at the end of
the long room. Glasses are filled, and "a song, a
song," is the cry, and the whole company join in the
chorus:

"Here's a health to old honest John Bull,
 When he's gone we shan't find such another,
 And with hearts and with glasses brim full,
 We will drink to old England, his mother!"

And a few weeks after this convivial meeting Tom
Spring was laid beneath the slopes of Norwood
Cemetery. But here is the description of Tom to which
we have alluded above:—" You might see him, this
fine Boniface of the ' Castle,' in Holborn, of a morning
in a white smock, busy in his cellar or about the
premises, whilst at three o'clock in the afternoon he
was always to be seen behind the bar or in his parlour,
dressed in an evening black suit, with a white neck
cloth, a brooch in his snowy shirt frill, and his
boots polished until they shone like a mirror. It was
a treat to see him at cattle show time among the prize
beasts, surrounded by an admiring crowd of top-
booted farmers, who listened to his opinions with sin-
gular deference, for Tom was as good a judge of a
bullock, a horse, a dog, or gamecock as you would
find in a day's march. There was nothing of the
Cockney about him. Keen for all country sports he
was always, and when some of his aristocratic friends
invited him, as they often did, to come over to their
country seats and have a turn at the pheasants, they
found that the ex-champion could handle a double-
barrel with the best of them. But, popular as he was,
Tom Spring never made the "Castle" pay as Belcher had
done, for the latter retired after fourteen years with
a handsome independence, and lived like a gentleman
in his villa over at Finchley. Spring was too fond of
' backing his fancy ' on the Turf, and executing com-
missions for so-called friends, who left him in the
lurch when they found it inconvenient to pay their
loans."

Yes, Tom Spring's death was undoubtedly a great
loss to the prize ring, and although it will be remembered that the match with Harry Broome and the
Tipton Slasher was delayed on account of his illness,
he did not live to see the first named become champion.
Harry having won his spurs, the Slasher naturally
wanted to have another bid for the position he had
lost, but they could never come to terms, and the
sports of the day had to glance round for another and
younger man to take up the gauntlet. Mr. Moore,
landlord of the " Old Rum Puncheon," Rose and Crown
Court, Moorfields, a good old sport particularly popular with the East Enders, and an excellent judge of a
pugilist, had seen a lad named Harry Orme fight, and,
indeed, had, in conjunction with Mr. Hunter, of the
" Weavers' Arms," Kingsland Road, backed him
against Jem Burns's protégé, Aaron Jones, a man
destined to shine in the ring, and subsequently to
prove a tough customer for Tom Sayers. They fought

for £20 aside, at 11st 4lb, on December 18th, 1849, and it proved to be an excellent combat, lasting two hours and a quarter. Orme's superior strength told at the finish, and he proved the victor. After this, Harry's friends were exceedingly proud of him, for he had defeated a man taller, heavier, with a longer reach, and with more experience. So his backers determined to bide their time, and not to match him again until they could do so for a larger stake. Eighteen months elapsed before that opportunity came, and the man selected for him to do battle with was none other than the redoubtable Nat Langham. Now, Nat was even then known as one of the trickiest and cleverest fighters amongst the middle weights, and had already defeated Tom Lowe, "Doctor" Campbell, George Gutteridge, and William Sparkes, the Australian, and had consequently taken a very high position.

Mr. Vincent Dowling declared that this fight was "one of the gamest the modern annals of the ring can boast." Langham was two inches taller, was longer in the reach, and 3lb heavier. Naturally, this battle does not find a place in these fights for the championship, but a good description is given of Harry Orme, as he appeared when he met Langham, which we may be permitted to quote:—

"The contrast between them was great: Nat tall, fair skinned, clean built, supple, elegant, symmetrical. Harry short, square, massive, large limbed, swarthy as a gipsy, hard as mahogany, his deep chest mottled with coarse black hair, his dark face set in an expression of dogged determination, as formidable and dangerous a gladiator as ever stepped into the ring."

Such was the description of Harry Orme, who was destined to make a bold bid for the championship of England. His fight with Nat Langham must, indeed, have been a desperate one. Nat's terrible "pick-axe" (his left), as Tom Sayers christened it after it blinded him, played havoc with Orme in the first few rounds— but the latter gave him a fearful fall in the eleventh bout, which shook up Langham considerably, and from that moment matters were more equalised. So desperately did the men fight, and with such tenacity did they stick to it, that no less than one hundred and seventeen rounds were fought, lasting over two hours and forty-six minutes. In the last round but two, both men had fought absolutely to a standstill, and it was but a question of making a draw of this splendid combat. However, Harry Orme had just enough left in him to come up for two more rounds, and wore his

man completely out, having scarcely an ounce left
himself.

This entitled Harry Orme to take the title of champion of the light weights, and for a whole twelve
months he rested on the laurels earned by this splendid
battle.   Then, in the early part of 1852, his old
opponent, Aaron Jones, threw down the gauntlet.   He
had undoubtedly much improved in both strength and
science, and his friends thought he was equal to lower-
ing the colours of the victor of Nat Langham.

HARRY ORME.

The match was made for £100 a-side. It was a most
unsatisfactory affair, as they were interrupted by the
police and chased from pillar to post, and at the finish
Aaron Jones refused to fight after two adjournments;
there was a question about Mr. Vincent Dowling
having resigned his post as referee, and the whole
affair ended in a most disagreeable manner by an
action at law brought against the stakeholder. Ulti-

mately, however, the money was handed to Harry Orme.

At this period there was very great rivalry between the East End and the West End schools, and the Broomes might be said to lead the former, with Johnny Broome, the celebrated light weight at their head. He had in 1842 married and gone into business at the "Rising Sun," Air Street, Piccadilly, the hostelry which old Ben Burn had kept for many years, and of which Jem himself had in his later days been Boniface. Johnny Broome was exceedingly popular as "mine host," and was well patronised by all the swells of that period. Not only was he a great enthusiast with respect to his profession as a pugilist, but he was a good all round sport. He would frequently ride to hounds whilst on visits to his noble patrons, and often followed the Atherstone and North Warwickshire. So good a horseman was he, that he rode his own steeplechaser "Eagle" fourth for the Grand National at Liverpool. In fact, Master Johnny Broome was a very great star in the pugilistic circles, and wonderfully clever, and made the "Rising Sun" the most popular sporting house in the West End. But he was rather selfish and very crafty; so if he made a number of friends and enlisted many admirers, he also made a great number of enemies, and amongst them was the popular bookmaker Harry Hill, and he, with another penciller, the aristocratic Tom Crommelin, who also had no affection for the Broomes, thought they could find somebody capable of taking down Harry's colours. So they put up Harry Orme to fight for £250 a-side and the championship.

Now Harry Orme weighed only 11st 4lb when at his best, so would have to give away no less than half a stone, which was considered in those times a considerable weight, so his friends wanted Harry Broome to come to that weight. This, of course, Johnny refused to do on behalf of his brother. He was quite agreeable to let Harry fight at a stipulated weight, but not for the championship. So, in consequence, a deal of time was wasted before the men could come to an understanding, but after much stupid wrangling, the match was made, the parties agreeing to fight for the championship on the 18th of April, 1853.

Harry Broome, during his career as a Boniface, had put on much flesh, and when out of training it readily accumulated. His brother put him under the wing of Levi Eckersley, one of the cleverest trainers of the day, and they went to Cleave Hill, the spot celebrated

for the Cheltenham Steeplechases. There he would
frequently have the gloves on with that clever left-
handed fighter Jem Edwards, who kept a tavern in
the town, whilst Levi gave Master Harry some exceedingly warm work according to all accounts, for Johnny
had given him orders that his brother was to be
brought down to 12st. Smothered in flannels he would
do his twenty or thirty miles a day at a swinging pace,
and when he got back to his quarters, every rag upon
him was wringing wet with perspiration, just as if his
clothes had come dripping from the wash tub. Dumb
bells, Indian clubs, punching at the sack, did wonders,
but Eckersley was never able to get him down to less
than 12st. 5lb, which Johnny Broome declared was
quite half a stone too heavy.

Harry Orme was taken in hand by the well known
long-distance ped Bob Fuller, and went to West
Malling, near Maidstone, and there was no difficulty
at all about getting him into perfect condition.

There was absolute secrecy kept as to the whereabouts of the fight, but it leaked out that it would
take place somewhere on the Eastern Counties line,
so everybody who thought they were knowing besieged
the approach to Shoreditch station. They were accompanied in many instances by the roughs of the
East End, and not a few light-fingered gents hailing
from the West. Anybody who looked in the least like
a "toff" would be hustled and bustled about whilst
they were "gone over" in a most bare-faced manner,
watches, money, pins, and even rings being annexed.
Most of the Corinthians, however, came under escort,
protected by such well known pugilists as Jem Burn,
Owen Swift, Johnny Hannen, Peter Crawley, Frank
Redmond, Dan Dismore, Bob Castles, Johnny Walker,
Jemmy Shaw, and many others.

The morning was delightful, and there was a bigger
muster than there had been at any championship fight
since that between Caunt and Bendigo. At eight
o'clock the special train steamed out, and did not stop
until it arrived at Bishop's Stortford, where Harry
Orme, his trainer, and Harry Hill were picked up, and
they then proceeded to Elsenham, where the Broomes
joined the train, and Fred Oliver was taken aboard.
He had been sent to select a suitable place,
and to keep a look-out upon the movements of the
"beaks." He reported that the authorities were on
the look-out, but that a young farmer had offered him
a capital piece of ground where there would be no fear
of interruption. He also informed the executive that
hundreds of people had arrived at Mildenhall from

London by the early parliamentary train, and were
anxiously awaiting the arrival of the men, concluding
that that would be the spot selected.

As the train moved through that station (for of
course under the circumstances there would be no
possibility of bringing the fight off there), the expression of rage and disappointment upon those who had
speculated as to where the battle would take place
must have been something to remember. At the next
station the train slowed up. This was Lakenheath,
where any number of constabulary, both on horseback
and on foot, were there ready to meet them. So on
they went until they arrived at a spot between Bran-
don and Thetford, some ninety miles from London,
where, guided by Fred Oliver's friend, they were conducted to a meadow, close to the railway, where the
ring was put up. The sale of tickets for the outer
ring was considerable, and Dismore and Owen Swift,
who had charge of that department, sold no less than
£50 worth at half-a-guinea apiece. There were present
several of the well-known patrons of the Ring—men
who were past the meridian of life, gray-haired, good
old sports—who rarely attended fights, but who never
missed a championship battle when it was possible to
be at the side of the ropes. We have no space to
describe the scene at the side of the ring, but by the
account before us we read the names of some whose
names have shone in our descriptions of the "fights
for the championship," many of them having seen
Jem Belcher do battle for the belt, as well as The
Game Chicken, Cribb, Molineux, Tom Spring, and
Jack Langan. Amongst those present were Mr. Sant,
the rich Wandsworth brewer; John Gully, the ex-
champion, then a wealthy colliery owner and a fine
old English gentleman, as we have already pictured
him in these "Memoirs." There were also Ned Painter
and Tom Oliver, and amongst the Corinthians could
be recognised the Dukes of Devonshire and Hamilton,
with many other noblemen. Unfortunately, however,
there were several East End roughs, who were, though,
well held in check by the special constables selected
from second and third rate pros. by the Pugilistic
Association.

Peter Crawley was selected as referee. He at once
took up his position at the ropes upon a chair which
had been brought from the farmhouse, and at a quarter
past one o'clock the men entered the arena. A strange
incident in connection with the selection of the seconds
was noticed, for Orme's esquires were Tom Sayers and
Jack Grant (both of whom will figure in these pages

anon), who had, less than a year previously, had a desperate set-to not far from this very spot, and oddly enough Harry Orme had been Grant's second upon that very occasion. They all three sported the East End colours — a green kerchief with white rings. Harry Orme looked in splendid condition as he stood laughing and chatting with his friends, for it was fully ten minutes before Harry Broome entered an appearance. In the meanwhile the "toffs" in the outer ring were having a regular banquet, for the "Bishop" of Bond Street had brought down a great hamper of the choicest viands, and well nigh all had come provided with baskets of wine, cold chicken, lobsters, and other delicacies. The beaming face of the Bishop, and his fund of anecdote, had the effect of creating much merriment in the ring, and the sun was shining gloriously, more as if it were June or July than May. At length a shout from the majority of the throats belonging to the 2,000 people assembled, announced the arrival of Harry Broome, who was, of course, accompanied by his brother Johnny, and had for his seconds Billy Hayman, of Birmingham, and Callaghan, of Derby, who at once proceeded to prepare for action, tying on the colours of the West Ender, which were blue with white spots. The betting was 7 to 4 on Broome, and was pretty brisk when the men were stripped and ready for the call of "Time."

But a description of the grand battle for the belt and the championship between the two Harrys we must defer for another chapter.

CHAPTER XLVII.

HARRY BROOME AND HARRY ORME.—THEIR DESPERATE BATTLE.—A TERRIBLE TRAGEDY AT BOW STREET.

In the last chapter we left Harry Broome and Harry Orme facing each other to do combat for the Championship of England and the coveted belt, surrounded by a company numbering no less than 2,000 sports of all classes, from the noble lord to the East End rough. The sun poured its rays down upon the gladiators and spectators almost fiercely for the time of year. It was half-past one o'clock when "Time" was called by Peter Crawley, and the battle commenced. With half

an eye one would detect the disparity in the size of
the men. Harry Broome stood 5ft 10½in, and weighed
12st 5lb, whilst Orme's height was but 5ft 7¾in, and
he scaled only 11st 6lb. But Orme was in the better
condition, for he had not had the tavern experience of
his opponent, and had always kept himself fit. A description of both men we have already given, so it
will be unnecessary to repeat. One account states
that " Harry Orme looked the embodiment of physical
strength and endurance; his thick-set, powerful frame,
his bull-neck, and huge, muscular arms, his immense
calves and thighs, his enormous round shoulders, made
him a picture of Herculean power, while his dark, determined visage and swarthy skin conveyed the idea
of exceptional courage and hardihood."

They both started very cautiously, Broome, with
his longer reach, trying, by feints and advances, to
draw his opponent, but the East Ender was not to be
caught. For two minutes it was a question of advance
and retreat, both sparring carefully, without a blow
being attempted. At length Orme seemed determined
to waste no more time manoeuvring, for he went
straight up to his man and let fly. But Broome, instead of meeting him, jumped back, laughing, and
did not seem inclined to come to work in real earnest.
Then the sparring was resumed, and the spectators
exhibited signs of impatience. Here is a description
of the fighting in the first round, written by an eye-
witness:—" Broome's game was to lure his adversary
on to hit, and not to open the ball himself. Finding,
however, that Orme was not to be kidded, Harry altered
his tactics, crept in carefully inch by inch, till he
thought he was within distance, then shot out his left,
followed by the right. Orme cleverly stopped the first,
but the latter caught him on the left side of the head;
in return, he slung in his sledge-hammer right on the
ribs, leaving a crimson mark there, napped a little one
on the forehead from Broome's left, and then the latter
closed; but Orme foiled his attempts to crook, and
they rolled over together. The round had lasted eight
minutes."

Without describing each round of this magnificent
battle, we may call attention to a few of the most
prominent episodes. In the fourth, the company were
treated to most sensational doings, which caused the
greatest excitement all round the ring. Broome opened
the bout with a terrific blow over the eye, which gashed
the flesh and produced first blood. Orme, however,
was more than even with him, delivering his right
three times in succession on the ribs with terrific force,

but Broome's turn came next; he struck the East Ender
heavily in the right eye and mouth. Orme lunged out
with his right, and as his hand came forward Broome
gave him an awful upper cut on the mark, which
doubled Orme completely up. He turned twice round,
and fell on his knees. His seconds rushed up in alarm,
and nine persons out of ten who saw the
effect of the terrible blow fancied it was all
over with Orme, and that he would not come up
again. Some even went so far as to express
their disappointment that the fight should be so soon
over. But those who thought so were agreeably disappointed, for the magnificent condition of the East
Ender and the splendid treatment by his seconds enabled him to pull himself together, and to respond to
the call of " Time," although he came up for the succeeding round in a somewhat groggy state.

In spite of the severity of the work in the fourth
round, the fifth was even more tremendous by all accounts. It lasted no less than six minutes, at the expiration of which time Harry Broome was in a very
queer state. His want of condition was telling upon him
badly, for he was bathed in perspiration and blowing
like a grampus. Besides, he had received some rough
treatment at the hands of the East Ender. One blow
delivered was with tremendous force upon the brow,
cutting it deeply to the bone, and the blood flowed
copiously. Harry Broome appeared quite dazed as he
staggered back and placed his hand involuntarily on
the damaged eye. This was Orme's chance. Many
judges present declared that had he availed himself of
it, and gone on punching with right and left with all
his great strength, it would have settled the battle in
his favour.

But he did nothing of the kind, whether it was a
desire not to take advantage of his distressed foe, or
that he was too excited to make use of the opportunity,
it is impossible to say, but it is quite certain that
Harry Broome profited by his inactivity.

When we learn that the eighth round lasted twelve
minutes, and the first nine occupied quite an hour, it
may be imagined in what a manly way they stood up
to each other. There certainly was no dropping to
avoid, and the fighting was of a most desperate character. Betting went to evens, and it was obvious that
Broome had discovered that he had a more difficult
customer to contend with than he had bargained for.

In the sixteenth round, Orme received another
dreadful upper-cut on the mark, which very nearly
decided the combat, and in the twenty-first he received

a very heavy fall, which half-dazed him, when Broome
set about him in real earnest, giving him some fearful
facers. Nearly blind, with his face streaming with
blood, Orme stuck to it gallantly. Then, in a wild
rally, one account says, "Orme stood up to Broome,
and exchanged hit for hit, the like to which few present
had ever witnessed before. These exchanges were terrific, each man staggering back from the effect of the
blows. Orme held his man well till just the close of
the round, when Broome, stepping back as his adversary came in, met him with a fearful smash on the left
eye, and Orme fell. Both men were so terribly exhausted that they lay on their backs on the ground
until 'Time' was called."

We have said enough to give an idea of the desperate
manner in which the two Harrys fought for the championship, and have little more to add, further than
that they kept at it until two hours and eighteen
minutes had elapsed, when Orme, completely blinded
and as weak as a rat, received a finishing blow straight
in the face, and fell, deaf to the call of "Time."

And so Harry Broome was entitled to dub himself
Champion of England, a title which, no doubt, he
would have held for a much longer period than he did
had it not been for a tragic event which made him
desire to disassociate himself from the Ring, although
he once more entered the lists, as in due course we shall
relate. Although the subject has nothing to do
with the history of the Champions, it created such a
sensation at the time in the sporting world, and con-
trolled the fortunes of the Ring to such an extent, so
far as Harry Broome was concerned, that we think
it should be recorded here.

It was a lovely morning, in June, 1855. It was just
that time of the day when, in the neighbourhood of
Covent Garden, there was a lull in the business, and
the market porters, who had finished their early work,
were taking refreshments in the various pubs of the
neighbourhood. A favourite house of theirs was a well-
known sporting hostelry, now swept away for the improvements in the vicinity of the New Bow Street Police
Court. It was known as the "Wrekin Tavern," in
Broad Court. Outside were several loafers, smoking
their short pipes, and in the public bar were a few
market porters, discussing some foaming pots of ale.
In the private compartments there were few customers, for the "Wrekin" was frequented by the Fancy
principally, and they did not usually make their appearance until the evening. Indeed, this was the
slackest part of the day.

Whilst all was quiet in the house, a short, muscular
man turned out of Bow Street into Broad Court, and
made for the "Wrekin." There was a wild, fierce expression upon his face, and so strange was his gait that
two gentlemen passing riveted their attention upon
him. "Why, that's Johnny Broome!" exclaimed one

JOHNNY BROOME.

of them. "How strange he looks. I'll follow him;
there's something wrong, I am sure." The speaker was
a Mr. Isaacs, a friend of the Broomes, and a customer
at the "Wrekin Tavern," where Johnny Broome had
taken up his quarters with the proprietor or manager,
Mr. John Mitchell Ellis. And here we may state that

24

Broome had been for some time previously under a cloud. His reputation had suffered badly. He had had a hand in the notorious Brighton card scandal, and his name was associated with several other shady transactions. He was consequently looked askance at by the tip-top members of the sporting world, and when he left the " Rising Sun," Air Street, Piccadilly, he was a ruined man, having lost a fortune on the Turf and in other gambling transactions. In fact, Johnny Broome was a broken-down man, and, added to all the misfortunes brought on by his own folly, he had a domestic trouble which broke his heart.

But, to return to Bow Street and the " Wrekin Tavern." Johnny Broome, with quickening step, made for the tavern, pushing open the door and passing through the bar into the kitchen, he seized a carving knife from the table, and drew it across his throat at the moment Mr. Isaacs entered the room. Johnny staggered back against the table, and the terrified gentleman endeavoured to seize the wrist of the hand which held the knife. Broome, however, with his left fist, for he was clutching a letter in that hand, pushed him with great force away, and then, once more drawing the knife across the throat, inflicted a fearful gash, and sank to the floor. There was a quiver throughout the once powerful frame, and, as Mr. Isaacs called for help and tried to staunch the great flow of blood with the table cloth, the once bright eyes of Johnny Broome glazed, and one of the greatest lights of the Prize Ring expired.

After this tragic end of the notorious and clever Johnny Broome, his brother Harry was broken down with grief, for the elder was the Champion's guide, philosopher, and friend, and there was nobody in his eyes like Brother John. It was a terrible blow to him, for they had been all but inseparable. So the survivor made no secret about the matter, and declared his intention to retire from the Ring. He had achieved the title and borne it honourably, and it was his wish, therefore, to settle down in the tavern of which he was Boniface, the " Bell's Life Tavern," afterwards known as the " Norfolk Arms," in the Strand, a house now condemned to be pulled down for the County Council improvements. Besides, Harry, after his long inactivity, had grown so corpulent that it was quite a question whether he would be able to bring himself into condition fit to enter the ring again.

But in the early part of 1855 a subscription was made by the leaders of the fistic art for a new belt, which was to be of greater value than any that pre-

viously existed. This was done as an inducement for
some of the heavy weights to throw down the gauntlet
and resuscitate the somewhat declining sport. It was,
indeed, absolutely necessary to provide another trophy,
for during the wrangle between Bendigo, Caunt, and
the Tipton Slasher, the other belt had gone astray. So
£100 was collected, and Mr. Hancock, the well-known
jeweller of Bond Street, was entrusted with the manu-
facture of a new one. The committee who represented
the subscribers were empowered to set forth the terms
upon which the Championship Belt was to be won and
held, which was done as follows:—

"That it should not be handed over to any person
claiming the Championship until he had proved his
right to it by a fight; that any pugilist having held it
against all comers for three years without a defeat
should become the absolute possessor; that the holder
should be bound to meet every challenger of any weight
who should challenge him for the sum of £200 a-side
within six months after the issue of such challenge,
during the three years; that he should not be bound
to fight for less than £200 a-side; that on the final
deposit for every match within the three years the belt
should be delivered up to the committee until after
the battle; and finally that on the belt being given
to the winner of any champion fight, he should deposit
such security as should be deemed necessary in the
hands of the committee to ensure the above regulations
being carried out."

At this period there were only five men who were
probable pugilists to compete for this new trophy.
They were the old Tipton Slasher, Harry Broome,
Harry Orme, Tom Paddock, and Aaron Jones. But as
Harry Broome had resigned and Jones had been beaten
by Tom Paddock twice, and Orme displayed no signs
of activity, it looked as if the new belt would be contested for between the Slasher and Paddock. The
latter had so far improved that his friends believed that
he could easily defeat the Tipton, although that
worthy had turned the tables upon him before, it will
be remembered. Then, to the disgust of Tom, Aaron
Jones made a match with the Tipton for £200 a-side,
and so forestalled him.

But on the 2nd of December, 1855, there appeared
the following in *Bell's Life*, which created a murmur of
astonishment throughout all sporting circles:—

"Mr. Editor—It was my intention never to have
entered the roped arena again, but the persuasions of
my old friends and backers have determined me to pull

off my shirt once more. I now come forward for the
satisfaction of the public and the Prize Ring, in order
to determine who's the better man, Tom Paddock or
myself. I will fight him for £200 a-side for the
Champion's Belt, which I feel I am entitled to, for both
the Tipton Slasher and Aaron Jones have been beaten
by me or men that I have beaten, and, therefore, I
claim it, and shall do so until fairly beaten in a roped
ring, as a trophy of that description ought to be contested for man to man, and never obtained upon mere
challenge. To prove that I mean to carry out what I
state, I will meet Paddock at your office on Wednesday,
December 12th, to sign articles, to which the following
conditions must be attached:—The money not under
any circumstances to be parted with until *fairly won or
lost* in a 24ft ring. Should this not suit Paddock (not
that I wish to interfere with the match between the
Tipton Slasher and Aaron Jones), I will fight Aaron
Jones for £200 a-side, whether he wins or loses with the
Tipton Slasher. By inserting this you will oblige
yours, etc.,   Henry Broome.

   " Bell's Life Tavern,
      November 28th, 1855."

And so Harry Broome could not resist the temptation of having another cut in to win the new and handsome belt. He most assuredly had a right to consider
himself the best man of the period. But Tom Paddock had asserted that *he* was the Champion, and that,
perhaps, was the reason for Broome coming from his
self-appointed retirement. Anyhow, the challenge of
Harry was at once responded to, for Tom Paddock
called upon *Bell's Life,* and left a tenner, on the understanding that if he could not raise the £200, Broome
should fight him for £100.

But the progress of the match and the battle for
the new belt under the conditions mentioned above
we must reserve until another chapter.

CHAPTER XLVIII

AND now we come to the opening chapters of one of
the most brilliant pugilists in the annals of the Ring.
Tom Sayers was, if not the most scientific, certainly
the pluckiest of modern gladiators, and his name will
be for ever remembered in connection with the roped
arena for the great battle which it will shortly be our
duty to describe, which took place at Farnborough,
between Sayers and Heenan. It was this fight that
originated a hot debate in the House of Parliament,
and a part of Lord Palmerston's reply to Lord Lovaine
upon the subject is worth quoting, showing, as it
does, the fine old English gentleman's appreciation of
honest, manly British sport. "He would not question
the technical legal question that a fight between two
men, not a fight of enmity, but a trial of strength, is
legally a breach of peace and an act that renders the
parties liable to prosecution; nor whether the persons
who go to witness it are not technically involved in
the charge. But, as far as they are concerned, they
may conceive it to be a very harmless pursuit. Some
persons like what takes place. There may be a difference of opinion, as a matter of taste, whether it is a
spectacle one would wish to see, or whether it is calculated to excite disgust. Some people look upon it as
an exhibition of manly courage characteristic of the
people of this country. I saw the other day," said his
Lordship, "a long extract from a French newspaper describing this fight as a type of the national character
for endurance, patience under suffering, of indomitable

perseverance in determined effort, and holding it up as
a specimen of the manly, admirable qualities of the
British race. All this, of course, is entirely a matter
of opinion; but, really, setting aside the legal techni-
calities of the case, I do not perceive why any number
of persons—say one thousand, if you please—who assemble to witness a prize fight are in their own persons
more guilty of a breach of peace than an equal number
of persons who assemble to witness a balloon ascent.
There they stand. There is no breach of the peace.
They go to see a sight, and when that sight is over
they return, and there is no injury done to anyone.
They only stand or sit on the grass to witness the performance, and as to the danger to those who perform
themselves, I imagine the danger to life in the case of
those who go up in balloons is certainly greater than
that of two combatants who hit each other as hard as
they can, but inflict no permanent injury upon each
other."

Good old Lord Palmerston! Where is the noble lord
who would now, in the House of Parliament, express
such true English sentiment to-day? But this is
digression, so let us return to the brave little hero who
called for these remarks.

Tom Sayers was born at Pimlico, near Brighton, on
May 25th, 1828, and was what is termed an Irish Cockney, the best fighting breed. The trade selected for
him to follow was that of a bricklayer, and the first
work of any note that he was employed upon was at the
Preston Viaduct, near Brighton. He shortly afterwards, however, came to London, and. getting employment at the building of the North Western Railway
Company, took up his residence in Camden Town, where
he spent the greater part of his life, and where he
died. Tom, when handling the trowel, was a failure,
and giving up bricklaying got an engagement at the
old White Conduit Gardens, Islington, where he was
employed to keep away intruders who attempted to
climb the palings around the old suburban pub.

Tom Sayers was about twenty-one years of age when
he fought his first battle. This was with Aby Couch,
and took place near Greenhithe in the March of 1849.
He disposed of Couch in less than a quarter of an hour,
and after this encounter Tom's backers looked around
in vain for any man who would confront him at 10st.
About twelve months of inactivity had passed when
Dan Collins, who was recognised as a smart, active
sparrer at Tom Spring's, where he was employed as
waiter, induced his patrons to throw out a challenge to
Sayers to fight him for £25 a side, the combat to come

off in October, 1850. This engagement turned out to
be a drama in three acts, for when Sayers and Collins
had been at it for half an hour the police interfered,
and stopped the fight. This was at Edenbridge, in
Kent, and for the purpose of finishing the " mill " they
adjourned to Redhill, where they fought thirty-nine
rounds, making a total of forty-eight. Then darkness
came on, and hostilities ceased for the day. The last
act was postponed until the following April, when they
again met to decide which should take the small stake
of £25. Poor Collins was on this occasion over-matched
to a degree, so rapidly had Sayers improved in his style
and physique, that he went in and won with the
greatest of ease.

After this Tom found it still more difficult to get an
opponent, for he was just that awkward weight, some
10st, making him too heavy for the light weights and
too light for the heavies, so it was nearly another year
before he found anybody to meet him. At length one
Jack Grant, the " Pet of the Borough," threw down the
gauntlet to Sayers, and a match was made for £100
a-side, the date being fixed for June 29, 1852. The
place selected for the fight was Mildenhall, Suffolk.

It is our intention to describe this combat as a specimen of Tom Sayers' earlier efforts, for Jack Grant was,
save his engagements with Langham and Heenan, undoubtedly the coming champion's most formidable
opponent. But before doing so let us introduce the
" Pet " to our readers, to do which we must ask them
to accompany us to the neighbourhood of the Borough.

Some forty odd years ago there resided near Gravel
Lane one Jack Grant. He was by occupation a porter
in the market of that neighbourhood, and had frequent
opportunities of testing his stamina and skill in settling
the many little disputes which were sure to crop up
from time to time amongst such men whose livelihood
depended upon their activity and energetic qualities.
It soon became evident to all who had seen him put
up his hands with the gloves that there was material
enough to make a first-class gladiator. At the " Prince
and Princess of Wales," a tavern in Gravel Lane,
Grant, with his friends and patrons, used to meet.
There, at the back, was a large club room, afterwards
turned into a skittle alley. In this room many a lively
little spar took place with the mittens, and Grant was
looked upon as champion of the district, getting christened the " Borough Market Pet."

When he commenced his pugilistic career it became
evident that the Southwark Fancy had not mistaken
their man, and had something to be proud of. His

first combat was with James, of Nottingham, who was easily defeated. He was then matched with Haggerty, of the East-End. This was a severe battle, resulting in another victory for Grant. Then came Jack's memorable fight with Mike Madden, notorious for having been the longest battle but one on record. It took place in 1848 at Woking, and lasted for five hours and threequarters. Daylight failed after the combatants had got through 140 rounds. Although Jack Grant did not come off best in this encounter he lost none of his prestige, for Madden was handy with his fists, and was, indeed, a very hard nut to crack. The next match made for the Market "Pet" was with Alec Keene. So excellent a performer was Keene considered that long odds were offered against Grant; but after fighting about an hour Jack was proclaimed the victor. Naturally this last performance placed Jack high up in the fistic world, and he became the chosen one of the Southwark Fancy.

Jack Callaghan, of Derby, was his next selected, but the match fell through. About this time Grant, whether elated by the success of his career, or because the temptations surrounding were irresistible, he foolishly raised his elbow too frequently, and gave way to dissipation.

Grant had some extraordinary notions of training, and we fear his penchant for "blue ruin" and his dissipated habits prevented him on more than one occasion from being victorious. After his fight with Madden he had a pretty good rest, and while his backers were looking around for someone likely to take him on, a challenge appeared in *Bell's Life* from Tom Sayers, which was immediately taken up by Grant.

Without going into details of the men's training or of the journey to the ring side on that June morning, we will briefly describe the encounter which brought Tom Sayers, the champion in embryo, so much to the front. Jack Grant was attended by Jemmy Welsh and Harry Orme, whilst Sayers was looked after by Ned Adams and Bob Fuller, the pedestrian. Tom's improvement in appearance since his battle with Dan Collins was very marked, and he looked the pink of perfection. His dark, tan-coloured skin covered limbs as muscular and well modelled as a sculptor would have wished to look upon, and his easy grace as he shaped on coming to the scratch must have pleased his supporters. Grant, with his long, strong arms, looked the more powerful of the two, and apparently had made up his mind to force the pace, for immediately "Time" was called he dashed in, but was neatly stopped by

Sayers in the coolest possible manner. Coming together some smart exchanges were given, when Sayers
slipped and fell, closing the initial round, but proving
to those present that the Borough man, upon whom
odds had been laid, had all his work cut out for him.

The succeeding half dozen rounds were productive of
some scientific displays on the part of Grant, but the

JACK GRANT.

activity of the younger and less experienced man and
his punishing blows called forth cheers from his supporters; and in the seventh round, Tom having gauged
his opponent to a nicety, changed his tactics, and
took the initiative. Still forcing the fighting, Sayers
delivered a couple of terrific blows on Grant's face, and
jumped back from the return. Renewing the attack,

he caught Grant with the right and left on the side of the head and a terrible punch in the ribs. The " Pet," who looked very savage, swinging round his right, gave Tom a stinger on his ear that sent him reeling. Grant followed him up, and closed with his man, but Sayers declining any more that round, slipped down.

As they came together again the pace they put on was a deal too hot to last. Grant placed a straight blow on Tom's forehead, and was answered by an upper cut, when a lively rally ensued. Grant, acting on Jemmy Welsh's advice, again tried to force the fighting; but Sayers, displaying marvellous quickness upon his legs, hit and got away in splendid style, and it was evident before the battle was half over that the " Pet " had caught a Tartar, and that Tom Sayers' brilliant performance with a man of Jack's experience and strength gave promise of greater things to come.

It would be but wearisome to follow the sixty-four rounds which were fought. The battle was virtually over at the end of the sixty-third, for Grant had been thrown several times badly, and his want of condition and the result of his dissipation began to tell. Both were slow to time. Grant was very rocky. He appeared to be in pain from the damage sustained by the last two or three throws. Grant led off, but his action was feeble, and now, for the first time, Jack put himself entirely on the defensive. Tom Sayers, however, was not to be denied, and he set about his man in real earnest, then closed with him, threw him, and fell heavily upon his prostrate body. Both men were assisted to their corners by their seconds, and Jemmy Welsh, discovering that poor Jack Grant had received an injury to his inside by the last fall, threw up the sponge in token of defeat after one of the toughest fights, lasting two hours and a half, that had been contested in the twenty-four foot ring for many a long day.

By this victory over such a man as Jack Grant, a natural and experienced fighter, who had vanquished such men as Alec Keene and Mike Madden, Tom Sayers came right to the front, and was looked upon as the coming man amongst the middle weights. Nobody, however, ever dreamed that he would ever aspire to Championship honours, for at that period it would have been laughed at had a 10st man matched himself against a 12-stoner. But how Tom Sayers climbed the ladder of fame, and to the surprise of the whole sporting world became one of our most admired champions, we must leave to future chapters.

CHAPTER XLIX.

AFTER the "Little Wonder," as Tom Sayers was nick-named, defeated Jack Grant, he became somewhat inflated with success, and leaving his old haunts in Camden Town spent most of his time at the "Coach and Horses" in St. Martin's Lane, where Ben Caunt, it will be remembered, ruled the roast as host. The big ex-champion had taken quite a fancy for the novice, and it was in the parlour of the above-mentioned house that Sayers presided very frequently at Ben's harmonic meetings. But Tom, to tell the truth, was not over-burdened with brains, and the class who sought his society throughout his career were not like those who had kept company with Tom Spring and some of the older lights of the Ring.

But where Sayers was most admired was at Saville House, in Leicester Square, and his boxing bouts at this establishment, under the organisation of the Pugilistic Benevolent Association, attracted no end of attention. It was not, however, until many months after his engagement with Grant that, in the October of 1852, he issued a challenge to fight anybody at 10st 8lb for £50 or £100 a-side, and the challenge was taken up by Lee, of the "York Arms," on behalf of one Jack Masters. The latter had never been in the metro-politan ring, but had distinguished himself with no little success in the provinces, having beaten Bates of Birmingham and Harrison of Manchester. Tom Sayers was backed by Ben Caunt and his party, and the fight took place at Long Reach on January 26, 1853, the Brighton man winning in 23 rounds, lasting 55 minutes.

It is not our intention to write full particulars of this early battle in which the coming champion was engaged, for his long and brilliant career was productive of more interesting combats, and to describe them all would occupy too much space. It will be sufficient to state that the combat was productive of a splendid exhibition of courage on the part of both men, and brought the name of Tom Sayers more prominent than ever with the Fancy. Rarely had there been such a magnificent natural fighter, and the punishment he meted out to his adversary was fearful, knocking him clean out of time in the last round with a blow upon the jaw which rendered him insensible for more than five minutes.

This battle established Tom's reputation as a middle weight of no ordinary calibre, and that he was able to take the lead at that weight everybody who had seen him fight believed. For two years the championship of the middle weights had been held by Nat Langham, that clever and scientific boxer who, although he had been beaten by Harry Orme, a man much heavier than himself, was looked upon as invincible as a 10st man. Nat at this time was residing in Cambridge, and kept the Ram Inn, Bridge Street, close to Magdalen College. He was in no way anxious to enter the Ring again, for he had numerous pupils amongst the Cantabs, and did an excellent business at his tavern ; so he was content to rest on his laurels and enjoy the title of champion of the middle weights. There was one though who had a wonderful opinion of Tom Sayers and a very poor estimate of Nat Langham, and he was Alec Keene, who had enjoyed a brilliant career in the P.R., and retired from active service in the roped arena, having gone into business at the "Three Tuns" in Moor Street, Soho. Alec Keene was one of the finest fighters of his weight, 9st 7lb, and had defeated Bill Cain, Joe Philps, Young Sambo, and Bill Hayes, and there was no better judge of a man's fighting capabilities anywhere. Besides his great appreciation for Tom Sayers' ability as a fighter, he liked the simple "Brighton Boy," as he called him, and did much to help him. Alec Keene was an enormous favourite, for his pleasing manner and gentlemanly appearance were suited to the customers and frequenters of the "Three Tuns," who numbered amongst them some of the *élite* of the sporting world. To mention a few, Sir Robert Peel, his brother William, both splendid boxers and lovers of the manly art ; Lord Ongley, Lord Drumlanrig, Mr. Wilbraham, the brothers Rosemount, Lord Winchelsea, Sir Edward Kent, Colonel Ouseley Hig-

gins, and many other votaries of the sport, were in the
habit of visiting Alec Keene's house; so Master Tom
Sayers was in good company, and for his exhibition
with the gloves found many admirers. It was principally through mine host of the " Three Tuns," therefore, that Tom found the money for his battles with
Dan Collins, Grant, and Jack Masters, and as Alec
Keene had backed him for all these fights and seconded
him in the last-named, he felt justified in continuing
to pin his faith to the rising young novice, and determined that he should if possible be matched against
the so-called invincible Nat Langham.

So Keene had no difficulty in getting Tom Sayers to
agree to fight, and the gauntlet was thrown down to
Langham to do battle for £100 a-side and the Championship of the Middle Weights. The Cambridge
men laughed at the audacity of Sayers, and were only
too anxious to find the money, so the challenge was
at once accepted, and articles were signed to fight on
the 18th of October, 1853. Such confidence did Nat's
supporters have in him that odds of 6 to 4 were freely
laid to a considerable amount. The limit of weight
was 11st, and Langham had all his work cut out at
training to get down, but under the guidance of Jemmy
Welsh he got through his preparation successfully, and
was never in better condition. Not so with Tom
Sayers though, for although he went down to his native
place, Brighton, under charge of Bob Fuller, he was
taken with a severe attack of influenza, followed by
an eruption of the skin. His condition became so
alarming that Alec Keene went down with a doctor
from London, who prescribed for him, and he speedily
recovered, much to the relief of his backers, who had
invested a deal of money upon his chance, and by the
morning of the fight was pronounced as fit as could be.

Tuesday, the 18th of October, was a glorious day,
and the muster at Shoreditch Station was considerable.
The special which had been chartered started about
8.30 with about 400, amongst them several Corinthians
under the wing of Alec Keene and Jem Burn. Through
Cambridge, Ely, and Mildenhall the train arrived at
Lakenham, where, some half a mile from the station, it
pulled up, and the company alighted.

Tom Oliver soon had the inner and outer rings
formed, and quite fifty " swells " paid their half-guinea
each for the reserved places within the two enclosures.
At 12.30 all was in readiness, and Sayers entered the
ring, waited upon by Alec Keene and Bob Fuller. He
was soon followed by Nat Langham, who had as his
esquires Jemmy Welsh and Jerry Noon. The men

shook hands cordially, and after the preliminary arrangements had been gone through the men stepped to the scratch at the call of " Time," and the combat commenced. Of Langham we have had much to say in a previous chapter, so it will be unnecessary to describe him and his performances. Until he lost the battle with Orme he had an unbeaten record, and his scientific and clever style was admired by all who saw him in the ring. By all accounts, the difference in the con-

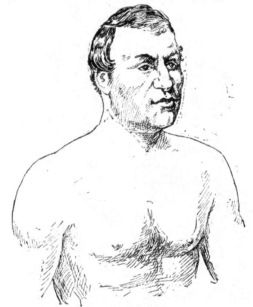

TOM SAYERS.

dition of the men was very great, for in spite of what had been said about Tom's recovery he looked dull about the complexion, and was at least 5lb over his proper fighting weight; whilst his opponent appeared to be trained to the hour. Both men commenced very cautiously, Nat showing great activity in getting out of the way. But Sayers meant business, and at length dashed in, but Langham stopped a blow, and delivered

first his right and then his left, marking Tom on the
nose and cheek, and before the first round was finished
cut Sayers on the chin, and produced first blood. The
Brighton man, amidst wild cheering, caught Nat a
terrific blow upon the forehead, which knocked him
clean off his legs.

After this Langham showed his craftiness by getting
down on every available occasion, which annoyed Tom
to no little extent, for he had always been accustomed
to stand-up fights, and knew little of the trickery of
the Ring, so much played by Langham when he desired to weary a foe. In the fourth round they treated
the spectators to a lively display, and Sayers managed
to get in some ugly blows with that celebrated " auctioneer," as his right was termed; but Nat was much
cleverer in the countering, and one blow, which caught
Tom between the eyes, seemed to daze him for the time,
and his bad condition caused the flesh to immediately
puff up. Langham, no doubt, made up his mind to
play for the optics after this, and he constantly got
over Tom's guard, getting on the nose, eye, and mouth,
and the balance of the betting was greatly in favour
of the elder man.

Round after round Langham managed to get the
blows in on the same spot, whilst Sayers rarely managed
to land the return, save now and again upon the ribs.
In the twentieth though, Sayers was much the stronger
of the two, whilst Nat seemed to be falling off and
losing strength, when Sayers went for him hammer and
tongs, and again knocked him down. Johnny Gideon,
who was one of Tom's principal backers all through his
career, offered 5 to 4 on Sayers at this juncture, and the
bet was at once taken. In the next round, however,
again the tables were turned, for Nat showed his superior science, and managed to get in hit after hit on the
eyes, and it was evident that Tom's peepers were
closing.

To give full details of this most exciting combat will
be unnecessary, for there were in all sixty rounds
fought, during which Langham showed wonderful ring-
craft, and, although weaker than his adversary, played
for the eyes in such a clever manner that Sayers became all but blind, and rushed in madly. Langham
stepped aside, and lashed out with the left on the eye
and nose, and then peppered his man with both hands.
" Take him away, he's stone blind!" cried somebody
at the ring side, and Alec Keene caught him by the arm
and was about to throw up the sponge. Sayers, however, shook him off, and went towards the scratch.
He lunged out where he supposed Langham to be, but

the latter stepped aside, and then measuring his distance struck him a smashing blow in the face, and he rolled over.

It was now evident that Sayers was blind, so the battle was awarded to Langham, who was dreadfully punished about the body, for Tom had delivered some terrific blows, and had it not been for the blindness would certainly not have suffered this, his first and last defeat.

Although Tom Sayers was deprived of victory, he was by no means disgraced, and so gallantly had he fought that a sum of £50 was subscribed in the train going home, and his friends declared their willingness to find the money for another match. Nat Langham, however, had no desire to try conclusions with the brave Tom again, although when the latter's eyes got well, which took a considerable time, he threw the gauntlet down again, offering to fight Nat for another £100, or twice that amount. Langham about this time married a niece of Ben Caunt's, and came from Cambridge to London, and took the "Cambrian Stores" in Castle Street, Leicester Square, and declared his intention of never entering the Ring again, much to Sayers' annoyance, although, through the refusal of Langham, he was entitled to call himself Champion of the Middle Weights.

Langham went into the Ring but once after this, when, it will be remembered, he met Ben Caunt over a personal quarrel. He settled down as a sporting publican, and was for a time very successful, being patronised by the Corinthians. He will be remembered by many as the originator of the celebrated convivial sporting club called the Rum-Pum-Pas, Mr. John Rosemount being the first president. Amongst the members were Lord Caledon (afterwards Lord Verulam), his brother, the Hon. "Bob" Grimston, Captain Hope-Johnstone, the Hon. "Billy" Duff, Lord Edward Russell, Major William Peel, "Fatty" Sutherland, and others.

The members used to meet on Wednesday evenings and dine in a twenty-four-foot square ring. Nat Langham was M.C., and the chief songster of the club was Bill Benjamin, who had a capital voice. The principal dish for which the club was famous was plum pudding. Two of these puddings, one hot and the other cold, were regularly supplied by Mrs. Burnell, of the "King's Arms," Hanwell. They were brought to the "Cambrian" punctually every Wednesday in time for dinner, the hot one wrapped in flannel upon a water plate. The company would frequently make a night

of it, for Nat Langham would promise them a little
mill in the early morning between two lads for a purse,
and frequently conduct them early on a summer's
morning down Epsom way, and give them a treat.
Much profit accrued to Langham out of this club, and
when he died in 1871 it was removed to Alec Keene's,
where it continued to hold its meetings until the year
1853.

But enough of the Rum-Pum-Pas. Let us return to
the coming champion, Tom Sayers. As we have said,
he was very much vexed at Langham refusing to meet
him a second time, and to his disgust nobody would
respond to his persistent challenges. At this time,
too, he had left the " Bricklayers' Arms," in Camden
Town, where he had had but a short tenancy, for Tom
had no head for business, and as he seemed unable to
get a match on, he thought seriously of giving prize-
fighting up and returning to his old trade. At length,
however, a foeman cropped up unexpectedly at the
house of his friend, Alec Keene. One evening Harry
Orme came over from the East-End with a few friends,
amongst them a young chap named George Sims. He
was a tall, thin young fellow, who had fought a couple
of times in the Ring, but was not looked upon by any
means as a top sawyer. Tom Sayers happened to be
there on this particular evening, and the two men got
chaffing each other, Sims using some very unpleasant
remarks about Tom's fight with Nat Langham. Sayers
was one of the best tempered fellows imaginable, but
the East-Ender was so offensive that it came to a
wrangle, Sims at the finish offering to fight Tom for
£25. This was too ridiculously small a sum for the
Champion of the Middle Weights, and for that evening
the whole thing fell through. In the next issue of
Bell's Life though, Sims renewed his challenge, and
Sayers determined upon accepting, the stakes being
made £50 to £25, and it was agreed that they should
fight on the 2nd of February. The East-Enders thought
a good deal of their man, for he had licked a big fellow
named Waldron, who weighed over 12st, and had shown
some knowledge of the art.

They went down the river near Long Reach, and it
was such a damp, cold, foggy morning that the steamer
was by no means crowded, although a great number of
"toffs" came down with Jem Burn, anxious to see the
plucky Tom, who had made such a gallant fight with
Langham. The ring was pitched near the bank of the
river, Sayers being waited upon by Jemmy Shaw and
Bob Fuller, Sims being looked after by Jemmy Welsh
and Harry Orme. Sayers was the shorter and lighter

man of the two, weighing at this time 10st 6lb, and standing 5ft 8½in, whilst Sims stood 5ft 10in, and weighed over 11st.

It must have been an extraordinary battle to have witnessed, although, no doubt, those who travelled all that distance on such a morning thought the game hardly worth the candle. Directly the East-Ender put up his hands anybody could see that he knew little or nothing about the game, and the natty attitude of Sayers must have been in strange contrast as he stood grinning before his lanky opponent. Tom feinted, and drew his man, shot his left in upon the nose, got his head in chancery, and pegged away at him unmerci-fully until the East-Ender slipped down.

In the next round Sims was all abroad, and Tom planted his left on the nose, which gushed with blood, and he was in a pretty plight. Orme sponged him down, and he was sent to the scratch again. Tom at once met him with a terrific blow over the eye, cutting it deeply, and sending him reeling back, and as Sayers went for the close he fell backwards. It must have been a terrible hit, for when Welsh and Orme picked the man up and tried to stanch the blood his head rolled back, and he was found to be senseless, so Tom had polished Mr. George Sims off in just five minutes.

CHAPTER L.

LIMMER'S HOTEL AND ITS PATRONS,—TOM SAYERS AND HARRY
PAULSON, AND HIS TWO BATTLES WITH AARON JONES.

AFTER the exhibition Sayers made of Sims he issued
a challenge; but nobody responded. He travelled
throughout England on boxing tours and in search of a
foeman; but none would oblige him who were any way
near his weight. At length he astonished the sporting
world by offering to fight Tom Paddock at catch-weight
if he would find £200 to Tom's £100. Although Paddock was a much heavier man, his friends thought the
odds were too great, and the offer was not accepted.
Tom Sayers at length became despondent, and made up
his mind to go to Australia. This he most certainly
would have done, and then in all probability we should
not have his name enrolled amongst the illustrious
champions had not one more chance been offered him
from an unexpected quarter.

Harry Paulson, of Nottingham, who had beaten Tom
Paddock once and been defeated by him twice, and who
had been idle for a considerable time, made overtures to
Sayers. Now, Paulson's weight was over 12st, so that
Sayers would be giving away something like 2st, a thing
unheard of at that period. Nevertheless the plucky
little coming champion agreed to take the heavy man on
for £50 a-side. But Tom had been a little too fast in
putting down the deposit of £5, for his friends hesitated
with the money, thinking that, confident and capable as
he was, to give away so much was preposterous.

Nat Langham had the matter in hand for Sayers, for
they had made it up and were good friends, and it was
due to him that the affair was arranged. He went
straight to Sir Edward Kent, one of the staunchest of
the Corinthian sportsmen, and informed him of Tom's
desertion by his backers. Sir Edward in the cause of
sport thought it a pity that such a plucky effort on the
part of Sayers to take on the big 'un should be thwarted,
that he called a meeting of friends at Limmer's Hotel,
the great rendezvous of racing men and aristocratic
followers of every sport, to meet upon the subject of the
proposed fight.

And here we may be permitted to digress for a few

moments to have a word or two to say about the
celebrated and historic hotel. Limmer's from the time
of the Regency was the most celebrated of all the
sporting houses, for although Tom Spring's, Jem
Burns', and Nat Langham's were houses patronised by
the Fancy, there were more prize-fights arranged at
Limmer's than all the others put together. Here is a
quotation from the writing of one who frequented it in
the good old days:—"Many may remember the dark
brown coffee-room of that most celebrated of sporting
hotels, where in the good old days of the Regency, the
Prince himself drank bumpers of old port with Sheridan
and Beau Brummel. Many a jolly orgie did that coffee-
room witness in its day. Some survivors, too, there may
be who can recall the famous head-waiter of that coffee-
room who invented a wonderful drink composed of gin,
soda water, ice, lemon, and sugar, which enraptured
drinkers declared to be the genuine nectar of the gods."

It was at Limmer's that Nat Langham met Sir
Edward Kent, and came back with a cheque for £50,
because that good sport would not allow the fight to
fall through for the sake of that amount. So the match
between Harry Paulson and Tom Sayers was made.
Tom had taken matters a little too easily, and had
allowed himself to get very much out of condition, and
there was insufficient time between the making of the
match and the date of the fight for him to get fit.

On the other hand, Harry Paulson was in splendid
fettle, for he had been looked after by his fellow-townsman, the Bold Bendigo, the first-named being a Nottingham man, and a great friend of Bendigo. Bendigo had
backed Harry very heavily, and Jem Burn was so certain
that Tom Sayers could not give all the weight away that
he had induced several of his Corinthian patrons to go
for the Nottingham man, so that there was quite a pile
of money on the result of the fight both in London and
the provinces. Harry Paulson came to London accompanied by Bendigo, and made Jem Burn's house, the
Rising Sun, Air Street, Piccadilly, his headquarters.
What a famous house this was, to be sure, in the old days
of the Prize Ring. It was kept by Ben Burn, who
fought Tom Spring and Tom Oliver. Then the house
went to Jem Burn, old Ben's nephew, passing afterwards into Johnny Hannan's hands, the celebrated
light-weight pugilist, and then to Johnny Broome. The
house, which is very little altered, is now quite famous,
but not as a sporting crib, being now kept by our old
friend, Mr. C. O. Thurston, a gentleman exceedingly
well-known in the Trade.

There was a merry meeting at the Rising Sun on the

eve of the battle under notice, and Bendigo was full of
his fun, whilst the callers to see Harry Paulson were
very numerous, Jem Burn doing a rousing trade. At
Nat Langham's, too, there was a big audience to see
Tom Sayers, who had come up from his training
quarters at Brighton on the day before that set down
for the battle, which was January 29, 1856.

HARRY PAULSON.

That morning was bitterly cold, the frost being **very
severe.** Cabs were at a premium, for the roads were
very slippery, and a great number who had intended to
have witnessed the battle were too late for the " special."
Amongst those who nearly missed the train was Tom
Sayers himself, for Nat Langham found it impossible to
hire a vehicle, having neglected to order one overnight,
and had he not met with an old friend with his dog-cart,

who drove them to the station, they would have certainly missed the train, and there would have been no fight.

However, the train steamed away with both Tom and the Nottingham man, their destination being Appledore, a village about eight miles from Ashford, in Kent. The journey of some sixty-four miles occupied over three hours, so it was eleven o'clock before the party arrived and the ring was formed. Paulson was attended by his friends, Bendigo and Bob Fuller, whilst Tom Sayers was looked after by Nat Langham and Jemmy Massey. The odds were 7 to 4 on Paulson, and as the men stood in the ring surrounded by the shivering spectators, the wonderful difference in size was very apparent. John Gideon, who was a friend of Sayers, and afterwards his backer, declared that Paulson weighed no less than 12st 4lb, whilst Sayers was only 10st 9lb.

We have no space to describe this long and grand battle, which really was Tom's stepping-stone to the Championship, for it is quite certain that had he not met Paulson and defeated him he would never have been backed to beat the heavy-weights and become possessor of the belt and title of Champion. It was a critical time for Tom all throughout the fight, and at one period 3 to 1 was laid against him. His splendid physique, his indomitable courage, and his marvellously accurate deliveries, however, served him, and although Harry Paulson was the stronger man of the two, Sayers managed to win, after standing up to his foe for three hours and eight minutes.

It was one of the grandest displays of endurance ever known in the Prize Ring, and at several periods of the battle it looked as if Paulson must win. In the forty-first round the Nottingham man completeley closed one of Tom's eyes, and from that period to the end of the battle he could see through but one eye. In the sixty-second, the two men countered so heavily simultaneously, Tom on the right eye and Harry on the jaw, that both were knocked to grass. Again and again was Sayers floored, but such a glutton did he prove that he always came to the scratch. Towards the end, however, Tom's repeated blows upon the face closed both the Nottingham man's eyes, and after they had been at it three hours he could see but a glimmer of daylight. During the next eight minutes Tom Sayers managed to completely blind him, and, having him at his mercy, finished him off.

As we have said, this victory was the link in the chain which led to the Championship. To thrash a man like Paulson, who was considerably over 12st, was indeed a feat, and the Little Wonder was made as a pugilist. It created quite a revolution in the Ring. Nothing of the kind had ever been attempted before.

At this time the Tipton Slasher had received forfeit from Tom Paddock, and was looked upon as Champion, though the new belt was still in abeyance. At the time that the Slasher came to London to receive his forfeit of £160 at the Coal Hole Tavern, in the Strand, where Baron Nicholson held his "Judge and Jury;" and when a "Champion Dinner" was given there was another match pending, which was thought would eventually have something to do with the future of the Belt. This was between Aaron Jones and Tom Sayers. The former, who had met with an accident, which interrupted his match with the Tipton, to the astonishment of the sporting world, had been challenged by Tom Sayers. There had been some surprise, as we have already shown, by the presumption on the part of Sayers to fight Harry Paulson; but the latter was ten years his senior. On the other hand, Aaron Jones was five years his junior, there was great disparity in their weights, Jones was 8in taller, was a punishing hitter, and a scientific boxer, who aspired to the Championship. As in the other case, numbers of Tom's friends thought he was at last playing too high a game. Still there were some backers who, having seen him dispose of Paulson, thought he might succeed with Jones, so the match was made for £100 a-side, and the date fixed for January 9, 1857.

About this time there had been such a dead set against prize-fighting by the provincial magistrates that it was really risky to attempt to bring a battle off at all, and there was no little difficulty in finding a suitable place to pitch a ring. The Eastern Counties had been a favourite venue, but it became too dangerous for the party to congregate at Shoreditch Station, so it was decided to make a trip on the Great Northern, and bills were printed to the effect that a train would leave King's Cross on the morning of Tuesday, January 6. At the eleventh hour, however, it was discovered that the authorities were on the alert, and that it would be next to impossible to bring the battle off on that line. Ultimately it was decided to proceed as far as Tilbury by train, and embark on a steamer which would take the party to some secluded spot on the banks of old Father Thames. In consequence of these changes only a few were actually in the know, and the small party was principally composed of Corinthians who had been looked up by Jem Burn and Nat Langham, the rough element being conspicuous by its absence.

At eight o'clock the train steamed out of Fenchurch
Street station, by nine it was at Tilbury, and before ten
the boat was making way down river. The weather, as
when Sayers fought Harry Paulson, was bitterly cold,
and there having been a great quantity of rain, there
was no little difficulty in fixing upon a suitable spot
upon which to form the ring. At length it was decided
to disembark at a place opposite Canvey Island, and
there, after some difficulty, the passengers were landed
and the ring formed. It must have been a dreadful day,
for one account before us states that a keen north-east
wind was blowing, and the men when they stripped were
sc cold that they had to be wrapped in blankets whilst
the preliminary arangements were being made. It was
so sharp indeed that it was feared that the men would
suffer considerably. We never could understand why
tights should have been so frequently brought off on
these winter mornings. Surely the summer time would
be more agreeable both to men and spectators, yet rain,
frost, and even snow have been the accompaniments to a
" merry mill."

The betting was 5 to 4 against Sayers, and he himself
staked £8 to £10 with Aaron Jones. The latter weighed
twenty-three pounds more than his opponent, and stood
three inches taller. He had fought some good men,
amongst them Harry Orme and Tom Paddock, and was
thought to have vastly improved. That in this battle
under notice he displayed more science than with
Paddock is certain, for frequently he puzzled Sayers.
But Tom was in splendid condition, and although he
received some severe punishment he stood it well, and
managed to land Jones time after time in the eyes, for
that was his practice, as will be found in the accounts of
most of his battles. He had learned it from Nat Langham, and never forgot it.

It is not our intention to describe the rounds of this
battle, for, although it was fiercely fought at the onset,
it finished up in a most unsatisfactory manner. They
had been fighting for three hours, and Jones was nearly
blind, whilst Tom had fought himself to a standstill,
and both being too done up to do any damage, and darkness setting in, the referee made a draw of it, having
power to appoint another meeting.

The backers of Tom Sayers were anxious to settle the
matter that week, and Mr. Johnny Gideon and Tom
Sayers waited upon the referee, Mr. Frank Dowling, of
Bell's Life, to ask him to fix the following Saturday
This he would not do, however, as Aaron Jones had
injured his arm, and both men were much punished.
Jones wanted to postpone it for a couple of months, but

the Sayers party strongly objected to such a delay, and
so Mr. Dowling split the difference, and ordered them
into the Ring on February 10. There was much
interest displayed in this second meeting, and three
steamers were chartered to take the party down the
river.

There was a remarkable falling off with Aaron Jones,
who had declared his intention of taking the lead at the
commencement of the battle and forcing the fighting.
But he did nothing of the sort, and Tom Sayers,
profiting by his experience of the first meeting, went in
fearlessly, and punished his adversary in the first few
rounds. Jones' backers were much disappointed, and
the only fear that Tom's friends had was that he was
fighting too fast. But his condition was splendid, and
early in the fight he delighted his friends by planting
his left on Aaron's right eye, and then, bringing his
" auctioneer " across his jaw, knocking him clean off his
legs. This very nearly put him out, and he was very
slow to time. Up to the thirty-third round the tide of
fortune was all in favour of Tom Sayers, but at that
point he appeared to come over weak, and showed un
mistakable symptoms of fatigue. He had been fight
ing too fast, in spite of "Farmer" Bennett's and
Johnny Gideon's advice.

Jones saw his chance, and dashed in to avail himself
of it, but his strength was giving out too, and his blows
had little effect. Then Tom pulled himself together in
that extraordinary manner for which he was so celebrated, and planted his well-known double on Jones'
face as the latter fell. They continued until the eighty-
fifth, when Jones, dazed and half-stunned, received his
coup de grâce, and Tom Sayers was once more proclaimed victor. This battle brought the plucky Brighton
Boy still nearer to the coveted title, and it was evident
that giving away weight made very little matter to him
and he proved by his conquering of the two heavy
weights that he must have some chance for the Championship, so his friends were determined that he
should have a try when the opportunity offered itself.

CHAPTER LI.

A LIVELY EVENING AT LANGHAM'S.—OLD JOHN GIDEON.—
TOM SAYERS AND THE TIPTON SLASHER.—BATTLE FOR
THE BELT AND £400,

AFTER the Tipton Slasher's defeat by Harry Broome,
through his delivery of a foul blow, in the August of
1853, he received forfeit from Broome and reclaimed the
Championship. Aaron Jones and Tom Paddock having
forfeited to him, he found it most difficult to make a match
with anybody, and it was not until four years afterwards that he managed to get an offer from Tom Sayers.
And this is how it all came about.

On February 16, 1857, there was a sporting dinner
given at Nat Langham's to celebrate the victory of the
Little Wonder over Aaron Jones, and a great number of
Tom's backers and friends were present as a matter of
course. Amongst the former was Mr. Johnny Gideon
(who, by-the-bye, we believe to be still in the land of the
living, for it is not so long ago that we met him in
Paris, where he had been residing for many years).
Besides Gideon there were "Farmer" Bennett, Mr.
Lupton, and Tom Sayers' seconds in his last fight, Bill
Hayes and Jemmy Massey. Now the latter was a great
friend of the Tipton's, and when the cloth had been
cleared, the pipes lighted, and the grogs served, naturally
there was only one topic of conversation, and that was
prize-fighting. Massey was singing the praises of the
old Tipton, and declared that there was no other man
amongst the heavy-weights capable of holding a candle
to him. To this Johnny Gideon differed, saying that it
was his opinion that the Slasher was too old and stale,
and really had no right to hold the belt, knowing that
Tom Sayers had for a long time been anxious to have a
cut at Tom Paddock or the Slasher. But many ridiculed
the idea of a comparative shrimp, like Sayers, standing
before the Herculean form of the Tipton. But Sayers
knew his man, and was all anxiety to have a try.

In the first place he knew, as all who were well
acquainted with him were aware, that Mr. William Perry

had during these few years been taking very little care
of himself. He was always a rackety sort of a fellow,
and when he became Boniface of the Champion Inn,
Spoon Lane, Tipton, he lived an exceedingly unsteady
life. The business he did was very good, for he acted as
purveyor of refreshments at many of the Midland race
meetings, and he was very popular in the Black Country.
There are any number of anecdotes told about the Tipton,
some as interesting as those in connection with the Bold
Bendigo's career, for Perry was nearly as eccentric. Mr.
David Christie Murray, the celebrated novelist, in an
autobiography published some six or seven years ago,
records some of his recollections of the Slasher about
this period, which may be worth repeating. On one
occasion, Mr. Christie Murray tells us, as a boy he played
truant, and followed the Slasher (the idol of his boyhood) to a little race meeting held at a place called The
Roughs, on the side of the Birmingham Road, in the parish
of Handsworth. The Slasher was surrounded by his usual
tag-rag and bob-tail of admirers, and was in his most
swaggering mood, aggravated no doubt by alcohol. As
he roamed over the course the old warrior's eyes lighted
upon a machine for trying the strength—one of those
apparata where you pay a penny and smite your
hardest, and a dial records the force of the blow. There
was the figure of a circus clown, with a buffer about his
midriff, at which you were invited to strike. The Slasher
tossed a penny to the proprietor, and prepared to strike,
when the latter cried out, " Don't strike. Not you, Mr.
Perry ! Not you !" " Gerrout," said he, as he spat on his
hand, clenched his fist, and smote. Crash went the whole
machine into ruin ; the wooden uprights splintered, and
the iron supports doubled into uselessness. The destroyer
rolled on rejoicing ; but the crowd made a subscription,
and the owner of the machine stowed away his damaged
property, well pleased.

The notorious Morris Roberts had a boxing booth at
these races, and standing on the platform outside, was
calling out, " Walk up, gentlemen, walk up, and see the
noble art of self-defence practised by Englishmen. Not
like the cowardly Frenchman or Italian, as uses sticks,
knives, and pistils, and other fire-arms, but the weapons
pervided by nature. I've got a nigger inside as won't
say ' No ' to no man. Also George Gough, as has fought
fifteen knuckle fights within the last two years, and won
'em all. One man down and the next come on. If
there's any sportsman 'ere as cares to 'ave a turn, there's
half a crown and a glass of sperrits for the man who stands
before George Gough five minutes, no matter where he
comes from." Up goes the wicked Slasher's old silk hat

upon the stage. Morris Roberts, who was bawling
"Twopence does it—first-rate sample of the noble
art for twopence!" froze at the approach of Perry.
"Come, come, Mr. Perry," he exclaimed when he had
recovered himself a little, "you can't expect George to
stand up agin the Champion of all England. That
doesn't stand to reason, that doesn't; now does it, Mr.
Perry?" The Slasher smiled. "All right, hand down
that half a crown and that there glass o' sperrits." "You
don't mean it, Mr. Perry?" said Mr. Morris Roberts.
"Don't I?" cried the Slasher. A sudden inspiration
illumined Mr. Morris' mind. "All right, come up, Mr.
Perry; sixpence does it, sixpence does it." It was no
sooner known that the Champion was really resolved on
business than the booth was besieged. It turned out
that Mr. Gough had been impertinent to the Slasher, and
the offended dignitary punched him, it was thought, a
little unmercifully. At the close of the first round
the man of the booth said, truthfully enough no doubt,
that he had had enough of it, and the entertainment came
to a premature end.

These stories told by the well-known novelist give a
pretty good idea of how the Slasher carried on as Champion. He certainly took too much to drink, and Sayers
and Gideon knew it.

But, to return to the evening at Nat Langham's.
Jemmy Massey had great faith in his friend, and
declared that there was only one man capable of standing up against the Tipton, and that was Tom Paddock,
and he'd have a bellyful before he had finished.

Johnny Gideon mentioned Sayers' name. Now that
worthy was sitting next to him, and immediately
joined in the conversation, and declared that he was quite
willing to meet the Slasher. Thereupon Jemmy Massey
jumped up and banged his fist upon the table, shouting
"Then I'll back the Tipton against you for £200 a-side,
and here's a fiver to bind the match."

Sayers turned to his friend Gideon, and said, "Take
him, Mr. Gideon, take him; down with a fiver to cover
his; it's a bargain, and I won't back out of it." This
was instantly done, and the match was made. At this
time Massey kept the Crown, in Cranbourn Passage,
Leicester Square, and there it was arranged they should
meet that day week and sign articles. But most of Tom's
friends looked upon the whole thing as an after-dinner
bit of bravado on his part, and that he never intended to
meet the great Tipton. So universal was the opinion
that Massey was convinced that such was the case, and
failed to communicate with the Slasher. So when Tom
Sayers and Johnny Gideon arrived on the appointed day,

they found that nothing had been done in the matter.
This made Sayers very angry, and he told Massey that if
the match was not proceeded with immediately he should
draw the first instalment, and then publish a challenge
to the Tipton.

Seeing that Tom was very much in earnest, Massey
communicated with Perry, who came to London, and a
meeting took place at Nat Langham's, on Monday,
March 3, 1857, when articles were signed to fight for
£200 a-side and the new Championship Belt, within 100
miles of London, upon June 16, 1857. £20 was at once
deposited with Mr. Frank Dowling, editor of *Bell's Life*,
and it was arranged that other deposits should be made
at the following sporting houses :—Owen Swift's, the
Horse Shoe, Tichborne Street; Dan Dismore's, the King's
Arms, Smart's Buildings, Holborn; Mr. Jackson's, the
King's Head, King Street Mews; Joe Phelps', the Green
Dragon, Villiers Street, Strand; Mr. Watkin's, the Horse
and Groom, George Yard, Grosvenor Square; Nat Lang-
ham's, the Cambrian Stores, Leicester Square; Jemmy
Massey's, the Crown, Cranbourn Passage, Leicester
Square; Mr. Newham's, the Ship Tavern, Hanover
Court, Long Acre; and Mr. Lipman's, the King of
Prussia, Middlesex Street, Whitechapel.

When the match had been properly made there was
much discussion as to the relative chances of the two men.
Those of the old school declared that a man under 11st
could have no possible chance with the Slasher, who was
not only a tricky, clever fighter, up to all the moves in the
ring, but was undoubtedly the best heavy-weight in the
kingdom, topped six foot by half an inch, and weighed
14½st. True, Sayers had, as we have already chronicled,
given away a stone and a half or so, but this was very
different to giving something like 4st. The Tipton himself laughed at the idea. He wanted to know how the
little 'un could get at him, and declared that he did not
mean to caper about all over the ring, but that he should
just wait for Sayers to come on, and then how was he
going to reach him?

On the other hand, Sayers was very confident. He
declared that the Slasher was worn out and incapable of
long exertion, and that he should wear him out. So
sanguine were the two men about winning, that they
invested every shilling they had on the result, the Tipton
selling his public-house immediately the articles were
signed. So defeat meant absolute ruin to either of the
men.

Sayers was in comparative good condition owing to his
recent battle, but the Slasher was very much out of
form. So after he had disposed of his business he came

from Tipton to Boxmoor, in Hertfordshire, where he settled down steadily to work. Tom starred about the country boxing. So opposed were the authorities about this time to a fight, that a warrant was issued for Tom's arrest, and executed at a house where he had been lodging, but fortunately he had timely warning, and did a bolt, and afterwards had to use every precaution by moving from county to county to avoid arrest.

An aquatic trip was decided upon, and a steamer chartered to carry a limited number (200) from Southend, the excursionists going by train to that place from Fenchurch Street. The accounts before us of that journey are somewhat startling, and some of them must have had a rough time of it. They went, it appears, down by ordinary train, and the crush was terrific, whilst the roughs were very much in evidence, and the railway officials had all their work cut out to keep them from breaking through the barriers. The Slasher went down to Tilbury overnight, but Sayers travelled with his friends, but was so well disguised that nobody recognised him. This was fortunate, as all down the line officers were on the alert to arrest them and spoil the fun. At Southend there was a regular stampede down to the beach, and the people had to get off in small boats to the steamer—no little risky matter, for the craft were overcrowded, and the sea was lumpy. Nobody was allowed aboard the steamer but those provided with tickets, or who were willing to pay a couple of sovereigns, and the consequence was that numbers had to return to the shore.

We have no space to quote from the descriptions of the voyage to the field of battle. How Barney Aaron, " Admiral " Coobidy and Pinxton provided the banquet in the cabin, consisting of cold chicken, ribs of beef and salad, of the nips of brandy at 6d. a little glass, and of the effect the rolling steamer had upon some of the hardy sportsmen (for it was blowing half a gale) as they rounded the Nore Lightship, and they " shipped it green " over and over again, and more than half the voyagers were suffering with *mal de mer.* Off the Isle of Grain the skipper let go the anchor, and the disembarkation took place, attended with as much danger as before, for swarms of little boats came around the steamer, and were immediately overcrowded. The marvel was that there were no mishaps.

Tom Oliver and his assistants soon had the ring formed, and the crowd took their places. At this moment a man galloped up on horseback, and wanted to know what they were doing on his master's land. He was, however, squared with a sovereign. During the preliminaries, whilst the men were tossing for corners, another scare took place. There was no question about it this time, there were some half-dozen police-officers running towards them. The alarm was at once given, and the men made a bolt for the shore, with the crowd after them, and hurried into the boats. In an extraordinary

JACK MACDONALD,
THE FAMOUS SECOND.

short space of time they were all once more aboard the steamer, waving adieu to the constables on the shore.

By this time it was nearly four o'clock in the afternoon, as they made for the opposite side of the river, and landing again formed the ring; this time in the

meadow of a friendly farmer. Sayers and the Slasher
were soon in the ring, the former esquired by Nat Langham and Bill Hayes; the Tipton by Tass Parker and Jack
Macdonald. The colours were tied to the stakes—blue,
with large white spots, for Tom, and blue birdseye for
Perry. As " Time " was called several bets were made,
6 to 5 on the Tipton Slasher being the closing price. It is
our intention to give but a skeleton account of this, Tom
Sayers' maiden fight for the Championship, for we shall
have several more opportunities of describing the Little
Wonder's handiwork.

We have already stated that it was the Tipton's intention to play a waiting game, and to let Sayers come for
him, but to the surprise of everybody present the Tipton
opened the ball. He let go his huge fists one after the
other, but the wily Tom had only to step nimbly back
and the blows wasted themselves in the air.

In the next round the Slasher followed the same
tactics, and again reached Sayers a sounding whack on
the ribs; but Tom as quick as lightning countered, dealing a terrific blow on the mouth, cutting the Slasher's
lips and drawing a copious supply of blood. The Tipton
looked dumfounded. He stood gazing at Sayers for a
few seconds, as if he was uncertain as to the best thing
to do; then, swinging his great arms about like the sails
of a windmill, rushed at his small adversary. Tom,
quick on his pins, was away before the blow could get
near him, and then springing in nailed the Slasher on
the bridge of the nose and got away unharmed. Then
the old 'un pursued Tom, who danced about all over the
ring, until the Slasher fairly lost his head. Here is an
account by an eye-witness at this period of the battle,
which will fairly describe the remainder of the combat :—
" An ugly look came over the Slasher's face; he dashed
savagely at his man, slung out his right and followed it
up with a terrific upper-cut from his left, which if it
had got home, would have pretty well lifted Tom's head
off his shoulders, but needless to say Tom's head did
not happen to be in the way—both blows missed, and
Sayers again dropped his left heavily on the Slasher's
bleeding beak. The Slasher then was guilty of the very
folly which he had solemnly assured us previously that
he meant to avoid. He stupidly played into his opponent's hands by chasing him all over the ring. This was
exactly what Tom wanted; it was his only chance of
winning—to tire the Slasher out until he was unable to
strike an effective blow, and then go in and finish him
off. So Sayers proceeded to make a fool of the veteran,
now dancing round him like a wild Indian, now running
from him as if he were in dread of his life. And that

dunder-headed old Tipton couldn't see that he was being made game of."

And so the combat proceeded much after the above style. One round lasted half an hour, and it was by no means an idle one; the Slasher at one period nearly getting hold of Tom, and finishing the bout up by sending him heavily to grass. Had he stood his ground and not gone chasing his nimble foe all over the ring, he might have won. But he would not stand his ground, in spite of the advice of his seconds and orders of his backers. At the close of the eighth round, however, he began to see the folly of his ways. But it was too late. He had tired himself out. The excitement was intense, and the Tipton's followers threatened to break into the ring on more than one occasion.

In the ninth the Slasher came up to time very slowly. He had evidently done himself up, and was badly damaged. He had never fought a man like this before. In this round Sayers was able to take greater liberties and he delivered three terrific facers in rapid succession, which fairly dazed the old 'un. One account says, "The last of the three caught him in the mouth and ripped his lip open like paper! whilst his jaw was suddenly bulged out like that of an ape. He staggered and fell, Sayers falling over him in an attempt to hit him as he went down."

This practically settled the fight. He was in such a state that cries came from all parts of the surrounding crowd to take him away, and after Sayers had hit him all over the face again and again, and he could hardly stand, Owen Swift entered the ring and threw up the sponge. So Tom Sayers, the Little Wonder, was proclaimed Champion of England.

26

CHAPTER LII.

AFTER the poor old Tipton's defeat by Tom Sayers,
which had brought about quite a revolution in Championship fights, nobody dared say that it was weight
alone that should be considered. Undoubtedly, good
generalship, activity, pluck, and endurance counted for
more than size and strength. Tom possessed all these
qualifications, and was looked upon as the marvel of
his age.

The old Slasher was done for, he had lost his all as
well as his position that he had held for some seven years.
Every farthing he possessed had been invested in the
fight, and he was utterly ruined. Tom Sayers on the
way home collected £25 for him, and the sum was raised
to over £100 in London, and a further subscription was
started in the Midlands. These sums enabled him to
take a beerhouse in his native place. He, however, did
no good, but gave way to drink, and was never known to
refuse a drink for the good of the house. Mr. Christie
Murray, the novelist, who has given many reminiscences
of the Tipton, some of which we have retold, writes of
him in his declining years as follows:—"He was
dying when I saw him again, and his vast chest
and shoulders were shrunk and bowed, so that
one wondered where the giant frame of the man had
fallen to. He was despised and forgotten and left alone,
and he sat on the side of his bed with an aspect altogether
dejected and heartless. In his better days he had
liked what he used to call 'a stripe of white satin,'
which was the poetic for a glass of Old Tom gin. I
carried a bottle of that liquor with me as a peace offer
ing, and a quarter of a pound of birdseye. He did not
know me, and there was no speculation in his look. But
after a drink he brightened. When I entered the room
he sat in he was twirling an empty clay with a weary,
listless thumb and finger, and the tobacco was welcome."
He died suddenly, being attacked with a fit in his house,
near Wolverhampton, on January 18, 1881.

But to return to Tom Sayers. After he had so decisively polished off Aaron Jones and the Tipton, there was only one other man with which to link his name that they might try conclusions, and that was Tom Paddock. It was not long before the Redditch man challenged the Champion for the new belt, which, it will be remembered, had to be defended against all comers for a period of three years before becoming his own property. So Tom Paddock forthwith challenged the Little Wonder for the trophy and from £100 to £500 a side. Unfortunately, however, just as the match was being ratified Tom Paddock was taken ill with rheumatic fever, and was removed to Westminster Hospital. Of course, the fight had to remain in abeyance; but Sayers visited his would-be combatant, left him a five-pound note, and promised to raise a subscription, which certainly showed a kindness of heart.

Indeed, Tom Sayers was one of the most generous fellows to any of his less fortunate fraternity, and rarely refused to give his services at a benefit. And now we think we may be permitted to quote a description of the Champion as he appeared in private, for it was written some years ago by one who knew him personally, and it was a first impression. The meeting took place just about the time that Tom Paddock was taken ill, and was at a circus at Dale End, which was being run by Bob Brettle, who then kept the White Lion, at Digbeth, and who afterwards tried conclusions with Tom Sayers. The gentleman who describes the interview says:—
"The performance began at eight o'clock in the evening, and Sayers had promised to be there, but at 9.30 he had failed to put in an appearance. However, a few minutes after this time Bob Brettle touched me on the arm, causing me to turn round, and before I scarcely knew I was being introduced and shaking hands with the Champion of England. In front of me stood a man about 5ft 8in or 5ft 9in in height, dressed in an old-fashioned coachman's top-coat, one of those with any quantity of small capes hanging from the neck down over the shoulders. On his head was a kind of skull-cap, and his face was not improved by the three or four days' growth of hair which so thickly covered his cheeks and chin. I had scarcely time to express the pleasure I had at seeing him, and the fear I had been in that by his non-arrival the pleasure would have been denied me, when Brettle hurried him off to introduce him to the public from the sawdust-covered arena. Before moving away Bob told me they were going to have a quiet supper upstairs at his house, and invited me to come, an invitation I accepted readily. Two minutes later Tom Sayers was introduced to the Birmingham public, who cheered

the Champion most lustily, a cry, however, being raised
that Tom should set-to with their hero. To the applause
Tom bowed his acknowledgments, and to the demands
for him to set-to with Brettle, he explained that he had
just come off a long journey by rail, which had been
aggravated by a stoppage on the road ; so that he was
not in the condition he should like to be when sparring
before a Birmingham audience. He, however, begged
to assure them that as he meant taking a benefit in the
town before long, they would then have an opportunity
of seeing him and his friend Brettle set-to. I may state
that Tom in the rough, as I had seen him, had not made
a very favourable impression upon me. In fact, his
whole make-up reminded me more of the stage highway-
man than of what he really was ; in short, he looked
more like Jerry Abershaw to my fancy than the Champion of England. But when I got to the White Lion,
at Digbeth, and walked up to Brettle's private sitting-
room, Sayers was quite another man. The barber had
removed all superfluous hair from his face ; he had got
on a clean shirt, a black coat and waistcoat, and a pair
of dark elastic cord inexpressibles, which set off his
well-shaped legs to advantage. Sayers was now not only
presentable in appearance, but fairly good-looking. In
his manner he was quiet and very unassuming, saying
very little, but what he said was to the point ; and what
I also noted was his language being quite free from oaths.
I believe had it not been for the unmistakably fighting-
looking mug, so far as conversation went, he might have
passed for a bishop. As to fighting, very little ' shop '
was spoken. After supper we stuck to the bottle very
close, but I remember Sayers drank very sparingly."

The above is a life-like picture of Tom Sayers when
ne was at his best, and that time was when the match fell
through with Tom Paddock, referred to above. With
Paddock incapacitated, and the Tipton and Jones licked,
there was nobody to dispute the title with Sayers, but
there was one man who was jealous of Tom, and he
determined that if he could help it the Championship
and belt should go into other hands. This was our old
friend Harry Broome. He had given up fighting himself,
but he announced that he had a "dark horse" that
would be one too many for the Little Wonder, and that
this "Unknown" was willing to make a match for
the Championship and £200 a-side. Sayers was quite
willing, so when the match was made great speculation
was rife as to who the mysterious one could be. Some
said it was Bendigo, others Caunt or Nat Langham, and
some declared that it would be Harry Broome himself.
But they were all wrong, for the "Unknown" turned out

to be one Bill Bainge, who was better known in sporting circles as Bill Benjamin. Although it was hinted that this was only a game of "spoof" on the part of Mr. Harry, the match turned out to be genuine enough. Mr. Bainge was the son of a farmer near Northfleet, and his ambition was to perform in the ring. He was a fine-built young fellow, and could certainly spar a bit, but what Harry Broome could have been thinking about when he allowed him to fly at such high game as Sayers

BILL BENJAMIN.

and the belt we never could understand. The fight, if fight it could be termed, came off on the Isle of Grain on January 3, 1858, on a bitterly cold day. Those who went had cause to regret it, for after a long and tedious river journey the Champion settled Bill Benjamin in three rounds, which occupied exactly 6½ minutes.

After this it looked as if Sayers would have a long rest, but in the spring of the same year Paddock, having recovered, again threw down the gauntlet to Tom,

who of course was only too glad to take it up. Alec
Keene, who was formerly such a great friend of Sayers,
for some reason or other, threw him over and became
the supporter of Tom Paddock. It was the kind-hearted
landlord of the Three Tuns who visited the Redditch
man whilst he was in the hospital, found him luxuries,
and kept his wife and children. And when he came out
cured it was Alec Keene who helped him to make the
match with Tom Sayers. There is no doubt that Alec had
great belief in Paddock, and he was undoubtedly a good
man, a fearfully hard hitter, and an equally good general.
So the match was made, to fight for £100 and the belt,
the battle to take place on Tuesday, June 16, 1858, the
anniversary of Tom's fight with the Tipton Slasher.

Many thought, with Alec Keene, that the Redditch
Tom would prove more than a match for the Brighton
Tom, and there was a deal of excitement in sporting
circles over the affair, and a tremendous lot of money at
stake. But at the eleventh hour Alec Keene and Tom
Paddock quarrelled, the former declaring that the latter
had shown such ingratitude that he would have no more
to do with him. He even went so far as to swear that
he would spoil the match, and did even go to *Bell's Life*
and demand the money he had put down, refusing to be
answerable for the last deposit. However, Paddock
managed to get a friend, a bookie, to find the balance of
the money, and the forfeit was saved. Keene, however,
declared that he would spoil the sport by putting the
" blues " on their track on the day of the fight. The
place selected for the mill was down the river—train
from London Bridge to Gravesend—thence by steamer.
An enormous crowd gathered at the station on that
memorable morning, and there hadn't been so much
interest displayed in a Championship battle for many a
long day. It was a lovely day, and the steamboat accommodation was first-class, more than four hundred people
going by the special steamer, the other boats following up
closely packed. An excellent bit of pasture land on the
Kentish shore was selected, and everything was made
comfortable for the great battle. The only thing feared
was an interruption, for knowing what a short-tempered
man Alec Keene was, and how he had on the platform
told that he would spoil the sport, some feared that he
would in reality send the police.

The men had put on their fighting costumes whilst on
the steamer, so they were soon ready to enter the ring ;
Tom Sayers with Harry Brunton and Bill Hayes, and
Paddock with Jemmy Massey and Jack Macdonald. As
they went to the centre of the ring to shake hands, it was
noticeable that the Redditch man was, although in

splendid condition, somewhat pinched about the face and there were palpable signs of his late illness. Sayers never looked better in his life. He was in the pink of condition ; his good-natured " mug " smiling all over, and his dark-brown skin shining in the sunlight.

All in readiness, they faced each other to fight out the most important battle of the year. Cautiously they commenced, for both knew that no liberties could be taken. Paddock was the first to try, and he let go the left, but Sayers adroitly jumped back and avoided the blow. Again the Redditch man tried and managed to get lightly on Tom's forehead. And they got at it in a very lively manner. Sayers in half a dozen exchanges got home heavily upon Paddock's left cheek, but received a couple of nasty blows between the eyes. He then tried his favourite double, and succeeded in getting upon his opponent's cheek. After a rally they by mutual consent in the middle of the round went to their respective corners and had a sponge down, for the sun was blazing away fiercely. Paddock now tried one of his rushes, but Sayers met him stoutly, and stopped his blows as he broke ground. Some lively work was then put in, and both displayed great activity, as the exchanges came in rapid succession. That it was going to be a fair stand-up fight and no flinching, everybody could see at half a glance. Again and again Paddock tried his fierce rushes, which had been so successful in his former fights, but Tom Sayers heeded them not, and they seemed to lack that dash and vigour of days gone by, and the remark was made that the Redditch man was no longer the warrior of former times. The first round lasted fifteen minutes, and at the finish 2 to 1 was laid on Sayers.

Paddock showed signs of punishment, whilst Tom was comparatively scatheless. Number two was a very severe bout, and thus early in the battle the respective powers and abilities of the men were shown. After some exciting exchanges Tom Sayers caught his man a well-measured blow with his dangerous right and brought him fairly to grass.

Then came a little excitement that was not in the programme. A tug was noticed coming towards the shore near where the fighting was going on, and immediately there was an alarm of " Police !" shouted, but as a boat put off some very familiar figures were seen to be its occupants. Amongst them was Alec Keene. A tremendous cheer rent the air, and the penitent host of the Three Tuns came towards the ring, and at once went to Tom Paddock. Here is an account of that happy little episode, described by one who was present :—" Pushing the crowd Alec Keene made his way to Tom Paddock's corner, and held out his hand to his old friend and *protégé*, who took it with a firm grip. And those who were near enough might have seen a couple of bright tears start from Paddock's eyes as he made it up with his old patron and benefactor, whilst Alec coughed and blew his nose loudly to hide the watery appearance at the flood-gates of his visionary organs."

Alec Keene then, seeing that Paddock was getting the worst of it, whipped off his coat and took his place in Tom's corner. After this the Redditch man seemed to have more confidence, and he made desperate efforts to get at his slippery opponent ; but it was no good, the Little Wonder was too nimble and clever for him. He indulged in all sorts of acrobatic feats when Paddock tried to force the fighting, dodging under his arm and bobbing up behind him in a most extraordinary manner. At length, having winded his adversary, Sayers found an opportunity, and again put in his wonderful double one under the chin, the other between the optics, and Paddock went down like a ninepin.

We have described sufficient of this battle to indicate how the men fought ; Tom Sayers never better in his life, and Paddock never so badly. In the thirteenth round the Redditch man tried another rush, and Sayers in jumping back fell. There was an immediate call of " Foul," but the verdict was " Fight on." Paddock was at this period holding out signals of distress, and Harry Brunton told Tom Sayers to go in and win, and so cut the matter short. He did, and from the eighteenth to the twentieth round punished the Redditch man fearfully about the face. In the twenty-first he came up very groggy, and was all but blind. Still he would not be persuaded to give in, and tried rush after rush, whilst Sayers pegged away at him every time in a most effective manner. Then he thought it time to give him his *coup de grace*, for he was quite blind, and would not give in. But the final act in this Championship drama had better be told by an eye-witness :—

" Sayers, drawing back the right, was about to smash it full in the poor fellow's face. His good feelings, however, at the last moment getting the better of him, Tom, the brave and honourable Champion of England, stayed the blow, and seizing Paddock's outstretched hand, gave him a hearty shake, and conducted him to his corner, when his seconds, seeing that all was over, skied the sponge in token of his defeat."

And so Tom Sayers retained the new belt and the title, after having contested one of the gamest and most exciting contests for the Championship.

CHAPTER LIII.

AFTER the defeat of Tom Paddock by the Little Wonder, he had placed himself fairly at the top of the tree, and for nine months he had an easy time of it, for there was not a man who cared to try conclusions with him. And here we may mention that Master Tom Sayers, although of a somewhat retiring disposition, was very fond of enjoying himself in his own sort of way, and when not upon business bent was fond of a bit of travel. It was sometime before the events which we are about to relate that Tom paid a visit to the Channel Islands, and as we have before us a reminiscence of the stalwart little Champion in which he figured in a battle that does not appear in the long list printed in "Fistiana," and of which few of our readers may have heard, we will take this opportunity of quoting the story, which is a true one, and was related by a Mr. "Brown" some twenty years ago. Furthermore, it goes to give us another capital portrait of the noble Sayers, who was perhaps, one of the most popular amongst the long line of champions.

Mr. "Brown" had gone over to the pleasant little island, Capua, St. Heliers, Jersey, in his friend's (Captain Lear) cutter yacht, the *Fenella*, the crew consisting of Messrs. Jack, Joe, and Jem, sons of the above-named skipper, a cabin-boy, and a cook. But let us tell the story in Mr. "Brown's" own words : —

"We landed at St. Heliers, met some friends who belonged to the garrison, and who gave us luncheon at Fort Regent, above the town. In the course of a stroll through the streets afterwards we came upon a quaint little tavern, in a square not far from the pier, called the Prince of Wales, and kept by one Harry Phelps, hailing from Brighton, where his brother Joe was well known as the landlord of a sporting club. Another brother, I need scarcely say, was the celebrated and unfortunate pugilist, "Brighton Bill," killed in a desperate fight with Owen Swift, in 1838. We had a smoke and a long chat with our host—an agreeable, pleasant-mannered young

fellow, who seemed a perfect walking dictionary or
encyclopædia in regard to the annals and traditions of
the P.R. Phelps informed us that he gave lessons in
the noble art of self-defence to the nobility and gentry
and officers of the island. And amongst his pupils were
not a few whose names are now famous in military and
sporting circles. A pressing invitation from other
Jersey friends was accepted by our *Fenella* crew, and
during our prolonged visit to St. Heliers we saw much
of Harry Phelps, who was always a welcome guest at
Fort Regent and the other barracks on the island.

"After spending one glorious evening at Lionel's Café
and Billiard Saloon with my friend Lord Lurgan, whose
guest I was, my host said to me as we lit our cigars and
buttoned our coats before mounting the hill leading to
Fort Regent, where we were to sup, 'I have asked a
friend to meet you to-night.' 'May I ask his name?'
said I. 'His name is Captain Smith,' replied Lord
Lurgan, 'and you'll find him a very jolly fellow.'
Captain Smith was waiting for us when we arrived.
We all know that it has been the custom from the days
of G. P. R. James to those of Miss Braddon to describe
one's hero, and I cannot do better than follow such
good examples. A well-built, able-bodied personage,
apparently about five - and - twenty years of age, of
medium height and stout build; about 5ft 8in, in a
pair of neat high-lows and worsted socks, and with a
compact, well-put-together frame, calculated to stand a
deal of hard work. A round-cropped, bullet head, which
is so seldom seen out of our little island; a fresh, healthy
mahogany-tinted skin, brown and clear as a glass of old
ale, and which painters would indicate with a mixture of
madder brown and burnt sienna. His shoulders, chest,
and back, square and substantial as a tower, deriving
their proportions from good English beef and floods of
nut-brown ale ; an honest-looking, somewhat bull-dog
face, with a square jaw, and light grey eyes, such as
denote an energetic and persevering temperament. Such
was our new arrival ; and as I took in these details at a
glance, Captain Smith struck me as a gentleman with
whom I would at any time rather drink than fight. The
' get up ' of our distinguished guest was a check suit
of the ' Stunner tartan,' with a preternaturally short
coat, a hat of that 'five to one bar one,' ' down the road '
shape, which invariably suggests, as Whyte-Melville so
well says, ' an amount of astuteness bordering on dis-
honesty.' The usual introductions were performed by
our host. 'Mr. Smith, my friend Mr. Brown. Brown, my
friend Captain Smith. You ought to know each other,
and you do. Is supper ready?' (to the mess-room waiter).

"We were indeed, a merry party. Alas! that I
should have to say, with Bret Harte, 'Vere is dat barty
now ?' Captain Smith, as the guest of ' my lord,' the
founder of the feast, occupied the post of honour, and
sitting on the right of the chair received marked attention from the rest of the party. Everybody took wine
with the Captain, who, not to be outdone in politeness,
returned the compliment by challenging each in return.
As our supper party consisted of fifteen, the number of
bumpers of champagne thus consumed in interchanging
compliments would make a nice arithmetical problem.
The conversation soon became general, and as each man
had lit his cigar, the wreaths of smoke curling upwards
gave a cloudy appearance to the room, so that it became
difficult to distinguish one face from another. Every
possible subject was discussed—politics, racing, hunting,
prize-fighting, cock-fighting, the opera, wine, women,
and scandal. There were lots of songs, heaps of cigars,
uncounted bottles of wine and spirits, plenty of chaff,
fun, and laughter, and had it not been for the morning
parade at 7 a.m., I believe we should have seen ' twice
round the clock.' But at length the jovial meeting
came to an end, and, amidst a volley of invitations all
round, we took our departure from our hospitable host
As our road was the same, Captain Smith, who was
staying at the Prince of Wales (Harry Phelps' house)
the Lears, who always slept on board the *Fenella*, and I
who lived in lodgings, went off together, and should no
doubt have reached our destination in safety had it not
been for the larking propensities of Jack Lear, who
would insist upon chaffing some drunken sailors, who
were standing at the corner of the market square. Words
led to blows, and Jack was knocked down by an iron bar,
which one of the fellows wrenched out of some iron rail-
ings. We dashed to the rescue and found ourselves
assailed from front and rear by a score of stout ruffians
who, luckily for us, were ' half seas over.' Our party
consisted of the four Lears, Captain Smith, a Yankee
captain, and myself ; and it would have fared ill with us
had not our military friend been with us. Just as we
managed to get our backs to a wall and floor a couple of
of the leaders, the Captain commenced by suddenly
catching the biggest of our assailants, an enormous
Dutchman, by the collar and seat of his breeches, and
literally flinging him into the crowd of his friends, and
then dashed in and let them have it right and left, a
man going down like a ninepin at each straight one he
delivered. The odds were, as I have explained, three to
one, less a fraction, against us ; but encouraged with
such a commencement, we all went in in a manner

which considerably flummuxed our foes, who were sent down one after another, and then, I am ashamed to say, we made a clean bolt of it. As it was considerably more than daylight, and the sea looked inviting, we accepted an invitation to breakfast on board the yacht, and afterwards took a short cruise in her, returning to St. Heliers in time for dinner.

" Captain Smith stayed about a fortnight with Phelps, who was often a visitor to Fort Regent, and there he often gave me lessons in the ' noble art,' and considerably astonished everybody who put on the gloves with him. All the time he stayed in Jersey after the memorable night, I noticed how singularly abstemious he was, and asking him the reason, he informed me that he was in training for a little match he had on. More than this he would not say, nor could I get information from Lurgan or Phelps, and not until I returned to London, and called at an address the Captain had given me, did I discover that he was Tom Sayers, who had run over to Jersey *incog.* to spend a week or so with his pal, a Brighton townsman, Harry Phelps."

But we could relate any number of reminiscences similar to that told by Mr. Brown had we but space, but we must return to the Little Wonder's career as Champion of England.

Nine months after his battle with Paddock, to the surprise of everybody in the sporting world, Bill Benjamin (alias Bainge), to whose very ridiculous performance with Sayers we have already called attention, was again matched with Tom by Broome for £400 and the belt. We cannot imagine what Broome could have been thinking about, and we have always believed that with Harry " the wish was father to the thought," that he might get the Champion beaten by such a man as Bainge. However, the match was made and articles were signed for them to fight on April 5, 1859, for the amount above mentioned.

Although the battle was for the Championship, and should find a place here, it was of no great importance in the career of Tom Sayers, so we shall content ourselves with the very briefest description of the affair. Tom thought he had such an easy thing on that he took very little pains with his training, and although when there was business on he was fairly abstemious, he had during the interval between his fight with Paddock and that which we are now referring to dissipated a good deal, and was when he came from Brighton to London on the Sunday before the battle, and showed himself at Owen Swift's, the Horseshoe, in Titchborne Street, in anything but condition.

Bill Benjamin, on the other hand, was a very different man to what he was when he fought Sayers some fifteen months previously, and appeared to be in splendid condition. London Bridge was the rendezvous at 6.30 in the morning, and although it was delightful weather, quite a limited number of excursionists took their places in the train. The trip was made to near Ashford, and between two stations the men and their friends alighted, a ring was soon put up, the combatants entered, and by twenty-two minutes past eleven they were delivered to the

CAPTAIN SMITH.

scratch. The first blow that was struck caught Benjamin smartly on the cheek ; then, to the surprise of everybody, and no less Sayers himself, Bill countered with a smasher full on the nozzle, and first blood was awarded to the novice. This made Sayers brighten up, so he went in, and delivering his left on the body and right on the cheek, knocked Benjamin clean off his feet.

The Champion, however, had discovered that Bill was a very different opponent to what he was on the occasion of their first meeting, and found it necessary to

play cautiously, for in the second round there was a deal
of give and take, Benjamin getting home several severe
blows, and as the battle progressed those who had
thought that it would have been an altogether one-sided
affair were agreeably disappointed. Frequently Sayers'
hitting was very wild, and he constantly missed his
man, and in the seventh round both were blowing hard,
and the way in which Bill Benjamin stood to the clever
Champion called forth the greatest praise from all who
witnessed this, perhaps one of the worst fights in which
Tom Sayers ever figured. He was, however, too good
for the novice, and in the eighth round Tom knocked his
man down with a fearful crack on the jaw, and repeated
it again and again. Still Benjamin, although nearly
blind, stuck gamely to it, and even when he was absolutely
defeated and his seconds threw up the sponge in the
eleventh round, he would go up again and face Sayers,
who gave the poor fellow, who was quite blind, a smart
tap on the nose and down he went. Again he wanted to
continue, but his friends hurried him from the ring, and
Tom Sayers, therefore, netted the £200, retained the
belt, and won a fairly good amount in bets. It was, of
course, a comparatively easy walk-over for him, but he
certainly on that occasion took liberties with himself by
not getting properly fit.

But during the progress of this match another " Richmond " had entered the field and thrown the gauntlet to
Tom Sayers, and this was no other than his old friend,
Bob Brettle, the Birmingham Champion. The Londoners
hardly believed Bob to be in earnest, but he was ready
with his money, and wanted Sayers to meet him for
£600 and the belt, only that Sayers should put down
£400 to his £200. Now this was all very well, and his
backers were quite willing to lay the odds, but Tom could
not see the fun of throwing in the belt as well, so after
much correspondence upon the matter, it was agreed
that this should not be a Championship fight, but that
they should meet upon a date to be named by Sayers
after his battle with Bill Benjamin. The date he fixed
was September 25, 1859, which gave him ample time to
go round the country on a sparring tour during the
summer months, and enable him to return for a few
weeks to get into condition. John Gideon was Tom's
principal backer at this time, and when they met to sign
articles at Owen Swift's, he was there amongst several
of Sayers' supporters, and such was the certainty
amongst them that Tom would defeat the Brum that
offers of bets to take £100 to £10, and back the Little
Wonder to knock Brettle out in ten minutes.

As the time drew nigh for the contest the greatest

excitement prevailed, for the Birmingham men had come up in great force, with their pockets well lined. Sayers had been training at Newmarket, under the care of Joey Jones, the clever little pedestrian, and there he became quite a lion amongst the jockeys and racing men. Brettle got himself fit at Ashbourne, in Derbyshire, where Bob Travers waited upon him and got him along splendidly, he, after the finishing touches had been put to him, bringing down the beam at 10st 4lb, or 5lb lighter than Sayers.

And now we must not omit just to give a list of the men who fought the Birmingham man, who had such an opinion of himself that he thought he might successfully try conclusions with the Champion. Bob Brettle was born at Portobello, near Edinburgh, in the January of 1832, so was six years junior to Sayers, and was by calling a glass-blower, and came to Birmingham as a youngster to practise the art. His first battle was with Malpas for £50 a-side, which resulted in a draw. He was then beaten by the redoubtable Jack Jones of Portsmouth, for £100 a-side, the contest taking place on November 21, 1854. His next effort was successful, he defeating Roger Coyne, at Combe, in Warwickshire, for £200 a-side, in twelve rounds, at Didcot, on June 3, 1856. He then beat Job Cobley, in forty-seven rounds, for £100 a-side. After this he fought Bob Travers twice, for £100, the police interfering the first time, and Brettle winning on the second occasion on account of Travers falling without a blow. He then beat Jem Mace for £100 a-side, on September 21, 1858, for £100, and that brings us down to his meeting with Tom Sayers. So it will be seen that the Birmingham man had met some good exponents of the fistic art, and had always fought for heavy stakes, and many people thought that his record was almost as good as that of the Champion.

The excursion started from London Bridge at 7 a.m. on Tuesday, September 25, 1859, and there had not been such a muster of the " swells " for many a long day. The train was so long and heavy that two engines were attached, and away they went down the line some sixty miles, to a place in Sussex, a capital piece of meadow land being fixed upon, and the ring, under the constables of the Pugilistic Benevolent Association, being pitched, all was soon in readiness.

There was a marked difference in the appearance of the men as they faced each other, Tom standing in that easy, graceful attitude which he always adopted ; and Brettle somewhat stooping and too square. Tom was grinning all over his pleasant-looking mug, but Brettle looked very serious. They were soon at it, and the

exchanges were fast and furious, Brettle getting a nasty
cut on the mouth and a lump raised on the forehead,
Tom catching some heavy blows about the ribs. Brettle
was annoyed at the cheering for Tom, and rushed in
regardless of consequences, when Tom hit him with his
wonderful "auctioneer" again on the lump, and down
he went. There could be no doubt who had been
receiver, for Bob's mouth and nose were cut and bleeding,
whilst Sayers was but a little flushed.

It will be unnecessary to follow the rounds all through.
In the second and third there was some exceedingly
rapid fighting, and Brettle dashed in time after time,
and the infighting was very severe. By the end of the
third round ten minutes had expired, and several bets
that Tom Sayers would win in that period were won by
the Brummagem boys. The excitement grew intense
amongst them as Bob took a decided lead, and Tom,
pulling himself together, they got at it with a vengeance.
Here is one account :—" Hits were exchanged as they
hammered each other all over the ring, Tom missing his
man and losing his perpendicular. Then Bob, as quick
as lightning, delivered his left—a stinger—on the peeper,
and then the right upon the side of the jaw, which,
amidst the wild cheers of the multitude, knocked the
Champion clean off his legs. Bob's corner claimed first
knock-down, which was allowed.

In spite of all this Johnny Gideon yelled out, " I'll
lay 3 to 1 Sayers wins." There were no takers, when
Tom's backer increased it a point, and Bob Travers took
£40 to £10. In the fifth, after some smart work,
Sayers knocked Brettle down, and also grassed him in
the next. Sayers seemed to be in no hurry to force the
fighting, and was exceedingly cautious. In the seventh
round, however, the end came. Tom, evidently on mischief bent, followed Bob up quickly to the ropes, the
Brum made a stand and lashed out furiously. Sayers
cleverly avoided, and hit his man a tremendous blow
upon the shoulder. Bob staggered back with an expression of pain upon his face, and with his hand up to
where he had been hit, and then went down and finished
the round.

It was evident that something was seriously wrong,
and a gentleman pushed his way into the ring. He was
a surgeon, who, on examining Brettle, found his shoulder
dislocated. His seconds assisted the doctor to pull the
limb in, and, of course, the battle was finished, and
Sayers still remained Champion.

CHAPTER LIV.

AND now we come to the closing scene of Tom Sayers'
pugilistic career, memorable as the greatest battle of
modern times, supported by our greatest sportsmen and
many of our most prominent politicians of the day.
Before, however, taking our readers to the ring-side, we
must devote a chapter to the introduction of John C.
Heenan, and to the origin of the fight which created such
excitement, both in the Old and New Worlds. It will also
be advisable to briefly sketch the American Championships, and trace the careers of those who climbed to the
top rung.

Of course, pugilism in its professional form was introduced to the States long after it had flourished in this
country, for it will be remembered that it was started in
England by Figg, in 1719, and in the New World we have
no record of the P.R. until 1812, or nearly one hundred
years after that time when Tom Cribb held the Championship of England. It was then that Jacob Hyer was
acknowledged to be the American "Father of the Ring."
His battle with Tom Beasley, in 1816, is the first
recognised Ring fight, and resulted in a draw, after but
a few rounds had been contested. About twenty years
later Tom Hyer came to the front. He was a son of
Jacob, and by all accounts a very fine fellow, and it was
he who made pugilism popular in the States. Of course,
the Irish settlers took a prominent part in establishing
the Ring, and when "Yankee" Sullivan, who had fought
several battles in England, went out to New York, he
was at once seized upon as their Champion. And so
there was a split in the party, the American Irishmen
standing by Sullivan, and the American party by Tom
Hyer. The latter kept a sporting house in Park Row,
New York, and was a great favourite amongst the better
class of sports. Sullivan had taken another den in
Division Street, and there was a sort of rivalry between
the two pugilists. Sullivan had a great friend named
McChiester, but better known as Country McClosky, a
bully of a fellow, and a terror to the city. In due course
Tom Hyer sent out offering to fight any man in America.

27

thinking that Sullivan would respond. Instead of
which, however, his pal McClosky went down to Hyer's
saloon and offered to fight him then and there. Of course
that was out of the question, and a match was made
to fight at Albany, N.Y., on September 9, 1841. This
was by all accounts a desperate affair, one hundred and
one rounds being fought, lasting two hours and forty
minutes; Hyer knocking his man about in a fearful
manner. Shortly after this Sullivan appeared at Hyer's
bar, and being rude, words came to blows, and they had
a set-to then and there, Sullivan getting the worst of it.
This led to a match. January 7, 1849, was the date
fixed, and they went to Rock Point, Kent County, Mary-
land. The battle lasted only seventeen minutes, when
Tom Hyer was again victorious. Sullivan was so much
punished that he had to be taken to hospital, and Tom
was arrested and kept in prison until his opponent was
out of danger. After this Sullivan took a house in
Chatham Street, where there were nightly brawls and
fights. A frequenter there was one John Morrissey, an
Irishman, who was born at Templemore, Tipperary.
His friends wanted to match him against " Yankee"
Sullivan, but just as arrangements were about to be satisfactorily made, Morrissey went to San Francisco when
the gold fever was on in California. There he met George
Thompson, an Englishman, who had been brought
up by Peter Crawley. It was the same Thompson who
had trained Tom Hyer, and Morrissey for that reason
showed some ill-feeling, which developed into a quarrel,
which they determined to settle in the 24ft ring for
2,000 dollars, according to the rules of the London Prize
Ring. It was a terrible affair, for the Irishman's friends
came armed with revolvers and knives. It was evident
that they meant to make it a win, tie, or wrangle. This
was fixed for August 31, 1852. Thompson was getting
all the best of it, having knocked Morrissey down six
times in ten rounds, when the scoundrels round the ring
threatened to shoot him. He therefore did the only
thing possible, dropped without a blow, and gave the
fight away on a foul. On the Irishman's return there
was a talk of a meeting between him and Hyer, but the
latter named the stakes at 10,000 dols, and Morrissey
backed out. Shortly after this the Champion retired,
and both the Irishmen—Sullivan and Morrissey—
claimed the title, and decided to fight for it. They met
on October 5, 1853, for 2,000 dols, and the betting was
100 to 80 on Sullivan. This was another disgraceful
affair, and ended in a free fight. Sullivan, although
having the best of it, had it given against him for leaving the ring during the *mêlée*. When John Morrissey

came back to New York, he did so with a great reputation for having beaten (save the mark) Thompson and Sullivan.

And now let us turn our attention to John Heenan. He was born at West Troy, on May 2, 1833. His father, Timothy Heenan, was a most respectable man, who held an important position in the Ordnance Department of the Watervilet Arsenal at Troy, N.Y. According to his American biographer, young John became a great favourite amongst his schoolfellows and companions, owing to his generous, open disposition, pluck, and natural athletic aptitude. He at a very early age developed an extraordinary aptitude for boxing, and was the leader of the West Troy boys. Now at Troy was another gang who were constantly coming in contact with young Heenan's following, and free fights were continuous. The leader of this lot was no other than John Morrissey, then a lad about the same age as Heenan. Little did those two think at the time that they were destined to become notorious as professional pugilists, and that one at least of them would do battle for the Championship of the World.

As Heenan grew up he was apprenticed as an engineer at the age of eighteen; having mastered his trade he left his native place and went to the Pacific Slope, sailing for San Francisco in 1850. On arriving there he soon found employment, being admitted to the Benicia workshops belonging to the Pacific Mail Steamship Company. That is the origin of his nickname, the " Benicia Boy.' So powerful did he become, and so smart was he with the mawleys that he soon attracted attention, especially after he had had a dust-up with a bully who had for a long while been the terror of the place. He gave him a rare thrashing, and was looked upon as the Champion of the weak ever after that event. Shortly after this Heenan, taking the " yellow fever," went up to the gold mines of California, and had a rough time. He was looked upon as the strongest man on the Slope, and able to take down the colours of any pugilist in America. "Yankee" Sullivan came to California, and Heenan's friends hearing of it, wished to back him against the new comer. But when Sullivan met the " Benicia Boy " he cried off. During the period that he was on the Slope he figured in many sparring exhibitions, and delighted everybody who was interested in sport to such an extent that he was persuaded by his friends to pay a visit to New York City and get matched. This he did, and threw down the gauntlet to John Morrissey, the man whom he had met in his juvenile days at Troy. On July 18, 1858, they met and signed articles to fight for

5 0 dols at Long Point, Canada, on the 20th of the following October. It was a fiercely - fought battle, Heenan getting all the best of it until he unfortunately struck his fist against one of the stakes, which gave Morrissey a great advantage. With the latter's constant rushes he wore Heenan down and finished the fight, after it had lasted only twenty - one minutes. Morrissey was then justified in claiming to be Champion of America, but John Heenan was not satisfied with the result of the battle, and challenged him again, maintaining that had it not been for the accident he would most assuredly have won. Morrissey, however, dec'ined to meet him, and as the affair between Sayers and the "Benicia Boy" was on the *tapis*, he determined to come over to England and fight for the British belt, having an understanding with Morrissey that if he should succeed they were then to do battle for the Championship of the World.

So much for the American Prize Ring, so far as the Champions were concerned. We have devoted some space to the subject, so that our readers may comprehend the reason why John C. Heenan was sent forth as their Champion. We will now give brief details of how the match was made.

Towards the end of 1858 there were rumours in the air that the Yankees had determined to send a representative over to this country to endeavour to take down the colours of our Little Wonder, and everybody on this side of the Atlantic thought that man would be John Morrissey. But in the early part of 1859 Mr. Wilkes, of *Wilkes' Spirit of the Times*, of New York, wrote to the editor of *Bell's Life*, in which he requested to know upon what terms John C. Heenan could be accepted as a candidate for the English Championship. Mr. Wilkes was informed that Heenan could be at once accommodated, but that the new belt could not be permitted to go out of England, supposing Heenan won, without the latter remained in this country for three years, so that he could defend it against all comers. Whether this did not suit them on the other side we are unable to say, but a letter came by the next mail enclosing a draft for £200 from Mr. Wilkes, which was to be deposited in favour of Aaron Jones, who had been in the States some time. This was very annoying, for it looked like postponing the International battle indefinitely, and as Sayers had thrashed Aaron Jones, and felt that he could do it again, little interest would be created in such a match.

Then, to complicate matters, Mr. Wilkes wrote again enclosing £50 as a deposit for Heenan to fight Sayers, begging that he might be accommodated before Jones.

This was, of course, impossible, as Jones had had £50
out of the £200 placed down by the editor of *Bell's Life*,
and it was a question of first come first served. It was
generally thought, after all this weathercock sort of
business, that it was nothing but Yankee bluff, and that
the whole thing would drop through.

Nothing was heard of the matter until October of
1859 (just about nine months after the receipt of Mr.
Wilkes' first letter), when another epistle came to hand
from that gentleman, which stated that Aaron Jones

JOHN HEENAN.

was desirous of forfeiting the £50, so that Heenan might
take his place. This was indeed good news, and the
international fight looked as if it were in measurable
distance after all. Again, however, there was a misunderstanding. Heenan did not mean that he should take
Aaron Jones' place and fight upon the same day as fixed
by Sayers and him, but desired that it should be treated
as an entirely new match, and that he should have six
months to get fit after articles were signed. This, of
course, meant great delay, but it could not be avoided,

and as Sayers was satisfied, having drawn his £50, it was determined to agree to the American's proposals. So in the December, Mr. Falkland, who was entrusted with the arrangement of affairs by the Americans, arrived in this country, and articles were drawn and signed at Owen Swift's, when it was decided by the Americans that the stakes should be limited to £200 a-side, as they anticipated being able to lay out their money on the day to greater advantage, for, without doubt, Sayers would be favourite.

When all was settled, Heenan started for England; but again there was very nearly a hitch, for the " Benicia Boy " was wanted for some serious breach of the peace which he had committed, and there was a warran' out for his arrest. He was, however, so well disguised that his friends took him aboard without detection. On arriving at Liverpool he met a few friends, and was taken thence to the neighbourhood of Salisbury, where he settled down to work with his friend Mr. Falkland and Cusick to look after his training arrangement. They had not been there long, however, when the peace-at-any-price party tried to get hold of him, and they first begged of him not to fight, and when they found him obdurate they threatened. This did not suit John Heenan, and they changed their quarters. Coming up to London, they stayed with Macdonald a short time, and then went to Box by the Great Western Railway, and fixed upon Bathampton as a secluded spot. Here they were again in trouble, for some blithering idiot swore before a magistrate that there was going to be a prize-fight upon the spot, and asked for a warrant against Heenan. It was issued, but a friendly " tip " put them on their guard, and before anything could be done they were off again to fields and pastures new, and out of harm's way. The extraordinary part about the whole thing was that Tom Sayers was left quite unmolested. From Bathampton Heenan went to a place near Bedford, but there again he was threatened and had to move, going to Nottingham, where they were advised to take up their quarters at Trent Lock, that being on the borders of Derbyshire, Nottingham, and Leicester. Here they rested in peace for a time, but the Bedford warrant was transferred, and poor Heenan was betrayed in a most disgraceful manner by a supposed friend who intro-duced the policeman in disguise. He made a desperate effort to escape, and ran along the road for a mile and a half in his stockings only. He was captured and taken to gaol. The next day he was bailed, himself in £50 and two sureties in £25. What the stranger could have thought of all this hunting about we often wonder.

Tom Sayers, after enjoying the sea breezes of Brighton, went to Newmarket, and did a fine spell of training. Whilst there the magistrates were asked to sign a warrant, but, like good sportsmen that they were, they positively declined to do so. Mr. Wilkes, of the *Spirit of the Times,* Dr. Rawlings, of *Frank Leslie's,* and Mr. Bergham, of the same paper, together with many other American gentlemen, made an excursion to the town of gee-gees, in order to be introduced to the Little Wonder, and were much struck with his appearance. Both men, indeed, trained on splendidly. As the day drew near— Tuesday, April 17, 1860—the excitement kept increasing, and never had there been such interest taken in a prize-fight before. Amongst youngsters at school, in all the Universities, at clubs, in military circles, in the lobby of the House of Commons, at the Stock Exchange, and indeed everywhere, was the great prize-fight the topic of conversation. The management had great responsibility in getting the great show through, for they were beset by difficulties, and it was thought that possibly at the last moment the authorities might interfere. But of the neat manner in which all was carried out, and an introduction to the field of battle, we must leave for another chapter.

CHAPTER LV.

A MEMORABLE MORNING.—A FIELD DAY AT FARNBOROUGH.—SAYERS AND HEENAN.—THE GREAT INTERNATIONAL BATTLE.

As the date for the great International fight drew near the most intense excitement prevailed. It had been arranged that the two men should be conveyed to London on the Sunday evening. Heenan arrived in good time and without adventure; but Sayers, curiously enough, who had been unmolested all through the weeks of his training, was less fortunate. At Newmarket, at the eleventh hour, detectives had been sent down from Scotland Yard, with instructions not to lose sight of the Champion, and they paid him the closest attention, having instructions to arrest him on his attempting to journey to London. On the Saturday he made no effort to hide or dodge his watchers, for he walked down the High Street in his sweaters, and took gentle

exercise upon the Heath, but in the evening he paid a
visit to Sam Rogers, and there the subject of how to
elude the minions of the law was discussed. Rogers
struck upon a happy idea. He had some horses going
away on the Sunday to fulfil their engagements, and he
suggested that Tom Sayers should be " boxed " with
them. Acccordingly, on Sunday evening the Champion
went down to Sam's place and, disguised as a stable-
help, accompanied the racehorses to the train, and hid
himself in one of the boxes. Although the 'tecs were
planted at every station all along the line from Newmarket to London where the train stopped, and
eagerly sought their man, they failed to discover
him. But on arrival at Shoreditch on the Sunday
night, it was expected that he would be certain to fall
into the officers' hands, for a tremendous crowd had
congregated at the station, and it was supposed that
somebody amongst them would be sure to recognise
Tom.

However, the game was well played, and Sayers remained with the gee-gees from Newmarket until the
crowd had dispersed, and the officers had come to the
conclusion that he was not there, and, as it was the last
train, believed that he had come to town by some other
route. When they had exhausted their patience, and
the coast was clear, the Little Wonder was released,
put into a cab, and driven off to his town quarters. Sunday was lively enough at the sporting houses, but Monday night, April 16, 1860, will be ever remembered as
one of the greatest and most exciting in the annals of
sport. Every "drum" was packed by the Fancy, and
at Alec Keene's and Nat Langham's the scenes were
particularly lively, whilst at Owen Swift's and Harry
Brunton's they kept the "ball rolling" until it was
time to "make tracks" to the station.

London Bridge, four o'clock a.m., was the order given
out for the rendezvous, and those who were there on
that memorable morning will never forget it. All
classes of society were represented, and coachmen in
livery and tigers with natty boots and shining top-hats
were nearly as plentiful as hackney coachmen. It was
indeed a sight. The low East End sportsman hustled
the Corinthian, who had left his carriage—with coronets
upon the panels—and the Israelite, who was there
" to make a bit," rubbed shoulders with the cream of our
aristocracy. The arrangements on the part of the railway company were admirable, and the first train, consisting of no less than thirty-three carriages, was soon filled
and awaited the signal to start immediately the two
warriors should arrive. It was an anxious ten minutes,

for there was still the chance of an arrest, and a possibility of the whole thing collapsing. But at exactly twenty minutes past four there was a cheering heard outside the station, which swelled into a great roar as Tom Sayers, dressed very flashily in a kind of seaside suit, appeared upon the platform. In a few minutes another great shout rent the air and proclaimed the appearance of the Benicia Boy. So far all was well, and the first train steamed out of the terminus. It took very little time after this for number two consignment to get off, and the great crowd were speeding away, nobody but the pilot on the first engine and a select few knew where. The day was just dawning as they rattled along with a clear line towards Reigate Junction, where they branched off towards Guildford. The morning was delightful, with a clear blue sky, and everybody in the happiest of moods.

Never, perhaps, in the history of the Prize Ring had such a representative crowd foregathered to witness a fight. There were men of letters, members of Parliament (both Commons and Lords, Palmerston himself being present), the cream of the artistic, literary, dramatic, and musical world, and many of the foremost military men, and leaders of fashion of the day. The trip was made more delightful by the brilliant conversation, and the popping of corks was very frequent, for many of the "toffs" had provided themselves with hampers, and brought their servants with them to look after their comforts. At Guildford the trains stopped to water the engines, and then away they went again until they approached Aldershot, when it was discovered that the spot selected for the battle was Farnborough.

The two trains were soon unloaded of their human freight, and in an incredibly short space of time Billy Duncan, who had charge of the ropes and stakes, had the ring formed, and the vast multitude fell into their places without the slightest disorder. There was a reserved enclosure for the "swells" who cared to pay, and there had been provided stools, chairs, and trusses of straw for seats, whilst the mob gathered around, some climbing trees in their immediate vicinity, others getting on to waggons and carts which had mysteriously sprung up. Where the people had all come from it is difficult to surmise, for the number present was estimated to exceed 12,000, and certainly nothing approaching that number came down by train.

All being in readiness, a cheer announced the appearance of Tom Sayers, who entered the ring accompanied by his seconds, Harry Brunton and Jemmy Welsh. He was immediately followed by Heenan, who received an

SAYERS AND HEENAN.
(From a sketch made at the time of the battle.)

enthusiastic reception. This was the first time that
Sayers had met the American, and when they shook
hands cordially another hearty cheer went up. Both
men looked as well as could be, and had a most cheerful
expression upon their faces as they had a quiet little
chat all to themselves before they placed themselves in
their seconds' hands in order to have the finishing
touches put to their toilets, for they had entered the
ring in their fighting costumes covered with their overcoats. John C. Heenan was the first to show himself in
the " buff," and a murmur of admiration went forth
at his finely-proportioned shoulders, chest, and arms.
He was in the pink of condition, and was certainly a
fine specimen of a man. Every muscle upon his splendid torso stood out in relief, and he looked a tower
of strength.

Tom Sayers, with his reddish brown skin and well-
knit figure, also looked in perfect form, and although
a totally different class of figure to his American opponent, there was something very formidable about his
appearance, and he presented a perfect picture of an
athlete. Their respective sizes as they faced each
other was very marked, for the Benicia Boy had the
advantage of $4\frac{1}{2}$in in height, and his long arms gave him
an enormous advantage, and there could be no two
opinions about the fact that Tom Sayers had met on
this occasion a more formidable foeman than he had
ever faced before. There was very little time wasted,
for the umpires and referee had been chosen, so the
audience was not kept waiting. During a breathless
silence "Time" was called, and the great battle to decide
who should claim the Championship of the World commenced.

Heenan was the first to move quickly in sparring
attitude, whilst Tom threw himself into that easy, well-
known position of his, the right well across the body,
and the left loosely at play. He smiled at the American,
and as the latter advanced he slowly retired, and
nodded and grinned. Heenan let go the left, but Tom
jumped out of distance and playfully shook his head.
Again the Benicia Boy put out a feeler, but Tom was too
quick for him, and he was out of reach. The American
had won the toss, so the sun was in the Champion's eyes,
and it seemed to bother him somewhat, but as Heenan
came to him he stood his ground, and bang, bang, bang
went some sharp exchanges about the body, and Tom let
go his left full on Heenan's nose, and a shout from the
multitude went up as it was seen that thus early in the
battle Sayers had scored the first event by drawing blood
from the American's nasal organ. A brief pause and

they came together again, Tom planting once more
upon the same tender place, but received a heavy blow
on the head. Some cautious sparring led to the men
coming to close quarters, when Heenan got his arm
round Tom's neck, but the latter rattled some half-arm
blows on to the American's neck, which caused him to
let go his hold, and the Champion slipped to grass
laughing.

They both showed that the work had been lively, as
they came up for the second round, for their faces were
flushed, and there were distinct signs of the hitting upon
their bodies. Heenan, as Sayers advanced, slowly fell
back to his corner ; but Tom was not to be denied, so
followed his man up fearlessly. When in distance
Heenan let go the left, but Sayers stopped it cleverly,
but missed the return, when the Yankee rushed in and
closed on the Champion, getting him firmly in his iron
grip, and after a brief struggle threw him and fell on to
him. There was a yell of delight from the Americans
present (and they were quite numerous), who offered
2 to 1 on their man, but only a few bets were made,
for it was evident that the Englishman was no match
for the powerful stranger at wrestling. Sayers had
quickly discovered that, and as he always fought with his
head, altered his tactics, and kept clear of his ponderous
antagonist. A deal of fiddling and dodging about the
ring took place, and Sayers, who at every point checkmated Heenan, soon proved that at good generalship he
was nowhere with him. Yet in this round Tom held
his man too cheaply in attempting to draw him, for
Heenan found an opening and lashed out his left, catching Sayers full on the nose sending him to grass, a fair
knock-down blow, so the American scored the second
event.

As Tom came up for the third round the accustomed
grin upon his good-natured looking mug was missing.
Indeed, he had a very serious and perplexed expression as
he blinked in the sun. The American, evidently encouraged by his success, was anxious to get to work, and
advanced upon Sayers, following him up nearly to the
ropes, where the Champion made a stand. It was only
for a moment though, for Heenan, again letting the left
go, caught him a terrific blow on the jaw, and down he
went a second time. There was silence for a few
seconds, until it was broken by the American party, who
now cheered and felt that the Little Wonder had at
last found his match. This opinion was also shared
by some of Tom's friends, and undoubtedly Heenan was
the best man that Sayers had ever faced in the 24ft
ring. Tom was very cautious, and kept out of his oppo-

nent's reach. But the Boy was not to be denied, for he bored in and again caught the Champion a smack on the mouth, but Sayers countered beautifully on the nose, which once more turned on the purple stream. Heenan then tried to close, but Tom was too quick for him, lashed out his left on to the American's nasal organ, and slipped down to finish the round.

The succeeding bout was perhaps the most important throughout the whole of the battle. It was in this that Sayers received a blow which undoubtedly influenced the result of the fight, and which would, with any other man save Tom, have lost him the fight. It was evident that Sayers at this period had made up his mind to stand his ground and fight, so with that determined look which always meant mischief he unflinchingly took up a position in the centre of the ring. Heenan led, and some severe blows were exchanged. Then one of the American's terrific blows at Tom's head drove the latter's guard back upon the face. It was a tremendous blow, and the arm at once became swollen and purple, and it was evident to those who were near that the Champion was suffering. He held the right arm that had been damaged close to his body, and then dashed in the left smartly on Heenan's cheek. The American countered on the forehead, and Sayers went down.

Without describing all the rounds of this memorable battle, for the tale has been told o'er and o'er again, it will be sufficient to summarise. Sayers warmed to his work, and astonished the American by his wonderful agility and quickness on his legs. He was in and out of distance in an instant, and generally managed to land one before getting away. As in many of his other battles, he was fighting to blind his opponent, and time after time did he hit his man over the eyes until they became painfully swollen. In the twenty-ninth round Sayers seemed to have obtained his second wind, and was much fresher than his opponent, whose eyes were in a sorry plight; one was all but closed, and the other was following suit. They had been fighting desperately, and both had suffered, for Tom's arm was twice its normal size, and his face and body were much bruised. Yet his eyes were all right, and it was seen that the Englishman's chance lay in his being able to blind the Yankee. Persevering, he again hit Heenan over the good optic, and Jemmy Welsh shouted out, " That's it Tom—put up his shutters, and the show is over." And Sayers did all he could to follow this advice, for in the thirtieth round the American was all but blind. There was a consultation in his corner, and he was told to go in and make the best use of his time and force the fight-

ing. This he did, and the battle was fast and furious.
Sayers, however, was the quicker of the two, although
Heenan was the stronger. But the Boy's face by this
time presented an awful picture —swollen, bruised, and
bleeding, with the eyes all but closed. Had Sayers
been able to use his right, there could at this period
have been little doubt as to who would have finished
the battle. The Champion could have won easily.

The excitement was terrific, which was added to by
the arrival of the police. In spite of this, however, the
men were sent up again and again. In the thirty-sixth
round Heenan rushed at his man and catching him round
the neck, tried to hold him on the ropes; but Tom
slipped from him like an eel, and rolled over on the
grass. " Time " was called for the thirty-seventh, and
the men again faced each other. All this while the
police were struggling in the crowd to get to the ring-
side. Nevertheless the men went on fighting. Heenan's
hands were puffed up like boxing-gloves, and did little
damage to his opponent. Sayers in this round twice
landed on the eyes, and those who were able to see
declared that this made the American totally blind, and
had it not been for the disturbance that followed, the
battle would certainly have gone to the Britisher. It was
most unfortunate for Sayers. Unable to see, Heenan
rushed at Tom and managed by more luck than judgment to get a grip of him. They were near the ropes,
and the police had nearly made their way to the ring-
side. Heenan managed to get Tom's head over the
rope, and pressed it there until he was nearly black in
the face, and there is no doubt that he would have been
strangled had somebody not cut the ropes. Then the
scene that ensued beggars description. The referee,
umpires, seconds, and all were scattered, the mob was
trying to keep the officers back, so that the fight should
end; but that was impossible, for the referee could not
see the men. It was stated that he ordered them to
cease hostilities, but they disregarded it, and a series of
supplementary rounds were fought. The crowd had
broken into the ring, and the ropes and stakes were
knocked down, so there was little room for them to continue, and no doubt they should have been stopped. Yet
at it they went in a mad, reckless manner, disregarding
time and every regulation. Sayers was knocked down
and nearly trampled upon, and Heenan's name was
shouted as victor; but Tom was on his feet dealing blows
upon the wet, bleeding face of his adversary, and then
his name was shrieked out, as scramble after scramble
went on in the midst of this surging sea of humanity.
During a brief cessation Sayers was on his second's

knee, when Heenan rushed across the ring and, proving that he was not quite so blind as he appeared, struck Jemmy Welsh a blow in the face and knocked him over. Then seizing Sayers, the two men rolled over together. As they got to their feet a wild scramble went on between them, when fortunately the referee managed to get near and ordered them to cease fighting. By this time the police were present in force, and as there was no possibility of re-erecting the ring and continuing the battle, the men left the arena. Heenan was like a madman, and rushed off through the crowd, and was within five minutes as blind as a bat and had to be led. Sayers, although a good deal damaged, was strong, and could have fought on for a considerable time, so the interruption was fatal to his success.

And so ended the great international fight, which had caused such excitement throughout the whole of Great Britain and America, and which had attracted the best in the land to the ring-side. It had ended in a disgraceful and most unsatisfactory manner, and was undoubtedly the cause of the early downfall of the Prize Ring.

CHAPTER LVI.

A WRANGLE.—TWO NEW BELTS.—SAYERS AND HEENAN — ANECDOTE OF SAYERS.—HIS DEATH AND FUNERAL.

In the last chapter we described the disgraceful conclusion to the great international fight. It was a pity that the police should have interfered at that particular moment, for had the men been allowed but a quarter of an hour longer there would have been a satisfactory result to the Britisher. Of course, a force of police such as that sent to Farnborough could do very little with a crowd of, say 12,000, but when they made their way to the ring-side it was impossible for the referee to defy the law, so there was no alternative but to stop the battle, which, as we have described, degenerated into a rough and tumble.

The police had made up their minds to arrest Sayers, but he managed to get away and hide in a van, which took him some distance down the road, when in a complete disguise he was able to join the special (which had been considerably delayed on his account) at the railway station. The great crowd arrived at London Bridge about three o'clock, and nobody present will forget the scene at the terminus. All sporting London seemed to have turned out to meet the men on their return, and to learn the news and details of the great battle. Of course both parties declared that, save for the interruption, their man would have won. But had the referee not been hustled away there is little doubt but that the fight would have been awarded to Sayers. Some dozen gentlemen, whose words could be relied upon, declared that Heenan struck Sayers twice when he was upon his two knees, which would, of course, be foul. He also struck and kicked Jemmy Welsh, and knocked Sayers off the latter's knee, and also struck Brunton. All these acts would have been "foul," and the referee would have had no alternative than but to award the fight to Sayers had he witnessed them. No doubt these statements were perfectly true, for Mr. Wilkes himself wrote in a special edition of *Frank Leslie's Illustrated Paper*, which was published in London on the following day :— "Heenan, finding that Sayers could not or would not rise from his seat in the corner, and his seconds refused to award him the victory that belonged to him by throwing up the sponge, he advanced upon him in the middle of his seconds, and struck him where he sat."

Yet in spite of this admission, the Americans called upon the Englishmen in the cause of fair play to award the new belt to Heenan. Then they asked that the referee should call upon the men to meet again during the same week, so that it should not end in a draw. But this the referee refused to do until the matter had been fully discussed, for the two men were neither in condition to renew the combat. Sayers had the small bone of his arm broken, and Heenan's eyes were in a dreadful state. Suffice it to say that the result of the discussion was that no other meeting was decided upon, and that the battle was to be pronounced a draw, and that each man should be awarded a belt.

Never in the annals of the Prize Ring had there been such excitement over a Championship fight. On the following day papers were full of it. A detailed account of the rounds, occupying columns, appeared in the *Times*, and it is by far away the best description extant. *Blackwood's Magazine* had a long article, as did also the *Saturday Review*, and one of the cleverest set of verses that ever appeared in *Punch* was devoted to the subject. It was entitled "'The Combat of Sayerius and Heenanus,' a Lay of Ancient London, supposed to be recounted to his great grandchildren, April 17, 1920, by an Ancient

FRANK DOWLING ESQ

EDITOR OF *Bell's Life.*

Gladiator." It was written by H. Cholmondeley Pennell, and, of course, is a parody upon Lord Macaulay's "Horatius," in his "Lays of Ancient Rome." It is well worth reading, and we should like to reprint it had we but space. Here, however, is a sample :—

> " How nine times in that desperate mill
>   Heenanus in his strength
> Knocked stout Sayerius off his pins,
>   And laid him all at length :
> But how in each succeeding round
>   Sayerius smiling came,
> With head as cool, and wind as sound
> As his first moment on the ground,
>   Still confident and game.
> How from Heenanus' sledge-like fist
> Striving a smasher to resist,
>   Sayers' stout right arm gave way.
> Yet the maimed hero still made play,
> And when ' in-fighting ' threatened ill,
> Was nimble in ' out-fighting ' still—
>   And still his own maintain—
> In mourning put Heenanus' glims.
> Till blinded eyes and helpless limbs
>   The chances squared again."

Never had the British Press printed so much about a prize-fight, and it really looked as if the waning fortunes of the Ring were about to return. Our hero had done much in that direction, for his brave combats, which we have described, shed glory on the sport. His battles with Jack Grant, Harry Paulson, and Aaron Jones had done much, but that between the Little Wonder and the Benicia Boy had eclipsed them all. In the Houses of Parliament, on 'Change, in clubs, taverns, and sporting kens, and even in the pulpit, the great fight was discussed. In fact, the talk was of nothing else.

The amount of money subscribed for Sayers reached £3,000. This was invested in the names of trustees Sayers was to have the interest during his life, condition, ally that he did not fight again. Should he do so or die, then the interest was to go to his children until they became of age, when the principal was to be divided amongst them. They were only two: Tom, aged at the time, nine, and Sarah, twelve. Besides this very generous subscription Tom Sayers had many other presents in the way of plate, jewellery, &c. What has become of most of those articles we know not, but Johnny Gideon, who was Tom's warmest friend, had in his possession the spiked boots in which the Champion fought at Farnborough.

Sayers never entered the ring as a principal again, but went in for the show business, becoming at first a shareholder and then proprietor of Howes and Cushing's Circus, under the management of Jem Meyers. But Tom, good general as he was in the ring, had no know-ledge of business, and he soon got out of his depth, and the show had to be sold. After this the ex-Champion led an idle life, and could be found hanging about Camden Town, frequenting the Britannia, the Mother Red-Cap, and other pubs. In 1863 he appeared in public as Heenan's second, when the American fought Tom King, and which battle we shall describe in due course. Tom Sayers, however, did not know how to enjoy life, and after his Ring career he imbibed too much, and mixed in company that was no good to him. He loafed about the north-west of London, wearing high boots with tassels, and across the knees in large letters were the words "Tom Sayers, Champion," whilst his constant companion was a fine mastiff, called "Lion."

And now a few words about the belt. After Sayers had decided to fight no more, the question came as to what was to be done about the belt. On May 18, follow-ing the great fight, a meeting was held at *Bell's Life* office in the Strand, to decide what should be done about the trophy. All kinds of suggestions had been made——one was that the belt should be cut in half, and a sub-scription raised in order to supply the halves wanted, but that was too ridiculous. Then it was suggested that two new belts should be subscribed for, one for Sayers, and one for Heenan, whilst the original belt should still be up for competition. On the day mentioned above Sayers, accompanied by Johnny Gideon, and Jack Mac-donald, representing Heenan, met Mr. Frank Dowling at his office. There was a deal of talk, and ultimately the men agreed to accept new belts, the old one to be left in the possession of *Bell's Life* until won three times, so that if Heenan wished to become possessed of it he must remain in England and fight for it. Then compli-ments were freely exchanged, but we doubt whether the men sincerely meant what they said. Heenan stated that if he had won the old belt he would have given it back to Sayers, a statement that nobody believed, whilst Sayers assured Heenan that he was the best man he had ever met, and that he considered him worthy to hold the Championship of England—another statement that must have been positively untrue. Anyhow, it was a most amicable meeting between the two men, and it was decided that the belts should be at once manufactured and presented publicly to the men at the Alhambra, although it had at first been suggested that the presenta-tion should take place at Cremorne Gardens. Mr. Han-cock, the silversmith, was entrusted with the order, and

he undertook to have the trophies ready in six days.
There was a pretty good muster of the Fancy on the
particular evening at the Alhambra, although, curiously
enough, the public took very little interest in the affair
for some unknown reason, the house being barely half
full. The presentation was timed to take place at nine
o'clock, and the men shortly after entered the ring (it
must be remembered that at this time a circus was run
at the Alhambra) arm-in-arm with the M C., who introduced them. The belts were in red morocco cases, and
upon the outside in gold letters were the words "Champion
of England," although for the life of us we could never
understand how there could be two claiming the title.
The M.C. then proceeded to read the address, and
handed each man a cheque for his part of the battle-
money, and a vellum, upon which was written the
address. Heenan's belt was then presented by Mr. John
Gideon, who made a short speech, finishing up with the
following remarks:—"Meanwhile take this token—
cherish it as a well-earned, well-deserved memento of
the admiration of the people of this country—and rest
assured that while pugilism remains a sport of
Great Britain (and long may that period be)
so long will the name of John C. Heenan be
remembered with respect as one of the bravest men
that ever entered a four-and-twenty foot roped ring."
Heenan having received his belt, Mr. Wilkis made Tom
Sayers his presentation in a somewhat long-winded
speech, in which he called attention to the qualities of the
Englishman, saying to him, "Buckle it about your
loins and treasure it, and be proud of it, for it is a sure
expression of the admiration of two nations such as
a man of your humble standing never had the proud
fortune to receive before."

Sayers at once took off his coat and put on the belt, a
task which he found none too easy, for since the fight he
had put on quite a corporation. Neither Tom nor
Heenan were orators, but they mumbled out a few words
of thanks, and then, linked arm in arm, walked round
the circus, whilst those who were present cheered them
to the echo, and the ceremony was at an end. This was
certainly a farce, for what value could those belts have
been, neither of them being fairly won in fight. Still
they seemed to satisfy the men, and left the original
open for anybody to try to win.

Of Heenan we shall have more to say in future
chapters, so we will, for the present, say *au revoir*. But
Sayers we shall meet but casually, so it will be a fitting
place here to record the remainder of his career.
Tom, as we have said, fell into dissipated habits,

and the splendid constitution that he once
possessed soon gave signs of breaking up, and he
would not take care of himself. No doctor could induce
him to take physic if it happened to be at all nasty,
and that reminds me of one more anecdote about the
ex-champion which we may tell here. The incident
happened whilst he was travelling with Howes and
Cushing's circus. Tom was right out of sorts, and Mr.
Cushing prescribed some medicine for him in the way
of a stiff dose of castor oil, and brought it to him

TOM SAYERS' TOMB.

floating about on the top of half a cupful of brandy.
"Drink it, Tom," he said in a persuasive tone, "it'll
put you right in no time." Tom held it in his hand,
looked at it, and made awful grimaces. "Drink it, I tell
you," said his friend, but Tom raised it to his lips, and
put it back with a shudder. "Damn it, I can't," said he.
Then, making another attempt, he put the cup down.
" —— — if I *can* take it—there now—and one word is
as good as a hundred. Look here," he cried, eyeing the
tea cup. "If I could only get my beak through that

beastly stuff at the top and swig the brandy underneath it, there'd be some sense in it; but no, I can't." "No oil, no brandy," said Cushing. "Drink it, Tom. Be a man." Tom jumped up as if he had been galvanised. "Be a man, indeed," he growled with some amount of bitterness, and then he swore that he would rather fight fifty Heenans than be drenched with that infernal stuff. No, he couldn't take it, and he wouldn't take it. Tom Sayers had found his master. The man who had been brave enough to stand and be punched and bruised, and suffered the greatest agony, was beaten by a little dose of castor oil.

But Tom went from bad to worse, and when Dr. Adams attended him at his sister's house, 161, Claremont Square, Pentonville, he took his medicine readily enough, for his symptoms became alarming. He had diabetes, and consumption had set in. He, for a time, rallied, and went down to Brighton, where it was thought he would mend, for breathing his native air seemed to do him much good. This was in the April of 1865; but by the August he was as bad as ever, and had to come up to London, where his friends called in Dr. Gull, who at once declared that nothing could be done to save him. He desired to go to his old friend, Mr. Menseley, of High Street, Camden Town, in the October, and again a change for the better apparently set in. It was but temporary, however, and he had a relapse, with unconsciousness, from which he recovered only at intervals, and it was evident that he was fighting his last round. The end came in the presence of his father and two children, who witnessed him pass peacefully away. He was buried at Highgate Cemetery on the 15th of November, 1865, when some time afterwards a handsome tomb was erected to his memory. The attendance at the funeral was enormous, one of his mourners being his dog Lion, who followed in his pony trap. All the sporting world was represented, and many distinguished people were present to see the last of the plucky little British Champion who had fought so bravely and so honestly in all his battles, and who had saved the belt from being taken from our shores.

CHAPTER LVII.

After the presentation of the two belts to Sayers and
Heenan, at the Alhambra, the latter, never appreciating
this country very much, determined upon journeying
back to the land of the Stars and Stripes. It seemed a
pity that he should have made up his mind to this, for
there would have been piles of money to have been
made through the country had the American gone on a
boxing tour with Tom Sayers and other stars of the
Ring. He was, however, restless and discontented, and
nothing would induce him to remain. His departure was
particularly provoking to one man, and that was Mr.
Samuel Hurst, better known as the Stalybridge Infant,
his original title being the " Chicken," for he had challenged Heenan, before his fight with Sayers, to do battle
with him, whether the Yankee should prove successful
with Tom or not. Hurst had put down £50, with a like
amount from Heenan, but there had been no stipula-
tions as to forfeiture, so that when the American decided
to leave England he picked up his £50 and went.

Then came the question as to who would be likely to
meet the Stalybridge Infant for the belt which Sayers
and Heenan had left. The title of Champion had been
buffeted about between Ben Caunt, Bendigo, Harry
Orme, Tipton Slasher, Con Parker, Tom Paddock, and
Harry Broome, and it was difficult to say who was most
entitled to the distinctive office. It was clear that
neither of the above could lay claim to the belt, and that
it would have to be won by somebody and held for three
years, as stipulated. So when the " Infant" threw
down the gauntlet to fight any man in the world for the
trophy and £400, the sporting fraternity anxiously
awaited a response. But the year 1860 passed on and
nobody accepted Sam Hurst's challenge. At length, to

the surprise and satisfaction of all, Tom Paddock, the
Redditch man, who has figured in these pages before,
came to the front and, accompanied by Nat Langham,
journeyed to *Bell's Life* and covered Hurst's deposit of
£50.   Although Tom was in the "sere and yellow," and
had been vainly endeavouring to get to the top of the
tree for the past ten years, he thought himself good
enough to meet a novice like the Stalybridge Infant, in
spite of that worthy's youth, size, and reputed strength.

It will be remembered that Paddock was born near
Redditch, in Worcestershire, in 1824, and that although
in several biographies he has been described as a needle
" pointer," he was in reality an agricultural labourer.
He, however, was always ready for a " dust up," and
it was amongst these " pointers " that he graduated in
the art of self-defence.   By all accounts these gentlemen were a pugnacious lot, and were always engaged in
fisticuffs.   Here is a description of them by a Redditch
man, who lived amongst them and knew them well.   He
says:—

" The most terrible fighting I ever saw was at the
White Hart, when a lot of the ' pointers ' who, having
met there to spend a quiet day, found that time hung
rather heavily on their hands, and so by way of variety
turned out to fight.   They paired themselves according
to weight, and made the arrangement that no one should
be permitted to fight more than three rounds, but those
rounds might be as long as they could make them.
Knowing, therefore, how little time they had to do business in, you may imagine the manner they went to
work, and the execution they did.   I never in my life saw
heavier hitting or more bloodshed.   Some of the men's
faces were battered out of all recognition, yet after it was
all over they didn't seem to mind it a bit, but sat and
drank their liquor quite kindly, cheek by jowl, with their
recent antagonists."

Such was the school that Tom Paddock was nursed in,
and he proved himself to be, as we have already had
occasion to describe, a fine natural fighter.   Of his
career there is no need to say more here.   It would
be but a repetition.   Fred Peace, Jack Stagg, a man
named Sam Hurst (no relation to the Stalybridge
Infant), Parsons, Nobby Clarke (twice), all fell beneath
the powerful arm of the young Redditch man.   But when
he flew at higher game, and entered the ring with the
Bold Bendigo, he met his master and his first defeat.
Then he fought a draw with the Tipton Slasher, and was
afterwards defeated by Harry Paulson, of Nottingham.
However, he turned the tables on Paulson in the December of 1851 ,when a disgraceful riot took place, and when

both men were apprehended, and they were sentenced to ten months' imprisonment with hard labour. Again Paddock met Paulson and beat him. This was in 1854, and in the same year he met and defeated Aaron Jones. He was then matched on two occasions with Harry Broome, from whom Paddock received forfeit on both occasions. In the June of 1855 he defeated Aaron Jones again for £100 a-side, and followed up this victory by beating Harry Broome. He then forfeited to the Tipton Slasher, and was beaten by Tom Sayers.

It will be seen by the above brilliant performances that the Redditch man was quite entitled to defend the title against all comers, for he had proved himself superior to the ex-Champion, Harry Broome, and more than held his own against some of the best men of the day. It was believed that Paddock, after his fight with Tom Sayers, would never enter the ring again. He could not, however, stand the presumption of Sam Hurst, and he determined to have another cut for the belt, for, Sayers having retired, and Heenan having left the country, Tom was justified in considering himself as the best man left. When the match was made Nat Langham took Paddock round the country with him, and their exhibition sparring before provincial audiences brought plenty of grist to the mill. Alec Keene took Sam Hurst on tour, with Brettle to pair off with him, and they also did remarkably well.

Hurst had never fought in the legitimate ring, but had proved himself a good man with the gloves, and a terror in the town where he was born. He was just thirty years of age at this period, and was a mountain of flesh, standing 6ft 2in in his stockings. After the sparring tour was over he went into training under the watchful eye of Jem Hodgkiss, near Stalybridge, and put in some stiff work in order to bring himself down a stone or so, for he was very " beefy." After a spell there, Hodgkiss took his man to Polesworth, near Tamworth, where he succeeded in getting him down to the respectable weight of 15st.

Paddock trained near London, with Nat Langham to look after him, and as he was a most abstemious man, and lived regularly, there was little difficulty in getting him into perfect form, and when he came to town on the eve of the fight, November 5, 1860, and dropped into the Rotunda, in the Blackfriars Road, where Bob Travers was taking his benefit, he was much admired by the Fancy, for he never looked better in his life. Sam Hurst made Harry Brunton's house, the George and Dragon, Barbican, his headquarters, and there on the day before the battle was a big assembly, many of

the "Infant's" friends having come up from Stalybridge to see their man fight for the Championship of
England. Amongst them were his two principal backers,
Mr. Woolley and Mr. Hyde, the latter host of the White
Horse, Stalybridge. There had been such a fuss made
over the great Farnborough fight between Sayers and
Heenan by the authorities, that the supporters of the
P.R. were very shy in identifying themselves with a
fight, and the Corinthians particularly held aloof. Besides it was really a risky affair to bring off a mill after
what had transpired. So it might be imagined there
was some difficulty in deciding where the fight for the
Championship should take place, and how it should be
managed so as to avoid interference by the police. All
kinds of places had been suggested, but each had its
danger, so at last it was determined to consult old Jem
Burn. The grand old sporting "bung" at this time
lived at the Rising Sun, Air Street, Piccadilly, and was
suffering dreadfully with his old enemy the gout. The
old warrior strongly urged that they should make an
aquatic trip of it, but there were objections to this,
owing to the difficulty in keeping the rough element
away, for it was they who did all the mischief.

Ultimately it was decided by Mr. Johnny Gideon and
those who had so successfully organised the Sayers-
Heenan arrangements, that a very select few should
engage a special on the Great Western Railway, and
proceed to a spot to be determined upon *en route,*
and far from the "madding crowd." The company
had no objection to provide the train, conditionally that
those proceeding to the field of battle should be limited
in number and quite select. The Pugilistic Benevolent
Association, represented by several well-known sporting
gents, undertook that this should be, so two hundred
railway tickets were issued, and although Paddington
presented an animated appearance at four a.m. on the
morning of the fight—hundreds of "the lads" having come
over to try what they could make, and with an idea of
forcing themselves to the front—so well had everything
been managed, and so numerous were the officials, that
the ticket holders were enabled to walk quietly on to
the platform, and take their seats comfortably.

It was just after five a.m. that the train moved off.
It had been decided to make a long trip, but at the last
moment information had come to hand that the blues
were mustering in great force at the proposed spot ; so
it was arranged that it would be better to risk a place
nearer home. So the pilot had instructions to slacken
speed after passing through Reading, where the lines
branch off to Hungerford and Basingstoke. There the

train was shunted, and after proceeding about two miles
past Mortimer Street Station, we came to a standstill
Although it was early November the day had dawned,
so without loss of time the ring was formed, and the
men getting ready soon entered the arena. Jem Hodgkiss and a well known " East End bung " whose name

TOM PADDOCK.

we are unable to remember, officiated for Sam Hurst,
and Jerry Noon and Bob Travers did the amiable for
Tom Paddock.

All was in readiness and " Time " was about to he
called, instead of which the cry of " Police " saluted
the car, and there sure enough, marching quickly in the

direction of the ring, were an inspector and four constables. He must have been a good sport, for the officer
apologised for his presence, and said that he had no
intention of interfering, as no breach of the peace had
been observed by him. Nevertheless, his instructions
were to allow no fighting, and suggested that the company should proceed to another county out of his jurisdiction. His advice was at once acted upon, and the
train was once more boarded. Arriving at Mortimer, it
was discovered that the blues were in great force, so
the excursionists proceeded to Reading, and there ascertained that the officers had gone thence to Streat ley,
but that the Hungerford branch was clear. So they
made their way in that direction, and when a short
distance from Newbury the train stopped, the company
once more alighted, and the ring was again formed.

Everything was ready very quickly, for the men were
in their fighting costume, and had only to throw off
their greatcoats; so at eighteen minutes past eleven,
or six hours after the start from Paddington, "Time"
was called, and Tom Paddock and Sam Hurst stood
before each other to do battle for the Championship of
England. We have gone to some length in describing
the journey and interruptions, for it gives one an idea
of the toil and dangers of following the Ring in its later
periods, and did undoubtedly detract greatly from the
sport, and helped in no small degree to bring about its
collapse.

As they faced each other there was noticeable a great
disparity in the size and height of the two men. The
"Infant" towered some three inches over the Redditch
man, and his fine muscular frame and enormously long
arms, together with his more youthful appearance, all
tended to give him what would seem many advantages.
As they shaped, however, it was evident that Hurst had
not the cultivation or experience of his antagonist.
and he seemed a bit flurried. Tom Paddock was very
much at home, and placed himself in easy position.
The first round was very uninteresting, a few slight
blows being exchanged, when Hurst closed, and Tom
slipped down on both knees. Facing each other again,
Hurst, who had received instructions to force the fighting,
dashed in and delivered two or three severe body blows,
and catching his man on the chin, opened an old scar,
which had been left there by Tom Sayers, and produced
first blood. They then closed, and after a short struggle,
rolled over together.

The fighting to commence with was anything but
Championship form. Paddock's weakness was his
hastiness. He played right into Hurst's hands, for

with a wicked look upon his usually pleasant looking face he rushed in, but Sam with his long arms swinging about like the sails of a windmill, caught Paddock an awful blow on the cheek. This caused the Redditch man to lose all control of himself, and he once more rushed in, but was caught round the waist by Hurst, and Tom, not desiring to test the "Infant's" wrestling powers, about which so much had been said, slipped down and finished the round.

The Novice was feeling quite at home by this time, and faced his more experienced adversary fearlessly in the centre of the ring. There were some very heavy exchanges, Tom getting all the worst of it, until for the fourth time he was knocked down. In the next bout rather an extraordinary incident happened, which brought to a close one of the least interesting battles for the Championship ever fought in a twenty-four-foot ring. After some severe exchanges Paddock, who was showing signs of fatigue, slipped down, and everybody, Hurst included, thought that the Redditch man had fallen upon both knees and finished the round. Hurst had turned his back, and was walking to his corner, when Paddock jumped to his feet and pursued his man. He was just about to launch out from behind, when Sam's seconds shouted a warning which induced him to turn round quickly enough to meet his foe. Swinging his right with a round-arm blow, he brought his great fist with a fearful thud upon Tom's ribs just below the armpit. It was a terrific blow, and it brought Paddock down upon his face. His seconds rushed to him and picked him up, carrying him to his corner. On examination it was found that the "Infant's" great fist had fractured two of Paddock's ribs, and he was in a helpless state, quite unable to come up again. He was carried to the railway carriage suffering the greatest agony, and so Sam Hurst was proclaimed Champion of England after fighting his first battle in the ring, which had lasted only nine minutes and a half.

This was Tom Paddock's last appearance in the arena, for, after a somewhat lingering illness, he died within three years of his fight with Sam Hurst, expiring on June 30, 1863.

CHAPTER LVIII.

INTRODUCING JEM MACE.—HIS EARLY CAREER.—HIS ENGAGE-
MENTS WITH THORPE, MADDEN, PRICE, TRAVERS, AND
BRETTLE.

And now we come to a period which marks the beginning of the end of the Prize Ring. From the time of
Figg and Broughton we have traced the long line of
Champions down to Jem Mace, to whom we introduce
our readers in this chapter. During his active career as
a bruiser, the once fine old manly sport became degene-
rate, and at last extinct. To quote the words of a well-
known sporting writer, we shall tell how the sport had
decayed:—" When the patronage of the P.R. had fallen
from noblemen, gentlemen, and the admirers of courage
and fair play into the hands of the keepers of nighthouses, 'hells,' and even resorts yet more detestable,
whose sole object was to fleece the dissipated and un-
wary by the sale of high-priced railway passes for
'special excursions,' and bring customers and victims to
their dens of debauchery and robbery, could it be
expected that boxers would remain honest and brave, the
encouragement of bravery and skill being as nothing to
these debased speculators?"

Such was the state of affairs at the period we are fast
approaching, which foreshadow the closing scenes of our
"Fights for the Championship," the state of affairs
which existed when Jem Mace made a bid for the belt
and the title. Of Mace himself (who, by-the-bye, is still
living and mine host of the Black Bull, Colville Street,
Birmingham), we can afford space but for a brief outline
of his career, as we shall have to find room for his fights
for the Championship. That he was a scientific boxer
and bruiser endowed with a marvellous knowledge of
ringcraft, there can be but one opinion. Jem Mace may,
indeed, be compared with any or all of the great Champions who were his predecessors, and we doubt if he has
ever been surpassed. Perhaps his only two equals were
the other Jameses—Jem Belcher and Jem Ward. The
first-named must have been a marvel in his way, as all
who have read our history of him will have gathered.
He was a genius in his way—a natural fighter, and a

punishing hitter, if we can believe the ablest critic of the Ring of the period, who wrote of him :—" Considered merely as a bruiser, I should say he was not so much a man of science, according to the rules of the pugilistic art, as that he possessed a style peculiar or rather natural to himself, capable of baffling all regular science, and what appeared self-taught and invented, rather than acquired by practice. He was remarkably quick, springing backwards and forwards with the rapidity of lightning. You heard his blows, but did not see them. At the conclusion of a round his antagonist was struck and bleeding; but he threw in his hits with such adroitness that you could not discern how the damage was done. His style, like that of great masters in every line, was truly his own—perfectly original and extremely difficult to avoid or withstand. Add to this that a braver boxer never pulled off a shirt, and we need hardly wonder at his eminent success, until an accident deprived him of one of the most wonderful organs of man's complex frame."

Jem Ward must be ranked next to Jem Belcher as a scientific fighter, even if he were not his superior. Ward was indeed a marvel, and was undoubtedly one of the best men the British Prize Ring has ever seen. Tom Spring, perhaps, had the finest defence of any of the big 'uns, but his hitting powers were not too great, and he carried caution to excess. No, in looking through the list of our Champions, the three Jems stand out as scientific boxers right to the front, and the living pugilist, Jem Mace has shown as much talent as either of the other two, and that, surely, is according him the very highest praise.

Bill Richardson, mine host of the Blue Anchor, Shoreditch, was a wonderful judge, and his opinion of Mace was, that he was the most punishing fighter he had ever seen, and old Bill had seen a few. To quote his words :—" Whatever may have been some persons' opinion of Mace, no grander bit of fighting was ever seen than that in the sixteen-foot ring, when Mace fought Goss the second time. When Nat Langham's mob of swells were on the beat, they all cried, ' Give the —— no rest, Joe !' But I know who had no rest that day, and it wasn't Jem. When they faced each other for the fight, Joe Goss stood with his arms well forward and his head back. You would have thought no boxer could have reached him, but Jem Mace, with a ' Look to yourself, Joe,' ducked, and hit him a heavy punch in the mouth. Joe tried all he knew to suck in the claret, for heavy wagering was on first blood, but another banger on the cheek-bone cut it to the chin. Jem then

cross-buttocked his man, and out spurted the blood like
a little fountain, and in a quarter of an hour Joe was
licked. I'll tell you what was the matter with Jem in
the other twenty-four foot ring—his ankles gave way, but
still the young 'un dare not touch him."

So much for the opinions of Jem Mace as a sparrer
and boxer. It will now be our duty to briefly sketch
his career before he fought Sam Hurst for the belt and
Championship.

Mace was born at Beeston, near Swaffham, in Norfolk,
in the May of 1831, so he will be now in his seventieth
year. He is a marvellously preserved man, as upright as a
dart, and as active and quick with arms and eye now as
many a youngster. But then Jem always led a sober life,
ate well, and went to bed early. Anybody who knows Jem
personally will readily believe that there is Gipsy blood
in his veins, although he is certainly not a true Romany,
and does not belong to that nomadic sect who never have
slept in a house, never entered a church, and who left
an undying curse upon any of their people who would
permit them to be buried in a churchyard. Gipsy or no
gipsy, Jem Mace's early life was spent in roving about
the country, having the nomadic disposition of a true
Bohemian. Before he was twenty-one years of age
he became associated with a travelling booth, from
which, at fairs and races, he provided refreshments,
played on the violin, and gave exhibitions in sparring.

During one of these displays with a man named
Bunney Blythe, who was another showman, Nat Langham happened to be passing by, and was struck with the
elegant way in which Jem put up his "dukes." So
pleased was Nat, indeed, that he at once offered to take
Mace in hand, offering him a situation in his boxing
booth. This Mace at once agreed to, so he donned the
regulation guernsey and prepared to meet all comers
with the mittens. Jem has stated to us: "This was
the proudest moment of my life. They could hardly
get the guernsey off me. I strutted about the fair as
vain as a peacock." Accompanying Langham to Horncastle Fair, he was put up with the gloves to take down
the local champion, a much bigger and heavier man than
himself, which he did most successfully, after a terrible
struggle, the Horncastle man being licked to a complete
standstill.

To quote Jem again: "My most formidable opponent
with the gloves at that time was a giant, whose face was
as hard as an anvil—harder, I believe, than the old Deaf
'Un's. His mates admitted that they could break a stick
across his jib without leaving a mark. Well, I tried first
at his nut, but I might as well have banged away at a

marble mantelpiece. So I gave it up, and let *him* do all the hitting, whilst I just dodged him. He couldn't touch me, and when I had him winded I just let him have one on the mark, and doubled him up."

Mace's first battle in the ring was with "Licker"

BILL THORPE.

Pratt, who defeated Jem. We believe that Pratt is still alive, and keeps a tavern in Norwich, or did so until a few years ago. Pratt, who was some five years older and much heavier, succeeded in defeating Mace. After this Mace did not enter the ring for four years, when he

29

met and defeated Slack, giving him a dreadful hiding in
nine rounds. After this Dan Dismore took Mace in
hand, and introduced him to the London Ring, and the
Norwich man was matched with Bill Thorpe, who hailed
from the Borough. This took place on February 17, 1857,
up the Medway, and resulted in a victory for Mace in
eighteen rounds, lasting only twenty-seven minutes,
and so decisive was the victory that Mace at once
came to the front in the London Ring. Mr.
Dowling, editor of *Bell's Life*, wrote about the novice
in the following manner:—" He is one of the best
boxers we have seen for many a day. He is a
quick and rapid fighter, and hits with judgment, precision, and remarkable force, as the condition of poor
Thorpe's head strikingly manifested. . . . . He
fights remarkably well, and when in danger has the
ability to get out of it in clever style. . . . . If his
pluck and bottom are in any way equal to his other
qualifications, we can only say that it will require an
opponent of first-rate ability to beat him."

After this Mike Madden was selected as the most
likely man to take down the youngster's colours, and
a match was made for £50 a-side, articles were signed,
and as was customary, the selection of referee was left
to the editor of *Bell's Life*. Mr. Dowling appointed Dan
Dismore. This proved to be an unfortunate selection,
for Nat Langham and Dan had quarrelled, and Mace
being under the wing of Ould Nat, at his instigation
declined to accept Dismore. There was a wrangle
over the matter, and in the end there was no fight. Mace,
having refused to accept the nomination, of course forfeited the stakes, and there was consequently a dreadful
row over the affair. Mace was accused of cowardice by Mr.
Dowling, and the young Norfolk man thereupon offered
to fight Madden when he liked, and for what he liked—
even for nothing, if that would suit him. At length
they agreed to fight for £15 to £10, and the time and
place were fixed. For some unaccountable reason, however, Mace did not turn up at the rendezvous, so there
was no fight. Now Mace was abused right and left,
Bell's Life taking the lead. We believe that Nat Langham
was at the bottom of all this disappointment, and had
some good reason, best known to himself, for preventing
Mace from fighting, for, although Jem was accused of
showing the white feather, he certainly was no coward, as
his subsequent battles proved. They tried to make a third
match, but Mr. Dowling would have nothing whatever
to do with Mace, so for about a year he was on the
shelf. At length, in the latter part of 1858, George
Brown notified to the sporting public that he had a

novice who was good enough to do battle with Bob Brettle, whose name just about this time had become famous, both in London as well as Birmingham. Of course the Brum accepted the challenge, and it then transpired that the young novice was Jem Mace. The fight took place down the river, and although it was short and sweet, it did away with all the suggestions that Mace was a coward. Here is a brief description of the battle. In the opening round they both came eagerly to the scratch, amidst the greatest excitement, for there had been some heavy betting upon the ground. To the utter dismay of the Brum, Mace went straight for him without attempting to spar, and the hitting became very fast and furious. Jem drew first blood by splitting Bob's ear, and in a scramble they both went down. On facing each other for round number two, Brettle tried to lead, when Mace countered heavily with the right on the left ear. Some terrific exchanges followed, during which Brettle, measuring his man, struck a fearful blow with his right upon Jem's jaw, and he went down as if he had been poleaxed. Everything was done to get him round; but all was in vain, so the Birmingham man was hailed the winner in the short space of three minutes.

This was a surprise to all Mace's patrons. That a man of his acknowledged scientific attainments should fight so recklessly was inexplicable. Jem Mace has often told us the reason that he made such a fiasco. On the journey down Mr. Dowling addressed Jem by saying, " What! you don't mean to say that you really have entered an appearance?" This so upset Jem that he worked himself up into a pitch of anger—so much so that he declared that he bit his lip through and made it bleed, to keep himself from boiling over with rage. He kept on saying to himself, " I'll show the —— to-day whether I'm a coward or not, damn them!" He excited himself so much that when he entered the ring he had lost his self-possession, and to make matters worse, whilst they were getting ready he heard Mr. Dowling say to George Brown, " What, George, do you mean to say that you have brought that cur out without a chain?" Jem's blood was literally boiling when "Time" was called, and, instead of displaying his usual coolness and caution, he rushed in heedless of everything, and with the result as above described.

Bob Brettle over this became very friendly with Mace, took him to Birmingham, and found a man to match him against. This was Posh Price. It was decided that the fight should take place on January 25, 1859. It was a desperately fought battle, lasting only seventeen minutes, during which time, however, Jem Mace had ample time to prove that he possessed any amount of pluck, science, and power, and was class enough to take his place in the front rank amongst the pugilists of the day, putting the statements of the editor of *Bell's Life* to the blush.

Mace's next engagement was with Bob Travers, the Black (also living). The match was made just about the same time as that between Sayers and Heenan, and articles were drawn for the men to fight on February 21, 1860, the amount of the stakes being £100 a-side. It was a most unsatisfactory affair, for the men and spectators, having been landed on the Essex shore, were interfered with by the police, and an adjournment until next day had to be arranged. The men met, and after fighting fifty-seven rounds in ninety-one minutes, Travers fell without a blow, and lost the fight.

Mace's next appearance in the ring was with his former antagonist—Bob Brettle. They had signed articles to fight for £200, and the battle came off partly in Oxfordshire on September 9, 1860, and partly down the river on the 20th of the same month. Mace had marvellously improved since his first appearance with the Birmingham man, and furthermore he fought at greater advantage, for he had nothing to upset him on the second occasion. He proved in a very short time his superiority over Bob, who was certainly very lucky to have beaten his man at their first meeting. The battle lasted only nineteen minutes, but during that period Jem Mace put in some splendid work. In the last round Jem opened the ball, and went for his man with both hands, raining in the blows with marvellous rapidity. Bob fought desperately, and they got to the ropes, when Mace, measuring his distance and putting all his weight behind the blow, delivered a punisher, which sent Master Bob down "all of a heap," and as Mace sprang lightly to the scratch to the call of "Time," Brettle lay unconscious.

Passing over a few episodes of Mace's eventful career, we come to his first fight for the Championship, the details of which we must reserve for another chapter.

CHAPTER LIX.

JEM MACE AND SAM HURST.—COLLAPSE OF THE INFANT.—
THE GAUNTLET AGAIN THROWN DOWN.—TOM KING.

After Jem Mace's defeat of Bob Brettle, and he became Champion of the Middle Weights, nothing short of an attempt for the belt would satisfy him, so accordingly he threw down the gauntlet to Sam Hurst, the Stalybridge Infant, who, it will be remembered, had beaten Tom Paddock and won the title of Champion of England. Now Sam was a veritable Anak, for he stood 6ft 2½in in height, and weighed no less than 16st 10lb at the time Mace challenged him. But although he held the Championship and the belt he had done really very little in the ring, his only battle of note being that with Paddock, referred to above, and that was undoubtedly a fluke. Nevertheless, Sam was an enormously strong man, and was looked upon as a wonderful wrestler, being dubbed Champion of Lancashire, and his hitting power was exceedingly great, as Paddock found to his cost, having two of his ribs broken by one of Sam's blows.

But Jem Mace had determined to become Champion of England, so he challenged Hurst, and the fight was arranged to come off on June 18, 1861. Mace at the time kept the King John, Holywell Lane, Shoreditch, and soon after articles were signed he made an engagement with Pablo Fanque, and travelled with his circus throughout the country. Amongst the places at which they pitched their tent was Stalybridge, and there they attracted enormous audiences from all around the country, everybody being anxious to see what sort of a man the "Infant" was about to take on. Jem at this time weighed under 11st, and when he boxed in the arena at Stalybridge, the Lancashire lads to a man laughed at the idea of such a David slaying their Goliath. The Norfolk man, who was always a bit of a "kidder" too, did not put on his best style before the Stalybridge audiences, so their impression of him as a scientific performer was by no means great, and long before the fight they were offering odds on the Infant. But Sam Hurst was by no means in a fit condition, for just eight months before the day upon which the battle was to be fought he slipped down some steps which were covered with ice, and broke his leg just above the ankle. Naturally this deterred him from taking the necessary exercise to bring him to the proper weight, and he had to reduce by means of Turkish baths and other artificial resources. In spite of this nearly everybody believed that Mace stood a poor chance, and Sam's friends declared that if their Infant could only get hold of the Norfolk man, he would "Squeeze the wee chap like a cooked turnip."

Mace took his final training at Swaffham, near his home, and Hurst put the finishing touches to himself at Stalybridge. Two or three days before the battle the Lancashire man came to London, and put up at Harry Brunton's, whilst Mace made Bill Richardson's, the Blue Anchor, Shoreditch, his headquarters. The morning of the 18th of June was glorious, and the crowd at Fenchurch Street Station was very great, that being selected at the last moment as the rendezvous. Not so many of the Corinthians were present, for at this particular period there had been a dead set at pugilism, for since the Sayers and Heenan battle the authorities had determined to put a stop to these fistic encounters. To be sure a certain section of the public advocated the continuance of the manly art, and one of the papers, which was foremost in championing the cause was the *Saturday Review*. This high-class journal admired the national sport and the manly, true British bull-dog spirit which has always been the prominent characteristic of the Anglo-Saxon, and which has undoubtedly helped us to gain and hold our Empire. This particular paper, in defending the Ring, declared that there was no more danger or disgrace in the manly art than in exhibitions upon the high rope and the trapeze. Just about the time of the fight we are about to record, Blondin had taken the town by storm, and was performing at the Crystal Palace. He had just come from America, having crossed the Niagara Falls, in the presence of our present Sovereign, with a man upon his back. The hero of Niagara was going through a similar performance, and wheeling a man along the rope in a wheelbarrow. The *Saturday Review* compared these exhibitions with those of the Prize Ring, and pointed out that one was neither more nor less likely to cause death than the other, and a disaster to either would bring equal reproach upon the law which permitted and the spectators who applauded the performance of the adventurer who lost his life trying to gain a living. Certainly there were more lives lost from the high rope and trapeze than in the roped arena, yet the goody-goody people would go to the Crystal Palace and look out for and expect a man to fall from a height to become a maimed and mangled mass of humanity, knocked out of all shape—more so than it would ever be possible to accomplish in the prize-ring.

However, prize-fighting was to be put down, and naturally the difficulty of bringing a mill off proved greater every year, and of course the whereabouts of a fight had to be kept a profound secret. So but very few knew the destination when Sam Hurst and Jem Mace and their followers took train from Fenchurch Street upon this beautiful June morning. Passing through Plaistow and the verdant Essex meadows, the excursionists were taken past Tilbury and on to Southend. There a steamer was in waiting and the crowd embarked and were taken over to the Medway, where they were landed on one of the small islands, about nine o'clock in the morning.

Oliver soon had the ring formed, and all the preliminaries being arranged the men entered to do battle for the Championship of England. Boss Tyler and Woody looked after Mace, and Jerry Noon and Jem Hodgkiss attended upon Sam Hurst. Mace's elegant style we have already described, and the colossal Infant has also appeared before us. But although Mace could scarcely be designated but a fine man, his figure sank into insignificance before the great body of the Infant. Yet there was no comparison as to their symmetry, the Norfolk man being perfect, whilst his opponent looked unwieldy and disproportioned in limb and figure. Mace had won the toss, so he, of course, selected the position which gave him his back to the sun. They soon got to work. Mace creeping in cautiously, feinting and placing a smart blow upon Sam's cheek, and jumping back with surprising activity out of harm's way. Again he approached and put in a slashing blow upon the big 'un's eye and avoided the return. Hurst dashed in after him, but Jem was too quick, landing two more blows upon the face and receiving a slight tap on the head, when he went down.

In the fourth round there was evidence of Hurst's want of condition, for one report says he presented a shocking appearance thus early in the battle. His flesh was flabby, and became bruised and swollen from every blow delivered by the sledgehammer-like arms of the Norwich man. He followed the example of a mad bull and persistently rushed at Mace, who nimbly got out of his way, and each time pinked him smartly in the face, until his optics puffed up and almost blinded him. He became furious, and Jem, as cool as a cucumber, had but to await his coming to hit him as he chose.

In the sixth round the battle was practically decided

for the punishment Mace inflicted was terrible. So badly was Hurst knocked about that people shouted for him to be taken out of the ring. But Sam would not listen to it, and again rushed in. His intention was each time to catch hold of his opponent and throw him, but Mace had never given him a chance to grip. In this round, however, the Norwich man had the temerity to accept the Infant's challenge, and they both got a good hold. Imagine the surprise, then, of all assembled, and particularly the Stalybridgeites, who had such faith in their man's wrestling powers, when they saw the Norwich man throw Hurst by what many declared was a cross-buttock. He was so dreadfully shaken and so badly hurt that Bob Brettle went into the ring and begged him to give it up ; but Sam would listen to none of his advisers, and would come again and again.

Here is a graphic description of the finish of this unequal fight for the Championship, which brought Jem Mace to the top of the ladder of his fistic fame, and ended the pugilistic career of the Stalybridge Infant. In the next round Mace dashed in with a delivery full on the smashed face. Hurst presented a sorry spectacle, the blood pouring in torrents down his chest, whilst Jem was besmeared and bespattered with the Infant's gore, until he had the appearance of a Red Indian. Yells of "Take him away!" were raised from outside the ring. Hodgkiss, Sam's second, wanted to throw up the sponge, but Hurst wouldn't hear of it, so he was sent up again until the eighth round, when Brettle once more tried to induce him to desist, for he was as blind as a bat, and wandering all over the ring. "Look where he's going, Jerry," shouted Mace to Noon, whereupon Hurst turned to the direction whence the voice came, and made a rush. As he passed, Jem dealt him a crashing blow on the battered face, which sounded sickening as he fell to the ground. Yet the plucky fellow would come up again, but Jem refrained from punishing him, thinking that his seconds would give in for him. At last, however, there was nothing for it, as Hurst kept rushing about trying to discover Mace's whereabouts in a mad sort of manner. So Jem met him, and with right and left hit the big fellow all over the ring, and then, throwing all his weight into a blow upon the chest, stretched him out upon his back. It was all over, and Mace was hailed victor.

Immediately the battle was finished a fine young fellow entered the ring, and formally threw down the gauntlet to the new Champion. This was Tom King, who had already challenged Sam Hurst, but Mace had a good claim upon the Stalybridge man, so the novice

bad to await the result of the battle just described.
Now young Tom King had only appeared twice before
in the roped arena, but he had fought and defeated two
who were looked upon as hard nuts to crack. But as
he will play a prominent part amongst our Champions, it
will be as well to give a brief history of his early career.

SAM HURST.

Tom King was born at Silver Street, Stepney, in 1836,
and as a youngster went to sea. Not caring for a life on
the ocean wave, he obtained employment at the docks,
where for a considerable time he was engaged in the
exceedingly unpleasant occupation of landing guano
from the vessels. At this time he lived at 21, London

Street, off the Commercial Road, lodging with an old lady named Wingrove. He was a very quiet, respectable young fellow, and, anxious to improve his education, during the evenings he would go round to a baker named Brabach, a German, who taught Tom reading, writing, and arithmetic, accomplishments which proved invaluable to him in after life, as we shall in due course describe. Although devoting a deal of time to his books, young King was always fond of manly sports, and if some of his mates thought him a bit soft (for he was very reserved) they soon found out their mistake, for about this time a great hulking bully, called Brighton Bill, came across his path, and insulted the boss of the stevedores to whom King was attached, and amongst whom Bill worked. After the day's labour was over Tom gave the bully a bit of his mind, and the latter pulled off his coat to fight the cheeky youngster, declaring that he would shut up his mouth once and for all by breaking his jaw. In a very few minutes a crowd consisting of stevedores, 'longshoremen, sailors, dock officials, and even police collected and formed a ring. Brighton Bill, who had been unmercifully chaffed, was in a towering rage as he faced Tom King, but the latter was perfectly cool and determined. Everybody thought that the youngster would get a fearful hiding, for Bill was a terror to the docks. The veteran rushed at Tom as if to annihilate him, but to the surprise of all, King met him with a straight, slashing blow full in the face, which sent him staggering back on his heels. Again and again did he serve the bully in the same way, Tom hitting away without receiving a single blow. Bill got frantic with rage as the crowd hurrahed. When Tom found that his temper had got the better of him he went for him with a vengeance, hitting him in a business-like manner with both hands, until " Brighton Bill" was, as one eye-witness stated, "a bruised and bleeding half-senseless, quivering mass in the dust, and Tom King was proclaimed conqueror over the ' terror of Wapping.' "

His fame in the East End soon became known, and attracted the attention of Jem Ward, who then kept the George Tavern, in the Ratcliff Highway. The old " Black Diamond " sent for King, and put the gloves on with him. He soon found out what he was made of and declared that he was a wonder, and (with the exception of Jem Mace) the best man of the period. So well did Tom get on under his experienced old tutor that the latter advertised in *Bell's Life* that he had found an " Unknown " who had never fought in the prize ring, but who was ready to fight anybody in the world at catch-weight for £50 a-side. This was a tall order, but the

Fancy knowing whence it came, felt confident that Ward had really discovered something good, and were not over anxious to take up the challenge. At length, however, a man named Clamp responded. Before the match was made, this gentleman went to the George and had the gloves on with Tom on the quiet. This was quite enough : no more was heard of Mr. Clamp. Some months elapsed, when he at last found a man to take up the gauntlet. This was Tommy Truckle, of Portsmouth, several officers having subscribed the money to match the latter. The fight came off down the river on November 27, 1860. The Portsmouth lad being thoroughly thrashed in the space of one hour. So delighted was Ward and his friends at this performance, that they had no hesitation in putting the money down for him to fight Young Broome, who was anxious for a job, and to follow this up by matching him for the Champinoship. Broome (whose real name was William Evans Pato) was a fine made, well-behaved fellow, who stood 5ft 10in, was born in 1836, and weighed 11st 2lb. He had fought several times, and proved himself a first-class man, having astonished the sporting world by his vigorous style of fighting. They were matched at catch-weight for £50 a-side, and King scored another victory, beating his man in forty-two minutes.

And that brings us down to Tom King's challenge to Jem Mace to fight for the belt, as described above.

January 28, 1862, was the day appointed, and not for a long time had there been so much interest taken in a Championship fight, for this was to be with two good ones, there could be no doubt, for Mace had proved his fine science, and King his pluck, physique, and clever-ness. The morning of the fight, however, was as bad as it could be, and no doubt kept many away from the appointed place—London Bridge, 6 a.m. Anyhow, it appears that there was a pretty good muster and all went well, although the authorities had threatened to arrest the principals. The train, which did not leave until seven o'clock, rattled away to Godstone, in Surrey, some thirty miles down the line. There the company disembarked, and in less than an hour everything was ready, and the two men were in the ring.

We cannot devote much space to the description of this fight, as both men will appear in other contests, so must be content with a brief outline of the combat. Jem Mace discovers that he has a very different man to deal with to Sam Hurst, and he has to be very careful, for Tom King is 6ft 2in, and towers over the compact form of the Norfolk man. Besides, he has a much longer reach and is as quick as lightning. They

open cautiously and get to work quickly, but although
the exchanges are very smart they are light. King,
after a round or two, forces the fighting, and cuts out
the pace with a vengeance. He gets home several blows
but without much force, but Mace cross counters with
great effect, and King receives heavily upon the cheek.
Tom then manages to get a hold, but Jem, with a
wriggle, gets away.

By the fifth round Mace has received some severe
visitations and he is bleeding from nose and mouth,
whilst his left eye is much discoloured. After some
sharp work they get together, a struggle ensues, and
they both roll over on the wet grass. The rain still
falls, and the ground is very slippery. Twice Mace
falls, and it is with great difficulty that either can
keep his feet. In spite of these unfavourable conditions, however, they give a fine display of true, manly
British sport, with no small amount of science. In the
twenty-seventh round King knocks Mace clean off his
pins, but the latter is in far better condition, and King
is distressed about the wind, and seems quite pumped.
About half-way through the fight Jem unfortunately
knocks his wrist up, and is evidently suffering pain.
He is such a good general though that he is able to give
his arm a good rest by dodging his opponent. The fight
progresses until the forty-third round, and although the
hopes of King's supporters are frequently raised, Jem
outfights him at every move, and appears, instead of
tiring, to warm to his work. It is evident that the Champion has made up his mind to bring the battle swiftly
to a close, for King is much distressed. Mace
goes to his man, finds an opening, and strikes him a
fearful blow upon the neck, and closes. They struggle
desperately, but Mace brings his man down with a crash
upon the ground, and there he remains until his seconds
carry him in an unconscious state to his corner.
"Time" is called, but still the great form of Tom King
lies limp and inanimate. There is a painful silence as
the referee counts him out and calls "Time" again.
King does not hear, and with a wild "Hurrah!" Jem
Mace is hailed victor, and still remains Champion of
England.

CHAPTER LX.

MACE AGAIN CLAIMS THE TITLE.—HIS MYSTERIOUS MATCH
WITH GOSS.—TWO HUNDRED MILES TO SEE A MILL.—A
DESPERATE ENCOUNTER.

After King's defeat for the Championship by Jem
Mace, in which the latter had proved himself undoubtedly the best man of his time, there was litt'e
chance of getting a match on, so Jem led an idle life for
many months. At length, Tom King's friends thought
that he was entitled to another try for the honoured
title, and with pleasure the Norfolk man agreed that he
should be accommodated. But King hesitated, saying
that he and Mace had arranged to go touring together.
Tom's disinclination to meet his former antagonist
created some surprise, and it looked as if Jem were going
to have a walk-over for the belt, and that in the following year it would become his own property.

In the month of May, 1862, however, there appeared
an advertisement in *Bell's Life* to the effect that Mace
was matched to fight Brettle's " Unknown," and that
the articles had been signed and a deposit made. This
so nettled Tom King that he at once threw down the
gauntlet and taunted Mace for not having an understanding with him first, for it would appear that they
had mutually arranged that Mace should not make a
match with anybody else without first letting King
know. There was a lengthy paper warfare, and so riled
did Jem become that he gave Brettle a sum of money so
that he could be off with the new love and on with the
old. Then came about a curious revelation, which gave
rise to all kinds of accusations and distrusts. It transpired that Nat Langham and his Corinthian friends
had found the money for Mace instead of for King, as was
done for the previous battle, and that Tom had gone
back to his home at the East End, and was being backed
from Bill Richardson's house, the Blue Anchor, in
Shoreditch. This was a curious arrangement, for it
was well known that Richardson had an interest in the
Old King John, the house which was kept by Mace.

Those behind the scenes, however, knew that Jem and Old Bill had quarrelled, and that Tom King had been deserted by Langham and his friends at the West End after being beaten by Mace. And so there was quite a complication, and all sorts of ugly rumours about the affair being a " cross."

Anyhow, the match was made and articles signed for them to fight on November 26, 1862. Both Mace and King continued their sparring tour and kept in perfect condition, so it was only necessary for them to go into training for a few weeks. We cannot possibly devote space to a description of the fight, but must hurry on with Mace's other performances. Suffice it to say, that the mill took place on the banks of the river, not far from Thames Haven, and, to the surprise of everybody, Tom King turned the tables upon his former conqueror, beating the Champion, and winning the Belt and £200, finishing the battle in thirty-eight minutes, during which they fought 31 rounds. This was a dreadful shock to Nat Langham and his party, whilst the East-Enders were frantic with delight.

Tom King, however, as soon as he had earned the Championship, determined to retire from the Ring, so Mace came forward again and claimed the title. Of course he had a perfect right to do so, but the Belt was handed back to *Bell's Life*, who were to hold it until somebody had fought Mace again. But nobody for a time seemed inclined to face the Norwich hero.

In the December of 1862, however, Joe Goss, of Wolverhampton, an unbeaten warrior, who fought at 10st 10lb, threw down the gauntlet. There was something rather unsatisfactory about the whole affair though, for there was no definite time fixed in the articles ; they simply said that the fight should take place nine months after date. Then so large a sum as £1,000 was looked upon as indicating something "fishy" about it, Mace's backers having to find £600 to the Wolverhampton man's £400. Another thing was the Belt was not to be included. Meanwhile Bill Ryall, of Birmingham, observing that Goss did not ask for the Belt to be thrown in, offered himself to Jem Mace to fight for £200 a-side and the trophy. This Jem readily assented to and a deposit of £25 was made, Bob Brettle backing Ryall. The latter, however, paid forfeit, and the match between the Champion and Goss held good.

But when in the August Bill Richardson handed in his cheque for £330, and the same was covered by Goss with £220, matters began to take a serious turn, and a deal of interest was at once centred in the match, and

when the final deposits were posted, and the men met
to weigh at Mr. Tupper's, the Greyhound, Webber
Street, Waterloo Road, the pent-up excitement burst
forth in all its intensity.

The meeting place to take the journey was Paddington
Station, and the crowd that congregated there as early
as 3.30 a.m. must have astonished the residents of the
neighbourhood. There was a long train, consisting of
first and second-class carriages, provided, the fares of
which were two guineas and one guinea respectively.
At four o'clock the crowded train steamed out, and ran,
without stopping, to Didcot Junction, where they took
water for the engine, and then proceeded to Swindon.
There they came to a standstill to pick up Nat Langham
and his friends, who had travelled most unwisely to
the place on the previous day, and thereby put the police
on the alert. Journeying some five miles further, in
order to get outside Oxfordshire, they found themselves
in the vicinity of Wooten Bassett, North Wilts. The
morning was delightful, for it was September 1, the day
of St. Partridge. The place selected to form the ring
was about a mile from the line, and it must have been a
strange sight for the natives to watch the mixed crowd
making their way across the fields at that early hour, for
it was only just past six.

And now, whilst the men who are to meet for this
large stake are getting ready, it will be as well to introduce Joe Goss, who met Jem Mace no less than three
times, and who has not yet been presented to our
reader. He was born at Wolverhampton on August 16,
1838, and first entered the arena when twenty-one years
of age, meeting Jack Rooke, of Birmingham, for the
sum of £25 a-side. This was on September 20, 1859,
and Goss was victorious after sixty-four rounds had
been fought in one hour forty minutes. This was considered an excellent performance, for the Birmingham
lad had only just before defeated Tom Lane, brother to
the notorious "Hammer" of that ilk. His next engagement was with Price, of Bilston. This, however,
ended in a forfeit, Joe Goss having been arrested at the
instigation of his father. Goss was so annoyed with his
parent that he determined to meet Price, if only for
love, and the lads made a match for £10 a-side of their
own money. They met on February 10, 1860, and Goss'
hard hitting and fearless style had the effect of knocking his man out in twenty minutes, and when only
fifteen rounds had been fought. Bodger Crutchley was
the next, a man who was thought a deal of in the Midlands, for he had defeated George Lane, Bos Tyler, Sam
Millard, and Smith, of Manchester. He met Goss on

July 17, 1860, near Oxford, for £100 a-side. After a tremendous battle, lasting three hours and twenty minutes, during which 120 rounds were fought, Goss was once more proclaimed victor. Then in the September of the following year Goss met and defeated Ryall for £50 a-side in two hours fifty minutes, fighting thirty-seven rounds. He again met the same antagonist for £100 a-side on February 11, 1862, but the fight was unfinished after a stubborn and prolonged combat lasting three hours eighteen minutes, the referee declaring it to be a draw. That brings his most creditable list of performances down to the fight we are about to briefly relate.

The referee having been selected and all the preliminaries gone through, the men entered the ring. Mace never looked better in his life. Goss was a fine, fresh-looking young fellow, with immense power about his arms and legs. He was twenty-five years whilst Mace had entered his thirty-third year, so the Wolverhampton man had the advantage of youth on his side.

Those who had seen Goss fight his previous battles thought that he would have forced the fighting, and have depended upon his strength to finish his man off quickly, but he did nothing of the kind. Mace, with great caution, sparred round his opponent until four minutes had been cut to waste. Mace at length made up his mind to attack, when a shout of "Police" was heard, and five boys in blue appeared upon the field. There was nothing for it, the stakes were pulled up and a dash was made for the trains. Unfortunately the "special" had been sent to Swindon, so the multitude had four miles to walk, and at the villages they passed through there was no small surprise at the moving mass. Arrived at Swindon a consultation took place, but it was found that the railway company had only agreed to take the train from London to one place selected and back to town. There was no possibility of pitching the ring upon fields and pastures new, so there was nothing for it but to return to the metropolis. The referee then called the men, their seconds and backers together, and said: "I shall order, as I am empowered to order by the rules, that the men meet again *this day* at Fenchurch Street Station, and go down to Purfleet. When there we must be guided by circumstances, but we will have the fight off to-day if possible."

This was a surprise, for by the time the train returned to London they had journeyed no less than 166 miles. Arrived at Paddington, all the cabs in the yard and outside the station were chartered for the enthusiasts who were determined to see the matter through. By

1.30 most of those intending to make the second journey
had arrived at Fenchurch Street, and the ticket-office
was beseiged, a marvellous run on "returns" for
Purfleet being the result. Some delay took place in the
start, so it was 3 o'clock before the second journey was
completed. From Purfleet it was decided to make for
Plumstead Marshes, and quite a flotilla of boats were
engaged to convey the weary travellers to the spot where
the ring was to be finally pitched. From start to finish

JOE GOSS.

these lovers of the manly sport had been exactly fifteen
hours on the journey, and we have gone into these
particulars to show how great was the fascination at
this period for a good prize-fight.

At five o'clock in the afternoon all was ready, and the
men entered the ring. Goss had been instructed on the
journey to make the running, so that it was believed
that the "terrible Joe" would give a taste of his
qualities. It was not to be, however, and he hung fire as

in the first ring. Mace sparred beautifully and pressed
him until he was right on the ropes, when the Norwich
man let go the left and caught him over the eye, cutting
it deeply and calling forth first blood. They then
fought very rapidly, Mace receiving some nasty taps,
but generally getting the best of the hitting, and
avoiding in a remarkably clever manner. After the first
half-dozen rounds had been fought both showed signs
of the conflict. Jem had received a nasty blow upon the
right eye, and that organ of vision was very much
puffed. Goss at this seemed to be much encouraged,
and followed his opponent up vigorously. Mace
retreated before the attack of this young Hercules, and
the friends of Goss yelled, "The young 'un wins! The
young 'un wins! I'll take 5 to 4!" But they soon
withdrew their offers, for a change came o'er the
scene. Mace, steadying himself, put in some splendid
two-handed fighting, and, measuring his man, caught
him on the ear with his left and knocked him clean off
his pins, thus gaining the second event.

After this the punishment meted out on both sides
was great, and Mace was very serious, for Goss
commenced to adopt the tactics he had employed in all
his other combats. He tried again and again to get at
Jem; but he was neatly stopped, or Jem got nimbly out
of the way, until Joe became perplexed and ill-tempered,
whilst Mace was perfectly cool and laughing at the
difficulties his man was in. Jem, in the twelfth round,
hit Goss a fearful smash on the cheek-bone with his left,
and, before he could recover, sent the right in with
terrific force full upon the nasal organ. One account
says: "His face was pitiable to look upon; the mouth
swollen, eyebrow cut, gash on the cheek, and tinted
proboscis, developed to a Bardolphian dimension, whilst
Mace was unmarked, save the bump over the eye, which
gave him a curiously disreputable appearance."

Round after round was fought, and Goss kept getting
all the worst of it. Mace was showing his usual good
generalship by playing with him, and endeavouring to
tire him out before giving him his *coup de grâce*. Here
is a description of the finish of the great battle by an
eye-witness, which gives a vivid picture of the men's
manner of fighting: —

"In the seventeenth round Goss made a desperate
effort, and for a time there were some slashing
exchanges, Joe sticking to the work bravely, but suffering dreadfully. He finally made the circuit of the ring
in his endeavour to avoid his clever opponent, who was
all over him directly they got into distance. The pace
had been exceedingly warm. Mace steadily pursued

him, and, getting him to the ropes, nailed him with the
left on the side of the "nut," and before Joe could
attempt the return a slashing right from Mace caught
him in the neck, which made his eyes start from their
sockets. Goss with the greatest pluck then dashed at
his opponent, who retired to the centre of the ring,
where some fierce, rapid, two-handed fighting took
place. Again and again did Jem—now with the left,
now with the right—get all over his man's head and
body, each blow being delivered with stinging effect.
Goss fought unflinchingly, but the superior qualities of
Jem as a tactician became fully demonstrated in this
grandly fought round. The excitement was intense as
the crowd yelled and pressed about the ring, until they
threatened to break in upon the men. At length both
got to close quarters, and Goss, rushing in, put on the
hug, and they wrestled for some minutes, at length
going down together, amidst deafening applause.

"In the eighteenth Goss came up blinded with the
blood that, in spite of his seconds' efforts to stop it, ran
freely from the gash over his eye, which had been
bruised and lacerated by the constant visitations of
Jem's sharp knuckles. The Champion was a dead shot,
and seemed to be able to hit where he chose. The ruby
was also streaming from poor Joe's nose and cut lips, the
crimson trickling down his neck and chest. Altogether
he looked a study in bright red. Mace was again all
over him, and in attempting to close Goss overbalanced.

"At the opening of the nineteenth round, the Gos-
sites looked very blue, for their man was slow to
'Time,' whilst Mace came up in a sprightly manner and
took stock of his opponent just as if he were commencing the fight. He worked his left backwards and
forwards nervously. Goss retreated when the latter
could go no further on account of the ropes. Mace
lunged straight from the shoulder a terrific blow, which
could be heard by those who didn't see it. It struck
with a crack against Joe's jaw, and the effect was
instantaneous. Goss's head fell forward with his chin
on his chest, and he pitched with his forehead upon the
ground and rolled over senseless, Mace being proclaimed
victor after fighting for fifty-five minutes and thirty
seconds."

CHAPTER LXI.

THE MEETING OF GIANTS.—TOM KING AND JOHN C. HEENAN. —BATTLE FOR A BIG STAKE.

We now have to chronicle one of the last great fights which was attended by the Corinthians or noble supporters of the Prize Ring. True, several other good battles were fought before pugilism actually suffered its death-blow; but the great encounter for the enormous stakes of £2,000 was the finish of the two giants' careers—the two men who had created such a sensation, but whose battles could be counted upon the fingers of one hand. Tom King and John C. Heenan were both mighty gladiators, but neither of them had his heart and soul in the profession, and after their meeting which we shall presently describe they both retired, the Britisher to make his fortune in another path of life and the Yankee to come to utter grief and shuffle off this mortal coil just in the prime of manhood.

Of both men we have had something to say in previous chapters, and it will be scarcely worth while to give another list of their battles. It will be remembered that Tom King was an East Ender by birth, having been born in Silver Street, Stepney, on August 11, 1835. After leading a seaman's life for some time he returned to his native place and worked in the docks, where his abilities as a pugilist were soon recognised by Jem Ward, who first took him in hand. As we have told, his fights were few, the two most important being those with Jem Mace, already referred to, in which he was defeated the first time, but turned the tables at their next meeting. There had been a good deal of ill-feeling between Mace and King after the first fight, but when they had each scored one they buried the hatchet, and were firm friends; and that reminds us of an anecdote which goes to show the humble way in which King, then Champion of England, lived. When he was at work in the docks he had lodgings with an old lady named Winburne, and she was, by all accounts, like a mother to him—looked upon him with pride as her boy. So as Tom mounted the ladder to fame, he kept on his little room and received

his friends at the old lady's humble little domicile.
Tom Sayers, Tom King, and Jem Mace were well-nigh
inseparable about this time, and one evening, whilst the
distinguished trio were at Massey's house, the White
Swan, in the Commercial Road, Sayers asked his two
friends to run down that night to Brighton with him.
Mace was agreeable, but King declined, having other
business on. Mace declared that he would go down to
Tom's diggings and get his portmanteau, and that he
would have to go with them. King laughingly said,
"All right; if you'll do that, I'm with you; but I'll bet
you a couple of bottles of 'fiz' that you don't bring my
traps back." "Done," said Mace, and off he went.
Arrived at London Street, he knocked at the door, and
Mrs. Winburne put her head out of the bedroom window,
demanding who was there. Mace told her that Tom
King had sent him to get his portmanteau, and she was
to pack a few things in it, as Tom was off to Brighton,
where he had a little business which would bring him in
some £50. "Not if I know it," said the old dame. "If
Tom wants his portmanteau let him come for it. You
don't get anything belonging to him out of me. Don't
tell me rubbish. I know Tom too well for that." Mace
pleaded, expostulated, and even threatened; but Mrs.
Winburne was obdurate, and eventually put the window
down with a bang. So Master Jem had to return, pay
for the wine, and Tom had the laugh at him.

But to return to King's ring career. After his second
battle with Mace he announced his retirement from the
ring, and handed back the belt to *Bell's Life*. But even
the strong resolution of a man like Tom King was
capable of being overcome, for pride and a heavy bait in
the way of £1,000 induced him to once more strip in the
24ft ring. Heenan challenged any man in the world to
fight him for the stake of £2,000, and Charlie Bush and
several other sports determined to find the money and
put up King if he would agree. With little persuasion he
yielded and the match was made, the following articles
being drawn up and duly signed, and as this is the
last and greatest modern battle that we shall record we
may be permitted to quote the document, especially as
appearing therein are some names in the sporting world
which were once famous, and which it will be our pleasure to hand down in this complete history of the fights
for the championship :—

"Articles of agreement entered into 17th day of
March, 1863, between John Carmel Heenan and Thomas
King. The said John Carmel Heenan agrees to fight
the said Thomas King a fair stand-up fight according to
the new rules of the Ring, by which the said John

Carmel Heenan and the said Thomas King agree to be bound. The said fight shall be for the sum of £1,000 a-side, and shall take place on the eighth day of December, 1863, within 100 miles of London. In pursuance of this agreement £100 a-side are now deposited in the hands of Mr. John Coney, who shall transmit the same to the editor of *Bell's Life.* The second deposit of £50 a-side shall be made at Mr. William Richardson's, the Blue Anchor, Shoreditch, on Thursday, March 26th; the third of £50 a-side to be made on April the 9th; the fourth £50 a-side on April 23rd; the fifth of £50 a-side on May 2nd; the sixth of £50 on May the 21st; the seventh of £50 a-side on June 4th; the eighth of £50 a-side on June 18th; the ninth of £50 a-side on July 2nd; the tenth of £50 a-side on July 16th; the eleventh of £50 a-side on July 30th; the twelfth of £50 a-side on August 13th; the thirteenth of £50 a-side on August 27th; the fourteenth of £50 a-side on Sept. the 10th; the fifteenth of £50 a side on Sept. the 24th; the sixteenth of £50 a-side on Oct. 27th; the seventeenth of £50 a-side on Nov. 5th; and the final deposit of £100 a-side on Nov. 26th at Mr. William Richardson's, Blue Anchor, as above, when the men shall mutually agree to the place of fighting. The said deposits to be made between the hours of eight and ten p.m. on the days and at the houses named. Either part failing, to forfeit the money down. The houses at which deposits shall be made shall be named by each party alternately and be made in London. The place of the next deposit to be named at the staking of the previous one, Heenan having to name the place of the third deposit. The men to be in the ring between the hours of 10 a.m. and 1 p.m. on the day named, or the man absent to forfeit the money. But in the event of magisterial interference the referee shall decide the next time and place of meeting, the same day if possible. The expenses of the ropes and stakes shall be borne mutually, Mr. Dowling, the editor of *Bell's Life in London*, to be referee. Two umpires to be chosen on the ground; and, in case of dispute between them, the decision of the referee to be final. In pursuance of this agreement we hereunto attach our names.

" Witness: H. A. REED.   JOHN CARMEL HEENAN,
                          CHARLES BUSH, for
                          THOMAS KING."

So everything went on merrily, the deposits being paid regularly, and Heenan and King went on a sparring tour, making money literally hand over fist.

And now a few words about the American. He was born on May 4, 1835, and was a smith by trade. His

American battles we have already referred to, his battle
with Morrissey being the most important, although he
suffered defeat. This was in 1858. A year later Aaron
Jones went to America, and, meeting Heenan, became
his trainer, and was partly instrumental in bringing
about the big match with Tom Sayers, which we
have already described at some length. Perhaps this

TOM KING.

great fight was the most exciting of the past
century; but it had a very unsatisfactory finish, and
Heenan was much displeased, and he shortly afterwards
returned to America with the intention of retiring from
the ring unless he could get a match for £1,000 a-side.
Although he never issued a challenge really his backers
put it about that he was willing to enter the ring again

on those terms and the news was spread to England,
with the result of the match being made as described
above. We believe, too, it was somewhere about this
time that Heenan was married to Adah Isaac Menken,
the fascinating woman who later broke the hearts of
half the fast youths of London when she came over
here and played Mazeppa at Astley's Theatre, Westminster, and John Heenan did not lead a very happy
life with the lady.

He was, however, one of the nicest fellows you could
possibly meet, and nobody would have imagined him to
have been a pugilist, or that he had been brought up in
the rough trade of a smith and miner. Like Tom King
he was one of nature's gentlemen, and proved himself
so after he finished his pugilistic career with the battle
we are about to describe.

We might here digress a moment and give a word
picture of him, sketched by Mr. John Hawthorne, who
was at Harvard University when Heenan returned
after his battle with King. Mr. Hawthorne says:—He
was a tall, grave, urbane gentleman, with reddish-brown
hair and a dark moustache. He wore black broadcloth
and a tall hat, and diamonds sparkled here and there.
A sand bag was hung up in the college gymnasium.
It was suspended by a long rope to a horizontal bar,
half way from floor to ceiling. The strongest man in
the college—and he was pretty strong—had once hit the
bag so hard that it swung up on a level with the bar.
It was suggested that Heenan should hit the bag. He
glanced at it, then stripped off his black broadcloth,
and laid it, with its silk lining outward, on the back of
a chair. Then he walked up to the bag, poised himself
for a moment, and his arm shot out. The bag flew up
with an impetus that carried it completely round the
bar once and nearly round a second time. As it fell,
Heenan sadly shook his head and turned away. No one
spoke ; but as he slowly invested himself into the silk
lining he remarked, "Boys, you should have seen me
when I was fit ! "

He was as fit as a fiddle when he came over to meet
Tom King, so it can be imagined what a punch from
that brawny arm must have meant. He trained at
Newmarket, in company with his brother, who came
to England with him, and Jack Macdonald, and his
feats as a pedestrian during his training were extraordinary. One writer who visited him at the metropolis
of gee-gees writes: " I saw the American champion
stripped, and could not help thinking that his muscular
development was overdone, and he appeared consequently somewhat shoulder-tied. Every muscle was

developed to a gigantic size, every tendon and sinew was distinctly visible, and it was generally accepted that such a specimen of a herculean frame had not been seen in the ranks of fistic warriors for many a long year."

King also made magnificent progress, and as the day drew near for the settlement the excitement both in the East and West became intense. Nothing had been settled as to the rendezvous in the early part of the week, and so well had the secret as to arrangements been kept that the outsiders, who at that time infested these meetings, were totally in the dark.

London Bridge was ultimately given out as the place to meet, at the last moment, and 5 a.m. the hour of Thursday, December 8, 1863. Here is a description of the absence of the "ugly" element written by Mr. Henry Downton Miles, a well-known sporting writer of the time, who attended all prize fights, and was a reporter upon *Bell's Life*: "The cut-purse family were wiping the frosty icicles from their noses in the West, when they should have been looking out for squalls in the South-Eastern horizon. The delightful result was that the congregation of the fistic art passed the thin dark line of worn and weary 'snapper-badgers.' The arrangements of the 'illegitimate conveyancers' were most excellent; everybody was comfortably taken in and done for, whilst the presence of the King volunteers set the foot of authority down with a crash upon all attempts at 'rigging the market.' In fact, one might have thought that he was going to an early ploughing match, whilst the 'Yahoo' business didn't run so high as the song of an old tea-kettle. Indeed, the ugly element was wise in the course it was constrained to adopt, for had it done otherwise, there was force enough present to have brought every atom of it to grief."

The railway company had taken every precaution for the preservation of order, and Superintendent Bradford, with a powerful body of police, occupied the yard and approaches to the station. Altogether it was a most comfortable send-off by the train, consisting of thirty carriages and two engines.

CHAPTER LXII.

A PLEASURABLE EXCURSION. — DESCRIPTION BY AN EYE-
WITNESS. — TOM KING AND J. C. HEENAN. — A TERRIFIC
INTERNATIONAL BATTLE.

Although it was December 8 of the year 1863 that the
start was made from London Bridge, the weather was so
mild that it might have been mistaken for an April
morning, for it was damp and clammy, something
like the weather that bowed out the last century, and
which, according to the old woman's saying, that "a
green Christmas makes a fat churchyard," must have
been accountable for many shuffling off their mortal
coils before the year 1864 had far advanced.

One writer gives a graphic description of the journey
to the battlefield, which we will condense. All being
aboard, and ample time having been given for the
stragglers to come up, at a quarter-past six o'clock we
glided out of the station into the dark, clammy, muggy
morning, with the weather so mild that it was difficult
to believe that we were in the month of December.
We were an orderly lot, for as the train trailed
along over the housetops, through Bermondsey, and on
to New Cross, there was an absence of the noisy singing
and shouting which usually accompany these excursions,
making the early morning hideous, and awakening the
peacefully slumbering inhabitants along the route. On
we dashed at a rattling pace, and by the dim light of
the primitive oil lamp (what a contrast to the electric
light of to-day!) we were enabled to take stock of our
fellow-passengers. Amongst them we recognised several
of the Corinthian contingent, and as the conversation
opened up we could tell by the "dwal, don't yer
know," that we were in the company of lordlings and
swells of high degree. As the grey dawn in the east
broke before us, and trees and solitary houses on the
wayside appeared in a spectre-like manner, we slackened
pace, and glided noiselessly, but exceedingly cautiously,
through Reigate Junction; and there we disturbed a
fine strong covey of early "blue birds," evidently there
assembled for anything but our entertainment. There
was a look of disappointment upon the mugs of these

gentry belonging to the Surrey County Constabulary as
we showed them the red bull's-eye on the tail of the
last carriage and continued our journey. The day was
then breaking, a white mist hanging over the
landscape, and the gravest fears existed as to the
morning turning into a soaker, and that gamps and water
proofs would be in requisition, when the heavy clouds
were chased away with a stiff breeze and patches
of blue appeared upon the sky where King Sol was
about to ascend his throne. We were then travelling at
a speed of nearly fifty miles an hour, dashing
past hamlet, village, and farmhouse, and as we
shot through Tunbridge Wells we shortly after
slackened speed and drew up at a secluded spot
where the command was given to dismount. As we
scrambled down the embankment the sun burst forth in
all the magnificence of a May morning. It was a
quarter past nine as the straggling crowd followed my
leader up a steep hill, which necessitated a lot of collar-
work, and made Falstaffian sections of the company puff
and blow, our hearts being as light as a batch of school-
boys out for a treat. "Halt" was called after walking
about half a mile, and the staff-officers drove the stakes
into a capital piece of turf covering a field at Wadhurst,
near Frant, just below Tunbridge Wells.

So according to accounts this was quite an agreeable
excursion, unlike most of the expeditions which
led so frequently to disgust and disappointment
at this particular period of the history of the Ring.
There was little time lost, and the men were soon
in the twenty-four foot enclosure, Tom King being
seconded by Jerry Noon and Bos Tyler, and Heenan by
Jack Macdonald and Tom Sayers. All was ready and
the men were stripped in their corners, when there came
an objection as to the choice of the referee. Three-
quarters of an hour was wasted in the endeavour to find
one who would undertake the ticklish job. They were
unsuccessful in finding anybody to undertake the post,
so it was decided that *Bell's Life* representative should
officiate, and everything was arranged for the great
battle, which proved to be second only to that between
the Benicia Boy and Tom Sayers, and was one of the
most stubbornly fought encounters that we have had to
record.

The journals of the day were full of the battle, and
we cannot do better than cull from some of the principal
organs, which as a rule ignored prize fights but could not
resist the temptations to report this great fight, for it
was the one battle that will remain in the annals of
championship fights as the last and greatest of all save

that between Heenan and Sayers. Yet it was more
satisfactory, for in the latter no decision was come to,
but in this we had the undoubted supremacy of the
Londoner over the splendid American pugilist proved
without question.

But to the ring-side with the reporters of the day.
One says : "Never did a handsomer, finer brace of
pugilists ever step into the arena. King was the taller
of the two, but was quite a stone lighter, for Heenan
had filled up considerably since his fight with Sayers,
and in our opinion to the detriment of his chances of
success, for he seemed clumsy, and his limbs were
unwieldly. He also wore a jaded appearance upon
close inspection, although he kept up a cheerful expression, whilst King was as serious as a mute at a funeral.
Notwithstanding this the Londoner looked better than
ever we had seen him, his smooth, white skin glisten-
ing like polished ivory in the morning sun. He was
perhaps hardly of the build of the ideal pugilist, but
his symmetry was perfect, especially his arms, a cast
of one which is, by-the-bye, in the College of Surgeons
and pronounced by anatomists as being superb."

Now we will give extracts from the several descriptions of the fight itself, although in the space at our disposal it would be impossible to describe round after
round :--

"Quickly sparring, whilst the spectators kept silently
watching every move, they almost imperceptibly came
closer and closer until well within distance. A hurried
movement on the part of Heenan as he moved off
enabled King to get just out of distance ; but he likewise
was not near enough for the return. Wasting no time
after these failures, they came together, and whack !
whack ! told of a couple of counter hits. Again the
sounds of blows were heard, and King jumped back, but
Heenan dashed after him with such force that they were
both quickly on the ropes, and the Benicia Boy's arm
was round Tom's neck. But King lurched forward,
and again they were in the centre of the ring, the
American holding him still round the throat. 'Get
down, Tom ; he'll choke you if you don't,' was yelled
out by the crowd. But King peppered away at his
opponent's ribs, and Heenan let go his hold, when they
gripped each other and rolled over, Tom underneath.
Mr. Dowling, the referee, then entered the ring and
cautioned Heenan as to hugging, pointing out that it
might lead to disqualification on a question of foul.

"King had received a rare shaking, and Heenan was
blowing like a grampus, and in the next round the
former was thrown heavily. The Britisher was intent

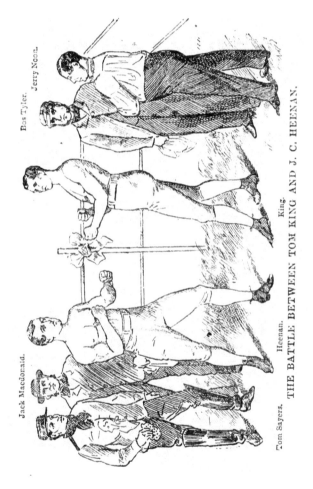

THE BATTLE BETWEEN TOM KING AND J. C. HEENAN.

upon outfighting, whilst it was evident that the
American's line of business was wrestling, and threw his
opponent so severely that had the ground been hard
instead of yielding Tom King would certainly, after one
fall early in the fight, never have faced his man again, so
severe was it."

Here is a description of the fifth round, King having
been thrown heavily in the two previous bouts :—Heenan
was much distressed, and his efforts .had undoubtedly
told upon him, for his great chest was heaving as if it
would burst. Tom worked around him until the sun
was dazzling in the Yankee's eyes, and for the moment
the boy seemed at a loss, when King, seeing his
opportunity, stepped in, and with the swiftness
of lightning put in a crushing blow full in the face
of Heenan, sending the whole of his weight behind
it. "It sounded like the splash of a wet fish thrown upon
a marble slab, and the blood poured in streams from
Heenan's mouth and nose."

And so the great fight progressed, King getting all the
best of the hitting; but Heenan, throwing his man frequently and with fearful force, so in the fourteenth round
everybody thought the battle was over. They fought
desperately for some time, and here is a description of
the finish of the round by an eye witness :—"Heenan
threw his arm round the Londoner, and with sheer
force raised him off his legs, whilst we fancied we could
almost hear his bones crush, as, like a bear or a boa
constrictor, he hugged and nipped his helpless antagonist.
He then in his quivering grasp wheeled him round
and gave him such a cross-buttock as never was seen
beo re, and Tom came down with a thud that seemed
to make the very earth where we stood tremble. King
lay senseless. As his seconds rolled him over to carry
him to the corner, his head fell back, and his half-closed
eyes had a vacant, glazed look belonging to the
lifeless, whilst his arms swung limply at his side.
'It's all over !' was the cry from every part of the
ring."

Not so, however, for Bob Tyler bit his ear, and did
everything in his power to resuscitate the fallen warrior,
and the astute Jerry Noon rushed across the ring and made
an appeal to the referee, declaring that King had been
kicked. There was naturally a fearful dispute and
wrangle, which gave King considerably more than the
allotted time to come round, and as he showed symptoms of recovery, Tyler shouted into his ear, "For
God's sake, Tom, pull yourself together before it's too
late! .Remember, for your mother's sake, Tom, £200
will save her from want." This did it, as "Time !

Time! Time!" was called, he staggered to his feet and faced his opponent once more. Neither seemed in a hurry to recommence, for Heenan was nearly blind, but in the succeeding round he managed to deliver a tremendous blow full in the face, which sent Tom staggering, and he fell upon his back. The Americans were frantic with delight, and it certainly seemed to be long odds on the Boy.

Again and again King was thrown, but the efforts on the part of Heenan seemed to take more out of him than King, and at length they faced each other like two drunken men, the Yankee apparently in a state of stupor. Then King amidst the encouraging shouts of his party, saw how matters stood and pulled himself together, and to quote another account, "His nostrils dilated, his lips quivering, and his eyes starting from his head with the last flicker of excitement, went to his helpless foe and administered blow after blow upon the face, which resembled now a raw buttock of beef. Heenan's head swayed to and fro as Tom hit him, first one side then the other, and the blood spurted from nose, mouth, and eyes, until his visage presented a sickening spectacle."

It was all over, the brave American dropped to the ground, deaf to the call of "Time," and Tom King was proclaimed conqueror. . . . Neither entered the Ring again; but how different their successes in after life. King became a rich man, having become one of the leading bookmakers of the day and died in affluence. Poor Heenan had a rough time of it, for his domestic life was very unhappy, and would form quite a romance had we space to go into it at length. It will be remembered that his wife was the beautiful Ada Isaac Menkin, a woman with a strange mixture of love and infidelity—a woman who won the hearts of men wherever she went, and was a great favourite with the public in London in the sixties. Amongst her greatest admirers was one of the greatest living poets, for the charming Ada wrote verse herself which was admired by Charles Dickens. It will be interesting to quote from her poem and print the great novelist's letter in acknowledgment for a copy of the book which was dedicated to Dickens. And this was the wife of a pugilist !

Visions of Beauty, of Light, and of Love;
  Born in the soul of a dream,
Lost like the phantom bird, under the dove,
  When she flies over the stream.

Leaves pallid, and sombre and ruddy,
  Dead fruits of the fugitive years ;
Some stained as with wine and made bloody,
  And some as with tears.

Here is a copy of the letter written to her by Charles
Dickens :—

Gads Hill Place,
Higham, by Rochester, Kent,
Monday, October 21, 1867.

Dear Miss Menkin,—I shall have great pleasure in
accepting your dedication, and I thank you for your portrait
as a highly remarkable specimen of photography. I also
thank you for the verse enclosed in your note. Many such
enclosures come to me, but few so pathetically written, and
fewer still so modestly sent.--Faithfully yours,

CHARLES DICKENS.

CHAPTER LXIII.

A YANKEE FIZZLE.—JEM MACE V. COBURN AND JOE GOSS.—
ONE ROUND FOR THE BELT. — A SLASHING BATTLE IN A
SIXTEEN FEET RING.

After Mace had met and defeated Joe Goss, within
two months he was challenged by Joe Coburn, who had
come over from America. Although a naturalised
citizen of New York he was really a native of Middleton,
in County Armagh, Ireland, having been born in
that place on July 30, 1835. This Irish-American, it
would seem, was thought a great deal of in the land of
Stars and Stripes, although his performances in the ring
were of no particular consequence. His first appearance
was with Ned Price, with whom he fought a draw after
going through seventy rounds in three hours. In 1857 he
fought Harry Gubben, for £100 a-side, defeating him in
less than half an hour.

Coburn then retired for six years, making a re-appear-
ance with Mike M. Coole, of St. Louis, a big fellow of
little or no science. Coburn easily defeated him, and was
dubbed champion of America. After this, Heenan
having retired, Mike found nobody willing to try conclusions with him, so he took a bar saloon in Grand
Street, New York. In the January of 1864 he sent a
challenge over to England offering to fight Mace, who at
once accepted, and the Irishman came across the
Atlantic. No little interest was centred in the affair,
for the stakes decided upon were the then large sum of
£1,000, but owing to the dead set that had been made

against prize fighting it was thought safer to bring the
battle off in Ireland.

Many ardent votaries of sport journeyed with Mace
to Dublin, but the affair turned out to be a regular sell,
and after much shuffling about on the part of Coburn
the affair ended in smoke, because the parties could not
agree as to who was a fitting person to take office,
as referee. The representative of *Bell's Life* was chosen
but the Americans would not accept him, and desired
that a friend of Coburn's, named James Bowler, should
be appointed. Harry Brunton, who represented Jem
Mace, naturally would not agree to this, and a stormy
half hour ensued. This was the day before the fight
was to take place, and the meeting being held at Mr.
Woodruff's house in Dublin. No decision could be come
to, and the company separated.

In the meantime Jem Mace quarrelled with Brunton,
and the latter washed his hands of the whole affair, and
came back to England, and on the day when the fight
should have taken place he sailed for Holyhead.
Coburn and his party went out with the ropes and
stakes, but were followed by a posse of Irish constabulary, who threatened to arrest them if a breach of
the peace were committed. But as it takes two men to
bring off a prize fight, and Mace was absent, the police
had nothing to do but to look on. The ring was formed,
Coburn entered, and after the stipulated time had elapsed
claimed the stakes. Of course this was not allow-
able, as the articles specified that a referee was to be
appointed before 3 p.m. on the day before the battle, and
that had not been done. Jem Mace, in accordance with
the aforesaid article had to forfeit £100 towards Joe
Coburn's expenses of visiting this country, and the rest
of the money was returned to the two men. But this is
a long and somewhat uninteresting story which, however, must be told to link up our history of the fights
for the Championship, so we must devote a little space
to the doings of the two gladiators.

Here is the letter Mace sent to *Bell's Life* upon the
subject :—"Sir, I take the earliest opportunity of
informing you that I am greatly disappointed at not
being permitted to meet Coburn. I have, for the sake of
my backers, taken every pains in training, and to-day I
was never more fit or better in my life, as my trainer,
Milner, will certify. I do not consider myself well
treated, and Mr. Brunton, who never found a shilling of
my money, has taken everything to himself, and asserts
that he was solely responsible in getting gentlemen to
find me the amount required. Mr. Brunton suddenly
left me in Dublin, on Monday, with no xplanation,

Coburn had every opportunity if he wished to meet me,
and would, only through his representative choosing Mr.
Bowler, of whom I know nothing, and is also said to be a
brother-in-law to Coburn. I am most disappointed, and
how on earth could it be supposed that I should fight
with a referee who was a hundred miles away even when
proposed? I wished any representative of the press to
act, and Milner asked even Coburn's friend, Mr. Edwin
James, of the *New York Clipper*, when Mr. Smith of
Bell's Life was objected to, if he (Mr. James) would
stand, but he would not do so. Now as to the money
business. Every shilling that has been found me has
come from sportsmen who put their names down, I
trust, owing to my public reputation. Coburn placed an
insurmountable obstacle against our fighting, and, as I
have reason to suppose, Coburn was not even training, and
evaded his engagement with no intention of fighting,
I consider myself entitled to the stakes.—James Mace."

Anyhow the stakes were returned, and the collapse of
the "Great Windbag," as the match was called, became
complete, Jem being a hundred pounds poorer. To give
Mace his due, however, he met all his supporters at the
following Newmarket races, and offered them back their
money, although in most cases it was not accepted.

After this fizzle, which took place in 1864, Jem waived
all claim to the championship, and settled down to
business, determining that if he went in for fighting
again it would be in America. During the period that
Mace was getting "rusty" two young aspirants for
championship honours met. Their names were Joe
Wormald and Andrew Marsden, the first-named winning
and claiming the title. An account of this battle, to
make our series of Fights for the Championship complete, will appear in a future chapter, together with a
short notice of the men's careers, but at present we
shall deal only with Mace's battles. Well, on Wormald
making claim for the first position in the ring, the old
champion's warlike spirit returned to him, and Jem
could not rest until he had thrown down the gauntlet to
the successful novice, and articles were duly signed for the
men to fight on September 26, 1865, just two years after
Mace's previous appearance in the Ring, which it will be
remembered was with Joe Goss, in the September of 1863.

There was a good deal of surprise at Jem's reappear-
ance, and many thought that the battle would never
come off, and that there was a screw loose somewhere.
Mace was very confident, and at Doncaster races, a week
before they were to meet, he said to his numerous friends:
" If you are going to lay out any money upon the event,
mind, back me, for if young Wormald should meet me,

it's a guinea to a gooseberry that I beat him, for good as
he may be you must remember that he is not a Tom King."
"*If* young Wormald should meet me," seemed a strange
remark for Mace to make only a few days before the
contest was to come off. The fact was there had been
a rumour to the effect that he would *not* face the ex-
champion, and Jem had heard it. This turned out to
be only too true, for within a few days of the Doncaster
St. Leger there appeared the following certificate in
the sporting journals :—

"St. Bartholomew's Hospital, September 21, 1865.

"I do hereby certify that Joseph Wormald is
under my care at St. Bartholomew's Hospital as an out-
patient, suffering with periostitis of the right humerus,
consequent upon injury.

"John Astley Bloxham, House Surgeon."

He had whilst using some heavy dumb bells strained
the muscles of his arm so seriously that going into
the ring was quite out of the question. On the 27th of
the month Mace called upon the stakeholder, and received
the nice little sum of £120, forfeit money. After this
Jem was determined to have another try for the belt, so
he issued a challenge to fight anybody in the world on
the usual terms, £200 a-side, and the belt, within twelve
months, money ready at Harry Montague's (a great
friend of Jem's, who afterwards became his secretary),
the Ship Inn, Briggate, Leeds.

To Jem's amazement, the gauntlet was taken up by
his old antagonist, Joe Goss, who had been so decisively
beaten by Mace a couple of years previously. Mace was
at this period proprietor of the Strawberry Recrea-
tion Grounds, Liverpool, where he had foot-racing, a
gymnasium, and, of course, boxing. He had made many
friends in the great seaport, and when it became known
that he was matched again with Goss, he could have
had four times the money for the stakes had he needed
it. Mace trained at his own grounds, and Goss remained
at his native town, Wolverhampton. The arrangements
were left in the hands of Jack Lawley and Nat Langham,
for the start was to be made from London, and The
Mitre (Nat's house in St. Martin's Lane) was to be the
headquarters of the Norwich man.

The matter was kept very dark, and the men did not
come to London until the evening before the fight, and
the greatest secrecy was preserved as to the whereabouts,
as the authorities were down more than ever on prize
fighting. Those who got the "office" from Nat Langham had to be away by 5.30.

But to describe the journey to this miserable meeting
will be only waste of space, and to give details of the

farce would but worry our readers. After entering the ring they stood fencing and sparring for some considerable time, and in spite of the calls from the spectators for the men to fight neither would open the ball. Mace at last caught Goss lightly on the cheek-bone, and was countered by Joe on the nose. Then came more spar-

JOE WORMALD.

ring and fooling about the ring, and after thirty minutes, during which time but two blows had been struck, the audience became impatient and declared that it was a "cross." The referee, however, exhibited great patience, and declared that he would remain there until the next morning, so long as the men faced each other and sparred. But neither would go for the other, and at length they

stood still, folded their arms, and looked at each other.
Preposterous as the idea was that a championship
battle should end in a draw, there was no help for it,
and the referee, after repeatedly calling on the men to
fight, reluctantly, and amidst the indignant yells of the
crowd, pronounced the "Great Fight," consisting of one
unfinished round, to be a draw.

Of course there was an undisguised feeling of disgust
throughout the sporting world, and both men's reputation suffered to no little extent. Goss declared that he
fought to the orders of his backers, and that it would
have been madness on his part to go to close quarters
and fight Mace ; whilst the latter explained matters in a
long letter, portions of which we quote in justice to the old
champion, who is still alive. He wrote :—" In taking my
accustomed training in company with Brighton and
Thomas (the Northern Deer), my instep gave way, and
I found that strong rubbing must be resorted to ; a
medical man examined it and ordered embrocation to
be used, and an elastic stocking to be worn. For three
weeks my leg was most painful, and prevented me from
taking exercise, so necessary to insure a victory.
Only imagine what my feelings were, knowing as I did
any information of my breakdown reaching the ears of
my opponent, or any show of lameness in the ring, would
be sure to add a stimulus to him more than ever, and
in his accustomed manner cause him to harass and tire
me, by delay and dwelling. Hence I had to be quiet
and passive, afraid it should get out. My trainer used
every means in his power to bring me to a cure. I dared
not even tell my friends and backers, lest it should get
before the public, and hence have lost their money as
well as my own . . . I have gained nothing, but have
been a great loser, by what appears to have disappointed
you, and many others, except this, that I have the satisfaction of knowing that those who backed me have,
through my sheer generalship, been recouped the sums
they laid out upon me, which had my opponent known
of my lameness might not have been the case . . . I
have the full satisfaction of knowing that I held the belt
for five years against all comers, great or small ; that I
have taken more money from your office [*Bell's Life*]
than any man who ever entered the ring ; and that my
conscience tells me that in my last encounter I did that
which was right, although to my own loss, in saving the
money of my backers and friends. For me to have
forced the fight would have been sheer madness. I can
only compare my breakdown to that of a favourite horse,
but in my case it is not p.p."

This we must take as sufficient for an explanation, for

it is quite certain that Jem Mace did sprain his foot badly. Nevertheless it was a most unsatisfactory performance, and they both came in for a deal of abuse. It was suggested that the only thing left was for them to meet once more, and fight it out in a manly straightforward manner. Joe Goss, who was certainly more to blame than Mace for the *fiasco*, was looked upon as the right man to make the first move, and his friends urged him to such an extent that Joe issued the following challenge :—
" I will make a match to fight anyone from £100 to £500 a-side, from 11st to 12st (thus giving away nearly a stone), to come off in six weeks or six months. Mace has boasted of what he can do with me if he is well. Let him get well, and I will meet him at any time, any weight, and for any sum."

This was a fearless sort of a challenge, and was greatly approved by the sporting fraternity, and of course Jem Mace at once replied by saying that he was quite prepared to fight Goss for anything from one to five hundred, but on the understanding that they should do battle in a 16ft ring instead of a 24ft, and that he should have £10 for expenses. Mace sent up £50 deposit, which was immediately covered by Goss, and the two men met at Mr. Kelley's house in Liverpool, where articles were signed. Besides the clause about the size of the arena another was inserted stipulating that the seconds should get out of the ring immediately the men were delivered at the scratch. Their names were affixed on June 20, 1866, and the date selected for the battle August 6.

There was plenty of time for Goss to get fit, but Mace had more difficulty, as his foot turned out to be worse than was anticipated. However, he went to Llandudno and took plenty of sea baths, and all went well with him. Goss went to Northampton and made fair progress, although he did not take the care of himself that he might, having too many visitors. Besides he had a great difficulty in getting the whole of the money, and had to make two or three journeys to Wolverhampton in order to have a whip round amongst his friends there.

There was some anxiety as to how this, their third meeting, would turn out, but everything looked fair and above board, so there was a very good muster at St. Paul's Wharf, where the steamer was to start. Unfortunately it was a miserable day, with the wind howling, making it a very unpleasant journey to Purfleet, where the ring was formed without interruption.

Directly they commenced the battle it was seen that both were in earnest, for Goss in his old dashing style rushed into close quarters, but the scientific Mace was too quick for him, and cleverly avoiding,

dealt Joe blow after blow until he literally fought him
on to his knees. Throughout it was a manfully fought
battle, with no flinching on either side. Indeed, we
have heard Mace say that it was one of the hardest
contests in which he had ever been engaged, and the
perusal of the accounts of it in the journals of the day
prove it to have been a slashing affair.

We have no space to follow the combat through, for
we have already devoted many pages to Mace's fights,
and must finish with his career as champion in the
next chapter. The 16ft ring made a wonderful difference, and the pace was much smarter. In the fifth round
Mace proved his superiority, and Goss was dreadfully
punished, and in the fourteenth he had taken a long
lead, victory being his, bar accidents.

Although Joe Goss fought pluckily it was no good he was
over-matched, and in the nineteenth round the sponge
should have been thrown up, but the brave fellow would
come again, only to be knocked down. In the twenty-
first there were shouts of "take him away." But he
made one final rush at Jem, who hit him with both
fists upon his disfigured face, and Joe fell forward
senseless. It was a fine battle and atoned for the former
fiasco, and Jem Mace was looked upon as a veritable hero
on his return to Liverpool, being received by thousands of
people, and taken from the station in a carriage and four,
accompanied by a brass band.

CHAPTER LXIV.

BATTLE IN A BEDROOM.—A CLEVER CAPTURE.—JEM MACE AND NED BALDWIN.—A SCENE IN COURT.

And now we come to the closing fights for the Championship by the most scientific and cleverest fighter of his
time, for there can be but one opinion, Jem Mace,
by his several contests that we have already described, had proved himself far above any of his con-
temporaries as a boxer. Endowed with a magnificent constitution, great strength, and marvellous
agility, he was the ideal man for a champion. Besides
which he had his heart and soul in the sport, and
although a few times in his career he proposed to throw
up the sponge, we still find him to-day as enthusiastic as

ever, and a marvel for his age. We have seen him not
so long ago put in a few blows with the gloves that
would astonish some of the youngsters, and had he but
the wind no better demonstrator of the fistic art could
be found to give displays at the "National Sporting,"
for Jem Mace would not descend to the hugging habits,
which we regret to say is a canker in boxing of the
present day. Even now, though, Jem for a quick dust
up would be an ugly customer, and although he is
on the verge of three score years and ten, he is as
straight as a dart and (let me tell you in a whisper) the
father of a young family.

After the old champion's fight in the sixteen foot ring
with Joe Goss, that being their third meeting, Jem
Mace had a long rest, for that event, it will be remembered, took place in the August of 1865, and it was not
until the October of 1867 that he threw down the
gauntlet to Ned Baldwin (of whom we shall have more
to say in future chapters), of Waterford, known as
the Irish giant. Baldwin had been an aspirant for the
championship, had been beaten by Andrew Marsden,
and had defeated George Isles. He then met Marsden
a second time and turned the tables, but forfeited to Joe
Wormald. Then Jem Mace, who had never got his
ankle quite well, and was unable for a long period to
train, challenged the Irishman, and the following
articles were drawn up and signed:—

"Articles of agreement entered into on June 17, 1867,
between James Mace and Edward Baldwin. The said
Edward Baldwin agrees to fight the said James Mace
for £200 a-side and the Belt (open to £500 a-side) on
Tuesday, October 15, 1867, within a hundred miles of
London, according to the new rules of the Prize Ring,
the money not to be given up unless fairly won by a
fight. In pursuance of this agreement £26 a-side is now
staked in the hands of the editor of *Bell's Life*, who shall
be final stakeholder, and name a referee, it being
mutually agreed that two persons now named by the
men alternately receive, until the last deposit,
which shall be made at a house named by
Mace, when the whole of the money is to be made up.
The place of fighting to be agreed upon between the
backers of the men at a meeting to be held at the office
of the stakeholder on Wednesday, 4th, between two and
four o'clock,

"Witness, G. ROBERTS.   Signed, EDWARD BALDWIN.
      WILLIAM RILEY.   JAMES MACE."

Baldwin went into training with Jack Hicks at
Surbiton; but he had to remove to Walton-on-Thames,
and afterwards shift to Epsom, so much were the

authorities on the alert and determined to stop the fight.
Mace first went into training at Hammersmith, then to
Margate, Yarmouth, and finally Newmarket. He was,
however, so much harassed that he came nearer town,
and stayed at Woodford, eventually making his escape
from there to Herne Hill, where he was arrested. But
as this will form a somewhat amusing episode in Mace's
career, we will tell it in the words of his cousin, Pooley
Mace, who gave us the description from his own lips,
and who is, we believe, still alive, and residing in New
York. Here it is:—

" Well, you want me to tell you what happened to the
police, and that Baldwin affair. It was about the
warmest ten minutes I ever had to do with, and I shall
never forget it as long as I live. It all ended happily
enough, but I've often thought since that it might have
meant the next public appearance for Jem, myself,
and Young Gus (another cousin of ours) in
front of the Newgate Prison ; for, you know,
they used to string them up outside at that
time, and I've often wondered whether the good old
patrons of the ring and the cream of Corinthians would
have been present to have witnessed the champion's last
fight against a chap they call Death, who would certainly have knocked him out in no time and claimed
the colours—a black flag tied to the stakes. But, seriously
though, to this day I don't know how it was Jem did
not do for that Inspector Silverton. But there, I'll tell
you all about it. You will remember that the authorities
had sworn that they'd put down all the big meetings
that attracted the roughs. The little ones they didn't
trouble their heads about, and, of course, the fight for
the Championship which was to come off between
Jem and the Big 'Un, Ned Baldwin, was the talk
of the town and the country too. In fact, nothing
so important had been on the cards since the
battle between Sayers and Heenan and Jem's two
turns with King and Sam Hurst. The consequence
was we were chevied all over the place, and I
don't know how many shifts we had to make from our
various training quarters. We heard that there was a
warrant out for Baldwin ; but, curiously enough,
nothing of the kind had been applied for against Jem.
By dint of dodging about and being posted daily as to
the movements of the ' coppers,' we managed to keep
out of harm's way, and a few days before the fight (bar
accidents on the day) we felt pretty safe and sure that the
affair so far as we were concerned, would come off all
right. Our only anxiety was about Baldwin ; but we
knew that Jack Hicks had him in hand, and

that Jack was as wide as they're made, and could dodge the blues. Well, on the Monday, the day before the fight, Jack Coney, who was, with his pals, finding the £200 for Jem's stakes, thought it would be better for us to move from Woodford, where we had finally taken up our quarters, to a station down the line, so as to avoid running the gauntlet through London on the morning of the fight. So a four-wheeled cab was chartered, and Jem, Gus, Bos Tyler, and I were driven right away from Woodford to Herne Hill, for it was decided that we were to make our trip upon the London, Chatham, and Dover line. We didn't stop on the road—that is, we didn't get out to show ourselves—and arrived at our new quarters about half-past five in the afternoon. The house where we were to stop belonged to the station-master, whom we knew we could trust. So we felt quite snug in our new drum. There was a nice apartment furnished as a bed-sitting-room for Jem on the first floor, and the rest of us were to sleep upstairs. I suppose it would have been about eight o'clock when Jem, who had taken his rations, said he would turn in for the night, and he was soon in bed driving his pigs to market, and looking in his sleep as happy and contented as if the battle was over, that he was wearing the belt and pocketing the stakes. Tyler had gone up to bed too, and Gus and I had taken off our boots and coats, and were having a quiet game at cards in Jem's room. Presently I heard a knock—not a very loud knock—at the street door, which was at the end of the landing just outside the room where we were sitting. The landlady opened the door, and I heard voices, but I could not hear what was said, for we were shut in. Somehow or other I felt as if all wasn't quite right, and I said to Gussie, 'As sure as my name's Pooley, there's something wrong. Listen!' But before I could tell him anything further there was the devil of a row in the hall, a tramp of feet which there was no mistaking, and our door opened and in walked the Inspector, followed by I don't know how many officers. 'I want Jem Mace,' said he. Jem, who had been as sound as a bell all this time, sat up in bed rubbing his eyes and looking dazed, whilst I out with the light. In a second Jem was up. 'You want Jem Mace, you ——, do you? Here he is, and you'll know it, too. Get out, you —— ——, or I'll break every —— jaw in the rooms.' I never heard Jem swear so much before, and I knew by the tone of his voice that he meant business. One of the bobbies struck a light, and there was Jem standing up in his shirt with a chair over his head, and I thought there would be brains all over the wall-paper in a trip. As the officers came towards him (fortunately, as it turned out) he hurled the chair at one of their heads, and just missed, but it went smash into the wash-stand and crockery, breaking the lot, and kicking up a devil of a noise. What occurred then I can hardly make out, for the room was full of men. Jem was shouting for Bos Tyler, and squaring himself up on the defensive, and the bobbies made a rush, tearing Jem's shirt off, and leaving him as naked as when he was born. I've often thought what a funny sight he presented—the Champion of England shaping, stark naked. But you could see all his points, and he looked wonderfully fit, I can tell you.

JEM MACE

Well, there was a short parley, and Jem was quiet for a bit, when he commenced swearing again and declared that he would not be taken alive. But it was no go, there were too many of them and before he knew where he was they had slipped on the bracelets, and declared him their prisoner. This was the signal for another fierce outburst of temper, and Jem with an oath broke away and made for the window, through which he would have certainly gone into the street, just as he was without a rag on, if it hadn't been for me persuading him, and the officers getting in front of him. Well, to cut a long story short we were all three formally arrested, athough Silverton had no warrant. Jem quieted down, got

dressed, and the three of us were walked off, taken in a
cab to Marlborough Street Police Station, it being then
getting on for midnight. The inspector on duty refusing to listen to the production of bail, we were
politely conducted to the cells, and, as you may
imagine, had a pretty pleasant night of it, for we knew
that the 'special' would leave Ludgate at an early
hour in the morning. So now you know the true story
of how we were 'copped' on the night before the Ned
Baldwin affair."

But to resume the story of the match. Baldwin
had gone on the previous day to Beckenham, and
when the train came along and stopped there to
pick Mace up Ned was waiting on the platform. But there
was no Jem, and by that time the news had spread, for
somebody had wired down the line notifying his arrest.
So the train brought back its ill-tempered freight, and
many who had been disappointed over the fight on their
return to London proceeded to Marlborough Street
Station to await Jem's appearance before the " beak."
On that morning of October 15, 1867, there was a
mixed crowd at the court, and when the magistrate
took his seat the place presented a strange appearance.
The Mace triplet of cousins were put in the dock, and
Inspector Silverton entered the witness-box. He described
his visit to the house at Herne Hill, and the scene enacted
therein, which we have already related in the words
of Pooley Mace. He further told of the journey to
town, and what James Mace replied to the charge.
Mace declared that he could get forty gentlemen who
would find five hundred pounds each to bail him,
that he would fight in spite of all the police and magistrates in the country, and that before the week was
over, too. Silverton also declared that Mace had sworn
to knock his (the inspector's) life out for arresting
him the very first chance he got. He further stated
that he had gone to Ludgate Hill Station at 3 a.m., and
had witnessed a disgraceful scene. Prize fighters were
using sticks, people were having their clothes torn off,
and windows of cabs were being smashed.

Mr. Lewis, Mace's counsel, objected to the evidence,
and said that Mace had no right legally to have
been taken without a warrant. But the magistrate
remarked that he should not consider that part of the
transaction. The prisoners were before him and he
intended to deal with them. He should require £500 in
himself and £250 in two sureties each. He observed
that there must be a deal of money made out of these
affairs, when the tickets cost £2, £3, and £4 for the
journey. Mace's counsel pleaded hard for him and said

that his pecuniary position was very bad, and for a long time he had only obtained his living by teaching the noble art of self-defence, and asking for such bail meant really sending him to prison for twelve months. His worship, however, disagreed with counsel, asserting that it was in his power to release him when he thought proper, saying " How do I know whether you will fight or not even if I release you on bail ? You have not pledged yourself." Jem, in a most evasive manner, replied " Yes, I do. I can't afford to pay, so I can't fight." " What is that you say ? " smartly rejoined the " beak." " I won't fight. I won't fight now under these circumstances." The bail was then reduced to £300 in himself, and £150 in two others ; whilst Pooley and Augustus were to find £100 and two in £50. The prisoners were then sent down, the two youngsters were immediately set at liberty, and later in the day Jemmy Shaw and Jack Cowey helped Jem Mace out.

Of course Mace was bound over, and Baldwin's warrant held good, so it was impossible for the men to meet. Baldwin declared that he would have the money if Mace would not go to France with him and carry out the engagement there or in the Channel Islands. It was then found that they and their sureties were just as liable, so that was out of the question. So Ned Baldwin claimed the money (which was a mean thing to do), declaring that he had fulfilled his part of the contract. Mace then retorted that the Baldwin party had given away his whereabouts to Inspector Silverton because they knew their man would be licked, whilst the other side accused Mace of getting himself caught and arrested.

And so another fight for the Championship came to grief, and Mace found himself in a very awkward position. Baldwin behaved in a disgraceful manner, and went to *Bell's Life* office, and threatened the stakeholder with a bludgeon. But the future destiny of the belt we must reserve to another chapter.

CHAPTER LXV.

FIELDS AND PASTURES NEW.—MACE IN AMERICA AND FIGHT
WITH TOM ALLEN.—TWO THOUSAND MILES TO SEE A
MILL.—LIFE IN THE CRESCENT CITY.

After Mace's persecution by Inspector Silverton, and
his harsh treatment by the magistrate, he thought his
native land was no place for him; so he determined to
journey to fields and pastures new, and take a trip to the
New World. It was in 1869 that Jem found himself in
New York. Although here in England the Ring was at
its lowest ebb, over there things pugilistic were looking up,
and our British Champion found no difficulty in making
a match. This he did with Tom Allen, who at that
time dubbed himself champion of America. Now
Tom was no more an American than Jem himself, for
he had fought many times in England, and had only
been away from his mother country a very short time.
Still he had proved himself an exceedingly good man
over there, for he had defeated Bill Davies, Gallagher,
and the notorious M'Coole, the latter having laid claim
to the British Championship during 1869.

Tom Allen had however, before going to America
done fairly well in the ring. Entering it in 1864 he beat
Rose for £25 a-side on January 28, after fighting ten
rounds in twenty-nine minutes. His next meeting was
with J. Parkinson, when after fighting eleven rounds,
only lasting twenty-three minutes, the police interfered
and the battle was adjourned. Another meeting was
arranged, but Parkinson failed to enter an appearance,
and Allen claimed the stakes. Tom's next match was
with Price for £25 a-side, at Holly Lane, Staffordshire,
on November 28, 1865; but the latter got himself
arrested, and Allen received the stakes. Then on
June 13, 1866, Allen fought George Iles, at Kings-
wood, near Birmingham, at catch weights, and defeated
him in a battle consisting of seventeen rounds lasting
sixty-two minutes. Then followed Tom's farewell performance with Joe Goss. The match was made for
£100 a-side, and they fought in the Bristol district on
March 5, 1867, but after making a brilliant stand they
were interrupted by the police.

Of course Jem Mace had seen his countryman fight on
several occasions, and knew his strength and form to

an ounce. The Americans, however, believed that his best fighting had been done with them, and he was acknowledged as their champion at the time that Jem visited New York. That the Yankees did have faith in Allen was proved by their readiness to back him. When it became known over here that they were to be matched the idea that Tom Allen could lick Jem Mace was ridiculed, and Jem himself thought that he had a very soft thing on. Anyhow Allen issued the challenge from Pittsburg on the Ohio river. Then came a difficulty about the signature of articles. Allen wanted Mace to visit him for the purpose, but Jem did not feel inclined to leave New York, so there was a deal of time out to waste over correspondence upon the subject, and much comment in the columns of the sporting papers, suggesting that the two Britishers were having a barney, and never meant fighting at all. But Mace at least was in earnest, as witness the following letter which was dated from New York, December 27, 1869:—

"Tom Allen,—Sir,—In the latest issue of the *Clipper*, I observe your rather debating reply to my acceptance of your challenge, and I was somewhat astonished at the tenour of a portion of it. You use the words 'put up or shut up;' but you should understand that being the challenging party it is your place to put up a deposit as an evidence of sincerity and mine to cover it. To show that I mean precisely what I say, however, and do not court notoriety through the Press, I have this day deposited five hundred dollars at the *Clipper* office, which I desire you to come forward and cover without any more talk, with which the public do not wish to be bored. My business engagements render it altogether out of the question for me to meet you in Pittsburg as you propose; but I will meet you at the *Clipper* office any time you may name (the sooner the better), and will pay one-half of your expenses to this city, which I think is as reasonable as anyone could ask. In reference to the belt, which you say is shortly to be presented to you, I wish to say that my friends in New York propose to present me with a belt also, which I will put against yours and contest for in addition to the stakes. As I previously stated, I had no intention of re-entering the ring when I came to America, but as you have chosen to include me in your challenge, I am determined to afford you the opportunity you propose to desire, and will not throw any obstacle in the way of a match. Now, if, as you say, you are ready to defend the title of Champion against all comers, I wish you to prove it by covering my deposit, and meeting me as soon as possible and signing articles. Now is the time to show whether you are in earnest or merely bouncing. Hoping for a favourable reply immediately, I am, yours, &c., JEM MACE."

This brought Allen to the scratch, for he deputed Frank Burns, who kept the House of Commons Saloon, 25, Houston Street, to act for him, and he and Bill Edwards dropped into the *Clipper* office at the very moment Mace had the corrected draft of the articles handed to him. The agreement was for them to fight for the large sum of 10,000 dollars, and the battle was to take place in the following May.

The men went into strict training, and eventually the place was fixed for the fight, this being New Orleans, just a nice little trip of about a thousand miles from New York. What a journey! Over two thousand miles to witness a prize fight! Indeed, it was about the worst place that could have been selected for two Britishers to fight in, for we remember old Ludlow's descriptions of the feeling in the Crescent City towards the English which existed not many years before this time. Ludlow was an old actor, who was the first to take a travelling company through many of the towns of the New World, and the first to perform English drama in New Orleans, having gone there in 1817, when Cribb was Champion of England, and the Prize Ring was unknown in America. The old mummer tells us that the southern city on the Gulf of Mexico was by no means a desirable place to reside in, as in spite of its many natural beauties — its pretty little white residences adorned with honey-suckle, morning glories, and Virginia creepers, the picturesque dresses of the men and women, and the surrounding groves of orange trees, bearing rich golden fruit that contrasted so finely, so beautifully, with the rich green foliage — the people themselves were—that is to say, the majority—most undesirable associates. Two-thirds of the inhabitants didn't speak English, and those who did cared little for a Britisher, the dislike having been handed down from a very remote period. The feeling of animosity had existed among the French from the day that Louisiana or the east side of the Mississippi was ceded to England by the Treaty of Paris in February, 1763, and the dislike to us on the part of the Spanish when they were in possession of the west side of the French settlement in about 1766. The Spaniards and English were constantly at war to the knife. This feeling was undoubtedly diminished after the war, 1812-15, and practically ceased during the Civil War of 1861. But in the old actor's time New Orleans was not the place to spend a comfortable time,

for Britishers at any rate, and he told us that he had
known assassinations and robberies to take place in the
town at Bienville, and along Bourbon to St. Peter's
Street murders were very frequently committed. However, the sunny southern town of oranges, surrounded
by beautiful meadows and grand plantations, had somewhat improved in character by the time Mace took up
his quarters some miles from the Crescent City to put
the finishing touches to his condition. Mace has often
told us that he could not help thinking of the great
contrast of his training quarters there and those of
the dear old home where he used to take his
breathers over the heath at Newmarket or in
the vicinity of his native town, Norwich. Besides,
the weather was fearfully hot, and there was little
difficulty in getting down his weight. His cousin,
Pooley, and Abrahams looked after him whilst they
stayed at Mobile. Allen had also been hard at work
under the care of Goulding, and brought himself from
14st 8lb to 12st 7lb in less than two months.

To read the accounts in the American sporting papers
is very amusing, and the gush and big business puts our
own fights for the Championship quite into the shade.
But the British sport never had the possibility of
travelling a couple of thousand miles to witness a mill.
Here is a condensed description by one who made this
terrible journey :—" I will not worry you with an
account of our journey down South, which was a run of
over 1,000 miles. You know what railway travelling is
in the States, and how much more comfortable the
carriages are constructed, so that we can promenade
from end to end of the train. That this particular
journey was made agreeable, you bet, for we had some
of the right sort of boys with us, and very few skunks.
A number of skippers amounting to four figures suddenly arriving in a town like Orleans naturally created
a sort of sensation, and many and hearty were the
welcomes given us by old friends, for most of us had
some relation or acquaintance on the lookout for us on
our arrival. The first question asked was, of course,
whether the men were there and willing, for all kinds
of ugly rumours had been floating about on the journey
down, some stating that Tom Allen, thinking that he
had caught a Tartar, had made his way from St. Louis,
where he had been training, in an opposite direction, and
could be found if we wanted him at a well-known
saloon bar in the Bowery taking a cocktail. When
we knew that all was right and business meant it was
a great relief, as it wouldn't have been much of a joke
to have made even a short run like that, from New York

to New Orleans, and then discovered that one of the
men had skipped. However, there we were, and so were
the men, and the company being numerous, and all the
arrangements being complete, we looked like having a
high old time of it. But, there, without going into
particulars of the merry time we had upon our arrival
in the Southern City, and how we astonished the natives,
some of the New Yorkers going their fastest pace, let us
turn our attenton to the fight."

Then the writer goes on to say that after a nice
level bit of turf had been selected the crowd in a most
orderly manner encircled the ring with a cordon of
carriages and omnibuses. Allen was the first to show
up, and a ringing cheer went up, for Tom was an
immense favourite in America. But when Mace
followed the cheering was louder than ever, and he
must have felt delighted at the reception given him.
They gripped hands in the most friendly manner.
Joe Coburn and Thurston looked after Allen, whilst
Jerry Donovan and Cusick did the amiable for Jem
Mace, who looked in splendid condition. Very carefully
they went to work, sparring with the utmost caution.
Presently Mace, seeing an opening, lashed out
the left, and (to use the American reporter's
own words) "hit Allen over the right eye
with a crack sounding like the noise of a cowboy's
whip." Mace avoided the return, and followed up by
landing Allen bang on the nose, and fetched first blood.
But to go on with our reporter's account.

"Mace stepped back with a smile upon his good-looking countenance; but immediately advanced once more
with a crafty-like movement; then changing his tune
from 'andante' to 'allegretto' hit out heavily, and the
blow came uncomfortably right in the middle of Allen's
stomach, and he folded himself forward. Mace then let
fly, one, two, three, on the left eye, the chin, and the
lower lip. Tom then tried to punch Mace, and just
managed to get his fist on the forehead when Jem got a
grip of his man and threw him a buster, whilst the
cheering was great, and I thanked my stars and stripes
that I had backed the stranger."

And so he goes on giving every detail of the battle
from beginning to end, but it will be unnecessary to
describe them here. It would seem that Mace outfought
him in every round, and at one period so often did he
follow up his advantage that it looked as if the fight
would be of brief duration. Six times did Mace in
succession get on his opponent's face with his terrible
left, and at last Allen fell from sheer exhaustion.

By this time Tom's face was in a dreadful state. One

eye was closed, and he could scarcely see out of the
other. He was, however, still full of pluck, and proved
himself a perfect glutton. Jem was too quick for him
though, and at last making up his mind to bring the
fight to a conclusion he crept up, dashed in with right
and left until the men closed. Then a desperate struggle
ensued, and Tom Allen was employing all his strength
for the final effort. He seemed, with his immense
strength, to get the advantage over the supple form of
his antagonist. Down went Mace, Allen with him, but
the latter shot over his opponent's prostrate form
and struck himself violently against the stake. His
seconds picked him up, and it was discovered that his
shoulder was dislocated, so the sponge was skied,
Mace being declared the winner of the very handsome
sum of 10,000dols, besides many bets he had made.

After this Jem Mace became quite a lion in the States,
and was greeted most enthusiastically wherever he
went. He visited Canada, and was received there
most enthusiastically, boxing with Joe Wormald, who
had settled there after his failure in the British ring, as
described in a previous chapter.

And here we record the end of this not too successful
yet promising young pugilist, who has figured in our
list of Champions. Joe Wormald, it will be remembered, had commenced his career under Jack
Hicks in 1863, and within the short period of eight
years he had ended it and was no more. Settling in
Canada, he opened a sparring saloon at Montreal, afterwards going to Quebec, where he was stricken down by
an illness which affected his brain, and he became a
raving lunatic. So dreadfully unmanagable did he
become that he had to be strapped down upon a bed in
the Marine Hospital at the last-named town. His
immense strength, which had increased during his madness, was so great that before he could be secured he
had injured several of the attendants, and according to
accounts there was a dreadful scene, in which much
cruelty was used in the treatment of the poor fellow.

In the meanwhile Mace became more popular than
ever in the New World, and he thought seriously of
settling down there and retiring from the Ring. How
that determination was overthrown we must leave until
the next chapter, when we shall say adieu to the gallant
warrior in these pages.

CHAPTER LXVI.

A DEATH ROLL.— BATTLE AT LAST WITH JEM MACE AND
JOE COBURN.—AMERICAN CHAMPIONSHIP.

In our last chapter we called attention to the death of
Joe Wormald, who had a butterfly existence as Champion, and ended his days in a tragic manner in Canada.
But in England, too, the grim enemy was busy amongst
our fighting men. Two months after Wormald's death,
Jerry Noon (whose real name was John Calven) was
called over to the majority. Jerry was a prominent star
of the P.R., and, although he does not come under our
heading, he took part in all the Championship fights,
either as second or prime mover in matters pugilistic.
He was a black, curly-haired merry fellow, and was
looked upon as one of the straightest members of the
fistic fraternity. They dubbed him " The Unbought
and Undefeated." But poor Jerry shuffled off this
mortal coil in the ward of St. George's Hospital.
The death roll of 1871, however, was destined to be
added to by one who, although he never aspired to championship form, was the most scientific man of his day,
and the only fighter who beat Tom Sayers. This was
Ould Nat Langham, who at the time kept the Cambrian Stores. Nat was one of the busiest members of the
corps pugilistique, and a great favourite of the swell
sports of the time. He started the Rum-pum-Pas Club
to which we have already alluded, and had amongst his
patrons such men as Lord Caledon, Captain Hope
Johnstone, Lord Edward Russell, Captain W. Peel, Mr.
John Rosemont, and others. The Cambrian was the
rendezvous of all these swells and many more, and
when Nat died these Corinthians generously took charge
of his two daughters, Alice and Lizzie, and they had
erected a monument in Brompton Cemetery, his grave
being only a few feet from that of John Jackson, who
held the championship just over a hundred years ago.
The whole world of sport turned out to follow Nat to
his last resting place, and the following lines were
written to his memory :—

> He's gone, and death with sable wing
> Covers the hero of the Ring,
> A braver form, a manlier soul,
> Ne'er donned the gloves, ne'er drained the bowl.

Though classic lore he might disdain,
Nor love for Athen's sages fame,
Still was he from his earliest year
To charming " science " ever dear.
Unmatched for pluck or fistic skill,
Ne'er fought a cross nor shunned a mill,
E'en Sayers' self before him quailed,
Nought Sparkes or Ben Caunt might avail,
But ne'er again will the Fancy view
How Langham hit, and claret flew.
Fond memory will keep his name
Preserved on golden scrolls of fame,
To sing his praise, to gild his shrine,
I leave to abler pens than mine.

What with the warriors dropping off (particularly Nat Langham, who was really the link to the old pugilists), and the non-appearance of good men, the Ring looked like going to rack and ruin, and in this country during the early seventies it was in a rapid decline. No wonder, then, Jem Mace kept on the other side of the Atlantic, for there was little inducement for him to return to London. In America, though, matters were different. Popular as Mace had become, there was a certain amount of jealousy about his claim to the title, and a great deal of animosity was engendered amongst the Irish-American community. Indeed they made it so disagreeable for Jem that he had serious thoughts of returning to the old country in spite of the condition of affairs. Before doing so, however, he threw down a challenge, in order that he should not be accused of backing out of any engagement that might likely be made for him.

The response to this came from a very unexpected quarter. Joe Coburn, who had made the fizzle with Jem in Ireland, responded and planked down the money, offering to fight Mace in Canada for 5,000dols and the American Championship, to take place in the June of 1871. This, however, proved to be another fiasco, for what with the Canadian police interfering and the absence of Coburn at the time nominated, it all fell through, and Mace claimed the money in accordance with the referee's decision. Harry Hill, the stakeholder, was afraid to pay it over, and there was a terrible disturbance over the whole matter. At length, however, an amicable settlement was come to, and each drawing their own money a new match was made, and we will quote the articles, which will explain the situation.

" ARTICLES OF AGREEMENT BETWEEN JAMES MACE AND JOSEPH COBURN.—The undersigned agree to fight a fair stand-up fight, according to the new rules of the London and American Prize Rings on November 30, 1871, at a suitable place to be hereafter agreed upon between the pugilists, and such place to be within 100 miles of New Orleans, the stakes to be 2,500 dollars

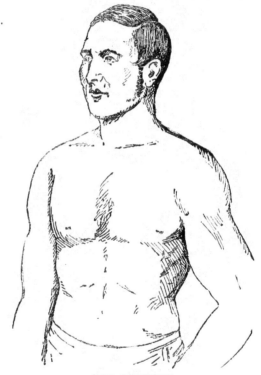

BOB BRETTLE.

a-side; 100 dollars is at the making of these articles deposited in the hands of Charles J. Foster, and the said Charles J. Foster is hereby authorised to demand and receive from Harry Hill the sum of 2,500 dollars, being money heretofore deposited with him by the said

Mace and Coburn, and to be treated as 1,000 dollars a-side for the match. The balance of the stakes, 1,500 dollars a-side, is to be deposited with the said Foster on Monday, July 31, 1871, at 3 o'clock p.m. The final stakeholder in the match to be   , and to him the said Charles J. Foster shall pay the stakes in his hands, or which shall come into his hands, whenever expected to do so by Mace or Coburn. The men to be in the ring on the day of fighting between the hours of 7 o'clock a.m. and 7 o'clock p.m. The referee shall be chosen on the ground. Either party failing to appear shall forfeit the stakes. The expenses of the ropes and stakes shall be borne by the parties equally, the money accruing from the excursion tickets to be equally divided between the principals. The said Charles J. Foster is empowered to insert the name of the final stakeholder to these articles when he is elected, and the principals shall designate him at least two weeks before the day set for the fight.

" Signed this 24th July, 1871.

" JOHN DWYER.	JOSEPH COBURN.
" POOLEY MACE.	JAMES MACE."

Coburn nominated Mr. George Mitchell, of New York, to be final stakeholder, who was immediately approved by Mace, but for some reason this gentleman refused to have anything to do with it. So Colonel Rube Hunt was selected, a very popular sportsman at New Orleans, and his name gave great satisfaction. Before going into training the men travelled through the States giving sparring exhibitions, but the expenses were so great that very little money was made out of the business.

Joe Coburn was the first to go into training, and he took up his quarters near the Crescent City, putting up at Dan Hickok's, at Carrolltown, with Johnny Dwyer, of Brooklyn, to attend to him. The work, however, proved too hard for Master Johnny, and he completely broke down, so Coburn had to send for the assistance of Tom M'Alpine. Mace did not go into training for some little time afterwards, and journeyed to Shady Grove, Cincinnati, with his cousin Pooley and Jem Cusick, where they remained for some time, travelling to New Orleans a few days before the date set down for the battle. Comparatively few people made the long journey from New York, for the fizzle over the Canadian affair made them suspicious, and it was a most expensive journey. It was, however, astonishing to find that some of the greatest roughs of New York city were able to purchase tickets and spoil the select company that was supposed to have things all their own way.

We have but recently described New Orleans in the account of Mace's fight with Tom Allen, so it will be unnecessary to say anything further about the Crescent City. An excursion had been arranged to travel by the Mobile and Chattanooga Railway, and there were about 600 people left New Orleans, the time taken being something over three hours when the train came to a standstill at Montgomery Station, about a mile from Bay St. Louis. There had gathered several hundred men from the surrounding districts, so altogether there was a very good muster, 1,000 spectators being around the ring.

Colonel Rufus Hart was appointed referee, and the umpires, A. Smith, of Chicago, for Mace, and a brother of Joe Coburn officiated for him. The seconds were—for Mace, Jem Cusick and Tom Allen ; Tom Kelly and Tom M'Alpine for Coburn. Betting was 2 to 1 on Mace.

This is the last fight we shall describe of Mace's, so we will give a condensed account of the bout that appeared in the American journals of the time. They both sparred cautiously, until Mace, seeing an opening, let drive straight at the mark, but was neatly stopped by Coburn, who returned low down—suspiciously low down—which made Mace look serious. Jem feinted with his left, and, crossing with the right, drove it into his opponent's bread-basket with such force that the latter caught his breath. As quick as lightning, however, he dashed his left on to Mace's ivories, which made them rattle again. Some fierce exchanges then took place, and in a few minutes lost time was made up, but the pace being too warm for the Yankee he closed, and in the struggle which followed succeeded in throwing Mace heavily, and as shouts went up from the home supporters, yells of " Even money on Coburn " met the ear.

Mace was not anxious to commence; but Joe, who was egged on by his seconds, and his fortunate opening encouraged him, and he made a dash, getting heavily on the body ; but Jem responded with one of his sharp clips on the mouth. Once more Mace landed on the face without a return, and then caught him a stinger on the nasal organ, and Coburn returned with another below, which those who were in a position to see declared was below the belt. After several exchanges the men closed once more, and Mace was thrown, the American party being in ecstasies of delight.

After this Mace kept out of harm's way, and a long bout of sparring ensued; at the finish Mace was down again. Although for several rounds Jem held his own, the battle seems to have gone dead in favour of Coburn, according to the Yankee reports before us, and the British party began to look blue. Then Jem rallied, but again fell off, and in the tenth round his seconds discovered that he had hurt his wrist badly in the first round, and that it had at length given way. Of course it would never have done for Mace to have let his opponent know the true state of affairs. He therefore fought on the defensive, and round after round lasted so long that it was evident that neither were inclined to

JOE COBORN.

make a fight of it. There was some excuse for Mace considering the state of his arm, but there was none for Joe Coburn, who had not the pluck to go in and lick his man right off. So after they had been in the ring for upwards of three hours and a half, and there was little prospect of a fight to a finish, Colonel Rufus Hart entered the ring and told the men that if they did not get to work he would declare it a draw. The same tiresome business continued, and the Colonel kept his word; so the second meeting of Mace and Coburn ended almost as unsatisfactoryily as the first.

We shall not follow Jem Mace through his Australian career and his more modern boxing encounters, practically after this fight with Coburn ended his battles for the Championship. He has been a marvellous man in his time, and to see him now you (1901) would scarcely believe that it was the same Jem Mace who fought Bill Thorpe nearly half a century ago, for he is well-preserved, and looked hale and hearty when we met him and had a glass of wine with the old warrior but a few months ago. He has now a tavern at Birmingham, and is, or was when last we visited there, as happy as a sandboy. He has lost the staying powers, but he is as quick with eye and fist as ever.

Perhaps before parting with old Jem Mace in these pages it may be amusing to relate the personal anecdote, when we shall leave the old-time fighters with the " raw 'uns," and after referring to the few more or less miserable exhibitions by the modern school of fighters, bring our history of the " Fights for the Championship " to a conclusion.

It would be a few years ago that in a well-known publishing office Jem Mace called upon business. His engagement was to sign his name beneath some fifty portraits of himself, which were to be bound up with a book upon boxing. One morning he drove up in a hansom, and swinging himself out with the activity of a young fellow of twenty he entered the premises. We never saw him look better. Clear complexion, black (we'll not answer for the natural colour), waxed-pointed moustache, long fur-lined coat, and a top hat shining like a mirror, Jem might have been mistaken for a distinguished nobleman.

Business first and a chat afterwards were the order of the day. So the great pugilist divested himself of his coat, sat at the writing table, and, pen in hand, commenced signing the portraits. Never shall we forget the expression upon the old warrior's face as he struggled in his efforts at caligraphy. Dabbing the pen into the ink-pot half a dozen times he commenced with a great blot upon picture number one, and with a grunt threw down the pen and called for another. Then, with tongue sticking out at the corner of his mouth, he commenced his signature, and looked for all the world like a schoolboy doing his first pothooks and hangers. Then executing (after a fashion) some half-dozen signatures, he threw down the pen and exclaimed, " Damn me if I wouldn't sooner fight a round for every one of those names I have put on there. I shall do no more. I'll come round again some other day."

Now, it so happened that a gentleman from the land

o' cakes called and was introduced to the ex-champion.
Our friend felt proud, and being a bit of a boxer and a
good all-round athlete, whispered to us if we would ask
Mace just to put up his hands with him, so that
he could truthfully say that he had sparred with the
Champion of England.

Jem at once agreed, and hands were up, and in an
instant the old champion feinted with the left and
caught our friend a pushing hit on the mark which sent
him staggering backwards until he fell all of a heap
into a pile of waste newspapers. Yes, Mace has lost
none of his quickness and cunning, and is a fine
specimen still of the old school of champions.

CHAPTER LXVII.

INTRODUCING ANDREW MARSDEN. — SOME AMERICAN BIG
GUNS.—O'BALDWIN, ALLEN, AND M'COOLE.

We have now arrived at a period when the bright
stars of the fistic firmament have set, and but a few
struggles for the championship will need to be recorded. Indeed, we fear that the interest in the
heroes of the Ring, about whom it has been our
pleasant duty to write during the many chapters of
this chronicle, will have somewhat lagged. Nevertheless, to complete our task, we must pursue the subject to the end, and ask our readers to accompany us
to our chapter of the present series, which will
shortly be marked "Finis."

We must now bring upon the scene Andrew Marsden, who was a promising pugilist, and regarded as a
likely man to win the championship. He stood
6ft 1½in, was a fine powerful fellow, and was
matched to fight Joe Wormald for the Belt and the
championship. We have referred to the latter previously. His first battle in England was with Jack
Smith, who was known as "Jem Mace's Wolf," which
took place down the river on May 26, 1863.

They fought for £25 a-side, and one hundred and
thirteen rounds were accomplished in four hours and

twenty-five minutes, when darkness came on and
the match ended in a draw. His next encounter
was with George Iles. It took place on June 25,
1864, and was for £50. Again Wormald was victorious, winning the battle in twenty-four rounds,
lasting two hours and eight minutes.

After his fight with Iles, Wormald was thought
good enough to be put up for the championship, and
he was matched with Marsden for £400 and the
Belt.   Joe knocked his opponent out in the
eighteenth round, and became acknowledged as
Champion of England.

It will be remembered that we mentioned in Mace's
combats that Joe Wormald was matched against the
Norfolk man, but he injured his hand whilst training, and forfeited £120 to Jem.

Wormald then went to America, and Mace re-
assumed the title. O'Baldwin, who had fought a
draw, was also in the land of Stars and Stripes, and
on the former's arrival, which was on August 4, 1868,
he immediately challenged O'Baldwin to fight for
£200 a-side and the title in America.

Edward O'Baldwin was an Irishman by birth,
having been born at Lismore in the year 1840.
Whilst quite a youngster, however, he went to Birmingham. He was a tremendous fellow, standing
6ft 5½in, and was known as " Tom Cooper's big 'un."
We have already referred to his first battle with
Marsden, for which Bob Travis and some Nottingham men put up the sum of £50 a-side. They fought
on October 21, 1863, when it was said that O'Baldwin
was nervous and bewildered at the start, and was
beaten in three rounds lasting 3½ minutes. This was
by no means a good beginning, yet he had many who
had the greatest confidence in him. So he was next
matched against George Iles, who had made such a
gallant stand against Joe Wormald. They fought on
February 19, 1864, for £50 a-side, O'Baldwin polishing off his opponent in fifty-seven minutes. After this
victory the Irish giant desired to try conclusions
once more with Marsden, and issued a challenge to
fight him for £100 a-side. The affair took place between Nottingham and London, but was a disgrace
to the Prize Ring, and no doubt helped to sound its
parting knell. Edward O'Baldwin turned the tables
upon his opponent, beating him in eleven rounds,
but the Nottingham lambs broke into the ring and
pelted O'Baldwin with stones before the verdict could
be given. But it was decided that the Irishman
should have the money, as he had virtually won the

fight before the disturbance. Ned's next match made was with Joe Goss, who was put up as "Mace's Unknown." The latter, however, was arrested, so Mace nominated another, who turned out to be Joe Wormald.

This was for £200 a-side and the Belt, and turned out a fiasco like so many others at this period, each one after the other shortening the existence of the Prize Ring. No doubt O'Baldwin was bamboozled out of the money, for although neither fought, the referee decided that Wormald was entitled to the stakes, although the ring had been formed, and the latter had not gone through the ceremony of entering it in his opponent's absence, which, according to the rules, was absolutely necessary before claiming the stakes.

After this O'Baldwin and Mace were matched. This also ended in a most unsatisfactory manner, as we have described in another chapter. The giant then followed the example of most of our British pugilists, and made a journey across the Atlantic, where he met Wormald as referred to above. This must have been an amusing, not to say a surprising, affair. The ring was formed upon the village green at Lynfield, Mass., on September 1, 1868. The spot chosen was facing the church, and a great crowd had gathered, placing themselves on every tombstone and fence where a good view could be obtained. Such sacrilege was, however, not to be permitted, for the Boston police had hidden themselves near the curiously selected battlefield, and before the first round was got through pounced down upon the principals and their seconds, and sent the crowd helter skelter in double quick time. O'Baldwin was arrested and imprisoned for eighteen months.

By this time Mace had arrived, and O'Baldwin issued a challenge to fight him, Tom Allen, or M'Coole. The result of that we have given in the chapter devoted to Mace's fights. It was another unsatisfactory affair, the stake money eventually being returned. A few months afterwards Edward O'Baldwin, the Irish giant who had aspired to the Championship of the World, was shot by his partner, Michael Finnell, in their bar saloon on September 27, 1875. He died two days afterwards, and was buried in Brookline, Mass.

And now, in order to make our list of champions complete, we must refer to Tom Allen and M'Coole. who in America did battle for the Championship of the World. Tom Allen, who also has appeared be-

fore in our description of his fight with Jem Mace,
was born at Birmingham in the April of 1840.
Allen's first fight was with Waggoner of Brum for
£5 a-side in the autumn of 1861, which Waggoner
won. His match with young Gould contributed him
a second victory some six months after for £20.
Posh Price then beat Allen in fifty-five minutes in
the July of 1862.   His next encounter was with
Bingley Rose of Nottingham for £25 a-side, whom he
defeated in twenty-nine minutes after fighting ten
rounds. This was in January, 1864. Six months
after this he met Bob Smith, the Liverpool Black,
who defeated Tom in two hours fifteen minutes. He
then fought Jack Parkinson, beating him easily in
twenty minutes for £25 a-side. Posh Price, who
had fought Allen once, could never hit it with him,
and the two men were always at loggerheads, so
they determined to have another turn together.
They met for £25 a-side. On this occasion Allen
had by far the best of the fight, and Price had, it was
proved, caused his own apprehension before the
battle was finished, and forfeited the stakes. They
fought for two hours five minutes in November of
1865. On June 12 of the next year Allen defeated
George Iles, and then came his meeting with Joe
Goss for £100 a-side at catch weight, in Monmouth-
shire, March 5, 1867. They fought a desperate battle,
lasting one hour and fifty-two minutes, of thirty-five
rounds. They were so exhausted then that neither
was able to finish, so the contest was pronounced a
draw. Allen then received forfeits of £50 from Bill
Thorne, Peter Millard, and Mike Cockelin.

Tom Allen arrived in America in the July of 1867
in company with Peter Morris of Birmingham
(looked upon then as our feather-weight champion)
and Bill Ryall. His first appearance in the ring in
America was as a second. It was upon the occasion of
the encounter between Tom Kelly of St. John's, New
Brunswick, then residing at Baltimore, and Billy
Parkinson of Pitsville.

The battle took place at Ucquia Creek, and Allen
and Billy Edwards of New York acted for Kelly.
The excitement of attending this affair must have
given Tom Allen a strange introduction to American
pugilism. It had been arranged by the gangs of
roughs from Philadelphia and Baltimore interested
in Kelly to either win, tie, or wrangle, and Tom
Allen, instead of insisting that the men should fight
on their merits and in accordance with the rules of
the Ring, early in the fight produced a revolver, and

with the assistance of the Philadelphian and Baltimore sports, threatened to kill the referee if he
would not declare Kelly the winner by an alleged
foul. From the start of the battle Parkinson had
all the best of it, and punished Kelly fearfully; and
the latter, according to all accounts, had not the
ghost of a chance of winning. Kelly's friends
crowded round the referee in nearly every round,

TOM ALLEN.

and Tom Allen was the most desperate. The referee,
however, was not inclined to be intimidated, and
Allen, followed by the roughs, cut the ropes, and
carried his man, who was much knocked about and
very weak, out of the ring, so of course amidst the
greatest uproar the battle ended. Parkinson was
justly declared the winner of the fight on the ground

that Allen broke up the ring before any decision was
given.

This was certainly a pretty nice start for the
British pugilist. But it showed that particular class
of American sports that he was a desperate and ugly
customer to deal with. In the Old World pugilism
and sticks and stones at that period went together,
but on the other side of the Atlantic the sporting
men who frequented the ring side were armed to a
man with knives and revolvers, and at very slight
provocation used them. We have heard Jem Mace
relate some of his experiences over there that would
appear almost incredible, nobody's life being safe:
for blazing away in a crowd several hundred strong
could scarcely be done without inflicting some injury.
And yet that is what really happened in bar saloon
and at prize fights at the time Tom Allen made his
début as a second.

The new arrival's first battle in America was with
Bill Davis at Chatteau Island, St. Louis, January 12,
1869. Allen won in forty-three rounds. Charlie
Gallagher of Cleveland next challenged him, and
They met on February 23, 1869, at Carroll Island,
near St. Louis. The combat terminated in Gallagher's favour, Tom receiving a fearful blow upon
the jugular vein which stretched him out insensible
after they had fought but two rounds.

Shortly after this Tom Allen and Mike M'Coole of
St. Louis then signed articles to fight within fifty
miles of the last named place for 1,000 dollars a-side
and travelling expenses. The battle took place on
Foster's Island in the Mississippi on July 15, 1869.
After the fight began, Allen outfought M'Coole at
all points, punishing him in a dreadful manner, and
when nine rounds had been gone through Allen was
pronounced victor. Then a disgraceful scene was
witnessed, nearly, if not quite, as bad as that described above. Here is an account of it from an
American source, which may be taken as a very mild
description :—

"The M'Coole party then cut the ropes, and the
excited mass covered the fighting ground. Clubs
were wielded promiscuously, while the referee was
besieged by enraged men, armed with murderous
weapons, who savagely and threateningly demanded
a decision in favour of the poor, bleeding, almost
powerless mass of humanity who had been a chopping
block for Allen."

Charlie Gallagher, who had defeated Allen, then
challenged him, and the match was fought at Fos-

ter's Island on August 16, 1869. Allen proved suc
cessful upon this occasion, beating his man in eleven
rounds, occupying twenty-five minutes. Again the
roughs interfered, and Larry Wessel, the referee,
declared Gallagher the victor, and Allen was robbed
of the stakes.

Tom then made a second match with M'Coole for
2,000 dollars, to fight on November 10, 1870; but
M'Coole failed to keep up his deposits, and the match
fell through. In the meanwhile, Jem Mace arrived
in America with his cousin, Pooley Mace, and his
backer, Fred Abrahams. Although Mace declared
that he did not come to fight, an insulting challenge
issued by Tom Allen caused him to alter his mind,
and they met at New Orleans as described in Mace's
career in another chapter. The result was Allen's
downfall, and Mace became Champion of the World.

Allen then after his defeat challenged Joe Coburn,
who declined, and then Tom finally, with Mace out
of the way, made a match with his old opponent for
2,000 dollars.   The fight took place at Chateau
Island, St. Louis, September 23, 1873, four years
after the previous battle between the men. Again
Tom Allen made short work of M'Coole, giving him a
terrible thrashing in twenty-nine rounds. Allen was
then declared to be Champion.

He was then matched to fight Ben Hogan (who
afterwards, like Bendigo, became a preacher) for
2,000 dollars. After a fizzle at St. Louis, by the
authorities interfering, and stopping the steamer
with the pugilists and their friends, a fresh match
was made. The fight took place, and Allen won.
Then came his fight in America with Joe Goss for
the Championship and 2,000 dollars. The battle took
place in Kentucky in 1876. They fought in two rings
for fifty-three minutes, when Goss was declared the
winner on a foul. Allen was arrested and put under
bonds. He did not stay in America after that, but
slipped off to England, leaving behind him a name as
a fearless hard-hitting pugilist and a desperate
character.

CHAPTER LXVIII.

UNDER THE STARS AND STRIPES.—J. L. SULLIVAN AND
CHARLIE MITCHELL.—AN EXCITING DAY AT CHANTILLY.

After the battles of Jem Mace we may almost say
that the Prize Ring in this country was extinguished,
although before we close the chapters of our long
history of the fights for the championship, our
chronicles would not be complete without devoting
space to the careers and battles of the modern warriors of the Ring. We shall, however, have to cast
our scenes away from home, for it was after the
decline of pugilism in this country that it was taken
up in the land of the "Stars and Stripes," and one of
the most energetic and prominent promoters of matters pugilistic was Mr. Richard K. Fox, who (as the
proprietor of the "Police Gazette" of New York) has
given such publicity to the modern gladiator and
found so much money for fistic competitions. Indeed, it would be but our duty to point out that this
gentleman forged the golden link which has connected
the old time fighters with the modern boxers, and
that it is principally due to his efforts that the professionals in the manly art have so far survived. We
are indebted considerably to the publications of
Mr. Fox for the events which took place in the
American Ring, and the battles with the raw 'uns,
which bring our champions down to date, for we have
now to deal with but very few, the principal amongst
them being John L. Sullivan. In Mr. Fox's preface
to the life of the celebrated pugilist, he speaks of
the rise of the Ring in America, and we think a
quotation from the work would prove interesting.
He says: "In America pugilism gained its first hold
rather on the principles of stern war than as a sport
or an art. It came to its highest degree under the
encouragement of race rivalry, and the native American movement brought it to its culmination with
Tom Hyer and Bill Poole as its bright particular
stars. Then, when that movement lost its interest,
Heenan and Morrissey took it up, and ran it as a
sport on the 'high art' principles of the Ring pure
and simple. It was the bitter rivalry of factions and

ersonal hatred that kept it going, however. Then came the culmination in the encounter with Heenan and Sayers, which commanded interest as an international event. After that there was a decline. The bellicose spirit of the nation was fully gratified in the awful slaughter of the Civil War, and, after it was over, the fighting element remaining worked off its residue of pugnacity in a score of minor matches, which gradually tapered off in interest in

JOHN L. SULLIVAN.

the course of ten years to an utter stagnation of their former sport."

Our American review of this interesting evolution in fistic displays goes on to tell us that "it was at this point that the 'Police Gazette' took it up, and by offering earnest money behind, its proprietor, Richard K. Fox, essayed to revive the Ring. A young man, John L. Sullivan, of Boston, came on the scene about this time (1881), and astonished all the experts who thought themselves great with the gloves by dealing out blows of such vigour that no one, not even the best of them, could withstand. He came forward like a meteor, working his way by downing with the gloves whoever had the hardihood to face him. It was at this moment that Mr. Fox had undertaken to revive the Ring, and here was a new prophet arisen as if by magic to lead the revival."

And now it is our intention to introduce Sullivan, give a short history of his career, and then briefly describe his two battles with Charlie Mitchell and Jake Kilrain, both of these pugilists having figured prominently in the latter-day fights for the Championships.

Sullivan was born on October 15, 1858. At the age of sixteen young Sullivan had developed the pluck and strength that had made him respected among the young men of his neighbourhood, and which brought him so rapidly to the very head and front of pugilism. He had several off-hand fights, and his chronicler says: "He had all the modesty and self-depreciation peculiar to genius in any form. He was his own sternest critic, and accorded himself superior qualities, only submitting himself to the most trying tests. He was induced to appear at boxing matches at Boston, and found that there was an especial pleasure afforded him by this form of sport. He set to on the platforms of these exhibitions, and soon had given the ordinary run of boxers such a taste of his quality that no casual youngster would set-to with him. Every time he appeared improvement was noted in him. There were several wise ones who had no hesitation in making early predictions that the young man would attain the highest point and become the Champion of the Prize Ring."

At this period Jim Keenan and Tom Earley were his greatest supporters, and it was when Joe Goss and Paddy Ryan were to fight for 1,000 dollars. Donaldson had arrived at Buffalo, and declared that he was willing to meet any of the heavy-weights, and the "Strong Boy," as Sullivan was nick-named, responded; but the man from the West, when he had clapped eyes on John L., retired. They, however, afterwards fought with the gloves, and Sullivan was victorious. In the April of 1881 he (the Bostonian) fought John Flood, a heavy-weight New Yorker, according to the rules of the London Prize Ring, and defeated him in sixteen minutes after fighting only eight rounds.

After this there was an attempt to make a match

with Ryan, but it fell through for the time. Sullivan
visited, amongst other places, Philadelphia, and
knocked out Crossley, following up his victory by
defeating M'Carthy, of Baltimore. After this, John
L. electrified the Chicago sports by polishing off his
opponents with the gloves in as quick a manner as
he had disposed of others with the " raw 'uns."

Then articles were signed for the great Bostonian
to fight Ryan on February 7, 1882, within 100 miles of
New Orleans. There was a big wrangle over the
affair at ring-side ` ,ore the battle commenced, but
when the men got together it was a desperate affair,
in which Sullivan knocked his man out in the ninth
round.

After several fights with the gloves, and his failure
to knock Long Wilson out in four three-minute
rounds, which he had undertaken to do, Sullivan
went on a sparring tour through Canada and the
United States with Billy Madden, who was acting
as the American's manager. During this tour he and
Madden quarrelled, and the latter came to England
and returned with Charlie Mitchell, who was then
at the zenith of his pugilistic career. The young
Englishman was put up to fight Sullivan for the
Championship of the World, but Sullivan refused to
meet the challenger except in a glove contest, which
was eventually arranged.

But of glove-fights at this particular period
we have nothing to do with here, so we must pass
by the several other contests of the American champion, including that with Charlie Mitchell, and come
to their fight with the " raw 'uns," which took place
on March 10, 1888, on Baron Rothschild's training
grounds, near Chantilly, France. The battle was for
£500 a-side, according to the London rules of the
Prize Ring. The party arrived upon the battle-
ground that had been selected by our old friend
Johnny Gideon (the great patron of Tom Sayers), at
eleven in the morning, both men being in the pink
of condition.

Here is the special " official " American report.
Sullivan stepped into the ring at twenty-five minutes
past twelve. In five minutes Mitchell followed.
Sullivan wore his stars and stripes silk handkerchief
on the left hand of which is an Irish harp. The rest
of his costume was the same which he wore in his
exhibition fights. Mitchell was similarly attired.
The latter was laughing, for he had won the toss, and
put Sullivan's face to the wind and sun. The seconds
for Mitchell were Jack Baldock, of London, and Jake

Kilrain, those for the American, Jack Ashton and McDonald. Mr. G. B. Angle was referee.

"As the two men stood facing each other in the centre of the ring the contrast in their height and appearance was most striking. Sullivan's tall and powerfully-built form towered far over the slighter but more elegant figure of his antagonist. But the condition of the latter was far superior. There was not an ounce of superfluous flesh on any part, but the muscles of his arms and shoulders as he stood watching his tremendous antagonist, every movement of his right guard close to his body, and his left in regular play ready to shoot in whenever opportunity offered or any opening appeared, showed like bundles of cord under his fair, almost transparent skin. Mitchell's loins and legs were very powerful, firm, and muscular, and his entire appearance that of a man of the highest form of physical development and in the perfection of condition.   Nothing could be more beautiful and artistic than his position, equally ready for offensive or defensive operations, as opportunity presented or necessity demanded. Sullivan, on the other hand, was the study of a sculptor. His round, close-cropped figure-head, well-shaped nose, thin determined lips, rounded chiselled chin, and well-formed neck were set upon a body divested of all its greatness.   With arms of rare muscular development, with legs of symmetrical beauty, he stood the very picture of an athlete.   Sullivan's position was also advantageous, but he evinced in every movement that his right hand was the 'sheet anchor' on which he relied to conquer his antagonist. His form compared with Mitchell was Herculean in its proportion, but his legs were not so large and muscular in their development as might have been expected by his great size. He was in the pink of condition, and his bright eye and clear complexion and firm elastic step showed that he was in the perfection of health.   Sullivan's stand was not so artistic as Mitchell's, but he stood well, keeping his left and right alternately in motion."

We have given the above full descriptions of the men, for the word-painting serves to show what fine fellows they were, as fine a brace as could be found amongst all the past champions who have passed through our previous chapters, and need but briefly give an account of this battle which ended in a very unsatisfactory manner.

Mitchell tried to draw his opponent, and succeeded, but with an unsatisfactory result, for Sullivan got

home effectively with his right, and at the finish
knocked his antagonist down. He did the same in the
second round, and repeated it in the third, fourth,
fifth and sixth. Mitchell was generally carried to his
corner, but Sullivan walked. The Englishman con-
tinuously went down to avoid, and in the fifteenth
looked like winning with hands down. Here is an
account of the last rounds, which must suffice. "The utmost fairness was shown on

CHARLIE MITCHELL.

both sides. It was at times most amusing
to see them, on closing and fibbing, by consent separating in the most polite manner. Mitchell
playfully tapping Sullivan, much talking was done,
usually followed by smack, smack, and a rush, Mitchell always laughing."

What a contrast to the old-time battles we have
already chronicled! Our account goes on to say:
"Sullivan did not seem to relish some of Mitchell's

hits, but was gracious enough to acknowledge some of them, 'That's a good one, Charlie,' and so on. Sullivan's right eye was getting in mourning, and his lips were swelling, while Mitchell's temple had a big lump, but there was no blood from the latter. Sullivan's nose and lips trickled crimson. He had not had his moustache removed. After thirty-nine rounds, which occupied 3hrs 11mins, the battle was declared a draw."

Just compare this exhibition with some of the Tom Spring, Tom Cribb, and Tom Sayers displays which we have already chronicled, and our readers will make their own deductions.

CHAPTER LXIX.

JEM SMITH AND HIS BATTLES.—MODERN BRITISH BOXERS.

And now, after our long spell in America, where we have witnessed some of the most disgraceful scenes that have ever been enacted at the ring-side, and our disappointing visits to France, let us return to Old England and take a glance at some of the modern British boxers, although we shall have to return anon to the land of Stars and Stripes in order to complete our biographies of the champions.

The name of the first of the present day boxers to whom we shall introduce our readers will be familiar to every ear, Jem Smith of London. He was born on January 21, 1863, in Red Lion Market, Whitecross Street, St. Luke's. For a considerable time he was employed in a London timber yard, where he soon showed that he had a taste for boxing, and that his hitting power was enormous, as those who stood before him in a few rough and tumbles found to their cost. His height was 5ft 8½in, and he weighed when in condition close upon fourteen stone. The first to take him in hand was Jack Knifton (the "Eighty-one Tonner," as he was called) and the veteran Goode (father to Jem and Chesterfield of that ilk), afterwards by Mr. F. Grimm, of the Central Club. His first success was at a competition at the Griffin, Shoreditch, but in the opinion of many good

judges, there was plenty of room for improvement,
for he shaped by no means well. After this he met
and defeated Snowy of Holloway, and was then
matched to box Harry Arnold with gloves for a ten
pound purse. The last-named was a stone and a half
lighter than Smith, was a good man, and had a good
deal of experience, having trained Jack Massey for an
important battle. The affair, however, was looked
upon as a good thing for Jem Smith; but it took him
nearly an hour to defeat his antagonist, who, by the
way, hailed from the Seven Dials.

After this old Goode deposited a sovereign on behalf of Smith to match him to fight Massey, but the

JEM SMITH.

affair fell through. Jem's next encounter was with
Wolf Bendorf to box to a finish with gloves for £20
a-side, which came off in the East End. Again Smith
was successful, although he fought at a great disadvantage, having injured his arm early in the
contest. He then won Tom Symmond's all-comers
competition at Bill Richardson's, the Blue Anchor,
Shoreditch. On this occasion he defeated Jack
Wannop and Tom Longer.

The above engagements were with the gloves,
but his next meeting was with Jack Davis, and the
men met in the old-fashioned style in the 24ft. ring

which was formed on the borders of Surrey and Sussex on Wednesday, September 17, 1885. They fought six rounds, which only occupied eight minutes, Davis being knocked out with Smith's tremendous right. This was for £100 a-side, and the result entitled Jem Smith to enroll his name amongst the champions of England.

Jem was then matched with Alf Greenfield for £300 a-side. The battle came off near Paris on Tuesday, February 17, 1886. The fight was all in favour of Smith, but after they had fought thirteen rounds the ropes were cut and the ring taken possession of by Greenfield's crowd. What followed was a disgrace to the British prize ring, and drove another long nail into the coffin of pugilism. Knuckle dusters and sticks were freely used, and a free fight went on, many of those who had journeyed to witness the encounter being set upon and seriously injured.

Smith was next matched with his old friend and mentor, Jack Knifton, and again a journey was made to France for the purpose of settling who should prove the better man. This was on December 1, 1886, and it was arranged that only ten people a-side should accompany them, including the principals and seconds. Instead of this, however, the number who assembled mounted to over a hundred, so the fight did not take place, both men returning to London. There was a general quarrel, for each side accused the other of breach of faith. So bitter did the feeling over the affair run between the two old friends that they mutually agreed to settle their differences in private, and met with that intention at a room in town. As they were arranging the necessary preliminaries, again there was a leakage somewhere, for the police surprised them, and the fight was abandoned.

After this Jem Smith devoted himself to sparring exhibitions, and then Charlie Mitchell suggested that he should accompany him to America to fight John L. Sullivan; but the project fell through. He was then matched to fight Jake Kilrain, who then held the championship of America, for £200, the "Police Gazette" Diamond Belt, and the Championship of the World. The battle was fought on an island in the Seine near Rouen, in the December of 1887. Jake Kilrain gained first blood, first fall, and first knock down, and it was agreed that he had by far the best of the fighting throughout. They fought 106 rounds, when darkness came on, and the match was declared to be a draw.

So far Jem Smith had never been beaten, and had certainly proved himself to be a tremendous hitter, and not devoid of science; but his enormous muscles on the arms were, in the opinion of many, no great advantage to him, some even declaring that he was shoulder-tied. Smith after this fought many times with the gloves; but it was not until 1889 that he entered the ring proper again, when he met Frank Slavin. But we shall come to that in due course. We must now have a few words to say about Charlie Mitchell, who was introduced to our readers in a previous chapter when upon the subject of John L. Sullivan's career.

Mitchell, one of the quickest, cleverest, and smartest men of his time, but, we fancy, always a bit unlucky, was born of Irish parents in Birmingham on November 24, 1861. His first battle was with Bob Cunningham at Selby Oak, near Birmingham, on January 11, 1878, for £5 a-side. He defeated his man in fifty minutes. After this he was victorious over C. Smithers, for £10 a-side, at Wolverhampton, on November 22, 1879, the time occupied being seventeen minutes. He then fought a draw with the gloves with Bill Kennedy, who was then light-weight champion. This was for a purse, and introduced Mitchell to London in 1879. He next met Bialy Gray, the black, who weighed 12st 7lb, Mitchell weighing only 9st 7lb. This was with the "raw 'uns" near Manchester, when Charlie defeated him for a purse in one round, occupying eleven minutes. He then fought Caryadoff, the Continental champion, better known as the Belgian Giant, who weighed between eighteen and nineteen stone. This took place at the El Dorado, Antwerp, in February, 1881, for 1,000 francs. This encounter was, of course, with gloves, and Master Charles defeated the foreigner in one round, which lasted sixteen minutes. He then defeated Tom Tully in a glove fight under the Marquis of Queensberry's rules in six rounds, and after that met Jack Burke.

This was with the knuckles, and the fight took place at Ascot on June 16, 1881, for £100. The battle lasted one hour and seventeen minutes, ending in a draw as darkness came on. Mitchell was giving away more than a stone, and held his own throughout the fight. Taking a long rest, he did not figure in the ring until April, 1882, when he was engaged in a middle weight competition, and carried off first prize. Then he won Billy Madden's London championship competition in December, 1882, which was open to all England. This was an exceedingly good test of his capabilities, for several heavy weights entered, such as Knifton, W. England, W. Wallis, and others. Mitchell, however, won all his heats without the slightest difficulty, and received a massive silver cup with the following inscription: "Won by Charles Mitchell, of Birmingham, Champion of England, December 10, 1882."

Charlie Mitchell then went to America, where he was matched to box Mike Cleary four rounds under the Queensberry rules. The contest was held at the American Institute, New York, on April 9, 1883, and the Birmingham man proved himself far superior to his antagonist. In the third round Cleary received a fearful body blow, and he was only just able to stagger to the scratch for the final bout, only to be knocked down, when the police came upon the platform and ordered the men to stop. After this Mitchell was matched to box John L. Sullivan with the gloves four rounds. and the men met at Madison Square Gardens on May 22, 1883. Although Mitchell succeeded in knocking the great American down, Sullivan proved too powerful for him, and Captain Williams, the referee, stopped the fight in the third round.

After this it was proposed that Mitchell should meet Herbert A. Slade for 2,500 dollars; but the match fell through, and his next appearance was with William Sheriff, the Prussian, when he boxed six rounds with the small gloves for 1,000 dollars a-side at Harry Hill's, at Flushing, Long Island, on October 2, 1883. Mitchell was proclaimed the winner. He then met Joe Denning, of Brooklyn, at Furn Hall, New York, to fight four rounds. Charlie was declared the winner. Jake Kilrain was the next to face him, and they fought a draw in the April of 1884. Then came Billy Edwards as Mitchell's opponent, who was acknowledged to be American light weight champion. They fought four rounds, Queensberry rules, for the gate money, in Madison Square Gardens in the May of 1884. After a capital display, Charlie was again victorious.

The Birmingham man was then matched to box four rounds with Dominick M'Caffrey. On this occasion it was not for the gate money, as M'Caffrey's backers, Messrs. George Bretherton and William P. Corney, paid Mitchell 1,200 dollars to enter the ring. The affair took place at Madison Square Gardens, New York, on October 13, 1884, when four rounds were fought, and although M'Caffrey displayed a fair amount of science, he proved that he was much inferior to Mitchell. Yet, to the astonishment and disgust of everybody present save those who had backed M'Caffrey, the referee decided in favour of the last-named.

John L. Sullivan was again matched against Mitchell at Madison Square Gardens, four rounds, Queensberry rules. John L. Sullivan appeared on the platform, and it was at once seen that something was amiss, for there was no doubt about it he was in a maudlin state of intoxication. He declared that ho was too unwell to box, and amidst the groans of the great audience retired. Mitchell and William Madden then gave a display, and the disappointed audience dispersed. Mitchell's next glove match was with Jack Burke, of England. It will be remembered that they had met before. On this occasion they met at Chicago on May 16, 1886. Mitchell proved himself by far the better man, as Burke was completely outclassed when six rounds had been fought. At the end of the tenth round Mitchell was declared the winner. His next match was with Patsey Cardiff, of Minneapolis. They fought with soft gloves at the above place, June 11, 1887. There was a difference in their weights of two stone, Mitchell scaling just over 11st and Cardiff 13st 3lb. Everybody agreed that Charlie had the best of the hitting, but the referee pronounced the battle to be a draw.

Mitchell then came back to England, where he gave boxing exhibitions with Jem Smith, and became very popular as a fine scientific boxer. In the spring of 1887 he once more returned to America, and with Billy Madden and Jake Kilrain gave boxing exhibitions until the last-named was matched to fight Smith, who was then English champion.

Mitchell's next fight was with Stephen Gallagher (better known as " Reddy " Gallagher. They fought in August, 1887, at Cleveland, when Charlie added another to his long list of victories. In the September of the same year, Mitchell, with Pony Moore and Jake Kilrain, returned to England, when he boxed with the American at the various music halls, and then assisted to train Kilrain for his battle with Jem Smith, acting as one of his seconds in the battle fought on December 19, 1887, at St. Pierre, in France.

On March 10, 1888, Charlie Mitchell fought John L. Sullivan, who at this time boasted that he was Champion of the World, for £500 a-side. The fight took place at Chantilly, near Paris, as we

have already described. Thirty-nine rounds
were gone through, and Mitchell would certainly have beaten the great American, for at the
expiration of three hours he had it all his own way.
Sullivan's backer, however, made overtures to Mitchell to make it a draw, which he unfortunately
consented to do.

Although the brief account of Charlie Mitchell's
career that we have given points to the fact that most
of his engagements were with the gloves, he was undoubtedly a rough customer with the " raw 'uns,"
and, had he been born in the palmy days of the prize
ring, would undoubtedly have held a high position
amongst the old pugilists as a punishing hitter and
scientific sparrer.

CHAPTER LXX.

JOHN L. SULLIVAN AND KILRAIN.—FRANK SLAVIN AND JEM
SMITH.—CONCLUSION.

We have already referred to the fight between
Jem Smith and Jake Kilrain, which ended in a draw
owing to darkness, and to bring our chronicle of the
fights for the championship to a conclusion, we shall
just refer to the battles between the last-mentioned
and John L. Sullivan, and finish our series by reference to the disgraceful affair between Frank P. Slavin
and Jem Smith, which put the extinguisher on the
Prize Ring so far as fighting with the knuckles is concerned.

Sullivan, after his failure to defeat Charlie Mitchell, was anxious to meet Kilrain, for he was desirous
to regain his lost prestige. He knew that Jake was
looked upon, after his battle with Jem Smith, as
being the best man, and Sullivan had on two occasions declined to meet Smith, although he had every
opportunity offered. Sullivan therefore induced a
syndicate of sporting men to back him against Kil-

rain, and they agreed to find the sum of 10,000 dollars to match him. This was made known on August 13. 1888. Kilrain's backer at once deposited 5,000 dollars at the "New York Herald" office in Paris, and agreed to match Kilrain against John L. Sullivan for 5,000 dollars a-side, the "Police Gazette" champion belt, and the championship of the world.

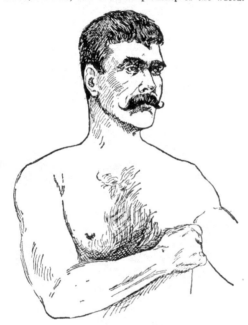

FRANK SLAVIN.

And now this will be, we think. a fitting opportunity of giving a description and history of the valuable trophy which was introduced by Mr. Richard K. Fox, for it will serve as a record of the several contests with which it was from time to time associated, and form a history of the modern American Prize Ring.

The "Police Gazette" champion belt was manufactured to be held specially by a fistic hero who was willing to defend the trophy against all challengers, and was the first to be offered in America. It was to be battled for according to the rules of the London Prize Ring, which govern all championship contests. John L. Sullivan and Paddy Ryan, after their battle for the championship for 5,000 dollars on February 7, 1882, were to have again met face to face within the roped arena, and battle again for a purse of 2,500 dollars, 1,000 dollars a-side, and the "Police Gazette" champion belt. A match was arranged, and the stakes posted with Harry Hill, but the match fell through.   John L. Sullivan was then offered the trophy to defend if he would agree to do so according to the rules governing the same.   He would not accept the conditions. At this time Jem Smith issued a challenge to do battle in the orthodox 24ft ring against any man in the world, and the donor of the trophy agreed to match Sullivan against the English champion for the "Police Gazette" belt and 10,000 dollars a-side. Sullivan agreed to fill the breach and battle with the English champion for the same.   But just when the match was being made a fixture, Sullivan backed out, and the Englishman began to talk about there being no pugilists in America who would enter the lists against him. Sullivan held the title of American Champion, but he would not defend it.   And then came Jake Kilrain on the scene.   He challenged Sullivan to battle for the belt, and after every fair inducement was made to bring the men together, Kilrain was declared champion, and in August, 1887, he was presented with the "Police Gazette" champion belt at Baltimore.   On receiving the trophy, he announced his intention of defending it against all challengers. Later, Jem Smith, who was then English Champion, issued a challenge to fight Kilrain for 5,000 dollars a-side, the belt, and the Championship of the World. The match was ratified, and as we have described in a previous chapter, the battle was fought, and the belt became the recognised championship emblem of the modern Prize Ring.   In arranging the match which we are about to describe between Kilrain and Sullivan, the latter declined to fight for the trophy, but on the jurists of the P.R. deciding that he must contend for the trophy, he waived all objections, and agreed to contest for the emblem.

The following is a description of the "Police Gazette" champion belt, which Sullivan had agreed to fight for. It is fifty inches long and eight inches wide, and weighs about 200 oz. in solid silver and gold. The design of this work of art is entirely different, as will be seen by the illustration, from any prize ring belt ever offered in America or England, and its intrinsic value has never been equalled. The work is laid out by solid silver plates and flexible woven silver chains, fortunately, so that the belt, notwithstanding its great and ponderous weight and size, can be adjusted to the body and worn with ease. The plates are richly ornamented with solid gold figures, and one of these ornaments is so made that a likeness of the winner can be put in a gold frame, encircled by a solid gold laurel leaf, suspended from the bill of a full-winged eagle. The centre of the belt represents a prize ring with two men facing each other in a fighting attitude. The whole of this part is solid gold. The men are represented in full ring costume.

Such was the trophy for which the men were to do battle, and the following conditions were agreed to: The fight to take place in February, the stake to be 5,000 dollars a-side, the "New York Herald" to be the final stakeholders, and the stakes to remain in Paris with the stakeholders until won or lost by either, the contest to be for the Championship of the World, the battle ground to be tossed for.

Meetings were held, but nothing definite was done, and it was said that Jake could not find the sinews of war; and after Kilrain's party agreed to all the propositions made by the representatives of Sullivan, the latter repudiated them. But on December 8, 1888, the sporting fraternity were startled by the announcement that John L. Sullivan, of Boston, had called at the "Clipper" office in New York and posted 5,000 dollars and issued a challenge to meet Kilrain to battle according to the new rules of the London Prize Ring for 10,000 dollars a-side. Sullivan also stated that if the challenge were not accepted within two weeks, Sullivan would claim the Championship of the World, which the latter by his challenge admitted that Kilrain held.

Everybody, on account of the large sum, imagined that it was only a piece of "bluff." But a letter from Kilrain in the "Clipper" and the deposit of his backers, soon pointed to the fact that the men were in earnest. Everything was arranged satisfactorily, but it was not until July 8, 1889, that the two men met in the 24ft ring to do battle for the largest stakes ever fought for, 20,000 dollars, the "Police

Gazette" Belt, and the Championship of the World.
The battlefield was Richburg, Missouri, and for a
week prior to the event New Orleans had been
crowding itself with men of sporting proclivities from
all parts of the world until the town was filled to
repletion. Richburg Mills, a borough a little more
than a hundred miles from New Orleans, had been
selected as the scene of the fight, and the crowd
started in that direction. "It was not a particular

JAKE KILRAIN.

crowd," says one report. "When it could not make
its way through the doors of the cars, it oozed
through the fractured windows, and when there was
not room inside it spread itself over the roofs of the
carriages and hung on by its eyelids to the sides of
the cars. Trainload after trainload arrived at the
scene of the anticipated disturbance, and all hurried
to the ring. It was estimated that 5,000 people
were present, and they gained every possible point of

vantage; and the coloured population took to the roof of their meeting-house hard by, and when the reserved seats were all taken, many of them had 'a boss circus without crawling under the tent.'

"It was 9.50 a.m. when Kilrain, accompanied by Pony Moore and Charlie Mitchell, pushed their way to the ring, and the Baltimorean followed the time-honoured custom of shying his castor over the ropes, followed it himself, and took a seat in his corner. Kilrain was hardly settled in his chair before the 5,000 throats were roaring like wild bulls. Then it was noticed that Kilrain was far from appearing well. This fact became more apparent afterwards. Sullivan, accompanied by Muldoon and Cleary, then jumped from a carriage, and walked rapidly to the enclosure. The first-named tossed his hat into the ring, and followed."

But the details before us are too long to repeat. There was a great fuss over the choice of referee, but ultimately Mr. Fitzpatrick was selected, and the men were in readiness. "Are you ready?" he asked, and at that moment Kilrain advanced and placed 1,000 dollars as a wager on himself into the referee's hands. This amount was immediately covered by Sullivan, and beneath a scorching sun "Time" was called and the fight commenced.

It is not our intention to follow the battle through. Let it be sufficient to say that seventy-five terrific rounds were fought, lasting two hours and sixteen minutes, and throughout Kilrain had the worst of it, Sullivan at the finish knocking him about as he pleased. It was a great battle, and brings our series of fights for the Championship to a close, for we will draw a veil over the shameful scene which occurred at the Slavin-Smith affair at Bruges in the same year. The mob behaved disgracefully, and this was the last dying gasp of the Prize Ring and of knuckle fights in the old style. True, there are glove fights with as much or more punishment given and taken than with the fists; but the old style of fighting in the twenty-four foot ring upon a patch of turf is over for ever. Perhaps it is as well.

THE END.

THE LICENSED VICTUALLERS' YEAR BOOK.

A REMEMBRANCER, RECORD, AND CALENDAR

FOR

LICENSED VICTUALLERS, HOTEL KEEPERS,
BREWERS, DISTILLERS, RECTIFIERS,
VINTNERS AND MINERAL WATER
MANUFACTURERS OF THE
UNITED KINGDOM.

Comprising a full and complete Summary of the Effects of the Licensing Act of 1902, the Act *in extenso*, with Explanatory Notes; a complete list of the Protection and Benevolent Societies connected with the Licensed Victuallers' interest throughout the kingdom, compiled from official sources; Notes upon Sport, both of the past and of the coming year, with selections for the Derby, Oaks, and Two and One Thousand Guineas; principal Jockey Mounts, &c.; Useful Memoranda, with carefully-compiled dates upon which interesting events happened in the past; a List of Public-House Sales for each year; of Public-House Changes, with dates of Transfer; Useful Legal Trade Points for Licensed Victuallers, alphabetically arranged; and numerous other matters of interest and value, together with full Almanack and Calendar Information, and various entertaining articles.

THE "WHITAKER" OF SPORT.

PUBLISHED BY THE

LICENSED VICTUALLERS' GAZETTE, LTD.,

AT THE OFFICES OF

"The Licensed Victuallers' Gazette and Hotel Courier,"

81, FARRINGDON STREET, LONDON, E.C.

PRICE 1s., or POST FREE 1s. 4d.

Broome & Hunner

of the
-seven
of the
Between
n and
man,

tions by
sy of
& Sons.

Ingram Content Group UK Ltd.
Milton Keynes UK
UKHW010757280423
420934UK00004B/234